Beowulf

An Introduction to the Study of the Poem with a Discussion of the Stories of Offa and Finn

R. W. Chambers

Alpha Editions

This edition published in 2021

ISBN : 9789354842412

Design and Setting By
Alpha Editions
www.alphaedis.com
Email - info@alphaedis.com

Contents

PREFACE

I have to thank various colleagues who have read proofs of this book, in whole or in part: first and foremost my old teacher, W. P. Ker; also Robert Priebsch, J. H. G. Grattan, Ernest Classen and two old students, Miss E. V. Hitchcock and Mrs Blackman. I have also to thank Prof. W. W. Lawrence of Columbia; and though there are details where we do not agree, I think there is no difference upon any important issues. If in these details I am in the right, this is largely due to the helpful criticism of Prof. Lawrence, which has often led me to reconsider my conclusions, and to re-state them more cautiously, and, I hope, more correctly. If, on the other hand, I am in the wrong, then it is thanks to Prof. Lawrence that I am not still more in the wrong.

From Axel Olrik, though my debt to him is heavy, I find myself differing on several questions. I had hoped that what I had to urge on some of these might have convinced him, or, better still, might have drawn from him a reply which would have convinced me. But the death of that great scholar has put an end to many hopes, and deprived many of us of a warm personal friend. It would be impossible to modify now these passages expressing dissent, for the early pages of this book were printed off some years ago. I can only repeat that it is just because of my intense respect for the work of Dr Olrik that, where I cannot agree with his conclusions, I feel bound to go into the matter at length. Names like those of Olrik, Bradley, Chadwick and Sievers carry rightly such authority as to make it the duty of those who differ, if only on minor details, to justify that difference if they can.

From Dr Bradley especially I have had help in discussing various of these problems: also from Mr Wharton of the British Museum, Prof. Collin of Christiania, Mr Ritchie Girvan of Glasgow, and Mr Teddy. To Prof. Brøgger, the Norwegian state-antiquary, I am indebted for permission to reproduce photographs of the {viii} Viking ships: to Prof. Finnur Jónsson for permission to quote from his most useful edition of the *Hrólfs Saga* and the *Bjarka Rímur*, and, above all, to Mr Sigfús Blöndal, of the Royal Library of Copenhagen, for his labour in collating with the manuscript the passages quoted from the *Grettis Saga*.

Finally, I have to thank the Syndics of the University Press for undertaking the publication of the book, and the staff for the efficient way in which they have carried out the work, in spite of the long interruption caused by the war.

R. W. C.
April 6, 1921.

PART I

CHAPTER I

THE HISTORICAL ELEMENTS

SECTION I. THE PROBLEM.

The unique MS of *Beowulf* may be, and if possible should be, seen by the student in the British Museum. It is a good specimen of the elegant script of Anglo-Saxon times: "a book got up with some care," as if intended for the library of a nobleman or of a monastery. Yet this MS is removed from the date when the poem was composed and from the events which it narrates (so far as these events are historic at all) by periods of time approximately equal to those which separate us from the time when Shakespeare's *Henry V* was written, and when the battle of Agincourt was fought.

To try to penetrate the darkness of the five centuries which lie behind the extant MS by fitting together such fragments of illustrative information as can be obtained, and by using the imagination to bridge the gaps, has been the business of three generations of scholars distributed among the ten nations of Germanic speech. A whole library has been written around our poem, and the result is that this book cannot be as simple as either writer or reader might have wished.

The story which the MS tells us may be summarized thus: Beowulf, a prince of the Geatas, voyages to Heorot, the hall of Hrothgar, king of the Danes; there he destroys a monster Grendel, who for twelve years has haunted the hall by night and slain all he found therein. When Grendel's mother in revenge makes an attack on the hall, Beowulf seeks her out and kills her also in her home beneath the waters. He then returns to his land with honour and is rewarded by his king Hygelac. Ultimately he himself becomes king of the Geatas, and fifty years later slays a dragon and is slain by it. The poem closes with an account of the funeral rites.

Fantastic as these stories are, they are depicted against a background of what appears to be fact. Incidentally, and in a number of digressions, we receive much information about the Geatas, Swedes and Danes: all which information has an appearance of historic accuracy, and in some cases can be proved, from external evidence, to be historically accurate.

SECTION II. THE GEATAS—THEIR KINGS AND THEIR WARS.

Beowulf's people have been identified with many tribes: but there is strong evidence that the Geatas are the Götar (O.N. *Gautar*), the inhabitants of what is now a portion of Southern Sweden, immediately to the south of the great lakes Wener and Wetter. The names *Geatas* and *Gautar* correspond exactly[3], according to the rules of O.E. and O.N. phonetic development, and all we can ascertain of the Geatas and of the Gautar harmonizes well with the identification[4].

We know of one occasion only when the Geatas came into violent contact with the world outside Scandinavia. Putting together the accounts which we receive from Gregory of Tours and from two other (anonymous) writers, we learn that a piratical raid was made upon the country of the Atuarii (the O.E. *Hetware*) who dwelt between the lower Rhine and what is now the Zuyder Zee, by a king whose name is spelt in a variety of ways, all of which readily admit of identification with that of the Hygelac of our poem[5]. From the land of the Atuarii this king carried much spoil to his ships; but, remaining on shore, he was overwhelmed and slain by the army which the Frankish king Theodoric had sent under his son to the rescue of these outlying provinces; the plunderers' fleet was routed and the booty restored to the country. The bones of this gigantic king of the "Getae" [presumably = Geatas] were long preserved, it was said, on an island near the mouth of the Rhine.

Such is the story of the raid, so far as we can reconstruct it from monkish Latin sources. The precise date is not given, but it must have been between A.D. 512 and 520.

Now this disastrous raid of Hygelac is referred to constantly in *Beowulf*: and the mention there of Hetware, Franks and the Merovingian king as the foes confirms an identification which would be satisfactory even without these additional data[6].

Our authorities are:

(1) Gregory of Tours (d. 594):

His ita gestis, Dani cum rege suo nomine Chlochilaico evectu navale per mare Gallias appetunt. Egressique ad terras, pagum unum de regno Theudorici devastant atque captivant, oneratisque navibus tam de captivis quam de reliquis spoliis, reverti ad patriam cupiunt; sed rex eorum in litus resedebat donec naves alto mare conpraehenderent, ipse deinceps secuturus. Quod cum Theudorico nuntiatum fuisset, quod scilicet regio ejus fuerit ab extraneis devastata, Theudobertum, filium suum, in illis partibus cum valido exercitu et magno armorum apparatu direxit. Qui, interfecto rege, hostibus navali proelio superatis opprimit, omnemque rapinam terrae restituit.

The name of the vanquished king is spelt in a variety of ways: *Chlochilaichum, Chrochilaicho, Chlodilaichum, Hrodolaicum.*

See *Gregorii episcopi Turonensis Historia Francorum*, p. 110, in *Monumenta Germaniae Historica (Scriptores rerum merovingicarum, I).*

(2) The *Liber Historiae Francorum* (commonly called the *Gesta Francorum*):

In illo tempore Dani cum rege suo nomine Chochilaico cum navale hoste per alto mare Gallias appetent, Theuderico paygo [i.e. pagum] Attoarios vel alios devastantes atque captivantes plenas naves de captivis alto mare intrantes rex eorum ad litus maris resedens. Quod cum Theuderico nuntiatum fuisset, Theudobertum filium suum cum magno exercitu in illis partibus dirigens. Qui consequens eos, pugnavit cum eis caede magna atque prostravit, regem eorum interficit, preda tullit, et in terra sua restituit.

The *Liber Historiae Francorum* was written in 727, but although so much later than Gregory, it preserves features which are wanting in the earlier historian, such as the mention of the Hetware (*Attoarii*). Note too that the name of the invading king is given in a form which approximates more closely to *Hygelac* than that of any of the MSS of Gregory: variants are *Chrochilaico, Chohilaico, Chochilago*, etc.

See *Monumenta Germaniae Historica (Scriptores rerum merovingicarum, II, 274).*

(3) An anonymous work *On monsters and strange beasts*, appended to two MSS of Phaedrus.

Et sunt [monstra] mirae magnitudinis: ut rex Huiglaucus qui imperavit Getis et a Francis occisus est. Quem equus a duodecimo anno portare non potuit. Cujus ossa in Reni fluminis insula, ubi in Oceanum prorumpit, reservata sunt et de longinquo venientibus pro miraculo ostenduntur.

This treatise was first printed (from a MS of the tenth century, in private possession) by J. Berger de Xivrey (*Traditions tératologiques*, Paris, 1836, p. 12). It was again published from a second MS at Wolfenbüttel by Haupt (see his *Opuscula* II, 223, 1876). This MS is in some respects less accurate, reading *Huncglacus* for *Huiglaucus*, and *gentes* for *Getis*. The treatise is assigned by Berger de Xivrey to the sixth century, on grounds which are hardly conclusive (p. xxxiv). Haupt would date it not later than the eighth century (II, 220).

The importance of this reference lies in its describing Hygelac as king of the Getae, and in its fixing the spot where his bones were preserved as near the mouth of the Rhine[7].

But if *Beowulf* is supported in this matter by what is almost contemporary evidence (for Gregory of Tours was born only some twenty years after the raid he narrates) we shall probably be right in arguing that the other stories from the history of the Geatas, their Danish friends, and their Swedish foes, told with what seems to be such historic sincerity in the different digressions of our poem, are equally based on fact. True, we have no evidence outside *Beowulf* for Hygelac's father, king Hrethel, nor for Hygelac's elder brothers, Herebeald and Hæthcyn; and very little for Hæthcyn's deadly foe, the Swedish king Ongentheow[8].

And in the last case, at any rate, such evidence might fairly have been expected. For there are extant a very early Norse poem, the *Ynglinga tal*, and a much later prose account, the *Ynglinga saga*, enumerating the kings of Sweden. The *Ynglinga tal* traces back these kings of Sweden for some thirty reigns. Therefore, though it was not composed till some four centuries after the date to which we must assign Ongentheow, it should deal with events even earlier than the reign of that king: for, unless the rate of mortality among early Swedish kings was abnormally high, thirty reigns should occupy a period of more than 400 years. Nothing is, however, told us in the *Ynglinga tal* concerning the deeds of any king Angantyr—which is the name we might expect to correspond to Ongentheow[9].

But on the other hand, the son and grandson of Ongentheow, as recorded in *Beowulf*, *do* meet us both in the *Ynglinga tal* and in the *Ynglinga saga*.

According to *Beowulf*, Ongentheow had two sons, Onela and Ohthere: Onela became king of Sweden and is spoken of in terms of highest praise[10]. Yet to judge from the account given in *Beowulf*, the Geatas had little reason to love him. He had followed up the defeat of Hygelac by dealing their nation a second deadly blow. For Onela's nephews, Eadgils and Eanmund (the sons of Ohthere), had rebelled against him, and had taken refuge at the court of the Geatas, where Heardred, son of Hygelac, was now reigning, supported by Beowulf. Thither Onela pursued them, and slew the young king Heardred. Eanmund also was slain[11], then or later, but Eadgils escaped.

It is not clear from the poem what part Beowulf is supposed to have taken in this struggle, or why he failed to ward off disaster from his lord and his country. It is not even made clear whether or no he had to make formal submission to the hated Swede: but we are told that when Onela withdrew he succeeded to the vacant throne. In later days he took his revenge upon Onela. "He became a friend to Eadgils in his distress; he supported the son of Ohthere across the broad water with men, with warriors and arms: he wreaked his vengeance in a chill journey fraught with woe: he deprived the king [Onela] of his life."

This story bears in its general outline every impression of true history: the struggle for the throne between the nephew and the uncle, the support given to the unsuccessful candidate by a rival state, these are events which recur frequently in the wild history of the Germanic tribes during the dark ages, following inevitably from the looseness of the law of succession to the throne.

Now the *Ynglinga tal* contains allusions to these events, and the *Ynglinga saga* a brief account of them, though dim and distorted[12]. We are told how Athils (=Eadgils) king of Sweden, son of Ottar (=Ohthere), made war upon Ali (=Onela). By the time the *Ynglinga tal* was written it had been forgotten that Ali was Athils' uncle, and that the war was a civil war. But the issue, as reported in the *Ynglinga tal* and *Ynglinga saga*, is the same as in *Beowulf*:

"King Athils had great quarrels with the king called Ali of Uppland; he was from Norway. They had a battle on the ice of Lake Wener; there King Ali fell, and Athils had the victory. Concerning this battle there is much said in the *Skjoldunga saga*."

From the *Ynglinga saga* we learn more concerning King Athils: not always to his credit. He was, as the Swedes had been from of old, a great horse-breeder. Authorities differed as to whether horses or drink were the death of him[13]. According to one account he brought on his end by celebrating, with immoderate drinking, the death of his enemy Rolf (the *Hrothulf* of *Beowulf*). According to another:

"King Athils was at a sacrifice of the goddesses, and rode his horse through the hall of the goddesses: the horse tripped under him and fell and threw the king; and his head smote a stone so that the skull broke and the brains lay on the stones, and that was his death. He died at Uppsala, and there was laid in mound, and the Swedes called him a mighty king."

There can, then, hardly be a doubt that there actually was such a king as Eadgils: and some of the charred bones which still lie within the gigantic "King's mounds" at Old Uppsala may well be his[14]. And, though they are not quite so well authenticated, there can also be little doubt as to the historic existence of Onela, Ohthere, and even of Ongentheow.

The Swedish Kings.

The account in the *Ynglinga saga* of the fight between Onela and Eadgils is as follows:

Aðils konungr átti deilur miklar við konung þann, er Áli hét inn upplenzki: hann var ór Nóregi. Þeir áttu orrostu á Vænis ísi; þar fell Áli konungr en Aðils hafði sigr; frá þessarri orrostu er langt sagt í Skjǫldunga sǫgu. (*Ynglinga saga* in *Heimskringla*, ed. Jónsson, Kjøbenhavn, 1893, I, 56.)

The *Skjoldunga saga* here mentioned is an account of the kings of Denmark. It is preserved only in a Latin abstract.

Post haec ortis inter Adilsum illum Sveciae regem et Alonem Opplandorum regem in Norvegia, inimicitiis, praelium utrinque indicitur: loco pugnae statuto in stagno Waener, glacie jam obducto. Ad illud igitur se viribus inferiorem agnoscens Rolphonis privigni sui opem implorat, hoc proposito praemio, ut ipse Rolpho tres praeciosissimas res quascunque optaret ex universo regno Sveciae praemii loco auferret: duodecim autem pugilum ipsius quilibet 3 libras auri puri, quilibet reliquorum bellatorum tres marcas argenti defecati. Rolpho domi ipse reses pugilos suos duodecim Adilso in subsidium mittit, quorum etiam opera is alioqui vincendus, victoriam obtinuit. Illi sibi et regi propositum praemium exposcunt, negat Adilsus, Rolphoni absenti ullum deberi praemium, quare et Dani pugiles sibi oblatum respuebant, cum regem suum eo frustrari intelligerent, reversique rem, ut gesta est, exponunt. (See *Skjoldungasaga i Arngrim Jonssons Udtog, udgiven af Axel Olrik*, Kjøbenhavn, 1894, p. 34 [116].)

There is also a reference to this battle on the ice in the *Kálfsvísa*, a mnemonic list of famous heroes and their horses. It is noteworthy that in this list mention is made of Vestein, who is perhaps the Wihstan of our poem, and of Biar, who has been thought (very doubtfully) to correspond to the O.E. Beaw.

Dagr reiþ Drǫsle   en Dvalenn Móþne...
Ále Hrafne   es til íss riþo,
enn annarr austr   und Aþilse
grár hvarfaþe   geire undaþr.
Bjǫrn reiþ Blakke   en Biarr Kerte,
Atle Glaume   en Aþils Slungne...
Lieder der Edda, ed. Symons and Gering, I, 221-2.

"Ale was on Hrafn when they rode to the ice: but another horse, a grey one, with Athils on his back, fell eastward, wounded by the spear." This, as Olrik points out, appears to refer to a version of the story in which Athils had his fall from his horse, not at a ceremony at Uppsala, but after the battle with Ali. (*Heltedigtning*, I, 203-4.)

For various theories as to the early history of the Swedish royal house, as recorded in *Beowulf*, see Weyhe, *König Ongentheows Fall*, in *Engl. Stud.*, XXXIX,

14-39; Schück, *Studier i Ynglingatal* (1905-7); Stjerna, *Vendel och Vendelkråka*, in *A.f.n.F.* XXI, 71, *etc.*

The Geatas.

The identification of Geatas and Götar has been accepted by the great majority of scholars, although Kemble wished to locate the Geatas in Schleswig, Grundtvig in Gotland, and Haigh in England. Leo was the first to suggest the Jutes: but the "Jute-hypothesis" owes its currency to the arguments of Fahlbeck (*Beovulfsqvädet såsom källa för nordisk fornhistoria* in the *Antiqvarisk Tidskrift för Sverige*, VIII, 2, 1). Fahlbeck's very inconclusive reasons were contested at the time by Sarrazin (23 *etc.*) and ten Brink (194 *etc.*) and the arguments against them have lately been marshalled by H. Schück (*Folknamnet Geatas i den fornengelska dikten Beowulf*, Upsala, 1907). It is indeed difficult to understand how Fahlbeck's theory came to receive the support it has had from several scholars (e.g. Bugge, *P.B.B.* XII, 1 *etc.*; Weyhe, *Engl. Stud.*, XXXIX, 38 *etc.*; Gering). For his conclusions do not arise naturally from the O.E. data: his whole argument is a piece of learned pleading, undertaken to support his rather revolutionary speculations as to early Swedish history. These speculations would have been rendered less probable had the natural interpretation of Geatas as Götar been accepted. The Jute-hypothesis has recently been revived, with the greatest skill and learning, by Gudmund Schütte (*Journal of English and Germanic Philology*, XI, 574 *etc.*). But here again I cannot help suspecting that the wish is father to the thought, and that the fact that that eminent scholar is a Dane living in Jutland, has something to do with his attempt to locate the Geatas there. No amount of learning will eradicate patriotism.

The following considerations need to be weighed:

(1) *Geatas* etymologically corresponds exactly with O.N. *Gautar*, the modern Götar. The O.E. word corresponding to Jutes (the Iutae of Bede) should be, not *Geatas*, but in the Anglian dialect *Eote, Iote*, in the West Saxon *Iete, Yte*.

Now it is true that in one passage in the O.E. translation of Bede (I, 15) the word "Iutarum" *is* rendered *Geata*: but in the other (IV, 16) "Iutorum" is rendered *Eota, Ytena*. And this latter rendering is supported (*a*) by the *Anglo-Saxon Chronicle* (*Iotum, Iutna*) and (*b*) by the fact that the current O.E. word for Jutes was *Yte, Ytan*, which survived till after the Norman conquest. For the name *Ytena land* was used for that portion of Hampshire which had been settled by the Jutes: William Rufus was slain, according to Florence of Worcester, in *Ytene* (which Florence explains as *prouincia Iutarum*).

From the purely etymological point of view the Götar-hypothesis, then, is unimpeachable: but the Jute-hypothesis is unsatisfactory, since it is based upon one passage in the O.E. Bede, where *Jutarum* is incorrectly rendered *Geata*, whilst it is invalidated by the other passage in the O.E. Bede, by the *Chronicle* and by Florence of Worcester, where *Jutorum* is correctly translated by *Ytena*, or its Anglian or Kentish equivalent *Eota, Iotna.*

(2) It is obvious that the Geatas of *Beowulf* were a strong and independent power—a match for the Swedes. Now we learn from Procopius that in the sixth century the Götar were an independent and numerous nation. But we have no equal evidence for any similar preponderant Jutish power in the sixth century. The *Iutae* are indeed a rather puzzling tribe, and scholars have not even been able to agree where they dwelt.

The Götar on the other hand are located among the great nations of Scandinavia both by Ptolemy (*Geog.* II, 11, 16) in the second century and by Procopius (*Bell. Gott.* II, 15) in the sixth. When we next get clear information (through the Christian missionaries) both Götar and Swedes have been united under one king. But the Götar retained their separate laws, traditions, and voice in the selection of the king, and they were constantly asserting themselves during the Middle Ages. The title of the king of Sweden, *rex Sveorum Gothorumque*, commemorates the old distinction.

From the historical point of view, then, the Götar comply with what we are told in *Beowulf* of the power of the Geatas much better than do the Jutes.

(3) Advocates of the Jute-hypothesis have claimed much support from the geographical argument that the Swedes and Geatas fight *ofer sǽ* (e.g. when Beowulf and Eadgils attack Onela, 2394). But the term *sǽ* is just as appropriate to the great lakes Wener and Wetter, which separated the Swedes from the Götar, as it is to the Cattegatt. And we have the evidence of Scandinavian sources that the battle between Eadgils and Onela actually *did* take place on the ice of lake Wener (see above, p. 6). Moreover the absence of any mention of ships in the fighting narrated in ll. 2922-2945 would be remarkable if the contending nations were Jutes and Swedes, but suits Götar and Swedes admirably: since they could attack each other by land as well as by water.

(4) There is reason to think that the old land of the Götar included a great deal of what is now the south-west coast of Sweden[15]. Hygelac's capital was probably not far from the modern Göteborg. The descriptions in *Beowulf* would suit the cliffs of southern Sweden well, but they are quite inapplicable to the sandy dunes of Jutland.

Little weight can, however, be attached to this last argument, as the cliffs of the land of the Geatas are in any case probably drawn from the poet's imagination.

(5) If we accept the identification Beowulf = Bjarki (see below, pp. 60-1) a further argument for the equation of Geatas and Götar will be found in the fact that Bjarki travels to Denmark from Gautland just as Beowulf from the land of the Geatas; Bjarki is the brother of the king of the Gautar, Beowulf the nephew of the king of the Geatas.

(6) No argument as to the meaning of *Geatas* can be drawn from the fact that Gregory calls Chlochilaicus (Hygelac) a Dane. For it is clear from *Beowulf* that, whatever else they may have been, the Geatas were not Danes. Either, then, Gregory must be misinformed, or he must be using the word *Dane* vaguely, to cover any kind of Scandinavian pirate.

(7) Probably what has weighed most heavily (often perhaps not consciously) in gaining converts to the "Jute-hypothesis" has been the conviction that "in ancient times each nation celebrated in song its own heroes alone." Hence one set of scholars, accepting the identification of the Geatas with the Scandinavian Götar, have argued that *Beowulf* is therefore simply a translation from a Scandinavian Götish original. Others, accepting *Beowulf* as an English poem, have argued that the Geatas who are celebrated in it must therefore be one of the tribes that settled in England, and have therefore favoured the "Jute theory." But the *a priori* assumption that each Germanic tribe celebrated in song its own national heroes only is demonstrably incorrect[16].

But in none of the accounts of the warfare of these Scandinavian kings, whether written in Norse or monkish Latin, is there mention of any name corresponding to that of Beowulf, as king of the Geatas. Whether he is as historic as the other kings with whom in our poem he is brought into contact, we cannot say.

It has been generally held that the Beowulf of our poem is compounded out of two elements: that an historic Beowulf, king of the Geatas, has been combined with a mythological figure Beowa[17], a god of the ancient Angles: that the historical achievements against Frisians and Swedes belong to the king, the mythological adventures with giants and dragons to the god. But there is no conclusive evidence for either of these presumed component parts of our hero. To the god Beowa we shall have to return later: here it is enough to note that the current assumption that there *was* a king Beowulf of the Geatas lacks confirmation from Scandinavian sources.

And one piece of evidence there is, which tends to show that Beowulf is not an historic king at all, but that his adventures have been violently inserted amid the historic names of the kings of the Geatas. Members of the families in *Beowulf* which we have reason to think historic bear names which alliterate the one with the other. The inference seems to be that it was customary, when a Scandinavian prince was named in the Sixth Century, to give him a name which had an initial letter similar to that of his father: care was thus taken that metrical difficulties should not prevent the names of father and son being linked together in song[18]. In the case of Beowulf himself, however, this rule breaks down. Beowulf seems an intruder into the house of Hrethel. It may be answered that since he was only the offspring of a daughter of that house, and since that daughter had three brothers, there would have been no prospect of his becoming king, when he was named. But neither does his name fit in with that of the other great house with which he is supposed to be connected. Wiglaf, son of Wihstan of the Wægmundingas, was named according to the familiar rules: but Beowulf, son of Ecgtheow, seems an intruder in that family as well.

This failure to fall in with the alliterative scheme, and the absence of confirmation from external evidence, are, of course, not in themselves enough to prove that the reign of Beowulf over the Geatas is a poetic figment. And indeed our poem *may* quite possibly be true to historic fact in representing him as the last of the great kings of the Geatas; after whose death his people have nothing but national disaster to expect[19]. It would be strange that this last and most mighty and magnanimous of the kings of the Geatas should have been forgotten in Scandinavian lands: that outside *Beowulf* nothing should be known of his reign. But when we consider how little, outside *Beowulf,* we know of the Geatic kingdom at all, we cannot pronounce such oblivion impossible.

What tells much more against Beowulf as a historic Geatic king is that there is always apt to be something extravagant and unreal about what the poem tells us of his deeds, contrasting with the sober and historic way in which other kings, like Hrothgar or Hygelac or Eadgils, are referred to. True, we must not disqualify Beowulf forthwith because he slew a dragon[20]. Several unimpeachably historical persons have done this: so sober an authority as the *Anglo-Saxon Chronicle* assures us that fiery dragons were flying in Northumbria as late as A.D. 793[21].

But (and this is the serious difficulty) even when Beowulf is depicted in quite historic circumstances, there is still something unsubstantial about his actions. When, in the midst of the strictly historical account of Hygelac's overthrow, we are told that Beowulf swam home bearing thirty suits of armour, this is as fantastic as the account of his swimming home from Grendel's lair with Grendel's head and the magic swordhilt. We may well doubt whether there is any more kernel of historic fact in the one feat than in the other[22]. Again, we are told how Beowulf defended the young prince Heardred, Hygelac's son. Where was he, then, when Heardred was defeated and slain? To protect and if necessary avenge his lord upon the battlefield was the essential duty of the Germanic retainer. Yet Beowulf has no part to play in the episode of the death of Heardred. He is simply ignored till it is over. True, we are told that in later days he *did* take vengeance, by supporting the claims of Eadgils, the pretender, against Onela, the slayer of Heardred. But here again difficulties meet us: for the Scandinavian authorities, whilst they agree that Eadgils overthrew Onela by the use of foreign auxiliaries, represent these auxiliaries as Danish retainers, dispatched by the Danish king Hrothulf. The chief of these Danish retainers is Bothvar Bjarki, who, as we shall see later, has been thought to stand in some relation to Beowulf. But Bothvar is never regarded as king of the Geatas: and the fact remains that *Beowulf* is at variance with our other authorities in representing Eadgils as having been placed on the throne by a Geatic rather than by a Danish force. Yet this Geatic expedition against Onela is, with the exception of the dragon episode, the only event which our poem has to narrate concerning Beowulf's long reign of fifty years. And in other respects the reign is shadowy. Beowulf, we are told, came to the throne at a time of utter national distress; he had a long and prosperous reign, and became so powerful that he was able to dethrone the mighty[23] Swedish king Onela, and place in his stead the miserable fugitive[24] Eadgils. Yet, after this half century of success, the kingdom is depicted upon Beowulf's death as being in the same tottering condition in which it stood at the time when he is represented as having come to the throne, after the fall of Heardred.

The destruction one after the other of the descendants of Hrethel sounds historic: at any rate it possesses verisimilitude. But the picture of the childless Beowulf, dying, after a glorious reign, in extreme old age, having apparently made no previous arrangements for the succession, so that Wiglaf, a youth hitherto quite untried in war, steps at once into the place of command on account of his valour in slaying the dragon—this is a picture which lacks all historic probability.

I cannot avoid a suspicion that the fifty years' reign of Beowulf over the Geatas may quite conceivably be a poetic fiction[25]; that the downfall of the Geatic kingdom and its absorption in Sweden were very possibly brought about by the destruction of Hygelac and all his warriors at the mouth of the Rhine.

Such an event would have given the Swedes their opportunity for vengeance: they may have swooped down, destroyed Heardred, and utterly crushed the independent kingdom of the Geatas before the younger generation had time to grow up into fighting men.

To the fabulous achievements of Beowulf, his fight with Grendel, Grendel's dam, and the dragon, it will be necessary to return later. As to his other feats, all we can say is that the common assumption that they rest upon an historic foundation does not seem to be capable of proof. But that they have an historic background is indisputable.

SECTION III. HEOROT AND THE DANISH KINGS.

Of the Danish kings mentioned in *Beowulf*, we have first Scyld Scefing, the foundling, an ancient and probably a mythical figure, then Beowulf, son of Scyld, who seems an intruder among the Danish kings, since the Danish records know nothing of him, and since his name does not alliterate with those of either his reputed father or his reputed son. Then comes the "high" Healfdene, to whom four children were born: Heorogar, Hrothgar, Halga "the good," and a daughter who was wedded to the Swedish king. Since Hrothgar is represented as an elder contemporary of Hygelac, we must date[26] Healfdene and his sons, should they be historic characters, between A.D. 430 and 520.

Now it is noteworthy that just after A.D. 500 the Danes first become widely known, and the name "Danes" first meets us in Latin and Greek authors. And this cannot be explained on the ground that the North has become more familiar to dwellers in the classical lands: on the contrary far less is known concerning the geography of the North Sea and the Baltic than had been the case four or five centuries before. Tacitus and Ptolemy knew of many tribes inhabiting what is now Denmark, but not of the Danes: the writers in Ravenna and Constantinople in the sixth century, though much less well informed on the geography of the North, know of the Danes as amongst the most powerful nations there. *Beowulf* is, then, supported by the Latin and Greek records when it depicts these rulers of Denmark as a house of mighty kings, the fame of whose realm spread far and wide. We cannot tell to what extent this realm was made by the driving forth of alien nations from Denmark, to what extent by the coming together (under the common name of Danes) of many tribes which had hitherto been known by other distinct names.

The pedigree of the house of Healfdene can be constructed from the references in *Beowulf*. Healfdene's three sons, Heorogar, Hrothgar, Halga, are presumably enumerated in order of age, since Hrothgar mentions Heorogar, but not Halga, as his senior[27]. Heorogar left a son Heoroweard[28], but it is in accordance with Teutonic custom that Hrothgar should have succeeded to the throne if, as we may well suppose, Heoroweard was too young to be trusted with the kingship.

The younger brother Halga is never mentioned during Beowulf's visit to Heorot, and the presumption is that he is already dead.

The Hrothulf who, both in *Beowulf* and *Widsith*, is linked with King Hrothgar, almost as his equal, is clearly the son of Halga: for he is Hrothgar's nephew[29], and yet he is not the son of Heorogar[30]. The mention of how Hrothgar shielded this Hrothulf when he was a child confirms us in the belief that his father Halga had died early. Yet, though he thus belongs to the youngest branch of the family, Hrothulf is clearly older than Hrethric and Hrothmund, the two sons of Hrothgar, whose youth, in spite of the age of their father, is striking. The seat of honour occupied by Hrothulf[31] is contrasted with the undistinguished place of his two young cousins, sitting among the *giogoth*[32]. Nevertheless Hrothgar and his wife expect their son, not their nephew, to succeed to the throne[33]. Very small acquaintance with the history of royal houses in these lawless Teutonic times is enough to show us that trouble is likely to be in store.

So much can be made out from the English sources, *Beowulf* and *Widsith*. Turning now to the Scandinavian records, we find much confusion as to details, and as to the characters of the heroes: but the relationships are the same as in the Old English poem.

Heorogar is, it is true, forgotten; and though a name Hiarwarus is found in Saxo corresponding to that of Heoroweard, the son of Heorogar, in *Beowulf*, this Hiarwarus is cut off from the family, now that his father is no longer remembered. Accordingly the Halfdan of Danish tradition (Haldanus in Saxo's Latin: = O.E. Healfdene) has only two sons, Hroar (Saxo's Roe, corresponding to O.E. Hrothgar) and Helgi (Saxo's Helgo: = O.E. Halga). Helgi is the father of Rolf Kraki (Saxo's Roluo: = O.E. Hrothulf), the type of the noble king, the Arthur of Denmark.

And, just as Arthur holds court at Camelot, or Charlemagne is at home *ad Ais, à sa capele*, so the Scandinavian traditions represent Rolf Kraki as keeping house at Leire (*Lethra, Hleiðar garðr*).

Accounts of all these kings, and above all of Rolf Kraki, meet us in a number of Scandinavian documents, of which three are particularly important:

(1) Saxo Grammaticus (the lettered), the earlier books of whose *Historia Danica* are a storehouse of Scandinavian tradition and poetry, clothed in a difficult and bombastic, but always amusing, Latin. How much later than the English these Scandinavian sources are, we can realize by remembering that when Saxo was putting the finishing touches to his history, King John was ruling in England.

There are also a number of other Danish-Latin histories and genealogies.

(2) The Icelandic *Saga of Rolf Kraki*, a late document belonging to the end of the middle ages, but nevertheless containing valuable matter.

(3) The Icelandic *Skjoldunga saga*, extant only in a Latin summary of the end of the sixteenth century.

SECTION IV. LEIRE AND HEOROT.

The village of Leire remains to the present day. It stands near the north coast of the island of Seeland, some five miles from Roskilde and three miles from the sea, in a gentle valley, through the midst of which flows a small stream. The village itself consists of a tiny cluster of cottages: the outstanding feature of the place is formed by the huge grave mounds scattered around in all directions.

The tourist, walking amid these cottages and mounds, may feel fairly confident that he is standing on the site of Heorot.

There are two distinct stages in this identification: it must be proved (*a*) that the modern Leire occupies the site of the Leire (*Lethra*) where Rolf Kraki ruled, and (*b*) that the Leire of Rolf Kraki was built on the site of Heorot.

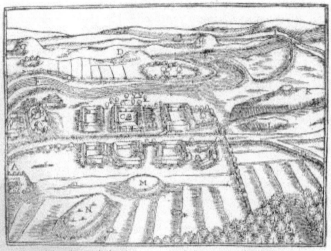

IN LIBRUM II. HISTORIÆ DANICÆ SAXONIS GRAMMATICI.

ANTIQUISSIMÆ IN DANIA
ARCIS ET OPPIDI
LETHRÆ
TOPOGRAPHIA

A. Sepulchrum Haraldi Hyldetan..
B. Sela Regiæ, Dronningstuen vulgò.
C. Locus, ubi Regia olim erat..
D. Dichen? forsan ubi homagia Regibus præstita..
H. Dichen? A Regia Olai sepulchrum.
I. Pons major, Maglebroe vulgò.
K. Equile olim regium, Heltbierg.
L. Stabulum pullis deputatum olim, Folehap, id. Kircchen.

Leire in the Seventeenth Century
From Saxo Grammaticus, ed. Stephanius, 1644.

(a) That the modern Leire occupies the site of the ancient Leire has indeed been disputed[34], but seems hardly open to doubt, in view of the express words of the Danish chroniclers[35]. It is true that the mounds, which these early chroniclers probably imagined as covering the ashes of 'Haldanus' or 'Roe,' and which later antiquaries dubbed with the names of other kings, are now thought to belong, not to the time of Hrothgar, but to the Stone or Bronze Ages. But this evidence that Leire was a place of importance thousands of years before Hrothgar or Hrothulf were born, in no wise invalidates the overwhelming evidence that it was their residence also.

The equation of the modern Leire with the Leire of Rolf Kraki we may then accept. We cannot be quite so sure of our thesis (b): that the ancient Leire was identical with the site where Hrothgar built Heorot. But it is highly probable: for although Leire is more particularly connected with the memory of Rolf Kraki himself, we are assured, in one of the mediæval Danish chronicles, that Leire was the royal seat of Rolf's predecessors as well: of Ro (Hrothgar) and of Ro's father: and that Ro "enriched it with great magnificence[36]." Ro also, according to this chronicler, heaped a mound at Leire over the grave of his father, and was himself buried at Leire under another mound.

Now since the Danish tradition represents Hrothgar as enriching his royal town of Leire, whilst English tradition commemorates him as a builder king, constructing a royal hall "greater than the sons of men had ever heard speak of"—it becomes very probable that the two traditions are reflections of the same fact, and that the site of that hall was Leire. That Heorot, the picturesque name of the hall itself, should, in English tradition, have been remembered, whilst that of the town where it was built had been forgotten, is natural[37]. For though the names of heroes survived in such numbers, after the settlement of the Angles in England, it was very rarely indeed, so far as we can judge, that the Angles and Saxons continued to have any clear idea concerning the *places* which had been familiar to their forefathers, but which they themselves had never seen.

Further, the names of both Hrothgar and Hrothulf are linked with Heorot in English tradition in the same way as those of Roe and Rolf are with Leire in Danish chronicles.

Yet there is some little doubt, though not such as need seriously trouble us, as to this identification of the site of Heorot with Leire. Two causes especially have led students to doubt the connection of Roe (Hrothgar) with Leire, and to place elsewhere the great hall Heorot which he built.

In the first place, Rolf Kraki came to be so intimately associated with Leire that his connection overshadowed that of Roe, and Saxo even goes so far in one place as to represent Leire as having been *founded* by Rolf[38]. In that case Leire clearly could not be the place where Rolf's predecessor built his royal hall. But that Saxo is in error here seems clear, for elsewhere he himself speaks of Leire as being a Danish stronghold when Rolf was a child[39].

In the second place, Roe is credited with having founded the neighbouring town of Roskilde (Roe's spring)[40] so that some have wished to locate Heorot there, rather than at Leire, five miles to the west. But against this identification of Heorot with Roskilde it must be noted that Roe is said to have built Roskilde, not as a capital for himself, but as a market-place for the merchants: there is no suggestion that it was his royal town, though in time it became the capital, and its cathedral is still the Westminster Abbey of Denmark.

What at first sight looks so much in favour of our equating Roskilde with Heorot—the presence in its name of the element *Ro* (Hrothgar)—is in reality the most suspicious thing about the identification. There are other names in Denmark with the element *Ro*, in places where it is quite impossible to suppose that the king's name is commemorated. Some other explanation of the name has therefore to be sought, and it is very probable that Roskilde meant originally not "Hrothgar's spring," but "the horses' spring," and that the connection with King Ro is simply one of those inevitable pieces of popular etymology which take place so soon as the true origin of a name is forgotten[41].

Leire has, then, a much better claim than Roskilde to being the site of Heorot: and geographical considerations confirm this. For Heorot is clearly imagined by the poet of *Beowulf* as being some distance inland; and this, whilst it suits admirably the position of Leire, is quite inapplicable to Roskilde, which is situated on the sea at the head of the Roskilde fjord[42]. Of course we must not expect to find the poet of *Beowulf*, or indeed any epic poet, minutely exact in his geography. At the same time it is clear that at the time *Beowulf* was written there were traditions extant, dealing with the attack made upon Heorot by the ancestral foes of the Danes, a tribe called the Heathobeardan. These accounts of the fighting around Heorot must have preserved the general impression of its situation, precisely as from the *Iliad* we know that Troy is neither on the sea nor yet very remote from it. A poet would draw on his imagination for details, but would hardly alter a feature like this.

In these matters absolute certainty cannot be reached: but we may be fairly sure that the spot where Hrothgar built his "Hart-Hall" and where Hrothulf held that court to which the North ever after looked for its pattern of chivalry was Leire, where the grave mounds rise out of the waving cornfields[43].

SECTION V. THE HEATHOBEARDAN.

Now, as *Beowulf* is the one long Old English poem which happens to have been preserved, we, drawing our ideas of Old English story almost exclusively from it, naturally think of Heorot as the scene of the fight with Grendel.

But in the short poem of *Widsith*, almost certainly older than *Beowulf*, we have a catalogue of the characters of the Old English heroic poetry. This catalogue is dry in itself, but is of the greatest interest for the light it throws upon Old Germanic heroic legends and the history behind them. And from *Widsith* it is clear that the rule of Hrothgar and Hrothulf at Heorot and the attack of the Heathobeardan upon them, rather than any story of monster-quelling, was what the old poets more particularly associated with the name of Heorot. The passage in *Widsith* runs:

"For a very long time did Hrothgar and Hrothwulf, uncle and nephew, hold the peace together, after they had driven away the race of the Vikings and humbled the array of Ingeld, had hewed down at Heorot the host of the Heathobeardan."

The details of this war can be reconstructed, partly from the allusions in *Beowulf*, partly from the Scandinavian accounts. The Scandinavian versions are less primitive and historic. They have forgotten all about the Heathobeardan as an independent tribe, and, whilst remembering the names of the leading chieftains on both sides, they see in them members of two rival branches of the Danish royal house.

We gather from *Beowulf* that for generations a blood feud has raged between the Danes and the Heathobeardan. Nothing is told us in *Beowulf* about the king Healfdene, except that he was fierce in war and that he lived to be old. From the Scandinavian stories it seems clear that he was concerned in the Heathobard feud. According to some later Scandinavian accounts he was slain by Frothi (=Froda, whom we know from *Beowulf* to have been king of the Heathobeardan) and this may well have been the historic fact[44]. How Hroar and Helgi (Hrothgar and Halga), the sons of Halfdan (Healfdene), evaded the pursuit of Frothi, we learn from the Scandinavian tales; whether the Old English story knew anything of their hair-breadth escapes we cannot tell. Ultimately, the saga tells us, Hroar and Helgi, in revenge for their father's death, burnt the hall over the head of his slayer, Frothi[45]. To judge from the hints in *Beowulf*, it would rather seem that the Old English tradition represented this vengeance upon Froda as having been inflicted in a pitched battle. The eldest brother Heorogar—known only to the English story— perhaps took his share in this feat. But, after his brothers Heorogar and Halga were dead, Hrothgar, left alone, and fearing vengeance in his turn, strove to compose the feud by wedding his daughter Freawaru to Ingeld, the son of Froda. So much we learn from the report which Beowulf gives, on his return home, to Hygelac, as to the state of things at the Danish court.

Beowulf is depicted as carrying a very sage head upon his young shoulders, and he gives evidence of his astuteness by predicting[46] that the peace which Hrothgar has purchased will not be lasting. Some Heathobard survivor of the fight in which Froda fell, will, he thinks, see a young Dane in the retinue of Freawaru proudly pacing the hall, wearing the treasures which his father had won from the Heathobeardan. Then the old warrior will urge on his younger comrade "Canst thou, my lord, tell the sword, the dear iron, which thy father carried to the fight when he bore helm for the last time, when the Danes slew him and had the victory? And now the son of one of these slayers paces the hall, proud of his arms, boasts of the slaughter and wears the precious sword which thou by right shouldst wield[47]."

Such a reminder as this no Germanic warrior could long resist. So, Beowulf thinks, the young Dane will be slain; Ingeld will cease to take joy in his bride; and the old feud will break out afresh.

That it did so we know from *Widsith*, and from the same source we know that this Heathobard attack was repulsed by the combined strength of Hrothgar and his nephew Hrothulf.

But the tragic figure of Ingeld, hesitating between love for his father and love for his wife, between the duty of vengeance and his plighted word, was one which was sure to attract the interest of the old heroic poets more even than those of the victorious uncle and nephew. In the eighth century Alcuin, the Northumbrian, quotes Ingeld as the typical hero of song. Writing to a bishop of Lindisfarne, he reproves the monks for their fondness for the old stories about heathen kings, who are now lamenting their sins in Hell: "in the Refectory," he says, "the Bible should be read: the lector heard, not the harper: patristic sermons rather than pagan songs. For what has Ingeld to do with Christ[48]?" This protest testifies eloquently to the popularity of the Ingeld story, and further evidence is possibly afforded by the fact that few heroes of story seem to have had so many namesakes in Eighth Century England.

What is emphasized in *Beowulf* is not so much the struggle in the mind of Ingeld as the stern, unforgiving temper of the grim old warrior who will not let the feud die down; and this is the case also with the Danish versions, preserved to us in the Latin of Saxo Grammaticus. In two songs (translated by Saxo into "delightful sapphics") the old warrior Starcatherus stirs up Ingellus to his revenge:

"Why, Ingeld, buried in vice, dost thou delay to avenge thy father? Wilt thou endure patiently the slaughter of thy righteous sire?...

Whilst thou takest pleasure in honouring thy bride, laden with gems, and bright with golden vestments, grief torments us, coupled with shame, as we bewail thine infamies.

Whilst headlong lust urges thee, our troubled mind recalls the fashion of an earlier day, and admonishes us to grieve over many things.

For we reckon otherwise than thou the crime of the foes, whom now thou holdest in honour; wherefore the face of this age is a burden to me, who have known the old ways.

By nought more would I desire to be blessed, if, Froda, I might see those guilty of thy murder paying the due penalty of such a crime[49]."

Starkath came to be one of the best-known figures in Scandinavian legend, the type of the fierce, unrelenting warrior. Even in death his severed head bit the earth: or according to another version "the trunk fought on when the head was gone[50]." Nor did the Northern imagination leave him there. It loved to follow him below, and to indulge in conjectures as to his bearing in the pit of Hell[51].

Who the Heathobeardan were is uncertain. It is frequently argued that they are identical with the Longobardi; that the words *Heatho-Bard* and *Long-Bard* correspond, just as we get sometimes *Gar-Dene*, sometimes *Hring-Dene*. (So Heyne; Bremer in *Pauls Grdr.* (2) III, 949 *etc.*) The evidence for this is however unsatisfactory (see Chambers, *Widsith*, 205). Since the year 186 A.D. onwards the Longobardi were dwelling far inland, and were certainly never in a position from which an attack upon the Danes would have been practicable. If, therefore, we accept the identification of Heatho-Bard and Long-Bard, we must suppose the Heathobeardan of *Beowulf* to have been not the Longobardi of history, but a separate portion of the people, which had been left behind on the shores of the Baltic, when the main body went south. But as we have no evidence for any such offshoot from the main tribe, it is misleading to speak of the Heathobeardan as identical with the Longobardi: and although the similarity of one element in the name suggests some primitive relationship, that relationship may well have been exceedingly remote[52].

It has further been proposed to identify the Heathobeardan with the Heruli[53]. The Heruli came from the Scandinavian district, overran Europe, and became famous for their valour, savagery, and value as light-armed troops. If the Heathobeardan are identical with the Heruli, and if what we are told of the customs of the Heruli is true, Freawaru was certainly to be pitied. The Heruli were accustomed to put to death their sick and aged: and to compel widows to commit suicide.

The supposed identity of the Heruli with the Heathobeardan is however very doubtful. It rests solely upon the statement of Jordanes that they had been driven from their homes by the Danes (*Dani ... Herulos propriis sedibus expulerunt*). This is inconclusive, since the growth of the Danish power is likely enough to have led to collisions with more than one tribe. In fact *Beowulf* tells us that Scyld "tore away the mead benches from *many* a people." On the other hand the dissimilarity of names is not conclusive evidence against the identification, for the word *Heruli* is pretty certainly the same as the Old English *Eorlas*, and is a complimentary nick-name applied by the tribe to themselves, rather than their original racial designation.

Nothing, then, is really known of the Heathobeardan, except that evidence points to their having dwelt somewhere on the Baltic[54].

The Scandinavian sources which have preserved the memory of this feud have transformed it in an extraordinary way. The Heathobeardan came to be quite forgotten, although maybe some trace of their name remains in *Hothbrodd*, who is represented as the foe of Roe (Hrothgar) and Rolf (Hrothulf). When the Heathobeardan were forgotten, Froda and Ingeld were left without any subjects, and naturally came to be regarded, like Healfdene and the other kings with whom they were associated in story, as Danish kings. Accordingly the tale developed in Scandinavian lands in two ways. Some documents, and especially the Icelandic ones[55], represent the struggle as a feud between two branches of the Danish royal house. Even here there is no agreement who is the usurper and who the victim, so that sometimes it is Froda and sometimes Healfdene who is represented as the traitor and murderer.

But another version[56]—the Danish—whilst making Froda and Ingeld into Danish kings, separates their story altogether from that of Healfdene and his house: in this version the quarrel is still thought of as being between two nations, not as between the rightful heir to the throne and a treacherous and relentless usurper. Accordingly the feud is such as may be, at any rate temporarily, laid aside: peace between the contending parties is not out of the question. This version therefore preserves much more of the original character of the story, for it remains the tale of a young prince who, willing to marry into the house of his ancestral foes and to forgive and forget the old feud, is stirred by his more unrelenting henchman into taking vengeance for his father. But, owing to the prince having come to be represented as a Dane, patriotic reasons have suggested to the Danish poets and historians a quite different conclusion to the story. Instead of being routed, Ingeld, in Saxo, is successful in his revenge.

See Neckel, *Studien über Froði* in *Z.f.d.A.* XLVIII, 182: Heusler, *Zur Skiöldungendichtung* in *Z.f.d.A.* XLVIII, 57: Olrik, *Skjoldungasaga*, 1894, 112 [30]; Olrik, *Heltedigtning*, II, 11 *etc.*: Olrik, *Sakses Oldhistorie*, 222-6: Chambers, *Widsith*, pp. 79-81.]

SECTION VI. HROTHULF.

Yet, although the Icelandic sources are wrong in representing Froda and Ingeld as Danes, they are not altogether wrong in representing the Danish royal house as divided against itself. Only they fail to place the blame where it really lay. For none of the Scandinavian sources attribute any act of injustice or usurpation to Rolf Kraki. He is the ideal king, and his title to the throne is not supposed to be doubtful.

Yet we saw that, in *Beowulf*, the position of Hrothulf is represented as an ambiguous one[57], he is the king's too powerful nephew, whose claims may prejudice those of his less distinguished young cousins, the king's sons, and the speech of queen Wealhtheow is heavy with foreboding. "I know," she says, "that my gracious Hrothulf will support the young princes in honour, if thou, King of the Scyldings, shouldst leave the world sooner than he. I ween that he will requite our children, if he remembers all which we two have done for his pleasure and honour, being yet a child[58]." Whilst Hrethric and Hrothmund, the sons of King Hrothgar, have to sit with the juniors, the *giogoth*[59], Hrothulf is a man of tried valour, who sits side by side with the king: "where the two good ones sat, uncle and nephew: *as yet* was there peace between them, and each was true to the other[60]."

Again we have mention of "Hrothgar and Hrothulf. Heorot was filled full of friends: *at that time* the mighty Scylding folk in no wise worked treachery[61]." Similarly in *Widsith* the mention of Hrothgar and Hrothulf together seems to stir the poet to dark sayings. "*For a very long time* did Hrothgar and Hrothulf, uncle and nephew, hold the peace together[62]."

The statement that "as yet" or "for a very long time" or "at that time" there was peace within the family, necessarily implies that, at last, the peace *was* broken, that Hrothulf quarrelled with Hrothgar, or strove to set aside his sons[63].

Further evidence is hardly needed; yet further evidence we have: by rather complicated, but quite unforced, fitting together of various Scandinavian authorities, we find that Hrothulf deposed and slew his cousin Hrethric.

Saxo Grammaticus tells us how Roluo (Rolf = O.N. Hrolfr, O.E. Hrothulf) slew a certain Røricus (or Hrærek = O.E. Hrethric) and gave to his own followers all the plunder which he found in the city of Røricus. Saxo is here translating an older authority, the *Bjarkamál* (now lost), and he did not know who Røricus was: he certainly did not regard him as a son or successor of Roe (Hrothgar) or as a cousin of Roluo (Hrothulf). "Roluo, who laid low Røricus *the son of the covetous Bøkus*" is Saxo's phrase (*qui natum Bøki Røricum stravit avari*). This would be a translation of some such phrase in the *Bjarkamál* as *Hræreks bani hnøggvanbauga*, "the slayer of Hrærek Hnøggvanbaugi[64]."

But, when we turn to the genealogy of the Danish kings[65], we actually find a *Hrærekr Hnauggvanbaugi* given as a king of Denmark about the time of Roluo. This *Røricus* or *Hrærekr* who was slain by Roluo was then, himself, a king of the Danes, and must, therefore, have preceded Roluo on the throne. But in that case Røricus *must* be son of Roe, and identical with his namesake Hrethric, the son of Hrothgar, in *Beowulf*. For no one but a son of King Roe could have had such a claim to the throne as to rule between that king and his all powerful nephew Roluo[65].

It is difficult, perhaps, to state this argument in a way which will be convincing to those who are not acquainted with Saxo's method of working. To those who realize how he treats his sources, it will be clear that Røricus is the son of Roe, and is slain by Roluo. Translating the words into their Old English equivalents, Hrethric, son of Hrothgar, is slain by Hrothulf.

The forebodings of Wealhtheow were justified.

Hrethric is then almost certainly an actual historic prince who was thrust from the throne by Hrothulf. Of Hrothmund[66], his brother, Scandinavian authorities seem to know nothing. He is very likely a poetical fiction, a duplicate of Hrethric. For it is very natural that in story the princes whose lives are threatened by powerful usurpers should go in pairs. Hrethric and Hrothmund go together like Malcolm and Donalbain. Their helplessness is thus emphasized over against the one mighty figure, Rolf or Macbeth, threatening them[67].

Yet this does not prove Hrothmund unhistoric. On the contrary it may well happen that the facts of history will coincide with the demands of well-ordered narrative, as was the case when Richard of Gloucester murdered *two* young princes in the Tower.

Two other characters, who meet us in *Beowulf*, seem to have some part to play in this tragedy.

It was a maxim of the old Teutonic poetry, as it is of the British Constitution, that the king could do no wrong: the real fault lay with the adviser. If Ermanaric the Goth slew his wife and his son, or if Irminfrid the Thuringian unwisely challenged Theodoric the Frank to battle, this was never supposed to be due solely to the recklessness of the monarch himself—it was the work of an evil counsellor—a Bikki or an Iring. Now we have seen that there is mischief brewing in Heorot—and we are introduced to a counsellor Unferth, the *thyle* or official spokesman and adviser of King Hrothgar. And Unferth is evil. His jealous temper is shown by the hostile and inhospitable reception which he gives to Beowulf. And Beowulf's reply gives us a hint of some darker stain: "though thou hast been the slayer of thine own brethren—thy flesh and blood: for that thou shalt suffer damnation in hell, good though thy wit may be[68]." One might perhaps think that Beowulf in these words was only giving the "countercheck quarrelsome," and indulging in mere reckless abuse, just as Sinfjotli (the Fitela of *Beowulf*) in the *First Helgi Lay* hurls at his foes all kinds of outrageous charges assuredly not meant to be taken literally. But, as we learn from the *Helgi Lay* itself, the uttering of such unfounded taunts was not considered good form; whilst it seems pretty clear that the speech of Beowulf to Unferth is intended as an example of justifiable and spirited self-defence, not, like the speech of Sinfjotli, as a storehouse of things which a well-mannered warrior should *not* say.

Besides, the taunt of Beowulf is confirmed, although but darkly, by the poet himself, in the same passage in which he has recorded the fears of Wealhtheow lest perhaps Hrothulf should not be loyal to Hrothgar and his issue: "Likewise there Unferth the counsellor sat at the foot of the lord of the Scyldingas: each of them [i.e. both Hrothgar and Hrothulf] trusted to his spirit: that his courage was great, *though he had not done his duty by his kinsmen at the sword-play*[69]."

But, granting that Unferth has really been the cause of the death of his kinsmen, some scholars have doubted whether we are to suppose that he literally slew them himself. For, had that been the case, they urge, he could not be occupying a place of trust with the almost ideal king Hrothgar. But the record of the historians makes it quite clear that murder of kin did happen, and that constantly[70]. Amid the tragic complexities of heroic life it often could not be avoided. The *comitatus*-system, by which a man was expected to give unflinching support to any chief whose service he had entered, must often have resulted in slaughter between men united by very close bonds of kin or friendship. Turning from history to saga, we find some of the greatest heroes not free from the stain. Sigmund, Gunnar, Hogni, Atli, Hrothulf, Heoroweard, Hnæf, Eadgils, Hæthcyn, Ermanaric and Hildebrand were all marred with this taint, and indeed were, in many cases, rather to be pitied than blamed. I doubt, therefore, whether we need try and save Unferth's character by suggesting that the stern words of the poet mean only that he had indirectly caused the death of his brethren by failing them, in battle, at some critical moment[71]. I suspect that this, involving cowardice or incompetence, would have been held the more unpardonable offence, and *would* have resulted in Unferth's disgrace. But a man might well have slain his kin under circumstances which, while leaving a blot on his record, did not necessitate his banishment from good society. All the same, the poet evidently thinks it a weakness on the part of Hrothgar and Hrothulf that, after what has happened, they still put their trust in Unferth.

Here then is the situation. The king has a counsellor: that counsellor is evil. Both the king and his nephew trust the evil counsellor. A bitter feud springs up between the king and his nephew. That the feud was due to the machinations of the evil adviser can hardly be doubted by those who have studied the ways of the old Germanic heroic story. But it is only an inference: positive proof we have none.

Lastly, there is Heoroweard. Of him we are told in *Beowulf* very little. He is son of Heorogar (or Heregar), Hrothgar's elder brother, who was apparently king before him, but died young[72]. It is quite natural, as we have seen, that, if Heoroweard was too young for the responsibility when his father died, he should not have succeeded to the throne. What is not so natural is that he does not inherit his father's arms, which one might reasonably have supposed Hrothgar would have preserved, to give to him when he came of age. Instead, Hrothgar gives them to Beowulf[73]. Does Hrothgar deliberately avoid doing honour to Heoroweard, because he fears that any distinction conferred upon him would strengthen a rival whose claims to the throne might endanger those of his own sons? However this may be, in any future struggle for the throne Heoroweard may reasonably be expected to play some part.

Turning now to Saxo, and to the *Saga of Rolf Kraki*, we find that Rolf owed his death to the treachery of one whose name corresponds exactly to that of Heoroweard—Hiarwarus (Saxo), Hjǫrvarthr (*Saga*). Neither Saxo nor the *Saga* thinks of Hiarwarus as the cousin of Rolf Kraki: they do not make it really clear *what* the cause of his enmity was. But they tell us that, after a banquet, he and his men treacherously rose upon Rolf and his warriors. The defence which Rolf and his men put up in their burning hall: the loyalty and defiance of Rolf's champions, invincible in death—these were amongst the most famous things of the North; they were told in the *Bjarkamál*, now unfortunately extant in Saxo's paraphrase only.

But the triumph of Hiarwarus was brief. Rolf's men all fell around him, save the young Wiggo, who had previously, in the confidence of youth, boasted that, should Rolf fall, he would avenge him. Astonished at the loyalty of Rolf's champions, Hiarwarus expressed regret that none had taken quarter, declaring that he would gladly accept the service of such men. Whereupon Wiggo came from the hiding-place where he had taken refuge, and offered to do homage to Hiarwarus, by placing his hand on the hilt of his new lord's sword: but in doing so he drove the point through Hiarwarus, and rejoiced as he received his death from the attendants of the foe he had slain. It shows how entirely the duty of vengeance was felt to outweigh all other considerations, that this treacherous act of Wiggo is always spoken of with the highest praise.

For the story of the fall of Rolf and his men see Saxo, Book II (ed. Holder, pp. 55-68): *Saga of Rolf Kraki*, caps. 32-34: *Skjoldunga Saga* (ed. Olrik, 1894, 36-7 [118-9]).

How the feud between the different members of the Danish family forms the background to *Beowulf* was first explained in full detail by Ludvig Schrøder (*Om Bjovulfs-drapen. Efter en række foredrag på folke-höjskolen i Askov*, Kjøbenhavn, 1875). Schrøder showed how the bad character of Unferth has its part to play: "It is a *weakness* in Hrothgar that he entrusts important office to such a man—a weakness which will carry its punishment." Independently the domestic feud was demonstrated again by Sarrazin (*Rolf Krake und sein vetter im Beowulfliede: Engl. Stud.* XXIV, 144-5). The story has been fully worked out by Olrik (*Heltedigtning*, 1903, I, 11-18 *etc.*).

These views have been disputed by Miss Clarke (*Sidelights*, 102), who seems to regard as "hypotheses" of Olrik data which have been ascertained facts for more than a generation. Miss Clarke's contentions, however, appear to me to be based upon a misunderstanding of Olrik.

The poem, then, is mainly concerned with the deeds of Geatic and Danish kings: only once is reference made to a king of Anglian stock—Offa.

The *Anglo-Saxon Chronicle* tells us of several kings named Offa, but two only concern us here. Still remembered is the historic tyrant-king who reigned over Mercia during the latter half of the eighth century, and who was celebrated through the Middle Ages chiefly as the founder of the great abbey of St Albans. This Offa is sometimes referred to as Offa *the Second*, because he had a remote ancestor, Offa I, who, if the Mercian pedigree can be trusted, lived twelve generations earlier, and therefore presumably in the latter half of the fourth century. Offa I, then, must have ruled over the Angles whilst they were still dwelling in Angel, their continental home, in or near the modern Schleswig.

Now the Offa mentioned in *Beowulf* is spoken of as related to Garmund and Eomer (MS *geomor*). This, apart from the abundant further evidence, is sufficient to identify him with Offa I, who was, according to the pedigree, the son of Wærmund and the grandfather of Eomer.

This Offa I, king of Angel, is referred to in *Widsith*. *Widsith* is a composite poem: the passage concerning Offa, though not the most obviously primitive portion of it, is, nevertheless, early: it may well be earlier than *Beowulf*. After a list of famous chieftains we are told:

Offa ruled Angel, Alewih the Danes; he was the boldest of all these men, yet did he not in his deeds of valour surpass Offa. But Offa gained, first of men, by arms the greatest of kingdoms whilst yet a boy; no one of equal age ever did greater deeds of valour in battle with his single sword: he drew the boundary against the Myrgingas at Fifeldor. The boundaries were held afterwards by the Angles and the Swæfe as Offa struck it out.

Much is obscure here: more particularly our ignorance as to the Myrgingas is to be regretted: but there is reason for thinking that they were a people dwelling to the south of the old continental home of the Angles.

After the lapse of some five centuries, we get abundant further information concerning Offa. The legends about him, though carried to England by the Anglian conquerors, must also have survived in the neighbourhood of his old kingdom of Angel: for as Angel was incorporated into the Danish kingdom, so these stories became part of the stock of Danish national legend. Offa came to be regarded as a Danish king, and his story is told at length by the two earliest historians of Denmark, Sweyn Aageson and Saxo Grammaticus. In Saxo the story runs thus:

Wermund, king of Denmark, had a son Uffo [Offa], tall beyond the measure of his age, but dull and speechless. When Wermund grew blind, his southern neighbour, the king of Saxony, laid claim to Denmark on the ground that he was no longer fit to rule, and, relying upon Uffo's incapacity, suggested that the quarrel should be decided by their two sons in single combat. Wermund, in despair, offered himself to fight, in spite of his blindness: this offer the envoys of the Saxon king refused with insult, and the Danes knew not what to say. Thereupon Uffo, who happened to be present, suddenly asked leave to speak. Wermund could not believe that it was really his son who had spoken, but when they all assured him that it *was*, he gave the permission. "In vain," then said Uffo, "does the king of Saxony covet the land of Denmark, which trusts to its true king and its brave nobles: neither is a son wanting to the king nor a successor to the kingdom." And he offered to fight not only the Saxon prince, but any chosen champion the prince might bring with him.

The Saxon envoys accepted the offer and departed. The blind king was at last convinced, by passing his hands over him, that the speaker had been in truth his son. But it was found difficult to arm him; for his broad chest split the rings of every coat of mail: the largest, his father's, had to be cleft down the side and fastened with a clasp. Likewise no sword was so well tempered that he did not shatter it by merely brandishing it, till the old king directed his men how they might find his ancient sword, *Skrep* (= ? stedfast) which he had buried, in despair, thinking his son unworthy of it. The sword, when found, was so frail from age that Uffo did not test it: for Wermund told him that, if he broke it, there was no other left strong enough for him.

So Uffo and his two antagonists were taken to the place of combat, an island in the river Eider. Crowds lined either bank, and Wermund stood prepared to throw himself into the river should his son be slain. Uffo held back at first, till he had discovered which of his antagonists was the more dangerous, since he feared the sword would only be good for one blow. Then, having by his taunts induced the champion to come to close quarters, he clove him asunder with one stroke. Wermund cried out that he had heard the sound of his son's sword, and asked where the blow had fallen: his attendants assured him that it had pierced, not any particular part, but the man's whole structure.

So Wermund drew back from the edge, desiring life now as keenly as before he had longed for death. Finally Uffo smote his second antagonist through, thus opening a career which after such a beginning we may well believe to have been glorious.

The story is told again by Sweyn Aageson in a slightly varying form. Sweyn's story has some good traits of its own—as when it makes Uffo enter the lists girt with *two* swords, intending to use his father's only in an emergency. The worthless sword breaks, and all the Danes quake for fear: whereupon Uffo draws the old sword and achieves the victory. But above all Sweyn Aageson tells us the *reason* of Uffo's dumbness and incapacity, which Saxo leaves obscure: it was the result of shame over the deeds of two Danes who had combined to avenge their father upon a single foe. What is the incident referred to we can gather from Saxo. Two Danes, Keto and Wigo, whose father Frowinus had been slain by a hostile king Athislus, attacked Athislus together, two to one, thus breaking the laws of the duel. Uffo had wedded the sister of Keto and Wigo, and it was in order to wipe out the stain left upon his family and his nation by their breach of duelling etiquette that he insisted upon fighting single-handed against two opponents.

That this incident was also known in England is rendered probable by the fact that Freawine and Wig, who correspond to Saxo's Frowinus and Wiggo, are found in the genealogy of English kings, and that an Eadgils, king of the Myrgingas, who is almost certainly the Athislus of Saxo[74], also appears in Old English heroic poetry. It is probable then that the two tales were connected in Old English story: the two brethren shamefully combine to avenge their father: in due time the family of the slain foe take up the feud: Offa saves his country and his country's honour by voluntarily undertaking to fight one against two.

About the same time that the Danish ecclesiastics were at work, a monk of St Albans was committing to Latin the English stories which were still current concerning Offa. The object of the English writer was, however, local rather than national. He wrote the *Vitae duorum Offarum* to celebrate the historic Offa, king of Mercia, the founder of his abbey, and that founder's ancestor, Offa I: popular tradition had confused the two, and much is told concerning the Mercian Offa that seems to belong more rightly to his forefather. The St Albans writer drew upon contemporary tradition, and it is evident that in certain cases, as when he gives two sets of names to some of the chief actors in the story, he is trying to harmonize two distinct versions: he makes at least one error which seems to point to a written source[75]. In one of the MSS the story is illustrated by a series of very artistic drawings, which might possibly be from the pen of Matthew Paris himself[76]. These drawings depict a version of the story which in some respects differs from the Latin text which they accompany.

Offa, miraculously restored, vindicates his Right. At the side, Offa is
represented in Prayer
From MS Cotton Nero D. I, fol. 2 b.

The story is located in England. Warmundus is represented as a king of the
Western Angles, ruling at Warwick. Offa, his only son, was blind till his
seventh, dumb till his thirtieth year. Accordingly an ambitious noble,
Riganus, otherwise called Aliel, claims to be recognized heir, in hope of
gaining the throne for his son, Hildebrand (Brutus). Offa gains the gift of
speech in answer to prayer; to the joy of his father and the councillors he
vindicates his right, much as in the Danish story. He is knighted with a
chosen body of companions, armed, and leads the host to meet the foe. He
dashes across the river which separates the two armies, although his
followers hang back. This act of cowardice on their part is not explained: it
is apparently a reminiscence of an older version in which Offa fights his duel
single handed by the river, and his host look on. The armies join battle, but
after a long struggle draw away from each other with the victory undecided.
Offa remaining in front of his men is attacked by Brutus (or Hildebrand) and
Sueno, the sons of the usurper, and slays them both (a second reminiscence
of the duel-scene). He then hurls himself again upon the foe, and wins the
victory.

Widsith shows us that the Danish account has kept closer to the primitive
story than has later English tradition. *Widsith* confirms the Danish view that
the quarrel was with a foreign, not with a domestic foe, and the combat a
duel, not a pitched battle: above all, *Widsith* confirms Saxo in representing
the fight as taking place on the Eider — *bī Fīfeldore*[77], whilst the account
recorded by the monk of St Albans had localised the story in England.

- 34 -

In *Beowulf* too we hear of Offa as a mighty king, "the best of all mankind betwixt the seas." But, although his wars are referred to, we are given no details of them. The episode in *Beowulf* relates rather to his wife Thryth, and his dealings with her. The passage is the most obscure in the whole poem, but this at least is clear: Thryth had an evil reputation for cruelty and murder: she wedded Offa, and he put a stop to her evil deeds: she became to him a good and loyal wife.

Now in the *Lives of the two Offas* quite a long space is devoted to the matrimonial entanglements of both kings. Concerning Offa I, a tale is told of how he succoured a daughter of the king of York, who had been turned adrift by her father; how when his years were advancing his subjects pressed him to marry: and how his mind went back to the damsel whom he had saved, and he chose her for his wife. Whilst the king was absent on his wars, a messenger whom he had sent with a letter to report his victories passed through York, where the wicked father of Offa's queen lived. A false letter was substituted, commanding that the queen and her children should be mutilated and left to die in the woods, because she was a witch and had brought defeat upon the king's arms. The order was carried out, but a hermit rescued and healed the queen and her children, and ultimately united them to the king.

This is a popular folk-tale which is scattered all over Europe, and which has many times been clothed in literary form: in France in the romance of the *Manekine*, in English in the metrical romance of *Emaré*, and in Chaucer's *Man of Lawes Tale*. From the name of the heroine in the last of these versions, the tale is often known as the *Constance*-story. But it is clear that this tale is not identical with the obscure story of the wife of Offa, which is indicated in *Beowulf*.

When, however, we turn to the *Life of Offa II*, we do find a very close parallel to the Thryth story.

Drida (Thryth) arrives in the land of King Offa, "in nauicula armamentis carente"
From MS Cotton Nero D. I, fol. 11a

This tells how in the days of Charles the Great a certain beautiful but wicked girl, related to that king, was condemned to death on account of her crimes, but, from respect for her birth, was exposed instead in a boat without sails or tackle, and driven ashore on the coast of King Offa's land. Drida, as she said her name was, deceived the king by a tale of injured innocence, and he committed her to the safe keeping of his mother, the Countess Marcellina. Later, Offa fell in love with Drida, and married her, after which she became known as *Quendrida*. But Drida continued her evil courses and compassed the death of St Æthelbert, the vassal king of East Anglia. In the end she was murdered by robbers—a just punishment for her crimes—and her widowed husband built the Abbey of St Albans as a thank-offering for her death.

The parallel here is too striking to be denied: for Drida is but another way of spelling Thryth, and the character of the murderous queen is the same in both stories. There are, however, striking differences: for whereas Thryth ceases from her evil deeds and becomes a model wife to Offa, Drida continues on her course of crime, and is cut off by violence in the midst of her evil career. How are we to account for the parallels and for the discrepancies?

As a matter of historical fact, the wife of Offa, king of Mercia, *was* named (not indeed Cwœnthryth, which is the form which should correspond to Quendrida, but) Cynethryth. The most obvious and facile way of accounting for the likeness between what we are told in *Beowulf* of the queen of Offa I, and what we are elsewhere told of the queen of Offa II, is to suppose that Thryth in *Beowulf* is a mere fiction evolved from the historic Cynethryth, wife of Offa II, and by poetic licence represented as the wife of his ancestor, Offa I. It was in this way she was explained by Professor Earle:

The name [Thrytho] was suggested by that of Cynethryth, Offa's queen.... The vindictive character here given to Thrytho is a poetic and veiled admonition addressed to Cynethryth[78].

Unfortunately this, like many another facile theory, is open to fatal objections. In the first place the poem of *Beowulf* can, with fair certainty, be attributed to a date *earlier* than that at which the historic Offa and his spouse lived. Of course, it may be said that the Offa episode in *Beowulf* is an interpolation of a later date. But this needs proof.

There are metrical and above all syntactical grounds which have led most scholars to place *Beowulf* very early[79]. If we wish to regard the *Offa-Thryth-*episode as a later interpolation, we ought first to prove that it is later in its syntax and metre. We have no right to assume that the episode is an interpolation merely because such an assumption may suit our theory of the development of *Beowulf*. So until reasons are forthcoming for supposing the episode of Thryth to be later than the rest of the poem, we can but note that what we know of the date of *Beowulf* forbids us to accept Earle's theory that Thryth is a reflection of, or upon, the historic Cynethryth.

But there are difficulties in the way of Earle's theory even more serious than the chronological one. We know nothing very definitely about the wife of Offa II, except her name, but from a reference in a letter of Alcuin it seems clear that she was a woman of marked piety: it is not likely that she could have been guilty of deliberate murder of the kind represented in the *Life of Offa II*. The St Albans *Life* depends, so far as we know, upon the traditions which were current four centuries after her death. There may be, there doubtless are, some historic facts concerning Offa preserved in it: but we have no reason to think that the bad character of Offa's queen is one of them. Indeed, on purely intrinsic grounds we might well suppose the reverse. As a matter of history we know that Offa *did* put to death Æthelberht, the vassal king of East Anglia. When in the *Life* we find Offa completely exonerated, and the deed represented as an assassination brought about by the malice and cruelty of his queen, it seems intrinsically likely that we are dealing with an attempt of the monks to clear their founder by transferring his cruel deeds to the account of his wife.

So far, then, from Thryth being a reflection of an historic cruel queen Cynethryth, it is more probable that the influence has been in the reverse direction; that the pious Cynethryth has been represented as a monster of cruelty because she has not unnaturally been confused with a mythical Thryth, the wife of Offa I.

To this it may be objected that we have no right to assume remarkable coincidences, and that such a coincidence is involved by the assumption that there was a story of a mythical Thryth, the wife of Offa I, and that this existed prior to, and independently of, the actual wedding of Offa II to a Cynethryth. But the exceeding frequency of the element *thryth* in the names of women robs this objection of all its point. Such a coincidence, far from being remarkable, would be the most natural in the world. If we look at the Mercian pedigree we find that almost half the ladies connected with it have that element *thryth* in their names. The founder of the house, Wihtlæg, according to Saxo Grammaticus[80], wedded Hermuthruda, the old English form of which would be Eormenthryth.

It is to this lady Hermuthruda that we must now devote our attention. She belongs to a type which is common in folk-tale down to the time of Hans Andersen—the cruel princess who puts her lovers to death unless they can vanquish her in some way, worsting her in a contest of wits, such as the guessing of riddles, or a contest of strength, such as running, jumping, or wrestling. The stock example of this perilous maiden is, of course, for classical story Atalanta, for Germanic tradition the Brunhilt of the *Nibelungen Lied*, who demands from her wooer that he shall surpass her in all three feats; if he fails in one, his head is forfeit[81].

Of this type was Hermuthruda: "in the cruelty of her arrogance she had always loathed her wooers, and inflicted upon them the supreme punishment, so that out of many there was not one but paid for his boldness with his head[82]," words which remind us strongly of what our poet says of Thryth.

Hamlet (Amlethus) is sent by the king of Britain to woo this maiden for him: but she causes Hamlet's shield and the commission to be stolen while he sleeps: she learns from the shield that the messenger is the famous and valiant Hamlet, and alters the commission so that her hand is requested, not for the king of Britain, but for Hamlet himself. With this request she complies, and the wedding is celebrated. But when Wihtlæg (Vigletus) conquers and slays Hamlet, she weds the conqueror, thus becoming ancestress of Offa.

It may well be that there is some connection between the Thryth of *Beowulf* and the Hermuthruda who in Saxo weds Offa's ancestor—that they are both types of the wild maiden who becomes a submissive though not always happy wife. If so, the continued wickedness of Drida in the *Life of Offa II* would be an alteration of the original story, made in order to exonerate Offa II from the deeds of murder which, as a matter of history, did characterize his reign.

CHAPTER II

THE NON-HISTORICAL ELEMENTS

Section I. The Grendel Fight.

When we come to the story of Beowulf's struggle with Grendel, with Grendel's mother, and with the dragon, we are faced by difficulties much greater than those which meet us when considering that background of Danish or Geatic history in which these stories are framed.

In the first place, it is both surprising and confusing that, in the prologue, before the main story begins, *another* Beowulf is introduced, the son of Scyld Scefing. Much emphasis is laid upon the upbringing and youthful fame of this prince, and the glory of his father. Any reader would suppose that the poet is going on to tell of *his* adventures, when suddenly the story is switched off, and, after brief mention of this Beowulf's son, Healfdene, we come to Hrothgar, the building of Heorot, Grendel's attack, and the voyage of Beowulf the Geat to the rescue.

Now "Beowulf" is an exceedingly rare name. The presence of the earlier Beowulf, Scyld's son, seems then to demand explanation, and many critics, working on quite different lines, have arrived independently at the conclusion that either the story of Grendel and his mother, or the story of the dragon, or both stories, were originally told of the son of Scyld, and only afterwards transferred to the Geatic hero. This has indeed been generally accepted, almost from the beginning of Beowulf criticism[83]. Yet, though possible enough, it does not admit of any demonstration.

Now Beowulf, son of Scyld, clearly corresponds to a Beow or Beaw in the West Saxon genealogy. In this genealogy Beow is always connected with Scyld and Scef, and in some versions the relations are identical with those given in *Beowulf*: Beow, son of Scyld, son of Scef, in the genealogies[84], corresponding to Beowulf, son of Scyld Scefing, in our poem. Hence arose the further speculation of many scholars that the hero who slays the monsters was originally called, not Beowulf, but Beow, and that he was identical with the hero in the West Saxon pedigree; in other words, that the original story was of a hero Beow (son of Scyld) who slew a monster and a dragon: and that this adventure was only subsequently transferred to Beowulf, prince of the Geatas.

This is a theory based upon a theory, and some confirmation may reasonably be asked, before it is entertained. As to the dragon-slaying, the confirmatory evidence is open to extreme doubt. It is dealt with in Section VII (Beowulf-

Frotho), below. As to Grendel, one such piece of confirmation there is. The conquering Angles and Saxons seem to have given the names of their heroes to the lands they won in England: some such names—'Wade's causeway,' 'Weyland's smithy'—have survived to modern times. The evidence of the Anglo-Saxon charters shows that very many which have now been lost existed in England prior to the Conquest. Now in a Wiltshire charter of the year 931, we have *Bēowan hammes hecgan* mentioned not far from a *Grendles mere*. This has been claimed as evidence that the story of Grendel, with Beow as his adversary, was localized in Wiltshire in the reign of Athelstan, and perhaps had been localized there since the settlement four centuries previously. Until recently this was accepted as definitely proving that the Beowulf-Grendel story was derived from an ancient Beow-myth. Yet one such instance of name-association is not conclusive. We cannot leave out of consideration the possibility of its being a mere chance coincidence, especially considering how large is the number of place names recorded in Old English charters. Of late, people have become more sceptical in drawing inferences from proper names, and quite recently there has been a tendency entirely to overlook the evidence of the charter, by way of making compensation for having hitherto overrated it.

All that can be said with certainty is that it *is* remarkable that a place named after Beowa should be found in the immediate proximity of a "Grendel's lake," and that this fact supports the possibility, though it assuredly does not prove, that in the oldest versions of the tale the monster queller was named Beow, not Beowulf. But it is only a possibility: it is not grounded upon any real evidence.

These crucial references occur in a charter given by Athelstan at Luton, concerning a grant of land at Ham in Wiltshire to his thane Wulfgar. [See Birch, *Cartularium Saxonicum*, 1887, vol. II, p. 363.]

... Ego Æðelstanus, rex Anglorum ... quandam telluris particulam meo fideli ministro Wulfgaro ... in loco quem solicolae *æt Hamme* vocitant tribuo ... Praedicta siquidem tellus his terminis circumcincta clarescit....

ðonne norð ofer dūne on mēos-hlinc westeweardne; ðonne adūne on ðā yfre on bēowan hammes hecgan, on brēmeles sceagan ēasteweardne; ðonne on ðā blācan grǣfan; ðonne norð be ðēm ondhēafdan tō ðǣre scortan dīc būtan ānan æcre; ðonne tō fugelmere tō ðān wege; ondlong weges tō ottes forda; ðonon tō wudumere; ðonne tō ðǣre rūwan hecgan; ðæt on langan hangran; ðonne on grendles mere; ðonon on dyrnan geat....

Ambiguous as this evidence is, I do not think it can be dismissed as it is by Lawrence (*Pub. Mod. Lang. Assoc. Amer.* XXIV, 252) and Panzer (*Beowulf*, 397), who both say "How do we know that it is not the merest chance?" It *may* of course be chance: but this does not justify us in basing an argument upon the assumption that it *is* the merest chance. Lawrence continues: "Suppose one were to set up a theory that there was a saga-relation between Scyld and Bikki, and offered as proof the passage in the charter for the year 917 in which there are mentioned, as in the same district, *scyldes treow* and *bican sell*.... How much weight would this carry?"

The answer surely is that the occurrence of the two names together in the charter would, by itself, give no basis whatever for starting such a theory: but if, on other grounds, the theory were likely, then the occurrence of the two names together would certainly have some corroborative value. Exactly how much, it is impossible to say, because we cannot estimate the element of chance, and we cannot be certain that the *grendel* and the *beowa* mentioned are identical with our Grendel and our Beowulf.

Miller has argued [*Academy*, May 1894, p. 396] that *grendles* is not a proper name here, but a common noun signifying "drain," and that *grendles mere* therefore means "cesspool."

Now "grindle" is found in modern dialect and even in Middle English[85] in the sense of "a narrow ditch" or "gutter," but I doubt if it can be proved to be an Old English word. Evidence would rather point to its being an East Anglian corruption of the much more widely spread *drindle*, or *dringle*, used both as a verb "to go slowly, to trickle," and as "a small trickling stream." And even if an O.E. *grendel* as a common noun meaning "gutter" were authenticated, it seems unlikely to me that places were named "the fen," "the mere," "the pit," "the brook"—"of the gutter." There is no ground whatever for supposing the existence of an O.E. *grendel* = "sewer," or anything which would lead us to suppose *grendles mere* or *gryndeles sylle* to mean "cesspool[86]." Surely it is probable, knowing what we do of the way in which the English settlers gave epic names to the localities around their settlements, that these places were named after Grendel because they seemed the sort of place where his story might be localized—like "Weyland's smithy" or "Wade's causeway": and that the meaning is "Grendel's fen," "mere," "pit" or "brook."

Again, both Panzer and Lawrence suggest that the Beowa who gave his name to the *ham* may have been, not the hero, but "an ordinary mortal called after him" ... "some individual who lived in this locality." But, among the numerous English proper names recorded, can any instance be found of any individual named Beowa? And was it in accordance with the rules of Old English nomenclature to give to mortals the names of these heroes of the genealogies[87]?

Recent scepticism as to the "Beow-myth" has been largely due to the fact that speculation as to Beow had been carried too far. For example, because Beow appeared in the West Saxon genealogy, it had been assumed that the Beow-myth belonged essentially to the Angles and Saxons. Yet Beow would seem to have been also known among Scandinavians. For in somewhat later days Scandinavian genealogists, when they had made the acquaintance of the Anglo-Saxon pedigrees, noted that Beow had a Scandinavian counterpart in a hero whom they called Bjar[88]. That something was known in the north of this Bjar is proved by the *Kálfsvísa*, that same catalogue of famous heroes and their horses which we have already found giving us the counterparts of Onela and Eadgils. Yet this dry reference serves to show that Bjar must once have been sufficiently famous to have a horse specially his own[89]. Whether the fourteenth century Scandinavian who made Bjar the Northern equivalent of Beow was merely guessing, we unfortunately cannot tell. Most probably he was, for there is reason to think that the hero corresponding to Beow was named, not *Bjár*, but *Byggvir*[90]: a correspondence intelligible to modern philologists as in agreement with phonetic law, but naturally not obvious to an Icelandic genealogist. But however this may be, the assumption that Beow was peculiarly the hero of Angles and Saxons seems hardly justified.

Again, since Beow is an ancestor of Woden, it was further assumed that he was an ancient god, and that in the story of his adventures we had to deal with a nature-myth of a divine deliverer who saved the people from Grendel and his mother, the personified powers of the stormy sea. It is with the name of Müllenhoff, its most enthusiastic and ablest advocate, that this "mythological theory" is particularly associated. That Grendel is fictitious no one, of course, would deny. But Müllenhoff and his school, in applying the term "mythical" to those portions of the *Beowulf* story for which no historical explanation could be found, meant that they enshrined *nature-myths*. They thought that those elements in heroic poetry which could not be referred back to actual fact must be traced to ancient stories in which were recorded the nation's belief about the sun and the gods: about storms and seasons.

The different mythological explanations of Beowulf-Beowa and Grendel have depended mainly upon hazardous etymological explanations of the hero's name. The most popular is Müllenhoff's interpretation. Beaw is the divine helper of man in his struggle with the elements. Grendel represents the stormy North Sea of early spring, flooding and destroying the habitations of men, till the god rescues them: Grendel's mother represents the depths of the ocean. But in the autumn the power of the god wanes: the dragon personifies the coming of the wild weather: the god sinks in his final struggle to safeguard the treasures of the earth for his people[91]. Others, remembering that Grendel dwells in the fen, see in him rather a demon of the sea-marsh than of the sea itself: he is the pestilential swamp[92], and the hero a wind which drives him away[93]. Or, whilst Grendel still represents the storms, his antagonist is a "Blitzheros[94]." Others, whilst hardly ranking Beowulf as a god, still see an allegory in his adventures, and Grendel must be a personification either of an inundation[95], or of the terror of the long winter nights[96], or possibly of grinding at the mill, the work of the enslaved foe[97].

Such explanations were till recently universally current: the instances given above might be increased considerably.

Sufficient allowance was not made for the influence upon heroic poetry of the simple popular folk-tale, a tale of wonder with no mythological or allegorical meaning. Now, of late years, there has been a tendency not only to recognize but even to exaggerate this influence: to regard the hero of the folk-tale as the original and essential element in heroic poetry[98]. Though this is assuredly to go too far, it is but reasonable to recognize the fairy tale element in the O.E. epic.

We have in *Beowulf* a story of giant-killing and dragon-slaying. Why should we construct a legend of the gods or a nature-myth to account for these tales? Why must Grendel or his mother represent the tempest, or the malaria, or the drear long winter nights? We know that tales of giant-killers and dragon-slayers have been current among the people of Europe for thousands of years. Is it not far more easy to regard the story of the fight between Beowulf and Grendel merely as a fairy tale, glorified into an epic[99]?

Those students who of late years have tried thus to elucidate the story of Beowulf and Grendel, by comparison with folk-tales, have one great advantage over Müllenhoff and the "mythological" school. The weak point of Müllenhoff's view was that the nature-myth of Beow, which was called in to explain the origin of the Beowulf story as we have it, was itself only an assumption, a conjectural reconstruction. But the various popular tales in which scholars have more recently tried to find parallels to *Beowulf* have this great merit, that they do indubitably exist. And as to the first step—the parallel between *Beowulf* and the *Grettis saga*—there can, fortunately, be but little hesitation.

The *Grettis saga* tells the adventures of the most famous of all Icelandic outlaws, Grettir the strong. As to the historic existence of Grettir there is no doubt: we can even date the main events of his life, in spite of chronological inconsistencies, with some precision. But between the year 1031, when he was killed, and the latter half of the thirteenth century, when his saga took form, many fictitious episodes, derived from folk-lore, had woven themselves around his name. Of these, one bears a great, if possibly accidental, likeness to the Grendel story: the second is emphatically and unmistakably the same story as that of Grendel and his mother. In the first, Grettir stops at a farm house which is haunted by Glam, a ghost of monstrous stature. Grettir awaits his attack alone, but, like Beowulf, lying down. Glam's entry and onset resemble those of Grendel: when Grettir closes with him he tries to get out. They wrestle the length of the hall, and break all before them. Grettir supports himself against anything that will give him foothold, but for all his efforts he is dragged as far as the door. There he suddenly changes his tactics, and throws his whole weight upon his adversary. The monster falls, undermost, so that Grettir is able to draw, and strike off his head; though not till Glam has laid upon Grettir a curse which drags him to his doom.

The second story—the adventure of Grettir at Sandhaugar (Sandheaps)— begins in much the same way as that of Grettir and Glam. Grettir is staying in a haunted farm, from which first the farmer himself and then a house-carl have, on two successive Yuletides, been spirited away. As before, a light burns in the room all night, and Grettir awaits the attack alone, lying down, without having put off his clothes. As before, Grettir and his assailant wrestle down the room, breaking all in their way. But this time Grettir is pulled put of the hall, and dragged to the brink of the neighbouring gorge. Here, by a final effort, he wrenches a hand free, draws, and hews off the arm of the ogress, who falls into the torrent below.

Grettir conjectures that the two missing men must have been pulled by the ogress into the gulf. This, after his experience, is surely a reasonable inference: but Stein, the priest, is unconvinced. So they go together to the river, and find the side of the ravine a sheer precipice: it is ten fathom down to the water below the fall. Grettir lets down a rope: the priest is to watch it. Then Grettir dives in: "the priest saw the soles of his feet, and then knew no more what had become of him." Grettir swims under the fall and gets into the cave, where he sees a giant sitting by a fire: the giant aims a blow at him with a weapon with a wooden handle ("such a weapon men then called a *hefti-sax*"). Grettir hews it asunder. The giant then grasps at another sword hanging on the wall of the cave, but before he can use it Grettir wounds him.

Stein, the priest, seeing the water stained with blood from this wound, concludes that Grettir is dead, and departs home, lamenting the loss of such a man. "But Grettir let little space come between his blows till the giant lay dead." Grettir finds the bones of the two dead men in the cave, and bears them away with him to convince the priest: but when he reaches the rope and shakes it, there is no reply, and he has to climb up, unaided. He leaves the bones in the church porch, for the confusion of the priest, who has to admit that he has failed to do his part faithfully.

Now if we compare this with *Beowulf*, we see that in the Icelandic story much is different: for example, in the *Grettis saga* it is the female monster who raids the habitation of men, the male who stays at home in his den. In this the *Grettis saga* probably represents a corrupt tradition: for, that the female should remain at home whilst the male searches for his prey, is a rule which holds good for devils as well as for men[100]. The change was presumably made in order to avoid the difficulty—which the *Beowulf* poet seems also to have realized—that after the male has been slain, the rout of the female is felt to be a deed of less note—something of an anti-climax[101].

The sword on the wall, also, which in the *Beowulf*-story is used by the hero, is, in the *Grettir*-story, used by the giant in his attack on the hero.

But that the two stories are somehow connected cannot be disputed. Apart from the general likeness, we have details such as the escape of the monster after the loss of an arm, the fire burning in the cave, the *hefti-sax*, a word which, like its old English equivalent (*hæft-mēce*, *Beowulf*, 1457), is found in this story only, and the strange reasoning of the watchers that the blood-stained water must necessarily be due to the hero's death[102].

Now obviously such a series of resemblances cannot be the result of an accident. Either the *Grettir*-story is derived directly or indirectly from the *Beowulf* epic, more or less as we have it, or both stories are derived from one common earlier source. The scholars who first discovered the resemblance believed that both stories were independently derived from one original[103]. This view has generally been endorsed by later investigators, but not universally[104]. And this is one of the questions which the student cannot leave open, because our view of the origin of the *Grendel*-story will have to depend largely upon the view we take as to its connection with the episode in the *Grettis saga*.

If this episode be derived from *Beowulf*, then we have an interesting literary curiosity, but nothing further. But if it is independently derived from a common source, then the episode in the *saga*, although so much later, may nevertheless contain features which have been obliterated or confused or forgotten in the *Beowulf* version. In that case the story, as given in the *Grettis saga*, would be of great weight in any attempt to reconstruct the presumed original form of the *Grendel*-story.

The evidence seems to me to support strongly the view of the majority of scholars—that the *Grettir*-episode is not derived from *Beowulf* in the form in which that poem has come down to us, but that both come from one common source.

It is certain that the story of the monster invading a dwelling of men and rendering it uninhabitable, till the adventurous deliverer arrives, did not originate with Hrothgar and Heorot. It is an ancient and widespread type of story, of which one version is localized at the Danish court. When therefore we find it existing, independently of its Danish setting, the presumption is in favour of this being a survival of the old independent story. Of course it is *conceivable* that the Hrothgar-Heorot setting might have been first added, and subsequently stripped off again so clean that no trace of it remains. But it seems going out of our way to assume this, unless we are forced to do so[105].

Again, it is certain that these stories—like all the subject matter of the Old English epic—did not originate in England, but were brought across the North Sea from the old home. And that old home was in the closest connection, so far as the passage to and fro of story went, with Scandinavian lands. Nothing could be intrinsically more probable than that a story, current in ancient Angel and carried thence to England, should also have been current in Scandinavia, and thence have been carried to Iceland.

Other stories which were current in England in the eighth century were also current in Scandinavia in the thirteenth. Yet this does not mean that the tales of Hroar and Rolf, or of Athils and Ali, were borrowed from English epic accounts of Hrothgar and Hrothulf, or Eadgils and Onela. They were part of the common inheritance—as much so as the strong verbs or the alliterative line. Why then, contrary to all analogy, should we assume a literary borrowing in the case of the *Beowulf-Grettir*-story? The compiler of the *Grettis saga* could not possibly have drawn his material from a MS of *Beowulf*[106]: he could not have made sense of a single passage. He conceivably *might* have drawn from traditions *derived* from the Old English epic. But it is difficult to see how. Long before his time these traditions had for the most part been forgotten in England itself. One of the longest lived of all, that of Offa, is heard of for the last time in England at the beginning of the thirteenth century. That a Scandinavian sagaman at the end of the century could have been in touch, in any way, with Anglo-Saxon epic tradition seems on the whole unlikely. The Scandinavian tradition of Offa, scholars are now agreed[107], was not borrowed from England, and there is no reason why we should assume such borrowing in the case of Grettir.

The probability is, then, considerable, that the *Beowulf*-story and the *Grettir*-story are independently derived from one common original.

And this probability would be confirmed to a certainty if we should find that features which have been confused and half obliterated in the O.E. story become clear when we turn to the Icelandic. This argument has lately been brought forward by Dr Lawrence in his essay on "The Haunted Mere in *Beowulf*[108]." Impressive as the account of this mere is, it does not convey any very clear picture. Grendel's home seems sometimes to be in the sea: and again it seems to be amid marshes, moors and fens, and again it is "where the mountain torrent goes down under the darkness of the cliffs—the water below the ground (i.e. beneath overhanging rocks)."

This last account agrees admirably with the landscape depicted in the *Grettis saga*, and the gorge many fathoms deep through which the stream rushes, after it has fallen over the precipice; not so the other accounts. These descriptions are best harmonized if we imagine an original version in which the monsters live, as in the *Grettis saga*, in a hole under the waterfall. This story, natural enough in a Scandinavian country, would be less intelligible as it travelled South. The Angles and Saxons, both in their old home on the Continent and their new one in England, were accustomed to a somewhat flat country, and would be more inclined to place the dwelling of outcast spirits in moor and fen than under waterfalls, of which they probably had only an elementary conception. "The giant must dwell in the fen, alone in the land[109]."

Now it is in the highest degree improbable that, after the landscape had been blurred as it is in *Beowulf*, it could have been brought out again with the distinctness it has in the *Grettis saga*. To preserve the features so clearly the *Grettir*-story can hardly be derived from *Beowulf*: it must have come down independently.

But if so, it becomes at once of prime importance. For by a comparison of *Beowulf* and *Grettir* we must form an idea of what the original story was, from which both were derived.

Another parallel, though a less striking one, has been found in the story of Orm Storolfsson, which is extant in a short saga about contemporary with that of Grettir, *Ormspáttr Stórólfssonar*[110], in two ballads from the Faroe Islands[111] and two from Sweden[112].

It is generally asserted that the *Orm*-story affords a close parallel to the episodes of Grendel and his mother. I cannot find close resemblance, and I strongly suspect that the repetition of the assertion is due to the fact that the *Orm*-story has not been very easily accessible, and has often been taken as read by the critics.

But, in any case, it has been proved that the *Orm*-tale borrows largely from other sagas, and notably from the *Grettis saga* itself[113]. Before arguing, therefore, from any parallel, it must first be shown that the feature in which Orm resembles Beowulf is not derived at second hand from the *Grettis saga*. One such feature there is, namely Orm's piety, which he certainly does not derive from Grettir. In this he with equal certainty resembles Beowulf. According to modern ideas, indeed, there is more of the Christian hero in Beowulf than in Orm.

Now Orm owes his victory to the fact, among other things, that, at the critical moment, he vows to God and the holy apostle St Peter to make a pilgrimage to Rome should he be successful. In this a parallel is seen to the fact that Beowulf is saved, not only by his coat of mail, but also by the divine interposition[114]. But is this really a parallel? Beowulf is too much of a sportsman to buy victory by making a vow when in a tight place. *Gǣð ā wyrd swā hīo sceł*[115] is the exact antithesis of Orm's pledge.

However, I have given in the Second Part the text of the *Orm*-episode, so that readers may judge for themselves the closeness or remoteness of the parallel.

The parallel between Grettir and Beowulf was noted by the Icelander Gudbrand Vigfússon upon his first reading *Beowulf* (see *Prolegomena to Sturlunga saga*, 1878, p. xlix: *Corpus Poeticum Boreale*, II, 501: *Icelandic Reader*, 1879, 404). It was elaborately worked out by Gering in *Anglia*, III, 74-87, and it is of course noticed in almost every discussion of *Beowulf*. The parallel with Orm was first noted by Schück (*Svensk Literaturhistoria*, Stockholm, 1886, *etc.*, I, 62) and independently by Bugge (*P.B.B.* XII, 58-68).

The best edition of the *Grettis saga* is the excellent one of Boer (Halle, 1900), but the opinions there expressed as to the relationship of the episodes to each other and to the Grendel story have not received the general support of scholars.

SECTION III. BOTHVAR BJARKI.

We have seen that there are in *Beowulf* two distinct elements, which never seem quite harmonized: firstly the historic background of the Danish and Geatic courts, with their chieftains, Hrothgar and Hrothulf, or Hrethel and Hygelac: and secondly the old wives' fables of struggles with ogres and dragons. In the story of Grettir, the ogre fable appears—unmistakably connected with the similar story as given in *Beowulf*, but with no faintest trace of having ever possessed any Danish heroic setting.

Turning back to the *Saga of Rolf Kraki*, we *do* find against that Danish setting a figure, that of the hero Bothvar Bjarki, bearing a very remarkable resemblance to Beowulf.

Bjarki, bent on adventure, leaves the land of the Gautar (Götar), where his brother is king, and reaches Leire, where Rolf, the king of the Danes, holds his court; [just as Beowulf, bent on adventure, leaves the land of the Geatas (Götar) where his uncle is king, and reaches Heorot, where Hrothgar and Hrothulf (Rolf) hold court].

Arrived at Leire, Bjarki takes under his protection the despised coward Hott, whom Rolf's retainers have been wont to bully. The champions at the Danish court [in *Beowulf* one of them only—Unferth] prove quarrelsome, and they assail the hero during the feast, in the *Saga* by throwing bones at him, in *Beowulf* only by bitter words. The hero in each case replies, in kind, with such effect that the enemy is silenced.

But despite the fame and splendour of the Danish court, it has long been subject to the attacks of a strange monster[116]—a winged beast whom no iron will bite [just as Grendel is immune from swords[117]]. Bjarki [like Beowulf[118]] is scornful at the inability of the Danes to defend their own home: "if one beast can lay waste the kingdom and the cattle of the king." He goes out to fight with the monster *by night*, accompanied only by Hott. He tries to draw his sword, but the sword is fast in its sheath: he tugs, the sword comes out, and he slays the beast with it. This seems a most pointless incident: taken in connection with the supposed invulnerability of the foe, it looks like the survival of some episode in which the hero was unwilling [as in Beowulf's fight with Grendel[119]] or unable [as in Beowulf's fight with Grendel's mother[120]] to slay the foe with his sword. Bjarki then compels the terrified coward Hott to drink the monster's blood. Hott forthwith becomes a valiant champion, second only to Bjarki himself. The beast is then propped up as if still alive: when it is seen next morning the king calls upon his retainers to play the man, and Bjarki tells Hott that now is the time to clear his reputation. Hott demands first the sword, Gullinhjalti, from Rolf, and with this he slays the dead beast a second time. King Rolf is not deceived by this trick; yet he rejoices that Bjarki has not only himself slain the monster, but changed the cowardly Hott into a champion; he commands that Hott shall be called Hjalti, after the sword which has been given him. We are hardly justified in demanding logic in a wild tale like this, or one might ask how Rolf was convinced of Hott's valour by what he knew to be a piece of stage management on the part of Bjarki. But, however that may be, it is remarkable that in *Beowulf* also the monster Grendel, though proof against all ordinary weapons, is smitten *when dead* by a magic sword of which the *golden hilt*[121] is specially mentioned.

In addition to the undeniable similarity of the stories of these heroes, a certain similarity of name has been claimed. That *Bjarki* is not etymologically connected with *Bēowulf* or *Bēow* is clear: but if we are to accept the identification of Beowulf and Beow, remembering that the Scandinavian equivalent of the latter is said to be *Bjár*, the resemblance to *Bjarki* is obvious. Similarity of sound might have caused one name to be substituted for another[122]. This argument obviously depends upon the identification *Bēow* = *Bjár*, which is extremely doubtful: it will be argued below that it is more likely that *Bēow* = *Byggvir*[123].

But force remains in the argument that the name Bjarki (little bear) is very appropriate to a hero like the Beowulf of our epic, who crushes or hugs his foe to death instead of using his sword; even if we do not accept explanations which would interpret the name "Beowulf" itself as a synonym for "Bear."

It is scarcely to be wondered at, then, that most critics have seen in Bjarki a Scandinavian parallel to Beowulf. But serious difficulties remain. There is in the Scandinavian story a mass of detail quite unparalleled in *Beowulf*, which overshadows the resemblances. Bjarki's friendship, for example, with the coward Hott or Hjalti has no counterpart in *Beowulf*. And Bjarki becomes a retainer of King Rolf and dies in his service, whilst Beowulf never comes into direct contact with Hrothulf at all; the poet seems to avoid naming them together. Still, it is quite intelligible that the story should have developed on different lines in Scandinavia from those which it followed in England, till the new growths overshadowed the original resemblance, without obliterating it. After nearly a thousand years of independent development discrepancies must be expected. It would not be a reasonable objection to the identity of *Gullinhjalti* with *Gyldenhilt*, that the word *hilt* had grown to have a rather different meaning in Norse and in English; subsequent developments do not invalidate an original resemblance if the points of contact are really there.

But, allowing for this independent growth in Scandinavia, we should naturally expect that the further back we traced the story the greater the resemblance would become.

This brings us to the second, serious difficulty: that, when we turn from the *Saga of Rolf Kraki*—belonging in its present form perhaps to the early fifteenth century—to the pages of Saxo Grammaticus, who tells the same tale more than two centuries earlier, the resemblance, instead of becoming stronger, almost vanishes. Nothing is said of Bjarki coming from Gautland, or indeed of his being a stranger at the Danish court: nothing is said of the monster having paid previous visits, visits repeated till king Rolf, like Hrothgar, has to give up all attempt at resistance, and submit to its depredations. The monster, instead of being a troll, like Grendel, becomes a commonplace bear. All Saxo tells us is that "He [Biarco, i.e. Bjarki] met a great bear in a thicket and slew it with a spear, and bade his comrade Ialto [i.e. Hjalti] place his lips to the beast and drink its blood as it flowed, that he might become stronger."

Hence the Danish scholar, Axel Olrik, in the best and most elaborate discussion of Bjarki and all about him, has roundly denied any connection between his hero and Beowulf. He is astonished at the slenderness of the evidence upon which previous students have argued for relationship. "Neither Beowulf's wrestling match in the hall, nor in the fen, nor his struggle with the firedrake has any real identity, but when we take a little of them all we can get a kind of similarity with the latest and worst form of the Bjarki saga[124]." The development of Saxo's bear into a winged monster, "the worst of trolls," Olrik regards as simply in accordance with the usual heightening, in later Icelandic, of these early stories of struggles with beasts, and of this he gives a parallel instance.

Some Icelandic ballads on Bjarki (the *Bjarka rímur*), which were first printed in 1904, were claimed by Olrik as supporting his contention. These ballads belong to about the year 1400. Yet, though they are thus in date and dialect closely allied to the *Saga of Rolf Kraki* and remote from Saxo Grammaticus, they are so far from supporting the tradition of the *Saga* with regard to the monster slain, that they represent the foe first as a man-eating she-wolf, which is slain by Bjarki, then as a grey bear [as in Saxo], which is slain by Hjalti after he has been compelled to drink the blood of the she-wolf. We must therefore give up the winged beast as mere later elaboration; for if the Bjarki ballads in a point like this support Saxo, as against the *Saga* which is so closely connected with them by its date and Icelandic tongue, we must admit Saxo's version here to represent, beyond dispute, the genuine tradition.

Accordingly the attempt which has been made to connect Bjarki's winged monster with Beowulf's winged dragon goes overboard at once. But such an attempt ought never to have been made at all. The parallel is between Bjarki and the Beowulf-Grendel episode, not between Bjarki and the Beowulf-dragon episode, which ought to be left out of consideration. And the monstrous bear and the wolf of the *Rímur* are not so dissimilar from Grendel, with his bear-like hug, and Grendel's mother, the 'sea-wolf[125].'

The likeness between Beowulf and Bjarki lies, not in the wingedness or otherwise of the monsters they overthrow, but in the similarity of the position—in the situation which places the most famous court of the North, and its illustrious king, at the mercy of a ravaging foe, till a chance stranger from Gautland brings deliverance. And here the *Rímur* support, not Saxo, but the *Saga*, though in an outworn and faded way. In the *Rímur* Bjarki is a stranger come from abroad: the bear has made previous attacks upon the king's folds.

Thus, whilst we grant the wings of the beast to be a later elaboration, it does not in the least follow that other features in which the *Saga* differs from Saxo—the advent of Bjarki from Gautland, for instance—are also later elaboration.

And we must be careful not to attach too much weight to the account of Saxo merely because it is earlier in date than that of the *Saga*. The presumption is, of course, that the earlier form will be the more original: but just as a late manuscript will often preserve, amidst its corruptions, features which are lost in much earlier manuscripts, so will a tradition. Saxo's accounts are often imperfect[126]. And in this particular instance, there is a want of coherency and intelligibility in Saxo's account, which in itself affords a strong presumption that it *is* imperfect.

What Saxo tells us is this:

At which banquet, when the champions were rioting with every kind of wantonness, and flinging knuckle-bones at a certain Ialto [Hjalti] from all sides, it happened that his messmate Biarco [Bjarki] through the bad aim of the thrower received a severe blow on the head. But Biarco, equally annoyed by the injury and the insult, sent the bone back to the thrower, so that he twisted the front of his head to the back and the back to the front, punishing the cross-grain of the man's temper by turning his face round about.

But who were this "certain Hjalti" and Bjarki? There seems to be something missing in the story. The explanation [which Saxo does not give us, but the *Saga* does] that Bjarki has come from afar and taken the despised Hott-Hjalti under his protection, seems to be necessary. Why was Hjalti chosen as the victim, at whom missiles were to be discharged? Obviously [though Saxo does not tell us so], because he was the butt of the mess. And if Bjarki had been one of the mess for many hours, his messmates would have known him too well to throw knuckle-bones either at him or his friend. This is largely a matter of personal feeling, but Saxo's account seems to me pointless, till it is supplemented from the *Saga*[127].

And there is one further piece of evidence which seems to clinch the whole matter finally, though its importance has been curiously overlooked, by Panzer and Lawrence in their arguments for the identification, and by Olrik in his arguments to the contrary.

We have seen above how Beowulf "became a friend" to Eadgils, helping him in his expedition against King Onela of Sweden, and avenging, in "chill raids fraught with woe," *cealdum cearsīðum*, the wrongs which Onela had inflicted upon the Geatas. We saw, too, that this expedition was remembered in Scandinavian tradition. "They had a battle on the ice of Lake Wener; there King Ali fell, and Athils had the victory. Concerning this battle there is much said in the *Skjoldunga saga*." The *Skjoldunga saga* is lost, but the Latin extracts from it give some information about this battle[128]. Further, an account of it *is* preserved in the *Bjarka rímur*, probably derived from the lost *Skjoldunga saga*. And the *Bjarka rímur* expressly mention Bjarki as helping Athils in this battle against Ali on the ice of Lake Wener[129].

Olrik does not seem to allow for this at all, though of course aware of it. The other parallels between Bjarki and Beowulf he believes to be mere coincidence. But is this likely?

To recapitulate: In old English tradition a hero comes from the land of the Geatas to the royal court of Denmark, where Hrothgar and Hrothulf hold sway. This hero is received in none too friendly wise by one of the retainers, but puts his foe to shame, is warmly welcomed by the king, and slays by night a monster which has been attacking the Danish capital and against which the warriors of that court have been helpless. The monster is proof against all swords, yet its dead body is mutilated by a sword with a golden hilt. Subsequently this same hero helps King Eadgils of Sweden to overthrow Onela.

We find precisely the same situation in Icelandic tradition some seven centuries later, except that not Hrothgar and Hrothulf, but Hrothulf (Rolf) alone is represented as ruling the Danes, and the sword with the golden hilt has become a sword named "Golden-hilt." It is *conceivable* for a situation to have been reconstructed in this way by mere accident, just as it is conceivable that one player may have the eight or nine best trumps dealt him. But it does not seem advisable to base one's calculations, as Olrik does, upon such an accident happening.

The parallel of Bjarki and Beowulf seems to have been first noted by Gisli Brynjulfsson (*Antiquarisk Tidsskrift*, 1852-3, p. 130). It has been often discussed by Sarrazin (*Beowulf Studien*, 13 *etc.*, 47: *Anglia*, IX, 195 *etc.*: *Engl. Stud.* XVI, 79 *etc.*, XXIII, 242 *etc.*, XXXV, 19 *etc.*). Sarrazin's over-elaborated parallels form a broad target for doubters: it must be remembered that a case, though it may be discredited, is not invalidated by exaggeration. The problem is of course noted in the Beowulf studies of Müllenhoff (55), Bugge (*P.B.B.* XII, 55) and Boer (*Die Beowulfsage*, II, in *Arkiv f. nord. filol.* XIX, 44 *etc.*) and discussed at length and convincingly by Panzer (364-386) and Lawrence (*Pub. Mod. Lang. Assoc. Amer.* XXIV, 1909, 222 *etc.*). The usual view which accepts some relationship is endorsed by all these scholars, as it is by Finnur Jónsson in his edition of the *Hrólfs Saga Kraka og Bjarkarímur* (København, 1904, p. xxii).

Ten Brink (185 *etc.*) denied any original connection, on the ground of the dissimilarity between *Beowulf* and the story given by Saxo. Any resemblances between *Beowulf* and the *Hrólfs Saga* he attributed to the influence of the English *Beowulf*-story upon the *Saga*.

For Olrik's emphatic denial of any connection at all, see *Danmarks Heltedigtning*, I, 134 *etc.* (This seems to have influenced Brandl, who expresses some doubt in *Pauls Grdr.* (2) II. 1. 993.) For arguments to the contrary, see Heusler in *A.f.d.A.* XXX, 32, and especially Panzer and Lawrence as above.

The parallel of *Gullinhjalti* and *gyldenhilt* was first noted tentatively by Kluge (*Engl. Stud.* XXII, 145).

SECTION IV. PARALLELS FROM FOLKLORE.

Hitherto we have been dealing with parallels to the Grendel story in written literature: but a further series of parallels, although much more remote, is to be found in that vast store of old wives' tales which no one till the nineteenth century took the trouble to write down systematically, but which certainly go back to a very ancient period. One particular tale, that of the Bear's Son[130] (extant in many forms), has been instanced as showing a resemblance to the *Beowulf*-story. In this tale the hero, a young man of extraordinary strength, (1) sets out on his adventures, associating with himself various companions; (2) makes resistance in a house against a supernatural being, which his fellows have in vain striven to withstand, and succeeds in mishandling or mutilating him. (3) By the blood-stained track of this creature, or guided by him in some other manner, the hero finds his way to a spring, or hole in the earth, (4) is lowered down by a cord and (5) overcomes in the underworld different supernatural foes, amongst whom is often included his former foe, or very rarely the mother of that foe: victory can often only be gained by the use of a magic sword which the hero finds below. (6) The hero is left treacherously in the lurch by his companions, whose duty it was to have drawn him up...

Now it may be objected, with truth, that this is not like the *Beowulf*-story, or even particularly like the *Grettir*-story. But the question is not merely whether it resembles these stories as we possess them, but whether it resembles the story which must have been the common origin of both. And we have only to try to reconstruct from *Beowulf* and from the *Grettis saga* a tale which can have been the common original of both, to see that it must be something extraordinarily like the folk-tale outlined above.

For example, it is true that the departure of the Danes homeward because they believe that Beowulf has met his death in the water below, bears only the remotest resemblance to the deliberate treachery which the companions in the folk-tale mete out to the hero. But when we compare the *Grettir*-story, we see there that a real breach of trust is involved, for there the priest Stein leaves the hero in the lurch, and abandons the rope by which he should have drawn Grettir up. This can hardly be an innovation on the part of the composer of the *Grettis saga*, for he is quite well disposed towards Stein, and has no motive for wantonly attributing treachery to him. The innovation presumably lies in the *Beowulf*-story, where Hrothgar and his court are depicted in such a friendly spirit that no disreputable act can be attributed to them, and consequently Hrothgar's departure home must not be allowed in any way to imperil or inconvenience the hero. A comparison of the *Beowulf*-story with the *Grettir*-story leads then to the conclusion that in the oldest version those who remained above when the hero plunged below *were* guilty of some measure of disloyalty in ceasing to watch for him. In other words we see that the further we track the *Beowulf*-story back, the more it comes to resemble the folk-tale.

And our belief that there is some connection between the folk-tale and the original of *Beowulf* must be strengthened when we find that, by a comparison of the folk-tale, we are able to explain features in *Beowulf* which strike us as difficult and even absurd: precisely as when we turn to a study of Shakespeare's sources we often find the explanation of things that puzzle us: we see that the poet is dealing with an unmanageable source, which he cannot make quite plausible. For instance: when Grendel enters Heorot he kills and eats the first of Beowulf's retinue whom he finds: no one tries to prevent him. The only explanation which the poet has to offer is that the retinue are all asleep[131]—strange somnolence on the part of men who are awaiting a hostile attack, which they expect will be fatal to them all[132]. And Beowulf at any rate is not asleep. Yet he calmly watches whilst his henchman is both killed and eaten: and apparently, but for the accident that the monster next tackles Beowulf himself, he would have allowed his whole bodyguard to be devoured one after another.

But if we suppose the story to be derived from the folk-tale, we have an explanation. For in the folk-tale, the companions and the hero await the foe singly, in succession: the turn of the hero comes last, after all his companions have been put to shame. But Beowulf, who is represented as having specially voyaged to Heorot in order to purge it, cannot leave the defence of the hall for the first night to one of his comrades. Hence the discomfiture of the comrade and the single-handed success of the hero have to be represented as simultaneous. The result is incongruous: Beowulf *has* to look on whilst his comrade is killed.

Again, both Beowulf and Grettir plunge in the water with a sword, and with the deliberate object of shedding the monster's blood. Why then should the watchers on the cliff above assume that the blood-stained water must necessarily signify the *hero's* death, and depart home? Why did it never occur to them that this deluge of blood might much more suitably proceed from the monster?

But we can understand this unreason if we suppose that the story-teller had to start from the deliberate and treacherous departure of the companions, whilst at the same time it was not to his purpose to represent the companions as treacherous. In that case some excuse *must* be found for them: and the blood-stained water was the nearest at hand[133].

Again, quite independently of the folk-tale, many *Beowulf* scholars have come to the conclusion that in the original version of the story the hero did not wait for a second attack from the mother of the monster he had slain, but rather, from a natural and laudable desire to complete his task, followed the monster's tracks to the mere, and finished him and his mother below. Many traits have survived which may conceivably point to an original version of the story in which Beowulf (or the figure corresponding to him) at once plunged down in order to combat the foe corresponding to Grendel. There are unsatisfactory features in the story as it stands. For why, it might be urged, should the wrenching off of an arm have been fatal to so tough a monster? And why, it has often been asked, is the adversary under the water sometimes male, sometimes female? And why is it apparently the blood of Grendel, not of his mother, which discolours the water and burns up the sword, and the head of Grendel, not of his mother, which is brought home in triumph? These arguments may not carry much weight, but at any rate when we turn to the folk-tale we find that the adventure beneath the earth *is* the natural following up of the adventure in the house, not the result of any renewed attack.

In addition, there are many striking coincidences between individual versions or groups of the folk-tale on the one hand and the *Beowulf-Grettir* story on the other: yet it is very difficult to know what value should be attached to these parallels, since there are many features of popular story which float around and attach themselves to this or that tale without any original connection, so that it is easy for the same trait to recur in *Beowulf* and in a group of folk-tales, without this proving that the stories as a whole are connected[134].

The hero of the Bear's son folk-tale is often in his youth unmanageable or lazy. This is also emphasized in the stories both of Grettir and of Orm: and though such a feature was uncongenial to the courtly tone of *Beowulf*, which sought to depict the hero as a model prince, yet it *is* there[135], even though only alluded to incidentally, and elsewhere ignored or even denied[136].

Again, the hero of the folk-tale is very frequently (but not necessarily) either descended from a bear, nourished by a bear, or has some ursine characteristic. We see this recurring in certain traits of Beowulf such as his bear-like method of hugging his adversary to death. Here again the courtly poet has not emphasized his hero's wildness[137].

Again, there are some extraordinary coincidences in names, between the *Beowulf-Grettir* story and the folk-tale. These are not found in *Beowulf* itself, but only in the stories of Grettir and Orm. Yet, as the *Grettir*-episode is presumably derived from the same original as the *Beowulf*-episode, any *original* connection between it and the folk-tale involves such connection for *Beowulf* also. We have seen that in *Grettis saga* the priest Stein, as the unfaithful guardian of the rope which is to draw up the hero, seems to represent the faithless companions of the folktale. There is really no other way of accounting for him, for except on this supposition he is quite otiose and unnecessary to the *Grettir*-story: the saga-man has no use for him. And his name confirms this explanation, for in the folk-tale one of the three faithless companions of the hero is called the Stone-cleaver, *Steinhauer, Stenkløver*, or even, in one Scandinavian version, simply *Stein*[138].

Again, the struggle in the *Grettis saga* is localized at Sandhaugar in Barthardal in Northern Iceland. Yet it is difficult to say why the saga-teller located the story there. The scenery, with the neighbouring river and mighty waterfall, is fully described: but students of Icelandic topography assert that the neighbourhood does *not* at all lend itself to this description[139]. When we turn to the story of Orm we find it localized on the island Sandey. We are forced to the conclusion that the name belongs to the story, and that in some early version this was localized at a place called Sandhaug, perhaps at one of the numerous places in Norway of that name. Now turning to one of the Scandinavian versions of the folk-tale, we find that the descent into the earth and the consequent struggle is localized in *en stor sandhaug*[140].

On the other hand, it must be remembered that if a collection is made of some two hundred folk-tales, it is bound to contain, in addition to the essential kernel of common tradition, a vast amount of that floating material which tends to associate itself with this or that hero of story. Individual versions or groups of versions of the tale may contain features which occur also in the *Grendel*-story, without that being any evidence for primitive connection. Thus we are told how Grendel forces open the door of Heorot. In a Sicilian version of the folk-tale the doors spring open of themselves as the foe appears. This has been claimed as a parallel. But, as a sceptic has observed, the extraordinary thing is that of so slight a similarity (if it is entitled to be called a similarity) we should find only one example out of two hundred, and have to go to Sicily for that[141].

The parallel between the *Beowulf*-story and the "Bear's son" folk-tale had been noted by Laistner (*Das Rätsel der Sphinx*, Berlin, 1889, II, 22 *etc.*): but the prevalent belief that the *Beowulf*-story was a nature-myth seems to have prevented further investigation on these lines till Panzer independently (p. 254) undertook his monumental work.

Yet there are other features in the folk-tale which are entirely unrepresented in the *Beowulf-Grettir* story. The hero of the folk-tale rescues captive princesses in the underworld (it is because they wish to rob him of this prize that his companions leave him below); he is saved by some miraculous helper, and finally, after adopting a disguise, puts his treacherous comrades to shame and weds the youngest princess. None of these elements[142] are to be found in the stories of Beowulf, Grettir, Orm or Bjarki, yet they are essential to the fairy tale[143].

So that to speak of *Beowulf* as a version of the fairy tale is undoubtedly going too far. All we can say is that some early story-teller took, from folk-tale, those elements which suited his purpose, and that a tale, containing many leading features found in the "Bear's son" story, but omitting many of the leading motives of that story, came to be told of Beowulf and of Grettir[144].

SECTION V. SCEF AND SCYLD.

Our poem begins with an account of the might, and of the funeral, of Scyld Scefing, the ancestor of that Danish royal house which is to play so large a part in the story. After Scyld's death his retainers, following the command he had given them, placed their beloved prince in the bosom of a ship, surrounded by many treasures brought from distant lands, by weapons of battle and weeds of war, swords and byrnies. Also they placed a golden banner high over his head, and let the sea bear him away, with soul sorrowful and downcast. Men could not say for a truth, not the wisest of councillors, who received that burden.

Now there is much in this that can be paralleled both from the literature and from the archaeological remains of the North. Abundant traces have been found, either of the burial or of the burning of a chief within a ship. And we are told by different authorities of two ancient Swedish kings who, sorely wounded, and unwilling to die in their beds, had themselves placed upon ships, surrounded by weapons and the bodies of the slain. The funeral pyre was then lighted on the vessel, and the ship sent blazing out to sea. Similarly the dead body of Baldr was put upon his ship, and burnt.

Haki konungr fekk svá stór sár, at hann sá, at hans lífdagar mundu eigi langir verða; þá lét hann taka skeið, er hann átti, ok lét hlaða dauðum mǫnnum, ok vápnum, lét þá flytja út til hafs ok leggja stýri í lag ok draga upp segl, en leggja eld í tyrvið ok gera bál á skipinu; veðr stóð af landi; Haki var þá at kominn dauða eða dauðr, er hann var lagiðr á bálit; siglði skipit síðan loganda út í haf, ok var þetta allfrægt lengi síðan.

(King Haki was so sore wounded that he saw that his days could not be long. Then he had a warship of his taken, and loaded with dead men and weapons, had it carried out to sea, the rudder shipped, the sail drawn up, the fir-tree wood set alight, and a bale-fire made on the ship. The wind blew from the land. Haki was dead or nearly dead, when he was placed on the pyre. Then the ship sailed blazing out to sea; and that was widely famous for a long time after.)

Ynglinga Saga, Kap. 23, in *Heimskringla*, udg. af Finnur Jónsson, København, 1893, vol. I, p. 43.

The *Skjoldunga Saga* gives a story which is obviously connected with this. King Sigurd Ring in his old age asked in marriage the lady Alfsola; but her brothers scorned to give her to an aged man. War followed; and the brothers, knowing that they could not withstand the hosts of Sigurd, poisoned their sister before marching against him. In the battle the brothers were slain, and Sigurd badly wounded.

Qui, Alfsola funere allato, magnam navim mortuorum cadaveribus oneratam solus vivorum conscendit, seque et mortuam Alfsolam in puppi collocans navim pice, bitumine et sulphure incendi jubet: atque sublatis velis in altum, validis a continente impellentibus ventis, proram dirigit, simulque manus sibi violentas intulit; sese ... more majorum suorum regali pompa Odinum regem (id est inferos) invisere malle, quam inertis senectutis infirmitatem perpeti....

Skjoldungasaga i Arngrim Jónssons udtog, udgiven af Axel Olrik, Kjøbenhavn, 1894, Cap. XXVII, p. 50 [132].

So with the death of Baldr.

En æsirnir tóku lík Baldrs ok fluttu til sævar. Hringhorni hét skip Baldrs; hann var allra skipa mestr, hann vildu goðin framm setja ok gera þar á bálfǫr Baldrs ... þá var borit út á skipit lík Baldrs,... Oðinn lagði á bálit gullhring þann, er Draupnir heitir ... hestr Baldrs var leiddr á bálit með ǫllu reiði.

(But the gods took the body of Baldr and carried it to the sea-shore. Baldr's ship was named Hringhorni: it was the greatest of all ships and the gods sought to launch it, and to build the pyre of Baldr on it.... Then was the body of Baldr borne out on to the ship.... Odin laid on the pyre the gold ring named Draupnir ... and Baldr's horse with all his trappings was placed on the pyre.)

Snorra Edda: Gylfaginning, 48; udg. af Finnur Jónsson, København, 1900.

We are justified in rendering *setja skip fram* by "launch": Olrik (*Heltedigtning,* I, 250) regards Baldr's funeral as a case of the burning of a body in a ship on land. But it seems to me, as to Mr Chadwick (*Origin,* 287), that the natural meaning is that the ship was launched in the sea.

But the case of Scyld is not exactly parallel to these. The ship which conveyed Scyld out to sea was *not* set alight. And the words of the poet, though dark, seem to imply that it was intended to come to land somewhere: "None could say who received that freight."

Further, Scyld not merely departed over the waves—he had in the first instance come over them: "Not with less treasure did they adorn him," says the poet, speaking of the funeral rites, "than did those who at the beginning sent him forth alone over the waves, being yet a child."

Scyld Scefing then, like Tennyson's Arthur, comes from the unknown and departs back to it.

The story of the mysterious coming over the water was not confined to Scyld. It meets us in connection with King Scef, who was regarded, at any rate from the time of Alfred, and possibly much earlier, as the remotest ancestor of the Wessex kings. Ethelwerd, a member of the West Saxon royal house, who compiled a bombastic Latin chronicle towards the end of the tenth century, traces back the pedigree of the kings of Wessex to Scyld *and his father Scef.* "This Scef," he says, "came to land on a swift boat, surrounded by arms, in an island of the ocean called Scani, when a very young child. He was unknown to the people of that land, but was adopted by them as if of their kin, well cared for, and afterwards elected king[145]." Note here, firstly, that the story is told, not of Scyld Scefing, but of Scef, father of Scyld. Secondly, that although Ethelwerd is speaking of the ancestor of the West Saxon royal house, he makes him come to land and rule, not in the ancient homeland of continental Angeln, but in the "island of Scani," which signifies what is now the south of Sweden, and perhaps also the Danish islands[146]—that same land of *Scedenig* which is mentioned in *Beowulf* as the realm of Scyld. The tone of the narrative is, so far as we can judge from Ethelwerd's dry summary, entirely warlike: Scef is surrounded by weapons.

In the twelfth century the story is again told by William of Malmesbury. "Sceldius was the son of Sceaf. He, they say, was carried as a small boy in a boat without any oarsman to a certain isle of Germany called Scandza, concerning which Jordanes, the historian of the Goths, speaks. He was sleeping, and a handful of corn was placed at his head, from which he was called 'Sheaf.' He was regarded as a wonder by the folk of that country and carefully nurtured; when grown up he ruled in a town then called Slaswic, and now Haithebi—that region is called ancient Anglia[147]."

William of Malmesbury was, of course, aware of Ethelwerd's account, and may have been influenced by it. Some of his variations may be his own invention. The substitution of the classical form *Scandza* for Ethelwerd's *Scani* is simply a change from popular to learned nomenclature, and enables the historian to show that he has read something of Jordanes. The alteration by which Malmesbury makes Sceaf, when grown up, rule at Schleswig in ancient Angel, may again be his own work—a variant added in order to make Sceaf look more at home in an Anglo-Saxon pedigree.

But William of Malmesbury was, as we shall see later, prone to incorporate current ballads into his history, and after allowing for what he may have derived from Ethelwerd, and what he may have invented, there can be no doubt that many of the additional details which he gives are genuine popular poetry. Indeed, whilst the story of Scyld's *funeral* is very impressive in *Beowulf*, it is in William's narrative that the story of the child coming over the sea first becomes poetic.

Now since even the English historians connected this tale with the Danish territory of *Scani, Scandza*, we should expect to find it again on turning to the records of the Danish royal house. And we do find there, generally at the head of the pedigree[148], a hero—Skjold—whose name corresponds, and whose relationship to the later Danish kings shows him to be the same as the *Scyld Scefing* of *Beowulf*. But neither Saxo Grammaticus, nor any other Danish historian, knows anything of Skjold having come in his youth or returned in his death over the ocean.

How are we to harmonize these accounts?

Beowulf and Ethelwerd agree in representing the hero as "surrounded by arms"; William of Malmesbury mentions only the sheaf; the difference is weighty, for presumably the spoils which the hero brings with him from the unknown, or takes back thither, are in harmony with his career. *Beowulf* and Ethelwerd seem to show the warrior king, William of Malmesbury seems rather to be telling the story of a semi-divine foundling, who introduces the tillage of the earth[149].

In *Beowulf* the child is Scyld Scefing, in Ethelwerd and William of Malmesbury he is Sceaf, father of Scyld.

Beowulf, Ethelwerd and William of Malmesbury agree in connecting the story with *Scedenig, Scani* or *Scandza*, yet the two historians and the *Anglo-Saxon Chronicle* all make Sceaf the ancestor of the West Saxon house. Yet we have no evidence that the English were regarded as having come from Scandinavia.

The last problem admits of easy solution. In heathen times the English traced the pedigree of most of their kings to Woden, and stopped there. For higher than that they could not go. But a Christian poet or genealogist, who had no belief in Woden as a god, would regard the All Father as a man—a mere man who, by magic powers, had made the heathen believe he was a god. To such a Christian pedigree-maker Woden would convey no idea of finality; he would feel no difficulty in giving this human Woden any number of ancestors. Wishing to glorify the pedigree of his king, he would add any other distinguished and authentic genealogies, and the obvious place for these would be at the end of the line, i.e., above Woden. Hence we have in some quite early (not West Saxon) pedigrees, five names given as ancestors of Woden. These five names end in Geat or Geata, who was apparently regarded as a god, and was possibly Woden under another name[150]. Somewhat later, in the *Anglo-Saxon Chronicle*, under the year 855, we have a long version of the West Saxon pedigree with yet nine further names above Geat, ending in Sceaf. Sceaf is described as a son of Noah, and so the pedigree is carried back to Adam, 25 generations in all beyond Woden[151].

But it is rash to assume with Müllenhoff that, because Sceaf comes at the head[152] of this English pedigree, Sceaf was therefore essentially an English hero. *All* these later stages above Woden look like the ornate additions of a later compiler. Some of the figures, Finn, Sceldwa, Heremod, Sceaf himself, we have reason to identify with the primitive heroes of other nations.

The genealogist who finally made Sceaf into a son born to Noah in the ark, and then carried the pedigree nine stages further back through Noah to Adam, merely made the last of a series of accretions. It does not follow that, because he made them ancestors of the English king, this compiler regarded Noah, Enoch and Adam as Englishmen. Neither need he have so regarded Sceaf or Scyld[153] or Beaw. In fact—and this has constantly been overlooked—the authority for Sceaf, Scyld and Beaw as Anglo-Saxon heroes is but little stronger than the authority for Noah and Adam in that capacity. No manuscript exists which stops at Scyld or Sceaf. There is no version which goes beyond Geat except that which goes up to Adam. Scyld, Beaw, Sceaf, Noah and Adam as heroes of English mythology are all alike doubtful.

We must be careful, however, to define what we mean when we regard these stages of the pedigree as doubtful. They are doubtful in so far as they are represented as standing above Woden in the Anglo-Saxon pedigree, because it is incredible that, in primitive and heathen times, Woden was credited with a dozen or more forefathers. The *position* of these names in the pedigree is therefore doubtful. But it is only their connection with the West Saxon house that is unauthentic. It does not follow that the names are, *per se*, unauthentic. On the contrary, it is because the genealogist had such implicit belief in the authenticity of the generations from Noah to Adam that he could not rest satisfied with his West Saxon pedigree till he had incorporated these names. They are not West Saxon, but they are part of a tradition much more ancient than any pedigree of the West Saxon kings. And the argument which applies to the layer of Hebrew names between Noah and Adam applies equally to the layer of Germanic names between Woden and Sceaf. From whatever branch of the Germanic race the genealogist may have taken them, the fact that he placed them where he did in the pedigree is a proof of his veneration for them. But we must not without evidence claim them as West Saxon or Anglo-Saxon: we must not be surprised if evidence points to some of them being connected with other nations—as Heremod, for example, with the Danes[154].

More difficult are the other problems. William of Malmesbury tells the story of Sceaf, with the attributes of a culture-hero: *Beowulf*, four centuries earlier, tells it of Scyld, a warrior hero: Ethelwerd tells it of Sceaf, but gives him the warrior attributes of Scyld[155] instead of the sheaf of corn.

The earlier scholars mostly agreed[156] in regarding Malmesbury's attribution of the story to Sceaf as the original and correct version of the story, in spite of its late date. As a representative of these early scholars we may take Müllenhoff[157]. Müllenhoff's love of mythological interpretation found ample scope in the story of the child with the sheaf, which he, with considerable reason, regarded as a "culture-myth." Müllenhoff believed the carrying over of the attributes of a god to a line of his supposed descendants to be a common feature of myth—the descendants representing the god under another name. In accordance with this view, Scyld could be explained as an "hypostasis" of his father or forefather Sceaf, as a figure further explaining him and representing him, so that in the end the tale of the boat arrival came to be told, in *Beowulf*, of Scyld instead of Sceaf.

Recent years have seen a revolt against most of Müllenhoff's theories. The view that the story originally belonged to Sceaf has come to be regarded with a certain amount of impatience as "out of date." Even so fine a scholar as Dr Lawrence has expressed this impatience:

"That the graceful story of the boy sailing in an open boat to the land of his future people was told originally of Sceaf ... needs no detailed refutation at the present day.

"The attachment of the motive to Sceaf must be, as an examination of the sources shows, a later development[158]."

Accordingly the view of recent scholars has been this: That the story belongs essentially to Scyld. That, as the hero of the boat story is obviously of unknown parentage, we must interpret *Scefing* not as "son of Sceaf" but as "with the sheaf" (in itself a quite possible explanation). That this stage of the story is preserved in *Beowulf*. That subsequently *Scyld Scefing*, standing at the head of the pedigree, came to be misunderstood as "Scyld, son of Sceaf". That consequently the story, which must be told of the earlier ancestor, was thus transferred from Scyld to his supposed father Sceaf—the version which is found in Ethelwerd and William of Malmesbury.

One apparent advantage of this theory is that the oldest version, that of *Beowulf*, is accepted as the correct and original one, and the much later versions of the historians Ethelwerd and William of Malmesbury are regarded as subsequent corruptions. This on the surface seems eminently reasonable. But let us look closer. *Scyld Scefing* in *Beowulf* is to be interpreted "Scyld with the Sheaf." But *Beowulf* nowhere mentions the sheaf as part of Scyld's equipment. On the contrary, we gather that the hero is connected rather with prowess in war. It is the same in Ethelwerd. It is not till William of Malmesbury that the sheaf comes into the story. So that the interpretation of *Scefing* as "with the sheaf" assumes the accuracy of William of Malmesbury's story even in a point where it receives no support from the *Beowulf* version. In other words this theory does the very thing to avoid doing which it was called into being[159].

Besides this, there are two fundamental objections to the theory that Sceaf is a late creation, a figure formed from the misunderstanding of the epithet *Scefing* applied to *Scyld*. One portion of the poem of *Widsith* consists of a catalogue of ancient kings, and among these occurs *Sceafa*, ruling the Langobards. Now portions of *Widsith* are very ancient, and this catalogue in which Sceafa occurs is almost certainly appreciably older than *Beowulf* itself.

Secondly, the story of the wonderful foundling who comes over the sea from the unknown and founds a royal line, must *ex hypothesi* be told of the first in the line, and we have seen that it is Sceaf, not Scyld, who comes at the head of the Teutonic names in the genealogy in the *Anglo-Saxon Chronicle*.

Now we can date this genealogy fairly exactly. It occurs under the year 855, and seems to have been drawn up at the court of King Æthelwulf. In any case it cannot be later than the latter part of Alfred's reign. This takes us back to a period when the old English epic was still widely popular. A genealogist at Alfred's court must have known much about Old English story.

These facts are simply not consistent with the belief that Sceaf is a late creation, a figure formed from a misunderstanding of the epithet *Scefing*, applied to Scyld[160].

To arrive at any definite conclusion is difficult. But the following may be hazarded.

It may be taken as proved that the Scyld or Sceldwa of the genealogists is identical with the Scyld Scefing of *Beowulf*. For Sceldwa according to the genealogy is also ultimately a *Sceafing*, and is the father of Beow; Scyld is *Scefing* and is father of Beowulf[161].

It is equally clear that the Scyld Scefing of *Beowulf* is identical with the Skjold of the Danish genealogists and historians. For Scyld and Skjold are both represented as the founder and head of the Danish royal house of Scyldingas or Skjoldungar, and as reigning in the same district. Here, however, the resemblance ceases. *Beowulf* tells us of Scyld's marvellous coming and departure. The only Danish authority who tells us much of Skjold is Saxo Grammaticus, who records how as a boy Skjold wrestled successfully with a bear and overcame champions, and how later he annulled unrighteous laws, and distinguished himself by generosity to his court. But the Danish and English accounts have nothing specifically in common, though the type they portray is the same—that of a king from his youth beloved by his retainers and feared by neighbouring peoples, whom he subdues and makes tributary. It looks rather as if the oldest traditions had had little to say about this hero beyond the typical things which might be said of any great king; so that Danes and English had each supplied the deficiency in their own way.

Now this is exactly what we should expect. For Scyld-Skjold is hardly a personality: he is a figure evolved out of the name *Scyldingas*, *Skjoldungar*, which is an old epic title for the Danes. Of this we may be fairly certain: the Scyldingas did not get their name because they were really descended from Scyld, but Scyld was created in order to provide an eponymous father to the Scyldingas[162]. In just the same way tradition also evolved a hero Dan, from whom the Danes were supposed to have their name. Saxo Grammaticus has combined both pedigrees, making Skjold a descendant of Dan; but usually it was agreed that nothing came before Skjold, that he was the beginning of the Skjoldung line[163]. At first a mere name, we should expect that he would have no characteristic save that, like every respectable Germanic king, he took tribute from his foes and gave it to his friends. He differs therefore from those heroic figures like Hygelac or Guthhere (Gunnar) which, being derived from actual historic characters, have, from the beginning of their story, certain definite features attached to them. Scyld is, in the beginning, merely a name, the ancestor of the Scyldings. Tradition collects round him gradually.

Hence it will be rash to attach much weight to any feature which is found in one account of him only. Anything we are told of Scyld in English sources alone is not to be construed as evidence as to his original story, but only as to the form that story assumed in England. When, for example, *Beowulf* tells us that Scyld is *Scefing*, or that he is father of Beowulf, it will be very rash of us to assume that these relationships existed in the Danish, but have been forgotten. This is, I think, universally admitted[164]. Yet the very scholars who emphasize this, have assumed that the marvellous arrival as a child, in a boat, surrounded by weapons, is an essential feature of Scyld's story. Yet the evidence for this is no better and no worse than the evidence for his relationship to Sceaf or Beow—it rests solely on the English documents. Accordingly it only shows what was told about Scyld in England.

Of course the boat arrival *might* be an original part of the story of *Scyld-Skjold*, which has been forgotten in his native country, but remembered in England. But I cannot see that we have any right to assert this, without proof.

What we can assert to have been the original feature of Scyld is this—that he was the eponymous hero king of the Danes. Both *Beowulf* and the Scandinavian authorities agree upon that. The fact that his name (in the form *Sceldwa*) appears in the genealogy of the kings of Wessex is not evidence against a Danish origin. The name appears in close connection with that of Heremod, another Danish king, and is merely evidence of a desire on the part of the genealogist of the Wessex kings to connect his royal house with the most distinguished family he knew: that of the Scyldingas, about whom so much is said in the prologue to *Beowulf*.

Neither do the instances of place-names in England, such as *Scyldes treow*, *Scildes well*, prove Scyld to have been an English hero. They merely prove him to have been a hero who was celebrated in England—which the Prologue to *Beowulf* alone is sufficient to show to have been the case. For place-names commemorating heroes of alien tribes are common enough[165] on English ground.

So much at least is gained. Whatever Müllenhoff[166] and his followers constructed upon the assumption that Scyld was an essentially Anglo-Saxon hero goes overboard. Scyld is the ancestor king of the Danish house—more than this we can hardly with safety assert.

Now let us turn to the figure of Sceaf. This was not necessarily connected with Scyld from the first.

The story of Sceaf first meets us in its completeness in the pages of William of Malmesbury. And William of Malmesbury is a twelfth century authority; by his time the Old English courtly epics had died out—for they could not have long survived the Norman Conquest and the overthrow of Old English court life. But the popular tradition[167] remained, and a good many of the old stories, banished from the hall, must have lingered on at the cross-roads— tales of Wade and Weyland, of Offa and Sceaf. For songs, sung by minstrels at the cross roads, William of Malmesbury is good evidence, and he owns to having drawn information from similar popular sources[168]. William's story, then, is evidence that in his own day there was a tradition of a mythical king Sheaf who came as a child sleeping in a ship with a sheaf of corn at his head How old this tradition may be, we cannot say. Ethelwerd knew the story, though he has nothing to say of the sheaf. But we have seen that when we get back to the ninth century, and the formation of the *Anglo-Saxon Chronicle*, at a court where we may be sure the old English heroic stories were still popular, it is Sceaf and not Sceldwa who is regarded as the beginning of things—the king whose origin is so remote that he is the oldest Germanic ancestor one can get back to[169]: "he was born in Noah's ark."

Whether or no Noah's ark was chosen as Sceaf's birthplace because legend represented him as coming in a boat over the water, we cannot tell. But the place he occupies, with only the Biblical names before him, as compared with Sceldwa the son of Heremod, clearly marks Sceaf rather than Sceldwa as the hero who comes from the unknown. Turning now to the catalogue of kings in *Widsith*, probably the oldest extant piece of Anglo-Saxon verse, some generations more ancient than *Beowulf*, we find a King Sceafa, who ruled over the Langobards. Finally, in *Beowulf* itself, although the story is told of Scyld, nevertheless this Scyld is characterized as *Scefing*. If this means "with the sheaf," then the *Beowulf*-story stands convicted of imperfection, of needing explanation outside itself from the account which William of Malmesbury wrote four centuries later. If it means "son of Sceaf," why should a father be given to Scyld, when the story demands that he should come from the unknown? Was it because, if the boat story was to be attributed to Scyld, it was felt that this could only be made plausible by giving him some relation to Sceaf?

When we find an ancient king bearing the extraordinary name of "Sheaf," it is difficult not to connect this with the honour done to the sheaf of corn, survivals of which have been found in different parts of England. In Herrick's time, the sheaves of corn were still kissed as they were carried home on the Hock-cart, whilst

Some, with great
Devotion, stroke the home-borne wheat.

Professor Chadwick argues, on the analogy of Prussian and Bulgarian harvest customs, that the figure of the "Harvest Queen" in the English ceremony is derived from a corn figure made from the last sheaf, and that the sheaf was once regarded as a religious symbol[170]. But the evidence for this is surely even stronger than would be gathered from Professor Chadwick's very cautious statement. I suppose there is hardly a county in England from Kent to Cornwall and from Kent to Northumberland, where there is not evidence for honour paid to the last sheaf—an honour which cannot be accounted for as merely expressing the joy of the reapers at having got to the end of their task. In Kent "a figure composed of some of the best corn" was made into a human shape: "this is afterwards curiously dressed by the women, and adorned with paper trimmings cut to resemble a cap, ruffles, handkerchief, etc., of the finest lace. It is brought home with the last load of corn[171]." In Northumberland and Durham a sheaf known as the "Kern baby" was made into the likeness of a human figure, decked out and brought home in triumph with dancing and singing[172]. But the most striking form of the sheaf ceremony is found in the honour done to the "Neck" in the West of England.

... After the wheat is all cut, on most farms in the north of Devon the harvest people have a custom of "crying the neck." I believe that this practice is seldom omitted on any large farm in that part of the country. It is done in this way. An old man, or someone else well acquainted with the ceremonies used on the occasion (when the labourers are reaping the last field of wheat), goes round to the shocks and sheaves, and picks out a little bundle of all the best ears he can find; this bundle he ties up very neat and trim, and plats and arranges the straws very tastefully. This is called "the neck" of wheat, or wheaten-ears. After the field is cut out, and the pitcher once more circulated, the reapers, binders, and the women, stand round in a circle. The person with "the neck" stands in the centre, grasping it with both his hands. He first stoops and holds it near the ground, and all the men forming the ring take off their hats, stooping and holding them with both hands towards the ground. They then all begin at once in a very prolonged and harmonious tone to cry "the neck!" at the same time slowly raising themselves upright, and elevating their arms and hats above their heads; the person with "the neck" also raising it on high. This is done three times. They then change their cry to "wee yen!"—"way yen!"—which they sound in the same prolonged and slow manner as before, with singular harmony and effect, three times. This last cry is accompanied by the same movements of the body and arms as in crying "the neck." ...

... After having thus repeated "the neck" three times, and "wee yen" or "way yen" as often, they all burst out into a kind of loud and joyous laugh, flinging up their hats and caps into the air, capering about and perhaps kissing the girls. One of them then gets "the neck," and runs as hard as he can down to the farm-house, where the dairy-maid, or one of the young female domestics, stands at the door prepared with a pail of water. If he who holds "the neck" can manage to get into the house, in any way, unseen or openly, by any other way than the door at which the girl stands with the pail of water, then he may lawfully kiss her; but, if otherwise, he is regularly soused with the contents of the bucket. On a fine still autumn evening, the "crying of the neck" has a wonderful effect at a distance, far finer than that of the Turkish muezzin, which Lord Byron eulogizes so much, and which he says is preferable to all the bells in Christendom. I have once or twice heard upwards of twenty men cry it, and sometimes joined by an equal number of female voices. About three years back, on some high grounds, where our people were harvesting, I heard six or seven "necks" cried in one night, although I know that some of them were four miles off[173].

The account given by Mrs Bray of the Devonshire custom, in her letters to Southey, is practically identical with this[174]. We have plenty of evidence for this ceremony of "Crying the Neck" in the South-Western counties in Somersetshire[175], in Cornwall[176], and in a mutilated form in Dorsetshire[177].

On the Welsh border the essence of the ceremony consisted in tying the last ears of corn—perhaps twenty—with ribbon, and severing this "neck" by throwing the sickle at it from some distance. The custom is recorded in Cheshire[178], Shropshire[179], and under a different name in Herefordshire[180]. The term "neck" seems to have been known as far afield as Yorkshire and the "little England beyond Wales"—the English-speaking colony of Pembrokeshire[181].

Whether we are to interpret the expression "the Neck," applied to the last sheaf, as descended from a time when "the corn spirit is conceived in human form, and the last standing corn is a part of its body—its neck[182] ..." or whether it is merely a survival of the Scandinavian word for sheaf—*nek* or *neg*[183], we have here surely evidence of the worship of the sheaf. "In this way 'Sheaf' was greeted, before he passed over into a purely mythical being[184]."

I do not think these "neck" customs can be traced back beyond the seventeenth century[185]. Though analogous usages are recorded in England (near Eton) as early as the sixteenth century[186], it was not usual at that time to trouble to record such things.

The earliest document bearing upon the veneration of the sheaf comes from a neighbouring district, and is contained in the Chronicle of the Monastery of Abingdon, which tells how in the time of King Edmund (941-946) a controversy arose as to the right of the monks of Abingdon to a certain portion of land adjoining the river. The monks appealed to a judgment of God to vindicate their claim, and this took the shape of placing a sheaf, with a taper on the top, upon a round shield and letting it float down the river, the shield by its movements hither and thither indicating accurately the boundaries of the monastic domain. At last the shield came to the field in debate, which, thanks to the floods, it was able to circumnavigate[187].

Professor Chadwick, who first emphasized the importance of this strange ordeal[188], points out that although the extant MSS of the *Chronicle* date from the thirteenth century, the mention of a *round* shield carries the superstition back to a period before the Norman Conquest. Therefore this story seems to give us evidence for the use of the sheaf and shield together as a magic symbol in Anglo-Saxon times. "An ordeal by letting the sheaf sail down the river on a shield was only possible at a time when the sheaf was regarded as a kind of supernatural being which could find the way itself[189]."

But a still closer parallel to the story of the corn-figure coming over the water is found in Finnish mythology in the person of Sämpsä Pellervoinen. Finnish mythology seems remote from our subject, but if the figure of Sämpsä was borrowed from Germanic mythology, as seems to be thought[190], we are justified in laying great weight upon the parallel.

Readers of the *Kalewala* will remember, near the beginning, the figure of Sämpsä Pellervoinen, the god of Vegetation. He does not seem to do much. But there are other Finnish poems in his honour, extant in varying versions[191]. It is difficult to get a collected idea from these fragmentary records, but it seems to be this: Ahti, the god of the sea, sends messengers to summon Sämpsä, so that he may bring fertility to the fields. In one version, first the Winter and then the Summer are sent to arouse Sämpsä, that he may make the crops and trees grow. Winter—

Took a foal swift as the spring wind,
Let the storm wind bear him forward,
Blew the trees till they were leafless,
Blew the grass till it was seedless,
Bloodless likewise the young maidens.

Sämpsä refuses to come. Then the Summer is sent with better results. In another version Sämpsä is fetched from an island beyond the sea:

It is I who summoned Sämpsä
From an isle amid the ocean,
From a skerry bare and treeless.

In yet another variant we are told how the boy Sämpsä

Took six grains from off the corn heap,
Slept all summer mid the corn heap,
In the bosom of the corn boat.

Now "It's a long, long way to" Ilomantsi in the east of Finland, where this last variant was discovered. But at least we have evidence that, within the region influenced by Germanic mythology, the spirit of vegetation was thought of as a boy coming over the sea, or sleeping in a boat with corn[192].

To sum up:

Sceafa, when the Catalogue of Kings in *Widsith* was drawn up—before *Beowulf* was composed, at any rate in its present form—was regarded as an ancient king. When the West Saxon pedigree was drawn up, certainly not much more than a century and a half after the composition of *Beowulf,* and perhaps much less, Sceaf was regarded as the primitive figure in the pedigree, before whom no one lived save the Hebrew patriarchs. That he was originally thought of as a child, coming across the water, with the sheaf of corn, is, in view of the Finnish parallel, exceedingly probable, and acquires some confirmation from the Chronicler's placing him in Noah's ark. But the definite evidence for this is late.

Scyld, on the other hand, is in the first place probably a mere eponym of the power of the Scylding kings of Denmark. He may, at a very early date, have been provided with a ship funeral, since later two Swedish kings, both apparently of Danish origin, have this ship funeral accorded to them, and in one case it is expressly said to be "according to the custom of his ancestors." But it seems exceedingly improbable that his original story represented him as coming over the sea in a boat. For, if so, it remains to be explained why this motive has entirely disappeared among his own people in Scandinavia, and has been preserved only in England. Would the Danes have been likely to forget utterly so striking a story, concerning the king from whom their line derived its name? Further, in England, *Beowulf* alone attributes this story to Scyld, whilst later historians attribute it to Sceaf. In view of the way in which the story of William of Malmesbury is supported by folklore, to regard that story as merely the result of error or invention seems perilous indeed.

On the other hand, all becomes straightforward if we allow that Scyld and Sceaf were both ancient figures standing at the head of famous dynasties. Their names alliterate. What more likely than that their stories should have influenced each other, and that one king should have come to be regarded as the parent or ancestor of the other? Contamination with Scyld would account for Sceaf's boat being stated to have come to land in Scani, Scanza—that Scedeland which is mentioned as the seat of Scyld's rule. Yet this explanation is not necessary, for if Sceaf were an early Longobard king, he would be rightly represented as ruling in Scandinavia[193].

SECTION VI. BEOW.

The Anglo-Saxon genealogies agree that the son of Sceldwa (Scyld) is Beow (Beaw, Beo). In *Beowulf*, he is named not Beow, but Beowulf.

Many etymologies have been suggested for *Bēow*. But considering that Beow is in some versions a grandson, in all a descendant of Sceaf, it can hardly be an accident that his name is identical with the O.E. word for grain, *bēow*. The Norse word corresponding to this is *bygg*[194].

Recent investigation of the name is best summed up in the words of Axel Olrik:

"New light has been cast upon the question of the derivation of the name Beow by Kaarle Krohn's investigation of the debt of Finnish to Norse mythology, together with Magnus Olsen's linguistic interpretation. The Finnish has a deity Pekko, concerning whom it is said that he promoted the growth of barley: the Esths, closely akin to the Finns, have a corresponding Peko, whose image—the size of a three-year-old child—was carried out into the fields and invoked at the time of sowing, or else was kept in the corn-bin by a custodian chosen for a year. This Pekko is plainly a personification of the barley; the form corresponding phonetically in Runic Norse would be *beggw-* (from which comes Old Norse *bygg*).

"So in Norse there was a grain *beggw-* (becoming *bygg*) and a corn-god *Beggw-* (becoming *Pekko*). In Anglo-Saxon there was a grain *béow* and an ancestral *Béow*. And all four are phonetically identical (proceeding from a primitive form *beuwa*, 'barley'). The conclusion which it is difficult to avoid is, that the corn-spirit 'Barley' and the ancestor 'Barley' are one and the same. The relation is the same as that between King Sheaf and the worship of the sheaf: the worshipped corn-being gradually sinks into the background, and comes to be regarded as an epic figure, an early ancestor.

"We have no more exact knowledge of the mythical ideas connected either with the ancestor Beow or the corn-god Pekko. But we know enough of the worship of Pekko to show that he dwelt in the corn-heap, and that, in the spring, he was fetched out in the shape of a little child. That reminds us not a little of Sämpsä, who lay in the corn-heap on the ship, and came to land and awoke in the spring[195]."

But it may be objected that this is "harking back" to the old mythological interpretations. After refusing to accept Müllenhoff's assumptions, are we not reverting, through the names of Sceaf and Beow, and the worship of the sheaf, to very much the same thing?

No. It is one thing to believe that the ancestor-king Beow may be a weakened form of an ancient divinity, a mere name surviving from the figure of an old corn-god Beow; it is quite another to assume, as Müllenhoff did, that what we are told about Beowulf was originally told about Beow *and that therefore we are justified in giving a mythological meaning to it.*

All we know, conjecture apart, about Beow is his traditional relationship to Scyld, Sceaf and the other figures of the pedigree. That Beowulf's dragon fight belonged originally to him is only a conjecture. In confirmation of this conjecture only one argument has been put forward: an argument turning upon Beowulf, son of Scyld—that obscure figure, apparently equivalent to Beow, who meets us at the beginning of our poem.

Beowulf's place as a son of Scyld and father of Healfdene is occupied in the Danish genealogies by Frothi, son of Skjold, and father of Halfdan. It has been urged that the two figures are really identical, in spite of the difference of name. Now Frothi slays a dragon, and it has been argued that this dragon fight shows similarities which enable us to identify it with the dragon fight attributed in our poem to Beowulf the Geat.

The argument is a strong one—if it really is the case that the dragon slain by Frothi was the same monster as that slain by Beowulf the Geat.

Unfortunately this parallel, which will be examined in the next section, is far from certain. We must be careful not to argue in a circle, identifying Beowulf and Frothi because they slew the same dragon, and then identifying the dragons because they were slain by the same hero.

Whilst, therefore, we admit that it is highly probable that Beow (grain) the descendant of Sceaf (sheaf) was originally a corn divinity or corn fetish, we cannot follow Müllenhoff in his bold attribution to this "culture hero" of Beowulf's adventures with the dragon or with Grendel.

SECTION VII. THE HOUSE OF SCYLD AND DANISH PARALLELS:
HEREMOD-LOTHERUS AND BEOWULF-FROTHO.

Scyld, although the source of that Scylding dynasty which our poem celebrates, is *not* apparently regarded in *Beowulf* as the earliest Danish king. He came to the throne after an interregnum; the people whom he grew up to rule had long endured cruel need, "being without a prince[196]." We hear in *Beowulf* of one Danish king only whom we can place chronologically before Scyld—viz. Heremod[197]. The way in which Heremod is referred to would fit in very well with the supposition[198] that he was the last of a dynasty; the immediate predecessor of Scyld; and that it was the death or exile of Heremod which ushered in the time when the Danes were without a prince.

Now there is a natural tendency in genealogies for each king to be represented as the descendant of his predecessor, whether he really was so or no; so that in the course of time, and sometimes of a very short time, the first king of a new dynasty may come to be reckoned as son of a king of the preceding line[199]. Consequently, there would be nothing surprising if, in another account, we find Scyld represented as a son of Heremod. And we *do* find the matter represented thus in the West Saxon genealogy, where Sceldwa or Scyld is son of Heremod. Turning to the Danish accounts, however, we do not find any *Hermóðr* (which is the form we should expect corresponding to *Heremōd*) as father to Skjold (Scyld). Either no father of Skjold is known, or else (in Saxo Grammaticus) he has a father Lotherus. But, although the names are different, there is some correspondence between what we are told of Lother and what we are told of Heremod. A close parallel has indeed been drawn by Sievers between the whole dynasty: on the one hand Lotherus, his son Skioldus, and his descendant Frotho, as given in Saxo: and on the other hand the corresponding figures in *Beowulf*, Heremod, Scyld, and Scyld's son, Beowulf the Dane.

The fixed and certain point here is the identity of the central figure, Skioldus-Scyld. All the rest is very doubtful; not that there are not many parallel features, but because the parallels are of a commonplace type which might so easily recur accidentally.

The story of Lother, as given by Saxo, will be found below: the story of Heremod as given in *Beowulf* is hopelessly obscure—a mere succession of allusions intended for an audience who knew the tale quite well. Assuming the stories of Lother and Heremod to be different versions of one original, the following would seem to be the most likely reconstruction[200], the more doubtful portions being placed within round brackets thus ( ):

The old Danish prince [Dan in Saxo] has two sons, one a weakling [*Humblus*, Saxo] the other a hero [*Lotherus*, Saxo: *Heremod*, *Beowulf*] (who was already in his youth the hope of the nation). But after his father's death the elder was (through violence) raised to the throne: and Lother-Heremod went into banishment. (But under the rule of the weakling the kingdom went to pieces, and thus) many a man longed for the return of the exile, as a help against these evils. So the hero conquers and deposes the weaker brother. But then his faults break forth, his greed and his cruelty: he ceases to be the darling and becomes the scourge of his people, till they rise and either slay him or drive him again into exile.

If the stories of Lother and Heremod *are* connected, we may be fairly confident that Heremod, not Lother, was the name of the king in the original story.

For Scandinavian literature does know a Hermoth (*Hermóðr*), though no such adventures are attributed to him as those recorded of Heremod in *Beowulf*. Nevertheless it is probable that this Hermoth and Heremod in *Beowulf* are one and the same, because both heroes are linked in some way or other with Sigemund. How these two kings, Heremod and Sigemund, came to be connected, we do not know, but we find this connection recurring again and again[201]. This *may* be mere coincidence: but I doubt if we are justified in assuming it to be so[202].

It has been suggested[203] that both Heremod and Sigemund were originally heroes specially connected with the worship of Odin, and hence grouped together. The history of the Scandinavian Sigmund is bound up with that of the magic sword which Odin gave him, and with which he was always victorious till the last fight when Odin himself shattered it.

And we are told in the Icelandic that Odin, whilst he gave a sword to Sigmund, gave a helm and byrnie to Hermoth.

Again, whilst in one Scandinavian poem Sigmund is represented as welcoming the newcomer at the gates of Valhalla, in another the same duty is entrusted to Hermoth.

It is clear also that the *Beowulf*-poet had in mind some kind of connection, though we cannot tell what, between Sigemund and Heremod.

We may take it, then, that the Heremod who is linked with Sigemund in *Beowulf* was also known in Scandinavian literature as a hero in some way connected with Sigmund: whether or no the adventures which Saxo records of Lotherus were really told in Scandinavian lands in connection with Hermoth, we cannot say. The wicked king whose subjects rebel against him is too common a feature of Germanic story for us to feel sure, without a good deal of corroborative evidence, that the figures of Lotherus and Heremod are identical.

The next king in the line, Skioldus in Saxo, is, as we have seen, clearly identical with Scyld in *Beowulf.* But beyond the name, the two traditions have, as we have also seen, but little in common. Both are youthful heroes[204], both force neighbouring kings to pay tribute[205]; but such things are commonplaces[206].

We must therefore turn to the next figure in the pedigree: the son of Skjold in Scandinavian tradition is Frothi (Frotho in Saxo)[207], the son of Scyld in *Beowulf* is Beowulf the Dane. And Frothi is the father of Halfdan (Haldanus in Saxo) as Beowulf the Dane is of Healfdene. The Frothi of Scandinavian tradition corresponds then in position to Beowulf the Dane in Old English story[208].

Now of Beowulf the Dane we are told so little that we have really no means of drawing a comparison between him and Frothi. But a *theory* that has found wide acceptance among scholars assumes that the dragon fight of Beowulf the Geat was originally narrated of Beowulf the Dane, and only subsequently transferred to the Geatic hero. Theoretically, then, Beowulf the Dane kills a dragon. Now certainly Frotho kills a dragon: and it has been generally accepted[209] that the parallels between the dragon slain by Frotho and that slain by Beowulf the Geat are so remarkable as to exclude the possibility of mere accidental coincidence, and to lead us to conclude that the dragon story was originally told of that Beowulf who corresponds to Frothi, i.e. Beowulf the Dane, son of Scyld and father of Healfdene; not Beowulf, son of Ecgtheow, the Geat.

But are the parallels really so close? We must not forget that here we are building theory upon theory. That the Frotho of Saxo is the same figure as Beowulf the Dane in Old English, is a theory, based upon his common relationship to Skiold-Scyld before him and to Haldanus-Healfdene coming after him: that Beowulf the Dane was the original hero of the dragon fight, and that that dragon fight was only subsequently transferred to the credit of Beowulf the Geat, is again a theory. Only if we can find real parallels between the dragon-slaying of Frotho and the dragon-slaying of Beowulf will these theories have confirmation.

Parallels have been pointed out by Sievers which he regards as so close as to justify a belief that both are derived ultimately from an old lay, with so much closeness that verbal resemblances can still be traced.

Unfortunately the parallels are all commonplaces. That Sievers and others have been satisfied with them was perhaps due to the fact that they started by assuming as proved that the dragon fight of Beowulf the Geat belonged originally to Beowulf the Dane[210], and argued that since Frotho in Saxo occupies a place corresponding exactly to that of Beowulf the Dane in *Beowulf*, a comparatively limited resemblance between two dragons coming, as it were, at the same point in the pedigree, might be held sufficient to identify them.

But, as we have seen, the assumption that the dragon fight of Beowulf the Geat belonged originally to Beowulf the Dane is only a theory that will have to stand or fall as we can prove that the dragon fight of Frotho is really parallel to that of Beowulf the Geat, and therefore must have belonged to the connecting link supplied by the Scylding prince Beowulf the Dane. In other words, the theory that the dragon in *Beowulf* is to be identified with the dragon which in Saxo is slain by Frotho the Danish prince, father of Haldanus-Healfdene, is one of the main arguments upon which we must base the theory that the dragon in *Beowulf* was originally slain by the Danish Beowulf, father of Healfdene, not by Beowulf the Geat. We cannot then turn round, and assert that the fact that they were both slain by a Danish prince, the father of Healfdene, is an argument for identifying the dragons.

Turning to the dragon fight itself, the following parallels have been noted by Sievers:

(1) A native (*indigena*) comes to Frotho, and tells him of the treasure-guarding dragon. An informer (*melda*) plays the same part in *Beowulf*[211].

But a dragon is not game which can be met with every day. He is a shy beast, lurking in desert places. Some informant has very frequently to guide the hero to his foe[212]. And the situation is widely different. Frotho knows nothing of the dragon till directed to the spot: Beowulf's land has been assailed, he knows of the dragon, though he needs to be guided to its *exact* lair.

(2) Frotho's dragon lives on an island. Beowulf's lives near the sea, and there is an island (*ēalond*, 2334) in the neighbourhood.

But *ēalond* in *Beowulf* probably does not mean "island" at all: and in any case the dragon did not live upon the *ēalond*. Many dragons have lived near the sea. Sigemund's dragon did so[213].

(3) The hero in each case attacks the dragon single-handed.

But what hero ever did otherwise? On the contrary, Beowulf's exploit differs from that of Frotho and of most other dragon slayers in that he is unable to *overcome* his foe single-handed, and needs the support of Wiglaf.

(4) Special armour is carried by the dragon slayer in each case.

But this again is no uncommon feature. The Red Cross Knight also needs special armour. Dragon slayers constantly invent some ingenious or even unique method. And again the parallel is far from close. Frotho is advised to cover his shield and his limbs with the hides of bulls and kine: a sensible precaution against fiery venom. Beowulf constructs a shield of iron[214]: which naturally gives very inferior protection[215].

(5) Frotho's informant tells him that he must be of good courage[216]. Wiglaf encourages Beowulf[217].

But the circumstances under which the words are uttered are entirely different, nor have the words more than a general resemblance. That a man needs courage, if he is going to tackle a dragon, is surely a conclusion at which two minds could have arrived independently.

(6) Both heroes waste their blows at first on the scaly back of the dragon.

But if the hero went at once for the soft parts, there would be no fight at all, and all the fun would be lost. Sigurd's dragon-fight is, for this reason, a one-sided business from the first. To avoid this, Frotho is depicted as beginning by an attack on the dragon's rough hide (although he has been specially warned by the *indigena* not to do so):

ventre sub imo
esse locum scito quo ferrum mergere fas est,
hunc mucrone petens medium rimaberis anguem[218].

(7) The hoard is plundered by both heroes.

But it is the nature of a dragon to guard a hoard[219]. And, having slain the dragon, what hero would neglect the gold?

(8) There are many verbal resemblances: the dragon spits venom[220], and twists himself into coils[221].

Some of these verbal resemblances may be granted as proved: but they surely do not prove the common origin of the two dragon fights. They only tend to prove the common origin of the school of poetry in which these two dragon fights were told. That dragons dwelt in mounds was a common Germanic belief, to which the Cottonian Gnomic verses testify. Naturally, therefore, Frotho's dragon is *montis possessor*. Beowulf's is *beorges hyrde*. The two phrases undoubtedly point back to a similar gradus, to a similar traditional stock phraseology, and to similar beliefs: that is all. As well argue that two kings must be identical, because each is called *folces hyrde*.

These commonplace phrases and commonplace features are surely quite insufficient to prove that the stories are identical—at most they only prove that they bear the impress of one and the same poetical school. If a parallel is to carry weight there must be something individual about it, as there is, for example, about the arguments by which the identity of Beowulf and Bjarki have been supported. That a hero comes from Geatland (Gautland) to the court where Hrothulf (Rolf) is abiding; that the same hero subsequently is instrumental in helping Eadgils (Athils) against Onela (Ali)—here we have something tangible. But when two heroes, engaged upon slaying a dragon, are each told to be brave, the parallel is too general to be a parallel at all. "There is a river in Macedon: and there is also moreover a river at Monmouth, and there is salmons in both."

And there is a fundamental difference, which would serve to neutralize the parallels, even did they appear much less accidental than they do.

Dragon fights may be classified into several types: two stand out prominently. There is the story in which the young hero begins his career by slaying a dragon or monster and winning, it may be a hoard of gold, it may be a bride. This is the type of story found, for instance, in the tales of Sigurd, or Perseus, or St George. On the other hand there is the hero who, at the end of his career, seeks to ward off evil from himself and his people. He slays the monster, but is himself slain by it. The great example of this type is the god Thor, who in the last fight of the gods slays the Dragon, but dies when he has reeled back nine paces from the "baleful serpent[222]."

Now the story of the victorious young Frotho is of the one type: that of the aged Beowulf is of the other. And this difference is essential, fundamental, dominating the whole situation in each case: giving its cheerful and aggressive tone to the story of Frotho, giving the elegiac and pathetic note which runs through the whole of the last portion of *Beowulf*[223]. It is no mere detail which could be added or subtracted by a narrator without altering the essence of the story.

In face of this we must pronounce the two stories essentially and originally distinct. If, nevertheless, there were a large number of striking and specific similarities, we should have to allow that, though originally distinct, the one dragon story had influenced the other in detail. For, whilst each poet who retold the tale would make alterations in detail, and might import such detail from one dragon story into another, what we know of the method of the ancient story tellers does not allow us to assume that a poet would have altered the whole drift of a story, either by changing the last death-struggle of an aged, childless prince into the victorious feat of a young hero, or by the reverse process.

Those, therefore, who hold the parallels quoted above to be convincing, may believe that one dragon story has influenced another, originally distinct[224]. To me, it does not appear that even this necessarily follows from the evidence.

It seems very doubtful whether any of the parallels drawn by Sievers between the stories of Lotherus and Heremod[225], Skioldus and Scyld, Frotho and Beowulf, are more than the resemblances inevitable in poetry which, like the Old Danish and the Old English, still retains so many traces of the common Germanic frame in which it was moulded.

Indeed, of the innumerable dragon-stories extant, there is probably not one which we can declare to be really identical with that of Beowulf. There is a Danish tradition which shows many similarities[226], and I have given this below, in Part II; but rather as an example of a dragon-slaying of the *Beowulf* type, than because I believe in any direct connection between the two stories.

CHAPTER III

THEORIES AS TO THE ORIGIN, DATE, AND STRUCTURE OF THE POEM

SECTION I. IS "BEOWULF" TRANSLATED FROM A SCANDINAVIAN ORIGINAL?

Our poem, the first original poem of any length in the English tongue, ignores England. In one remarkable passage (ll. 1931-62) it mentions with praise Offa I, the great king who ruled the Angles whilst they were still upon the Continent. But, except for this, it deals mainly with heroes who, so far as we can identify them with historic figures, are Scandinavian.

Hence, not unnaturally, the first editor boldly declared *Beowulf* to be an Anglo-Saxon version of a Danish poem; and this view has had many supporters. The poem *must* be Scandinavian, said one of its earliest translators, because it deals mainly with Scandinavian heroes and "everyone knows that in ancient times each nation celebrated in song its own heroes alone[227]." And this idea, though not so crudely expressed, seems really to underlie the belief which has been held by numerous scholars, that the poem is nothing more than a translation of a poem in which some Scandinavian minstrel had glorified the heroes of his own nation.

But what do we mean by "nation"? Doubtless, from the point of view of politics and war, each Germanic tribe, or offshoot of a tribe, formed an independent nation: the Longobardi had no hesitation in helping the "Romans" to cut the throats of their Gothic kinsmen: Penda the Mercian was willing to ally with the Welshmen in order to overthrow his fellow Angles of Northumbria. But all this, as the history of the ancient Greeks or of the ancient Hebrews might show us, is quite compatible with a consciousness of racial unity among the warring states, with a common poetic tradition and a common literature. For purposes of poetry there was only one nation—the Germanic—split into many dialects and groups, but possessed of a common metre, a common style, a common standard of heroic feeling: and any deed of valour performed by any Germanic chief might become a fit subject for the poetry of any Germanic tribe of the heroic age.

So, if by "nation" we mean the whole Germanic race, then Germanic poetry is essentially "national." The Huns were the only non-Germanic tribe who were received (for poetical purposes) into Germania. Hunnish chiefs seem to have adopted Gothic manners, and after the Huns had disappeared it often came to be forgotten that they were not Germans. But with this exception the tribes and heroes of Germanic heroic poetry are Germanic.

If, however, by "nation" we understand the different warring units into which the Germanic race was, politically speaking, divided, then Germanic poetry is essentially "international."

This is no theory, but a fact capable of conclusive proof. The chief actors in the old Norse Volsung lays are not Norsemen, but Sigurd the Frank, Gunnar the Burgundian, Atli the Hun. In Continental Germany, the ideal knight of the Saxons in the North and the Bavarians in the South was no native hero, but Theodoric the Ostrogoth. So too in England, whilst *Beowulf* deals chiefly with Scandinavian heroes, the *Finnsburg* fragment deals with the Frisian tribes of the North Sea coast: *Waldere* with the adventures of Germanic chiefs settled in Gaul, *Deor* with stories of the Goths and of the Baltic tribes, whilst *Widsith*, which gives us a catalogue of the old heroic tales, shows that amongst the heroes whose names were current in England were men of Gothic, Burgundian, Frankish, Lombard, Frisian, Danish and Swedish race. There is nothing peculiar, then, in the fact that *Beowulf* celebrates heroes who were not of Anglian birth.

In their old home in Schleswig the Angles had been in the exact centre of Germania: with an outlook upon both the North Sea and the Baltic, and in touch with Scandinavian tribes on the North and Low German peoples on the South. That the Angles were interested in the stories of all the nations which surrounded them, and that they brought these stories with them to England, is certain. It is a mere accident that the one heroic poem which happens to have been preserved at length is almost exclusively concerned with Scandinavian doings. It could easily have happened that the history of the *Beowulf* MS and the *Waldere* MS might have been reversed: that the *Beowulf* might have been cut up to bind other books, and the *Waldere* preserved intact: in that case our one long poem would have been localized in ancient Burgundia, and would have dealt chiefly with the doings of Burgundian champions. But we should have had no more reason, without further evidence, to suppose the *Waldere* a translation from the Burgundian than we have, without further evidence, to suppose *Beowulf* a translation from the Scandinavian.

To deny that *Beowulf*, as we have it, is a translation from the Scandinavian does not, of course, involve any denial of the Scandinavian origin of the *story* of Beowulf's deeds. The fact that his achievements are framed in a Scandinavian setting, and that the closest parallels to them have to be sought in Scandinavian lands, makes it probable on *a priori* grounds that the story had its origin there. On the face of it, Müllenhoff's belief that the story was indigenous among the Angles is quite unlikely. It would seem rather to have originated in the Geatic country. But stories, whether in prose or verse, would spread quickly from the Geatas to the Danes and from the Danes to the Angles.

After the Angles had crossed the North Sea, however, this close intimacy ceased, till the Viking raids again reminded Englishmen, in a very unpleasant way, of their kinsmen across the sea. Now linguistic evidence tends to show that *Beowulf* belongs to a time prior to the Viking settlement in England, and it is unlikely that the Scandinavian traditions embodied in *Beowulf* found their way to England just at the time when communication with Scandinavian lands seems to have been suspended. We must conclude then that all this Scandinavian tradition probably spread to the Angles whilst they were still in their old continental home, was brought across to England by the settlers in the sixth century, was handed on by English bards from generation to generation, till some Englishmen formed the poem of *Beowulf* as we know it.

Of course, if evidence can be produced that *Beowulf* is translated from some Scandinavian original, which was brought over in the seventh century or later, that is another matter. But the evidence produced so far is not merely inconclusive, but ludicrously inadequate.

It has been urged[228] by Sarrazin, the chief advocate of the translation theory, that the description of the country round Heorot, and especially of the journey to the Grendel-lake, shows such local knowledge as to point to its having been composed by some Scandinavian poet familiar with the locality. Heorot can probably, as we have seen, be identified with Leire: and the Grendel-lake Sarrazin identifies with the neighbouring Roskilde fjord. But it is hardly possible to conceive a greater contrast than that between the Roskilde fjord and the scenery depicted in ll. 1357 *etc.*, 1408 *etc.* Seen, as Sarrazin saw it, on a May morning, in alternate sun and shadow, the Roskilde fjord presents a view of tame and peaceful beauty. In the days of Hrothgar, when there were perhaps fewer cultivated fields and more beech forests, the scenery may have been less tame, but can hardly have been less peaceful. The only trace of accurate geography is that Heorot is represented as not on the shore, and yet not far remote from it (ll. 307 *etc.*). But, as has been pointed out above, we know that traditions of the attack by the Heathobeardan upon Heorot were current in England: and these would be quite sufficient to keep alive, even among English bards, some remembrance of the strategic situation of Heorot with regard to the sea. A man need not have been near Troy, to realize that the town was no seaport and yet near the sea.

Again, it has been claimed by Sarrazin that the language of *Beowulf* shows traces of the Scandinavian origin of the poem. Sarrazin's arguments on this head have been contested energetically by Sievers[229]. After some heated controversy Sarrazin made a final and (presumably) carefully-weighed statement of his case. In this he gave a list of twenty-nine words upon which he based his belief[230]. Yet of these twenty-nine, twenty-one occur in other O.E. writings, where there can be no possible question of translation from the Scandinavian: some of these words, in fact, are amongst the commonest of O.E. poetical expressions. There remain eight which do not happen to be found elsewhere in the extant remains of O.E. poetry. But these are mostly compounds like *heaðo-lāc, feorh-sēoc*: and though the actual compound is not elsewhere extant in English, the component elements are thoroughly English. There is no reason whatever to think that these eight rare words are taken from Old Norse. Indeed, three of them do not occur in Old Norse at all.

Evidence to prove *Beowulf* a translation from a Scandinavian original is, then, wanting. On the other hand, over and above the difficulty that the *Beowulf* belongs just to the period when intimate communication between the Angles and Scandinavians was suspended, there is much evidence against the translation theory. The earliest Scandinavian poetry we possess, or of which we can get information, differs absolutely from *Beowulf* in style, metre and sentiment: the manners of *Beowulf* are incompatible with all we know of the wild heathendom of Scandinavia in the seventh or eighth century[231]. *Beowulf*, as we now have it, with its Christian references and its Latin loan-words, *could* not be a translation from the Scandinavian. And the proper names in *Beowulf* which Sarrazin claimed were Old Norse, not Old English, and had been taken over from the Old Norse original, are in all cases so correctly transliterated as to necessitate the assumption that they were brought across early, at the time of the settlement of Britain or very shortly after, and underwent phonetic development side by side with the other words in the English language. Had they been brought across from Scandinavia at a later date, much confusion must have ensued in the forms.

Somewhat less improbable is the suggestion "that the poet had travelled on the continent and become familiar with the legends of the Danes and Geats, or else had heard them from a Scandinavian resident in England[232]." But it is clear from the allusive manner in which the Scandinavian tales are told, that they must have been familiar to the poet's audience. If, then, the English audience knew them, why must the poet himself have travelled on the continent in order to know them? There is, therefore, no need for this theory, and it is open to many of the objections of the translation theory: for example it fails, equally with that theory, to account for the uniformly correct development of the proper names.

The obvious conclusion is that these Scandinavian traditions were brought over by the English settlers in the sixth century. Against this only one cavil can be raised, and that will not bear examination. It has been objected that, since Hygelac's raid took place about 516, since Beowulf's accession was some years subsequent, and since he then reigned fifty years, his death cannot be put much earlier than 575, and that this brings us to a date when the migration of the Angles and Saxons had been completed[233]. But it is forgotten that all the historical events mentioned in the poem, which we can date, occur before, or not very long after, the raid of Hygelac, c. 516. The poem asserts that fifty years after these events Beowulf slew a dragon and was slain by it. But this does not make the dragon historic, nor does it make the year 575 the historic date of the death of Beowulf. We cannot be sure that there *was* any actual king of the Geatas named Beowulf; and if there was, the last known historic act with which that king is associated is the raising of Eadgils to the Swedish throne, c. 525: the rest of Beowulf's long reign, since it contains no event save the slaying of a dragon, has no historic validity.

It is noteworthy that, whereas there is full knowledge shown in our poem of those events which took place in Scandinavian lands during the whole period from about 450 to 530—the period during which hordes of Angles, Saxons and Jutes were landing in Britain—there is no reference, not even by way of casual allusion, to any continental events which we can date with certainty as subsequent to the arrival of the latest settlers from the continent. Surely this is strong evidence that these tales were brought over by some of the last of the invaders, not carried to England by some casual traveller a century or two later.

A full discussion of the dialect, metre and syntax of *Beowulf* forms no part of the scheme of this study. It is only intended in this section to see how far such investigations throw light upon the literary history of the poem.

Dialect.

Beowulf is written in the late West Saxon dialect. Imbedded in the poem, however, are a large number of forms, concerning which this at least can be said—that they are not normal late West Saxon. Critics have classified these forms, and have drawn conclusions from them as to the history of the poem: arguing from sporadic "Mercian" and "Kentish" forms that *Beowulf* is of Mercian origin and has passed through the hands of a Kentish transcriber.

But, in fact, the evidence as to Old English dialects is more scanty and more conflicting than philologists have always been willing to admit. It is exceedingly difficult to say with any certainty what forms are "Mercian" and what "Kentish." Having run such forms to earth, it is still more difficult to say what arguments are to be drawn from their *occasional* appearance in any text. Men from widely different parts of the country would be working together in the scriptorium of one and the same monastery, and this fact alone may have often led to confusion in the dialectal forms of works transcribed.

A thorough investigation of the significance of all the abnormal forms in *Beowulf* has still to be made. Whether it would repay the labour of the investigator may well be questioned. In the meantime we may accept the view that the poem was in all probability originally written in some non-West-Saxon dialect, and most probably in an Anglian dialect, since this is confirmed by the way in which the Anglian hero Offa is dragged into the story.

Ten Brink's attempt to decide the dialect and transmission of *Beowulf* will be found in his *Beowulf*, pp. 237-241: he notes the difficulty that the "Kentish" forms from which he argues are nearly all such as occur also sporadically in West Saxon texts. A classification of the forms by P. G. Thomas will be found in the *Modern Language Review*, I, 202 *etc.* How difficult and uncertain all classification must be has been shown by Frederick Tupper (*Pub. Mod. Lang. Assoc. Amer.* XXVI, 235 *etc.*; *J.E.G.P.* XI, 82-9).

"Lichtenheld's Test."

Somewhat more definite results can be drawn from certain syntactical usages. There can be no doubt that as time went on, the use of *se, sēo, þæt* became more and more common in O.E. verse. This is largely due to the fact that in the older poems the *weak adjective + noun* appears frequently where we should now use the definite article: *wīsa fengel*—"the wise prince"; *se wīsa fengel* is used where some demonstrative is needed—"that wise prince." Later, however, *se, sēo, þæt* comes to be used in the common and vague sense in which the definite article is used in Modern English.

We consequently get with increasing frequency the use of the *definite article + weak adjective + noun*: whilst the usage *weak adjective + noun* decreases. Some rough criterion of date can thus be obtained by an examination of a poet's usage in this particular. Of course it would be absurd—as has been done— to group Old English poems in a strict chronological order according to the proportion of forms with and without the article. Individual usage must count for a good deal: also the scribes in copying and recopying our text must to a considerable extent have obliterated the earlier practice. Metre and syntax combine to make it probable that, in line 9 of our poem, the scribe has inserted the unnecessary article *þāra* before *ymbsittendra*: and in the rare cases where we have an O.E. poem preserved in two texts, a comparison proves that the scribe has occasionally interpolated an article. But this later tendency to level out the peculiarity only makes it the more remarkable that we should find such great differences between O.E. poems, all of them extant in copies transcribed about the year 1000.

How great is the difference between the usage of *Beowulf* and that of the great body of Old English poetry will be clear from the following statistics.

The proportion of phrases containing the weak adjective + noun with and without the definite article in the certain works of Cynewulf is as follows[234]:

	With article	Without article
Juliana	27	3
Christ (II)	28	3
Elene	66	9

In *Guthlac* (A) (c. 750) the proportions are:

	With article	Without article
Guthlac (A)	42	6

Contrast this with the proportion in our poem:

	With article	Without article

Beowulf	13	65

The nearest approach to the proportions of *Beowulf* is in the (certainly very archaic)

	With article	Without article
Exodus	10	14

On the other hand, certain late texts show how fallible this criterion is. Anyone dating *Maldon* solely by "Lichtenheld's Test" would assuredly place it much earlier than 991.

It is easy to make a false use of grammatical statistics: and this test should only be applied with the greatest caution. But the difference between *Beowulf* and the works of Cynewulf is too striking to be overlooked. In *Beowulf*, to every five examples without the article (e.g. *heaðo-stēapa helm*) we have *one* with the article (e.g. *se hearda helm*): in Cynewulf to every five examples without the article we have *forty* with it.

A further test of antiquity is in the use of the weak adjective with the instrumental—a use which rapidly diminishes.

There are eighteen such instrumental phrases in *Beowulf* (3182 lines)[235]. In *Exodus* (589 lines) there are six examples[236]—proportionally more than in *Beowulf*. In Cynewulf's undoubted works (c. 2478 lines) there is one example only, *beorhtan reorde*[237].

This criterion of the absence of the definite article before the weak adjective is often referred to as Lichtenheld's Test (see article by him in *Z.f.d.A.* XVI, 325 *etc.*). It has been applied to the whole body of O.E. poetry by Barnouw (*Textcritische Untersuchungen*, 1902). The data collected by Barnouw are most valuable, but we must be cautious in the conclusions we draw, as is shown by Sarrazin (*Eng. Stud.* XXXVIII, 145 *etc.*), and Tupper (*Pub. Mod. Lang. Assoc.* XXVI, 274).

Exact enumeration of instances is difficult. For example, Lichtenheld gave 22 instances of definite article + weak adjective + noun in *Beowulf*[238]. But eight of these are not quite certain; *se gōda mæg Hygelāces* may be not "the good kinsman of Hygelac," but "the good one—the kinsman of Hygelac," for there is the half line pause after *gōda*. These eight examples therefore should be deducted[239]. One instance, though practically certain, is the result of conjectural emendation[240]. Of the remaining thirteen[241] three are variations of the same phrase.

The statistics given above are those of Brandl (*Sitzungsberichte d. k. Preuss. Akad. d. Wissenschaften*, 1905, p. 719) which are based upon those of Barnouw.

"Morsbach's Test."

Sievers' theories as to O.E. metre have not been accepted by all scholars in their entirety. But the statistics which he collected enable us to say, with absolute certainty, that some given types of verse were not acceptable to the ear of an Old English bard.

Sceptics may emphasize the fact that Old English texts are uncertain, that nearly all poems are extant in one MS only, that the MS in each case was written down long after the poems were composed, and that precise verbal accuracy is therefore not to be expected[242]. All the more remarkable then becomes the fact, for it is a fact, that there are certain types of line which never occur in *Beowulf*, and that there are other types which are exceedingly rare. Again, there are certain types of line which *do* occur in *Beowulf* as we have it, though they seem contrary to the principles of O.E. scansion. When we find that such lines consistently contain some word which had a different metrical value when our extant MS of *Beowulf* was transcribed, from that which it had at the earlier date when *Beowulf* was composed, and that the earlier value makes the line metrical, the conclusion is obvious. *Beowulf* must have been composed at a time or in a dialect when the earlier metrical values held good.

But we reach a certain date beyond which, if we put the language back into its older form, it will no longer fit into the metrical structure. For example, words like *flōd, feld, eard* were originally "u-nouns": with nom. and acc. sing. *flōdu*, etc. But the half-line *ofer fealone flōd* (1950) becomes exceedingly difficult if we put it in the form *ofer fealone flōdu*[243]: the half-line *fifelcynnes eard* becomes absolutely impossible in the form *fifelcynnes eardu*[244].

It can, consequently, with some certainty be argued that these half-lines were composed after the time when *flōdu, eardu* had become *flōd, eard*. Therefore, it has been further argued, *Beowulf* was composed after that date. But are we justified in this further step—in assuming that because a certain number of half-lines in *Beowulf* must have been composed after a certain date, therefore *Beowulf* itself must have been composed after that date?

From what we know of the mechanical way in which the Old English *scribe* worked, we have no reason to suppose that he would have consistently altered what he found in an older copy, so as to make it metrical according to the later speech into which he was transcribing it. But if we go back to a time when poems were committed to memory by a *scop*, skilled in the laws of O.E. metre, the matter is very different. A written poem may be copied word for word, even though the spelling is at the same time modernized, but it is obvious that a poem preserved orally will be altered slightly from time to time, if the language in which it is written is undergoing changes which make the poem no longer metrically correct.

Imagine the state of things at the period when final *u* was being lost after a long syllable. This loss of a syllable would make a large number of the half-lines and formulas in the old poetry unmetrical. Are we to suppose that the whole of O.E. poetry was at once scrapped, and entirely new poems composed to fit in with the new sound laws? Surely not; old formulas would be recast, old lines modified where they needed it, but the old poetry would go on[245], with these minor verbal changes adapting it to the new order of things. We can see this taking place, to a limited extent, in the transcripts of Middle English poems. In the transmission of poems by word of mouth it would surely take place to such an extent as to baffle later investigation[246].

Consequently I am inclined to agree that this test is hardly final except "on the assumption that the poems were written down from the very beginning[247]." And we are clearly not justified in making any such assumption. A small number of such lines would accordingly give, not so much a means of fixing a period before which *Beowulf* cannot have been composed, as merely one before which *Beowulf* cannot have been fixed by writing in its present form.

If, however, more elaborate investigation were to show that the *percentage* of such lines is *just as great* in *Beowulf* as it is in poems certainly written after the sound changes had taken place, it might be conceded that the test was a valid one, and that it proved *Beowulf* to have been written after these sound changes occurred.

This would then bring us to our second difficulty. At what date exactly did these sound changes take place? The chief documents available are the proper names in Bede's History, and in certain Latin charters, the glosses, and a few early runic inscriptions. Most important, although very scanty, are the charters, since they bear a date. With these we proceed to investigate:

A. The dropping of the *u* after a long accented syllable (*flṓ´du* becoming *flṓ´d*), or semi-accented syllable (*Stā´nfòrdu* becoming *Stā´nfòrd*).

There is evidence from an Essex charter that this was already lost in 692 or 693 (*uuidmundesfelt*)[248]. From this date on, examples without the *u* are forthcoming in increasing number[249]. One certain example only has been claimed for the preservation of *u*. In the runic inscription on the "Franks casket" *flodu* is found for *flod*. But the spelling of the Franks casket is erratic: for example *giuþeasu* is also found for *giuþeas*, "the Jews." Now *u* here is impossible[250], and we must conclude perhaps that the inscriber of the runes intended to write *giuþea su[mæ]*[250] or *giuþea su[na]*[251], "some of the Jews," "the sons of the Jews," and that having reached the end of his line at *u*, he neglected to complete the word: or else perhaps that he wrote *giuþeas* and having some additional space added a *u* at the end of his line, just for fun. Whichever explanation we adopt, it will apply to *flodu*, which equally comes at the end of a line, and the *u* of which may equally have been part of some following word which was never completed[252].

Other linguistic data of the Franks casket would lead us to place it somewhere in the first half of the eighth century, and we should hardly expect to find *u* preserved as late as this[253]. For we have seen that by 693 the *u* was already lost after a subordinate accent in the Essex charter. Yet it is arguable that the *u* was retained later after a long accented syllable (*flódu*) than after a subordinate accent (*uuídmùndesfèlt*); and, besides, the casket is Northumbrian, and the sound changes need not have been simultaneous all over the country.

We cannot but feel that the evidence is pitifully scanty. All we can say is that *perhaps* the *flodu* of the Franks casket shows that *u* was still preserved after a fully accented syllable as late as 700. But the *u* in *flodu* may be a deliberate archaism on the part of the writer, may be a local dialectal survival, may be a mere miswriting.

B. The preservation of *h* between consonant and vowel.

Here there is one clear example which we can date: the archaic spelling of the proper name *Welhisc*. *Signum manus uelhisci* occurs in a Kentish charter of 679[254]. The same charter shows *h* already lost between vowels: *uuestan ae* (*ae* dative of *ēa*, "river," cf. Gothic *ahwa*).

Not much can be argued from the proper name *Welhisc*, as to the current pronunciation in Kent in 679, for an old man may well have continued to spell his name as it was spelt when he was a child, even though the current pronunciation had changed[255]. But we have further evidence in the glosses, which show *h* sometimes preserved and sometimes not. These glosses are mechanical copies of an original which was presumably compiled between 680 and 720. We are therefore justified in arguing that at that date *h* was still preserved, at any rate occasionally.

Of "Morsbach's test" we can then say that it establishes something of an argument that *Beowulf* was composed after the date when final *u* after a long syllable, or *h* between consonant and vowel, were lost, and that this date was probably within a generation or so of the year 700 A.D. But there are too many uncertain contingencies involved to make the test at all a conclusive one.

Morsbach's *Zur Datierung des Beowulf-epos* will be found in the Göttingen *Nachrichten*, 1906, pp. 252-77. These tests have been worked out for the whole body of Old English poetry in the *Chronologische Studien* of Carl Richter, Halle, 1910.

Certain peculiarities in the structure of *Beowulf* can hardly fail to strike the reader. (1) The poem is not a biography of Beowulf, nor yet an episode in his life: it is two distinct episodes: the Grendel business and the dragon business, joined by a narrow bridge. (2) Both these stories are broken in upon by digressions: some of these concern Beowulf himself, so that we get a fairly complete idea of the life of our hero: but for the most part these digressions are not strictly apposite. (3) Even apart from these digressions, the narrative is often hampered: the poet begins his story, diverges and returns. (4) The traces of Christian thought and knowledge which meet us from time to time seem to belong to a different world from that of the Germanic life in which our poem has its roots.

Now in the middle of the nineteenth century it was widely believed that the great epics of the world had been formed from collections of original shorter lays fitted together (often unskilfully) by later redactors. For a critic starting from this assumption, better material than the *Beowulf* could hardly be found. And it *was* with such assumptions that Carl Müllenhoff, the greatest of the scholars who have dissected the *Beowulf*, set to work. He attended the lectures of Lachmann, and formed, a biographer tells us, the fixed resolve to do for one epic what his admired master had done for another[256].

Müllenhoff claimed for his theories that they were simple[257] and straightforward: and so they were, if we may be allowed to assume as a basis that the *Beowulf* is made up out of shorter lays, and that the only business of the critic is to define the scope of these lays. In the story of Beowulf's fight with Grendel (ll. 194-836: Müllenhoff's Sect. I) and with the dragon (ll. 2200-3183: Müllenhoff's Sect. IV) Müllenhoff saw the much interpolated remains of two original lays by different authors. But, before it was united to the dragon story, the Grendel story, Müllenhoff held, had already undergone many interpolations and additions. The story of Grendel's mother (ll. 837-1623: Sect. II) was added, Müllenhoff held, by one continuator as a sequel to the story of Grendel, and ll. 1-193 were added by another hand as an introduction. Then this Grendel story was finally rounded off by an interpolator (A) who added the account of Beowulf's return home (Sect. III, ll. 1629-2199) and at the same time inserted passages into the poem throughout. Finally came Interpolator B, who was the first to combine the Grendel story, thus elaborated, with the dragon story. Interpolator B was responsible for the great bulk of the interpolations: episodes from other cycles and "theologizing" matter.

Ten Brink, like Müllenhoff, regarded the poem as falling into four sections: the Grendel fight, the fight with Grendel's mother, the return home, the dragon fight. But Müllenhoff had imagined the epic composed out of one set of lays: incoherences, he thought, were due to the bungling of successive interpolators. Ten Brink assumed that in the case of all three fights, with Grendel, with Grendel's mother, and with the dragon, there had been two *parallel* versions, which a later redactor had combined together, and that it was to this combination that the frequent repetitions in the narrative were due: he believed that not only were the different episodes of the poem originally distinct, but that each episode was compounded of two originally distinct lays, combined together.

Now it cannot be denied that the process postulated by Müllenhoff *might* have taken place: a lay on Grendel and a lay on the dragon-fight might have been combined by some later compiler. Ten Brink's theory, too, is inherently not improbable: that there should have been two or more versions current of a popular story is probable enough: that a scribe should have tried to fit these two parallel versions together is not without precedent: very good examples of such attempts at harmonizing different versions can be got from an examination of the MSS of *Piers Plowman*.

It is only here and there that we are struck by an inherent improbability in Müllenhoff's scheme. Thus the form in which Müllenhoff assumes the poem to have existed before Interpolator A set to work on it, is hardly a credible one. The "original poet" has brought Beowulf from his home to the Danish court, to slay Grendel, and the "continuator" has taken him to the haunted lake: Beowulf has plunged down, slain Grendel's mother, come back to land. Here Müllenhoff believed the poem to have ended, until "Interpolator A" came along, and told how Beowulf returned in triumph to Hrothgar, was thanked and rewarded, and then betook himself home, and was welcomed by Hygelac. That it would have been left to an interpolator to supply what from the old point of view was so necessary a part of the story as the return to Hrothgar is an assumption perilous indeed. "An epic poem only closes when everything is really concluded: not, like a modern novel, at a point where the reader can imagine the rest for himself[258]."

Generally speaking, however, the theories of the "dissecting school" are not in themselves faulty, if we admit the assumptions on which they rest. They fail however in two ways. An examination of the short lay and the long epic, so far as these are represented in extant documents, does not bear out well the assumptions of the theorizers. Secondly, the minute scrutiny to which the poem has been subjected in matters of syntax, metre, dialect and tradition has failed to show any difference between the parts attributed to the different authors, such as we must certainly have expected to find, had the theories of the "dissecting school" been correct.

That behind our extant *Beowulf*, and connecting it with the events of the sixth century, there must have been a number of older lays, may indeed well be admitted: also that to these lays our poem owes its plot, its traditions of metre and its phraseology, and perhaps (but this is a perilous assumption) continuous passages of its text. But what Müllenhoff and ten Brink go on to assume is that these original oral lays were simple in outline and treated a single well-defined episode in a straightforward manner; that later redactors and scribes corrupted this primiti7777ve simplicity; but that the modern critic, by demanding it, and using its presence or absence as a criterion, can still disentangle from the complex composite poem the simpler elements out of which it was built up.

Here are rather large assumptions. What right have we to postulate that this primitive "literature without letters[259]," these short oral ballads and lays, dealt with a single episode without digression or confusion: whilst the later age,—the civilized, Christianized age of written literature during which *Beowulf* in the form in which we now have it was produced,—is assumed to have been tolerant of both?

No doubt, here and there, in different literatures, groups of short lays can be found which one can imagine might be combined into an orderly narrative poem, without much hacking about. But on the other hand a short lay will often tell, in less than a hundred lines, a story more complex than that of the *Iliad* or the *Odyssey*. Its shortness may be due, not to any limitation in the scope of the plot, but rather to the passionate haste with which it rushes through a long story. It is one thing to admit that there must have been short lays on the story of Beowulf: it is another to assume that these lays were of such a character that nothing was needed but compilers with a taste for arrangement and interpolation in order to turn them into the extant epic of *Beowulf*.

When we find nearly five hundred lines spent in describing the reception of the hero in Hrothgar's land, we may well doubt whether this passage can have found its way into our poem through any such process of fitting together as Müllenhoff postulated. It would be out of scale in any narrative shorter than the *Beowulf* as we have it. It suggests to us that the epic is developed out of the lay, not by a process of fitting together, but rather by a retelling of the story in a more leisurely way.

A comparison of extant short lays or ballads with extant epics has shown that, if these epics were made by stringing lays together, such lays must have been different from the great majority of the short lays now known. "The lays into which this theory dissects the epics, or which it assumes as the sources of the epics, differ in two ways from extant lays: they deal with short, incomplete subjects and they have an epic breadth of style[260]."

It has been shown by W. P. Ker[261] that a comparison of such fragments as have survived of the Germanic short lay (*Finnsburg, Hildebrand*) does not bear out the theory that the epic is a conglomeration of such lays. "It is the change and development in style rather than any increase in the complexity of the themes that accounts for the difference in scale between the shorter and the longer poems."

A similar conclusion is reached by Professor Hart: "It might be illuminating to base a *Liedertheorie* in part, at least, upon a study of existing *Lieder*, rather than wholly upon an attempt to dismember the epic in question. Such study reveals indeed a certain similarity in kind of Ballad and Epic, but it reveals at the same time an enormous difference in degree, in stage of development. If the *Beowulf*, then, was made up of a series of heroic songs, strung together with little or no modification, these songs must have been something very different from the popular ballad[262]."

And subsequent investigations into the history and folk-lore of our poem have not confirmed Müllenhoff's theory: in some cases indeed they have hit it very hard. When a new light was thrown upon the story by the discovery of the parallels between *Beowulf* and the *Grettis saga*, it became clear that passages which Müllenhoff had condemned as otiose interpolations were likely to be genuine elements in the tale. Dr Olrik's minute investigations into the history of the Danish kings have shown from yet another point of view how allusions, which were rashly condemned by Müllenhoff and ten Brink as idle amplifications, are, in fact, essential.

How the investigation of the metre, form, and syntax of *Beowulf* has disclosed an archaic strictness of usage has been explained above (Sect. II). This usage is in striking contrast with the practice of later poets like Cynewulf. How far we are justified in relying upon such differences of usage as criteria of *exact* date is open to dispute. But it seems clear that, had Müllenhoff's theories been accurate, we might reasonably have expected to have been able to differentiate between the earlier and the later strata in so composite a poem.

The composite theory has lately been strongly supported by Schücking[263]. Schücking starts from the fact, upon which we are all agreed, that the poem falls into two main divisions: the story of how Beowulf at Heorot slew Grendel and Grendel's mother, and the story of the dragon, which fifty years later he slew at his home. These are connected by the section which tells how Beowulf returned from Heorot to his own home and was honourably received by his king, Hygelac.

It is now admitted that the ways of Old English narrative were not necessarily our ways, and that we must not postulate, because our poem falls into two somewhat clumsily connected sections, that therefore it is compounded out of two originally distinct lays. But, on the other hand, as Schücking rightly urges, instances *are* forthcoming of two O.E. poems having been clumsily connected into one[264]. Therefore, whilst no one would now urge that *Beowulf* is put together out of two older lays, *merely* because it can so easily be divided into two sections, this fact does suggest that a case exists for examination.

Now if a later poet had connected together two old lays, one on the Grendel and Grendel's mother business, and one on the dragon business, we might fairly expect that this connecting link would show traces of a different style. It is accordingly on the connecting link, the story of *Beowulf's Return* and reception by Hygelac, that Schücking concentrates his attention, submitting it to the most elaborate tests to see if it betrays metrical, stylistic or syntactical divergencies from the rest of the poem.

Various tests are applied, which admittedly give no result, such as the frequency of the repetition in the *Return* of half verse formulas which occur elsewhere in *Beowulf*[265], or the way in which compound nouns fit into the metrical scheme[266]. Metrical criteria are very little more helpful[267]. We have seen that the antiquity of *Beowulf* is proved by the cases where metre demands the substitution of an older uncontracted form for the existing shorter one. Schücking argues that no instance occurs in the 267 lines of the *Return*. But, even if this were the case, it might well be mere accident, since examples only occur at rare intervals anywhere in *Beowulf*. As a matter of fact, however, examples are to be found in the *Return*[268] (quite up to the normal proportion), though two of the clearest come in a portion of it which Schücking rather arbitrarily excludes.

Coming to syntax in its broadest sense, and especially the method of constructing and connecting sentences, Schücking enumerates several constructions which are found in the *Return*, but not elsewhere in *Beowulf*. Syntax is a subject to which he has given special study, and his opinion upon it must be of value. But I doubt whether anyone as expert in the subject as Schücking could not find in every passage of like length in *Beowulf* some constructions not to be exactly paralleled elsewhere in the poem.

The fact that we find here, and here only, passages introduced by the clauses *ic sceal forð sprecan*[269], and *tō lang ys tō reccenne*[270], is natural when we realize that we have here the longest speech in the whole poem, which obviously calls for such apologies for prolixity.

The fact that no parentheses occur in the *Return* does not differentiate it from the rest of *Beowulf*: for, as Schücking himself points out elsewhere, there are three other passages in the poem, longer than the *Return*, which are equally devoid of parentheses[271].

There remain a few *hapax legomena*[272], but very inconclusive.

There are, in addition, examples which occur only in the *Return*, and in certain other episodic passages. These episodic passages also, Schücking supposes, may have been added by the same reviser who added the *Return*. But this is a perilous change of position. For example, a certain peculiarity is found only in the *Return* and the introductory genealogical section[273]; or in the *Return* and the *Finn Episode*[274]. But when Schücking proceeds to the suggestion that the *Introduction* or the *Finn Episode* may have been added by the same reviser who added *Beowulf's Return*, he knocks the bottom out of some of his previous arguments. The argument from the absence of parentheses (whatever it was worth) must go: for according to Schücking's own punctuation, such parentheses are found both in the *Introduction* and in the *Finn Episode*. If these are by the author of the *Return*, then doubt is thrown upon one of the alleged peculiarities of that author; we find the author of the *Return* no more averse *on the whole* to parentheses than the author or authors of the rest of the poem.

Peculiar usages of the moods and tenses are found twice in the *Return*[275], and once again in the episode where Beowulf recalls his youth[276]. Supposing this episode to be also the work of the author of the *Return*, we get peculiar constructions used three times by this author, which cannot be paralleled elsewhere in *Beowulf*[277].

Now a large number of instances like this last might afford basis for argument; but they must be in bulk in order to prove anything. By the laws of chance we might expect, in any passage of three hundred lines, taken at random anywhere in *Beowulf*, to find something which occurred only in one other passage elsewhere in the poem. We cannot forthwith declare the two passages to be the work of an interpolator. One swallow does not make a summer.

And the arguments as to style are not helped by arguments as to matter. Even if it be granted—which I do not grant—that the long repetition narrating Beowulf's contest with Grendel and Grendel's mother is tedious, there is no reason why this tedious repetition should not as well be the work of the original poet as of a later reviser. Must we find many different authors for *The Ring and the Book*? It must be granted that there are details (such as the mention of Grendel's glove) found in the Grendel struggle as narrated in *Beowulf's Return*, but not found in the original account of the struggle. Obviously the object is to avoid monotony, by introducing a new feature: but this might as well have been aimed at by the old poet retelling the tale as by a new poet retelling it.

To me, the fact that so careful and elaborate a study of the story of *Beowulf's Return* fails to betray any satisfactory evidence of separate authorship, is a confirmation of the verdict of "not proven" against the "dividers[278]." But there can be no doubt that Schücking's method, his attempt to prove differences in treatment, grammar, and style, is the right one. If any satisfactory results are to be attained, it must be in this way.

Later students (like the man in Dante, placed between two equally enticing dishes) have been unable to decide in favour of either of the rival theories of Müllenhoff and ten Brink, and consequently the unity of the poem, which always had its champions, has of late years come to be maintained with increasing conviction and certainty.

Yet many recent critics have followed Müllenhoff so far at least as to believe that the Christian passages are inconsistent with what they regard as the "essentially heathen" tone of the rest of the poem, and are therefore the work of an interpolator[279].

Certainly no one can escape a feeling of incongruity, as he passes from ideas of which the home lies in the forests of ancient Germany, to others which come from the Holy Land. But that both sets of ideas could not have been cherished, in England, about the year 700, by one and the same poet, is an assumption which calls for examination.

As Christianity swept northward, situations were created which to the modern student are incongruous. But the Teutonic chief often had a larger mind than the modern student: he needed to have, if he was to get the best at the same time both from his wild fighting men and from his Latin clerks. It is this which gives so remarkable a character to the great men of the early centuries of converted Teutonism: men, like Theodoric the Great or Charles the Great, who could perform simultaneously the duties of a Germanic king and of a Roman Emperor: kings like Alfred the Great or St Olaf, who combined the character of the tough fighting chieftain with that of the saintly churchman. I love to think of these incongruities: to remember that the warrior Alfred, surrounded by *thegn* and *gesith*, listening to the "Saxon songs" which he loved, was yet the same Alfred who painfully translated Gregory's *Pastoral Care* under the direction of foreign clerics. It is well to remember that Charles the Great, the catholic and the orthodox, collected ancient lays which his successors thought too heathen to be tolerated; or that St Olaf (who was so holy that, having absent mindedly chipped shavings off a stick on Sunday, he burnt them, as penance, on his open hand) nevertheless allowed to be sung before him, on the morning of his last fight, one of the most wild and utterly heathen of all the old songs—the *Bjarkamál.*

It has been claimed that the account of the funeral rites of Beowulf is such as "no Christian poet could or would have composed[280]." Lately this argument has been stated more at length:

"In the long account of Beowulf's obsequies—beginning with the dying king's injunction to construct for him a lofty barrow on the edge of the cliff, and ending with the scene of the twelve princes riding round the barrow, proclaiming the dead man's exploits—we have the most detailed description of an early Teutonic funeral which has come down to us, and one of which the accuracy is confirmed in every point by archaeological or contemporary literary evidence[281]. Such an account must have been composed within living memory of a time when ceremonies of this kind were still actually in use[282]."

Owing to the standing of the scholar who urges it, this argument is coming to rank as a dogma[283], and needs therefore rather close examination.

Professor Chadwick *may* be right in urging that the custom of burning the dead had gone out of use in England even before Christianity was introduced[284]: anyhow it is certain that, wherever it survived, the practice was disapproved by ecclesiastics, and was, indeed, formally censured and suppressed by the church abroad.

The church equally censured and endeavoured to suppress the ancient "heathen lays"; but without equal success. Now, in many of these lays the heathen rites of cremation must certainly have been depicted, and, in this way, the memory of the old funeral customs must have been kept fresh, long after the last funeral pyre had died out in England. Of course there were then, as there have been ever since, puritanical people who objected that heathen lays and heathen ways were no fit concern for a Christian man. But the protests of such purists are just the strongest evidence that the average Christian did continue to take an interest in these things. We have seen that the very monks of Lindisfarne had to be warned by Alcuin. I cannot see that there is any such *a priori* impossibility that a poet, though a sincere Christian enough, would have described a funeral in the old style, modelling his account upon older lays, or upon tradition derived from those lays.

The church might disapprove of the practice of cremation, but we have no reason to suppose that mention of it was tabooed. And many of the old burial customs seem to have kept their hold, even upon the converted. Indeed, when the funeral of Attila is instanced as a type of the old heathen ceremony, it seems to be forgotten that those Gothic chieftains who rode their horses round the body of Attila were themselves probably Arian Christians, and that the historian who has preserved the account was an orthodox cleric.

Saxo Grammaticus, ecclesiastic as he was, has left us several accounts[285] of cremations. He mentions the "pyre built of ships" and differs from the poet of *Beowulf* chiefly because he allows those frankly heathen references to gods and offerings which the poet of *Beowulf* excludes. Of course, Saxo was merely translating. One can quite believe that a Christian poet composing an account of a funeral in the old days, would have omitted the more frankly heathen features, as indeed the *Beowulf* poet does. But Saxo shows us how far into Christian times the ancient funeral, in all its heathendom, was remembered; and how little compunction an ecclesiastic had in recording it. The assumption that no Christian poet would have composed the account of Beowulf's funeral or of Scyld's funeral ship, seems then to be quite unjustified.

The further question remains: Granting that he *would*, could he? Is the account of Beowulf's funeral so true to old custom that it must have been composed by an eye-witness of the rite of cremation? Is its "accuracy confirmed in every point by archaeological or contemporary literary evidence"?

As to the archaeological evidence, the fact seems to be that the account is archaeologically so inexact that it has given great trouble to one eminent antiquary, Knut Stjerna. That the pyre should be hung with arms, which are *burnt* with the hero (ll. 3139-40), and that then a second supply of unburnt treasures should be *buried* with the cremated bones (ll. 3163-8), is regarded by Stjerna as extraordinary[286].

Surely, any such inexactitude is what we should expect in a late poet, drawing upon tradition. He would know that in heathen times bodies were burnt, and that weapons were buried; and he might well combine both. It is not necessary to suppose, as Stjerna does, that the poet has combined two separate accounts of Beowulf's funeral, given in older lays, in one of which the hero was burnt, and in the other buried. But the fact that an archaeological specialist finds the account of Beowulf's funeral so inexact that he has to assume a confused and composite source, surely disposes of the argument that it is so exact that it must date back to heathen times.

As to confirmation from literary documents, the only one instanced by Chadwick is the account of the funeral of Attila. The parallel here is by no means so close as has been asserted. The features of Attila's funeral are: the lying in state, during which the chosen horsemen of the nation rode round the body singing the dead king's praises; the funeral feast; and the burial (not burning) of the body. Now the only feature which recurs in *Beowulf* is the praise of the dead man by the mounted thanes. Even here there is an essential difference. Attila's men rode round the dead body of their lord *before* his funeral. Beowulf's retainers ride and utter their lament around (not the body but) the grave mound of their lord, ten days after the cremation.

And this is perhaps no accidental discrepancy: it may well correspond to a real difference in practice between the Gothic custom of the time of the migrations and the Anglo-Saxon practice as it prevailed in Christian times[287]. For many documents, including the *Dream of the Rood*, tend to show that the *sorhlēoð*, the lament of the retainers for their dead lord, survived into Christian times, but as a ceremony which was subsequent not merely to the funeral, but even to the building of the tomb.

So that, here again, so far from the archaeological accuracy of the account of Beowulf's funeral being confirmed by the account of that of Attila, we find a discrepancy such as we might expect if a Christian poet, in later times, had tried to describe a funeral of the old heathen type.

Of course, the evidence is far too scanty to allow of much positive argument. Still, *so far as it goes*, and that is not far, it rather tends to show that the account of the funeral customs is not quite accurate, representing what later Christian times knew by tradition of the rite of cremation, rather than showing the observation of that rite by an eye-witness.

We must turn, then, to some other argument, if we wish to prove that the Christian element is inconsistent with other parts of the poem.

A second argument that *Beowulf* must belong either to heathen times, or to the very earliest Christian period in England, has been found in the character of the Christian allusions: they contain no "reference to Christ, to the Cross, to the Virgin or the Saints, to any doctrine of the church in regard to the Trinity, the Atonement, *etc.*[288]" "A pious Jew would have no difficulty in assenting to them all[289]." Hence it has been argued[290] that they are the work of an interpolator who, working upon a poem "essentially heathen," was not able to impose upon it more than this "vague and colourless Christianity." I cannot see this. If passages had to be rewritten at all, it was just as easy to rewrite them in a tone emphatically Christian as in a tone mildly so. The difficulties which the interpolator would meet in removing a heathen phrase, and composing a Christian half-line in substitution, would be metrical, rather than theological. For example, in a second half-line the interpolator could have written *ond hālig Crist* or *ylda nergend* just as easily as *ond hālig god*, or *ylda waldend*: he could have put in an allusion to the Trinity or to the Cross as easily as to the Lord of Hosts or the King of Glory. It would depend upon the alliteration which was the more convenient. And surely, if he was a monk deliberately sitting down to turn a heathen into a Christian poem, he would, of two alternatives, have favoured the more dogmatically Christian.

The vagueness which is so characteristic of the Christian references in *Beowulf* can then hardly be due to the poem having originally been a heathen one, worked over by a Christian.

Others have seen in this vagueness a proof "that the minstrels who introduced the Christian element had but a vague knowledge of the new faith[291]": or that the poem was the work of "a man who, without having, or wanting to have, much definite instruction, had become Christian because the Court had newly become Christian[292]." But, vague as it is, does the Christianity of *Beowulf* justify such a judgment as this? Do not the characters of Hrothgar or of Beowulf, of Hygd or of Wealhtheow, show a Christian influence which, however little dogmatic, is anything but superficial? This is a matter where individual feeling rather than argument must weigh: but the *Beowulf* does not seem to me the work of a man whose adherence to Christianity is merely nominal[293].

And, so far as the absence of dogma goes, it seems to have been overlooked that the Christian references in the *Battle of Maldon*, written when England had been Christian for over three centuries, are precisely of the same vague character as those in *Beowulf*.

Surely the explanation is that to a devout, but not theologically-minded poet, writing battle poetry, references to God as the Lord of Hosts or the Giver of Victory came naturally—references to the Trinity or the Atonement did not. This seems quite a sufficient explanation; though it may be that in *Beowulf* the poet has consciously avoided dogmatic references, because he realized that the characters in his story were not Christians[294]. That, at the same time, he allows those characters with whom he sympathizes to speak in a Christian spirit is only what we should expect. Just so Chaucer allows his pagans— Theseus for instance—to use Christian expressions about God or the soul, whilst avoiding anything strikingly doctrinal.

Finally I cannot admit that the Christian passages are "poetically of no value[295]." The description of Grendel nearing Heorot is good:

Ðā cōm of mōre under mist-hleoþum
Grendel gongan—

but it is heightened when the poet adds:

Godes yrre bær.

Yet here again it is impossible to argue: it is a matter of individual feeling.

When, however, we come to the further statement of Dr Bradley, that the Christian passages are not only interpolations poetically worthless, but "may be of any date down to that of the extant MS" (i.e. about the year 1000 A.D.), we have reached ground where argument *is* possible, and where definite results can be attained. For Dr Bradley, at the same time that he makes this statement about the character of the Christian passages, also quotes the archaic syntax of *Beowulf* as proving an early date[296]. *But this archaic syntax is just as prominent a feature of the Christian passages as of any other parts of the poem.* If these Christian passages are really the work of a "monkish copyist, whose piety exceeded his poetic powers[297]," how do they come to show an antique syntax and a strict technique surpassing those of Cynewulf or the *Dream of the Rood*? Why do they not betray their origin by metrical inaccuracies such as we find in poems undoubtedly interpolated, like *Widsith* or the *Seafarer*?

Dr Bradley is "our chief English seer in these matters," as Dr Furnivall said long ago; and it is only with the greatest circumspection that one should differ from any of his conclusions. Nevertheless, I feel that, before we can regard any portion of *Beowulf* as later than the rest, discrepancies need to be demonstrated.

Until such discrepancies between the different parts of *Beowulf* can be demonstrated, we are justified in regarding the poem as homogeneous: as a production of the Germanic world enlightened by the new faith. Whether through external violence or internal decay, this world was fated to rapid change, and perished with its promise unfulfilled. The great merit of *Beowulf* as a historic document is that it shows us a picture of a period in which the virtues of the heathen "Heroic Age" were tempered by the gentleness of the new belief; an age warlike, yet Christian: devout, yet tolerant.

PART II

DOCUMENTS ILLUSTRATING THE STORIES IN BEOWULF, AND THE OFFA-SAGA.

A. THE EARLY KINGS OF THE DANES ACCORDING TO SAXO GRAMMATICUS

Saxo, Book I, ed. Ascensius, fol. iii b; ed. Holder, p. 10, l. 25.

Uerum a Dan, ut fert antiquitas, regum nostrorum stemmata, ceu quodam deriuata principio, splendido successionis ordine profluxerunt. Huic filii Humblus et Lotherus fuere, ex Grytha, summæ inter Teutones dignitatis matrona, suscepti.

Lecturi regem ueteres affixis humo saxis insistere, suffragiaque promere consueuerant, subiectorum lapidum firmitate facti constantiam ominaturi. Quo ritu Humblus, decedente patre, nouo patriæ beneficio rex creatus, sequentis fortunæ malignitate, ex rege priuatus euasit. Bello siquidem a Lothero captus, regni depositione spiritum mercatus est; hæc sola quippe uicto salutis conditio reddebatur. Ita fraternis iniuriis imperium abdicare coactus, documentum hominibus præbuit, ut plus splendoris, ita minus securitatis, aulis quam tuguriis inesse. Ceterum iniuriæ tam patiens fuit, ut honoris damno tanquam beneficio gratulari crederetur, sagaciter, ut puto, regiæ conditionis habitum contemplatus. Sed nec Lotherus tolerabiliorem regem quam militem egit, ut prorsus insolentia ac scelere regnum auspicari uideretur; siquidem illustrissimum quemque uita aut opibus spoliare, patriamque bonis ciuibus uacuefacere probitatis loco duxit, regni æmulos ratus, quos nobilitate pares habuerat. Nec diu scelerum impunitus, patriæ consternatione perimitur; eadem spiritum eripiente, quæ regnum largita fuerat.

Cuius filius Skyoldus naturam ab ipso, non mores sortitus, per summam tenerioris ætatis industriam cuncta paternæ contagionis uestigia ingeniti erroris deuio præteribat. Igitur ut a paternis uitiis prudenter desciuit, ita auitis uirtutibus feliciter respondit, remotiorem pariter ac præstantiorem hereditarii moris portionem amplexus. Huius adolescentia inter paternos uenatores immanis beluæ subactione insignis extitit, mirandoque rei euentu futuræ eius fortitudinis habitum ominata est. Nam cum a tutoribus forte, quorum summo studio educabatur, inspectandæ uenationis licentiam impetrasset, obuium sibi insolitæ granditatis ursum, telo uacuus, cingulo, cuius usum habebat, religandum curauit, necandumque comitibus præbuit. Sed et complures spectatæ fortitudinis pugiles per idem tempus uiritim ab eo superati produntur, e quibus Attalus et Scatus clari illustresque fuere. Quindecim annos natus, inusitato corporis incremento perfectissimum humani roboris specimen præferebat, tantaque indolis eius experimenta fuere, ut ab ipso ceteri Danorum reges communi quodam uocabulo Skioldungi nuncuparentur....

Saxo then relates the adventures of Gram, Hadingus and Frotho, whom he represents as respectively son, grandson and great-grandson of Skioldus. That Gram and Hadingus are interpolated in the family is shewn by the fact that the pedigree of Sweyn Aageson passes direct from Skiold to his son Frothi.

Saxo, Book II, ed. Ascensius, fol. xi b; ed. Holder, p. 38, l. 4.

Hadingo filius Frotho succedit, cuius uarii insignesque casus fuere. Pubertatis annos emensus, iuuenilium præferebat complementa uirtutum, quas ne desidiæ corrumpendas præberet, abstractum uoluptatibus animum assidua armorum intentione torquebat. Qui cum, paterno thesauro bellicis operibus absumpto, stipendiorum facultatem, qua militem aleret, non haberet, attentiusque necessarii usus subsidia circunspiceret, tali subeuntis indigenæ carmine concitatur:

Insula non longe est præmollibus edita cliuis,
Collibus æra tegens et opimæ conscia prædæ.
Hic tenet eximium, montis possessor, aceruum

Implicitus giris serpens crebrisque reflexus
Orbibus, et caudæ sinuosa uolumina ducens,
Multiplicesque agitans spiras, uirusque profundens.
Quem superare uolens clypeo, quo conuenit uti,
Taurinas intende cutes, corpusque bouinis
Tergoribus tegito, nec amaro nuda ueneno
Membra patere sinas; sanies, quod conspuit, urit.
Lingua trisulca micans patulo licet ore resultet,
Tristiaque horrifico minitetur uulnera rictu,
Intrepidum mentis habitum retinere memento.
Nec te permoueat spinosi dentis acumen,
Nec rigor, aut rapida iactatum fauce uenenum.
Tela licet temnat uis squamea, uentre sub imo
Esse locum scito, quo ferrum mergere fas est;
Hunc mucrone petens medium rimaberis anguem.
Hinc montem securus adi, pressoque ligone
Perfossos scrutare cauos; mox ære crumenas
Imbue, completamque reduc ad littora puppim.

Credulus Frotho solitarius in insulam traiicit: ne comitatior beluam adoriretur, quam athletas aggredi moris fuerat. Quæ cum aquis pota specum repeteret, impactum Frothonis ferrum aspero cutis horrore contempsit. Sed et spicula, quæ in eam coniecta fuerant, eluso mittentis conatu læsionis irrita resultabant. At ubi nil tergi duritia cessit, uentris curiosius annotati mollities ferro patuit. Quæ se morsu ulcisci cupiens, clypeo duntaxat spinosum oris acumen impegit. Crebris deinde linguam micatibus ducens, uitam pariter ac uirus efflauit.

Repertæ pecuniæ regem locupletem fecere....

Saxo, Book II, ed. Ascensius, fol. xv b; ed. Holder, p. 51, l. 4.

His, uirtute paribus, æqua regnandi incessit auiditas. Imperii cuique cura extitit; fraternus nullum respectus astrinxit. Quem enim nimia sui caritas ceperit, aliena deserit: nee sibi quisquam ambitiose atque aliis amice consulere potest. Horum maximus Haldanus, Roe et Scato fratribus interfectis, naturam scelere polluit: regnum parricidio carpsit. Et ne ullum crudelitatis exemplum omitteret, comprehensos eorum fautores prius uinculorum pœna coercuit, mox suspendio consumpsit. Cuius ex eo maxime fortuna ammirabilis fuit, quod, licet omnia temporum momenta ad exercenda atrocitatis officia contulisset, senectute uitam, non ferro, finierit.

Huius filii Roe et Helgo fuere. A Roe Roskildia condita memoratur: quam postmodum Sueno, furcatæ barbæ cognomento clarus, ciuibus auxit, amplitudine propagauit. Hic breui angustoque corpore fuit: Helgonem habitus procerior cepit. Qui, diuiso cum fratre regno, maris possessionem sortitus, regem Sclauiæ Scalcum maritimis copiis lacessitum oppressit. Quam cum in prouinciam redegisset, uarios pelagi recessus uago nauigationis genere perlustrabat.

Saxo, Book II, ed. Ascensius, fol. xvi a; ed. Holder, p. 53, l. 16.

Huic filius Roluo succedit, uir corporis animique dotibus uenustus, qui staturæ magnitudinem pari uirtutis habitu commendaret.

Ibid., ed. Ascensius, fol. xvii a; ed. Holder, p. 55, l. 40.

Per idem tempus Agnerus quidam, Ingelli films, sororem Roluonis, Rutam nomine, matrimonio ducturus, ingenti conuiuio nuptias instruit. In quo cum pugiles, omni petulantiæ genere debacchantes, in Ialtonem quendam nodosa passim ossa coniicerent, accidit, ut eius consessor, Biarco nomine, iacientis errore uehementem capite ictum exciperet. Qui dolore pariter ac ludibrio lacessitus, osse inuicem in iacientem remisso, frontem eius in occuput reflexit, idemque loco frontis intorsit, transuersum hominis animum uultus obliquitate mulctando. Ea res contumeliosam ioci insolentiam temperauit, pugilesque regia abire coegit. Qua conuiuii iniuria permotus, sponsus ferro cum Biarcone decernere statuit, uiolatæ hilaritatis ultionem duelii nomine quæsiturus. In cuius ingressu, utri prior feriendi copia deberetur diutule certatum est. Non enim antiquitus in edendis agonibus crebræ ictuum uicissitudines petebantur: sed erat cum interuallo temporis etiam feriendi distincta successio; rarisque sed atrocibus plagis certamina gerebantur, ut gloria potius percussionum magnitudini, quam numero deferretur. Prælato ob generis dignitatem Agnero, tanta ui ictum ab eo editum constat, ut, prima cassidis parte conscissa, supremam capitis cuticulam uulneraret, ferrumque mediis galeæ interclusum foraminibus dimitteret. Tunc Biarco mutuo percussurus, quo plenius ferrum libraret, pedem trunco annixus, medium Agneri corpus præstantis acuminis mucrone transegit. Sunt qui asserant, morientem Agnerum soluto in risum ore per summam doloris dissimulationem spiritum reddidisse. Cuius ultionem pugiles auidius expetentes, simili per Biarconem exitio mulctati sunt. Utebatur quippe præstantis acuminis inusitatæque longitudinis gladio, quem Løui uocabat. Talibus operum meritis exultanti nouam de se siluestris fera uictoriam præbuit. Ursum quippe eximiæ magnitudinis obuium sibi inter dumeta factum iaculo confecit: comitemque suum Ialtonem, quo uiribus maior euaderet, applicato ore egestum belluæ cruorem haurire iussit. Creditum namque erat, hoc potionis genere corporei roboris incrementa præstari. His facinorum uirtutibus clarissimas optimatum familiaritates adeptus, etiam regi percarus euasit; sororem eius Rutam uxorem asciuit, uictique sponsam uictoriæ præmium habuit. Ab Atislo lacessiti Roluonis ultionem armis exegit, eumque uictum hello prostrauit. Tunc Roluo magni acuminis iuuenem Hiarthwarum nomine, sorore Sculda sibi in matrimonium data, annuoque uectigali imposito, Suetiæ præfectum constituit, libertatis iacturam affinitatis beneficio leniturus.

Hoc loci quiddam memoratu iucundum operi inseratur. Adolescens quidam Wiggo nomine, corpoream Roluonis magnitudinem attentiori contemplatione scrutatus, ingentique eiusdem admiratione captus, percontari per ludibrium cœpit, quisnam esset iste Krage, quem tanto staturæ fastigio prodiga rerum natura ditasset; faceto cauillationis genere inusitatum proceritatis habitum prosecutus. Dicitur enim lingua Danica 'krage' truncus, cuius semicæsis ramis fastigia conscenduntur, ita ut pes, præcisorum stipitum obsequio perinde ac scalæ beneficio nixus, sensimque ad superiora prouectus, petitæ celsitudinis compendium assequatur. Quern uocis iactum Roluo perinde ac inclytum sibi cognomen amplexus, urbanitatem dicti ingentis armillæ dono prosequitur. Qua Wiggo dexteram excultam extollens, læua per pudoris simulationem post tergum reflexa, ridiculum corporis incessum præbuit, præfatus, exiguo lætari munere, quem sors diutinæ tenuisset inopiæ. Rogatus, cur ita se gereret, inopem ornamenti manum nulloque cultus beneficio gloriantem ad aspectum reliquæ uerecundo paupertatis rubore perfundi dicebat. Cuius dicti calliditate consentaneum priori munus obtinuit. Siquidem Roluo manum, quæ ab ipso occultabatur, exemplo reliquæ in medium accersendam curauit. Nec Wiggoni rependendi beneficii cura defuit. Siquidem arctissima uoti nuncupatione pollicitus est, si Roluonem ferro perire contingeret, ultionem se ab eius interfectoribus exacturum. Nec prætereundum, quod olim ingressuri curiam proceres famulatus sui principia alicuius magnæ rei uoto principibus obligare solebant, uirtute tirocinium auspicantes.

Interea Sculda, tributariæ solutionis pudore permota, diris animum commentis applicans, maritum, exprobrata condicionis deformitate, propulsandæ seruitutis monitu concitatum atque ad insidias Roluoni nectendas perductum atrocissimis nouarum rerum consiliis imbuit, plus unumquenque libertati quam necessitudini debere testata. Igitur crebras armorum massas, diuersi generis tegminibus obuolutas, tributi more per Hiarthwarum in Daniam perferri iubet, occidendi noctu regis materiam præbituras. Refertis itaque falsa uectigalium mole nauigiis, Lethram pergitur, quod oppidum, a Roluone constructum eximiisque regni opibus illustratum, ceteris confinium prouinciarum urbibus regiæ fundationis et sedis auctoritate præstabat. Rex aduentum Hiarthwari conuiualis impensæ deliciis prosecutus ingenti se potione proluerat, hospitibus præter morem ebrietatis intemperantiam formidantibus. Ceteris igitur altiorem carpentibus somnum, Sueones, quibus scelesti libido propositi communem quietis usum ademerat, cubiculis furtim delabi cœpere. Aperitur ilico telorum occlusa congeries, et sua sibi quisque tacitus arma connectit. Deinde regiam petunt, irruptisque penetralibus in dormientium corpora ferrum destringunt. Experrecti complures, quibus non minus subitæ cladis horror quam somni stupor incesserat, dubio nisu discrimini restitere, socii an hostes occurrerent, noctis errore incertum reddente. Eiusdem forte silentio noctis Hialto, qui inter regios proceres spectatæ probitatis merito præeminebat, rus egressus, scorti se complexibus dederat. Hic cum obortum pugnæ fragorem stupida procul aure sensisset, fortitudinem luxuriæ prætulit, maluitque funestum Martis discrimen appetere, quam blandis Veneris illecebris indulgere. Quanta hunc militem regis caritate flagrasse putemus, qui, cum ignorantiæ simulatione excusationem absentiæ præstare posset, salutem suam manifesto periculo obicere, quam uoluptati seruare satius existimauit? Discedentem pellex percunctari cœpit, si ipso careat, cuius ætatis uiro nubere debeat. Quam Hialto, perinde ac secretius allocuturus, propius accedere iussam, indignatus amoris sibi successorem requiri, præciso naso deformem reddidit, erubescendoque uulnere libidinosæ percunctationis dictum mulctauit, mentis lasciuiam oris iactura temperandam existimans. Quo facto, liberum quæsitæ rei iudicium a se ei relinqui dixit. Post hæc, repetito ocius oppido, confertissimis se globis immergit, aduersasque acies mutua uulnerum inflictione prosternit. Cumque dormientis adhuc Biarconis cubiculum præteriret, expergisci iussum, tali uoce compellat:

Saxo's translation of the *Bjarkamál* follows. The part which concerns students of *Beowulf* most is the account of how Roluo deposed and slew Røricus.

Saxo, Book II, ed. Ascensius, fol. xix a; ed. Holder, p. 62, l. 1.

At nos, qui regem uoto meliore ueremur,
Iungamus cuneos stabiles, tutisque phalangem
Ordinibus mensi, qua rex præcepit, eamus
Qui natum Bøki Røricum strauit auari,
Implicuitque uirum leto uirtute carentem.
Ille quidem præstans opibus, habituque fruendi
Pauper erat, probitate minus quam fœnore pollens;
Aurum militia potius ratus, omnia lucro
Posthabuit, laudisque carens congessit aceruos
Æris, et ingenuis uti contempsit amicis.
Cumque lacessitus Roluonis classe fuisset,
Egestum cistis aurum deferre ministros
Iussit, et in primas urbis diffundere portas.

Dona magis quam bella parans, quia militis expers
Munere, non armis, tentandum credidit hostem;
Tanquam opibus solis bellum gesturus, et usu
Rerum, non hominum, Martem producere posset.
Ergo graues loculos et ditia claustra resoluit
Armillas teretes et onustas protulit arcas,
Exitii fomenta sui, ditissimus æris,
Bellatoris inops, hostique adimenda relinquens
Pignora, quæ patriis præbere pepercit amicis.
Annellos ultro metuens dare, maxima nolens
Pondera fudit opum, ueteris populator aceruI.
Rex tamen hunc prudens, oblataque munera spreuit,
Rem pariter uitamque adimens; nec profuit hosti
Census iners, quem longo auidus cumulauerat æuo.
Hunc pius inuasit Roluo, summasque perempti
Cepit opes, inter dignos partitus amicos,
Quicquid auara manus tantis congesserat annis;
Irrumpensque opulenta magis quam fortia castra,
Præbuit eximiam sociis sine sanguine prædam.

Cui nil tam pulchrum fuit, ut non funderet illud,
Aut carum, quod non sociis daret, æra fauillis
Assimulans, famaque annos, non fœnore mensus.
Unde liquet, regem claro iam funere functum
Præclaros egisse dies, speciosaque fati
Tempora, præteritos decorasse uiriliter annos.
Nam uirtute ardens, dum uiueret, omnia uicit,
Egregio dignas sortitus corpore uires.
Tam præceps in bella fuit, quam concitus amnis
In mare decurrit, pugnamque capessere promptus
Ut ceruus rapidum bifido pede tendere cursum.

Saxo, Book II, ed. Ascensius, fol. xxi a; ed. Holder, p. 67, l. 1.

Hanc maxime exhortationum seriem idcirco metrica ratione compegerim, quod earundem sententiarum intellectus Danici cuiusdam carminis compendio digestus a compluribus antiquitatis peritis memoriter usurpatur.

Contigit autem, potitis uictoria Gothis, omne Roluonis agmen occumbere, neminemque, excepto Wiggone, ex tanta iuuentute residuum fore. Tantum enim excellentissimis regis meritis ea pugna a militibus tributum est, ut ipsius cædes omnibus oppetendæ mortis cupiditatem ingeneraret, eique morte iungi uita iucundius duceretur.

Lætus Hiartuarus prandendi gratia positis mensis conuiuium pugnæ succedere iubet, uictoriam epulis prosecuturus. Quibus oneratus magnæ sibi ammirationi esse dixit, quod ex tanta Roluonis militia nemo, qui saluti fuga aut captione consuleret, repertus fuisset. Unde liquidum fuisse quanto fidei studio regis sui caritatem coluerint, cui superstites esse passi non fuerint. Fortunam quoque, quod sibi ne unius quidem eorum obsequium superesse permiserit, causabatur, quam libentissime se talium uirorum famulatu usurum testatus. Oblato Wiggone perinde ac munere gratulatus, an sibi militare uellet, perquirit. Annuenti destrictum gladium offert. Ille cuspidem refutans, capulum petit, hunc morem Roluoni in porrigendo militibus ense extitisse præfatus. Olim namque se regum clientelæ daturi, tacto gladii capulo obsequium polliceri solebant. Quo pacto Wiggo capulum complexus, cuspidem per Hiartuarum agit, ultionis compos, cuius Roluoni ministerium pollicitus fuerat. Quo facto, ouans irruentibus in se Hiartuari militibus cupidius corpus obtulit, plus uoluptatis se ex tyranni nece quam amaritudinis ex propria sentire uociferans. Ita conuiuio in exequias uerso, uictoriæ gaudium funeris luctus insequitur. Clarum ac semper memorabilem uirum, qui, uoto fortiter expleto, mortem sponte complexus suo ministerio mensas tyranni sanguine maculauit. Neque enim occidentium manus uiuax animi uirtus expauit, cum prius a se loca, quibus Roluo assueuerat, interfectoris eius cruore respersa cognosceret. Eadem itaque dies Hiartuari regnum finiuit ac peperit. Fraudulenter enim quæsitæ res eadem sorte defluunt, qua petuntur, nullusque diuturnus est fructus, qui scelere ac perfidia partus fuerit. Quo euenit ut Sueones, paulo ante Daniæ potitores, ne suæ quidem salutis potientes existerent. Protinus enim a Syalandensibus deleti læsis Roluonis manibus iusta exsoluere piacula. Adeo plerunque fortunæ sæuitia ulciscitur, quod dolo ac fallacia patratur.

B. *HRÓLFS SAGA KRAKA*, CAP. 23

(ed. Finnur Jónsson, København, 1904, p. 65 ff.)

Síðan fór Bǫðvarr leið sína til Hleiðargarðs. Hann kemr til konungs atsetu. Bǫðvarr leiðir síðan hest sinn á stall hjá konungs hestum hinum beztu ok spyrr engan at; gekk síðan inn í hǫllina, ok var þar fátt manna. Hann sez utarliga, ok sem hann hefir verit þar litla hríð, heyrir hann þrausk nǫkkut utar í hornit í einhverjum stað. Bǫðvarr lítr þangat ok sér, at mannshǫnd kemr upp úr mikilli beinahrúgu, er þar lá; hǫndin var svǫrt mjǫk. Bǫðvarr gengr þangat til ok spyrr, hverr þar væri í beinahrúgunni; þá var honum svarat ok heldr óframliga: "Hǫttr heiti ek, Bokki sæll." "Hví ertu hér, segir Bǫðvarr, eða hvat gerir þú?" Hǫttr segir: "ek geri mér skjaldborg, Bokki sæll." Bǫðvarr sagði: "vesall ertu þinnar skjaldborgar." Bǫðvarr þrífr til hans ok hnykkir honum upp úr beinahrúgunni. Hǫttr kvað þá hátt við ok mælti: "nú viltu mér bana, ger eigi þetta, svá sem ek hefi nú vel um búiz áðr, en þú hefir nú rótat í sundr skjaldborg minni, ok hafða ek nú svá gert hana háva utan at mér, at hún hefir hlíft mér við ǫllum hǫggum ykkar, svá *at* engi hǫgg hafa komit á mik lengi, en ekki var hún enn svá búin, sem ek ætlaði hún skyldi verða." Bǫðvarr mælti: "ekki muntu fá skjaldborgina lengr." Hǫttr mælti ok grét: "skaltu nú bana mér, Bokki sæll?" Bǫðvarr bað hann ekki hafa hátt, tók hann upp síðan ok bar hann út úr hǫllinni ok til vats nǫkkurs, sem þar var í nánd, ok gáfu fáir at þessu gaum, ok þó hann upp allan. Síðan gekk Bǫðvarr til þess rúms, sem hann hafði áðr tekit, ok leiddi eptir sér Hǫtt ok þar setr hann Hǫtt hjá sér, en hann er svá hræddr, at skelfr á honum leggr ok liðr, en þó þykkiz hann skilja, at þessi maðr vill hjálpa sér. Eptir þat kveldar ok drífa menn í hǫllina ok sjá Hrólfs kappar, at Hǫttr er settr á bekk upp, ok þykkir þeim sá maðr hafa gert sik ærit djarfan, er þetta hefir til tekit. Ilt tillit hefir Hǫttr, þá *er* hann sér kunningja sína, því *at* hann hefir ilt eitt af þeim reynt; hann vill lifa gjarnan ok fara aptr í beinahrúgu sína, en Bǫðvarr heldr honum, svá *at* hann náir ekki í burtu at fara, því *at* hann þóttiz ekki jafnberr fyrir hǫggum þeira, ef hann næði þangat at komaz sem hann er nú. Hirðmenn hafa nú sama vanda, ok kasta fyrst beinum smám um þvert gólfit til Bǫðvars ok Hattar. Bǫðvarr lætr, sem hann sjái eigi þetta. Hǫttr er svá hræddr, at hann tekr eigi mat né drukk, ok þykkir honum þá ok þá sem hann muni vera lostinn; ok nú mælti Hǫttr til Bǫðvars: "Bokki sæll, nú ferr at þér stór hnúta, ok mun þetta ætlat okkr til nauða." Bǫðvarr bað hann þegja; hann setr við holan lófann ok tekr svá við hnútunni; þar fylgir leggrinn með; Bǫðvarr sendi aptr hnútuna ok setr á þann, sem kastaði ok rétt framan í hann með svá harðri svipan, at hann fekk bana; sló þá miklum ótta yfir hirðmennina. Kemr nú þessi fregn fyrir Hrólf konung ok kappa hans upp í kastalann, at maðr mikilúðligr sé kominn til hallarinnar ok hafi drepit einn hirðmann hans, ok vildu þeir láta drepa manninn. Hrólfr konungr spurðiz eptir, hvárt hirðmaðrinn hefði verit saklauss drepinn. "Því var næsta," sǫgðu þeir. Kómuz þá fyrir Hrólf konung ǫll sannindi hér um. Hrólfr konungr sagði þat skyldu fjarri, at drepa skyldi manninn—"hafi þit hér illan vanda upp tekit, at berja saklausa menn beinum; er mér í því óvirðing, en yðr stór skǫmm, at gera slíkt; hefi ek jafnan rætt um þetta áðr, ok hafi þit at þessu engan gaum gefit, ok hygg ek, at þessi maðr muni ekki alllítill fyrir sér, er þér hafið nú á leitat, ok kallið hann til mín, svá *at* ek viti, hverr hann er." Bǫðvarr gengr fyrir konung ok kveðr hann kurteisliga. Konunga spyrr hann at nafni. "Hattargriða kalla mik hirðmenn yðar, en Bǫðvarr heiti ek." Konungr mælti: "hverjar bætr viltu bjóða mér fyrir hirðmann minn?" Bǫðvarr segir: "til þess gerði hann, sem hann fekk." Konungr mælti: "viltu vera minn maðr ok skipa rúm hans?" Bǫðvarr segir: "ekki neita ek, at vera yðarr maðr, ok munu vit ekki skiljaz svá búit, vit Hǫttr, ok dveljaz nær þér báðir, heldr en þessi hefir setit, elligar vit fǫrum burt báðir." Konungr mælti: "eigi sé ek at honum sæmd en ek spara ekki mat við hann." Bǫðvarr gengr nú til þess rúms, sem honum líkaði, en ekki vill hann þat skipa, sem hinn hafði áðr; hann kippir upp í einhverjum stað þremr mǫnnum, ok síðan settuz þeir Hǫttr þar niðr ok innar í hǫllinni en þeim var skipat. Heldr þótti mǫnnum ódælt við Bǫðvar, ok er þeim hinn mesti íhugi at honum. Ok sem leið at jólum, gerðuz menn ókátir. Bǫðvarr spyrr Hǫtt, hverju þetta sætti; hann segir honum, at dýr eitt hafi þar komit tvá vetr í samt, mikit ok ógurligt—"ok hefir vængi á bakinu ok flýgr þat jafnan; tvau haust hefir þat nú hingat vitjat ok gert mikinn skaða; á þat bíta ekki vápn, en kappar konungs koma ekki heim, þeir sem at eru einna mestir." Bǫðvarr mælti: "ekki er hǫllin svá vel skipuð, sem ek ætlaði, ef eitt dýr skal hér eyða ríki ok fé konungsins." Hǫttr sagði: "þat er ekki dýr, heldr er þat hit mesta trǫll." Nú kemr jólaaptann; þá mælti konungr: "nú vil ek, at menn sé kyrrir ok hljóðir í nótt, ok banna ek ǫllum mínum mǫnnum at ganga í nǫkkurn háska við dýrit, en fé ferr eptir því sem auðnar; menn mína vil ek ekki missa." Allir heita hér góðu um, at gera eptir því, sem konungr bauð. Bǫðvarr leyndiz í burt um nóttina; hann lætr Hǫtt fara með sér, ok gerir hann þat nauðugr ok kallaði hann sér stýrt til bana. Bǫðvarr segir, at betr mundi til takaz. Þeir ganga í burt frá hǫllinni, ok verðr Bǫðvarr at bera hann; svá er hann hræddr. Nú sjá þeir dýrit; ok því næst æpir Hǫttr slíkt, sem hann má, ok kvað dyrit mundu gleypa hann. Bǫðvarr bað bikkjuna hans þegja ok kastar honum niðr í mosann, ok þar liggr hann ok eigi með ǫllu óhræddr; eigi þorir hann heim at fara heldr. Nú gengr Bǫðvarr móti dýrinu; þat hæfir honum, at sverðit er fast í umgjǫrðinni, er hann vildi bregða því. Bǫðvarr eggjar nú fast sverðit ok þá bragðar í umgjǫrðinni, ok nú fær hann brugðit umgjǫrðinni, svá *at* sverðit gengr úr slíðrunum, ok leggr þegar undir bægi dýrsins ok svá fast, at stóð í hjartanu, ok datt þá dýrit til jarðar dautt niðr. Eptir þat ferr hann þangat sem Hǫttr liggr. Bǫðvarr tekr hann upp ok berr þangat, sem dýrit liggr dautt. Hǫttr skelfr ákaft. Bǫðvarr mælti: "nú skaltu drekka blóð dýrsins." Hann er lengi tregr, en þó þorir hann víst eigi annat. Bǫðvarr lætr hann drekka tvá, sopa stóra; hann lét hann ok eta nǫkkut af dýrshjartanu; eptir þetta tekr Bǫðvarr til hans, ok áttuz þeir við lengi. Bǫðvarr mælti: "helzt ertu nú sterkr orðinn, ok ekki vænti ek, et þú hræðiz nú hirðmenn Hrólfs konungs." Hǫttr sagði: "eigi mun ek þá hræðaz ok eigi þik upp frá þessu." "Vel er þá orðit, Hǫttr félagi; fǫru vit nú til ok reisum upp dýrit ok búum svá um, at aðrir ætli at kvikt muni vera." Þeir gera nú svá. Eptir þat fara þeir heim ok hafa kyrt um sik, ok veit engi maðr, hvat þeir hafa iðjat. Konungr spyrr um morguninn, hvat þeir viti til dýrsins, hvárt þat hafi nǫkkut þangat vitjat um nóttina; honum var sagt, at fé alt væri heilt í grindum ok ósakat. Konungr bað menn forvitnaz, hvárt engi sæi líkindi til, at þat hefði heim komit. Varðmenn gerðu svá ok kómu skjótt aptr ok sǫgðu konungi, at dýrit færi þar ok heldr geyst at borginni. Konungr bað hirðmenn vera hrausta ok duga nú hvern eptir því, sem hann hefði hug til, ok ráða af óvætt þenna; ok svá var gert, sem konungr bauð, at þeir bjuggu sik til þess. Konungr horfði á dýrit ok mælti síðan: "enga sé ek fǫr á dýrinu, en hverr vill nú taka kaup einn ok ganga í móti því?" Bǫðvarr mælti: "þat væri næsta hrausts manns forvitnisbót. Hǫttr félagi, rektu nú af þér illmælit þat, at menn láta, sem engi krellr né dugr muni í þer vera; far nú ok drep þú dýrit; máttu sjá, at engi er allfúss til annarra." "Já," sagði Hǫttr, "ek mun til þessa ráðaz." Konungr mælti: "ekki veit ek, hvaðan þessi hreysti er at þér komin, Hǫttr, ok mikit hefir um þik skipaz á skammri stundu." Hǫttr mælti: "gef mér til sverðit Gullinhjalta, er þú heldr á, ok skal ek þá fella dýrit eða fá bana." Hrólf konungr mælti: "þetta sverð er ekki beranda nema þeim manni, sem bæði er góðr drengr ok hraustr." Hǫttr sagði: "svá skaltu til ætla, at mér sé svá háttat." Konungr mælti: "hvat má vita, nema fleira hafi skipz um hagi þína, en sjá þykkir, en fæstir menn þykkjaz þik kenna, at þú sér enn sami maðr; nú tak við sverðinu ok njót manna bezt, ef þetta er til unnit." Síðan gengr Hǫttr at dýrinu alldjarfliga ok hǫggr til þess, þá *er* hann kemr í hǫggfæri, ok dýrit fellr niðr dautt. Bǫðvarr mælti: "sjáið nú, herra, hvat hann hefir til unnit." Konungr segir: "víst hefir hann mikit skipaz, en ekki hefir Hǫttr einn dýrit drepit, heldr hefir þú þat gert." Bǫðvarr segir: "vera má, at svá sé." Konungr segir: "vissa ek, þá *er* þú komt hér, at fáir mundu þínir jafningjar vera, en þat þykki mér þó þitt verk frægiligast, at þú hefir gert hér annan kappa, þar *er* Hǫttr er, ok óvænligr þótti til mikillar giptu; ok nú vil ek *at* hann heiti eigi Hǫttr lengr ok skal hann heita Hjalti upp frá þessu; skaltu heita eptir sverðinu Gullinhjalta."

Then Bothvar went on his way to Leire, and came to the king's dwelling.

Bothvar stabled his horse by the king's best horses, without asking leave; and then he went into the hall, and there were few men there. He took a seat near the door, and when he had been there a little time he heard a rummaging in a corner. Bothvar looked that way and saw that a man's hand came up out of a great heap of bones which lay there, and the hand was very black. Bothvar went thither and asked who was there in the heap of bones.

Then an answer came, in a very weak voice, "Hott is my name, good fellow."

"Why art thou here?" said Bothvar, "and what art thou doing?"

Hott said, "I am making a shield-wall for myself, good fellow."

Bothvar said, "Out on thee and thy shield-wall!" and gripped him and jerked him up out of the heap of bones.

Then Hott cried out and said, "Now thou wilt be the death of me: do not do so. I had made it all so snug, and now thou hast scattered in pieces my shield-wall; and I had built it so high all round myself that it has protected me against all your blows, so that for long no blows have come upon me, and yet it was not so arranged as I meant it should be."

Then Bothvar said, "Thou wilt not build thy shield-wall any longer."

Hott said, weeping, "Wilt thou be the death of me, good fellow?" Bothvar told him not to make a noise, and then took him up and bore him out of the hall to some water which was close by, and washed him from head to foot. Few paid any heed to this.

Then Bothvar went to the place which he had taken before, and led Hott with him, and set Hott by his side. But Hott was so afraid that he was trembling in every limb, and yet he seemed to know that this man would help him.

After that it grew to evening, and men crowded into the hall: and Rolf's warriors saw that Hott was seated upon the bench. And it seemed to them that the man must be bold enough, who had taken upon himself to put him there. Hott had an ill countenance when he saw his acquaintances, for he had received naught but evil from them. He wished to save his life and go back to his bone-heap, but Bothvar held him tightly so that he could not go away. For Hott thought that, if he could get back into his bone-heap, he would not be as much exposed to their blows as he was.

Now the retainers did as before; and first of all they tossed small bones across the floor towards Bothvar and Hott. Bothvar pretended not to see this. Hott was so afraid that he neither ate nor drank; and every moment he thought he would be smitten.

And now Hott said to Bothvar, "Good fellow, now a great knuckle bone is coming towards thee, aimed so as to do us sore injury." Bothvar told him to hold his tongue, and put up the hollow of his palm against the knuckle bone and caught it, and the leg bone was joined on to the knuckle bone. Then Bothvar sent the knuckle bone back, and hurled it straight at the man who had thrown it, with such a swift blow that it was the death of him. Then great fear came over the retainers.

Now news came to King Rolf and his men up in the castle that a stately man had come to the hall and killed a retainer, and that the retainers wished to kill the man. King Rolf asked whether the retainer who had been killed had given any offence. "Next to none," they said: then all the truth of the matter came up before King Rolf.

King Rolf said that it should be far from them to kill the man: "You have taken up an evil custom here in pelting men with bones without quarrel. It is a dishonour to me and a great shame to you to do so. I have spoken about it before, and you have paid no attention. I think that this man whom you have assailed must be a man of no small valour. Call him to me, so that I may know who he is."

Bothvar went before the king and greeted him courteously. The king asked him his name. "Your retainers call me Hott's protector, but my name is Bothvar."

The king said, "What compensation wilt thou offer me for my retainer?"

Bothvar said, "He only got what he asked for."

The king said, "Wilt thou become my man and fill his place?"

Bothvar said, "I do not refuse to be your man, but Hott and I must not part so. And we must sit nearer to thee than this man whom I have slain has sat; otherwise we will both depart together." The king said, "I do not see much credit in Hott, but I will not grudge him meat." Then Bothvar went to the seat that seemed good to him, and would not fill that which the other had before. He pulled up three men in one place, and then he and Hott sat down there higher in the hall than the place which had been given to them. The men thought Bothvar overbearing, and there was the greatest ill will among them concerning him.

And when it drew near to Christmas, men became gloomy. Bothvar asked Hott the reason of this. Hott said to him that for two winters together a wild beast had come, great and awful, "And it has wings on its back, and flies. For two autumns it has attacked us here and done much damage. No weapon will wound it: and the champions of the king, those who are the greatest, come not back."

Bothvar said, "This hall is not so well arrayed as I thought, if one beast can lay waste the kingdom and the cattle of the king." Hott said, "It is no beast: it is the greatest troll."

Now Christmas-eve came; then said the king, "Now my will is that men to-night be still and quiet, and I forbid all my men to run into any peril with this beast. It must be with the cattle as fate will have it: but I do not wish to lose my men." All men promised to do as the king commanded. But Bothvar went out in secret that night; he caused Hott to go with him, but Hott did that only under compulsion, and said that it would be the death of him. Bothvar said that he hoped that it would be better than that. They went away from the hall, and Bothvar had to carry Hott, so frightened was he. Now they saw the beast; and thereupon Hott cried out as loud as he could, and said that the beast would swallow him. Bothvar said, "Be silent, thou dog," and threw him down in the mire. And there he lay in no small fear; but he did not dare to go home, any the more.

Now Bothvar went against the beast, and it happened that his sword was fast in his sheath when he wished to draw it. Bothvar now tugged at his sword, it moved, he wrenched the scabbard so that the sword came out. And at once he plunged it into the beast's shoulder so mightily that it pierced him to the heart, and the beast fell down dead to the earth. After that Bothvar went where Hott lay. Bothvar took him up and bore him to where the beast lay dead. Hott was trembling all over. Bothvar said, "Now must thou drink the blood of the beast." For long Hott was unwilling, and yet he did not dare to do anything else. Bothvar made him drink two great sups; also he made him eat somewhat of the heart of the beast.

After that Bothvar turned to Hott, and they fought a long time.

Bothvar said, "Thou hast now become very strong, and I do not believe that thou wilt now fear the retainers of King Rolf."

Hott said, "I shall not fear them, nor thee either, from now on."

"That is good, fellow Hott. Let us now go and raise up the beast, and so array him that others may think that he is still alive." And they did so. After that they went home, and were quiet, and no man knew what they had achieved.

In the morning the king asked what news there was of the beast, and whether it had made any attack upon them in the night. And answer was made to the king, that all the cattle were safe and uninjured in their folds. The king bade his men examine whether any trace could be seen of the beast having visited them. The watchers did so, and came quickly back to the king with the news that the beast was making for the castle, and in great fury. The king bade his retainers be brave, and each play the man according as he had spirit, and do away with this monster. And they did as the king bade, and made them ready.

Then the king faced towards the beast and said, "I see no sign of movement in the beast. Who now will undertake to go against it?"

Bothvar said, "That would be an enterprise for a man of true valour. Fellow Hott, now clear thyself of that ill-repute, in that men hold that there is no spirit or valour in thee. Go now and do thou kill the beast; thou canst see that there is no one else who is forward to do it."

"Yea," said Hott, "I will undertake this."

The king said, "I do not know whence this valour has come upon thee, Hott; and much has changed in thee in a short time."

Hott said, "Give me the sword Goldenboss, Gullinhjalti, which thou dost wield, and I will fell the beast or take my death." Rolf the king said, "That sword cannot be borne except by a man who is both a good warrior and valiant." Hott said, "So shalt thou ween that I am a man of that kind." The king said, "How can one know that more has not changed in thy temper than can be seen? Few men would know thee for the same man. Now take the sword and have joy of it, if this deed is accomplished." Then Hott went boldly to the beast and smote at it when he came within reach, and the beast fell down dead. Bothvar said, "See now, my lord, what he has achieved." The king said, "Verily, he has altered much, but Hott has not killed the beast alone, rather hast thou done it." Bothvar said, "It may be that it is so." The king said, "I knew when thou didst come here that few would be thine equals. But this seems to me nevertheless thy most honourable work, that thou hast made here another warrior of Hott, who did not seem shaped for much luck. And now I will that he shall be called no longer Hott, but Hjalti from this time; thou shalt be called after the sword Gullinhjalti (Goldenboss)."

C. EXTRACTS FROM *GRETTIS SAGA*

(ed. G. Magnússon, 1853; R. C. Boer, 1900)

(*a*) *Glam episode* (caps. 32-35)

Þórhallr hét maðr, er bjó á Þórhallsstǫðum í Forsæludal. Forsæludalr er upp af Vatnsdal. Þórhallr var Grímsson, Þórhallssonar, Friðmundarsonar, er nam Forsæludal. Þórhallr átti þá konu, er Guðrún hét. Grímr hét sonr þeira, en Þuríðr dóttir; þau váru vel á legg komin. Þórhallr var vel auðigr maðr, ok mest at kvikfé, svá at engi maðr átti jafnmart ganganda fé, sem hann. Ekki var hann hǫfðingi, en þó skilríkr bóndi. Þar var reimt mjǫk, ok fekk hann varla sauðamann, svá at honum þœtti duga. Hann leitaði ráðs við marga vitra menn, hvat hann skyldi til bragðs taka; en engi gat þat ráð til gefit, er dygði. Þórhallr reið til þings hvert sumar. Hann átti hesta góða. Þat var eitt sumar á alþingi, at Þórhallr gekk til búðar Skapta lǫgmanns, Þóroddssonar. Skapti var manna vitrastr, ok heilráðr, ef hann var beiddr. Þat skildi með þeim feðgum: Þóroddr var forspár ok kallaðr undirhyggjumaðr af sumum mǫnnum, en Skapti lagði þat til með hverjum manni, sem hann ætlaði at duga skyldi, ef eigi væri af því brugðit; því var hann kallaðr betrfeðrungr. Þórhallr gekk í búð Skapta; hann fagnaði vel Þórhalli, því hann vissi, at hann var ríkr maðr at fé, ok spurði hvat at tíðendum væri.

Þórhallr mælti: "Heilræði vilda ek af yðr þiggja."

"Í litlum fœrum em ek til þess," sagði Skapti; "eða hvat stendr þik?"

Þórhallr mælti: "Þat er svá háttat, at mér helz lítt á sauðamǫnnum. Verðr þeim heldr klakksárt, en sumir gera engar lyktir á. Vill nú engi til taka, sá er kunnigt er til, hvat fyrir býr."

Skapti svarar: "Þar mun liggja meinvættr nǫkkur, er menn eru tregari til at geyma síðr þíns fjár en annarra manna. Nú fyrir því, at þú hefir at mér ráð sótt, þá skal ek fá þér sauðamann, þann er Glámr heitir, ættaðr ór Svíþjóð, ór Sylgsdǫlum, er út kom í fyrra sumar, mikill ok sterkr, ok ekki mjǫk við alþýðu skap."

Þórhallr kvaz ekki um þat gefa, ef hann geymdi vel fjárins; Skapti sagði ǫðrum eigi vænt horfa, ef hann geymdi eigi fyrir afls sakir ok áræðis; Þórhallr gekk þá út. Þetta var at þinglausnum.

Þórhalli var vant hesta tveggja ljósbleikra, ok fór sjálfr at leita; af því þykkjaz menn vita, at hann var ekki mikilmenni. Hann gekk upp undir Sleðás ok suðr með fjalli því, er Ármannsfell heitir. Þá sá hann, hvar maðr fór ofan ór Goðaskógi ok bar hrís á hesti. Brátt bar saman fund þeira; Þórhallr spurði hann at nafni, en hann kvez Glámr heita. Þessi maðr var mikill vexti ok undarligr í yfirbragði, bláeygðr ok opineygðr, úlfgrár á hárslit. Þórhalli brá nǫkkut í brún, er hann sá þenna mann; en þó skildi hann, at honum mundi til þessa vísat.

"Hvat er þér bezt hent at vinna?" segir Þórhallr.

Glámr kvað sér vel hent at geyma sauðfjár á vetrum.

"Viltu geyma sauðfjár míns?" segir Þórhallr; "gaf Skapti þik á mitt vald."

"Svá mun þér hentust mín vist, at ek fari sjálfráðr; því ek em skapstyggr, ef mér líkar eigi vel," sagði Glámr.

"Ekki mun mér mein at því," segir Þórhallr, "ok vil ek, at þú farir til mín."

"Gera má ek þat," segir Glámr; "eða eru þar nǫkkur vandhœfi á?"

"Reimt þykkir þar vera," sagði Þórhallr.

"Ekki hræðumz ek flykur þær," sagði Glámr, "ok þykkir mér at ódauflig[r]a."

"Þess muntu við þurfa," segir Þórhallr, "ok hentar þar betr, at vera eigi alllítill fyrir sér."

Eptir þat kaupa þeir saman, ok skal Glámr koma at vetrnóttum. Siðan skildu þeir, ok fann Þórhallr hesta sína, þar sem hann hafði nýleitat. Reið Þórhallr heim, ok þakkaði Skapta sinn velgerning.

Sumar leið af, ok frétti Þórhallr ekki til sauðamanns, ok engi kunni skyn á honum. En at ánefndum tíma kom hann á Þórhallsstaði. Tekr bóndi við honum vel, en ǫllum ǫðrum gaz ekki at honum, en húsfreyju þó minst. Hann tók við fjárvarðveizlu, ok varð honum lítit fyrir því; hann var hljóðmikill ok dimmraddaðr, ok féit stǫkk allt saman, þegar hann hóaði. Kirkja var á Þórhallsstǫðum; ekki vildi Glámr til hennar koma; hann var ósǫngvinn ok trúlauss, stirfinn ok viðskotaillr; ǫllum var hann hvimleiðr.

Nú leið svá þar til er kemr atfangadagr jóla. Þá stóð Glámr snemma upp ok kallaði til matar síns.

Húsfreyja svarar: "Ekki er þat háttr kristinna manna, at mataz þenna dag, þvíat á morgin er jóladagr hinn fyrsti," segir hon, "ok er því fyrst skylt at fasta í dag."

Hann svarar: "Marga hindrvitni hafi þér, þá er ek sé til enskis koma. Veit ek eigi, at mǫnnum fari nú betr at, heldr en þá, er menn fóru ekki með slíkt. Þótti mér þá betri siðr, er menn váru heiðnir kallaðir; ok vil ek mat minn en engar refjur."

Húsfreyja mælti: "Víst veit ek, at þér mun illa faraz í dag, ef þú tekr þetta illbrigði til."

Glámr bað hana taka mat í stað; kvað henni annat skyldu vera verra. Hon þorði eigi annat, en at gera, sem hann vildi. Ok er hann var mettr, gekk hann út, ok var heldr gustillr. Veðri var svá farit, at myrkt var um at litaz, ok flǫgraði ór drífa, ok gnýmikit, ok versnaði mjǫk sem á leið daginn. Heyrðu menn til sauðamanns ǫndverðan daginn, en miðr er á leið daginn. Tók þá at fjúka, ok gerði á hríð um kveldit; kómu menn til tíða, ok leið svá fram at dagsetri; eigi kom Glámr heim. Var þá um talat, hvárt hans skyldi eigi leita; en fyrir því, at hríð var á ok niðamyrkr, þá varð ekki af leitinni. Kom hann eigi heim jólanóttina; biðu menn svá fram um tíðir. At ærnum degi fóru menn í leitina, ok fundu féit víða í fǫnnum, lamit af ofviðri eða hlaupit á fjǫll upp. Þvínæst kómu þeir á traðk mikinn ofarliga í dalnum. Þótti þeim því líkt, sem þar hefði glímt verit heldr sterkliga, þvíat grjótit var víða upp leyst, ok svá jǫrðin. Þeir hugðu at vandliga ok sá, hvar Glámr lá, skamt á brott frá þeim. Hann var dauðr, ok blár sem Hel, en digr sem naut. Þeim bauð af honum óþekt mikla, ok hraus þeim mjǫk hugr við honum. En þó leituðu þeir við at færa hann til kirkju, ok gátu ekki komit honum, nema á einn gilsþrǫm þar skamt ofan frá sér; ok fóru heim við svá búit, ok sǫgðu bónda þenna atburð. Hann spurði, hvat Glámi mundi hafa at bana orðit. Þeir kváðuz rakit hafa spor svá stór, sem keraldsbotni væri niðr skelt þaðan frá, sem traðkrinn var, ok upp undir bjǫrg þau, er þar váru ofarliga í dalnum, ok fylgðu þar með blóðdrefjar miklar. Þat drógu menn saman, at sú meinvættr, er áðr hafði [þar] verit, mundi hafa deytt Glám; en hann mundi fengit hafa henni nǫkkurn áverka, þann er tekit hafi til fulls, þvíat við þá meinvætti hefir aldri vart orðit síðan. Annan jóladag var enn til farit at fœra Glám til kirkju. Váru eykir fyrir beittir, ok gátu þeir hvergi fœrt hann, þegar sléttlendit var ok eigi var forbrekkis at fara. Gengu nú frá við svá búit. Hinn þriðja dag fór prestr með þeim, ok leituðu allan daginn, ok Glámr fannz eigi. Eigi vildi prestr optar til fara; en sauðamaðr fannz, þegar prestr var eigi í ferð. Létu þeir þá fyrir vinnaz, at fœra hann til kirkju; ok dysjuðu hann þar, sem þá var hann kominn. Lítlu síðar urðu menn varir við þat, at Glámr lá eigi kyrr. Varð mǫnnum at því mikit mein, svá at margir fellu í óvit, ef sá hann, en sumir heldu eigi vitinu. Þegar eptir jólin þóttuz menn sjá hann heima þar á bœnum. Urðu menn ákafliga hræddir; stukku þá margir menn í brott. Þvínæst tók Glámr at ríða húsum á nætr, svá at lá við brotum. Gekk hann þá náliga nætr ok daga. Varla þorðu menn at fara upp í dalinn, þóat ætti nóg ørendi. Þótti mǫnnum þar í heraðinu mikit mein at þessu.

Um várit fekk Þórhallr sér hjón ok gerði bú á jǫrðu sinni. Tók þá at minka aptrgangr, meðan sólargangr var mestr. Leið svá fram á miðsumar. Þetta sumar kom út skip í Húnavatni; þar var á sá maðr, er Þorgautr hét. Hann var útlendr at kyni, mikill ok sterkr; hann hafði tveggja manna afl; hann var lauss ok einn fyrir sér; hann vildi fá starfa nǫkkurn, því(at) hann var félauss. Þórhallr reið til skips ok fann Þorgaut; spurði ef hann vildi vinna fyrir honum; Þorgautr kvað þat vel mega vera, ok kvez eigi vanda þat.

"Svá skaltu við búaz," segir Þórhallr, "sem þar sé ekki veslingsmǫnnum hent at vera, fyrir aptrgǫngum þeim, er þar hafa verit um hríð, en ek vil ekki þik á tálar draga."

Þorgautr svarar: "Eigi þykkjumz ek upp gefinn, þóat ek sjá smáváfur; mun þá eigi ǫðrum dælt, ef ek hræðumz; ok ekki bregð ek vist minni fyrir þat."

Nú semr þeim vel kaupstefnan, ok skal Þorgautr gæta sauðfjár at vetri.

Leið nú af sumarit. Tók Þorgautr við fénu at vetrnáttum. Vel líkaði ǫllum við hann. Jafnan kom Glámr heim ok reið húsum. Þat þótti Þorgauti allkátligt, ok kvað, "þrælinn þurfa mundu nær at ganga, ef ek hræðumz." Þórhallr bað hann hafa fátt um; "er bezt, at þit reynið ekki með ykkr."

Þorgautr mælti: "Sannliga er skekinn þróttr ór yðr; ok dett ek eigi niðr milli dœgra við skraf þetta."

Nú fór svá fram um vetrinn allt til jóla. Atfangakveld jóla fór sauðamaðr til fjár.

Þá mælti húsfreyja: "Þurfa þœtti mér, at nú fœri eigi at fornum brǫgðum."

Hann svarar: "Ver eigi hrædd um þat, húsfreyja," sagði hann; "verða mun eitthvert sǫguligt, ef ek kem ekki aptr." Síðan gekk hann aptr til fjár síns. Veðr var heldr kalt, ok fjúk mikit. Því var Þorgautr vanr, at koma heim, þá er hálfrøkkvat var; en nú kom hann ekki heim í þat mund. Kómu tíðamenn, sem vant var. Þat þótti mǫnnum eigi ólíkt á horfaz sem fyrr. Bóndi vildi leita láta eptir sauðamanni, en tíðamenn tǫlduz undan, ok sǫgðuz eigi mundu hætta sér út í trǫllahendr um nætr; ok treystiz bóndi eigi at fara, ok varð ekki af leitinni. Jóladag, er menn váru mettir, fóru menn til ok leituðu sauðamanns. Gengu þeir fyrst til dysjar Gláms, þvíat menn ætluðu af hans vǫldum mundi orðit um hvarf sauðamanns. En er þeir kómu nær dysinni, sáu þeir þar mikil tíðendi, ok þar fundu þeir sauðamann, ok var hann brotinn á háls, ok lamit sundr hvert bein í honum. Síðan fœrðu þeir hann til kirkju, ok varð engum manni mein at Þorgauti síðan. En Glámr tók at magnaz af nýju. Gerði hann nú svá mikit af sér, at menn allir stukku brott af Þórhallsstǫðum, útan bóndi einn ok húsfreyja. Nautamaðr hafði þar verit lengi hinn sami. Vildi Þórhallr hann ekki lausan láta fyrir góðvilja sakir ok geymslu. Hann var mjǫk við aldr, ok þótti honum mikit fyrir, at fara á brott; sá hann ok, at allt fór at ónytju, þat er bóndi átti, ef engi geymdi. Ok einn tíma eptir miðjan vetr var þat einn morgin, at húsfreyja fór til fjóss, at mjólka kýr eptir tíma. Þá var alljóst, þvíat engi treystiz fyrr úti at vera annarr en nautamaðr; hann fór út, þegar lýsti. Hon heyrði brak mikit í fjósit, ok beljan ǫskurliga; hon hljóp inn œpandi ok kvaz eigi vita, hver ódœmi um væri í fjósinu. Bóndi gekk út ok kom til nautanna, ok stangaði hvert annat. Þótti honum þar eigi gott, ok gekk innar at hlǫðunni. Hann sá, hvar lá, nautamaðr, ok hafði hǫfuðit í ǫðrum bási en fœtr í ǫðrum; hann lá á bak aptr. Bóndi gekk at honum ok þreifaði um hann; finnr brátt, at hann er dauðr ok sundr hryggrinn í honum. Var hann brotinn um báshelluna. Nú þótti bónda eigi vært, ok fór í brott af bœnum með allt þat, sem hann mátti í brott flytja. En allt kvikfé þat, sem eptir var, deyddi Glámr. Ok þvínæst fór hann um allan dalinn ok eyddi alla bœi upp frá Tungu. Var Þórhallr þá með vinum sínum þat [sem] eptir var vetrarins. Engi maðr mátti fara upp í dalinn með hest eðr hund, þvíat þat var þegar drepit. En er váraði, ok sólargangr var sem mestr, létti heldr aptrgǫngunum. Vildi Þórhallr nú fara aptr til lands síns. Urðu honum ekki auðfengin hjón, en þó gerði hann bú á Þórhallsstǫðum. Fór allt á sama veg sem fyrr; þegar at haustaði, tóku at vaxa reimleikar. Var þá mest sótt at bóndadóttur; ok svá fór, at hon léz af því. Margra ráða var í leitat, ok varð ekki at gǫrt. Þótti mǫnnum til þess horfaz, at eyðaz mundi allr Vatnsdalr, ef eigi yrði bœtr á ráðnar.

Nú er þar til at taka, at Grettir Ásmundarson sat heima at Bjargi um haustit, síðan þeir Vígabarði skildu á Þóreyjargnúpi. Ok er mjǫk var komit at vetrnóttum, reið Grettir heiman norðr yfir hálsa til Víðidals, ok gisti á Auðunarstǫðum. Sættuz þeir Auðunn til fulls, ok gaf Grettir honum øxi góða, ok mæltu til vináttu með sér. Auðunn bjó lengi á Auðunarstǫðum ok var kynsæll maðr. Hans sonr var Egill, er átti Úlfheiði, dóttur Eyjólfs Guðmundarsonar, ok var þeira sonr Eyjólfr, er veginn var á alþingi. Hann var faðir Orms, kapiláns Þorláks biskups. Grettir reið norðr til Vatnsdals ok kom á kynnisleit í Tungu. Þar bjó þá Jǫkull Bárðarson, móðurbróðir Grettis; Jǫkull var mikill maðr ok sterkr ok hinn mesti ofsamaðr. Hann var siglingamaðr, ok mjǫk ódæll, en þó mikilhœfr maðr. Hann tók vel við Gretti, ok var hann þar þrjár nætr. Þá var svá mikit orð á aptrgǫngum Gláms, at mǫnnum var ekki jafntíðrœtt sem þat. Grettir spurði inniliga at þeim atburðum, er hǫfðu orðit; Jǫkull kvað þar ekki meira af sagt en til væri hœft; "eða er þér forvitni á, frændi! at koma þar?"

Grettir sagði, at þat var satt.

Jǫkull bað hann þat eigi gera, "því þat er gæfuraun mikil; en frændr þínir eiga mikit í hættu, þar sem þú ert," sagði hann; "þykkir oss nú engi slíkr af ungum mǫnnum sem þú; en illt mun af illum hljóta, þar sem Glámr er. Er ok miklu betra, at fáz við mennska menn en við óvættir slíkar."

Grettir kvað sér hug á, at koma á Þórhallsstaði, ok sjá, hversu þar væri um gengit.

Jǫkull mælti: "Sé ek nú, at eigi tjáir at letja þik; en satt er þat sem mælt er, at sitt er hvárt, gæfa eða gervigleikr."

"Þá er ǫðrum vá fyrir dyrum, er ǫðrum er inn um komit; ok hygg at, hversu þér mun fara sjálfum, áðr lýkr," kvað Grettir.

Jǫkull svarar: "Vera kann, at vit sjáim báðir nǫkkut fram, en hvárrgi fái við gǫrt."

Eptir þat skildu þeir, ok líkaði hvárigum annars spár.

Grettir reið á Þórhallsstaði, ok fagnaði bóndi honum vel. Hann spurði, hvert Grettir ætlaði at fara; en hann segiz þar vilja vera um nóttina, ef bónda líkaði, at svá væri. Þórhallr kvaz þǫkk fyrir kunna, at hann væri þar, "en fám þykkir slœgr til at gista hér um tíma; muntu hafa heyrt getit um, hvat hér er at væla. En ek vilda gjarna, at þú hlytir engi vandræði af mér. En þóat þú komiz heill á brott, þá veit ek fyrir víst, at þú missir hests þíns; því engi heldr hér heilum sínum fararskjóta, sá er kemr."

Grettir kvað gott til hesta, hvat sem af þessum yrði.

Þórhallr varð glaðr við, er Grettir vildi þar vera, ok tók við honum báðum hǫndum. Var hestr Grettis læstr í húsi sterkliga. Þeir fóru til svefns, ok leið svá af nóttin, at ekki kom Glámr heim.

Þá mælti Þórhallr: "Vel hefir brugðit við þína kvámu, þvíat hverja nótt er Glámr vanr at ríða húsum eða brjóta upp hurðir, sem þú mátt merki sjá."

Grettir mælti: "Þá mun vera annathvárt, at hann mun ekki lengi á sér sitja, eða mun af venjaz meirr en eina nótt. Skal ek vera hér nótt aðra ok sjá, hversu ferr."

Síðan gengu þeir til hests Grettis, ok var ekki við hann glez. Allt þótti bónda at einu fara. Nú er Grettir þar aðra nótt, ok kom ekki þrællinn heim. Þá þótti bónda mjǫk vænkaz. Fór hann þá, at sjá hest Grettis. Þá var upp brotit húsit, er bóndi kom til, en hestrinn dreginn til dyra útar, ok lamit í sundr í honum hvert bein.

Þórhallr sagði Gretti, hvar þá var komit, ok bað hann forða sér: "þvíat víss er dauðinn, ef þú bíðr Gláms."

Grettir svarar: "Eigi má ek minna hafa fyrir hest minn, en at sjá þrælinn."

Bóndi sagði, at þat var eigi bati, at sjá hann, "þvíat hann er ólíkr nǫkkurri mannligri mynd; en góð þykki mér hver sú stund, er þú vilt hér vera."

Nú líðr dagrinn; ok er menn skyldu fara til svefns, vildi Grettir eigi fara af klæðum, ok lagðiz niðr í setit gegnt lokrekkju bónda. Hann hafði rǫggvarfeld yfir sér, ok knepti annat skautit niðr undir fœtr sér, en annat snaraði hann undir hǫfuð sér, ok sá út um hǫfuðsmáttina. Setstokkr var fyrir framan setit, mjǫk sterkr, ok spyrndi hann þar í. Dyraumbúningrinn allr var frá brotinn útidyrunum, en nú var þar fyrir bundinn hurðarflaki, ok óvendiliga um búit. Þverþilit var allt brotit frá skálanum, þat sem þar fyrir framan hafði verit, bæði fyrir ofan þvertréit ok neðan. Sængr allar váru ór stað fœrðar. Heldr var þar óvistuligt. Ljós brann í skálanum um nóttina. Ok er af mundi þriðjungr af nótt, heyrði Grettir út dynur miklar. Var þá farit upp á húsin, ok riðit skálanum ok barit hælunum, svá at brakaði í hverju tré. Því gekk lengi; þá var farit ofan af húsunum ok til dyra gengit. Ok er upp var lokit hurðunni, sá Grettir, at þrællinn rétti inn hǫfuðit, ok sýndiz honum afskræmiliga mikit ok undarliga stórskorit. Glámr fór seint ok réttiz upp, er hann kom inn í dyrnar; hann gnæfaði ofarliga við ræfrinu; snýr at skálanum ok lagði handleggina upp á þvertréit, ok gægðiz inn yfir skálann. Ekki lét bóndi heyra til sín, þvíat honum þótti œrit um, er hann heyrði, hvat um var úti. Grettir lá kyrr ok hrœrði sik hvergi. Glámr sá, at hrúga nǫkkur lá í setinu, ok réz nú innar eptir skálanum ok þreif í feldinn stundarfast. Grettir spyrndi í stokkinn, ok gekk því hvergi. Glámr hnykti í annat sinn miklu fastara, ok bifaðiz hvergi feldrinn. Í þriðja sinn þreif hann í með báðum hǫndum svá fast, at hann rétti Gretti upp ór setinu; kiptu nú í sundr feldinum í millum sín. Glámr leit á slitrit, er hann helt á, ok undraðiz mjǫk, hverr svá, fast mundi togaz við hann. Ok í því hljóp Grettir undir hendr honum, ok þreif um hann miðjan, ok spenti á honum hrygginn sem fastast gat hann, ok ætlaði hann, at Glámr skyldi kikna við. En þrællinn lagði at handleggjum Grettis svá fast, at hann hǫrfaði allr fyrir orku sakir. Fór Grettir þá undan í ýms setin. Gengu þá frá stokkarnir, ok allt brotnaði, þat sem fyrir varð. Vildi Glámr leita út, en Grettir fœrði við fœtr, hvar sem hann mátti. En þó gat Glámr dregit hann fram ór skálanum. Áttu þeir þá allharða sókn þvíat þrællinn ætlaði at koma honum út ór bœnum; en svá illt sem var at eiga við Glám inni, þá sá Grettir, at þó var verra, at fáz við hann úti; ok því brauz hann í móti af ǫllu afli at fara út. Glámr fœrðiz í aukana, ok knepti hann at sér, er þeir kómu í anddyrit. Ok er Grettir sér, at hann fekk eigi við spornat, hefir hann allt eitt atriðit, at hann hleypr sem harðast í fang þrælnum ok spyrnir báðum fótum í jarðfastan stein, er stoð í dyrunum. Við þessu bjóz þrællinn eigi; hann hafði þá togaz við at draga Gretti at sér; ok því kiknaði Glámr á bak aptr, ok rauk ǫfugr út á dyrnar, svá at herðarnar námu uppdyrit, ok ræfrit gekk í sundr, bæði viðirnir ok þekjan frerin; fell hann svá opinn ok ǫfugr út ór húsunum, en Grettir á hann ofan. Tunglskin var mikit úti ok gluggaþykkn; hratt stundum fyrir, en stundum dró frá. Nú í því, er Glámr fell, rak skýit frá tunglinu, en Glámr hvesti augun upp í móti. Ok svá, hefir Grettir sagt sjálfr, at þá eina sýn hafi hann sét svá, at honum brygði við. Þá sigaði svá at honum af ǫllu saman, mœði ok því, er hann sá at Glámr gaut sínum sjónum harðliga, at hann gat eigi brugðit saxinu, ok lá náliga í milli heims ok heljar. En því var meiri ófagnaðarkraptr með Glámi en flestum ǫðrum aptrgǫngumǫnnum, at hann mælti þá á þessa leið: "Mikit kapp hefir þú á lagit, Grettir," sagði hann, "at finna mik. En þat mun eigi undarligt þykkja, þóat þú hljótir ekki mikit happ af mér. En þat má ek segja þér, at þú hefir nú fengit helming afls þess ok þroska, er þér var ætlaðr, ef þú hefðir mik ekki fundit. Nú fæ ek þat afl eigi af þér tekit, er þú hefir áðr hrept; en því má ek ráða, at þú verðr aldri sterkari en nú ertu, ok ertu þó nógu sterkr, ok at því mun mǫrgum verða. Þú hefir frægr orðit hér til af verkum þínum; en heðan af munu falla til þín sektir ok vígaferli, en flest ǫll verk þín snúaz þér til ógæfu ok hamingjuleysis. Þú munt verða útlægr gǫrr, ok hljóta jafnan úti at búa einn samt. Þá legg ek þat á við þik, at þessi augu sé þér jafnan fyrir sjónum, sem ek ber eptir; ok mun þér erfitt þykkja, einum at vera; ok þat mun þér til dauða draga."

Ok sem þrællinn hafði þetta mælt, þá rann af Gretti ómegin, þat sem á honum hafði verit. Brá hann þá saxinu ok hjó hǫfuð af Glámi ok setti þat við þjó honum. Bóndi kom þá út, ok hafði klæz, á meðan Glámr lét ganga tǫluna; en hvergi þorði hann nær at koma, fyrr en Glámr var fallinn. Þórhallr lofaði guð fyrir, ok þakkaði vel Gretti, er hann hafði unnit þenna óhreina anda. Fóru þeir þá til, ok brendu Glám at kǫldum kolum. Eptir þat [báru þeir ǫsku hans í eina hít ok] grófu þar niðr, sem sízt váru fjárhagar eða mannavegir. Gengu heim eptir þat, ok var þá mjǫk komit at degi. Lagðiz Grettir niðr, þvíat hann var stirðr mjǫk. Þórhallr sendi menn á næstu bœi eptir mǫnnum; sýndi ok sagði, hversu farit hafði. Ǫllum þótti mikils um vert um þetta verk, þeim er heyrðu. Var þat þá almælt, at engi væri þvílíkr maðr á ǫllu landinu fyrir afls sakir ok hreysti ok allrar atgervi, sem Grettir Ásmundarson.

Þórhallr leysti Gretti vel af garði ok gaf honum góðan hest ok klæði sœmilig, því[at] þau váru ǫll sundr leyst, er hann hafði áðr borit. Skildu þeir með vináttu. Reið Grettir þaðan í Ás í Vatnsdal, ok tók Þorvaldr við honum vel ok spurði inniliga at sameign þeira Gláms; en Grettir segir honum viðskipti þeira, ok kvaz aldri í þvílíka aflraun komit hafa, svá langa viðreign sem þeir hǫfðu saman átt.

Þorvaldr bað hann hafa sik spakan, "ok mun þá vel duga, en ella mun þér slysgjarnt verða."

Grettir kvað ekki batnat hafa um lyndisbragðit, ok sagðiz nú miklu verr stiltr en áðr, ok allar mótgerðir verri þykkja. Á því fann hann mikla muni, at hann var orðinn maðr svá myrkfælinn, at hann þorði hvergi at fara einn saman, þegar myrkva tók. Sýndiz honum þá hvers kyns skrípi; ok þat er haft síðan fyrir orðtœki, at þeim ljái Glámr augna eðr gefi glámsýni, er mjǫk sýniz annan veg, en er. Grettir reið heim til Bjargs, er hann hafði gǫrt ørendi sín, ok sat heima um vetrinn.

(b) *Sandhaugar episode* (caps. 64-66)

Steinn hét prestr, er bjó at Eyjardalsá í Bárðardal. Hann var búþegn góðr ok ríkr at fé. Kjartan hét son hans, rǫskr maðr ok vel á legg kominn. Þorsteinn hvíti hét maðr, er bjó at Sandhaugum, suðr frá Eyjardalsá. Steinvǫr hét kona hans, ung ok glaðlát. Þau áttu bǫrn, ok váru þau ung í þenna tíma. Þar þótti mǫnnum reimt mjǫk sakir trǫllagangs. Þat bar til, tveim vetrum fyrr en Grettir kom norðr í sveitir, at Steinvǫr húsfreyja at Sandhaugum fór til jólatíða til Eyjardalsár eptir vana, en bóndi var heima. Lǫgðuz menn niðr til svefns um kveldit; ok um nóttina heyrðu menn brak mikit í skálann, ok til sængr bónda. Engi þorði upp at standa at forvitnaz um, þvíat þar var fáment mjǫk. Húsfreyja kom heim um morguninn, ok var bóndi horfinn, ok vissi engi, hvat af honum var orðit. Liðu svá hin næstu misseri. En annan vetr eptir, vildi húsfreyja fara til tíða; bað hon húskarl sinn heima vera. Hann var tregr til; en bað hana ráða. Fór þar allt á sǫmu leið, sem fyrr, at húskarl var horfinn. Þetta þótti mǫnnum undarligt. Sáu menn þá blóðdrefjar nǫkkurar í útidyrum. Þóttuz menn þat vita, at óvættir mundu hafa tekit þá báða. Þetta fréttiz víða um sveitir. Grettir hafði spurn af þessu. Ok með því at honum var mjǫk lagit at koma af reimleikum eða aptrgǫngum, þá gerði hann ferð sína til Bárðardals, ok kom atfangadag jóla til Sandha[u]ga. Hann duldiz ok nefndiz Gestr. Húsfreyja sá, at hann var furðu mikill vexti, en heimafólk var furðu hrætt við hann. Hann beiddiz þar gistingar. Húsfreyja kvað honum mat til reiðu, "en ábyrgz þik sjálfr."

Hann kvað svá vera skyldu. "Mun ek vera heima," segir hann, "en þú far til tíða, ef þú vilt."

Hon svarar: "Mér þykkir þú hraustr, ef þú þorir heima at vera."

"Eigi læt ek mér at einu getit," sagði hann.

"Illt þykkir mér heima at vera," segir hon, "en ekki komumz ek yfir ána."

"Ek skal fylgja þér yfir," segir Gestr.

Síðan bjóz hon til tiða, ok dóttir hennar með henni, lítil vexti. Hláka mikil var úti, ok áin í leysingum; var á henni jakafǫr.

Þá mælti húsfreyja: "Ófœrt er yfir ána, bæði mǫnnum ok hestum."

"Vǫð munu á vera," kvað Gestr; "ok verið eigi hræddar."

"Ber þú fyrst meyna," kvað húsfreyja, "hon er léttari."

"Ekki nenni ek at gera tvær ferðir at þessu," segir Gestr, "ok mun ek bera þik á handlegg mér."

Hon signdi sik ok mælti: "Þetta er ófœra; eða hvat gerir þú þá af meyjunni?"

"Sjá mun ek ráð til þess," segir hann; ok greip þær upp báðar ok setti hina yngri í kné móður sinnar, ok bar þær svá á vinstra armlegg sér; en hafði lausa hina hœgri hǫnd ok óð svá, út á vaðit. Eigi þorðu þær at œpa, svá váru þær hræddar. En áin skall þegar upp á brjósti honum. Þá rak at honum jaka mikinn; en hann skaut við hendi þeiri, er laus var, ok hratt frá sér. Gerði þá svá djúpt, at strauminn braut á ǫxlinni. Óð hann sterkliga, þar til er hann kom at bakkanum ǫðrum megin, ok fleygir þeim á land. Síðan sneri hann aptr, ok var þá hálfrøkkvit, er hann kom heim til Sandhauga; ok kallaði til matar. Ok er hann var mettr, bað hann heimafólk fara innar í stofu. Hann tók þá borð ok lausa viðu, ok rak um þvera stofuna, ok gerði bálk mikinn, svá at engi heimamaðr komz fram yfir. Engi þorði í móti honum at mæla, ok í engum skyldi kretta. Gengit var í hliðvegginn stofunnar inn við gaflhlaðit; ok þar þverpallr hjá. Þar lagðiz Gestr niðr ok fór ekki af klæðunum. Ljós brann í stofunni gegnt dyrum. Liggr Gestr svá fram á nóttina.

Húsfreyja kom til Eyjardalsár til tíða, ok undruðu menn um ferðir hennar yfir ána. Hon sagðiz eigi vita, hvárt hana hefði yfir flutt maðr eða trǫll. Prestr kvað mann víst vera mundu, þóat fárra maki sé; "ok látum hljótt yfir," sagði hann; "má vera, at hann sé ætlaðr til at vinna bót á vandræðum þínum." Var húsfreyja þar um nóttina.

Nú er frá Gretti þat at segja, at þá er dró at miðri nótt, heyrði hann út dynur miklar. Þvínæst kom inn í stofuna trǫllkona mikil. Hon hafði í hendi trog, en annarri skálm, heldr mikla. Hon litaz um, er hon kom inn, ok sá, hvar Gestr lá, ok hljóp at honum, en hann upp í móti, ok réðuz á grimmliga ok sóttuz lengi í stofunni. Hon var sterkari, en hann fór undan kœnliga. En allt þat, sem fyrir þeim varð, brutu þau, jafnvel þverþilit undan stofunni. Hon dró hann fram yfir dyrnar, ok svá í anddyrit; þar tók hann fast í móti. Hon vildi draga hann út ór bœnum, en þat varð eigi fyrr en þau leystu frá allan útidyraumbúninginn ok báru hann út á herðum sér. Þœfði hon þá ofan til árinnar ok allt fram at gljúfrum. Þá var Gestr ákafliga móðr, en þó varð annathvárt at gera: at herða sik, ella mundi hon steypa honum í gljúfrin. Alla nóttina sóttuz þau. Eigi þóttiz hann hafa fengiz við þvílíkan ófagnað fyrir afls sakir. Hon hafði haldit honum svá fast at sér, at hann mátti hvárigri hendi taka til nǫkkurs, útan hann helt um hana miðja k[ett]una. Ok er þau kómu á árgljufrit, bregðr hann flagðkonunni til sveiflu. Í því varð honum laus hin hœgri hǫndin. Hann þreif þá skjótt til saxins, er hann var gyrðr með, ok bregðr því; hǫggr þá á ǫxl trǫllinu, svá at af tók hǫndina hœgri, ok svá, varð hann lauss. En hon steyptiz í gljúfrin ok svá í fossinn. Gestr var þá bæði stirðr ok móðr, ok lá þar lengi á hamrinum. Gekk hann þá heim, er lýsa tók, ok lagðiz í rekkju. Hann var allr þrútinn ok blár.

Ok er húsfreyja kom frá tíðum, þótti henni heldr raskat um hýbýli sín. Gekk hon þá til Gests ok spurði, hvat til hefði borit, er allt var brotit ok bælt. Hann sagði allt, sem farit hafði. Henni þótti mikils um vert, ok spurði, hverr hann var. Hann sagði þá til hit sanna, ok bað sœkja prest ok kvaz vildu finna hann. Var ok svá gǫrt. En er Steinn prestr kom til Sandhauga, varð hann brátt þess víss, at þar var kominn Grettir Ásmundarson, er Gestr nefndiz. Prestr spurði, hvat hann ætlaði af þeim mǫnnum mundi vera orðit, er þar hǫfðu horfit. Grettir kvaz ætla, at í gljúfrin mundu þeir hafa horfit. Prestr kvaz eigi kunna at leggja trúnað á sagnir hans, ef engi merki mætti til sjá. Grettir segir, at síðar vissi þeir þat gǫrr. Fór prestr heim. Grettir lá í rekkju margar nætr. Húsfreyja gerði við hann harðla vel; ok leið svá af jólin. Þetta er sǫgn Grettis, at trǫllkonan steyptiz í gljúfrin við, er hon fekk sárit; en Bárðardalsmenn segja, at hana dagaði uppi, þá er þau glímdu, ok spryngi, þá er hann hjó af henni hǫndina, ok standi þar enn í konu líking á bjarginu. Þeir dalbúarnir leyndu þar Gretti.

Um vetrinn eptir jól var þat einn dag, at Grettir fór til Eyjardalsár. Ok er þeir Grettir funduz ok prestr, mælti Grettir: "Sé ek þat, prestr," segir hann, "at þú leggr lítinn trúnað á sagnir mínar. Nú vil ek at þú farir með mér til árinnar, ok sjáir, hver líkendi þér þykkir á vera."

Prestr gerði svá. En er þeir kómu til fossins, sáu þeir skúta upp undir bergit; þat var meitilberg svá mikit, at hvergi mátti upp komaz, ok nær tíu faðma ofan at vatninu. Þeir hǫfðu festi með sér.

Þá mælti prestr: "Langt um ófært sýniz mér þér niðr at fara."

Grettir svarar: "Fært er víst; en þeim mun bezt þar, sem ágætismenn eru. Mun ek forvitnaz, hvat í fossinum er, en þú skalt geyma festar."

Prestr bað hann ráða, ok keyrði niðr hæl á berginu, ok bar at grjót, [ok sat þar hjá].

Nú er frá Gretti at segja, at hann lét stein í festaraugat ok lét svá síga ofan at vatninu.

"Hvern veg ætlar þú nú," segir prestr, "at fara?"

"Ekki vil ek vera bundinn," segir Grettir, "þá er ek kem í fossinn; svá boðar mér hugr um."

Eptir þat bjó hann sik til ferðar, ok var fáklæddr, ok gyrði sik með saxinu, en hafði ekki fleiri vápn. Síðan hljóp hann af bjarginu ok niðr í fossinn. Sá prestr í iljar honum, ok vissi síðan aldri, hvat af honum varð. Grettir kafaði undir fossinn, ok var þat torvelt, þvíat iða var mikil, ok varð hann allt til grunns at kafa, áðr en hann kœmiz upp undir fossinn. Þar var forberg nǫkkut, ok komz hann inn þar upp á. Þar var hellir mikill undir fossinum, ok fell áin fram af berginu. Gekk hann þá inn í hellinn, ok var þar eldr mikill á brǫndum. Grettir sá, at þar sat jǫtunn ǫgurliga mikill; hann var hræðiligr at sjá. En er Grettir kom at honum, hljóp jǫtunninn upp ok greip flein einn ok hjó til þess, er kominn var, þvíat bæði mátti hǫggva ok leggja með [honum]. Tréskapt var í; þat kǫlluðu menn þá heptisax, er þannveg var gǫrt. Grettir hjó á móti með saxinu, ok kom á skaptit, svá at í sundr tók. Jǫtunninn vildi þá seilaz á bak sér aptr til sverðs, er þar hekk í hellinum. Í því hjó Grettir framan á brjóstit, svá at náliga tók af alla bringspelina ok kviðinn, svá at iðrin steyptuz ór honum ofan í ána, ok keyrði þau ofan eptir ánni. Ok er prestr sat við festina, sá hann, at slyðrur nǫkkurar rak ofan eptir strengnum blóðugar allar. Hann varð þá lauss á velli, ok þóttiz nú vita, at Grettir mundi dauðr vera. Hljóp hann þá frá festarhaldinu ok fór heim. Var þá komit at kveldi, ok sagði prestr vísliga, at Grettir væri dauðr; ok sagði, at mikill skaði væri eptir þvílíkan mann.

Nú er frá Gretti at segja; hann lét skamt hǫggva í milli, þar til er jǫtunninn dó. Gekk Grettir þá innar eptir hellinum. Hann kveikti ljós ok kannaði hellinn. Ekki er frá því sagt, hversu mikit fé hann fekk í hellinum; en þat ætla menn, at verit hafi nǫkkut. Dvaldiz honum þar fram á nóttina. Hann fann þar tveggja manna bein, ok bar þau í belg einn. Leitaði hann þá ór hellinum ok lagðiz til festarinnar, ok hristi hana, ok ætlaði, at prestr mundi þar vera. En er hann vissi, at prestr var heim farinn, varð hann þá at handstyrkja upp festina, ok komz hann svá upp á bjargit. Fór hann þá heim til Eyjardalsár ok kom í forkirkju belginum þeim, sem beinin váru í, ok þar með rúnakefli því, er vísur þessar váru forkunnliga vel á ristnar:

"Gekk ek í gljúfr et dǫkkva
gein veltiflug steina,
viþ hjǫrgæþi hríþar
hlunns úrsvǫlum munni,
fast lá framm á brjósti
flugstraumr í sal naumu
heldr kom á herþar skáldi
hǫrþ fjón Braga kvónar."

Ok en þessi:

"Ljótr kom mér í móti
mellu vinr ór helli;
hann fekz, heldr at sǫnnu
harþfengr, viþ mik lengi;
harþeggjat lét ek hǫggvit
heptisax af skepti;
Gangs klauf brjóst ok bringu
bjartr gunnlogi svarta[298]."

Þar sagði svá, at Grettir hafi bein þessi ór hellinum haft. En er prestr kom til kirkju um morgininn, fann hann keflit ok þat sem fylgdi, ok las rúnarnar. En Grettir hafði farit heim til Sandhauga.

En þá er prestr fann Gretti, spurði hann inniliga eptir atburðum; en hann sagði alla sǫgu um ferð sína, ok kvað prest ótrúliga hafa haldit festinni. Prestr lét þat á sannaz. Þóttuz menn þat vita, at þessar óvættir mundu valdit hafa mannahvǫrfum þar í dalnum. Varð ok aldri mein af aptrgǫngum eða reimleikum þar í dalnum síðan. Þótti Grettir þar gǫrt hafa mikla landhreinsan. Prestr jarðaði bein þessi í kirkjugarði.

TRANSLATION OF EXTRACTS FROM *GRETTIS SAGA*

The *Grettis saga* was first printed in the middle of the eighteenth century, in Iceland (Marcússon, *Nockrer Marg-frooder Sogu-patter*, 1756, pp. 81-163). It was edited by Magnússon and Thordarson, Copenhagen, 1853, with a Danish translation, and again by Boer (*Altnordische Saga-bibliothek*, Halle, 1900). An edition was also printed at Reykjavik in 1900, edited by V. Ásmundarson.

There are over forty MSS of the saga: *Cod. Arn. Mag. 551 a* (quoted in the notes below as A) forms the basis of all three modern editions. Boer has investigated the relationship of the MSS (*Die handschriftliche überlieferung der Grettissaga*, Z.f.d.Ph. XXXI, 40-60), and has published, in an appendix to his edition, the readings of five of the more important, in so far as he considers that they can be utilized to amend the text supplied by A.

The reader who consults the editions of both Magnússon and Boer will be struck by the differences in the text, although both are following the same MS. Many of these differences are, of course, due to the fact that the editors are normalizing the spelling, but on different principles: many others, however, are due to the extraordinary difficulty of the MS itself. Mr Sigfús Blöndal, of the Royal Library of Copenhagen, has examined *Cod. Arn. Mag. 551 a* for me, and he writes:

"It is the very worst MS I have ever met with. The writing is small, almost every word is abbreviated, and, worst of all, the writing is in many places effaced, partly by smoke (I suppose the MS needs must have been lying for years in some smoky and damp *baðstofa*) rendering the parchment almost as black as shoe-leather, but still more owing to the use of chemicals, which modern editors have been obliged to use, to make sure of what there really was in the text. By the use of much patience and a lens, one can read it, though, in most places. Unfortunately, this does not apply to the *Glámur* episode, a big portion of which belongs to the very worst part of the MS, and the readings of that portion are therefore rather uncertain."

The Icelandic text given above agrees in the main with that in the excellent edition of Boer, to whom, in common with all students of the *Grettis saga*, I am much indebted: but I have frequently adopted in preference a spelling or wording nearer to that of Magnússon. In several of these instances (notably the spelling of the verses attributed to Grettir) I think Prof. Boer would probably himself agree.

The words or letters placed between square brackets are those which are not to be found in *Cod. Arn. Mag. 551 a.*

To Mr Blöndal, who has been at the labour of collating with the MS, for my benefit, both the passages given above, my grateful thanks are due.

There are English translations of the *Grettis saga* by Morris and E. Magnússon (1869, and in Morris' *Works*, 1911, vol. VII) and by G. A. Hight (*Everyman's Library*, 1914).

For a discussion of the relationship of the *Grettis saga* to other stories, see also Boer, *Zur Grettissaga*, in *Z.f.d.Ph.* XXX, 1-71.

(*a*) *Glam episode* (p. 146 above)

There was a man called Thorhall, who lived at Thorhall's Farm in Shadow-dale. Shadow-dale runs up from Water-dale. Thorhall was son of Grim, son of Thorhall, son of Frithmund, who settled Shadow-dale. Thorhall's wife was called Guthrun: their son was Grim, and Thurith their daughter—they were grown up.

p. 147

Thorhall was a wealthy man, and especially in cattle, so that no man had as much live stock as he. He was not a chief, yet a substantial yeoman. The place was much haunted, and he found it hard to get a shepherd to suit him. He sought counsel of many wise men, what device he should follow, but he got no counsel which was of use to him. Thorhall rode each summer to the All-Thing; he had good horses. That was one summer at the All-Thing, that Thorhall went to the booth of Skapti Thoroddsson, the Law-man.

Skapti was the wisest of men, and gave good advice if he was asked. There was this difference between Skapti and his father Thorodd: Thorodd had second sight, and some men called him underhanded; but Skapti gave to every man that advice which he believed would avail, if it were kept to: so he was called 'Better than his father.' Thorhall went to the booth of Skapti. Skapti greeted Thorhall well, for he knew that he was a prosperous man, and asked what news he had.

Thorhall said, "I should like good counsel from thee." "I am little use at that," said Skapti. "But what is thy need?"

Thorhall said, "It happens so, that it is difficult for me to keep my shepherds: they easily get hurt, and some will not serve their time. And now no one will take on the task, who knows what is before him."

Skapti answered, "There must be some evil being about, if men are more unwilling to look after thy sheep than those of other folk. Now because thou hast sought counsel of me, I will find thee a shepherd, who is named Glam, a Swede, from Sylgsdale, who came out to Iceland last summer. He is great and strong, but not much to everybody's taste."

Thorhall said that he would not mind that, if he guarded the sheep well. Skapti said that if Glam had not the strength and courage to do that, there was no hope of anyone else. Then Thorhall went out; this was when the All-Thing was nearly ending.

Thorhall missed two light bay horses, and he went himself to look for them—so it seems that he was not a great man. He went up under Sledge-hill and south along the mountain called Armannsfell.

Then he saw where a man came down from Gothashaw, bearing faggots on a horse. They soon met, and Thorhall asked him his name, and he said he was called Glam. Glam p. 148 was tall and strange in bearing, with blue[299] and glaring eyes, and wolf-grey hair. Thorhall opened his eyes when he saw him, but yet he discerned that this was he to whom he had been sent.

"What work art thou best fitted for?" said Thorhall.

Glam said he was well fitted to watch sheep in the winter.

"Wilt thou watch my sheep?" said Thorhall. "Skapti gave thee into my hand."

"You will have least trouble with me in your house if I go my own way, for I am hard of temper if I am not pleased," said Glam.

"That will not matter to me," said Thorhall, "and I wish that thou shouldst go to my house."

"That may I well do," said Glam, "but are there any difficulties?"

"It is thought to be haunted," said Thorhall.

"I am not afraid of such phantoms," said Glam, "and it seems to me all the less dull."

"Thou wilt need such a spirit," said Thorhall, "and it is better that the man there should not be a coward."

After that they struck their bargain, and Glam was to come at the winter-nights [14th-16th of October]. Then they parted, and Thorhall found his horses where he had just been searching. Thorhall rode home and thanked Skapti for his good deed.

Summer passed, and Thorhall heard nothing of his shepherd, and no one knew anything of him; but at the time appointed he came to Thorhall's Farm. The yeoman greeted him well, but all the others could not abide him, and Thorhall's wife least of all. Glam undertook the watching of the sheep, and it gave him little trouble. He had a great deep voice, and the sheep came together as soon as he called them. There was a church at Thorhall's Farm, but Glam would not go to it. He would have nothing to do with the service, and was godless; he was obstinate and surly and abhorred by all.

Now time went on till it came to Yule eve. Then Glam rose early and called for meat. The yeoman's wife answered, "That is not the custom of Christian men to eat meat today, because tomorrow is the first day of Yule," said she, "and therefore it is right that we should first fast today."

He answered, "Ye have many superstitions which I see are good for nothing. I do not know that men fare better now p. 149 than before, when they had nought to do with such things. It seemed to me a better way when men were called heathen; and I want my meat and no tricks."

The yeoman's wife said, "I know for a certainty that it will fare ill with thee today, if thou dost this evil thing."

Glam bade her bring the meat at once, else he said it should be worse for her. She dared not do otherwise than he willed, and when he had eaten he went out, foul-mouthed.

Now it had gone so with the weather that it was heavy all round, and snow-flakes were falling, and it was blowing loud, and grew much worse as the day went on. The shepherd was heard early in the day, but less later. Then wind began to drive the snow, and towards evening it became a tempest. Then men came to the service, and so it went on to nightfall. Glam did not come home. Then there was talk whether search ought not to be made for him, but because there was a tempest and it was pitch dark, no search was attempted. That Yule night he did not come home, and so men waited till after the service [next, i.e. Christmas, morning]. But when it was full day, men went to search, and found the sheep scattered in the snow-drifts[300], battered by the tempest, or strayed up into the mountains. Then they came on a great space beaten down, high up in the valley. It looked to them as if there had been somewhat violent wrestling there, because the stones had been torn up for a distance around, and the earth likewise. They looked closely and saw where Glam lay a little distance away. He was dead, and blue like Hel and swollen like an ox. They had great loathing of him, and their souls shuddered at him. Nevertheless they strove to bring him to the church, but they could get him no further than the edge of a ravine a little below, and they went home leaving matters so, and told the yeoman what had happened. He asked what appeared to have been the death of Glam. They said that, from the trodden spot, up to a place beneath the rocks high in the valley, they had tracked marks as big as if a cask-bottom had been stamped down, and great drops of blood with them. So men concluded from this, that the evil thing which had been there before must have killed Glam, but Glam must have done it damage which had been enough, in that nought has ever happened since from that evil thing.

The second day of Yule it was again essayed to bring Glam to the church.

Beasts of draught were harnessed, but they could not move him where it was level ground and not down hill, so they departed, leaving matters so.

The third day the priest went with them, and they searched p. 150 all day, but Glam could not be found. The priest would go no more, but Glam was found when the priest was not in the company. Then they gave up trying to carry him to the church, and buried him where he was, under a cairn.

A little later men became aware that Glam was not lying quiet. Great harm came to men from this, so that many fell into a swoon when they saw him, and some could not keep their wits. Just after Yule, men thought they saw him at home at the farm. They were exceedingly afraid, and many fled away. Thereupon Glam took to riding the house-roofs at nights, so that he nearly broke them in. He walked almost night and day. Men hardly dared to go up into the dale, even though they had business enough. Men in that country-side thought great harm of this.

In the spring Thorhall got farm-hands together and set up house on his land. Then the apparition began to grow less frequent whilst the sun's course was at its height; and so it went on till midsummer. That summer a ship came out to Hunawater. On it was a man called Thorgaut. He was an outlander by race, big and powerful; he had the strength of two men. He was in no man's service, and alone, and he wished to take up some work, since he had no money. Thorhall rode to the ship, and met Thorgaut. He asked him if he would work for him. Thorgaut said that might well be, and that he would make no difficulties.

"But thou must be prepared," said Thorhall, "that it is no place for weaklings, by reason of the hauntings which have been going on for a while, for I will not let thee into a trap."

Thorgaut answered, "It does not seem to me that I am undone, even though I were to see some little ghosts. It must be no easy matter for others if I am frightened, and I will not give up my place for that."

So now they agreed well, and Thorgaut was to watch the sheep when winter came.

Now the summer passed on. Thorgaut took charge of the sheep at the winter-nights. He was well-pleasing to all. Glam ever came home and rode on the roofs. Thorgaut thought it sporting, and said that the thrall would have to come nearer in order to scare him. But Thorhall bade him keep quiet: "It is best that ye should not try your strength together." Thorgaut said, "Verily, your courage is shaken out of you: I shall not drop down with fear between day and night over such talk."

Now things went on through the winter up to Yule-tide. On Yule evening the shepherd went out to his sheep. Then p. 151 the yeoman's wife said, "It is to be hoped that now things will not go in the old way."

He answered, "Be not afraid of that, mistress; something worth telling will have happened if I do not come back."

Then he went to his sheep. The weather was cold, and it snowed much. Thorgaut was wont to come home when it was twilight, but now he did not come at that time. Men came to the service, as was the custom. It seemed to people that things were going as they had before. The yeoman wished to have search made for the shepherd, but the church-goers excused themselves, and said they would not risk themselves out in the hands of the trolls by night. And the yeoman did not dare to go, so the search came to nothing.

On Yule-day, when men had eaten, they went and searched for the shepherd. They went first to Glam's cairn, because men thought that the shepherd's disappearance must have been through his bringing-about. But when they came near the cairn they saw great things, for there they found the shepherd with his neck broken and not a bone in him whole. Then they carried him to the church, and no harm happened to any man from Thorgaut afterwards; but Glam began to increase in strength anew. He did so much that all men fled away from Thorhall's Farm, except only the yeoman and his wife.

Now the same cattle-herd had been there a long time. Thorhall would not let him go, because of his good-will and good service. He was far gone in age and was very unwilling to leave: he saw that everything went to waste which the yeoman had, if no one looked after it. And once after mid-winter it happened one morning that the yeoman's wife went to the byre to milk the cows as usual. It was quite light, because no one dared to go out before, except the cattle-herd: he went out as soon as it dawned. She heard great cracking in the byre and a hideous bellowing. She ran back, crying out, and said she did not know what devilry was going on in the byre.

The yeoman went out, and came to the cattle, and they were goring each other. It seemed to him no good to stay there, and he went further into the hay-barn. He saw where the cattle-herd lay, and he had his head in one stall and his feet in the next. He lay on his back. The yeoman went to him and felt him. He soon found that he was dead, and his back-bone broken in two; it had been broken over the partition slab.

Now it seemed no longer bearable to Thorhall, and he left his farm with all that he could carry away; but all the live-stock p. 152 left behind Glam killed. After that he went through all the dale and laid waste all the farms up from Tongue. Thorhall spent what was left of the winter with his friends. No man could go up into the dale with horse or hound, because it was slain forthwith. But when spring came, and the course of the sun was highest, the apparitions abated somewhat. Now Thorhall wished to go back to his land. It was not easy for him to get servants, but still he set up house at Thorhall's Farm.

All went the same way as before. When autumn came on the hauntings began to increase. The yeoman's daughter was most attacked, and it fared so that she died. Many counsels were taken, but nothing was done. Things seemed to men to be looking as if all Water-dale must be laid waste, unless some remedies could be found.

Now the story must be taken up about Grettir, how he sat at home at Bjarg that autumn, after he had parted from Barthi-of-the-Slayings at Thorey's Peak. And when it had almost come to the winter-nights, Grettir rode from home, north over the neck to Willow-dale, and was a guest at Authun's Farm. He was fully reconciled to Authun, and gave him a good axe, and they spake of their wish for friendship one with the other. (Authun dwelt long at Authun's Farm, and much goodly offspring had he. Egil was his son, who wedded Ulfheith, daughter of Eyjolf Guthmundson; and their son was Eyjolf, who was slain at the All-Thing. He was father of Orm, chaplain to Bishop Thorlak.) Grettir rode north to Water-dale and came on a visit to Tongue. At that time Jokul Barthson lived there, Grettir's uncle. Jokul was a man great and strong and very proud. He was a seafaring man, and very over-bearing, yet of great account. He received Grettir well, and Grettir was there three nights.

There was so much said about the apparitions of Glam that nothing was spoken of by men equally with that. Grettir inquired exactly about the events which had happened. Jokul said that nothing more had been spoken than had verily occurred. "But art thou anxious, kinsman, to go there?"

Grettir said that that was the truth. Jokul begged him not to do so, "For that is a great risk of thy luck, and thy kinsmen have much at stake where thou art," said he, "for none of the young men seems to us to be equal to thee; but ill will come of ill where Glam is, and it is much better to have to do with mortal men than with evil creatures like that."

Grettir said he was minded to go to Thorhall's Farm and p. 153 see how things had fared there. Jokul said, "I see now that it is of no avail to stop thee, but true it is what men say, that good-luck is one thing, and goodliness another."

"Woe is before one man's door when it is come into another's house. Think how it may fare with thee thyself before the end," said Grettir.

Jokul answered, "It may be that both of us can see somewhat into the future, but neither can do aught in the matter."

After that they parted, and neither was pleased with the other's foreboding.

Grettir rode to Thorhall's Farm, and the yeoman greeted him well. He asked whither Grettir meant to go, but Grettir said he would stay there over the night if the yeoman would have it so. Thorhall said he owed him thanks for being there, "But few men find it a profit to stay here for any time. Thou must have heard what the dealings are here, and I would fain that thou shouldst have no troubles on my account; but though thou shouldst come whole away, I know for certain that thou wilt lose thy steed, for no one who comes here keeps his horse whole."

Grettir said there were plenty of horses, whatever should become of this one.

Thorhall was glad that Grettir would stay there, and welcomed him exceedingly.

Grettir's horse was strongly locked in an out-house. They went to sleep, and so the night passed without Glam coming home. Then Thorhall said, "Things have taken a good turn against thy coming, for every night Glam has been wont to ride the roofs or break up the doors, even as thou canst see."

Grettir said, "Then must one of two things happen. Either he will not long hold himself in, or the wonted haunting will cease for more than one night. I will stay here another night and see how it goes."

Then they went to Grettir's horse, and he had not been attacked. Then everything seemed to the yeoman to be going one way. Now Grettir stayed for another night, and the thrall did not come home. Then things seemed to the yeoman to be taking a very hopeful turn. He went to look after Grettir's horse. When he came there, the stable was broken into, and the horse dragged out to the door, and every bone in him broken asunder.

Thorhall told Grettir what had happened, and bade him save his own life— "For thy death is sure if thou waitest for Glam."

Grettir answered, "The least I must have in exchange for my horse is to see the thrall."

The yeoman said that there was no good in seeing him: p. 154 "For he is unlike any shape of man; but every hour that thou wilt stay here seems good to me."

Now the day went on, and when bed-time came Grettir would not put off his clothes, but lay down in the seat over against the yeoman's sleeping-chamber. He had a shaggy cloak over him, and wrapped one corner of it down under his feet, and twisted the other under his head and looked out through the head-opening. There was a great and strong partition beam in front of the seat, and he put his feet against it. The doorframe was all broken away from the outer door, but now boards, fastened together carelessly anyhow, had been tied in front. The panelling which had been in front was all broken away from the hall, both above and below the cross-beam; the beds were all torn out of their places, and everything was very wretched[301].

A light burned in the hall during the night: and when a third part of the night was past, Grettir heard a great noise outside. Some creature had mounted upon the buildings and was riding upon the hall and beating it with its heels, so that it cracked in every rafter. This went on a long time. Then the creature came down from the buildings and went to the door. When the door was opened Grettir saw that the thrall had stretched in his head, and it seemed to him monstrously great and wonderfully huge. Glam went slowly and stretched himself up when he came inside the door. He towered up to the roof. He turned and laid his arm upon the cross-beam and glared in upon the hall. The yeoman did not let himself be heard, because the noise he heard outside seemed to him enough. Grettir lay quiet and did not move.

Glam saw that a heap lay upon the seat, and he stalked in up the hall and gripped the cloak wondrous fast. Grettir pressed his feet against the post and gave not at all. Glam pulled a second time much more violently, and the cloak did not move. A third time he gripped with both hands so mightily that he pulled Grettir up from the seat, and now the cloak was torn asunder between them.

Glam gazed at the portion which he held, and wondered much who could have pulled so hard against him; and at that moment Grettir leapt under his arms and grasped him round the middle, and bent his back as mightily as he could, reckoning that Glam would sink to his knees at his attack. But the thrall laid such a grip on Grettir's arm that he recoiled at the might of it. Then Grettir gave way from one seat to another. The beams[302] started, and all that came in their way was broken. p. 155 Glam wished to get out, but Grettir set his feet against any support he could find; nevertheless Glam dragged him forward out of the hall. And there they had a sore wrestling, in that the thrall meant to drag him right out of the building; but ill as it was to have to do with Glam inside, Grettir saw that it would be yet worse without, and so he struggled with all his might against going out. Glam put forth all his strength, and dragged Grettir towards himself when they came to the porch. And when Grettir saw that he could not resist, then all at once he flung himself against the breast of the thrall, as powerfully as he could, and pressed forward with both his feet against a stone which stood fast in the earth at the entrance. The thrall was not ready for this, he had been pulling to drag Grettir towards himself; and thereupon he stumbled on his back out of doors, so that his shoulders smote against the cross-piece of the door, and the roof clave asunder, both wood and frozen thatch. So Glam fell backwards out of the house and Grettir on top of him. There was bright moonshine and broken clouds without. At times they drifted in front of the moon and at times away. Now at the moment when Glam fell, the clouds cleared from before the moon, and Glam rolled up his eyes; and Grettir himself has said that that was the one sight he had seen which struck fear into him. Then such a sinking came over Grettir, from his weariness and from that sight of Glam rolling his eyes, that he had no strength to draw his knife and lay almost between life and death.

But in this was there more power for evil in Glam than in most other apparitions, in that he spake thus: "Much eagerness hast thou shown, Grettir," said he, "to meet with me. But no wonder will it seem if thou hast no good luck from me. And this can I tell thee, that thou hast now achieved one half of the power and might which was fated for thee if thou hadst not met with me. Now no power have I to take that might from thee to which thou hast attained. But in this may I have my way, that thou shalt never become stronger than now thou art, and yet art thou strong enough, as many a one shall find to his cost. Famous hast thou been till now for thy deeds, but from now on shall exiles and manslaughters fall to thy lot, and almost all of thy labours shall turn to ill-luck and unhappiness. Thou shalt be outlawed and doomed ever to dwell alone, away from men; and then lay I this fate on thee, that these eyes of mine be ever before thy sight, and it shall seem grievous unto thee to be alone, and that shall drag thee to thy death."

And when the thrall had said this, the swoon which had p. 156 fallen upon Grettir passed from him. Then he drew his sword and smote off Glam's head, and placed it by his thigh.

Then the yeoman came out: he had clad himself whilst Glam was uttering his curse, but he dare in no wise come near before Glam had fallen. Thorhall praised God for it, and thanked Grettir well for having vanquished the unclean spirit.

Then they set to work and burned Glam to cold cinders. After, they put the ashes in a skin-bag and buried them as far as possible from the ways of man or beast. After that they went home, and by that time it was well on to day. Grettir lay down, for he was very stiff. Thorhall sent people to the next farm for men, and showed to them what had happened. To all those who heard of it, it seemed a work of great account; and that was then spoken by all, that no man in all the land was equal to Grettir Asmundarson for might and valour and all prowess. Thorhall sent Grettir from his house with honour, and gave him a good horse and fit clothing; for all the clothes which he had worn before were torn asunder. They parted great friends. Grettir rode thence to Ridge in Water-dale, and Thorvald greeted him well, and asked closely as to his meeting with Glam. Grettir told him of their dealings, and said that never had he had such a trial of strength, so long a struggle had theirs been together.

Thorvald bade him keep quiet, "and then all will be well, otherwise there are bound to be troubles for thee."

Grettir said that his temper had not bettered, and that he was now more unruly than before, and all offences seemed worse to him. And in that he found a great difference, that he had become so afraid of the dark that he did not dare to go anywhere alone after night had fallen. All kinds of horrors appeared to him then. And that has since passed into a proverb, that Glam gives eyes, or gives "glam-sight" to those to whom things seem quite other than they are. Grettir rode home to Bjarg when he had done his errand, and remained at home during the winter.

There was a priest called Stein who lived at Eyjardalsá (Isledale River) in Barthardal. He was a good husbandman and rich in cattle. His son was Kjartan, a doughty man and well grown. There was a man called Thorstein the White who p. 157 lived at Sandhaugar (Sandheaps), south of Isledale river; his wife was called Steinvor, and she was young and merry. They had children, who were young then.

People thought the place was much haunted by reason of the visitation of trolls. It happened, two winters before Grettir came North into those districts, that the good-wife Steinvor at Sandhaugar went to a Christmas service, according to her custom, at Isledale river, but her husband remained at home. In the evening men went to bed, and during the night they heard a great rummage in the hall, and by the good-man's bed. No one dared to get up to look to it, because there were very few men about. The good-wife came home in the morning, but her husband had vanished, and no one knew what had become of him.

The next year passed away. But the winter after, the good-wife wished again to go to the church-service, and she bade her manservant remain at home. He was unwilling, but said she must have her own way. All went in the same manner as before, and the servant vanished. People thought that strange. They saw some splashes of blood on the outer door, and men thought that evil beings must have taken away both the good-man and the servant.

The news of this spread wide throughout the country. Grettir heard of it; and because it was his fortune to get rid of hauntings and spirit-walkings, he took his way to Barthardal, and came to Sandhaugar on Yule eve. He disguised himself[303], and said his name was Guest. The good-wife saw that he was great of stature; and the farm-folk were much afraid of him. He asked for quarters for the night. The good-wife said that he could have meat forthwith, but "You must look after your own safety."

He said it should be so. "I will be at home," said he, "and you can go to the service if you will."

She answered, "You are a brave man, it seems to me, if you dare to remain at home."

"I do not care to have things all one way[304]," said he.

"It seems ill to me to be at home," said she, "but I cannot get over the river."

"I will see you over," said Guest.

Then she got ready to go to the service, and her small daughter with her. It was thawing, the river was in flood, and there were ice-floes in it. Then the good-wife said, "It is impossible for man or horse to get across the river."

"There must be fords in it," said Guest, "do not be afraid."

p. 158

"Do you carry the child first," said the good-wife, "she is the lighter."

"I do not care to make two journeys of it," said Guest, "and I will carry thee on my arm."

She crossed herself and said, "That is an impossible way; what will you do with the child?"

"I will see a way for that," said he; and then he took them both up, and set the child on her mother's knee and so bore them both on his left arm. But he had his right hand free, and thus he waded out into the ford.

They did not dare to cry out, so much afraid were they. The river washed at once up against his breast; then it tossed a great icefloe against him, but he put out the hand that was free and pushed it from him. Then it grew so deep that the river dashed over his shoulder; but he waded stoutly on, until he came to the bank on the other side, and threw Steinvor and her daughter on the land.

Then he turned back, and it was half dark when he came to Sandhaugar and called for meat; and when he had eaten, he bade the farm folk go to the far side of the room. Then he took boards and loose timber which he dragged across the room, and made a great barrier so that none of the farm folk could come over it. No one dared to say anything against him or to murmur in any wise. The entrance was in the side wall of the chamber by the gable-end, and there was a dais there. Guest lay down there, but did not take off his clothes: a light was burning in the room over against the door: Guest lay there far into the night.

The good-wife came to Isledale river to the service, and men wondered how she had crossed the river. She said she did not know whether it was a man or a troll who had carried her over. The priest said, "It must surely be a man, although there are few like him. And let us say nothing about it," said he, "it may be that he is destined to work a remedy for your evils." The good-wife remained there through the night.

Now it is to be told concerning Grettir that when it drew towards midnight he heard great noises outside. Thereupon there came into the room a great giantess. She had in one hand a trough and in the other a short-sword, rather a big one. She looked round when she came in, and saw where Guest lay, and sprang at him; but he sprang up against her, and they struggled fiercely and wrestled for a long time in the room. She was the stronger, but he gave way warily; and they broke all that was before them, as well as the panelling of the room. She dragged him forward through the door and so[305] into the porch, and he p. 159 struggled hard against her. She wished to drag him out of the house, but that did not happen until they had broken all the fittings of the outer doorway and forced them out on their shoulders. Then she dragged him slowly down towards the river and right along to the gorge.

By that time Guest was exceedingly weary, but yet, one or other it had to be, either he had to gather his strength together, or else she would have hurled him down into the gorge. All night they struggled. He thought that he had never grappled with such a devil in the matter of strength. She had got such a grip upon him that he could do nothing with either hand, except to hold the witch by the middle; but when they came to the gorge of the river he swung the giantess round, and thereupon got his right hand free. Then quickly he gripped his knife that he wore in his girdle and drew it, and smote the shoulder of the giantess so that he cut off her right arm. So he got free: but she fell into the gorge, and so into the rapids below.

Guest was then both stiff and tired, and lay long on the rocks; then he went home when it began to grow light, and lay down in bed. He was all swollen black and blue.

And when the good-wife came from the service, it seemed to her that things had been somewhat disarranged in her house. Then she went to Guest and asked him what had happened, that all was broken and destroyed[306]. He told her all that had taken place. She thought it very wonderful, and asked who he was. He told her the truth, and asked her to send for the priest, and said he wished to meet him; and so it was done.

Then when Stein the priest came to Sandhaugar, he knew soon that it was Grettir Asmundarson who had come there, and who had called himself Guest.

The priest asked Grettir what he thought must have become of those men who had vanished. Grettir said he thought they must have vanished into the gorge. The priest said that he could not believe Grettir's saying, if no signs of it were to be seen. Grettir said that they would know more accurately about it later. Then the priest went home. Grettir lay many days in bed. The good-wife looked after him well, and so the Christmas-time passed.

Grettir's account was that the giantess fell into the gulf when she got her wound; but the men of Barthardal say that day came upon her whilst they wrestled, and that she burst when he smote her hand off, and that she stands there on the cliff yet, a rock in the likeness of a woman[307].

The dwellers in the dale kept Grettir in hiding there. But after Christmas time, one day that winter, Grettir went to Isledale river. And when Grettir and the priest met, Grettir p. 160 said "I see, priest, that you place little belief in my words. Now will I that you go with me to the river and see what the likelihood seems to you to be."

The priest did so. But when they came to the waterfall they saw that the sides of the gorge hung over[308]: it was a sheer cliff so great that one could in nowise come up, and it was nearly ten fathoms[309] from the top to the water below. They had a rope with them. Then the priest said, "It seems to me quite impossible for thee to get down."

Grettir said, "Assuredly it is possible, but best for those who are men of valour. I will examine what is in the waterfall, and thou shalt watch the rope."

The priest said it should be as he wished, drove a peg into the cliff, piled stones against it, and sat by it[310].

Now it must be told concerning Grettir that he knotted a stone into the rope, and so let it down to the water.

"What way," said the priest, "do you mean to go?"

"I will not be bound," said Grettir, "when I go into the water, so much my mind forebodes me."

After that he got ready for his exploit, and had little on; he girded himself with his short sword, and had no other weapon.

Then he plunged from the cliff down into the waterfall. The priest saw the soles of his feet, and knew no more what had become of him. Grettir dived under the waterfall, and that was difficult because there was a great eddy, and he had to dive right to the bottom before he could come up behind the waterfall. There was a jutting rock and he climbed upon it. There was a great cave behind the waterfall, and the river fell in front of it from the precipice. He went into the cave, and there was a big fire burning. Grettir saw that there sat a giant of frightful size. He was terrible to look upon: but when Grettir came to him, the giant leapt up and seized a pike, and hewed at the new-comer: for with the pike he could both cut and stab. It had a handle of wood: men at that time called a weapon made in such a way a *heptisax*. Grettir smote against it with his short sword, and struck the handle so that he cut it asunder. Then the giant tried to reach back for a sword which hung behind him in the cave. Thereupon Grettir smote him in the breast, and struck off almost all the lower part of his chest and his belly, so that the entrails gushed out of him down into the river, and were swept along the current.

And as the priest sat by the rope he saw some lumps, clotted p. 161 with blood, carried down stream. Then he became unsteady, and thought that now he knew that Grettir must be dead: and he ran from keeping the rope and went home. It was then evening, and the priest said for certain that Grettir was dead, and added that it was a great loss of such a man.

Now the tale must be told concerning Grettir. He let little space go between his blows till the giant was dead. Then he went further into the cave; he kindled a light and examined it. It is not said how much wealth he took in the cave, but men think that there was something. He stayed there far into the night. He found there the bones of two men, and put them into a bag. Then he left the cave and swam to the rope and shook it, for he thought that the priest must be there. But when he knew that the priest had gone home, then he had to draw himself up, hand over hand, and so he came up on to the cliff.

Then he went home to Isledale river, and came to the church porch, with the bag that the bones were in, and with a rune-staff, on which these verses were exceedingly well cut:

There into gloomy gulf I passed,
O'er which from the rock's throat is cast
The swirling rush of waters wan,
To meet the sword-player feared of man.
By giant's hall the strong stream pressed
Cold hands against the singer's breast;
Huge weight upon him there did hurl
The swallower of the changing whirl[311].

And this rhyme too:

- 153 -

The dreadful dweller of the cave
Great strokes and many 'gainst me drave;
Full hard he had to strive for it,
But toiling long he wan no whit;
For from its mighty shaft of tree
The heft-sax smote I speedily;
And dulled the flashing war-flame fair
In the black breast that met me there.

p. 162

These verses told also that Grettir had taken these bones out of the cave. But when the priest came to the church in the morning he found the staff, and what was with it, and read the runes; but Grettir had gone home to Sandhaugar.

But when the priest met Grettir he asked him closely as to what had happened: and Grettir told him all the story of his journey. And he added that the priest had not watched the rope faithfully. The priest said that that was true enough.

Men thought for certain that these monsters must have caused the loss of men there in the dale; and there was never any loss from hauntings or spirit-walkings there afterwards.

Grettir was thought to have caused a great purging of the land. The priest buried these bones in the churchyard.

D. EXTRACTS FROM *BJARKA RÍMUR*

(*Hrólfs saga Kraka og Bjarkarímur* udgivne ved F. Jónsson, København, 1904)

58. Flestir ǫmuðu Hetti heldr,
hann var ekki í máli sneldr,
einn dag fóru þeir út af hǫll,
svó ekki vissi hirðin ǫll.

59. Hjalti talar er felmtinn fær,

"fǫrum við ekki skógi nær,
hér er sú ylgr sem etr upp menn,
okkr drepr hún báða senn."

60. Ylgrin hljóp úr einum runn,
ógurlig með gapanda munn,
hǫrmuligt varð Hjalta viðr,
á honum skalf bæði leggr og liðr.

61. Ótæpt Bjarki að henni gengr,
ekki dvelr hann við það lengr,
hǫggur svó að í hamri stóð,
hljóp úr henni ferligt blóð.

62. "Kjóstu Hjalti um kosti tvó,"
kappinn Bǫðvar talaði svó,
"drekk nú blóð eða drep eg þig hér,
dugrinn líz mér engi í þér."

63. Ansar Hjalti af ærnum móð,
"ekki þori eg að drekka blóð,
nýtir flest ef nauðigr skal,
nú er ekki á betra val."

64. Hjalti gjǫrir sem Bǫðvar biðr,
að blóði frá eg hann lagðist niðr,
drekkur síðan drykki þrjá,
duga mun honum við einn að rjá.
IV, 58-64.

4. Hann hefr fengið hjartað snjalt
af hǫrðum móði,
fekk hann huginn og aflið alt
af ylgjar blóði.

5. Í grindur vandist grábjǫrn einn
í garðinn Hleiðar,
var sá margur vargrinn beinn
og víða sveiðar.

6. Bjarka er kent, að hjarðarhunda
hafi hann drepna,

ekki er hónum allvel hent
við ýta kepna.

7. Hrólfur býst og hirð hans ǫll
að húna stýri,
"Sá skal mestr í minni hǫll
er mætir dýri."

8. Beljandi hljóp bjǫrninn framm
úr bóli krukku,
veifar sínum vónda hramm,
svó virðar hrukku.

9. Hjalti sér og horfir þá á,
er hafin er róma,
hafði hann ekki í hǫndum þá
nema hnefana tóma.

10. Hrólfur fleygði að Hjalta þá
þeim hildar vendi,
kappinn móti krummu brá
og klótið hendi.

11. Lagði hann síðan bjǫrninn brátt
við bóginn hægra,
bessi fell í brúðar átt
og bar sig lægra.

12. Vann hann það til frægða fyst
og fleira síðar,
hans var lundin lǫngum byst
í leiki gríðar.

13. Hér með fekk hann Hjalta nafn
hins hjartaprúða,
Bjarki var eigi betri en jafn
við býti skrúða.
V, 4-13.

23. Aðals var glaðr afreksmaðr,
austur þangað kómu,
fyrðar þeir með fránan geir

flengja þegar til rómu.

24. Ýtar býta engum frið,
unnu vel til mála,
þar fell Áli og alt hans lið
ungr í leiki stála.

25. Hestrinn beztur Hrafn er kendr,
hafa þeir tekið af Ála,
Hildisvín er hjálmrinn vendr,
hann kaus Bjarki í mála.

26. Qðling bað þá eigi drafl
eiga um nǫkkur skipti,
það mun kosta kóngligt afl,
hann kappann gripunum svipti.

27. Ekki þótti Bǫðvar betr,
í burtu fóru þeir Hjalti,
létust áðr en liðinn er vetr
leita að Fróða malti.

28. Síðan ríða seggir heim
og sǫgðu kóngi þetta,
hann kveðst mundu handa þeim
heimta slíkt af létta.
VIII, 23-28.

TRANSLATION OF EXTRACTS FROM *BJARKA RÍMUR*

58. Most [of Rolf's retainers] much tormented Hott [Hjalti]; he was not cunning in speech. One day Hjalti and Bothvar went out of the hall, in such wise that none of the retainers knew thereof.

59. Hjalti spake in great terror, "Let us not go near the wood; here is the she-wolf who eats up men; she will kill us both together."

60. The she-wolf leapt from a thicket, dread, with gaping jaws. A great terror was it to Hjalti, and he trembled in every limb.

61. Without delay or hesitation went Bjarki towards her, and hewed at her so that the axe went deep; a monstrous stream of blood gushed from her.

62. "Choose now, Hjalti, of two things"—so spake Bothvar the champion—"Drink now the blood, or I slay thee here; it seems unto me that there is no valour in thee."

63. Hjalti replied stoutly enough, "I cannot bring myself to drink blood; but if I needs must, it avails most [to submit], and now is there no better choice."

64. Hjalti did as Bothvar bade: he stooped down to the blood; then drank he three sups: that will suffice him to wrestle with one man.

IV, 58-64.

4. He [Hjalti] has gained good courage and keen spirit; he got strength and all valour from the she-wolf's blood.

5. A grey bear visited the folds at Hleithargarth; many such a ravager was there far and wide throughout the country.

6. The blame was laid upon Bjarki, because he had slain the herdsmen's dogs; it was not so suited for him to have to strive with men[312].

7. Rolf and all his household prepared to hunt the bear; "He who faces the beast shall be greatest in my hall."

8. Roaring did the bear leap forth from out its den, swinging its evil claws, so that men shrank back.

9. Hjalti saw, he turned and gazed where the battle began; nought had he then in his hands—his empty fists alone.

10. Rolf tossed then to Hjalti his wand of war [his sword]; the warrior put forth his hand towards it, and grasped the pommel.

11. Quickly then he smote the bear in the right shoulder; Bruin fell to the earth, and bore himself in more lowly wise.

12. That was the beginning of his exploits: many followed later; his spirit was ever excellent amid the play of battle.

13. Herefrom he got the name of Hjalti the stout-hearted: Bjarki was no more than his equal.

V, 4-13.

23. Joyful was the valiant Athils when they [Bjarki and Rolf's champions] came east to that place [Lake Wener]; troops with flashing spears rode quickly forthwith to the battle.

24. No truce gave they to their foes: well they earned their pay; there fell Ali and all his host, young in the game of swords.

25. The best of horses, Hrafn by name, they took from Ali; Bjarki chose for his reward the helm Hildisvin.

26. The prince [Athils] bade them have no talk about the business; he deprived the champions[313] of their treasures—that will be a test of his power.

27. Ill-pleased was Bothvar: he and Hjalti departed; they declared that before the winter was gone they would seek for the treasure [the malt of Frothi].

28. Then they rode home and told it to the king [Rolf]; he said it was their business to claim their due outright.

VIII, 23-28.

E. EXTRACT FROM ÞÁTTR ORMS STÓRÓLFSSONAR

(*Fornmanna Sǫgur*, Copenhagen, 1827, III. 204 *etc.*; *Flateyarbók*, Christiania, 1859-68, I. 527 *etc.*)

7. Litlu síðarr enn þeir Ormr ok Ásbjǫrn hǫfðu skilit, fýstist Ásbjǫrn norðr í Sauðeyjar, fór hann við 4 menn ok 20 á skipi, heldr norðr fyrir Mæri, ok leggr seint dags at Sauðey hinni ytri, gánga á land ok reisa tjald, eru þar um nóttina, ok verða við ekki varir; um morgininn árla rís Ásbjǫrn upp, klæðir sik, ok tekr vópn sín, ok gengr uppá land, en biðr menn sína bíða sín; en er nokkut svá var liðit frá því, er Ásbjǫrn hafði í brott gengit, verða þeir við þat varir, at ketta ógrlig var komin í tjaldsdyrnar, hon var kolsvǫrt at lit ok heldr grimmlig, þvíat eldr þótti brenna or nǫsum hennar ok munni, eigi var hon ok vel eyg; þeim brá mjǫk við þessa sýn, ok urðu óttafullir. Ketta hleypr þá innar at þeim, ok grípr hvern at ǫðrum, ok svá er sagt at suma gleypti hon, en suma rifi hon til dauðs með klóm ok tǫnnum, 20 menn drap hon þar á lítilli stundu, en 3 kvómust út ok undan ok á skip, ok héldu þegar undan landi; en Ásbjǫrn gengr þar til, er hann kemr at hellinum Brúsa, ok snarar þegar inn í; honum

varð nokkut dimt fyrir augum, en skuggamikit var í hellinum; hann verðr eigi fyrr var við, enn hann er þrifinn álopt, ok færðr niðr svá hart, at Ásbirni þótti furða í, verðr hann þess þá varr, at þar er kominn Brúsi jǫtun, ok sýndist heldr mikiligr. Brúsi mælti þá: þó lagðir þú mikit kapp á at sækja híngat; skaltu nú ok eyrindi hafa, þvíat þú skalt hér lífit láta með svá miklum harmkvælum, at þat skal aðra letja at sækja mik heim með ófriði; fletti hann þá Ásbjǫrn klæðum, þvíat svá, var þeirra mikill afla munr, at jǫtuninn varð einn at ráða þeirra í milli; bálk mikinn sá Ásbjǫrn standa um þveran hellinn ok stórt gat á miðjum bálkinum; járnsúla stór stóð nokkut svá fyrir framan bálkinn. Nú skal prófa þat, segir Brúsi, hvárt þú ert nokkut harðari enn aðrir menn. Lítit mun þat at reyna, segir Ásbjǫrn....

Síðan lét Ásbjǫrn líf sitt með mikilli hreysti ok dreingskap.

8. Þat er at segja at þeir þrír menn, er undan kómust, sóttu knáliga róðr, ok léttu eigi fyrr enn þeir kómu at landi, sǫgðu þau tíðindi er gerzt hǫfðu í þeirra fǫrum, kvóðust ætla Ásbjǫrn dauðan, en kunnu ekki frá at segja, hversu at hefði borizt um hans líflát; kvómu þeir sér i skip með kaupmǫnnum, ok fluttust svá suðr til Danmerkr; spurðust nú þessi tíðindi víða, ok þóttu mikil. Þa var orðit hǫfðíngja skipti í Noregi, Hakon jarl dauðr, en Ólafr Tryggvason í land kominn, ok bauð ǫllum rétta trú. Ormr Stórólfsson spurði út til Íslands um farar ok líflát Ásbjarnar, er mǫnnum þótti sem vera mundi; þótti honum þat allmikill skaði, ok undi eigi lengr á Íslandi, ok tók sér far í Reyðarfirði, ok fór þar utan; þeir kvómu norðarliga við Noreg, ok sat hann um vetrinn í Þrándheimi; þá hafði Ólafr ráðit 3 vetr Noregi. Um vórit bjóst Ormr at fara til Sauðeya, þeir vóru því nærr margir á skipi, sem þeir Ásbjǫrn h[,]fðu verit; þeir lǫgðu at minni Sauðey síð um kveldit, ok tjǫlduðu á landi, ok lágu þar um náttina....

9. Nú gengr Ormr þar til er hann kemr at hellinum, sér hann nú bjargit þat stóra, ok leizt úmátuligt nokkurum manni þat í brott at færa; þó dregr hann á sik glófana Menglaðarnauta, tekr síðan á bjarginu ok færir þat burt or dyrunum, ok þikist Ormr þá aflraun mesta sýnt hafa; hann gekk þá inní hellinn, ok lagði málajárn í dyrnar, en er hann var inn kominn, sá hann hvar kettan hljóp með gapanda ginit. Ormr hafði boga ok ǫrvamæli, lagði hann þá ǫr á streing, ok skaut at kettunni þremr ǫrum, en hon hendi allar með hvoptunum, ok beit í sundr, hefir hon sik þá at Ormi, ok rekr klærnar framan í fángit, svá at Ormr kiknar við, en klærnar gengu í gegnum klæðin svá at í beini stóð; hon ætlar þá at bíta í andlit Ormi, finnr hann þá at honum mun eigi veita, heitir þá á sjálfan guð ok hinn heilaga Petrum postula, at gánga til Róms, ef hann ynni kettuna ok Brúsa, son hennar; síðan fann Ormr at mínkaðist afl kettunnar, tekr hann þá annarri hendi um kverkr henni, en annarri um hrygg, ok gengr hana á bak, ok brýtr ísundr í henni hrygginn, ok

gengr svá af henni dauðri. Ormr sá þá, hvar bálkr stórr var um þveran hellinn; hann gengr þá innar at, en er hann kemr þar, sér hann at fleinn mikill kemr utar í gegnum bálkinn, hann var bæði digr ok lángr; Ormr grípr þá í móti fleininum, ok leggr af út; Brúsi kippir þá at sér fleininum ok var hann fastr svá at hvergi gekk; þat undraðist Brúsi, ok gægdist upp yfir bálkinn, en er Ormr sér þat, þrífr hann í skeggit á Brúsa báðum hǫndum, en Brúsi bregzt við í ǫðrum stað, sviptast þeir þá fast um bálkinn. Ormr hafði vafit skegginu um hǫnd sér, ok rykkir til svá fast, at hann rífr af Brúsa allan skeggstaðinn, hǫkuna, kjaptana báða, vángafyllurnar upp alt at eyrum, gekk hér með holdit niðr at beini. Brúsi lét þá síga brýnnar, ok grettist heldr greppiliga. Ormr stǫkkr þá innar yfir bálkinn, grípast þeir þá til ok glíma lengi, mæddi Brúsa þá fast blóðrás, tekr hann þá heldr at gángast fyrir, gefr Ormr þá á, ok rekr Brúsa at bálkinum ok brýtr hann þar um á bak aptr. Snemma sagði mér þat hugr, sagði Brúsi, at ek munda af þér nokkut erfitt fá, þegar ek heyrða þín getit, enda er þat nú fram komit, muntu nú vinna skjótt um, ok hǫggva hǫfuð af mér, en þat var satt, at mjǫk pínda ek Ásbjǫrn prúða, þá er ek rakta or honum alla þarmana, ok gaf hann sik ekki við, fyrrenn hann dó. Illa gerðir þú þat, segir Ormr, at pína hann svá mjǫk jafnrǫskvan mann, skaltu ok hafa þess nokkurar menjar. Hann brá þá saxi ok reist blóðǫrn á baki honum, ok skar ǫll rifin frá hryggnum, ok dró þar út lúngun; lét Brúsi svá líf sitt með litlum dreingskap; síðan bar Ormr eld at, ok brendi upp til ǫsku bæði Brúsa ok kettuna, ok er hann hafði þetta starfat, fór hann burt or hellinum með kistur tvær fullar af gulli ok silfri, en þat sem meira var fémætt, gaf hann í vald Menglaðar, ok svá eyna; skildu þau með mikilli vináttu, kom Ormr til manna sinna í nefndan tíma, héldu síðan til meginlands. Sat Ormr í Þrándheimi vetr annan.

TRANSLATION OF EXTRACT FROM ÞÁTTR ORMS STÓRÓLFSSONAR

7.

A little after Orm and Asbiorn had parted, Asbiorn wished to go north to Sandeyar[314]; he went aboard with twenty-four men, went north past Mæri, and landed late in the day at the outermost of the Sandeyar[314]. They landed and pitched a tent, and spent the night there, and met with nothing.

Early in the morning Asbiorn arose, clothed himself, took his arms, went inland, and bade his men wait for him.

But when some time had passed from Asbiorn's having gone away, they were aware that a monstrous[315] cat had come to the door of the tent: she was coal-black in colour and very fierce, for it seemed as if fire was burning from her nostrils and mouth, and her eyes were nothing fair: they were much startled at this sight, and full of fear. Then the cat leapt within the tent upon them, and gripped one after the other, and so it is said that some she swallowed and some she tore to death with claws and teeth. Twenty men she killed in a short time, and three escaped aboard ship, and stood away from the shore.

But Asbiorn went till he came to the cave of Brusi, and hastened in forthwith. It was dim before his eyes, and very shadowy in the cave, and before he was aware of it, he was caught off his feet, and thrown down so violently that it seemed strange to him. Then was he aware that there was come the giant Brusi, and he seemed to him a great one.

Then said Brusi, "Thou didst seek with great eagerness to come hither—now shalt thou have business, in that thou shalt here leave thy life with so great torments that that shall stay others from attacking me in my lair."

Then he stripped Asbiorn of his clothes, forasmuch as so great was their difference in strength that the giant could do as he wished. Asbiorn saw a great barrier standing across the cave, and a mighty opening in the midst of it; a great iron column stood somewhat in front of the barrier. "Now it must be tried," said Brusi, "whether thou art somewhat hardier than other men." "Little will that be to test," said Asbiorn....

[Asbiorn then recites ten stanzas, Brusi tormenting him the while. The first stanza is almost identical with No. 50 in the *Grettis saga*.]

Then Asbiorn left his life with great valour and hardihood.

8.

Now it must be told concerning the three men who escaped; they rowed strongly, and stopped not until they came to land. They told the tidings of what had happened in their journey, and said that they thought that Asbiorn was dead, but that they could not tell how matters had happened concerning his death. They took ship with merchants, and so went south to Denmark: now these tidings were spread far and wide, and seemed weighty.

There had been a change of rulers in Norway: jarl Hakon was dead, and Olaf Tryggvason come to land: and he proclaimed the true faith to all. Orm Storolfson heard, out in Iceland, about the expedition of Asbiorn, and the death which it seemed to men must have come upon him. It seemed to him a great loss, and he cared no longer to be in Iceland, and took passage at Reytharfirth and went abroad. They reached Norway far to the north, and he stayed the winter at Thrandheim: Olaf at that time had reigned three years in Norway.

In the spring Orm made ready for his journey to Sandeyar, and there were nearly as many in the ship as the company of Asbiorn had been.

They landed at Little Sandey late in the evening, and pitched a tent on the land, and lay there the night....

9.

Now Orm went till he came to the cave. He saw the great rock, and thought it was impossible for any man to move it. Then he drew on the gloves that Menglath had given him, and grasped the rock and moved it away from the door; this is reckoned Orm's great feat of strength. Then he went into the cave, and thrust his weapon against the door. When he came in, he saw a giantess (she-cat) springing towards him with gaping jaws. Orm had a bow and quiver; he put the arrow on the string, and shot thrice at the giantess. But she seized all the arrows in her mouth, and bit them asunder. Then she flung herself upon Orm, and thrust her claws into his breast, so that Orm stumbled, and her claws went through his clothes and pierced him to the bone. She tried then to bite his face, and Orm found himself in straits: he promised then to God, and the holy apostle Peter, to go to Rome, if he conquered the giantess and Brusi her son. Then Orm felt the power of the giantess diminishing: he placed one hand round her throat, and the other round her back, and bent it till he broke it in two, and so left her dead.

Then Orm saw where a great barrier ran across the cave: he went further in, and when he came to it he saw a great shaft coming out through the barrier, both long and thick. Orm gripped the shaft and drew it away; Brusi pulled it towards himself, but it did not yield. Then Brusi wondered, and peeped up over the barrier. But when Orm saw that, he gripped Brusi by the beard with both hands, but Brusi pulled away, and so they tugged across the barrier. Orm twisted the beard round his hand, and tugged so violently that he pulled the flesh of Brusi away from the bone—from chin, jaws, cheeks, right up to the ears. Brusi knitted his brows and made a hideous face. Then Orm leapt in over the barrier, and they grappled and wrestled for a long time. But loss of blood wearied Brusi, and he began to fail in strength. Orm pressed on, pushed Brusi to the barrier, and broke his back across it. "Right early did my mind misgive me," said Brusi, "even so soon as I heard of thee, that I should have trouble from thee: and now has that come to pass. But now make quick work, and hew off my head. And true it is that much did I torture the gallant Asbiorn, in that I tore out all his entrails—yet did he not give in, before he died." "Ill didst thou do," said Orm, "to torture him, so fine a man as he was, and thou shalt have something in memory thereof." Then he drew his knife, and cut the "blood eagle" in the back of Brusi, shore off his ribs and drew out his lungs. So Brusi died in cowardly wise. Then Orm took fire, and burned to ashes both Brusi and the giantess. And when he had done that, he left the cave, with two chests full of gold and silver.

And all that was most of value he gave to Menglath, and the island likewise. So they parted with great friendship, and Orm came to his men at the time appointed, and then they sailed to the mainland. Orm remained a second winter at Thrandheim.

F. A Danish Dragon-slaying of the Beowulf-type

Paa den Tid, da kong Gram Guldkølve regierede i Leire, vare der ved Hoffet to Ministre, Bessus og Henrik. Og da der paa samme Tid indkom idelige klager fra Indbyggerne i Vendsyssel, at et grueligt Udyr, som Bønderne kaldte Lindorm, ødelagde baade Mennesker og Kreaturer, gav Bessus det Raad, at Kongen skulde sende Henrik did hen, efterdi ingen i det ganske Rige kunde maale sig med ham in Tapperhed og Mod. Da svarede Henrik, at han vel vilde paatage sig dette, dog tilføiede han, at han ansaae det for umuligt at slippe fra saadan Kamp med Livet. Og belavede han sig da strax til Reisen, tog rørende Afsked med sin Herre og Konge og sagde iblandt andet: "Herre! om jeg ikke kommer tilbage, da sørg for min kone og for mine Børn!" Da han derefter var kommen over til Vendsyssel, lod han sig af Bønderne vise det Sted, hvor Uhyret havde sit Leie, og fik da at vide, at Ormen endnu den samme Dag havde været ude af Hulen og borttaget en Hyrde og en Oxe, og at den efter Sædvane nu ikke vilde komme ud, førend om tre Timer, naar den skulde ned til Vandet for at drikke efter Maaltidet. Henrik iførte sig da sin fulde Rustning, og eftersom Ingen vovede at staae ham bi i dette Arbeide, lagde han sig ganske alene ved Vandet, dog saaledes, at Vinden ikke bar fra ham henimod Dyret. Da udsendte han først en vældig Piil fra sin Bue, men uagtet den rammede nøie det sted, hvortil han havde sigtet, tørnede den dog tilbage fra Ormens haarde Skæl. Herover blev Uhyret saa optændt af Vrede, at det strax gik henimod ham, agtende ham kun et ringe Maaltid; men Henrik havde iforveien hos en Smed ladet sig giøre en stor Krog med Gjenhold, hvilken han jog ind i Beestets aabne Gab, saa at det ikke kunde blive den qvit, ihvormeget det end arbeidede, og ihvorvel Jernstangen brast i Henriks Hænder. Da slog det ham med sin vældige Hale til Jorden, og skiøndt han havde fuldkommen Jernrustning paa, kradsede det dog med sine forfærdelige Kløer saa at han, næsten dødeligt saaret, faldt i Besvimelse. Men da han, efterat Ormen i nogen Tid havde haft ham liggende under sin Bug, endelig kom lidt til sin Samling igien, greb han af yderste Evne en Daggert, af hvilke han førte flere med sig i sit Bælte, og stak Dyret dermed i underlivet, hvor Sksællene vare blødest, saa at det tilsidst maate udpuste sin giftige Aande, medens han selv laae halv knust under dens Byrde. Da Bønderne i Vendsyssel som stode i nogen Afstand, under megen Frygt og lidet Haab omsider mærkede, at Striden sagtnede, og at begge Parter holdte sig rolige, nærmede de sig og fandt Hr. Henrik næsten livløs under det dræbte Udyr. Og efterat de i nogen Tid havde givet ham god Pleie, vendte han tilbage for at dø hos sin Konge, til hvem han gientagende anbefalede sin Slægt. Fra ham nedstammer Familien Lindenroth, som til Minde om denne vældige Strid fører en Lindorm i sit Vaaben.

MS 222. 4º. Stamme och Slectebog over den høiadelige Familie af Lindenroth, in *Danmarks Folkesagn*, samlede af J. M. Thiele, 1843, I, 125-7.

A DANISH DRAGON-SLAYING OF THE BEOWULF-TYPE.

Translation.

In the days when King Gram Guldkølve ruled in Leire, there were two ministers at court, Bessus and Henry. And at that time constant complaints came to the court from the inhabitants of Vendsyssel, that a dread monster, which the peasants called a Drake, was destroying both man and beast. So Bessus gave counsel, that the king should send Henry against the dragon, seeing that no one in the whole kingdom was his equal in valour and courage. Henry answered that assuredly he would undertake it; but he added that he thought it impossible to escape from such a struggle with his life. And he made himself ready forthwith for the expedition, took a touching farewell of his lord and king, and said among other things: "My lord, if I come not back, care thou for my wife and my children."

Afterwards, when he crossed over to Vendsyssel, he caused the peasants to show him the place where the monster had its lair, and learnt how that very day the drake had been out of its den, and had carried off a herdsman and an ox; how, according to its wont, it would now not come out for three hours, when it would want to go down to the water to drink after its meal. Henry clothed himself in full armour, and inasmuch as no one dared to stand by him in that task, he lay down all alone by the water, but in such wise that the wind did not blow from him toward the monster. First of all he sent a mighty arrow from his bow: but, although it exactly hit the spot at which he had aimed, it darted back from the dragon's hard scales. At this the monster was so maddened, that it attacked him forthwith, reckoning him but a little meal. But Henry had had a mighty barbed crook prepared by a smith beforehand, which he thrust into the beast's open mouth, so that it could not get rid of it, however much it strove, although the iron rod broke in Henry's hands.

Then it smote him to the ground with its mighty tail, and although he was in complete armour, clutched at him with its dread claws, so that he fell in a swoon, wounded almost to death. But when he came somewhat to his senses again, after the drake for some time had had him lying under its belly, he rallied his last strength and grasped a dagger, of which he carried several with him in his belt, and smote it therewith in the belly, where the scales were weakest. So the monster at last breathed out its poisoned breath, whilst he himself lay half crushed under its weight. When the Vendsyssel peasants, who stood some distance away, in great fear and little hope, at last noticed that the battle had slackened, and that both combatants were still, they drew near and found Henry almost lifeless under the slain monster. And after they for some time had tended him well, he returned to die by his king, to whom he again commended his offspring. From him descends the family Lindenroth, which in memory of this mighty contest carries a drake on its coat of arms.

This story resembles the dragon fight in *Beowulf*, in that the hero faces the dragon as protector of the land, with forebodings, and after taking farewell; he attacks the dragon in its lair, single-handed; his first attack is frustrated by the dragon's scales; in spite of apparatus specially prepared, he is wounded and stunned by the dragon, but nevertheless smites the dragon in the soft parts and slays him; the watchers draw near when the fight is over. Yet these things merely prove that the two stories are of the same type; there is no evidence that this story is descended from *Beowulf*.

G. The Old English Genealogies.

I. *THE MERCIAN GENEALOGY.*

Of the Old English Genealogies, the only one which, in its stages *below* Woden, immediately concerns the student of *Beowulf* is the Mercian. This contains three names which also occur in *Beowulf*, though two of them in a corrupt form—Offa, Wermund (Garmund, *Beowulf*), and Eomær (Geomor, *Beowulf*).

This Mercian pedigree is found in its best form in *MS Cotton Vesp. B. VI*, fol. 109 *b*,[316] and in the sister MS at Corpus Christi College, Cambridge (*C.C.C. 183*)[317]. Both these MSS are of the 9th century. They contain lists of popes and bishops, and pedigrees of kings. By noting where these lists stop, we get a limit for the final compilation of the document. It must have been drawn up in its present form between 811 and 814[318]. But it was obviously compiled from lists already existing, and some of them were even at that date old. For the genealogy of the Mercian kings, from Woden, is not traced directly down to this period 811-814, but in the first place only as far as Æthelred (reigning 675-704), son of Penda: that is to say, it stops considerably more than a century before the date of the document in which it appears. Additional pedigrees are then appended which show the subsequent stages down to and including Cenwulf, king of Mercia (reigning 796-821). It is difficult to account for such an arrangement except on the hypothesis that the genealogy was committed to writing in the reign of Æthelred, the monarch with whose name it terminates in its first form, and was then brought up to date by the addition of the supplementary names ending with Cenwulf. This is confirmed when we find that precisely the same arrangement holds good for the accompanying Northumbrian pedigree, which terminates with Ecgfrith (670-685), the contemporary of Æthelred of Mercia, and is then brought up to date by additional names.

Genealogies which draw from the same source as the *Vespasian* genealogies, and show the same peculiarities, are found in the *Historia Brittonum* (§§ 57-61). They show, even more emphatically than do the *Vespasian* lists, traces of having been originally drawn up in the time of Æthelred of Mercia (675-704) or possibly of his father Penda, and of having then been brought up to date in subsequent revisions[319].

One such revision must have been made about 796[320]: it is a modification of this revision which is found in the *Historia Brittonum*. Another was that which, as we have seen, must have been made between 811-814, and in this form is found in *MS Cotton Vespasian B. VI*, *MS C.C.C.C. 183*, both of the 9th century, and in the (much later) *MS Cotton Tiberius B. V*.

The genealogy up to Penda is also found in the *A.-S. Chronicle* under the year 626 (accession of Penda).

This Mercian list, together with the Northumbrian and other pedigrees which accompany it, can claim to be the earliest extant English historical document, having been written down in the 7th century, and recording historic names which (allowing thirty years for a generation) cannot be later than the 4th century A.D. In most similar pedigrees the earliest names are meaningless to us. But the Mercian pedigree differs from the rest, in that we are able from *Beowulf*, *Widsith*, Saxo Grammaticus, Sweyn Aageson and the *Vitae Offarum*, to attach stories to the names of Wermund and Offa. How much of these stories is history, and how much fiction, it is difficult to say—but, with them, extant English history and English poetry and English fiction alike have their beginning.

MS Cotton Vesp. B. VI.		MS C.C.C.C. 183.	
Aeðilred	Peding	Æðelred	Pending
Penda	Pypbing	Penda	Pybbing
Pypba	Crioding	Pybba	Creoding
Crioda	Cynewalding	Creoda	Cynewalding
Cynewald	Cnebbing	Cynewald	Cnebbing
Cnebba	Icling	Cnebba	Icling
Icil	Eamering	Icel	Eomæring
Eamer	Angengeoting	Eomær	Angengeoting
Angengeot	Offing	Angengiot	Offing
Offa	Uærmunding	Offa	Wærmunding
Uermund	Uihtlaeging	Wærmund	Wihtlæging
Uihtlaeg	Wioðulgeoting	Wihtlæg	Wioþolgeoting
Weoðulgeot	Wodning	Weoþolgiot	Wodning
Woden	Frealafing	Woden	Frealafing

Historia Brittonum[321].		Anglo-Saxon Chronicle.	
MS Harl 3859.		MSS Cotton Tib. A. VI. and B.I.[322]	
Penda		Penda	Pybbing
Pubba		Pybba	Creoding
		Creoda	Cynewalding
		Cynewald	Cnebbing
		Cnebba	Iceling
		Icel	Eomæring
Eamer		Eomær	Angelþeowing
Ongen		Angelþeow	Offing
Offa		Offa	Wærmunding
Guerdmund		Wærmund	Wihtlæging
Guithleg		Wihtlæg	Wodening
Gueagon			
Guedolgeat			
[U]Uoden			

II. *THE STAGES ABOVE WODEN.*

(1) *WODEN TO GEAT.*

The stages above Woden are found in two forms: a short list which traces the line from Woden up to Geat: and a longer list which carries the line from Geat to Sceaf and through Noah to Adam.

The line from Woden to Geat is found in the *Historia Brittonum*, not with the other genealogies, but in § 31, where the pedigree of the Kentish royal family is given, when the arrival of Hengest in Britain is recounted. Notwithstanding the dispute regarding the origin and date of the *Historia Brittonum*, there is a pretty general agreement that this *Woden to Geat* pedigree is one of the more primitive elements, and is not likely to be much later than the end of the 7th century[323]. The original nucleus of the *Historia Brittonum* was revised by Nennius in the 9th century, or possibly at the end of the 8th[324]. The earliest MS of the *Historia*, that of Chartres, belongs to the 9th or 10th century—this is fragmentary and already interpolated; the received text is based upon *MS Harleian* 3859, dating from the end of the 11th century[325], or possibly somewhat later.

I give the pedigree in four forms:

A. The critical text of the *Historia Brittonum* as edited by Th. Mommsen (*Monumenta Germaniae Historica, Auct. Antiq., Chronica Minora*, III, Berolini, 1898, p. 171).

B. *MS Harl.* 3859, upon which Mommsen's text is based, fol. 180.

C. The *Chartres MS.*

D. Mommsen's critical text of the later revision, *Nennius interpretatus*, which he gives parallel to the *Historia Brittonum*.

A	B	C	D
Hors et Hengist	Hors & Hengist	Cors et Haecgens	Hors et Hengist
filii Guictgils	filii Guictgils	filii Guictils	filii Guictgils
Guigta	Guitta	Guicta	Guigta
Guectha	Guectha	Gueta	Guectha
VVoden	VVoden	VVoden	Voden
Frealaf	Frealaf	Frelab	Frealaf
Fredulf	Fredulf	Freudulf	Fredolf
Finn	Finn	Fran	Finn

			Frenn
Fodepald	Fodepald	Folcpald	Folcvald
Geta	Geta	G[e]uta	Gaeta
qui fuit, ut aiunt, filius dei	qui fuit, ut aiunt, filius dei	qui sunt [sic], ut aiunt, filius dei	Vanli
			Saxi
			Negua

MS Cotton Vespasian B. VI (9th century) contains a number of Anglo-Saxon genealogies and other lists revised up to the period 811-14[326]. The genealogy of the kings of Lindsey in this list has the stages from Woden to Geat. This genealogy is also found in the sister list in the 9th century MS at Corpus Christi College, Cambridge (*MS C.C.C.C.* 183).

A similar list is to be found in the *Anglo-Saxon Chronicle* (entered under the year 547). But there it is appended to the genealogy of the Northumbrian kings. This genealogy has been erased in the oldest MS (Parker, end of the 9th century) to make room for later additions, but is found in *MSS Cotton Tiberius A. VI* and *B. I.*

Cotton (Vespasian) MS.	Corpus MS.	A.-S. Chronicle
UUoden	Woden Frealafing	Woden
Frealafing		Freoþolafing
Frealaf	Frealaf	Freoþelaf
Frioðulfing	Frioþowulsing (*sic*)	Freoþulfing
Frioðulf	Freoþowulf	
Finning	Godwulfing	Friþulf Finning
Finn		
Goduulfing		Finn Godulfing
Godulf Geoting	Godwulf Geating	Godulf Geating

The *Fodepald* or *Folcpald* who, in the *Historia Brittonum*, appears as the father of Finn, is clearly the *Folcwalda* who appears as Finn's father in *Beowulf* and *Widsith*. The Old English w (ƿ) has been mistaken for þ, just as in *Pinefred* for *Winefred* in the *Life of Offa II*. In the *Vespasian MS* and in other genealogies Godwulf is Finn's father. It has been very generally held that Finn and his father Godwulf are mythical heroes, quite distinct from the presumably historic Finn, son of Folcwalda, mentioned in *Beowulf* and *Widsith*: and that by confusion *Folcwald* came to be written instead of *Godwulf* in the genealogy, as given in the *Historia Brittonum*. I doubt whether there is sufficient justification for this distinction between a presumed historic Finn

Folcwalding and a mythical Finn Godwulfing. Is it not possible that Godwulf was a traditional, probably historic, king of the Frisians, father of Finn, and that *Folcwalda*[327] was a *title* which, since it alliterated conveniently, in the end supplanted the proper name in epic poetry?

III. *THE STAGES ABOVE WODEN.*

(2) *WODEN TO SCEAF.*

The stages above Geat are found in the genealogy of the West-Saxon kings only[328]. This is recorded in the *Chronicle* under the year 855 (notice concerning Æthelwulf) and it was probably drawn up at the court of that king. Though it doubtless contains ancient names, it is apparently not so ancient as the *Woden-Geat* list. It became very well known, and is also found in Asser and the *Textus Roffensis*. It was copied by later historians such as William of Malmesbury, and by the Icelandic genealogists[329].

The principal versions of this pedigree are given in tabular form below (pp. 202-3); omitting the merely second-hand reproductions, such as those of Florence of Worcester.

H. EXTRACT FROM THE CHRONICLE ROLL.

This roll was drawn up in the reign of Henry VI, and its compiler must have had access to a document now lost.

There are many copies of the roll extant—the "Moseley" Roll at University College, London (formerly in the Phillipps collection); at Corpus Christi College, Cambridge (No. 98 A); at Trinity College, Cambridge; and in the Bibliothèque Nationale, Paris[330]; and one which recently came into the market in London.

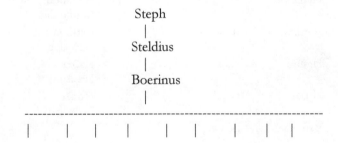

Cinrinicius Gothus Iutus Wandalus Gethius Fresus Suethedus Dacus
Geate

WEST-SAXON GENEALOGY—STAGES ABOVE WODEN

CHRONICLE PARKER MS	ASSER	TEXTUS ROFFENSIS I	ETHELWERD	CHRONICLE MSS COTT. TIB. A. VI [& B. I]
Woden Fribowalding	Uuoden	Woden	Uuothen	Woden Frealafing
Friþuwald Freawining	Frithowald	Friþewold	Frithouuald	
Frealaf Friþuwulfing	Frealaf	Frealaf	Frealaf	
Friþuwulf Finning	Frithuwulf	Friþewulf	Frithouulf	Frealaf Fin[n]ing
Fin Godwulfing	Fingodwulf	Finn	Fin	Finn Godwulfing [Godulfing]
Godwulf Geating		Godwulf	Goduulfe	Godulf Geat[t]ing
Geat Tætwaing	Geata* ...	Geata* ...	Geat	Geata [Geatt] Tætwaing
Tætwa Beawing	Caetuua	Teþwa	Tetuua	Tætwa Beawing
Beaw Sceldwaing	Beauu	Beaw	Beo	Beaw Sceldweaing [Scealdwaing]
Sceldwea Heremoding	Sceldwea	Scaldwa	Scyld	Scyldwa [Scealdwa] Heremoding
Heremod Itermoning	Heremod	Heremod	Heremod	Heremod Itermoning
Itermon Hraþraing	Itermod	Iterman		Itermon Haðraing
	Hathra	Haþra		Haðra Hwalaing
	Huala	Hwala		Hwala Bedwiging
	Beduuig	Bedwig		

se wæs geboren in þære earce Noe etc.	Seth Noe, etc.	Scyf, se wæs in ðam arken geboran [but son of Sem, not Noe]	Scef. Ipse Scef cum uno dromone advectus est in insula oceani quae dicitur	Bedwig Sceafing, [i]d est filius Nóe, se wæs geboren on þære earce Nóes
	* quem Getam iamdudum pagani pro deo venerabantur	* ðene ða hæþena wuþedon for god	Scani, armis circundatus, eratque valde recens puer, et ab incolis illius terrae ignotus; attamen ab eis suscipitur et ut familiarem diligenti animo eum custodierunt et post in regem eligunt; de cuius prosapia ordinem trahit Athulf [i.e. Æthelwulf] rex.	

Chronicle MS Cott. Tib. B. IV	Textus Roffensis II	MS Cott. Tib. B. V	Langfeðgatal Langebek, 1, 3	Flateyarbók Christiania, 1860, 1, 27
Woden Frealafing	Woden Frealafing	Woden Frealafing	Voden þan kollvm ver Oden	Voden, *er ver kollum* Odinn

Frealaf	Frealaf	Frealaf	Frealaf	Frilafr, *e.v.k.*
Finning	Finning	Finning		Bors
Fin	Finn	Finn	Finn	Burri, *e.v.k.*
Godulfing	Godulfing	Godulfing		Finn
Godulf	Godulf	Godulf	Godvlfi	Godolfr
Gating	Eating	Eating		
Geat	Eata	Eat Beawing	Eat	
Tætwaing	Teþwafing			
Tætwa	Teþwa			
Beawing	Beawing			
Beaw	Beaw	Beaw	Beaf	Beaf, *e.v.k.*
Scealdwaing	Scealdwaging	Scealdwaging		Biar
Scealdhwa	Scealwa	Scealwa	Scealdna	Skialldin,
Heremoding	Heremoding	Heremoding		*e.v.k.* Skiolld
Heremod	Heremod	Heremod	Heremotr	Heremoth,
Itermoning	Hermanning	Itermanning		*e.v.k.*
				Hermod
Itermon	Herman	Iterman	Itermann	Trinaan
Haðrahing	Haþraing	Haðraing		
Haþra	Haðra	Haðra	Athra	Atra
	Hwalaing	Bedwiging		
Hwala	Hwala			
Beowung	Bedwining			
Beowi	Beadwig	Bedwig	Bedvig	Beduigg
Sceafing, id	Sceafing	Sceafing		
est filius	Se Scef wæs	se Scef wæs	Seskef vel	Seseph
Noe, se wæs	Noes sunu	Nóes sunu	Sescef	
geboren on	and he wæs	and he wæs		
þære arce	innan ðære	innan þære		
Nones ...	earce	earce		
	geboren	geboren		

William of Malmesbury. Wodenius fuit filius Fridewaldi, Fridewaldus Frelafii, Frelafius Finni, Finnus Godulfi, Godulfus Getii, Getius Tetii, Tetius Beowii, Beowius Sceldii, Sceldius Sceaf. Iste, ut ferunt, in quandam insulam Germaniae Scandzam ... appulsus, navi sine remige, puerulus, posito ad caput frumenti manipulo, dormiens, ideoque Sceaf nuncupatus, ab hominibus regionis illius pro miraculo exceptus et sedulo nutritus, adulta aetate regnavit in oppido quod tunc Slaswic, nunc vero Haithebi appellatur ... Sceaf fuit filius Heremodii, Heremodius Stermonii, Stermonius Hadrae, Hadra Gwalae, Gwala Bedwigii, Bedwegius Strephii; hic, ut dicitur, fuit filius Noae in arca natus.

The following marginal note occurs:

Iste Steldius *primus* inhabitator Germanie fuit. Que Germania sic dicta erat, quia instar ramor*um* germina*n*cium ab arbore, sic nome*n* regnaq*ue* germania nuncupa*n*tur. In nouem filiis diuisa a radice Boerini geminaueru*n*t. Ab istis nouem filiis Boerini descenderu*n*t nouem gentes septentrionalem p*ar*tem inhabitantes, qui quondam regnu*m* Brita*n*nie inuaseru*n*t et optinueru*n*t, videlicet Saxones, Angli, Iuthi, Daci, Norwagences, Gothi, Wandali, Geathi et Fresi[331].

I. EXTRACT FROM THE LITTLE CHRONICLE OF THE KINGS OF LEIRE

From the *Annales Lundenses*. These Annals are comparatively late, going up to the year 1307; but the short *Chronicle of the Kings of Leire*, which is incorporated in them, is supposed to date from the latter half of the 12th century. The text is given in Langebek, *Scriptores Rerum Danicarum*, I, 224-6 (under the name of *Annales Esromenses*) from *Cod. Arn. Mag.* 841. There is a critical edition by Gertz, *Scriptores Minores historiæ Danicæ*, Copenhagen, 1917, based upon *Cod. Arn. Mag.* 843. The text given below is mainly that of Langebek, with corrections from Gertz's fine edition. See below, p. 216.

Erat ergo Dan rex in Dacia[332] per triennium. Anno tandem tertio cognouit uxorem suam Daniam, genuitque ex ea filium nomine Ro. Qui post patris obitum hereditarie possidebat regnum. Patrem uero suum Dan colle apud Lethram tumulauit Sialandiæ, ubi sedem regni pro eo pater constituit, quam ipse post eum diuitiis multiplicibus ditauit. Tempore illo ciuitas magna erat in medio Sialandiæ, ubi adhuc mons desertus est, nomine Hekebiarch, ubi sita erat ciuitas quæ Høkekoping nuncupata est; ad quam ut mox Ro rex uidit, quod mercatores a nauibus in uia currus conducentes multum expenderent, a loco illo ciuitatem amoueri jussit ad portum, ubi tenditur Isæfiorth, et circa fontem pulcherrimum domos disponere. Ædificauit ibi Ro ciuitatem honestam, cui nomen partitiuum imposuit post se et Fontem, partem capiens fontis partemque sui, Roskildam Danice uocans, quæ hoc nomine uoca[bi]tur[333] in æternum. Uixit autem rex Ro ita pacifice, ut nullus ei aciem opponeret, nec ipse usquam expeditionem direxit[334]. Erat autem uxor eius fecunda sobole, ex qua genuit duos filios, nomen primi Helhgi et secundi Haldan[335]. Cumque cepissent pueri robore confortari et crescere, obiit pater eorum Ro, et sepultus est tumulo quodam Læthræ, post cuius obitum partiti sunt regnum filii, quod in duas partes diuidentes, alter terras, alter mare possidebat. Rexit itaque terras Haldanus, et genuit filium nomine Siwardum, cognomine Album, qui patrem suum Haldanum Læthræ tumulauit mortuum. Helgi autem rex erat marinus, et multos ad se traxit malificos, nauali bello bene adeptus diuersas partes, quasdam pace, quasdam cum piratica classe[336] petisse perhibetur....

The Chronicle then tells how Rolf was born, the son of Helgi and Yrse or Ursula: also of the death and burial of Helgi.

Filius autem eius et Ursulæ puer crescebat Rolf et fortitudine uigebat. Mater uero eius Ursula, uelo uiduitatis deposito, data est regi Suethiæ Athislo, qui ex ea filiam sibi genuit, Rolf uero ex matre eius sororem nomine Skuld. Interea dum hæc de rege marino Helgi agerentur, frater eius, rex Daciæ, mortuus est Haldanus. Post quem[337] rex Sweciæ Athisl a Danis suscepit tributum.

Interea ... confortabatur filius Helgi, Rolff, cognomine Krake. Quem post mortem Snyo[338] Dani [in][339] regem assumpserunt. Qui Sialandiæ apud Lethram, sicut antecessores sui, sæpissime moratus est. Sororem suam nomine Sculd secum habuit, Athisli regis filiam, et suæ matris Ursulæ, de qua superius dictum est; quam fraterno amore dilexit. Cui provinciam Hornshæræth Sialandiæ ad pascendas puellas suas in expensam dedit, in qua uillam ædificauit, nomine Sculdelef, unde nomen suscepit. Hoc tempore erat quidam Comes Scaniæ, nomine Hiarwarth, Teotonicus genere, Rolf tributarius, qui ad eum procos misit, ut sororem suam Sculd Hiarwardo daret uxorem. Quo nolente, propria ipsius uoluntate puellæ clanculo eam raptam sociauit sibi. Unde conspirauerunt inter se deliberantes Hiarwart et Sculd, quomodo Rolf interficeretur, et Hiarwardus superstes regni heres efficeretur. Non post multum vero temporis animosus ad uxoris exhortationem Hiarwart Sialandiam classe petiit. Genero suo Rolff tributum attulisse simulauit. Die quadam dilucescente ad Læthram misit, ut uideret tributum, Rolff nunciauit. Qui cum uidisset non tributum sed exercitum armatum, uallatus est Rolff militibus, et a Hyarwardo interfectus est. Hyarwardum autem Syalandenses et Scanienses, qui cum eo erant, in regem assumpserunt. Qui breui tempore, a mane usque ad primam, regali nomine potitus est. Tunc uenit Haky, frater Haghbardi, filius Hamundi; Hyarwardum interfecit et Danorum rex effectus est. Quo regnante, uenit quidam nomine Fritleff a partibus Septentrionalibus et filiam sibi desponsauit Rolff Crake, ex qua filium nomine Frothe genuit, cognomine Largus.

K. THE STORY OF OFFA IN SAXO GRAMMATICUS

Book IV, ed. Ascensius, fol. xxxii b; ed. Holder, pp. 106-7.

Cui filius Wermundus succedit. Hic prolixis tranquillitatis otiis felicissima temporum quiete decursis, diutinam domesticæ pacis constantiam inconcussa rerum securitate tractabat. Idem prolis expers iuuentam exegit; senior uero filium Uffonem sero fortunæ munere suscitauit, cum nullam ei sobolem elapsa tot annorum curricula peperissent. Hic Uffo coæuos quosque corporis habitu supergressus, adeo hebetis ineptique animi principio iuuentæ existimatus est, ut priuatis ac publicis rebus inutilis uideretur. Siquidem ab ineunte ætate nunquam Iusus aut ioci consuetudinem præbuit; adeoque humanæ delectationis uacuus fuit, ut labiorum continentiam iugi silentio premeret, et seueritatem oris a ridendi prorsus officio temperaret. Uerum ut incunabula stoliditatis opinione referta habuit, ita post modum conditionis contemptum claritate mutauit; et quantum inertiæ spectaculum fuit, tantum prudentiæ et fortitudinis exemplum euasit.

Book IV, ed. Ascensius, fol. xxxiv b; ed. Holder, pp. 113-7.

Cumque Wermundus ætatis uitio oculis orbaretur, Saxoniæ rex, Daniam duce uacuam ratus, ei per legatos mandat, regnum, quod præter ætatis debitum teneat, sibi procurandum committat, ne nimis longa imperii auiditate patriam legibus armisque destituat. Qualiter enim regem censeri posse, cui senectus animum, cæcitas oculum pari caliginis horrore fuscauerit? Quod si abnuat, filiumque habeat, qui cum suo ex prouocatione confligere audeat, uictorem regno potiri permittat. Si neutrum probet, armis secum, non monitis agendum cognoscat, ut tandem inuitus præbeat, quod ultroneus exhibere contemnat. Ad hæc Wermundus, altioribus suspiriis fractus, impudentius se ætatis exprobratione lacerari respondit, quem non ideo huc infelicitatis senectus prouexerit, quod pugnæ parcus timidius iuuentam exegerit. Nec aptius sibi cæcitatis uitium obiectari, quod plerunque talem ætatis habitum talis iactura consequi soleat, potiusque condolendum calamitati quam insultandum uideatur. Iustius autem Saxoniæ regi impatientiæ notam afferri posse, quem potius senis fatum operiri, quam imperium poscere decuisset, quod aliquanto præstet defuncto succedere, quam uiuum spoliare. Se tamen, ne tanquam delirus priscæ libertatis titulos externo uideatur mancipare

- 177 -

dominio, propria manu prouocationi pariturum. Ad hæc legati, scire se inquiunt, regem suum conserendæ cum cæco manus ludibrium perhorrere, quod tam ridiculum decernendi genus rubori quam honestati propinquius habeatur. Aptius uero per utriusque pignus et sanguinem amborum negotio consuli. Ad hæc obstupefactis animo Danis, subitaque responsi ignorantia perculsis, Uffo, qui forte cum ceteris aderat, responsionis a patre licentiam flagitabat, subitoque uelut ex muto uocalis euasit. Cumque Wermundus, quisnam talem a se loquendi copiam postularet, inquireret, ministrique eum ab Uffone rogari dixissent, satis esse perhibuit, ut infelicitatis suæ uulneribus alienorum fastus illuderet, ne etiam a domesticis simili insultationis petulantia uexaretur. Sed satellitibus Uffonem hunc esse pertinaci affirmatione testantibus, "Liberum ei sit," inquit, "quisquis est, cogitata profari." Tum Uffo, frustra ab eorum rege regnum appeti, inquit, quod tam proprii rectoris officio quam fortissimorum procerum armis industriaque niteretur: præterea, nec regi filium nec regno successorem deesse. Sciantque, se non solum regis eorum filium, sed etiam quemcunque ex gentis suæ fortissimis secum adsciuerit, simul pugna aggredi constituisse. Quo audito legati risere, uanam dicti animositatem existimantes. Nec mora, condicitur pugnæ locus, eidemque stata temporis meta præfigitur. Tantum autem stuporis Uffo loquendi ac prouocandi nouitate præsentibus iniecit, ut, utrum uoci eius an fiduciæ plus admirationis tributum sit, incertum extiterit.

Abeuntibus autem legatis, Wermundus, responsionis auctore laudato, quod uirtutis fiduciam non in unius, sed duorum prouocatione statuerit, potius se ei, quicunque sit, quam superbo hosti regno cessurum perhibuit. Uniuersis autem filium eius esse testantibus, qui legatorum fastum fiduciæ sublimitate contempserit, propius eum accedere iubet: quod oculis nequeat, manibus experturus. Corpore deinde eius curiosius contrectato, cum ex artuum granditate lineamentisque filium esse cognosset, fidem assertoribus habere cœpit, percontarique eum, cur suauissimum uocis habitum summo dissimulationis studio tegendum curauerit, tantoque ætatis spatio sine uoce et cunctis loquendi commerciis degere sustinuerit, ut se linguæ prorsus officio defectum natiuæque taciturnitatis uitio obsitum credi permitteret? Qui respondit, se paterna hactenus defensione contentum, non prius uocis officio opus habuisse, quam domesticam prudentiam externa loquacitate pressam animaduerteret. Rogatus item ab eo, cur duos quam unum prouocare maluit, hunc iccirco dimicationis modum a se exoptatum respondit, ut Athisli regis oppressio, quæ, quod a duobus gesta fuerat, Danis opprobrio extabat, unius facinore pensaretur, nouumque uirtutis specimen prisca ruboris monumenta conuelleret. Ita antiquæ crimen infamiæ recentis famæ litura respergendum dicebat. Quem Wermundus iustam omnium æstimationem fecisse testatus, armorum usum, quod eis parum assueuisset, prædiscere iubet. Quibus Uffo oblatis, magnitudine pectoris angustos loricarum nexus explicuit; nec erat ullam reperire, quæ eum iusto capacitatis spatio contineret. Maiore siquidem corpore erat, quam ut alienis armis uti posset. Ad ultimum, cum paternam quoque loricam uiolenta corporis astrictione dissolueret, Wermundus eam a læuo latere dissecari, fibulaque sarciri præcepit, partem, quæ clypei præsidio muniatur, ferro patere parui existimans. Sed et gladium, quo tuto uti possit, summa ab eo cura conscisci iussit. Oblatis compluribus, Uffo manu capulum stringens, frustatim singulos agitando comminuit; nec erat quisquam ex eis tanti rigoris gladius, quem non ad primæ concussionis motum crebra partium fractione dissolueret. Erat autem regi inusitati acuminis gladius, Skrep dictus, qui quodlibet obstaculi genus uno ferientis ictu medium penetrando diffinderet, nec adeo quicquam prædurum foret, ut adactam eius aciem remorari potuisset. Quem ne posteris fruendum relinqueret, per summam alienæ commoditatis inuidiam in profunda defoderat, utilitatem ferri, quod filii incrementis diffideret, ceteris negaturus. Interrogatus autem, an dignum Uffonis robore ferrum haberet, habere se dixit, quod, si pridem a se terræ traditum recognito locorum habitu reperire potuisset, aptum corporis eius uiribus exhiberet. In campum deinde perduci se iubens, cum, interrogatis per omnia comitibus, defossionis locum acceptis signorum indiciis comperisset, extractum cauo gladium filio porrigit. Quem Uffo nimia uetustate fragilem exesumque conspiciens, feriendi diffidentia percontatur, an hunc quoque priorum exemplo probare debeat, prius habitum eius, quam rem ferro geri oporteat, explorandum testatus. Refert Wermundus, si præsens ferrum ab ipso uentilando collideretur, non superesse, quod uirium eius habitui responderet. Abstinendum itaque facto, cuius in dubio exitus maneat.

Igitur ex pacto pugnæ locus expetitur. Hunc fluuius Eidorus ita aquarum ambitu uallat, ut earum interstitio repugnante, nauigii duntaxat aditus pateat. Quem Uffone sine comite petente, Saxoniæ regis filium insignis uiribus athleta consequitur, crebris utrinque turbis alternos riparum anfractus spectandi auiditate complentibus. Cunctis igitur huic spectaculo oculos inferentibus, Wermundus in extrema pontis parte se collocat, si filium uinci contigisset, flumine periturus. Maluit enim sanguinis sui ruinam comitari, quam patriæ interitum plenis doloris sensibus intueri. Uerum Uffo, geminis iuuenum congressibus lacessitus, gladii diffidentia amborum ictus umbone uitabat, patientius experiri constituens, quem e duobus attentius cauere debuisset, ut hunc saltem uno ferri impulsu contingeret. Quem Wermundus imbecillitatis uitio tantam recipiendorum ictuum patientiam præstare existimans, paulatim in occiduam pontis oram mortis cupiditate se protrahit, si de filio actum foret, fatum precipitio petiturus. Tanta sanguinis caritate flagrantem senem fortuna protexit. Uffo siquidem filium regis ad secum auidius decernendum hortatus, claritatem generis ab ipso conspicuo fortitudinis opere æquari iubet, ne rege ortum plebeius comes uirtute præstare uideatur. Athletam deinde, explorandæ eius fortitudinis gratia, ne domini sui terga timidius subsequeretur, admonitum fiduciam a regis filio in se repositam egregiis dimicationis operibus pensare præcepit, cuius delectu unicus pugnæ comes adscitus fuerit. Obtemperantem illum propiusque congredi rubore compulsum, primo ferri ictu medium dissecat. Quo sono recreatus Wermundus, filii ferrum audire se dixit, rogatque, cui potissimum parti ictum inflixerit. Referentibus deinde ministris, eum non unam corporis partem, sed totam hominis transegisse compagem, abstractum præcipitio corpus ponti restituit, eodem studio lucem expetens, quo fatum optauerat. Tum Uffo, reliquum hostem prioris exemplo consumere cupiens, regis filium ad ultionem interfecti pro se satellitis manibus parentationis loco erogandam impensioribus uerbis sollicitat. Quem propius accedere sua adhortatione coactum, infligendi ictus loco curiosius denotato, gladioque, quod tenuem eius laminam suis imparem uiribus formidaret, in aciem alteram uerso, penetrabili corporis sectione transuerberat. Quo audito Wermundus Screp gladii sonum secundo suis auribus incessisse perhibuit. Affirmantibus deinde arbitris, utrunque hostem ab eius filio consumptum, nimietate gaudii uultum fletu soluit. Ita genas, quas dolor madidare non poterat, lætitia rigauit. Saxonibus igitur pudore mœstis, pugilumque funus summa cum ruboris acerbitate ducentibus, Uffonem Dani iocundis excepere tripudiis. Quieuit tum Athislanæ cædis infamia, Saxonumque obprobriis expirauit.

Ita Saxoniæ regnum ad Danos translatum, post patrem Uffo regendum suscepit, utriusque imperii procurator effectus, qui ne unum quidem rite moderaturus credebatur. Hic a compluribus Olauus est dictus, atque ob animi moderationem Mansueti cognomine donatus. Cuius sequentes actus uetustatis uitio solennem fefellere notitiam. Sed credi potest, gloriosos eorum processus extitisse, quorum tam plena laudis principia fuerint.

L. FROM SKIOLD TO OFFA IN SWEYN AAGESON

In Langebek, *Scriptores*, i, 44-7; Gertz, I, 97.

CAP. I.

De primo Rege Danorum.

Skiold Danis primum didici præfuisse. Et ut eius alludamus uocabulo, idcirco tali functus est nomine, quia uniuersos regni terminos regiæ defensionis patrocinio affatim egregie tuebatur. A quo primum, modis Islandensibus,

"Skioldunger" sunt reges nuncupati. Qui regni post se reliquit hæredes, Frothi uidelicet et Haldanum. Successu temporum fratribus super regni ambitione inter se decertantibus, Haldan, fratre suo interempto, regni monarchiam obtinuit. Hic filium, scilicet Helghi, regni procreauit hæredem, qui ob eximiam uirtutum strenuitatem, pyraticam semper exercuit. Qui cum uniuersorum circumiacentium regnorum fines maritimos classe pyratica depopulatus, suo subiugasset imperio, "Rex maris" est cognominatus. Huic in regno successit filius Rolf Kraki, patria virtute pollens, occisus in Lethra, quæ tunc famosissima Regis extitit curia, nunc autem Roskildensi uicina ciuitati, inter abiectissima ferme uix colitur oppida. Post quem regnauit filius eius Rökil cognomento dictus "Slaghenback." Cui successit in regno hæres, agilitatis strenuitate cognominatus, quem nostro uulgari "Frothi hin Frökni" nominabant. Huius filius et hæres regni extitit Wermundus, qui adeo prudentiæ pollebat uirtute, ut inde nomen consequeretur. Unde et "Prudens" dictus est. Hic filium genuit Uffi nomine, qui usque ad tricesimum ætatis suæ annum fandi possibilitatem cohibuit, propter enormitatem opprobrii, quod tunc temporis Danis ingruerat, eo quod in ultionem patris duo Dani in Sueciam profecti, patricidam suum una interemerunt. Nam et tunc temporis ignominiosum extitit improperium, si solum duo iugularent; præsertim cum soli strenuitati tunc superstitiosa gentilitas operam satagebat impendere. Præfatus itaque Wermundus usque ad senium regni sui gubernabat imperium; adeo tandem ætate consumptus, ut oculi eius præ senio caligarent. Cuius debilitatis fama cum apud transalpinas[340] partes percrebuisset, elationis turgiditate Teotonica intumuit superbia, utpote suis nunquam contenta terminis. Hinc furoris sui rabiem in Danos exacuit Imperator, se iam Danorum regno conquisito sceptrum nancisci augustius conspicatus. Delegantur itaque spiculatores, qui turgidi principis jussa reportent præfato Danorum regi, scilicet Wermundo, duarum rerum præfigentes electionem, quarum pars tamen neutra extitit eligenda. Aut enim regnum jussit Romano resignare imperio, et tributum soluere, aut athletam inuestigare, qui cum Imperatoris campione monomachiam committere auderet. Quo audito, regis extitit mens consternata; totiusque regni procerum legione corrogata, quid facto opus sit, diligenti inquisitione percontabatur. Perplexam se namque regis autumabat autoritas, utpote cui et ius incumbebat decertandi, et qui regno patrocinari tenebatur. Uultum cœcitas obnubilauerat, et regni heres elinguis factus, desidia torpuerat, ita ut in eo, communi assertione, nulla prorsus species salutis existeret. Nam ab infantia præfatus Uffo uentris indulgebat ingluuiei, et Epicuræorum more, coquinæ et cellario alternum officiose impendebat obsequium. Corrogato itaque cœtu procerum, totiusque regni placito[341] celebrato, Alamannorum regis ambitionem explicuit, quid in hac optione haud eligenda facturus sit, indagatione cumulata senior sciscitatur. Et dum uniuersorum mens consternaretur angustia, cunctique indulgerent silentio, præfatus Uffo in media concione surrexit.

Quem cum cohors uniuersa conspexisset, satis nequibat admirari, ut quid elinguis uelut orationi gestus informaret. Et quia omne rarum dignum nouimus admiratione, omnium in se duxit intuitum. Tandem sic orsus cœpit: "Non nos minæ moueant lacessentium, cum ea Teotonicæ turgiditati innata sit conditio, ut uerborum ampullositate glorientur, minarumque uentositate pusillanimes et imbecilles calleant comminatione consternare. Me etenim unicum et uerum regni natura produxit heredem, cui profecto nouistis incumbere, ut monomachiæ me discrimini audacter obiiciam, quatenus uel pro regno solus occumbam, uel pro patria solus uictoriam obtineam. Ut ergo minarum cassetur ampullositas, hæc Imperatori referant mandata, ut Imperatoris filius et heres imperii, cum athleta præstantissimo, mihi soli non formidet occurrere." Dixit, et hæc verba dictauit voce superba. Qui dum orationem complesset, a collateralibus senior sciscitabatur, cuiusnam hæc fuisset oratio? Cum autem a circumstantibus intellexisset, quod filius suus, prius veluti mutus, hunc effudisset sermonem, palpandum eum jussit accersiri. Et cum humeros lacertosque, et clunes, suras atque tibias, cæteraque membra organica crebro palpasset: "Talem," ait, "me memini in flore extitisse iuuentutis." Quid multa? Terminus pugnæ constituitur et locus. Talique responso percepto, ad propria legati repedabant.

CAP. II.

De duello Uffonis.

Superest ergo, ut arma nouo militi congrua corrogentur. Allatisque ensibus, quos in regno præstantiores rex poterat inuestigare, Uffo singulos dextra uibrans, in partes confregit minutissimas. "Hæccine arma sunt," inquit, "quibus et uitam et regni tuebor honorem?" Cuius cum pater uiuidam experiretur uirtutem, "Unicum adhuc," ait, "et regni et uitæ nostræ superest asylum." Ad tumulum itaque ducatum postulauit, in quo prius mucronem experientissimum occultauerat. Et mox intersigniis per petrarum notas edoctus, gladium jussit effodi præstantissimum. Quem illico dextra corripiens, "Hic est," ait, "fili, quo numerose triumphaui, et qui mihi infallibile semper tutamen extitit." Et hæc dicens, eundem filio contradidit. Nec mora; terminus ecce congressioni præfixus arctius instabat. Tandem, confluentibus undique phalangis innumerabilibus, in Egdoræ fluminis mediamne[342] locus pugnæ constituitur: ut ita pugnatores ab utriusque cœtus adminiculo segregati nullius opitulatione fungerentur. Teotonicis ergo ultra fluminis ripam in Holsatia considentibus, Danis uero citra amnem dispositis, rex pontis in medio sedem elegit, quatenus, si unigenitus occumberet, in fluminis se gurgitem præcipitaret, ne pariter nato orbatus et regno cum dolore superstes canos deduceret ad inferos. Deinde emissis utrinque pugilibus, in medio amne conuenerunt. Ast ubi miles noster egregius Uffo, duos sibi conspexit occurrere, tanquam leo pectore robusto infremuit, animoque constanti duobus electis audacter se opponere non detrectauit, illo cinctus mucrone, quem patrem supra meminimus occuluisse, et alterum dextra strictum gestans. Quos cum primum obuios habuisset, sic singillatim utrumque alloquitur, et quod raro legitur accidisse, athleta noster elegantissimus, cuius memoria in æternum non delebitur, ita aduersarios animabat ad pugnam: "Si te," inquit, "regni nostri stimulat ambitio, ut nostræ opis, potentiæque, opumque capessere uelis opulentias, comminus te clientem decet præcedere, ut et regni tui terminos amplifices, et militibus tuis conspicientibus, strenuitatis nomen nanciscaris." Campionem uero hunc in modum alloquitur: "Uirtutis tuæ experientiam jam locus est propagare, si comminus accesseris, et eam, quam pridem Alamannis gloriam ostendisti, Danis quoque propalare non cuncteris. Nunc ergo famam tuæ strenuitatis poteris ampliare, et egregiæ munificentiæ dono ditari, si et dominum præcedas, et clypeo defensionis eum tuearis. Studeat, quæso, Teotonicis experta strenuitas variis artis pugillatoriæ modis Danos instruere, ut tandem optata potitus uictoria, cum triumphi ualeas exultatione ad propria remeare." Quam quum complesset exhortationem, pugilis cassidem toto percussit conamine, ita ut, quo feriebat, gladius in duo dissiliret. Cuius fragor per uniuersum intonuit exercitum. Unde cohors Teotonicorum exultatione perstrepebat: sed contra Dani desperationis consternati tristitia, gemebundi murmurabant. Rex uero, ut audiuit, quod filii ensis dissiliuisset, in margine se pontis jussit locari. Uerum Uffo, subito exempto, quo cinctus erat, gladio, pugilis illico coxam cruentauit, nec mora, et caput pariter amputauit. Sic ergo ludus fortunæ ad instar lunæ uarius, nunc his, nunc illis successibus illudebat, et quibus iamiam exultatione fauebat ingenti, eos nouercali mox uultu, toruoque conspexit intuitu. Hoc cognito, senior jam confidentius priori se jussit sede locari. Nec jam anceps diu extitit uictoria. Siquidem Uffo ualide instans, ad ripam amnis pepulit hæredem imperii, ibique eum haud difficulter gladio iugulauit. Sicque duorum solus uictor existens, Danis irrogatam multis retro temporibus infamiam gloriosa uirtute magnifice satis aboleuit. Atque ita Alamannis cum improperii uerecundia, cassatisque minarum ampullositatibus, cum probris ad propria remeantibus, postmodum in pacis tranquillitate præcluis Uffo regni sui regebat imperium.

M. NOTE ON THE DANISH CHRONICLES

The text of Saxo Grammaticus, given above, is based upon the magnificent first edition printed by Badius Ascensius (Paris, 1514). Even at the time when this edition was printed, manuscripts of Saxo had become exceedingly scarce, and we have now only odd leaves of MS remaining. One fragment, however, discovered at Angers, and now in the Royal Library at Copenhagen, comes from a MS which had apparently received additions from Saxo himself, and therefore affords evidence as to his spelling.

Holder's edition (Strassburg, 1886) whilst following in the main the 1514 text of Badius Ascensius, is accordingly revised to comply with the spelling of the Copenhagen fragments, and with any other traces of MS authority extant. I doubt the necessity for such revision. If the text were extant in MS, one might feel bound to follow the spelling of the MS, as in the case of the old English MSS of the *Vitae Offarum* below: but seeing that Saxo, with the exception of a few pages, is extant only in a 16th century printed copy, the spelling of which is almost identical with that now current in Latin text books, it seems a pity to restore conjecturally mediæval spellings likely to worry a student. Accordingly I have followed the printed text of 1514, modernizing a very few odd spellings, and correcting some obvious printers errors[343].

A translation of the first nine books of Saxo by Prof. O. Elton has been published by the Folk-Lore Society (No. XXXIII, 1893).

Saxo completed his history in the early years of the 13th century. His elder contemporary, Sweyn Aageson, had already written a *Brief History of the Kings of Denmark*. Sweyn's *History* must have been completed not long after 1185, to which date belongs the last event he records. The extracts given from it (pp. 211-15) are taken from Langebek's collection, with modifications of spelling. Langebek follows the first edition (Stephanius, 1642); the MS used in this edition had been destroyed in 1728. *Cod. Arn. Mag. 33*, recently printed by Gertz, although very corrupt, is supposed to give the text of Sweyn's *History* in a form less sophisticated than that of the received text (see Gertz, *Scriptores Minores Historiæ Danicæ*, 1917, p. 62). The *Little Chronicle of the Kings of Leire* is probably earlier than Sweyn's *History*. Gertz dates it c. 1170, and thinks it was written by someone connected with the church at Roskilde. It covers only the early traditional history. See above, pp. 17, 204.

For comparison, the following lists, as given in the roll of kings known as *Langfeðgatal*, in the *Little Chronicle*, in Sweyn, and in Saxo may be useful:

Langfeðgatal	*Little Chronicle*	*Sweyn*	*Saxo*	Names as given in *Beowulf*
	Dan		Dan	
				? =
		Humblus		Heremod

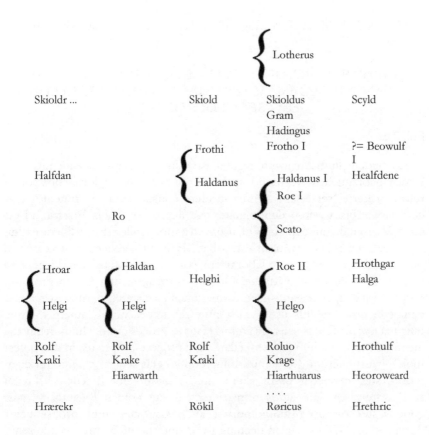

N. THE *LIFE OF OFFA I*, WITH EXTRACTS FROM THE *LIFE OF OFFA II*. EDITED FROM TWO MSS IN THE COTTONIAN COLLECTION

The text is given from *MS Cotton Nero D. I* (quoted in the footnotes as A), collated with *MS Claudius E. IV* (quoted as B). Minor variations of B are not usually noted. The two MSS agree closely.

The *Nero* MS is the more elaborate of the two, and is adorned with very fine drawings. *Claudius*, however, offers occasionally a better text; it has been read by a corrector whose alterations—contrary to what is so often the ease in mediæval MSS—seem to be authoritative.

The *Lives of the Offas* were printed by Wats in his edition of Matthew Paris (1639-40) from MS A. Miss Rickert has printed extracts from the two lives, in *Mod. Phil.* II, 14 *etc.*, following MS A, "as Wats sometimes takes liberties with the text."

INCIPIT HISTORIA DE OFFA PRIMO QUI STRENUITATE SUA SIBI ANGLIE MAXIMAM PARTEM SUBEGIT. CUI SIMILLIMUS FUIT SECUNDUS OFFA[344].

Fol. 2 *a*

Inter occidentalium Anglorum reges illustrissimos, precipua commendacionis laude celebratur Rex Warmundus, ab hiis qui historias Anglorum non solum relatu proferre, set eciam scriptis inserere consueuerant. Is fundator erat cuiusdam urbis a seipso denominate, que lingua Anglicana Warwic, id est curia Warmundi, nuncupatur. Qui usque ad annos seniles absque liberis extitit, preter unicum filium; quem, ut estimabat, regni sui heredem et successorem puerilis debilitatis incomodo laborantem, constituere non ualebat. Licet enim idem unicus filius eius, Offa uel Offanus nomine, statura fuisset procerus, corpore integer, et elegantissime forme iuuenis existeret, permansit tamen a natiuitate uisu priuatus usque ad annum septimum, mutus autem et uerba humana non proferens usque ad annum etatis sue tricesimum. Huius debilitatis incomodum non solum rex, sed eciam regni proceres, supra quam dici potest moleste sustinuerunt. Cum enim imineret patri etas senilis, et ignoraret diem mortis sue, nesciebat quem alium sibi[345] constitueret heredem et regni successorem. Quidam autem primarius regni, cui nomen Riganus[346], cum quodam suo complice Mitunno nomine, ambiciosus cum ambicioso, seductor cum proditore uidens regem decrepitum, et sine spe prolis procreande senio fatiscentem, de se presumens, cepit ad regie dignitatis culmen aspirare, contemptis aliis regni primatibus, se solum pre ceteris ad hoc dignum reputando.

Iccirco diebus singulis regi molestus nimis, proterue eum aggreditur, ut se heredis loco adoptaret. Aliquando cor regis blande alliciens, interim aspere minis et terroribus prouocans, persuadere non cessat regi quod optabat[347]. Suggerebat eciam regi per uiros potentes, complices cupiditatis et malicie sue, se regni sui summum apicem, uiolentia et terroribus et ui extorquere, nisi arbitrio uoluntatis sue rex ipse pareret, faciendo uirtutem de necessitate. Super hoc itaque et aliis regni negociis, euocato semel concilio, proteruus ille a rege reprobatus discessit a curie presentia, iracundie calore fremens in semetipso, pro repulsa quam sustinuit.

Riganus (or Aliel) comes before King Warmundus to claim that he should
be made King in place of the incompetent Offa
From MS Cotton Nero D. I, fol. 2 a.

Fol. 2 *b*

Nec mora, accitis m*u*ltis qui contr*a* regis i*m*pe*r*ium parte*m* sua*m* *con*fouebant,
infra paucos dies, copiosum i*mm*o infinitu*m* exce*r*citu*m* *con*gregauit: *et* sub spe
uictorie uirilit*er* optinende, regem *et* suos ad hostile p*re*lium prouocauit. Rex
au*tem* confectus senio, time*n*s rebellare, declinauit aliquocie*n*s impet*us*
adue*r*sarior*um*. Tandem uero, co*n*uocatis i*n* unum p*r*incipib*us* *et* magnatib*us*
suis, delibe*ra*re cep*it* q*uo* fa*c*to opus ha*be*ret. Dum igit*ur* tractarent i*n* co*m*mune
per aliq*uo*t dies, secu*m* deliberantes instantissime nece*s*citatis articulu*m*, affuit
int*er* se*r*moci | nantes natus *et* unigenitus regis, eo usq*ue* elinguis *et* absq*ue*
sermone, s*ed* aure purgata, singulorum uerba discernens. Cum aute*m* pa*t*ris
seniu*m*, *et* se ip*su*m ad regni negocia q*ua*si inutilem *et* min*us* efficacem despici
et reprobari ab om*n*ib*us* perpenderet, contritus est *et* humiliatus in semetip*s*o,
usq*ue* in lac*r*imarum aduberem profusionem. *Et* exitus aq*ua*rum dedux*er*unt
oculi eius; *et* estuabat dolore cordis intrinsecus amarissimo. Et q*ua*m ue*r*bis
no*n* pot*er*at, deo affe*c*tu int*r*inseco p*re*cordiali*ter* suggerebat, ingemiscens,
repone*n*sque lac*r*imabilem q*ue*relam coram ip*s*o, orabat ut a spiritu s*an*c*t*o
reciperet consolac*i*onem, a pa*t*re luminu*m* fortitudinem, *et* a filio pa*t*ris
unigenito sapi*enci*e salutaris donatiuum. In breui igitur, *con*triti cordis uota
prospiciens, is, cui nuda *et* aperta sunt omnia, resoluit os adolescentis in ue*r*ba
discreta *et* manifeste articulata. Sicq*ue* de regni principatu tumide *et* minaciter
contra se *et* pa*t*rem suu*m* perstrepentes, subito *et* ex insp*er*ato alloquitur:
"Quid adhuc me *et* pa*t*re meo supe*r*stite contra leges *et* iura uobis uendicatis

regni iudicium enormiter contrectare: *et* me excluso, herede geneali, alium degenerem facinorosum *eciam* in minas *et* diffiduciacionem superbe nimis prorumpentem, subrogare ut uos non immerito iniquitatis *et* prodicionis arguere valeamus. Quid, inquam, exteri, quid extranei contra nos agere debeant, cum nos affines *et* domestici nostri a patria quam hactenus generis nostri successio iure possedit hereditario, uelitis expellere?" Et dum hec Offanus uel Offa (hoc enim nomen adolescentulo erat) qui iam nunc primo eterno nomine cum bened[i]c[i]onis memoria meruit intitulari, ore facundo, sermone rethorico, uultu sereno prosequeretur, omnium audientium plus quam dici potest attonitorum oculos facies *et* corda in se conuertit. Et prosequens inceptum sermonem, continuando rationem, ait (intuens ad superna): "Deum testor, omnesque celestis curie primates, quod tanti sceleris *et* discidii incentores, (nisi qui ceperint titubare, uiriliter eriganter in uirtutem pristinam roborati) indempnes (pro ut desides *et* formidolosi promeruerunt) ac impunitos, non paciar. Fideles autem, ac strenuos, omni honore prosequar [et] confouebo."

Audito *igitur* adolescentis sermone, quem mutum estimabant vanum *et* inutilem, consternati admodum *et* conterriti, ab eius presencia discesserunt, qui contra patrem suum *et* ipsum, mota sedicione, ausu temerario conspirauerant. Riganus tamen, contumax *et* superbus, comitante Mittunno cum aliis complicibus suis, qui iam iram in odium conuerterant, minas minis recessit cumulando, regemque delirum cum filio suo inutili ac vano murione, frontose diffiduciauit. Econtra, naturales ac fideles regis, ipsius minas paruipendentes, *immo* Fol. 3 *a* | uilipendentes, inestimabili gaudio perfusi, regis *et* filii sui pedibus incuruati, sua suorumque corpora ad uindicandam regis iniuriam exponunt gratanter uniuersi. Nec mora, rex in sua *et* filii sui presentia generali edicto eos qui parti sue fauebant iubet assistere, uolens communi eorum consilio edoceri, qualiter in agendis suis procedere *et* negocia sua exequi habeat conuenienter. Qui super hiis diebus aliquot deliberantes, inprimis consulunt regi ut filium suum moribus *et* etate ad hoc maturum, militari cingulo faciat insigniri: vt ad bellum procedens, hostibus suis horrori fieret *et* formidini. Rex autem sano et salubri consilio suorum obtemperans, celebri[348] ad hoc condicto die, cum sollempni *et* regia pompa, gladio filium suum accinxit; adiunctis tirocinio suo strenuis adolescentibus generosis, quos rex ad decus *et* gloriam filii sui militaribus indui fecit, *et* honorari.

Cum autem post hec[349], aliquandiu cum sociis suis decertans, instrumenta tiro Offanus experiretur, omnes eum strenuissimum *et* singulos superantem uehementer[350] admirabantur. Rex igitur inde maiorem assumens audaciam, *et* in spem erectus alacriorem, communicato cum suis consilio, contra hostes regni sui insidiatores, *immo* iam manifeste contra regnum suum insurgentes, *et* inito certamine aduersantes, resumpto spiritu bellum instaurari precepit. Potentissimus autem ille, qui regnum sibi usurpare moliebatur, cum filiis suis iuuenib*us* duob*us*, uidelicet tironib*us* strenuissimis Otta *et* Milione nominatis, ascita quoq*ue* no*n* minima multitudine, n*ich*ilominu*s* audact*er* ad rebellandum, se suosq*ue* p*re*munire cepit, alacer *et* imp*er*territu*s*. Et preliandi diem *et* locum, hinc in*de* rex *et* eius emulus dete*r*minarunt.

Congregato itaq*ue* utrobiq*ue* copiosissimo *et* formidabili nimis exce*r*citu, parati ad congressum, fixerunt tentoria e regione, nichilq*ue* inte*r*erat nisi fluui*us* torrens in medio, qui utrumq*ue* exce*r*citu*m* sequestrabat. Et aliq*u*andiu hinc in*de* meticulosi *et* co*n*sternati, rapidi fluminis alueum inte*r*positu*m* (qui uix erat homini uel equo t*r*ansmeabil*is*) transire distulerunt. Tela tamen sola, cu*m* crebris co*m*minac*i*onibus *et* conuiciis, transuolarunt. Tande*m* indignatus Offa *et* egre ferens probrose more dispendia, electis de exce*r*citu suo robustiorib*us* *et* bello magis strenuis, q*u*os *eciam* credebat fideliores, subitus *et* improuisus flumen raptim p*er*transiens, fa*c*to impetu uehementi[351] *et* repentino, hostes ei obuiam occurre*n*tes, preocupatos *tam*en circa ripam flum*in*is, plurimos de adue*r*sario*rum* exce*r*citu cont*r*iuit, *et* i*n* ore gladii trucidauit. Primosq*ue* om*n*es t*r*ibunos *et* p*r*imicerios potenter dissipauit. Cu*m* tamen sui co*m*militones, forte uolentes p*re*scire in Offa p*re*uio Martis fortuna*m*, segnit*er* amne*m* t*r*ansmearent, q*u*i latus suu*m* tenebantur suffulcire, *et*[352] pocius Fol. 3 *b* | circumuallando roborare, et resu*m*pto sp*irit*u uiuidiore, reliquos om*n*es, hinc in*de* ad modu*m* nauis uelificantis *et* equora uelocit*er* sulcantis, impetuosissime diuisit, ense te*r*ribilit*er* fulminante, *et* hostium cruore sepius inebriato, don*ec* sue om*n*es acies ad ip*su*m illese *et* inde*m*pnes t*r*ansmeare*nt*. Quo cu*m* p*er*uenirent sui co*m*militones, congregati ci*r*ca ip*su*m domin*u*m suu*m*, exce*r*citu*m* magnu*m* et fortem co*n*flaue*r*unt. Duces aute*m* co*n*trarii exce*r*citus, sese densis agminib*us* *et* consertis aciebus, uiolent*er* opponu*n*t aduentantib*us*. Et congressu inito cruentissimo, acclamatu*m* *est* utrobiq*ue* et exhortatu*m*, ut res agatur pro capite, *et* ce*r*tamen pro sua *et* uxoru*m* sua*rum*, *et* libero*rum* suo*rum*, *et* possessionu*m* libe*r*ac*i*one, inea*n*t iustissimu*m*, auxilio diuino p*r*otegente. P*er*strepunt igitur tube cu*m* lituis, clamor exhortantiu*m*, equo*rum* hinnit*us*, morientiu*m* *et* uulnerato*rum* gemitus, fragor lancearum, gladioru*m* tinnit*us*, ictuu*m* tumultus, aera p*er*tu*r*bare uidebant*ur*. Adue*r*sarii tandem Offe legiones deiciunt, *et* i*n* fugam dissipatas co*n*ue*r*tunt.

Quod cum uideret Offa strenuissim*us*, *et* ex hostiu*m* cede cruent*us*, hausto sp*irit*u alac*r*iori, in hostes, more leonis *et* leene sublatis catulis, irruit truculent*er*, gladiu*m* suu*m* cruore hostili inebriando. Quod cu*m* uiderent t*r*ucida*n*di, fugitiui *et* meticulosi pudore confusi, reuersi su*n*t sup*er* hostes, et ut famam redime*r*ent, ferociores in obstantes fulminant *et* debacant*ur*.

Multoque tempore truculenter nimis decertatum est, et utrobique suspensa est uictoria; tandem post multorum ruinam, hostes fatigati pedem retulerunt, ut respirarent et pausarent post conflictum.

Similiter eciam et excercitus Offani. Quod tamen moleste nimis tulit Offanus, cuius sanguis in ulcionem estuabat, et indefessus propugnator cessare erubescebat. Hic casu Offe obuiant duo filii diuitis illius, qui regnum patris eius sibi attemptauit usurpare. Nomen primogenito Brutus [sive Hildebrandus][353] et iuniori Sueno. Hii probra et uerba turpia in Offam irreuerenter ingesserunt, et iuueni pudorato in conspectu excercituum, non minus sermonibus quam armis, molesti extiterunt. Offa igitur, magis lacessitus, et calore audacie scintillans, et iracundia usque ad fremitum succensus, in impetu spiritus sui in eosdem audacter irruit. Et eorum alterum, videlicet Brutum, unico gladii ictu percussit, amputatoque galee cono, craneum usque ad cerebri medullam perforauit, et in morte singultantem sub equinis pedibus potenter precipitauit. Alterum uero, qui hoc uiso fugam iniit, repentinus insequens, uulnere letali sauciatum, contempsit et prostratum. Post hec[354] deseuiens in ceteros contrarii excercitus duces, gladius Offe quicquid obuiam habuit prosternendo deuorauit, excercitu ipsius tali exemplo recencius in hostes insurgente, et iam gloriosius triumphante.

Fol. 4 *a*

Pater, uero, predictorum iuuenum, perterritus et dolore intrinseco sauciatus, subterfugiens amnem oppositum, nitebatur| pertransire: sed interfectorum sanguine torrens fluuius, eum loricatum et armorum pondere grauatum et multipliciter fatigatum, cum multis de suo excercitu simili incomodo prepeditis, ad ima submersit, et sine uulneribus, miseras animas exalarunt proditores, toti posteritati sue probra relinquentes. Amnis autem a Rigano ibi submerso sorciebatur uocabulum, et Riganburne, vt facti uiuat perpetuo memoria, nuncupatur. [Hiic alio nomine Auene dicitur.][355]

Reliqui autem omnes de excercitu Rigani [qui et Aliel dicebatur][355] qui sub ducatu Mitunni regebantur, in abissum desperacionis demersi, et timore effeminati, cum eorum duce in quo magis Riganus confidebat, in noctis crepusculo trucidati, cum uictoria gloriosa campum Offe strenuissimo (in nulla parte corporis sui deformiter mutilato, nec eciam uel letaliter uel periculose uulnerato, licet ea die multis se letiferis opposuisset periculis) reliquerunt[356].

Sicque Offe circa iuuentutis sue primicias, a Domino data est uictoria in bello nimis ancipiti, ac cruentissimo, et inter alienigenas uirtutis et industrie sue nomen celebre ipsius uentilatum, et odor longe lateque bonitatis ac ciuilitatis, nec non et strenuitatis eius circumfusus, nomen eius ad sidera subleuauit.

Porro in crastinum post uictoriam, hostium spolia interfectorum et fugitiuorum magnifice contempnens, nec sibi uolens aliquatenus usurpare, ne quomodolibet auaricie turpiter redargueretur, militibus suis stipendiariis, et naturalibus suis hominibus (precipue[357] hiis quos nouerat indigere) liberaliter dereliquit. Solos tamen magnates, quos ipsemet in prelio ceperat, sibi retinuit incarcerandos, redimendos, uel iudicialiter puniendos. Iussitque ut interfectorum duces et principes, quorum fama titulos magnificauit, et precipue eorum qui in prelio magnifice ac fideliter se habuerant (licet ei[358] aduersarentur) seorsum honorifice intumularentur, factis eis obsequiis, cum lamentacionibus. Excercitus autem popularis cadauera, in arduo et eminenti loco, ad posteritatis memoriam, tradi iussit sepulture ignobiliori. Vnde locus ille hoc nomine Anglico Qualmhul[359], a strage uidelicet et sepultura interfectorum merito meruit intitulari.

Multorum eciam et magnorum lapidum super eos struem excercitus Offe, uoce preconia iussus, congessit eminentem. Totaque circumiacens planicies[360] ab ipso cruentissimo certamine et notabili sepultura nomen et titulum indelebilem est sortita, et Blodiweld[361] a sanguine interfectorum denominabatur.

Deletis igitur et confusis hostibus, Offa cum ingenti triumpho ac tripudio et gloria reuertitur ad propria. Pater uero Warmundus, qui sese receperat in locis tucioribus rei euentum expectans, sed iam fausto nuncio certificatus, comperiensque et securus de carissimi filii sui uictoria, cum ingenti leticia ei procedit obuius[362]: et in amplexus eius diutissime commoratus, conceptum Fol. 4 b | interius de filii sui palma gaudium tegere non uolens set nec ualens, huius cum lacrimis exultacionis prorupit in vocem: "Euge fili dulcissime, quo affectu, quaue mentis leticia, laudes tuas prout dignum est prosequar? Tu enim es spes mea et subditorum iubilus ex insperato et exultacio. In te spes inopinata meis reuixit temporibus; in sinu tuo leticia mea, immo spes pocius tocius regni est reposita. Tu populi tocius firmamentum, tu pacis et libertatis mee basis et stabile, deo aspirante, fundamentum. Tibi debetur ruina proterui proditoris illius, quondam publici hostis nostri, qui regni fastigium quod mihi et de genere meo propagatis iure debetur hereditario, tam impudenter quam imprudenter, contra leges et ius gentium usurpare moliebatur. Sed uultus domini super eum et complices suos facientes mala, ut perderet de terra memoriam eorum, Deus ulcionum Dominus dissipauit consilium ipsius. Ipsum quoque Riganum in superbia rigentem, et immitem Mitunnum commilitonem ipsius, cum excercitu eorum proiecit in flumen rapacissimum. Descendunt quasi plumbum in aquis uehementibus; deuorauit gladius tuus hostes nostros fulminans et cruentatus, hostili sanguine magnifice inebriatus; non degener es fili mi genealis, sed patrissans, patrum tuorum uestigia sequeris magnificorum. Sepultus in inferno noster hostis et aduersarius, fructus viarum suarum condignos iam colligit, quos uiuus promerebatur. Luctum et miseriam quam senectuti mee malignus ille inferre disposuerat, uersa uice, clementia diuina conuertit in tripudium[363]. Quamobrem in presenti accipe, quod tuis meritis exigentibus debetur, eciam si filius meus non esses, et si mihi iure hereditario non succederes; ecce iam, cedo, et regnum Anglorum uoluntatis tue arbitrio deinceps committo; etas enim mea fragilis et iam decrepita, regni ceptrum ulterius sustinere non sufficit. Iccirco te fili desideratissime, uicem meam supplere te conuenit, et corpus meum senio confectum, donec morientis oculos clauseris, quieti tradere liberiori, vt a curis et secularibus sollicitudinibus, quibus discerpor liberatus, precibus uacem et contemplacioni. Armis hucusque materialibus dimicaui: restat ut de cetero uita mea que superest, militia sit super terram contra hostes spirituales.

"Ego uero pro incolumitate tua et regni statu, quod strenuitati tue, O anime mee dimidium, iam commisi, preces quales mea, sci[t][364] simplicitas et potest imbecillitas, Deo fundam indefessas. Sed quia tempus perbreue amodo mihi restat, et corpori meo solum superest sepulchrum, aurem benignam meis accomoda salutaribus consiliis, et cor credulum meis monitis inclina magnificis. Uerum ipsos qui nobiscum contra hostes publicos, Riganum videlicet et Mitunnum Fol. 5 a | et eorum complices emulos nostros fideliter steterunt, et periculoso discrimini pro nobis se opposuerunt, paterno amore tibi commendo, diligendos, honorandos, promouendos. Eos autem qui decrepite senectutis mee membra[365] debilia contemptui habere ausi sunt, asserentes uerba mea et regalia precepta esse sinilia deliramenta, presumentes temere apice regali me priuato te exheredare, suspectos habe et contemptibiles, si qui sint elapsi ab hoc bello, et a tuo gladio deuorante, eciam cum eorum posteritate: ne cum in ramusculos uirus pullulet, a radice aliquid consimile tibi generetur in posterum. Non enim recolo me talem eorum promeruisse, qui me et te filium meum gratis oderunt, persecucionem. Similiter eos, quos dici proditores pro eo quod nobis fideliter adheserant, exulare coegerunt, uel qui impotentes rabiem eorum fugiendo resistere, ad horam declinauerunt, cum omni mansuetudine studeas reuocare, et honores eorum cum possessionibus ex innata tibi regali munificentia, gracius ampliare. Laus industrie tue et fame preconia, et strenuitatis tue titulus, que adolescenciam tuam diuinitus illustrarunt, in posterum de te maiora promittunt. Desideranti animo sicienter affecto, ipsumque Deum, qui te tibi, sua mera gracia reddidit et restaurauit, deprecor affectuose, vt has iuuentutis tue primicias, hoc inopinato triumpho subarratas, melior semper ac splendidior operum gloria subsequatur. Et procul dubio post mortem meam (que non longe abest, iubente Domino) fame tue magnitudo per orbem uniuersum dilatabitur, et felix suscipiet incrementum. Et que Deo placita sunt, opere felici consumabis, que diuinitus prosperabuntur."

Hec autem filius deuotus et mansuetus, licet magnificus triumphator exaudisset et intenta aure intellexisset, flexis genibus et iunctis manibus, et exundantibus oculis, patri suo grates[366] rettulit accumulatas. Rex itaque per fines Anglie missis nunciis expeditissimis, qui mandata regia detulerunt, tocius dicionis sue conuocat nobilitatem. Que conuocata ex regis precepto, et persuasione, Offano filio suo unigenito ligiam fecerunt fidelitatem et homagium in patris presencia. Quod et omnes, animo uolenti, immo gaudenti, communiter perfecerunt.

Rex igitur quem pocius prona voluntas, quam uigor prouexit corporalis, per climata regni sui proficiscitur securus et letabundus, nullo contradicente, uel impediente, ut regni municiones et varias possessiones, diu per inimicos suos alienatas et iniuste ac uiolenter possessas, ad sue dicionis reacciperet iure potestatem. Que omnia sibi sunt sine difficultate uel more dispendio restituta. Statimque pater filium eorum possessionibus corporaliter inuestiuit; et paterno contulit affectu ac gratuito, proceribus Fol. 5 *b* congauden | tibus super hoc uniuersis. Post hec autem, Rex filio suo Offano erarium suum adaperiens, aurum suum et argentum, uasa concupiscibilia, gemmas, oloserica omnia, sue subdidit potestati. Sicque subactis et subtractis hostibus[367] cunctis, aliquandiu per uniuersum regnum uiguit pax et securitas diu desiderabilis.

Rex igitur filii sui prosperitate gauisus, qui *eciam* diatim de bono in melius gradatim ascendit, aliquo tempore uite sue metas distulit naturales: iubilus quoque in corde senis conceptus languores seniles plurimum mitigauit. Tandem Rex plenus dierum, cum benediccione omnium, qui ipsum *eciam* a remotis[368] partibus per famam cognouerunt[369], nature debita persoluens decessit. Et decedens, filio suo apicem regni sui pacatum et quietum reliquit: Offanus autem oculos patris sui pie claudens, lamentaciones mensurnas cum magnis eiulatibus, lacrimis et specialibus planctibus (prout moris tunc erat principibus magnificis) lugubriter pro tanto funere continuauit. Obsequiisque cum exequiis, magnifice tam in ecclesia quam in locis forinsecis conpletis, apparatu regio et loco celeberrimo et nominatissimo.

regibus condigno, videlicet in eminenciori ecclesia penes Glouerniam urbem egregiam, eidem exhiberi iubet sepulturam. Offanus autem cum moribus omnibus foret redimitus, elegans corpore, armis strenuus, munificus et benignus, post obitum patris sui magnifici Warmundi[370], cuius mores tractatus exigit speciales, plenarie omnium principum Regni dominium suscipit, et debitum cum omni deuocione, et mera uoluntate, famulatum. Cum igitur cuiusdam solempnitatis arrideret serenitas, Offanus cum sollempni tripudio omnibus applaudentibus et faustum omen acclamantibus, Anglie diademate feliciter est insignitus.

Adquiescens *igitur* seniorum consiliis et sapientum persuasionibus, cepit tocius regni irreprehensibiliter, immo laudabiliter, habenas[371] modernanter et

- 193 -

sapienter gubernare. Sic igitur, subactis hostibus regni uniuersis, uiguit pax secura et firmata in finibus Anglorum, per tempora longa; precipue tamen per spacium temporis quinquennale. Erat autem iam triginta quatuor annos etatis attingens, annis prospere pubescentibus.

Et cum Rex, more iuuenili, venatus gracia per nemora frequenter, cum suis ad hoc conuocatis uenatoribus et canibus sagacibus, expeditus peragrasset, contigit die quadam quod aere turbato, longe a suorum caterua semotus, solus per nemoris opaca penitus ipsorum locorum, necnon et fortune ignarus, casu deambulabat. Dum autem sic per ignota diuerticula incaucius oberraret, et per inuia, uocem lacrimabilem et miserabiliter querulam haut longe a se audiuit. Cuius sonitum secutus, inter densos frutices Fol. 6 a | virginem singularis forme et regii apparatus, sed decore uenustissimam, ex insperato repperit. Rex uero rei euentum admirans, que ibi ageret et querele causas, eam blande alloquens, cepit sciscitari. Que ex imo pectoris flebilia trahens suspiria, regi respondit (nequaquam in auctorem sed in seipsam reatum retorquens): "Peccatis meis" inquit "exigentibus infortunii huius calamitas mihi accidit." Erat autem reguli cuiusdam filia qui Eboracensibus preerat. Huius incomparabilis pulchritudinis singularem eminentiam pater admirans, amatorio demone seductus, cepit eam incestu libidinoso concupiscere, et ad amorem illicitum sepe sollicitare ipsam puellam, minis, pollicitis, blanditiis, atque muneribus adolescentule temptans emollire constantiam. Illa autem operi nephario nullatenus adquiescens, cum pater tamen minas minis exaggeraret[372], et promissa promissis accumularet, munera muneribus adaugeret, iuxta illud poeticum:

Imperium, promissa, preces, confudit in unum:

elegit magis incidere in manus hominum, et eciam ferarum qualiumcunque, vel gladii subire sententiam, quam Dei offensam incurrere, pro tam graui culpa manifestam. Pater itaque ipsam sibi parere constanter renuentem, euocatis quibusdam maligne mentis hominibus quos ad hoc elegerat, precepit eam in desertum solitudinis remote duci, uel pocius trahi, et crudelissima morte condempnatam, bestiis ibidem derelinqui. Qui cum in locum horroris et vaste solitudinis peruenissent, trahentes eam seductores illi, Deo ut creditur inspirante, miserti pulchritudinis[373] illius eam ibidem sine trucidacione et membrorum mutilacione, uiuam, sed tamen sine aliquorum uictualium alimento (exceptis talibus qui de radicibus et frondibus uel herbis colligi, urgente ultima fame, possunt) dimiserunt.

Cum hac rex aliquandiu habens sermonem, comitem itineris sui illam habuit, donec solitarii cuiusdam habitacionem reperissent, ubi nocte superueniente quiescentes pernoctauerunt. In crastinum autem solitarius ille uiarum et semitarum peritus, regem cum comite sua usque ad fines domesticos, et loca regi non ignota[374] conduxit. Ad suos itaque rex rediens, desolate illius quam nuper inuenerat curam gerens, familiaribus et domesticis generis sui sub diligenti custodia commisit.

Post hec aliquot annis elapsis, cum rex celibem agens uitam, mente castus et corpore perseueraret, proceres dicionis sue, non solum de tunc presenti, sed de futuro sibi periculo precauentes, et nimirum multum solliciti, dominum suum de uxore ducenda unanimiter conuenerunt: ne sibi et regno successorem et heredem non habens, post obitum ipsius iminens periculum generaret. Etatis enim iuuenilis pubertas, morum maturitas, et urgens regni necessitas, necnon et honoris dignitas, itidem postularunt. Fol. 6 b | Et cum super hoc negocio, sepius regem sollicitarentur, et alloquerentur, ipse multociens ioculando, et talia uerba asserendo interludia fuisse uanitatis, procerum suorum constantiam dissimulando differendoque delusit. Quod quidam aduertentes, communicato cum aliis consilio, regem ad nubendum incuntabiliter urgere ceperunt. Rex uero more optimi principis, cuius primordia iam bene subarrauerat, nolens uoluntati magnatum suorum resistere, diu secum de thori socia, libra profunde rationis, studiose cepit deliberare. Cumque hoc in mente sua sollicicius tractaret, uenit forte in mentem suam illius iuuencule memoria, quam dudum inter uenandum inuenit uagabundam, solam, feris et predonibus miserabiliter expositam: quam ad tuciora ducens, familiaribus generis sui commiserat alendam, ac carius custodiendam. Que, ut rex audiuit, moribus laudabiliter redimita, decoris existens expectabilis, omnibus sibi cognitis amabilem exhibuit et laudabilem; hec igitur sola, relictis multis, eciam regalis stematis sibi oblatis, complacuit; illamque solam in matrimonium sibi adoptauit.

Cum autem eam duxisset in uxorem, non interueniente multa mora, elegantissime forme utriusque sexus liberos ex eadem procreauit. Itaque cum prius esset rex propria seueritate subditis suis formidabilis, magnates eius, necnon et populus eius uniuersus, heredum et successorum apparentia animati, regni robur et leticiam geminarunt. Rex quoque ab uniuersis suis, et non solum prope positis, immo alienigenis et remotis, extitit honori, ueneracioni, ac dileccioni. Et cum inter se in Britannia, (que tunc temporis in plurima regna multiphariam diuisa fuisset) reguli sibi finitimi hostiliter se impeterent, solus Rex Offa pace regni sui potitus feliciter, se sibique subditos in pace regebat et libertate. Unde et adiacencium prouinciarum reges eius mendicabant auxilium, et in neccessitatis articulo, consilium.

Rex itaque Northamhimbrorum, a barbara Scotorum gente, et eciam aliquibus suorum, grauiter et usque ferme ad internecionem percussus, et proprie defensionis auxilio destitutus, ad Offam regem potentem legatos destinat; et pacificum supplicans, ut presidii eius solacio contra hostes suos roboretur. Tali mediante condicione, ut Offe filiam sibi matrimonio copularet, et non se proprii regni, *sed* Offam, primarium ac principem preferr*et*, *et* se cu*m* suis om*n*ib*us* ip*s*i subiugaret. Nichil itaq*ue* dotis cum Offe filia rogitauit, hoc sane contentus premio, ut a regni sui finibus barbaros illos potenter *et* frequenter experta fugaret strenuitate.

Cum autem legatorum uerba rex Offa succepisset, consilio suorum fretus Fol. 7 *a* sup | plicantis uoluntati ac precibus adquieuit si t*am*en rex ille pactum huiusmodi, tactis sac*ro*sanc*t*is euuangeliis[375], *et* obsidum tradic*i*one, fideliter tenendum confirmaret. Sic igitur Rex Offa, super hiis condic*i*onib*us* sub c*er*ta forma co*n*firmatus, *et* ad plenum certificatus, in partes illas cu*m* equitum numerosa multitudine proficiscitur. Cum autem illuc peruenisse*t*, timore eius consternata pars aduersa cessit, fuge presidio se saluando. Quam t*am*en rex Offa audacter prosecutus, non prius destitit fugare fugientem, donec eam ex integro contriuisset; *sed* nec eo contentus, ulteri*us* progreditur, barbaros expugnaturus. Inter*e*a ad patriam suam nunciu*m* imp*er*itu*m* destinau*i*t, ad primates et precipuos regni sui, quib*us* tocius dic*i*onis sue regimen commendau*er*at, et liter*as* regii sigilli sui munimine co*n*signatas[376], eidem nunc*i*o commisit, deferendas. Q*u*i autem destinatus fuit, iter arripiens u*er*sus Offe regnum, ut casu accidit int*er* eundu*m*, hospitandi gr*ac*i*a* aulam regiam introiuit illi*us* regis, cuius filiam Offa sibi m*a*trimo*n*io copulau*er*at. Rex au*tem* ille, cum de statu *et* causa itineris sui subdole requirendo cognouisset, u*u*ltus sui serenitate animi u*er*suciam mentitus, specie ten*us* illum amantissime suscepit: *et* uelamen sceleris sui querens, a conspectu publico sub quodam dilecc*i*onis pretexu, ad regii thalami secreta penetralia ip*su*m nuncium nichil sinist*r*i suspicantem introduxit: magnoq*ue* studio elaborauit, ut ip*su*m, uino estuanti madentem, redderet temulentum, et ip*s*o nuncio uel dormiente uel aliquo alio modo ignorante, mandata d*om*ini sui regis Offe tacit*us* ac subdolus apertis *et* explicatis liter*is* persc*r*utabatur; cepitq*ue* perniciose immutare et p*er*uertere sub Offe nomine sigillu*m* adultera*n*s, fallacesq*ue* *et* perniciosas literas loco inuentarum occultauit. Forma autem adulterinar*um* [*l*i*t*erar*um*][377] hec est q*ue* subscribitur[378]:

[379]"Rex Offa, maioribus et pr*e*cipuis regni sui, salutis et prosperitatis augmentu*m*. Uniu*er*sitati u*es*t*r*e notum facio, i*n* itine*r*e quod arripui infortunia *et* adu*er*sa plurima tam michi q*ua*m subditis meis accidisse, *et* maiores excercitus mei, non ignauia propria, u*e*l hostium oppugnantium uirtute, set pocius peccatis n*os*t*r*is iusto Dei iudicio interisse. Ego autem instantis periculi causam p*er*tracta*n*s, *et* consciencie mee intima perscrutatus, i*n* memetip*s*o nichil aliud conicio altissimo displicere, nisi quod perditam *et* maleficam illa*m* absq*ue* meorum consensu uxorem imperito *et* infelici duxi matrimonio. Ut ergo de malefica memorata, uoluntati u*es*t*r*e ad plenum q*ua*m temere offendi satisfiat, asportetur cum liber*is* ex ea genitis ad loca deserta, ho*m*i*n*ib*us*

incognita[380], Fol. 7 *b* | feris *et* auib*us* aut siluestribus predonibus frequentata: ubi cum pueris suis puerpera, truncata manus et pedes, exemplo pereat inaudito."

Nuncius autem mane facto, uino quo maduerat digesto, co*m*pos iam sui effectus, discessit: et post aliquot dies peruieniens ad propria, magnatib*us* qui regno regis Offe p*r*ærant literas do*m*ini sui sigillo signatas exposuit. In quar*um* auditu perlecta mandati serie, in stuporem *et* uehementissimam admirac*i*one*m* uniu*er*si, plus q*u*am dici possit, rapiuntur. Et super hiis, aliquot diebus co*m*municato cum magnatibus consilio deliberantes, periculosum ducebant[381] mandatis ac iussionib*us* regiis non obtemperare. Misera *igitur* seducta, deducta est in remotissimu*m* *et* i*n*habitabilem locum horroris et uaste solitudinis: cu*m* qua eciam liberi ei*u*s miseri *et* miserabiles queruli *et* uagientes, absq*ue* mi*s*e*r*icordi*a*, ut cu*m* ea t*r*ahere*n*tur occidendi, iudiciu*m* acceperu*n*t.

Nec mora, memorati apparitores matre*m* cu*m* pignorib*us* suis in dese*r*tu*m* uastissimu*m* t*r*aheba*n*t. Mat*r*i uero p*r*opter ei*u*s forma*m* admirabile*m* pa*r*ce*n*tes, libe*r*os ei*u*s, n*e*c forme, n*e*c sexui, etati u*e*l *con*dic*i*oni pa*r*centes, d*e*truncarunt menbratim, i*m*mo poci*u*s frustatim[382] crudeliter in bestialem feritate*m* seuientes. Completaq*ue* tam crudeli sente*n*cia, cruenti apparitores ocius reuertunt*ur*. Nec mora, solitarius quidam uitam in omni sanc*t*itate, uigiliis assiduis, ieiuniis crebris, *et* continuis o*rat*ionib*us*, ducens heremiticam, circa noctis crepusculum eo p*er*transie*n*s, mulieris cuiusdam luctus lac*r*imabiles *et* querelas usq*ue* ad intima cordis *et* ossuum[383] medullas penetratiuas, quas Do*m*inu*s* ex mortuorum corporib*us* licet lace*r*atis elicuit, audiuit. Infantulorumq*ue* uagitus lugubres nimis cu*m* doloris ululatibus quasi in materno sinu audiendo similiter annotauit. Mise*r*icordia autem s*a*nctus Dei motus, usq*ue* ad lacrimaru*m* aduberem effusionem, quo ipsa uox ip*su*m* uocabat, Domino ducente peruenit. Et cu*m* illuc peruenisset, nec aliud q*u*am corpo*r*a humana in frusta detruncata reperisset, cognouit[384] in sp*irit*u ip*s*a alicuius innocentis corp*u*s, uel aliquorum i*n*nocentiu*m* corpuscula extitisse, que tam inhumanam sentenciam subierunt. Nec sine martirii palma, ipsos quorum hee fuerunt exuuie, ab ho*c*[385] sec*u*lo t*r*ansmigrasse suspicabatur. Auxiliu*m* tam*e*n pro D*e*i amore *et* caritatis intuitu postulatu*m* non denegans, se pro illorum repara*ci*one prostrauit in deuotissima*m* cum lacrimis o*r*a*ci*onem, maxime propter uocem celitus emissam, quam profecto cognou*i*t[384] p*er* De*um* li*n*gu*a*s cadaue*r*u*m* p*r*otulisse. Piis *igitur* s*a*nct*u*s co*m*motus uisce*r*ib*us*, igneq*ue* succe*n*su*s* caritatis, ex cogni*ci*one[386] ei*u*s, qu*a*m, ut ia*m* d*i*c*tu*m, dudum uiderat, ha*b*uit, fa*c*tu*s* hilarior, pro ipsis Fol. 8 *a* | flexis genib*us*, inundantibus oculis, iunctisq*ue* palmis orauit, dicens: "Do*m*i*n*e Jesu Ch*r*ist*e*, q*ui* Lazarum quatriduanum ac fetidum resuscitasti, immo qui omniu*m* nost*r*o*r*um corpora i*n* ex*tr*emo examine suscitabis, uest*r*am oro mise*r*icordiam, ut non habens ad me peccatorem, s*e*d ad horum innocentum pressuras respectu*m* piissimu*m*, corpuscula he*c* iubeas resuscitari, ad laudem *et* gloriam

- 197 -

tuam i*n* se*m*piter*num*, vt om*n*es qui mortis horum causam *et* forma*m* audierint, te glorificent Deum *et* Dominum mundi Saluatorem."

Sic igitur s*an*ctus iste, Do*m*ini de fidei sue[387] uirtute i*n* Domino presumens *et* co*n*fidens, inter orandum, membra p*re*cisa recollige*n*s, *et* sibi particulas adaptans *et* coniungens, *et* i*n* q*u*antum potuit redintegrans, in parciu*m* q*u*amplurimu*m*, set in integritate*m* pocius delectat*us*, Domino rei consummac*i*onem q*ui* mortificat *et* uiuificat co*m*mendauit. Coniuncta igitur corpora, signo crucis triumphali consignauit. Mira fidei uirtus et efficacia, signo c*r*ucis uiuifice et or*ati*onis ac fidei serui D*ei* uirtute, no*n* solu*m* ma*t*ris orbate anim*us* reparat*ur*, s*e*d *et* filior*um* corp*us*cula in pristinu*m* *et* integrum nature sunt reformata decorem, necnon *et* anime mortuor*um* ad sua pristina domicilia sunt reuerse. Ad mansiuncule igitur sue septa (a qua elongatus fuerat, gr*ac*ia lignor*um* ad pulmentaria deq*u*oquenda colligendor*um*) ip*s*e senex: qui prius detruncati fuerant, Domino iubente integ*r*i uiui *et* alacres sunt reuersi, ducem s*an*ctu*m* suum sequentes pedetentim. Ubi more patris, ip*s*am desolatam cum liberis sibi ip*s*is restitutis, alimentis quibus potuit, *et* q*ue* ad manum habuit, pie ac misericorditer *con*fouebat.

Nesciens *er*go quo migraret regina, cu*m* suis infantulis intra uastissimam heremum cum memorato solitario, diu moram ibidem or*ati*onib*us*, uigiliis, ac aliis s*an*ct*i*s operibus eius intenta *et* iamiam conuenienter informata, *et* edulio siluestri sustentata, co*n*tinuabat. Post duoru*m* uero mensium curricula, Rex Offa uictoriosissimus domu*m* let*us* remeauit, spolia deuictorum suis magnatib*us* regali munificentia gloriose distribuendo; ueruntam*en*, ne lacrime gaudia regis, *et* eorum q*ui* cum eo adue*n*erant, miserabiliter inter*r*ump*er*ent, consiliarii regii q*ue* de regina *et* liberis ei*us* accide*r*ant, diu sub silenc*i*o caute dissimulando, *et* causas absencie eius fictas annectendo, *con*celabant. Tandem cu*m* rex uehement*er* admiraretur ubinam regina delituisset, q*ue* ip*s*i regi ab ancipiti bello reue*r*tenti occurrisse gaudenter teneretur, *et* in oscul*is* et amplexib*us* ceteris gaudentius triumphatore*m* aduentante*m* suscepisse, sciscitabatur instanti*us*, *et* toruius *et* p*ro*te*r*uius, quid de ip*s*a fieret uel euenisset. Suspicabatur eni*m* eam morbo detenta*m*, ipsa*m*que cu*m* liberis Fol. 8 *b* | suis, regis *et* aliorum hominu*m*, ut quieti uacaret, frequentiam declinasse. Tande*m* cum iratus nullatenus se uelle ampli*us* ignorare, cu*m* iuramento, q*ui*d de uxore sua *et* liberis euenisset, uultu toruo asseruisset, unus ex edituis omnia q*ue* accide*r*ant, de tirannico ei*us* mandato, *et* mandati plenaria execuc*i*one, seriatim enarrauit.

Hiis auditis, risus in luctu*m*, gaudium i*n* lamenta, iubilus in singultus flebilit*er* conu*er*tuntur, totaq*ue* regia ululatibus personuit *et* merorib*us*. Lugensq*ue* rex diu ta*m* i*m*mane infortuniu*m*, induit se sacco cilicino, aspersum cin*er*e, ac multiplicit*er* deformatum. Tandem monitu suorum, qui dicebant n*on* uiror*um* magnificor*um* s*e*d pocius effeminator*um*, dolorem inte*r*iecto solacio nolle temperare[388], e*s*se propriu*m* *et* *con*suetudine*m*, rex cepit respirare, *et* dolori modum imponere. Consilio igitur peritorum, qui nouerant regem libenter in tempore prospero in studio uenatico plurimum delectari, conuocantur uenatores, ut rex spaciaturus uenando, dolorem suum diminueret et luctum solacio demulceret. Qui inter uenandum dum per siluarum abdita, Deo misericordiarum et tocius consolac[i]onis ducente, feliciter solus per inuia oberrauit, et tandem ad heremitorium memorati heremite directe peruenit, eiusque exiguum domicilium subintrans, humaniss[im]e et cum summo gaudio receptus est. Et cum humili residens sedili, membra[389] fatigata quieti daret ad horam, recolens qualiter uxorem suam ibidem quondam diuinitus reperisset, et feliciter educasset, et educatam duxisset in uxorem, et quam elegantem ex ea prolem protulisset, eruperunt lacrime cum gemitibus, et in querelas lugubres ora resoluens, hospiti suo sinistrum de uxore sua qui[390] infausto sidere nuper euenerat quam et ipse quondam uiderat, enarrauit. At senex sereno uultu, factus ex intrinsecus concepto gaudio alacrior, consolatus est regem, et in uocem exultacionis eminus prorumpens: "Eia domine mi rex, eia, ait; uere Deus misericordiarum, Dominus, famulos suos quasi pater filios in omni tribulacione post pressuras consolatur, percutit et medetur, deicit ut gloriosius eleuet pregrauatum. Uiuit uxor tua, cum liberis tuis in omni sospitate restauratis: non meis meritis, sed pocius tuis, integritati, sanitati et leticie plenius qui trucidabantur restituuntur. Recognosce[391] quanta fecit tibi Dominus, et in laudes et graciarum acciones totus exurge." Tunc prosiliens sanctus pre gaudio, euocauit reginam, que in interiori diuerticulo, pueros suos balneo micius materno studio confouebat. Que cum ad regem introisset, uix se Fol. 9 a | gaudio capiens, pedibus mariti sui prouoluta, in lacrimis exultacionis inundauit. In cuius amplexus desideratissimos ruens rex, ipsam in maius quam dici possit gaudium suscepit. Interim senex, pueros elegantissimos et ex ablucione elegantiores, uestit, comit, et paterno more et affectu componit, et ad presentiam patris et matris introducit. Quos pater intra brachia suscipiens, et ad pectus arctioribus amplexibus applicans, roseis uultibus infantum oscula imprimit multiplicata; quos tamen rore lacrimarum, pre nimia mentis exultacione, madefecit. Et cum diucius eorum colloquiis pasceretur, conuersus rex ad senem, ait: "O pater sancte, pater dulcissime[392], mentis mee reparator, et gaudii cordis mei restaurator, qua merita uestra, caritatis officia, pietatisque beneficia, prosequar remunerac[i]one? Accipe ergo, licet multo maiora exigant merita tua, quicquid erarium meum ualet effundere; me, meos, et mea, tue expono uoluntati." At sanctus, "Domine mi rex, non decet me peccatorem conuersum ad Dominum, ad insanias quas reliqui falsas respicere. Tu uero pocius pro animabus patris tui et matris tue, quibus quandoque carus fueram ac familiaris, et tua, et uxoris tue, et liberorum tuorum corporali sanitate, et salute spirituali, regni tui soliditate, et successorum tuorum prosperitate, Deo gratus, qui tot in te congessit beneficia, cenobium quoddam fundare, uel aliquod dirutum studeas restaurare: in quo digne et laudabiliter Deo in perpetuum seruiatur; et tui memoria cum precibus ad Dominum fusis, cum benediccionibus semper recenter recolatur." Et conuersus ad reginam, ait, "Et tu, filia, quamuis mulier, non tamen muliebriter, ad hoc regem accendas et admoneas diligenter, filiosque tuos instrui facias, ut[393] et Dominum Deum, qui eos uite reparauit, studeant granter honorare, et eidem fideliter famulando fundandi cenobii possessiones ampliare, et tueri libertates."

Descensus ad secundum Offam.

Sanctus autem ad cellam reuersus, post paucum temporis ab incolatu huius mundi migrauit ad Dominum, mercedem eternam pro labore temporali recepturus. Rex autem, cito monita ipsius salubria dans obliuioni et incurie, ex tunc ocio ac paci uacauit: prolemque copiosam utriusque sexus expectabilis pulchritudinis procreauit. Unde semen regium a latere et descensu felix suscepit incrementum. Qui completo uite sue tempore, post etatem bonam quieuit in pace, et regaliter sepultus, appositus est ad patres suos; in eo multum redarguendus, quod cenobium[394] uotiuo affectu repromissum, thesauris parcendo non construxit. Post uictorias enim a Domino[395] sibi collatas, amplexibus et ignauie necnon auaricie plus equo indulsit. Prosperitas enim secularis, animos, licet Fol. 9 b uir|iles, solet frequenter effeminare. Ueruntamen hoc onus humeris filii sui moriturus apposuit: qui cum deuota assercione, illud sibi suscepit. Sed nec ipse Deo auerso pollicita, prout patri suo promiserat, compleuit; set filio suo huius uoti obligacionem in fine uite sue dereliquit. Et sic memorati uoti uinculum, sine efficacia complementi de patre in filium descendens, usque ad tempora Pineredi filii Tuinfreth suspendebatur. Quibus pro pena negligentie, tale euenit infortunium, ut omnes principes, quos Offa magnificus edomuerat, a subieccione ipsius Offe et posteritatis sue procaciter recesserunt, et ipsum morientem despexerunt. Quia ut predictum est, ad mortem uergens, deliciis et senii ualitudine marcuit eneruatus.

De ortu secundi Offe.

Natus est igitur memorato Tuinfred[o][396] (et qui de stemate regum fuit) filius, videlicet Pineredus, usque ad annos adolescentie inutilis, poplitibus contractis, qui nec oculorum uel aurium plene officio naturali fungeretur. Unde patri suo Tuinfredo et matri sue Marcelline, oneri fuit non honori, confusioni et non exultacioni. Et licet unicus eis fuisset, mallent prole caruisse, quam talem habuisse. Ueruntamen memorie reducentes euentum Offe magni, qui in tenera etate penitus erat inutilis, et postea, Deo propicio, penitus sibi restitutus, mirabili strenuitate omnes suos edomuit aduersarios, et bello prepotens, gloriose multociens de magnis hostibus triumphauit: spem conceperunt, quod eodem medico medente (Christo uidelicet, qui eciam mortuos suscitat, propiciatus) posset similiter uisitari et sibi restitui. Pater igitur eius et mater ipsum puerum inito salubri consilio, in templo presentarunt Domino, votiua deuocione firmiter promittentes: "Ut si ipsum Deus restauraret, quod parentes eius negligenter omiserunt, ipse puer cum se facultas offerret fideliter adimpleret": videlicet de cenobio[397], cuius mencio prelibata est, honorifice construendo: uel de diruto restaurando. Et cum hec tam puer quam pater et mater deuotissime postularent, exaudita est oratio eorum a Deo, qui se nunquam difficilem exhibet precibus iustis supplicantium, hoc modo.

Quomodo prosperabatur.

Erat in eadem regione (Merciorum uidelicet) quidam tirannus, pocius destruens et dissipans regni nobilitatem, quam regens, nomine Beormredus[398]. Hic generosos, quos regius sanguis preclaros [fecerat][399], usque ad internecionem subdole persequebatur, relegauit, et occulta nece perdidit iugulandos. Sciebat enim, quod uniuersis de regno merito extitit odiosus; et ne aliquis loco ipsius subrogaretur (et presertim de sanguine regio propagatus) uehementer formidabat. Tetendit insuper laqueos Tuinfredo et uxori eius, ut ipsos de terra expelleret, uel pocius perderet trucidatos. Fol. 10 *a* | Puerum autem Pinefredum[400] spreuit, nec ipsum querere ad perdendum dignabatur; reputans eum inutilem et ualitudinarium. Fugientes igitur memoratus Tuinfredus et uxor eius et familia a facie persequentis, sese in locis tucioribus receperunt, ne generali calumpnie inuoluerentur. Quod comperiens Pinefredus adolescens, quasi a graui sompno expergefactus, erexit se: et compagibus neruorum laxatis, et miraculose protensis, sese de longa desidia redarguens, fecit alices, brachia, crura, pedes, extendendo. Et aliquociens oscitans, cum loqui conaretur, solutum est uinculum lingue eius, et loquebatur recte, uerba proferens ore facundo prompcius articulata. Quid plura? de contracto, muto, et ceco, fit elegans corpore, eloquens sermone, acie perspicax oculorum. Qui tempore modico in tantam floruit ac uiguit strenuitatem, ut nullus in regno Merciorum, ipsi in moribus et probitate multiplici ualuit comparari, unde ipsi Mercii, secundum Offam, et non Pinefredum, iam nominantes (quia a Deo respectus et electus fuisset, eodem modo quo et rex Offa filius regis Warmundi) ceperunt ipsi quasi Domino uniuersaliter adherere; ipsumque iam factum militem, contra regem Beormredum et eius insidias, potenter ac prudenter protegere, dantes ei dextras, et fedus cum ipso, prestitis iuramentis, ineuntes. Quod audiens Beormredus, doluit, et dolens timuit sibi vehementer. Penituitque eum amarissime, ipsum Pinefredum[400] (qui iam Offa nominabatur) cum ceteris fraudulenter non interemisse....

Fol. 11 *a*

Qualiter Offa rex uxorem duxerit.

Diebus itaque sub eisdem, regnante in Francia Karolo rege magno ac uictoriosissimo, quedam puella, facie uenusta, sed mente nimis inhonesta, ipsi regi consanguinea, pro quodam quod patrauerat crimine flagiciosissimo, addicta est iudicialiter morti ignominiose; uerum, ob regie dignitatis reuerentiam, igni uel ferro tradenda non iudicatur, sed in nauicula armamentis carente, apposito uictu tenui, uentis et mari, eorumque ambiguis casibus exponitur condempnata. Que diu uariis[401] procellis exagitata, tandem fortuna trahente, litori Britonum est appulsa, et cum in terra subiecta potestati regis Offe memorata cimba applicuisset, conspectui regis protinus presentatur. Interogata autem quenam esset, respondens, patria lingua affirmauit, se Karolo regi Francorum fuisse consanguinitate propinquam, Dridamque nominatam, sed per tirannidem Fol. 11 b | quorundam ignobilium (quorum nuptias ne degeneraret, spreuit) tali fuisse discrimini adiudicatam, abortisque lacrimis addidit dicens, "Deus autem qui innocentes a laqueis insidiantium liberat, me captiuam ad alas tue protecionis, o regum serenissime, feliciter transmisit, vt meum infortunium, in auspicium fortunatum transmutetur, et beatior in exilio quam in natali patria, ab omni predicer posteritate."

Rex autem uerborum suorum ornatum et eloquentiam, et corporis puellaris cultum et elegantiam considerans[402], motus pietate, precepit ut ad comitissam Marcellin[am][403] matrem suam tucius duceretur alenda, ac mitius sub tam honeste matrone custodia, donec regium mandatum audiret, confouenda. Puelle igitur infra paucos dies, macie et pallore per alimenta depulsis, rediit decor pristinus, ita ut mulierum pulcherima censeretur. Sed cito in uerba iactantie et elacionis (secundum patrie sue consuetudinem) prorumpens, domine sue comitisse, que materno affectu eam dulciter educauerat, molesta nimis fuit, ipsam procaciter contempnendo. Sed comitissa, pro amore filii sui regis, omnia pacienter tolerauit: licet et ipsa dicta puella, inter comitem et comitissam uerba discordie seminasset. Una igitur dierum, cum rex ipsam causa uisitacionis adiens, uerbis consolatoriis alloqueretur, incidit in retia amoris illius; erat enim iam species illius concupiscibilis. Clandestino igitur ac repentino matrimonio ipsam sibi, inconsultis patre et matre, necnon et magnatibus suis uniuersis, copulauit. Unde uterque parentum, dolore ac tedio in etate senili contabescens, dies uite abreuiando, sue mortis horam lugubriter anticiparunt; sciebant enim ipsam mulierculam fuisse et regalibus amplexibus prorsus indignam; perpendebantque iamiam ueracissime, non sine causa exilio lacrimabili, ipsam, ut predictum est, fuisse conde[m]pnatam. Cum autem annos longeue senectutis vixisset[404] comes Tuinfredus, et pre senectute caligassent oculi eius, data filio suo regi benedicione, nature debita persoluit; cuius corpus magnifice, prout decuit, tradidit sepulture. Anno quoque sub eodem uxor eius comitissa Marcellina, mater uidelicet regis, valedicens filio, ab huius incolatu secculi feliciter transmigrauit....

Fol. 19*a*

De s*anct*o Ælberto[405] cui te*r*cia filia regis Offe t*ra*de*n*da fuit nuptui.

Erat quoq*ue* quida*m* iuuenis, cui rex Offa regnu*m* Orientalium Anglo*rum*, q*uo*d eu*m* iure sanguinis *con*ti*n*gebat, co*n*cesserat, no*min*e Ælbertus. De cui*us* virtutibus[406] q*ui*da*m* ue*r*sificator, solitus regu*m* laudes *et* gesta describe*re*, elegant*er* ait;

Ælbe*r*tus iuuenis fuerat rex, fortis ad arma,
Pace pius, pulch*er* corpore, me*n*te sagax.

Cu*m*q*ue* Hu*m*be*r*tu*s* Archiep*iscopus* Lichefeld*en*sis, *et* Vnwona Ep*iscopus* Legrecestre*n*sis, uiri sanc*ti et* discreti, et de nobili stirpe Me*r*cio*rum* oriundi, speciales essent regis *con*siliarii, *et* semp*er* q*ue* honesta era*nt et* iusta atq*ue* utilia, regi Offe suggessissent, i*n*uidebat eis regina uxor Offe, q*ue* p*ri*us Drida, postea ue*ro* Quendrida, id est regina Drida, q*ui*a regi ex insp*er*ato nupsit, est app*e*llata: sicut i*n* p*re*cedentibu*s* pleni*us* enarrat*ur*. Mulier auara et subdola, supe*r*biens, eo q*uo*d ex stirpe Karoli origine*m* duxerat, et i*n*exorabili odio uiros memoratos pe*r*seq*ue*batur, tende*n*s eis muscipulas muliebres. Porro cu*m* ip*s*i reges sup*ra*di*c*tos regi Offe in sp*irit*u consilii salubrit*er* re*con*ciliassent, *et* ut eide*m* regi fede*re* ma*tr*imoniali speciali*us* co*n*iungerentur, diligent*er et* efficacit*er* p*ro*curassent, ip*s*a mulier fa*c*ta eo*rum* nitebat*ur* i*n* irritu*m* reuocare, n*e*c pot*er*at, quib*us* acriter inuidebat. Ip*s*as eni*m* puellas filias suas, ultramarinis, alienigenis, in regis supplantac*i*one*m* et regni Me*r*cio*rum* pe*r*niciem, credidit t*ra*didisse marita*n*das. Cui*us* rei p*re*scii d*ic*ti Ep*iscop*i, muliebre co*n*silium prudencie repagulis impediebant. Uerum et adhuc te*r*cia filia regis Offe i*n* thalamo regine remansit maritanda, Ælfleda no*min*e. Procurantibus *igitur* sup*ra*di*c*t*i*s ep*iscop*is, inclinatu*m* est[407] cor regis ad co*n*sensum, lic*et con*tradice*r*et regina, ut e*t*[408] h*e*c regi Ælberto nuptui trade*r*etu*r*: ut *et* sic speciali*us* regi O*ffe* teneretur i*n* fidelitate dilec*i*onis obligatus. Uocat*us igitur* rex Ælbertu*s*, a rege O*ffa*, ut filiam sua*m* desponsaret, affuit festiu*us* Fol. 19*b* | et gaudens, ob honorem sibi a tanto rege oblatum. Cui amicabiliter rex occurrens aduentanti, recepit ip*s*um in osculo *et* pate*r*no amplexu, dicens: "Prospere ueneris fili *et* gen*er*, ex ho*c*, iuuenis amantissime, te in filiu*m* adopto specialem." S*ed* h*e*c postq*ua*m efferate regine plenius i*n*notuer*it*[409], plus accensa est liuore ac furore, dole*n*s eu*m* pietatis i*n* manu[410] regis *et* suo*rum* fidelium prosperari. Vide*n*sque sue neq*ui*cie argumenta minime p*re*ualere, n*e*c hanc salte*m* te*r*ciam filiam sua*m*, ad uolu*n*tatem suam alic*ui* t*ra*nsmarino amico suo, i*n* regni subue*r*sione*m* (q*uo*d ce*r*tissime sperauerat) dare nuptui, cu*m* n*on* p*re*ualuisset i*n* d*i*ctos ep*iscop*os h*uius* rei auctores eminu*s* malignari, i*n* Ælbertu*m* regem uiru*s* sue malicie truculent*er* euomuit, hoc m*od*o.

Fraus muliebr*is* c*ru*delissima.

Rex huius rei ignarus tantam latitasse fraudem non credebat, immo pocius credebat hec ipsi omnia placitura. Cum igitur rex piissimus ipsam super premissis[411] secrecius conueniret, consilium querens qualiter et quando forent complenda, hec respondit: "Ecce tradidit Deus hodie inimicum tuum, tibi caute, si sapis, trucidandum, qui sub specie superficiali, uenenum prodicionis in te et regnum tuum exercende, nequiter, ut fertur, occultauit. Et te cupit iam senescentem, cum sit iuuenis et elegans, de regno supplantando precipitare; et posterum suorum, immo et multorum, ut iactitat, quos regnis et possessionibus uiolenter et iniuste spoliasti, iniurias uindicare. In cuius rei fidem, michi a meis amicis significatum est, quod regis Karoli multis muneribus et nunciis ocultis intermeantibus, implorat ad hoc patrocinium: se spondens ei fore tributarium. Illo igitur, dum se tibi fortuna prebet fauorabilem, extincto latenter, regnum eius in ius tuum et successorum tuorum transeat in eternum."

Cui rex mente nimium perturbatus, et de uerbis quibus credidit inesse ueraciter falsitatem et fraudem, cum indignacione ipsam increpando, respondit: "Quasi una de stultis mulieribus locuta es! Absit a me, absit, tam detestabile factum! Quo perpetrato, mihi meisque successoribus foret obprobrium sempiternum, et peccatum in genus meum cum graui uindicta diucius propagabile." Et hiis dictis, rex iratus ab ea recessit; detestans tantos ac tales occultos laqueos in muliere latitasse.

Interea mentis perturbacione paulatim deposita, et hiis ciuiliter dissimulatis, reges consederunt ad mensam pransuri: ubi regalibus esculentis et poculentis refecti, in timpanis, citharis, et choris, diem totum in ingenti gaudio expleuerunt. Sed regina malefica, interim a ferali proposito non recedens, iussit in dolo thalamum more regio pallis sericis et auleis sollempniter adornari, in quo rex Ælbertus nocturnum caperet sompnum; iuxta stratum quoque regium sedile preparari fecit, cultu nobilissimo extructum, et cortinis undique redimitum. Sub quo eciam fossam preparari fecit profundam, Fol. 20a | ut nephandum propositum perduceret ad effectum.

De martirio Sancti Ælberti, regis innocentissimi.

Regina uero uultu sereno conceptum scelus pallians, intrauit in palatium, ut tam regem Offanum quam regem Ælbertum exhilararet. Et inter iocandum, conuersa ad Ælbertum, nihil sinistri[412] suspicantem, ait, "Fili, ueni uisendi causa puellam tibi nuptu copulandam, te in thalamo meo sicienter expectantem, ut sermonibus gratissimis amores subarres profuturos." Surgens igitur rex Ælbertus, secutus est reginam in thalamum ingredientem: rege Offano remanente, qui nil mali formidabat. Ingresso igitur rege Ælberto cum regina, exclusi sunt omnes qui eundem e uestigio sequebantur sui commilitones. Et cum puellam expectasset, ait regina: "Sede fili dum ueniat aduocata."

Et cum in memorato sedili residisset, cum ipsa sella in fosse corruit profunditatem. In qua, subito a lictoribus quos regina non procul absconderat, rex innocens suffocatus expirauit. Nam ilico cum corruisset, proiecerunt super eum regina et sui complices nephandissimi puluinaria cum uestibus et cortinis, ne clamans ab aliquibus audiretur. Et sic elegantissimus iuuenis rex et martir Ælbertus, innocenter et sine noxa extinctus, accepit coronam uite, [quam][413] ad instar Johannis Baptiste mulieris laqueis irretitus, meruit optinere.

Puella uero regis filia Ælfleda uirguncula uenustissima, cum hec audisset, non tantum matris detestata facinora, sed tocius seculi pompam relinquens, habitum suscepit religionis, ut uirgo martiris uestigia sequeretur. [P]orro[414] ad augmentum[415] muliebris tirannidis[416], decollatum est corpusculum exanime quia adhuc palpitans uidebatur. Clam igitur delatum est corpus cum capite, usque ad partes remociores ad occultandum sub profundo terre, et dum spiculator cruentus ista ferret, caput obiter amissum est feliciter: nox enim erat, et festinabat lictor, et aperto ore sacci, caput cecidit euolutum, ignorante hoc portitore. Corpus autem ab ipso carnifice sine aliquo teste conscio ignobiliter est humatum. Contigit autem, Deo sic disponente, ut quidam cecus eadem via graderetur, baculo semitam pretemptante. Habens autem caput memoratum pro pedum offendiculo, mirabatur quidnam esset: erat enim pes eius irretitus in cincinnis capitis flauis et prolixis. Et palpans cercius cognouit[417] esse caput hominis decollati. Et datum est ei in spiritu intelligere, quod alicuius sancti caput esset, ac iuuenis. Et cum maduissent manus eius sanguine, apposuit et sanguinem faciei sue: et loco ubi quandoque oculi eius extiterant, et ilico restitutus est ei uisus; et quod habuerat pro pedum offendiculo, factum est ei felix luminis restitucio. Sed et in eodem loco quo caput sanctum iacuerat, fons erupit lucidissimus. Quod cum celebriter[418] fuerat diuulgatum, compertum est hoc fuisse caput sancti adolescentis Ælberti, quem regina in thalamo nequiter fecit sugillari ac decollari. Corpus autem ubinam locorum occultatum fuerat, penitus ignoratur. Hoc cum constaret Humberto Archiepiscopo, facta capside ex auro et argento, illud iussit in tesauro recondi precioso in Ecclesia Herefordensi.

Drida (Thryth) entraps Albertus (Æthelberht) of East Anglia, and causes
him to be slain
From MS Cotton Nero D. I, fol. 19 b.

hraþe seoþðan wæs
æfter mund-ȝripe mēce ȝepinȝed.
(*Beowulf*, ll. 1937-8.)

De predicti facinoris ulcione.

Cuius tandem detestabilis sceleris a regina perpetrati, ad commilitonum beati
regis et Martiris aures cum[419] peruenisset, fama celerius ante lucem aurore diei
sequentis clanculo recesserunt, ne de ipsis simile fieret iudicium metuentes.
Unde dolens regina, in thalamo ficta infirmitate decubans, quasi uulpecula
latitabat.

Rex uero Offa cum de commisso facinore certitudinem comperisset, sese
lugens, in cenaculo interiori recludens, pe[r][420] tres dies cibum penitus non
gustauit, animam suam lacrimis, lamentacionibus, et ieiunio uehementer
affligens. Et execrans mulieris impietatem, eam iussit omnibus uite sue diebus
inclusam in loco remotam secreciori peccata sua deplorare, si forte sibi celitus

collata gr*aci*a, penite*n*do tanti co*m*missi facinoris maculam posset abolere. Rex au*tem* ip*s*am postea ut sociam late*r*is in lecto suo dormire quasi suspecta*m* no*n* pe*r*misit[421].

De morte illi*us* facinorose regine.

In loco igitur sibi d*e*putato, co*m*morante regina annis aliq*u*ot, insidiis latronu*m* preuenta, auro *et* argento quo multu*m* habundabat spoliata[422], in puteo suo prop*r*io p*r*ecipitata, spiritu*m* exalauit; iusto d*e*i iudic*i*o sic *con*de*m*pnata, ut sicut regem Ælbe*r*tu*m* innocente*m* in foueam fecit p*r*ecipitari, *et* p*r*ecipitatum suffocari, sic i*n* putei profunditate s*u*bme*r*sa, uita*m* mise*r*am te*r*minaret.

O. *WIDSITH*, ll. 18, 24-49

18. Ætla, wēold Hūnum, Eormanrīc ȝotum,
   *   *   *   *   *   *

Þēodrīc wēold Froncum, þyle Rondinȝu*m*,
25. Breoca Brondinȝu*m*, Billinȝ Wernum.
Ōswine wēold Ēowum *ond* Ȳtum ȝefwulf,

Fin Folcwaldinȝ Frēsna cynne.
Siȝehere lenȝest Sǣ-Denum wēold,
Hnæf Hōcinȝum, Helm Wulfinȝu*m*,
30. Wald Wōinȝum, Wōd Þyrinȝu*m*,
Sǣferð Sycȝum, Swēom Onȝendþēow,
Sceafthere Ymbrum, Scēafa Lonȝ-Beardu*m*,
Hūn Hætwerum, *ond* Holen Wrosnum.
Hrinȝweald wæs hāten Herefarena cyning.
35. Offa wēold Ongle, Alewīh Denu*m*:
sē wæs þāra manna mōdȝast ealra;
nōhwæþre hē ofer Offan eorlscype fremede,
ac Offa ȝeslōȝ ǣrest monna
cniht wesende cynerīca mǣst;
40. nǣniȝ efen-eald him eorlscipe māran
on ōrette āne sweorde:
merce ȝemǣrde wið Myrȝinȝu*m*
bī Fīfeldore; hēoldon forð siþþan
Enȝle *ond* Swǣfe, swā hit Offa ȝeslōȝ.

45. Hrōþwulf *ond* Hrōðᵹār hēoldon lenᵹest
sibbe ætsomne suhtorfædran,
siþþan hȳ forwrǣcon wīcinᵹa cynn
ond Inᵹeldes ord forbīᵹdan,
forhēowan æt Heorote Heaðo-Beardna þrym.

PART III

THE FIGHT AT FINNSBURG

The *Finnsburg Fragment* was discovered two centuries ago in the library of Lambeth Palace by George Hickes. It was written on a single leaf, which was transcribed and published by Hickes: but the leaf is not now to be found. This is to be regretted for reasons other than sentimental, since Hickes' transcript is far from accurate[423].

The *Fragment* begins and breaks off in the middle of a line: but possibly not much has been lost at the beginning. For the first lines of the fragment, as preserved, reveal a well-loved opening motive—the call to arms within the hall, as the watcher sees the foes approach. It was with such a call that the *Bjarkamál*, the poem on the death of Rolf Kraki, began: "a good call to work" as a fighting king-saint thought it[424]. It is with a similar summons to business that the *Finnsburg Fragment* begins. The watchman has warned the king within the hall that he sees lights approaching—so much we can gather from the two and a half words which are preserved from the watchman's speech, and from the reply made by the "war-young" king: "This is not the dawn which is rising, but dire deeds of woe; to arms, my men." And the defending warriors take their posts: at the one door Sigeferth and Eaha: at the other Ordlaf and Guthlaf, and Hengest himself[425].

Then the poet turns to the foes, as they approach for the attack. The text as reported by Hickes is difficult: but it seems that Garulf[426] is the name of the warrior about to lead the assault on the hall. Another warrior, Guthere, whether a friend, kinsman, or retainer[427] we do not know, is dissuading him, urging him not to risk so precious a life in the first brunt. But Garulf pays no heed; he challenges the champion on guard: "Who is it who holds the door?"

"Sigeferth is my name," comes the reply, "Prince I am of the Secgan: a wandering champion known far and wide: many a woe, many a hard fight have I endured: from me canst thou have what thou seekest."

So the clash of arms begins: and the first to fall is Garulf, son of Guthlaf: and many a good man round him. "The swords flashed as if all Finnsburg were afire."

Never, we are told, was there a better defence than that of the sixty champions within the hall. "Never did retainers repay the sweet mead better than his bachelors did unto Hnæf. For five days they fought, so that none of the men at arms fell: but they held the doors." After a few more lines the piece breaks off.

There are many textual difficulties here. But these, for the most part, do not affect the actual narrative, which is a story of clear and straightforward fighting. It is when we try to fit this narrative into relationship with the *Episode* in *Beowulf* that our troubles begin. Within the *Fragment* itself one difficulty only need at present be mentioned. Guthlaf is one of the champions defending the hall. Yet the leader of the assault, Garulf, is spoken of as Guthlaf's son. Of course it is possible that we have here a tragic incident parallel to the story of Hildebrand and Hadubrand: father and son may have been separated through earlier misadventures, and now find themselves engaged on opposite sides. This would harmonize with the atmosphere of the *Finnsburg* story, which is one of slaughter breaking out among men near of kin, so that afterwards an uncle and a nephew are burnt on the same pyre. And it has been noted[428] that Garulf rushes to the attack only after he has asked "Who holds the door?" and has learnt that it is Sigeferth: Guthlaf had gone to the opposite door. Can Garulf's question mean that he knows his father Guthlaf to be inside the hall, and wishes to avoid conflict with him? Possibly; but I do not think we can argue much from this double appearance of the name Guthlaf. It is possible that the occurrence of Guthlaf as Garulf's father is simply a scribal error. For, puzzling as the tradition of *Finnsburg* everywhere is, it is peculiarly puzzling in its proper names, which are mostly given in forms that seem to have undergone some alteration. And even if *Gūðlāfes sunu* be correctly written, it is possible that the Guthlaf who is father of Garulf is not to be identified with the Guthlaf whom Garulf is besieging within the hall[429].

One or other of these rather unsatisfactory solutions must unfortunately be accepted. For no theory is possible which will save us from admitting that, according to the received text, Guthlaf is fighting on the one side, and a "son of Guthlaf" on the other.

Section II. The Episode in *Beowulf*

Further details of the story we get in the *Episode* of *Finnsburg*, as recorded in *Beowulf* (ll. 1068-1159).

Beowulf is being entertained in the court of the king of the Danes, and the king's harper tells the tale of Hengest and Finn. Only the main events are enumerated. There are none of the dramatic speeches which we find in the *Fragment*. It is evident that the tale has been reduced in scope, in order that it may be fitted into its place as an episode in the longer epic.

The tone, too, is quite different. Whereas the *Fragment* is inspired by the lust and joy of battle, the theme of the *Episode*, as told in *Beowulf*, is rather the pity of it all; the legacy of mourning and vengeance which is left to the survivors:

For never can true reconcilement grow
Where wounds of deadly hate have struck so deep.

It is on this note that the *Episode* in *Beowulf* begins: with the tragic figure of Hildeburh. Hildeburh is closely related to both contending parties. She is sister to Hnæf, prince of the "Half-Danes," and she is wedded to Finn, king of the Frisians. Whatever may be obscure in the story, it is clear that a fight has taken place between the men of Hnæf and those of Finn, and that Hnæf has been slain: probably by Finn directly, though perhaps by his followers[430]. A son of Finn has also fallen.

With regard to the peoples concerned there are difficulties. Finn's Frisians are presumably the main Frisian race, dwelling in and around the district still known as Friesland; for in the Catalogue of Kings in *Widsith* it is said that "Finn Folcwalding ruled the kin of the Frisians[431]." Hnæf and his people are called Half-Danes, Danes and Scyldings; Hnæf is therefore presumably related to the Danish royal house. But, in no account which has come down to us of that house, are Hnæf or his father Hoc ever mentioned as kings or princes of Denmark, and their connection with the family of Hrothgar, the great house of Scyldings who ruled Denmark from the capital of Leire, remains obscure. In *Widsith*, the people ruled over by Hnæf are called "children of Hoc" (*Hócingum*), and are mentioned immediately after the "Sea-Danes[432]."

Then there is a mysterious people called the *Eotens*, upon whom is placed the blame of the struggle: "Verily Hildeburh had little reason to praise the good faith of the Eotens." This is the typical understatement of Old English rhetoric: it can only point to deliberate treachery on the part of the Eotens. Our interpretation of the poem will therefore hinge largely upon our interpretation of this name. There have been two views as to the Eotens. The one view holds them to be Hnæf's Danes, and consequently places on Hnæf the responsibility for the aggression. This theory is, I think, quite wrong, and has been the cause of much confusion: but it has been held by scholars of great weight[433]. The other view regards the Eotens as subjects of Finn and foes of Hnæf. This view has been more generally held, and it is, as I shall try to show, only along these lines that a satisfactory solution can be found.

The poet continues of the woes of Hildeburh. "Guiltless, she lost at the war those whom she loved, child and brother. They fell as was fated, wounded by the spear, and a sad lady was she. Not for naught did the daughter of Hoc [i.e. Hildeburh] bewail her fate when morning came, when under the sky she could behold the murderous bale of her kinsfolk...."

Then the poet turns to the figure of Finn, king of the Frisians. His cause for grief is as deep as that of Hildeburh. For he has lost that body of retainers which to a Germanic chief, even as to King Arthur, was dearer than a wife[434]. "War swept away all the retainers of Finn, except some few."

What follows is obscure, but as to the general drift there is no doubt. After the death of their king Hnæf, the besieged Danes are led by Hengest. Hengest must be Hnæf's retainer, for he is expressly so called (*þēodnes þegn*) "the king's thegn." So able is the defence of Hengest, and so heavy the loss among Finn's men, that Finn has to come to terms. Peace is made between Finn and Hengest, and the terms are given fully in the *Episode*. Unfortunately, owing to the confusion of pronouns, we soon lose our way amidst the clauses of this treaty, and it becomes exceedingly difficult to say who are the people who are alluded to as "they." This is peculiarly unlucky because here again the critical word *Eotena* occurs, but amid such a tangle of "thems" and "theys" that it is not easy to tell from this passage to which side the Eotens belong[435].

But one thing in the treaty is indisputable. In the midst of these complicated clauses, it is said of the Danes, the retainers of Hnæf, that they are not to be taunted with a certain fact: or perhaps it may be that they are not, when speaking amongst themselves, to remind each other of a certain fact. However that may be, what *is* clear is the *fact*, the mention of which is barred. Nothing is to be said of it, even though "*they were following the slayer (bana) of their lord, being without a prince, since they were compelled so to do.*" Here, at least, are two lines about the interpretation of which we can be certain: and I shall therefore return to them. We must be careful, however, to remember that the word *bana*, "slayer," conveys no idea of fault or criminality. It is a quite neutral word, although it has frequently been mistranslated "murderer," and has thus helped to encourage the belief that Finn slew Hnæf by treachery. Of course it conveys no such implication: *bana* can be applied to one who slays another in self-defence: it implies neither the one thing nor the other.

Then the poet turns to the funeral of the dead champions, who are burned on one pyre by the now reconciled foes. The bodies of Hnæf and of the son (or sons)[436] of Hildeburh are placed together, uncle and nephew side by side, whilst Hildeburh stands by lamenting.

Then, we are told, the warriors, deprived of their friends, departed to Friesland, to their homes and to their high-city.

Hengest still continued to dwell for the whole of that winter with Finn, and could not return home because of the winter storms. But when spring came and the bosom of the earth became fair, there came also the question of Hengest's departure: but he thought more of vengeance than of his sea-journey: "If he might bring about that hostile meeting which he kept in his mind concerning the child (or children) of the Eotens." Here again the word *Eotena* is used ambiguously, but, I think, this time not without some indication of its meaning. It has indeed been urged that the child or children of the Eotens are Hnæf, and any other Danes who may have fallen with him, and that when it is said that Hengest keeps them in mind, it is meant that he is remembering his fallen comrades with a view to taking vengeance for them. But this would be a queer way of speaking, as Hengest and his living comrades would on this theory be also themselves children of the Eotens[437]. We should therefore need the term to be further defined: "children of the Eotens *who fell at Finnsburg.*" It seems far more likely, from the way in which the expression is used here, that the children of the Eotens are the people *upon* whom Hengest intends to take vengeance.

Then, we are further told, Hunlafing places in the bosom of Hengest a sword of which the edges were well known amongst the Eotens. Here again there has been ambiguity, dispute and doubt. Hunlafing has been even bisected into a chief "Hun," and a sword "Lafing" which "Hun" is supposed to have placed in the bosom of Hengest (or of someone else). Upon this act of "Hun" many an interpretation has been placed, and many a theory built. Fortunately it has become possible, by a series of rather extraordinary discoveries, such as we had little reason to hope for at this time of day, to put Hunlafing together again. We now know (and this I think should be regarded as outside the region of controversy) that the warrior who put the sword into Hengest's bosom *was* Hunlafing. And about Hunlafing we gather, though very little, yet enough to help us. He is apparently a Dane, the son of Hunlaf, and Hunlaf is the brother of the two champions Guthlaf and Ordlaf[438]. Now Guthlaf and Ordlaf, as we know from the *Fragment*, were in the hall together with Hengest: it was "Guthlaf, Ordlaf and Hengest himself" who undertook the defence of one of the doors against the assailants. Guthlaf and Ordlaf were apparently sons of the king of Denmark. As Scyldings they would be Hnæf's kinsmen, and accompanied him to his meeting with Finn. Hunlafing, then, is a nephew of two champions who were attacked in the hall, and it is possible, though we cannot prove this, that his father Hunlaf was himself also in the hall, and was slain in the struggle[439]. At any rate, when Hunlaf's son places a sword in the bosom of Hengest, this can only mean one thing. It means mischief. The placing of the sword, by a prince, in the bosom of another, is a symbol of war-service. It means that Hengest has accepted obligations to a Danish lord, a Scylding, a kinsman of the dead Hnæf, and consequently that he means to break the troth which he has sworn to Finn.

Further, we are told concerning the sword, that its edges were well known amongst the Eotens. At first sight this might seem, and to many has seemed, an ambiguous phrase, for a sword may be well known amongst either friends or foes. The old poets loved nothing better than to dwell upon the adornments of a sword, to say how a man, by reason of a fine sword which had been given to him, was honoured amongst his associates at table[440]. But if this had been the poet's meaning here, he would surely have dwelt, not upon the edges of the sword, but upon its gold-adorned hilt, or its jewelled pommel. When he says the *edges* of the sword were well known amongst the Eotens, this seems to convey a hostile meaning. We know that the ill-faith of the Eotens was the cause of the trouble. The phrase about the sword seems therefore to mean that Hengest used this sword in order to take vengeance on the Eotens, presumably for their treachery.

The *Eotenas*, therefore, far from being the men of Hnæf and Hengest, must have been their foes.

Then the poet goes on to tell how "Dire sword-bale came upon the valiant Finn likewise." The Danes fell upon Finn at his own home, reddened the floor of his hall with the life-blood of his men, slew him, plundered his town, and led his wife back to her own people.

Here the *Episode* ends.

Now our first task is to find what is the relation between the events told in the *Fragment* and the events told in the *Episode* in *Beowulf*. It can, I think, be shown that the events of the *Fragment* precede the events of the *Episode* in *Beowulf*; that is to say that the fight in the hall, of which we are told in the *Fragment*, is the same fight which has taken place before the *Episode* in *Beowulf* begins, the fight which has resulted in the slaughter over which Hildeburh laments, and which necessitates the great funeral described in the first part of the *Episode* (ll. 1108-24).

How necessary it is to place the *Fragment* here, before the beginning of the *Episode*, will be best seen, I think, if we examine the theory which has tried to place it elsewhere.

This is the theory, worked out elaborately and ingeniously by Möller[441], a theory which has had considerable vogue, and many of the assumptions of which have been widely accepted. According to Möller and his followers, the story ran something like this:

"Finn, king of the Frisians, had carried off Hildeburh, daughter of Hoc (1076), probably with her consent. Her father Hoc seems to have pursued the fugitives, and to have been slain in the fight which ensued on his overtaking them. After the lapse of some twenty years, the brothers Hnæf and Hengest, Hoc's sons, were old enough to undertake the duty of avenging their father's death. They make an inroad into Finn's country."

Up to this, all is Möller's hypothesis, unsupported by any evidence, either in the *Fragment* or the *Episode*. It is based, so far as it has any real foundation, upon a mythical interpretation of Finn, and upon parallels with the Hild-story, the Gudrun-story, and a North Frisian folk-tale[442]. Some of the parallels are striking, but they are not sufficient to justify Möller's reconstruction. The authenticity of large portions of the folk-tale is open to doubt[443]: and these portions are vital to any parallel with the story of *Finnsburg*; whilst we have no right to read into the Finn story details from the Hild or Gudrun stories, unless we can show that they are really versions of the same tale: and this cannot be shown. Möller's suppositions as to the events before the *Episode* in *Beowulf* opens, must therefore be dismissed. Möller's reconstruction then gets into relation with the real story, as narrated in *Beowulf*:

"A battle takes place in which many warriors, among them Hnæf and a son of Finn (1074, 1079, 1115), are killed. Peace is therefore solemnly concluded, and the slain warriors are burnt (1068-1124).

As the year is too far advanced for Hengest to return home (ll. 1130 ff.), he and those of his men who survive remain for the winter in the Frisian country with Finn. But Hengest's thoughts dwell constantly on the death of his brother Hnæf, and he would gladly welcome any excuse to break the peace which has been sworn by both parties. His ill-concealed desire for revenge is noticed by the Frisians, who anticipate it by themselves taking the initiative and attacking Hengest and his men whilst they are sleeping in the hall. *This is the night attack described in the Fragment.* It would seem that after a brave and desperate resistance Hengest himself falls in this fight[444], but two of his retainers, Guthlaf and Oslaf[444], succeed in cutting their way through their enemies and in escaping to their own land. They return with fresh troops, attack and slay Finn, and carry his queen Hildeburh off with them (1125-1159)[445]."

Now the difficulties of this theory will, I think, be found to be insuperable. Let us look at some of them.

Möller's view rests upon his interpretation of the Eotens as the men of Hnæf[446]. Since the Eotens are the aggressors, he *has* consequently to invent the opening, which makes Hnæf and Hengest the invaders of Finn's country: and he *has* therefore to relegate the *Fragment* (in which Hnæf's men are clearly not the attacking party but the attacked) to a later stage in the story. But we have already seen that this interpretation of the Eotens as the men of Hnæf is not the natural one.

Further, the assumption that Hnæf and Hengest are brothers, though still frequently met with[447], is surely not justifiable. There is nothing which demands any such relationship, and there is much which definitely excludes it. *After Hnæf's death*, Hengest is described as the thegn of Hnæf: an expression without parallel or explanation, if he was really his brother and successor. Again, we are expressly told in the *Episode* that the Danish retainers make terms with Finn, *the slayer of their lord, being without a prince.* How could this be said, if Hengest was now their lord and prince? These lines are, as we have seen, one of the few clear and indisputable things in the poem. An interpretation which contradicts them flatly, by making Hengest the lord of the Danish retainers, seems self-condemned.

Again, in *Beowulf*, the poet dwells upon the blameless sorrows of Hildeburh. We gather that she wakes up in the morning to find that the kinsfolk whom she loves have, during the night, come to blows. "Innocent, she lost son and brother[448]—a sad lady she." Are such expressions natural, if Hildeburh had eloped with Finn, and her father had in consequence been slain by him some twenty years before? If she has taken that calmly, and continued to live happily with Finn, would her equanimity be so seriously disturbed by the slaughter of a brother in addition?

But these difficulties are nothing compared to the further difficulties which Möller's adherents have to face when they proceed to find a place for the night attack as told in the *Fragment*, in the middle of the *Episode* in *Beowulf*, i.e. between lines 1145 and 1146. In the first place we have no right to postulate that such important events could have been passed over in silence in the summary of the story as given in *Beowulf*. For Möller has to assume that after the reconciliation between Hengest and Finn, Finn broke his pledges, attacked Hengest by night, slew most of the men who were with him, including perhaps Hengest himself; and that the *Beowulf*-poet nevertheless omitted all reference to these events, though they occur in the midst of the story, and are essential to an understanding of it.

But even apart from this initial difficulty, we find that by no process of explaining *can* we make the night attack narrated in the *Fragment* fit in at the point where Möller places it. In the night attack the men are called to arms by a "war-young king." This "war-young king" cannot be, as Möller supposes, Hengest, for the simple reason that Hengest, as I have tried to show above, far from being the brother of Hnæf, and his successor as king, is his servant and thegn. The king can only be Hnæf. But Hnæf has already been slain before the *Episode* begins: and this makes it impossible to place the *Fragment* (in which Hnæf appears) in the middle of the *Episode*. Further, it is said in the *Fragment* that never did retainers repay a lord better than did his men repay Hnæf. Now these words would only be possible if the retainers were fighting for their lord; that is, either defending him alive or avenging him dead. But Möller's theory assumes that we are dealing with a period when the retainers have definitely left the service of their lord Hnæf, after his death, and have entered the service of his slayer, Finn. They have thus dissolved all bonds with their former lord: they have taken Finn's money and become *his* men. If Finn then turns upon his new retainers and treacherously tries to slay them, it might be said that the retainers defended their own lives stoutly: but it would be far-fetched to say that in doing so they repaid their lord Hnæf. Their lord, according to Möller's view, is no longer Hnæf, but Finn, who is seeking their lives.

Against such difficulties as these it is impossible to make headway, and we must therefore turn to some more possible view of the situation[449].

Let us therefore examine the second theory, which is more particularly associated with the name of Bugge, though it was the current theory before his time, and has been generally accepted since.

According to this view, the *Eotenas* are the men of Finn, and since upon them is placed the blame for the trouble, it must be Finn that makes a treacherous attack upon his wife's brother Hnæf, who is his guest in Finnsburg[450]. This is the fight of which the *Fragment* gives us the beginning. Hnæf is slain, and then follow the events as narrated in the *Episode*: the treaty which Finn makes with Hengest, the leader of the survivors: and the ultimate vengeance taken upon Finn by these survivors.

Here I think we are getting nearer to facts, nearer to a view which can command general acceptance: at any rate, in so far as the fight narrated in the *Fragment* is placed before the beginning of the *Episode* in *Beowulf*. Positive evidence that this is the right place for the *Fragment* is scanty, yet not altogether lacking. After all, the fight in the *Fragment* is a night attack, and the fight which precedes the *Episode* in *Beowulf*, as I have tried to show, is a night attack[451]. But our reason for putting the *Fragment* before the commencement of the *Episode* is mainly negative: it lies in the insuperable difficulties which meet us when we try to place it anywhere else.

But, it will be objected, there are difficulties also in placing the *Fragment* before the *Episode*. Perhaps: but I do not think these difficulties will be found to survive examination.

The first objection to supposing that the *Fragment* narrates the same fight as precedes the *Episode* is, that the fight in the *Fragment* takes place at Finnsburg[452], whilst the fight which precedes the *Episode* apparently takes place away from Finn's capital: for after the fighting is over, the dead burned, and the treaty made, the warriors depart "to see Friesland, their homes, and their high-town (*hēa-burh*)[453]."

But I do not see that this involves us in any difficulty. It is surely quite reasonable that Finnsburg—Finn's castle—where the first fight takes place, is not, and was never meant to be, the same as Finn's capital, his *hēaburh*, his "own home." After all, when a king's name is given to a town, the presumption is rather that the town is *not* his capital, but some new settlement built in a newly acquired territory. *Ēadwinesburh* was not the capital of King Eadwine: it was the stronghold which he held against the Picts on the outskirts of his realm. Aosta was not the capital of Augustus, nor Fort

William of William III, nor Harounabad of Haroun al Raschid. So here: we know that the chief town of the Frisians was not Finnsburg, but Dorestad: "Dorostates of the Frisians[454]." The fight may have taken place at some outlying castle built by Finn, and named after him *Finnsburg*: then he returned, we are told, to his *hēaburh*: and it is here, *æt his sylfes hām*, "in his own home" (the poet himself seems to emphasize a distinction) that destruction in the end comes upon him. There is surely no difficulty here.

A second discrepancy has often been indicated. In the *Fragment* the fight lasts five days before any one of the defenders fall: in the *Episode* (it is argued) Hildeburh in the morning finds her brother slain[455]. Even were this so, I do not know that it need trouble us much. In a detail like this, which does not go to the heart of the story, there might easily be a discrepancy between two versions[456].

But the whole difficulty merely arises from reading more into the words of the *Episode* than the text will warrant. It is not asserted in the *Episode* that Hildeburh found her kinsfolk dead in the morning, but that in the morning she found "murderous bale amid her kinsfolk." Hildeburh woke up to find a fight in progress: how long it went on, the *Episode* does not say: but that it was prolonged we gather from ll. 1080-5: and there is no reason why the deadly strife which Hildeburh found in the morning might not have lasted five days or more, before it culminated in the death of Hnæf.

Thirdly, the commander in the *Fragment* is called a "war-young king." This, it has been said, is inapplicable to Hnæf, since he is brother of Hildeburh, who is old enough to have a son slain in the combat.

But an uncle may be very young. Beowulf speaks of his uncle Hygelac as young, even though he seems to imply that his own youth is partly past[457]. And no advantage, but the reverse, is gained, even in this point, if, following Möller's hypothesis, and assuming that the fight narrated in the *Fragment* takes place after the treaty with Finn, we make the "war-young king" Hengest. For those who, with Möller, suppose Hengest to be brother of Hnæf, will have to admit the avuncular difficulty in him also.

We may then, I think, accept as certain, that first come the events narrated in the *Fragment*, then those told in the *Episode* in *Beowulf*. But we are not out of our troubles yet. There are difficulties in Bugge's view which have still to be faced.

The cause of the struggle, according to Bugge and his adherents, is a treacherous attack made by Finn upon his brother-in-law Hnæf. According to the *Episode*, it is the Eotens who are treacherous; so Eotens must be another name for the Frisians.

The word occurs three times in the genitive, *Eotena*; once in the dative, *Eotenum*: as a common noun it means "giant," "monster": earlier in *Beowulf* it is applied to Grendel and to the other misbegotten creatures descended from Cain. But how "giant" can be applied to the Frisians, or to either of the contending parties in the Finnsburg fight, remains inexplicable[458]. *Eotena* must rather be the name of some tribe. But what tribe? The only people of whom we know, possessing a name at all like this, are the people who colonized Kent, whom Bede calls Jutes, but whose name would in Anglian be in the genitive *Ēotna*, but in the dative *Ēotum*, or perhaps occasionally *Ēotnum, Ēotenum*[459]. Now a scribe transliterating a poem from an Anglian dialect into West-Saxon should, of course, have altered these forms into the corresponding West-Saxon forms *Ȳtena* and *Ȳtum*. But nothing would have been more likely than that he would have misunderstood the tribal name as a common noun, and retained the Anglian forms (altering *eotum* or *eotnum* into *eotenum*) supposing the word to mean "giants." After all, the common noun *eotenum*, "giants," was quite as like the tribal name *Ēotum*, which the scribe presumably had before him, as was the correct West-Saxon form of that name, *Ȳtum*.

It is difficult therefore to avoid the conclusion that the "Eotens" are Jutes: and this is confirmed by three other pieces of evidence, not convincing in themselves, but helpful as subsidiary arguments[460].

(1) We should gather from *Widsith* that the Jutes were concerned in the *Finnsburg* business. For in that poem generally (though not always) tribes connected in story are grouped together; and the Jutes and Frisians are so coupled:

Ȳtum [weold] Gefwulf
Fin Folcwalding Frēsna cynne.

(2) There is another passage in *Beowulf* in which *Eotenas* is possibly used in the sense of "Jutes."

We have seen above[461] that according to a Scandinavian tradition Lotherus was exiled *in Jutiam*: and Heremod, who has been held to be the counterpart of Lotherus

mid Eotenum wearð
on fēonda geweald forð forlācen.

But the identification of Lotherus and Heremod is too hypothetical to carry the weight of much argument.

(3) Finn comes into many Old English pedigrees, which have doubtless borrowed from one another. But the earliest in which we find him, and the only one in which we find his father Folcwald, is that of the Jutish kings of Kent[462]. Here, too, the name Hengest meets us.

The view that the name "Eoten" in the *Finnsburg* story is a form of the word "Jute" is, then, one which is very difficult to reject. It is one which has in the past been held by many scholars and is, I think, held by all who have recently expressed any opinion on the subject[463]. But this renders very difficult the assumption of Bugge and his followers that the word "Eoten" is synonymous with "Frisian[464]." For Frisians were not Jutes. The tribes were closely related; but the two words were not synonymous. The very lines in *Widsith*, which couple Jutes and Frisians together, as if they were related in story, show that the names were regarded as those of distinct tribes. And this evidence from *Widsith* is very important, because the compiler of that list of names clearly knew the story of Finn and Hnæf.

But this is not the only difficulty in Bugge's interpretation of the Eotens as Frisians. The outbreak of war, we are told, is due to the treachery of the Eotens. This Bugge and his followers interpret as meaning that Finn must have treacherously attacked Hnæf. Yet the poet speaks of "the warriors of Finn when the sudden danger fell upon them": *þā hīe se fǣr begeat*. It is essential to *fǣr* that it signifies a sudden and unexpected attack[465]: and the unexpected attack must have come, not upon the assailants but upon the assailed.

Yet this difficulty, though it has been emphasized by Möller[466] and other opponents of Bugge's view, is not insuperable[467], and I hope to show below that there is no real difficulty. But it leads us to a problem not so easily surmounted. If Finn made a treacherous attack upon Hnæf, and slew him, how did it come that Hengest, and Hnæf's other men, made terms with their murderous host?

In the primitive heathen days it had been a rule that the retainer must not survive his vanquished lord[468]. The ferocity of this rule was subsequently softened, and, in point of fact, we *do* often hear, after some great leader has been slain, of his followers accepting quarter from a chivalrous foe, without being therefore regarded as having acted disgracefully[469]. But, if Finn had invited Hnæf and Hnæf's retainers to be his guests, and had fallen upon them by treachery, the action of the retainers in coming to terms with Finn, in entering his service, and stipulating how much of his pay they shall receive, would be contrary to all standards of conduct as understood in the Heroic Age, and would deprive Hnæf's men of any sympathy the audience might feel for them. But Hnæf's men are not censured: they are in fact treated most sympathetically in the *Episode*, and in the *Fragment*, at an earlier point in the story, they are enthusiastically applauded[470].

It is strange enough in any case that Hnæf's retainers should make terms with the slayer of their lord. But it is not merely strange, it is absolutely unintelligible, if we are to suppose that Finn has not merely slain Hnæf, but has lured him into his power, and then slain him while a guest.

It is to the credit of Bugge that he felt this difficulty: but his attempt to explain it is hardly satisfactory. He fell back upon a parallel between the story of the death of Rolf Kraki and the story of *Finnsburg*. We have already seen that the resemblance is very close between the *Bjarkamál*, which narrates the death of Rolf, and the opening of the *Finnsburg Fragment*. The parallel which Bugge invoked comes from the sequel to the Rolf story[471] which tells how Hiarwarus, the murderer of Rolf Kraki, astonished by the devotion of Rolf's retainers, lamented their death, and said how gladly he would have given quarter to such men, and taken them into his service. Thereupon Wiggo, the one survivor, who had previously vowed to avenge his lord, and had concealed himself with that object, came forward and offered to accept these terms. Accordingly he placed his hand upon the hilt of his new master's drawn sword, as if about to swear fealty to him: but instead of swearing, he ran him through.

"Glorious and ever memorable hero, who valiantly kept his vow," says Saxo[472]. Whether or no we share the exultation of that excellent if somewhat bloodthirsty ecclesiastic, we must admit that Wiggo's methods were sensible and practical. If, singlehanded, he was to keep his vow, and avenge his lord, he could only hope to do it by some such stratagem.

Bugge tries to explain Hengest's action on similar lines: "He does not hesitate to enter the service of Finn in order thereby to carry out his revenge[473]."

But the circumstances are entirely different. Wiggo was left alone, the only survivor of Rolf's household, to face a whole army. But Hengest is no single survivor: he and his fellows have made so good a defence that Finn cannot overcome them by conflict on the *meðel-stede*. Not only so, but, if we accept the interpretation that almost every critic and editor has put upon the passage (ll. 1184-5), Hengest's position is even stronger. Finn has lost almost all his thegns; the usual interpretation puts him at the mercy of Hengest: at best it is a draw[474]. If, then, Hengest wants vengeance upon Finn, why does he not pursue it? Instead of which, according to Bugge, he enters Finn's service in order that he may get an opportunity for revenge.

And note, that Wiggo did not swear the oath of fealty to the murderer of his master Rolf: he merely put himself in the posture to do so, and then, instead, ran the tyrant through forthwith. But Hengest *does* swear the oath, and *does not* forthwith slay the tyrant. He spends the winter with him, receives a sword from Hunlafing, after which his name does not occur again. Finn is ultimately slain, but the names which are found in that connection are those of Guthlaf and Oslaf [Ordlaf].

So Bugge's explanation comes to this: Hengest is fighting with success against Finn, but he refrains from vengeance: instead, he treacherously enters his service in order that he may take an opportunity of vengeance, which opportunity, however, it is never made clear to us that he takes.

Had Hengest been a man of that kind, he would not have been a hero of Old English heroic song.

It is one of the merits of Bugge's view—one of the proofs of its general soundness—that it admits of successive improvements at the hands of succeeding commentators. No one has done more in this way than has Prof. Ayres to clear up the story, particularly the latter part of the *Episode*. Ayres evolves unity out of what had been before "a rapid-fire of events that hit all around a central tragic situation and do not once touch it." Hengest does not, Ayres thinks, enter the service of Finn with any such well-formed plan of revenge as Bugge had attributed to him. Hengest was in a difficult situation. It is his mental conflict, "torn between his oath to Finn and his duty to the dead Hnæf," which gives unity to all that follows. It is a tragedy of Hengest, hesitating, like Shakespeare's Hamlet, over the duty of revenge. Prof. Ayres' statement here is too good to summarize; it must be quoted at length:

"How did he feel during that long, blood-stained winter? He naturally thought about home (*eard gemunde*, 1129), but there was no question of sailing then, no need yet of decision while the storm roared outside. By and by spring came round, as it has a way of doing. How did he feel then? Then, like any other Northerner, he wanted to put to sea:

fundode wrecca,
gist of geardum.

That is what he would naturally do. He would speak to Finn and be off; in the spring his business was on the sea. That is all right as to Finn, but as to the dead Hnæf it is very like running away; it is postponing vengeance sadly. Will he prove so unpregnant of his cause as that? No; though he would like to go to sea, he thought *rather* of vengeance, and staid in the hope of managing a successful surprise against Finn and his people:

hē tō gyrn-wræce
swīðor þōhte   þonne tō sǣ-lāde,
gif hē torn-gemōt   þurhtēon mihte,
þæt hē Eotena bēarn   inne gemunde.

All this says clearly that Hengest was thinking things over, whether he should or should not take vengeance upon Finn; it tells us also very clearly, with characteristic anticipation of the outcome of the story, that in the end desire for vengeance carried the day:

Swā hē ne-forwyrnde   worold-rǣdenne,

he did not *thus* prove recreant to his duty. But we have not been told the steps by which Hengest arrived at his decision. That seems to be what we should naturally want to know at this point, and that is precisely what we are about to be told. Occasions gross as earth informed against him[475]."

Then Ayres goes on to explain the "egging," through the presentation of a sword by Hunlafing. This feature of the story is now pretty generally so understood; but Ayres has an interpretation of the part played by Guthlaf and Oslaf, which is new and enlightening.

"Hengest's almost blunted purpose was not whetted by Hunlafing alone. The latter's uncles, Guðlaf and Oslaf [Ordlaf] took occasion to mention to Hengest the fierce attack (the one, presumably, in which Hnæf had fallen); cast up to him all the troubles that had befallen them ever since their disastrous sea-journey to Finnsburg; they had plenty of woes to twit him with:

siððan grimne gripe   Gūðlāf and Ōslāf
æfter sǣ-sīðe   sorge mǣndon,
ætwiton wēana dǣl.

The effect of all this on Hengest is cumulative. Where he was before in perfect balance, he is now wrought to action by the words of his followers; he can control himself no longer; the balance is destroyed. The restless spirit (Hengest's in the first instance, but it may be thought of as referring to the entire attacking party, now of one mind) could no longer restrain itself within the breast:

ne meahte wǣfre mōd
forhabban in hreðre.

Vengeance wins the day[476]."

By this interpretation Ayres has, as he claims, "sharpened some of the features" of the current interpretation of the Finn story. For, as he says, "in some respects the current version was very unsatisfactory; there seemed to be little relation between the presentation of the sword to Hengest and the spectacle of Guðlaf and Oslaf howling their complaints in the face of Finn."

That Ayres' interpretation enhances the coherency of the story is beyond dispute: that it does so at the cost of putting some strain upon the text in one or two places may perhaps be urged[477]. But that in its main lines it is correct seems to me certain: the story of Finnsburg is the tragedy of Hengest—his hesitation and his revenge. Keeping this well in view, many of the difficulties disappear.

SECTION VII. PROBLEMS STILL OUTSTANDING

Many of the difficulties disappear: but the two big ones remain. Firstly, if "Eoten" means "Jute," as it is usually agreed that it does, why should the Frisians be called Jutes, seeing that a Frisian is not a Jute? Secondly, when Hengest and the other thegns of Hnæf enter the service of the slayer of their lord, they are not blamed for so doing, but rather excused, *þā him swā gepearfod wæs*. Such a situation is unusual; but it becomes incredible if that slayer, whose service they enter, had fallen upon and slain their lord by treachery, when his guest.

It seems to me that neither of these difficulties is really inherent in the situation, but rather accidental, and owing to the way Bugge's theory, right enough in its main lines, has been presented both by Bugge and his followers. For it is not necessary to assume that Frisians *are* called *Eotenas* or Jutes. All that we are justified in deducing from the text is that Frisians and *Eotenas* are both under the command of Finn. If we suppose what the text demands, *and no more*, we are at one stroke relieved of both our difficulties. Though "Jute" can hardly have been synonymous with "Frisian," nothing is more probable, as I shall try to show[478], than that a great Frisian king should have had a tribe of Jutes subject to him, or should have had in his pay a band of Jutish mercenaries. Now if the trouble was due to these "Eotens"—and we are told that it was[479]—our second difficulty is also solved. It would be much more natural for Hengest to come to terms with Finn, albeit the *bana* of his lord, if Finn's conduct had not been stained by treachery, and if the blame for the original attack did not rest with him.

And, as I have said, there is nothing in the text which justifies us in assuming that *Eotenas* means "Frisians" and that therefore *Eotena trēowe* refers to Finn's breach of faith. It has indeed been argued that *Eotenas* and Frisians are synonymous, because in the terms of peace, whilst it is stipulated that Hengest and his comrades are to have equal control with the *Eotena bearn*, it is further stipulated that Finn is to give Hengest's men gifts equal to those which he gives to the *Frēsena cynn*[480]. Here then *Eotena bearn* and *Frēsena cynn* are certainly parallel, and are both contrasted with Hengest and his troops. But surely this in no wise proves *Eotena bearn* and *Frēsena cynn* synonymous: they may equally well be different sections of Finn's host, just as in *Brunanburh* the soldiers of Athelstan are spoken of first as *Westseaxe*, and then as *Myrce*.

Are we to argue that West-Saxons are Mercians? So in the account of Hygelac's fatal expedition[481] the opponents are called Franks, Frisians, *Húgas, Hetware*. A reader ignorant of the story might suppose these all synonymous terms for one tribe. But we know that they are not: the *Hetware* were the people immediately attacked—the Frankish overlord hastened to the rescue, and was apparently helped by the neighbouring Frisians, who although frequently at this date opposed to the Franks, would naturally make common cause against the pirate from overseas[482].

It was quite natural that the earlier students of the *Finnsburg Episode*, thinking of the two opposing forces as two homogeneous tribes, and finding mention of three tribal names, Danes, Eotens and Frisians, should have assumed that the Eotens must be exactly synonymous with *either* Danes *or* Frisians. But it is now recognized that the conditions of the time postulate not so much tribes as groups of tribes[483]. In the *Fragment* we have, on the side of the Danes, *Sigeferth*, prince of the *Secgan*. The *Secgan* are not necessarily Danes, because their lord is fighting on the Danish side. Neither need the *Eotenas* be Frisians, because they are fighting on the Frisian side.

We cannot, then, argue that two tribes are identical, because engaged in fighting a common foe: still less, because they are mentioned with a certain parallelism[484]. And anyway, it is impossible to find in the use of the expression *Eotena bearn* in l. 1088 any support for the interpretation which makes *Eotena trēowe* signify the treachery of Finn himself. For, assuredly, the proviso that Hengest and his fellows are to have half control as against the *Eotena bearn* does not mean that they are to have half control as against Finn himself. For the very next lines make it clear that they are to enter Finn's service and become his retainers. That Hengest and his men are to have equal rights with Finn's Jutish followers (*Eotena bearn*) is reasonable enough: but they obviously have not equal rights with Finn, their lord whom they are now to follow. *Eotena bearn* in l. 1088, then, does *not* include Finn: how *can* it then be used as an argument that *Eotena trēowe* must refer to *Finn's* faith and his breach of it?

Finn, then, is the *bana* of Hnæf, but there is nothing in the text which compels us to assume that he is the slayer of his guest.

The reader may regard my zeal to clear the character of Finn as excessive. But it is always worth while to understand a good old tale. And it is only when we withdraw our unjust aspersions upon Finn's good faith that the tale becomes intelligible.

This, I know, has been disputed, and by the scholars whose opinion I most respect.

The poet tells us that Finn was the *bana* of Hnæf, so, says Ayres, "it is hard to see how it helps matters[485]" to argue that Finn was not guilty of treachery. And Lawrence argues in the same way:

"How is it possible to shift the blame for the attack from Finn to the Eotenas when Finn is called the *bana* of Hnæf? It does not matter whether he killed him with his own hands or not; he is clearly held responsible; the lines tell us it was regarded as disgraceful for the Danes to have to follow him, and the revenge at the end falls heavily upon him. The insult and hurt to Danish pride would be very little lessened by the assumption that someone else started the quarrel; and for this assumption, too, the lines give no warrant[486]."

Let us take these objections in turn. I do not see how the fact that Finn is called the *bana* of Hnæf can prove *anything* as to "the blame for the attack." Of course the older editors may have thought so. Kemble translates *bana* "slaughterer," which implies brutality, and perhaps culpability. Bosworth-Toller renders *bana* "murderer," which certainly implies blame for attack. But we know that these are mere mistranslations. Nothing as to "blame for attack" is implied in the term *bana*: "*bana* 'slayer' is a perfectly neutral word, and must not be translated by 'murderer,' or any word connoting criminality. A man who slays another in self-defence, or in righteous execution of the law, is still his 'bane'[487]." Everyone admits this to be true: and yet at the same time *bana* is quoted to prove that Finn is to blame; because, for want of a better word, we half-consciously render *bana* "murderer": and "murderer" *does* imply blame. "Words," says Bacon, "as a Tartar's bow, do shoot back upon the understanding of the wisest."

Lawrence continues: "The lines tell us that it was regarded as disgraceful for the Danes to have to follow him." But surely this is saying too much. That the Frisians are not to taunt the Danes with following the slayer of their lord is only one of two possible interpretations of the ll. 1101-3. And even if we accept this interpretation, it does not follow that the Danes are regarded as having done anything with which they can be *justly* taunted. It is part of the settlement between Gunnar and Njal, that Njal's sons are not to be taunted: if a man repeats the taunts he shall fall unavenged[488]. Surely a man may be touchy about being taunted, without being regarded as having done anything disgraceful. Indeed, in our case, the poet implies that taunts would *not* be just, *þá him swá geþearfod wæs*. But, as I try to show below, no *þearf* could have excused the submission of retainers to a foe who had just slain their lord by deliberate treachery.

"The revenge at the end falls heavily upon Finn." It does; as so often happens where the feud is temporarily patched up, it breaks out again, as in the stories of Alboin, Ingeld or Bolli. But this does not prove that the person upon whom the revenge ultimately falls heavily had been a guest-slayer. The possibility of even temporary reconciliation rather implies the reverse.

"The insult and hurt to Danish pride would be very little lessened by the assumption that someone else [than Finn] started the quarrel; and for this assumption, too, the lines give no warrant." But they *do*: for they tell us that it was due to the bad faith of the Eotens. Commentators may argue, if they will, that "Eotens" means Finn. But the weight of proof lies on them, and they have not met it, or seriously attempted to meet it.

SECTION VIII. THE WEIGHT OF PROOF: THE EOTENS

Finn is surely entitled to be held innocent till he can be proved guilty. And the argument for his guilt comes to this: the trouble was due to the bad faith of the Eotens: "Eotens" means "Jutes": "Jutes" means "Frisians": "Frisians" means "Finn": therefore the trouble was due to the treachery of Finn.

Now I agree that it is probable that *Eotenas* means Jutes; and, as I have said, there is nothing improbable in a Frisian king having had a clan of Jutes, or a body of Jutish mercenaries, subject to him. But that the Frisians as a whole should be called Jutes is, *per se*, exceedingly improbable, and we have no shadow of evidence for it. Lawrence tries to justify it by the authority of Siebs:

"Siebs, perhaps the foremost authority on Frisian conditions, conjectures that ... the occupation by the Frisians of Jutish territory after the conquest of Britain assisted the confusion between the two names."

But *did* the Frisians occupy Jutish territory? When we ask what is Siebs' authority for the hypothesis that Frisians occupied Jutish territory, we find it to be this: that because in *Beowulf* "Jute" means "Frisian," some such event must have taken place to account for this nomenclature[489]. So it comes to this: the Frisians must have been called Jutes, because they occupied Jutish territory: the Frisians must have occupied Jutish territory because they are called Jutes. I do not think we could have a better example of what Prof. Tupper calls "philological legend."

Siebs rejects Bede's statement, which places the Jutes in what is now Jutland: he believes them to have been immediately adjacent to the Frisians. For this belief that the Jutes were immediate neighbours of the Frisians there is, of course, some support, though not of a very convincing kind: but the belief that the Frisians occupied the territory of these adjacent Jutes rests, so far as

I know, solely upon this identification of the *Eotenas*-Jutes with the Frisians, which it is then in turn used to prove.

But if by Jutes we understand (following Bede) a people dwelling north of the Angles, in or near the peninsula of Jutland, then it is of course true that (at a much later date) a colony of Frisians *did* occupy territory which is near Jutland, and which is sometimes included in the name "Jutland." But, as I have tried to show above, this "North Frisian" colony belongs to a period much later than that of the Finn-story: we have no reason whatever to suppose that the Frisians of the Finn story are the North Frisians of Sylt and the adjoining islands and mainland—the *Frisiones qui habitabant Juthlandie*[490].

And when we have assumed, without evidence, that, at the period with which we are dealing, Frisians had occupied Jutish territory, we are then further asked to assume that, from this settlement in Jutish territory, such Frisians came to be called Jutes. Now this is an hypothesis *per se* conceivable, but very improbable. Throughout the whole Heroic Age, for a thousand years after the time of Tacitus, Germanic tribes were moving, and occupying the territory of other people. During this period, how many instances can we find in which a tribe took the name of the people whose territory it occupied? Even where the name of the new home is adopted, the old tribal name is *not* adopted. For instance, the Bavarians occupied the territory of the Celtic Boii, but they did not call themselves Boii, but Bai(haim)varii, "the dwellers in the land of the Boii"—a very different thing. In the same way the Jutes who settled in the land of the Cantii did not call themselves *Kente*, but *Cantware*, "dwellers in Cantium." Of course, where the old name of a country survives, it does often *in the long run* come to be applied to its new inhabitants; but this takes many ages. It was not till a good thousand years after the English had conquered the land of the Britons, that Englishmen began to speak and think of themselves as "Britons." In feudal or 18th century days all the subjects of the ruler of Britain, Prussia, Austria, may come to be called British, Prussians, Austrians. But this is no argument for the period with which we are dealing. The assumption, then, that a body of Frisians, simply because they inhabited land which had once been inhabited by Jutes, should have called themselves Jutes, is so contrary to all we know of tribal nomenclature at this date, that one could only accept it if compelled by very definite evidence to do so. And of such evidence there is no scrap[491]. Neither is there a scrap of evidence for the underlying hypothesis that any Frisians *were* settled at this date in Jutish territory.

And as if this were not hypothetical enough, a further hypothesis has then to be built upon it: viz., that this name "Jutes," belonging to such of the Frisians as had settled in Jutish territory, somehow became applicable to Frisians as a whole. Now this might conceivably have happened, but only as a result of certain political events. If the Jutish Frisians had become the governing element in Frisia, it would be conceivable. But after all, we know something about Frisian history, and I do not think we are at liberty to assume any such changes as would have enabled the Frisian people, as a whole, to be called Jutes. How is it that we never get any hint anywhere of this Jutish preponderance and Jutish ascendancy?

The argument that the "treachery of the Jutes" means the treachery of Finn, King of the Frisians, has, then, no support at all.

One further argument there is, for attributing treason to Finn.

It has been urged that in other stories a husband entraps and betrays the brother of his wife. But we are not justified in reading pieces of one story into another, unless we believe the two stories to be really connected. The Signy of the *Vǫlsunga Saga* has been quoted as a parallel to Hildeburh[492]. Signy leaves the home of her father Volsung and her brother Sigmund to wed King Siggeir. Siggeir invites the kin of his wife to visit him, and then slays Volsung and all his sons, save Sigmund. But it is the difference of the story, rather than its likeness, which is striking. No hint is ever made of any possibility of reconciliation between Siggeir and the kin of the men he has slain. The feud admits of no atonement, and is continued to the utterance. Siggeir's very wife helps her brother Sigmund to his revenge.

How different from the attitude of Sigmund and Signy is the willingness of Hengest to come to terms, and the merely passive and elegiac bearing of Hildeburh! These things do not suggest that we ought to read a King Siggeir treachery into the story of Finn.

Again, the fact that Atli entices the brother of his wife into his power, has been urged as a parallel. But surely it is rather unfair to erect this into a kind of standard of conduct for the early Germanic brother-in-law, and to assume as a matter of course that, because Finn is Hnæf's brother-in-law, therefore he must have sought to betray him. The whole atmosphere of the Finn-Hnæf story, with its attempted reconciliation, is as opposed to that of the story of Atli as it is to the story of Siggeir.

The only epithet applied to Finn is *ferð-freca*, "valiant in soul." Though *freca* is not necessarily a good word, and is applied to the dragon as well as to Beowulf, yet it denotes grim, fierce, almost reckless courage. It does not suggest a traitor who invites his foes to his house, and murders them by night.

I interpret the lines, then, as meaning that the trouble arose from the Jutes, and, since the context shows that these Jutes were on Finn's side, and against the Danes, we must hold them to be a body of Jutes in the service of Finn[493].

But, as we have seen, it is objected that this interpretation of the situation, absolving Finn from any charge of treachery or aggression, does not "help matters[494]." Or, as Prof. Lawrence puts it, "the hurt to Danish pride [in entering the service of Finn] would be very little lessened by the assumption that someone else [than Finn] started the quarrel."

These objections seem to me to be contrary to the whole spirit of the old heroic literature.

I quite admit that there is a stage in primitive society when the act of slaying is everything, and the circumstances, or motives, do not count. In the Levitical Law, it is taken for granted that, if a man innocently causes the death of another, as for instance if his axe break, and the axe-head accidentally kill his comrade, then the avenger of blood will seek to slay the homicide, just as much as if he had been guilty of treacherous murder. To meet such cases the Cities of Refuge are established, where the homicide may flee till his case can be investigated; but even though found innocent, the homicide may be at once slain by the avenger, should he step outside the City of Refuge. And this "eye for eye" vengeance yields slowly: it took long to establish legally in our own country the distinction between murder and homicide.

For "The thought of man" it was held "shall not be tried: as the devil himself knoweth not the thought of man." Nevertheless, even the Germanic *wer-gild* system permits consideration of circumstances: it often happens that no *wer-gild* is to be paid because the slain man has been unjust, or the aggressor[495], or no *wer-gild* will be accepted because the slaying was under circumstances making settlement impossible.

Doubtless in Germanic barbarism there was once a stage similar to that which must have preceded the establishment of the Cities of Refuge in Israel[496]; but that stage had passed before the period with which we are dealing; in the Heroic Age the motive *did* count for a very great deal. Not but what there were still the literal people who insisted upon "an eye for an eye," without looking at circumstances; and these people often had their way; but their view is seldom the one taken by the characters with whom the poet or the saga-man sympathises. These generally hold a more moderate creed. One may almost say that the leading motive in heroic literature is precisely this difference of opinion between the people who hold that under any circumstances it is shameful to come to an agreement with the *bana* of one's lord or friend or kinsman, and the people who are willing *under certain circumstances* to come to such an agreement.

It happens not infrequently that after some battle in which a great chief has been killed, his retainers are offered quarter, and accept it; but I do not remember any instance of their doing this if, instead of an open battle, it is a case of a treacherous attack. The two most famous downfalls of Northern princes afford typical examples: after the battle of Svold, Kolbjorn Stallari accepts quarter from Eric, the chivalrous *bani* of his lord Olaf[497]; but Rolf's men refuse quarter after the treacherous murder of their lord by Hiarwarus[498].

That men, after a fair fight, could take quarter from, or give it to, those who had slain their lord or closest kinsman, is shown by abundant references in the sagas and histories. For instance, when Eric, after the fight with the Jomsvikings, offers quarter to his prisoners, that quarter is accepted, even though their leaders, their nearest kin, and their friends have been slain. The first to receive quarter is young Sigurd, whose father Bui has just been killed: yet the writer obviously does not the less sympathize with Sigurd, or with the other Jomsviking survivors, and feels the action to be generous on the part of Eric, and in no wise base on the part of the Jomsvikings[499]. But this is natural, because the Jomsvikings have just been defeated by Eric in fair fight. It would be impossible, if Eric were represented as a traitor, slaying the Jomsvikings by a treacherous attack, whilst they were his guests. Is it to be supposed that Sigurd, under such circumstances, would have taken quarter from the slayer of Bui his father?

In the *Laxdæla Saga*, Olaf the Peacock, in exacting vengeance for the slaying of his son Kjartan, shows no leniency towards the sons of Osvif, on whom the moral responsibility rests. But he accepts compensation in money from Bolli, who had been drawn into the feud against his will. Yet Bolli was the actual slayer of Kjartan, and he had taken the responsibility as such[500]. And Olaf is not held to have lowered himself by accepting a money payment as atonement from the slayer of his son—on the contrary "he was considered to have grown in reputation" from having thus spared Bolli. But after Olaf's death, the feud bursts out again, and revenge in the end falls heavily upon Bolli[501], as it does upon Finn.

On this question a fairly uniform standard of feeling will be found from the sixth century to the thirteenth. That it *does* make all the difference in composing a feud, whether the slaying from which the feud arises was treacherous or not, can be abundantly proved from many documents, from Paul the Deacon, and possibly earlier, to the Icelandic Sagas. Such composition of feuds may or may not be lasting; it may or may not expose to taunt those who make it; but the questions which arise are precisely these: Who started the quarrel? Was the slaying fair or treacherous? Upon the answer depends the possibility of atonement. There may be some insult and hurt to a man's pride in accepting atonement, even in cases where the other side has much to say for itself. But if the slaying has been fair, composition is felt to be possible, though not without danger of the feud breaking out afresh.

Prof. Lawrence has suggested that perhaps, in the original version of the *Finnsburg* story, the Danes were reduced to greater straits than is represented to be the case in the extant *Beowulf Episode*. He thinks that it is "almost incomprehensible" that Hengest should make terms with Finn, if he had really reduced Finn and his thegns to such a degree of helplessness as the words of the *Episode* state. It seems to me that the matter depends much more upon the treachery or the honesty of Finn. If Finn was guilty of treachery and slaughter of his guests, then it *is* "unintelligible" that Hengest should spare him: but if Finn was really a respectable character, then the fact that Hengest was making headway against him is rather a reason why Hengest should be moderate, than otherwise. To quote the *Laxdæla Saga* again: though Olaf the Peacock lets off Bolli, the *bani* of his son Kjartan, with a money payment, he makes it clear that he is master of the situation, before he shows this mercy. Paradoxical as it sounds, it was often easier for a man to show moderation in pursuing a blood feud, just *because* he was in a strong position. It is so again in the *Saga of Thorstein the White*. But the adversary must be one who deserves to be treated with moderation.

Of course it is quite possible that Prof. Lawrence is right, and that in some earlier and more correct version the Danes may have been represented as so outnumbered by the Frisians that they had no choice except to surrender to Finn, and enter his service, or else to be destroyed. But, whether this be so or no, all parallel incidents in the old literature show that their choice between these evil alternatives will depend upon whether Finn, the *bana* of their lord, slew that lord by deliberate and premeditated treachery whilst he was his guest, or whether he was embroiled with him through the fault of others, under circumstances which were perfectly honourable. If the latter is the case, then Hnæf's men *might* accept quarter. Their position is comparable with that of Illugi at the end of the *Grettis Saga*[502]. Illugi is a prisoner in the hands of the slayers of Grettir and he charges them with having overcome Grettir, when already on the point of death from a mortifying wound, which they had inflicted on him by sorcery and enchantment. The slayers propose to Illugi terms parallel to those made to the retainers of Hnæf. "I will give thee thy life," says their leader, "if thou wilt swear to us an oath not to take vengeance on any of those who have been in this business."

Now, note the answer of Illugi: "That might have seemed to me a matter to be discussed, if Grettir had been able to defend himself, and if ye had overcome him with valour and courage; but now it is not to be looked for that I will save my life by being such a coward as art thou. In a word, no man shall be more harmful to thee than I, if I live, *for never can I forget how it was that ye have vanquished Grettir.* Much rather, then, do I choose to die."

Now of course it would have been an "insult and hurt" to the pride of Illugi, or of any other decent eleventh century Icelander, to have been compelled to swear an oath not to avenge his brother, even though that brother had been slain in the most chivalrous way possible; and it would doubtless have been a hard matter, even in such a case, for Illugi to have kept his oath, had he sworn it. But the treachery of the opponents puts an oath out of the question, just as it must have done in the case of the followers of King Cynewulf[503] or of Rolf Kraki, and as it must have done in the case of the followers of Hnæf, had the slaying of Hnæf been a premeditated act of treachery on the part of Finn.

In the *Njáls Saga*, Flosi has to take up the feud for the slain Hauskuld. Flosi is a moderate and reasonable man, so the first thing he does is to enquire into the *circumstances* under which Hauskuld was slain. Flosi finds that the circumstances, and the outrageous conduct of the slayers, give him no choice but to prosecute the feud. So in the end he burns Njal's hall, and in it the child of Kari.

Now to have burned a man's child to death might well seem a deed impossible of atonement. Yet in the end Flosi and Kari are reconciled by a full atonement, *the father of the slain child actually taking the first step*[504]. And all this is possible because Flosi and Kari recognise that each has been trying to play his part with justice and fairness, and that each is dragged into the feud through the fault of others. When Flosi has said of his enemy, "I would that I were altogether such a man as Kari is," we feel that reconciliation is in sight.

Very similar is the reconciliation between Alboin and Thurisind in Longobard story, but with this difference, that here it is Alboin who seeks reconciliation by going to the hall of the man whose son he has slain, thus reversing the parts of Flosi and Kari; and reconciliation is possible—just barely possible.

Again, when Bothvar comes to the hall of Rolf, and slays one of Rolf's retainers, the other retainers naturally claim full vengeance. Rolf insists upon investigating the *circumstances*. When he learns that it was his own man who gave the provocation, he comes to terms with the slayer.

Of course it was a difficult matter, and one involving a sacrifice of their pride, for the retainers of Hnæf to come to any composition with the *bana* of their lord; but it is not unthinkable, if the quarrel was started by Finn's subordinates without his consent, and if Finn himself fought fair. But had the slaying been an act of premeditated treachery on the part of Finn, the atonement would, I submit, have been not only difficult but impossible. If the retainers of Hnæf had had such success as our poem implies, then their action under such circumstances is, as Lawrence says, "almost incomprehensible." If they did it under compulsion, and fear of death, then their action would be contrary to all the ties of Germanic honour, and would entirely deprive them of any sympathy the audience might otherwise have felt for them. Yet it is quite obvious that the retainers of Hnæf are precisely the people with whom the audience is expected to sympathise[505].

In any case, the feud was likely enough to break out again as it did in the case of Alboin and Thurisind, and equally in that of Hrothgar and Ingeld.

Indeed, the different versions of the story of the feud between the house of Hrothgar and the house of Froda are very much to the point.

Much the oldest version—probably in its main lines quite historical—is the story as given in *Beowulf*. Froda has been slain by the Danes in pitched battle. Subsequently Hrothgar, upon whom, as King of the Danes, the responsibility for meeting the feud has devolved, tries to stave it off by wedding his daughter Freawaru to Ingeld, son of Froda. The sympathy of the poet is obviously with the luckless pair, Ingeld and Freawaru, involved as they are in ancient hatreds which are not of their making. For it is foreseen how some old warrior, who cannot forget his loyalty to his former king, will stir up the feud afresh.

But Saxo Grammaticus tells the story differently. Froda (Frotho) is treacherously invited to a banquet, and then slain. By this treachery the whole atmosphere of the story is changed. Ingeld (Ingellus) marries the daughter of his father's slayer, and, for this, the old version reproduced by Saxo showers upon him literally scores of phrases of scorn and contempt. The whole interest of the story now centres not in the recreant Ingeld or his wife of treacherous race, but in the old warrior Starkad, whose spirit and eloquence is such that he can bring Ingeld to a sense of his "vast sin[506]," can burst the bonds of his iniquity, and at last compel him to take vengeance for his father.

In the *Saga of Rolf Kraki* the story of Froda is still further changed. It is a tale not only of treachery but also of slaying of kin. Consequently the idea of any kind of atonement, however temporary, has become impossible; there is no hint of it.

Now the whole atmosphere of the Hengest-story in *Beowulf* is parallel to that of the *Beowulf* version of the Ingeld-story: agreement is possible, though it does not prove to be permanent. There is room for much hesitation in the minds of Hengest and of Ingeld: they remain the heroes of the story. But if Finn had, as is usually supposed, invited Hnæf to his fort and then deliberately slain him by treachery, the whole atmosphere would have been different. Hengest could not then be the hero, but the foil: the example of a man whose spirit fails at the crisis, who does the utterly disgraceful thing, and enters the service of his lord's treacherous foe. The hero of the story would be some other character—possibly the young Hunlafing, who, loyal in spite of the treachery and cowardice of his leader Hengest, yet, remaining steadfast of soul, is able in the end to infuse his own courage into the heart of the recreant Hengest, and to inspire all the perjured Danish thegns to their final and triumphant revenge on Finn.

But that is not how the story is presented.

Section X. An Attempt at Reconstruction

The theory, then, which seems to fit in best with what we know of the historic conditions at the time when the story arose, and which fits in best with such details of the story as we have, is this:

Finn, King of Frisia, has a stronghold, Finnsburg, outside the limits of Frisia proper. There several clans and chieftains are assembled[507]: Hnæf, Finn's brother-in-law, prince of the Hocings, the Eotens, and Sigeferth, prince of the Secgan; whether Sigeferth has his retinue with him or no is not clear.

But the treachery of the Eotens causes trouble: they have some old feud with Hnæf and his Danes, and attack them by surprise in their hall. There is no proof that Finn has any share in this treason. It is therefore quite natural that in the *Episode*—although the treachery of the Eotens is censured—Finn is never blamed; and that in the *Fragment*, Finn has apparently no share in the attack on the hall, at any rate during those first five days to which the account in the *Fragment* is limited.

The attack is led by Garulf (*Fragment*, l. 20), presumably the prince of the Eotens: and some friend or kinsman is urging Garulf not to hazard so precious a life in the first attack. And here, too, the situation now becomes clearer: if Garulf is the chief of the attacking people, we can understand one of his kinsmen or friends expostulating thus: but if he is merely one of a number of subordinates despatched by Finn to attack the hall, the position would not be so easily understood.

Garulf, however, does not heed the warning, and falls, "first of all the dwellers in that land." The *Fragment* breaks off, but the fight goes on: we can imagine that matters must have proceeded much as in the great attack upon the hall in the *Nibelungen lied*[508]. One man after another would be drawn in, by the duty of revenge, and Finn's own men would wake to find a battle in progress. "The sudden bale (*fǽr*) came upon them." Finn's son joins in the attack, perhaps in order to avenge some young comrade in arms; and is slain, possibly by Hnæf. Then Finn *has* to intervene, and Hnæf in turn is slain, possibly, though not certainly, by Finn himself. But Hengest, the thegn of Hnæf, puts up so stout a defence, that Finn is unable to take a full vengeance upon all the Danes. He offers them terms. What are Hengest and the thegns to do?

Finn has slain their lord. But they are Finn's guests, and they have slain Finn's son in his own house. Finn himself is, I take it, blameless. *It is here that the tragic tension comes in.* We can understand how, even if Hengest had Finn in his power, he might well have stayed his hand. So peace is made, and all is to be forgotten: solemn oaths are sworn. And Finn keeps his promise honestly. He resumes his position of host, making no distinction between Eotens, Frisians and Danes, who are all, for the time at least, his followers.

I think we have here a rational explanation of the action of Hengest and the other thegns of Hnæf, in following the slayer of their lord.

The situation resembles that which takes place when Alboin seeks hospitality in the hall of the man whose son he has slain, or when Ingeld is reconciled to Hrothgar. Very similar, too, is the temporary reconciliation often brought about in an Icelandic feud by the feeling that the other side has something to say for itself, and that both have suffered grievously. The death of Finn's son is a set off against the death of Hnæf[509]. But, as in the case of Alboin and of Ingeld, or of many an Icelandic Saga, the passion for revenge is too deep to be laid to rest permanently. This is what makes the figure of Hengest tragic, like the figure of Ingeld: both have plighted their word, but neither can keep it.

The assembly breaks up. Finn and his men go back to Friesland, and Hengest accompanies them: of the other Danish survivors nothing is said for the moment: whatever longings they may have had for revenge, the poet concentrates all for the moment in the figure of Hengest.

Hengest spends the winter with Finn, but he cannot quiet his conscience: and in the end, he accepts the gift of a sword from a young Danish prince Hunlafing, who is planning revenge. The uncles of Hunlafing, Guthlaf and Oslaf [Ordlaf], had been in the hall when it was attacked, and had survived. It is possible that the young prince's father, Hunlaf, was slain then, and that his son is therefore recognised as having the nominal leadership in the operations of vengeance[510]. Hengest, by accepting the sword, promises his services in the work of revenge, and makes a great slaughter of the treacherous Eotens. Perhaps he so far respects his oath that he leaves the simultaneous attack upon Finn to Guthlaf and Oslaf [Ordlaf]. Here we should have an explanation of *swylce*: "in like wise[511]"; and also an explanation of the omission of Hengest's name from the final act, the slaying of Finn himself. Hengest made the Eotens feel the sharpness of his sword: and in like wise Guthlaf and Oslaf conducted their part of the campaign. Of course this is only a guess: but it is very much in the manner of the Heroic Age to get out of a difficulty by respecting the letter of an oath whilst breaking its spirit—just as Hogni and Gunnar arrange that the actual slaying of Sigurd shall be done by Guttorm, who had not personally sworn the oath, as they had.

SECTION XI. GEFWULF, PRINCE OF THE JUTES

Conclusive external evidence in favour of the view just put forward we can hardly hope for: for this reason, amongst others, that the names of the actors in the Finn tragedy are corrupted and obscured in the different versions. Hnæf and Hengest are too well known to be altered: but most of the other names mentioned in the *Fragment* do not agree with the forms given in other documents. Sigeferth is the Sæferth of *Widsith*: the Ordlaf (correct) of the *Fragment* is the Oslaf of the *Episode*. The first Guthlaf is confirmed by the Guthlaf of the *Episode*: the other names, the second Guthlaf, Eaha and Guthere, we cannot control from other sources: but they have all, on various grounds, been suspected.

Tribal names are equally varied. Sigeferth's people, the Secgan, are called Sycgan in *Widsith*. And he would be a bold man who would deny (what almost all students of the subject hold) that *Eotena, Eotenum* in the *Episode* is yet another scribal error: the copyist had before him the Anglian form, *eotna*, *eotnum*, and miswrote *eotena*, *eotenum*, when he should have written the West-Saxon equivalent of the tribal name, *Ȳtena*, *Ȳtum*—the name we get in *Widsith*:

Ȳtum [weold] Gefwulf
Fin Folcwalding Frēsna cynne.

But in *Widsith* names of heroes and tribes are grouped together (often, but not invariably) according as they are related in story. Consequently Gefwulf is probably (not certainly) a hero of the Finn story. What part does he play? If, as I have been trying to show, the Jutes are the aggressors, then, as their chief, Gefwulf would probably be the leader of the attack upon the hall.

This part, in the *Fragment*, is played by Garulf.

Now *Gārulf* is not *Gefwulf*, and I am not going to pretend that it is. But *Gārulf* is very near *Gefwulf*: and (what is important) more so in Old English script than in modern script[512]. It stands to *Gefwulf* in exactly the same relation as *Heregār* to *Heorogār* or *Sigeferð* to *Sǣferð* or *Ordlāf* to *Ōslāf*: that is to say the initial letter and the second element are identical. And no serious student, I think, doubts that *Heregār* and *Heorogār*, or *Sigeferð* and *Sǣferð*, or *Ordlāf* and *Ōslāf* are merely corruptions of one name. And if it be admitted to be probable that *Gefwulf* is miswritten for *Gārulf*, then the theory that Garulf was prince of the Jutes, and the original assailant of Hnæf, in addition to being the only theory which satisfactorily explains the internal evidence of the *Fragment* and the *Episode*, has also powerful external support.

Section XII. Conclusion

But, apart from any such confirmation, I think that the theory offers an explanation of the known facts of the case, and that it is the only theory yet put forward which does. It enables us to solve many minor difficulties that hardly otherwise admit of solution. But, above all, it gives a tragic interest to the story by making the actions of the two main characters, Finn and Hengest, intelligible and human: they are both great chiefs, placed by circumstances in a cruel position. Finn is no longer a treacherous host, plotting the murder of his guests, without even having the courage personally to superintend the dirty work: and Hengest is not guilty of the shameful act of entering the service of a king who had slain his lord by treachery when a guest. The tale of *Finnsburg* becomes one of tragic misfortune besetting great heroes—a tale of the same type as the stories of Thurisind or Ingeld, of Sigurd or Theodric.

FRISIA IN THE HEROIC AGE

It is now generally recognised that loose confederacies of tribes were, at the period with which we are dealing, very common. Lawrence says this expressly: "The actors in this drama are members of two North Sea tribes, or *rather groups of tribes*[513]"; and again[514]: "At the time when the present poem was put into shape, we surely have to assume for the Danes and Frisians, not compact and unified political units, but groups of tribes held somewhat loosely together, and sometimes known by tribal names."

This seems to me a quite accurate view of the political situation in the later Heroic Age. The independent tribes, as they existed at the time of Tacitus, tended to coalesce, and from such coalition the nations of modern Europe are gradually evolved. In the seventh and eighth centuries a great king of Northumbria or Frisia is likely to be king, not of one only, but of many allied tribes. I cannot therefore quite understand why some scholars reject so immediately the idea that the Eotens are not necessarily Frisians, but rather a tribe in alliance with the Frisians. For if, as they admit, we are dealing not with two compact units, but with two groups of tribes, why must we assume, as earlier scholars have done, that *Eotenas* must be synonymous either with Frisians or Danes? That assumption is based upon the belief that we *are* dealing with two compact units. It has no other foundation. I can quite understand Kemble and Ettmüller jumping at the conclusion that the Eotens *must* be identical with the one side or the other. But once we have recognised that confederacies of tribes, rather than individual tribes, are to be expected in the period with which we are dealing, then surely no such assumption should be made.

I think we shall be helped if we try to get some clear idea of the nationalities concerned in the struggle. For to judge by the analogy of other contemporary Germanic stories, there probably is some historic basis for the *Finnsburg* story: and even if the fight is purely fictitious, and if Finn Folcwalding never existed, still the Old English poets would represent the fictitious Frisian king in the light of what they knew of contemporary kings.

Now the Frisians were no insignificant tribe. They were a power, controlling the coasts of what was then called the "Frisian Sea[515]." Commerce was in Frisian hands. Archaeological evidence points to a lively trade between the Frisian districts and the coast of Norway[516]. From about the sixth century, when "Dorostates of the Frisians" is mentioned by the Geographer of Ravenna (or the source from which he drew) in a manner which shows it to have been known even in Italy as a place of peculiar importance[517], to the ninth century, when it was destroyed by repeated attacks of the Vikings, the Frisian port of Dorestad[518] was one of the greatest trade centres of Northern

Europe[519]. By the year 700 the Frisian power had suffered severely from the constant blows dealt to it by the Frankish Mayors of the Palace. Yet evidence seems to show that even at that date the Frisian king ruled all the coast which intervened between the borders of the Franks on the one side and of the Danes on the other[520]. When a zealous missionary demonstrated the powerlessness of the heathen gods by baptizing three converts in the sacred spring of Fosetisland, he was carried before the King of Frisia for judgement[521].

At a later date the "Danes" became the controlling power in the North Sea; but in the centuries before the Viking raids began, the Frisians appear to have had it all their own way.

Finn, son of Folcwald, found his way into some English genealogies[522] just as the Roman Emperor did into others. This also seems to point to the Frisian power having made an impression on the nations around.

We should expect all this to be reflected in the story of the great Frisian king. How then would a seventh or eighth century Englishman regard Finn and his father Folcwalda? Probably as paramount chiefs, holding authority over the tribes of the South and East coast of the North Sea, similar to that which, for example, a Northumbrian king held over the tribes settled along the British coast. Indeed, the whole story of the Northumbrian kings, as given in Bede, deserves comparison: the relation with the subordinate tribes, the alliances, the feuds, the attempted assassinations, the loyalty of the thegns— this is the atmosphere amid which the Finn story grew up in England, and if we want to understand the story we must begin by getting this point of view.

But, if this be a correct estimate of tribal conditions at the time the *Finnsburg* story took form, we no longer need far-fetched explanations to account for Finnsburg not being in Friesland. It is natural that it should not be, just as natural as that the contemporary Eadwinesburg should be outside the ancient limits of Deira. Nor do we need any far-fetched explanations why the Frisians should be called *Eotenas*. That the King of Frisia should have had Jutes under his rule is likely enough. And this is all that the words of the *Episode* demand.

PART IV

APPENDIX

A. A POSTSCRIPT ON MYTHOLOGY IN *BEOWULF*

(1) *Beowulf the Scylding and Beowulf son of Ecgtheow*

It is now ten years since Prof. Lawrence attacked the mythological theories which, from the time when they were first enunciated by Kemble and elaborated by Müllenhoff, had wielded an authority over *Beowulf* scholars which was only very rarely disputed[523].

Whilst in the main I agree with Prof. Lawrence, I believe that there *is* an element of truth in the theories of Kemble. It would, indeed, be both astonishing and humiliating if we found that a view, accepted for three-quarters of a century by almost every student, had no foundation. What is really remarkable is, not that Kemble should have carried his mythological theory too far, but that, with the limited information at his disposal, he at once saw certain aspects of the truth so clearly.

The mythological theories involve three propositions:

(*a*) That some, or all, of the supernatural stories told of Beowulf the Geat, son of Ecgtheow (especially the Grendel-struggle and the dragon-struggle), were originally told of Beowulf the Dane, son of Scyld, who can be identified with the Beow or Beaw[524] of the genealogies.

(*b*) That this Beow was an ancient "god of agriculture and fertility."

(*c*) That therefore we can allegorize Grendel and the dragon into culture-myths connected with the "god Beow."

Now (*c*) would not necessarily follow, even granting (*a*) and (*b*); for though a hero of story be an ancient god, many of his most popular adventures may be later accretion. However, these two propositions (*a*) and (*b*) would, together, establish a very strong probability that the Grendel-story and the dragon-story were ancient culture-myths, and would entitle to a sympathetic hearing those who had such an interpretation of them to offer.

That Beow is an ancient "god of agriculture and fertility," I believe to be substantially true. We shall see that a great deal of evidence, unknown to

Kemble and Müllenhoff, is now forthcoming to show that there *was* an ancient belief in a corn-spirit Beow: and this Beow, whom we find in the genealogies as son of Scyld or Sceldwa and descendant of Sceaf, is pretty obviously identical with Beowulf, son of Scyld Scefing, in the *Prologue* of *Beowulf*.

So far as the *Prologue* is concerned, there is, then, almost certainly a remote mythological background. But before we can claim that this background extends to the supernatural adventures attributed to Beowulf, son of Ecgtheow, we must prove our proposition (*a*): that these adventures were once told, not of Beowulf, son of Ecgtheow, but of Beowulf or Beow, son of Scyld.

When it was first suggested, at the very beginning of *Beowulf*-criticism, that Beowulf was identical with the Beow of the genealogies, it had not been realized that there were in the poem *two* persons named Beowulf: and thus an anonymous scholar in the *Monthly Review* of 1816[525], not knowing that Beowulf the slayer of Grendel is (at any rate in the poem as it stands) distinct from Beowulf, son of Scyld, connected both with Beow, son of Scyld, so initiating a theory which, for almost a century, was accepted as ascertained fact.

Kemble's identification was probably made independently of the work of this early scholar. Unlike him, Kemble, of course, realized that in our poem Beowulf the Dane, son of Scyld, is a person distinct from, is in fact not related to, Beowulf son of Ecgtheow. But he deliberately identified the two: he thought that two distinct traditions concerning the same hero had been amalgamated: in one of these traditions Beowulf may have been represented as son of Scyld, in the other as son of Ecgtheow, precisely as the hero Gunnar or Gunter is in one tradition son of Gifica (Giuki), in another son of Dankrat.

Of course such duplication as Kemble assumed is conceivable. Kemble might have instanced the way in which one and the same hero reappears in the pages of Saxo Grammaticus, with somewhat different parentage or surroundings, as if he were a quite different person. The *Lives of the Two Offas* present another parallel: the adventures of the elder Offa have been transferred to the younger, so that, along with much that is historical or semi-historical, we have much in the *Life of Offa II* that is simply borrowed from the story of Offa I. In the same way it is conceivable that reminiscences of the mythical adventures of the elder Beowulf (Beow) might have been mingled with the history of the acts of the younger Beowulf, king of the Geatas. A guarantee of the intrinsic reasonableness of this theory lies in the fact that recently it has been put forward again by Dr Henry Bradley. But it is not enough that a theory should be conceivable, and be supported by great names. I cannot see that there is any positive evidence for it at all.

The arguments produced by Kemble are not such as to carry conviction at the present day. The fact that Beowulf the Geat, son of Ecgtheow, "is represented throughout as a protecting and redeeming being" does not necessarily mean that we must look for some god or demigod of the old mythology—Frey or Sceaf or Beow—with whom we can identify him. This characteristic is strongly present in many Old English monarchs and magnates of historic, Christian, times: Oswald or Alfred or Byrhtnoth. Indeed, it might with much plausibility be argued that we are to see in this "protecting" character of the hero evidence of Christian rather than of heathen influence[526].

Nor can we argue anything from the absence of any historic record of a king Beowulf of the Geatas; our records are too scanty to admit of argument from silence: and were such argument valid, it would only prove Beowulf fictitious, not mythological—no more necessarily an ancient god than Tom Jones or Mr Pickwick.

There remains the argument of Dr Bradley. He points out that

"The poem is divided into numbered sections, the length of which was probably determined by the size of the pieces of parchment of which an earlier exemplar consisted. Now the first fifty-two lines, which are concerned with Scyld and his son Beowulf, stand outside this numbering. It may reasonably be inferred that there once existed a written text of the poem that did not include these lines. Their substance, however, is clearly ancient. Many difficulties will be obviated if we may suppose that this passage is the beginning of a different poem, the hero of which was not Beowulf the son of Ecgtheow, but his Danish namesake[527]."

In this Bradley sees support for the view that "there were circulated in England two rival poetic versions of the story of the encounters with supernatural beings: the one referring them to Beowulf the Dane" [of this the *Prologue* to our extant poem would be the only surviving portion, whilst] "the other (represented by the existing poem) attached them to the legend of the son of Ecgtheow."

But surely many objections have to be met. Firstly, as Dr Bradley admits, the mention of Beowulf the Dane is not confined to the *Prologue*; this earlier Beowulf "is mentioned at the beginning of the first numbered section" and consequently Dr Bradley has to suppose that "the opening lines of this section have undergone alteration in order to bring them into connection with the prefixed matter." And why should we assume that the "passus" of *Beowulf* correspond to pieces of parchment of various sizes of which an earlier exemplar consisted? These "passus" vary in length from 43 lines to 142, a disproportion by no means extraordinary for the sections of one and the same poem, but very awkward for the pages of one and the same book, however roughly constructed. One of the "passus" is just twice the average length, and 30 lines longer than the one which comes next to it in size. Ought we to assume that an artificer would have made his book clumsy by putting in this one disproportionate page, when, by cutting it in two, he could have got two pages of just about the size he wanted? Besides, the different "passus" do not seem to me to show signs of having been caused by such mechanical reasons as the dimensions of the parchment upon which they were written. On the contrary, the 42 places where sections begin and end almost all come where a reader might reasonably be expected to pause: 16 at the beginning or end of a speech: 18 others at a point where the narrative is resumed after some digression or general remark. Only eight remain, and even with these, there is generally some pause in the narrative at the point indicated. In only two instances does a "passus" end at a flagrantly inappropriate spot; in one of these there is strong reason to suppose that the scribe may have caused the trouble by beginning with a capital where he had no business to have done so[528]. Generally, there seems to be some principle governing the division of chapter from chapter, even though this be not made as a modern would have made it. But, if so, is there anything extraordinary in the first chapter, which deals with events three generations earlier than those of the body of the poem, being allowed to stand outside the numbering, as a kind of prologue?

The idea of a preface or prologue was quite familiar in Old English times. The oldest MSS[529] of Bede's *History* have, at the end of the preface, *Explicit praefatio incipiunt capitula.* So we have in one of the two oldest MSS[530] of the *Pastoral Care* "Ðis is seo forespræc." On the other hand, the prologue or preface might be left without any heading or colophon, and the next chapter begin as No. I. This is the case in the other MS of the *Pastoral Care*[531]. Is there, then, such difficulty in the dissertation on the glory of the ancient Danish kings being treated as what, in fact, it is: a prologue or preface; and being, as such, simply left outside the numbering?

Still less can we argue for the identification of our hero, the son of Ecgtheow, with Frotho, and through him with Beow, from the supposed resemblances between the dragon fights of Beowulf and Frotho. Such resemblances have been divined by Sievers, but we have seen that it is the dissimilarity, not the resemblance, of the two dragon fights which is really noteworthy[532].

To prove that Beow was the original antagonist of Grendel there remains, then, only the mention in the charter of a *Grendles mere* near a *Bēowan hamm*[533]. Now this was not known to Kemble at the time when he formed his theory that the original slayer of Grendel was not Beowulf, but Beow. And if the arguments upon which Kemble based his theory had been at all substantial, this charter would have afforded really valuable support. But the fact that two names occur near each other in a charter cannot confirm any theory, unless that theory has already a real basis of its own.

(2) *Beow*

Therefore, until some further evidence be discovered, we must regard the belief that the Grendel and the dragon stories were originally myths of Beow, as a theory for which sufficient evidence is not forthcoming.

But note where the theory breaks down. It seems indisputable that Beowulf the Dane, son of Scyld Scefing, is identical with Beo(w) of the genealogies: for Beo(w) is son of Scyld[534] or Sce(a)ldwa[535], who is a Scefing. But here we must stop. There is, as we have seen, no evidence that the Grendel or dragon adventures were transferred from him to their present hero, Beowulf the Geat, son of Ecgtheow. It would, of course, be quite possible to accept such transference, and *still* to reject the mythological interpretation of these adventures, just as it would be possible to believe that Gawain was originally a sun-hero, whilst rejecting the interpretation as a sun-myth of any particular adventure which could be proved to have been once told concerning Gawain. But I do not think we need even concede, as Boer[536] and Chadwick[537] do, that adventures have been transferred from Beowulf the Dane to Beowulf the Geat. We have seen that there is no evidence for such transference, however intrinsically likely it may be. Till evidence *is* forthcoming, it is useless to build upon Kemble's conjecture that Beowulf the Scylding sank into Beowulf the Wægmunding[538].

But it is due to Kemble to remember that, while he only put this forward as a tentative conjecture, what he *was* certain about was the identity of Beowulf the Scylding with Beow, and the divinity of these figures. And here all the evidence seems to justify him.

"The divinity of the earlier Beówulf," Kemble wrote, "I hold for indisputable.... Beo or Beow is ... in all probability a god of agriculture and fertility.... It strengthens this view of the case that he is the grandson of Sceáf, *manipulus frumenti*, with whom he is perhaps in fact identical[539]."

Whether or no Beow and Sceaf were ever identical, it is certain that Beow (grain) the descendant of Sceaf (sheaf) suggests a corn-myth, some survival from the ancient worship of a corn-spirit.

Now *bēow*, 'grain, barley,' corresponds to Old Norse *bygg*, just as, corresponding to O.E. *trīewe*, we have O.N. *tryggr*, or corresponding to O.E. *glēaw*, O.N. *glǫggr*. Corresponding to the O.E. proper name *Bēow*, we might expect an O.N. name, the first letters in which would be *Bygg(v)-*.

And pat he comes, like the catastrophe of the Old Comedy. When Loki strode into the Hall of Ægir, and assailed with clamour and scandal the assembled gods and goddesses, there were present, among the major gods, also Byggvir and his wife Beyla, the servants of Frey, the god of agriculture and fertility. Loki reviles the gods, one after the other: at last he exchanges reproaches with Frey. To see his lord so taunted is more than Byggvir can endure, and he turns to Loki with the words:

Know thou, that were my race such as is that of Ingunar-Frey, and if I had so goodly a seat, finer than marrow would I grind thee, thou crow of ill-omen, and pound thee all to pieces[540].

Byggvir is evidently no great hero: he draws his ideas from the grinding of the homely hand-mill, with which John Barleycorn has reason to be familiar:

A miller used him worst of all,
For he crushed him between two stones[541].

Loki, who has addressed by name all the other gods, his acquaintances of old, professes not to know who is this insignificant being: but his reference to the hand-mill shows that in reality he knows quite well:

What is that little creature that I see, fawning and sneaking and snuffling: ever wilt thou be at the ears of Frey, and chattering at the quern[542].

Byggvir replies with a dignity which reminds us of the traditional characteristics of Sir John Barleycorn, or Allan O'Maut. For:

Uskie-bae ne'er bure the bell
Sae bald as Allan bure himsel[543].

Byggvir adopts the same comic-heroic pose:

Byggvir am I named, and all gods and men call me hasty; proud am I, by reason that all the children of Odin are drinking ale together[544].

But any claims Byggvir may make to be a hero are promptly dismissed by Loki:

Hold thou silence, Byggvir, for never canst thou share food justly among men: thou didst hide among the straw of the hall: they could not find thee, when men were fighting[545].

Now the taunts of Loki, though we must hope for the credit of Asgard that they are false, are never pointless. And such jibes as Loki addresses to Byggvir *would* be pointless, if applied to one whom we could think of as in any way like our Beowulf. Later, Beyla, wife of Byggvir, speaks, and is silenced with the words "Hold thy peace—wife thou art of Byggvir." Byggvir must have been a recognized figure of the old mythology[546], but one differing from the monster-slaying Beow of Müllenhoff's imagination.

Byggvir is a little creature (*et lítla*), and we have seen above[547] that Scandinavian scholars have thought that they have discovered this old god in the Pekko who "promoted the growth of barley" among the Finns in the sixteenth century, and who is still worshipped among the Esthonians on the opposite side of the gulf as a three year old child; the form *Pekko* being derived, it is supposed, from the primitive Norse form *Beggwuz*. This is a corner of a very big subject: the discovery, among the Lapps and Finns, of traces of the heathendom of the most ancient Teutonic world, just as Thomsen has taught us to find in the Finnish language traces of Teutonic words in their most antique form.

The Lappish field has proved the most successful hunting ground[548]: among the Finns, apart from the Thunder-god, connection with Norse beliefs is arguable mainly for a group of gods of fruitfulness[549]. The cult of these, it is suggested, comes from scattered Scandinavian settlers in Finland, among whom the Finns dwelt, and from whom they learnt the worship of the spirits of the seed and of the spring, just as they learnt more practical lessons. First and foremost among these stands Pekko, whom we know to have been especially the god of barley, and whose connection with Beow or Byggvir (*Beggwuz*) is therefore a likely hypothesis enough[550]. Much less certain is the connection of Sämpsä, the spirit of vegetation, with any Germanic prototype;

he may have been a god of the rush-grass[551] (Germ. *simse*). Runkoteivas or Rukotivo was certainly the god of rye, and the temptation to derive his name from Old Norse (*rugr-tivorr*, "rye-god") is great[552]. But we have not evidence for the worship among Germanic peoples of such a rye-god, as we have in the case of the barley-god Byggvir-Beow. These shadowy heathen gods, however, do give each other a certain measure of mutual support.

And, whether or no Pekko be the same as Byggvir, his worship is interesting as showing how the spirit of vegetation may be honoured among primitive folk. His worshippers, the Setukese, although nominally members of the Greek Orthodox Church, speak their own dialect and often hardly understand that of their Russian priests, but keep their old epic and lyric traditions more than almost any other section of the Finnish-Esthonian race. Pekko, who was honoured among the Finns in the sixteenth century for "promoting the growth of barley," survives among the present-day peasantry around Pskoff, not only as a spirit to be worshipped, but as an actual idol, fashioned out of wax in the form of a child, sometimes of a three year old child. He lives in the corn-bin, but on certain occasions is carried out into the fields. Not everyone can afford the amount of wax necessary for a Pekko—in fact there is usually only one in a village: he lodges in turn with different members of his circle of worshippers. He holds two moveable feasts, on moonlight nights—one in spring, the other in autumn. The wax figure is brought into a lighted room draped in a sheet, there is feasting, with dancing hand in hand, and singing round Pekko. Then they go out to decide who shall keep Pekko for the next year—his host is entitled to special blessing and protection. Pekko is carried out into the field, especially to preside over the sowing[553].

I doubt whether, in spite of the high authorities which support it, we can as yet feel at all certain about the identification of Beow and Pekko. But I think we can accept with fair certainty the identification of Beow and Byggvir. And we can at any rate use Pekko as a collateral example of the way in which a grain-spirit is regarded. Now in either case we find no support whatever for the supposition that the activities of Beow, the spirit of the barley, could, or would, have been typified under the guise of battles such as those which Beowulf the Geat wages against Grendel, Grendel's mother, and the dragon. In Beowulf the Geat we find much that suggests the hero of folk-tale, overlaid with much that belongs to him as the hero of an heroic poem, but nothing suggestive of a corn-myth. On the other hand, so long as we confine ourselves to Beow and his ancestor Sceaf, we *are* in touch with this type of myth, however remotely. The way that Sceaf comes over the sea, as recorded by William of Malmesbury, is characteristic. That "Sheaf" should be, in the language of Müllenhoff, "placed in a boat and committed to the winds and waves in the hope that he will return new-born in the spring" is exactly what we might expect, from the analogy of harvest customs and myths of the coming of spring.

In Sætersdale, in Norway, when the ice broke up in the spring, and was driven ashore, the inhabitants used to welcome it by throwing their hats into the air, and shouting "Welcome, Corn-boat." It was a good omen if the "Corn-boats" were driven high and dry up on the land[554]. The floating of the sheaf on a shield down the Thames at Abingdon[555] reminds us of the Bulgarian custom, in accordance with which the venerated last sheaf of the harvest was floated down the river[556]. But every neighbourhood is not provided with convenient rivers, and in many places the last sheaf is merely drenched with water. This is an essential part of the custom of "crying the neck."

The precise ritual of "crying the neck" or "crying the mare" was confined to the west and south-west of England[557]. But there is no such local limitation about the custom of drenching the last sheaf, or its bearers and escort, with water. This has been recorded, among other places, at Hitchin in Hertfordshire[558], in Cambridgeshire[559], Nottinghamshire[560], Pembrokeshire[561], Wigtownshire[562] as well as in Holstein[563], Westphalia[564], Prussia[565], Galicia[566], Saxon Transsylvania[567], Roumania[568] and perhaps in ancient Phrygia[569].

Now it is true that drenching the last sheaf with water, as a rain charm, is by no means the same thing as floating it down the river, in the expectation that it will come again in the spring. But it shows the same sense of the continued existence of the corn-spirit. That the *seed*, when sown, should be sprinkled with water as a rain charm (as is done in places) seems obvious and natural enough. But when the *last sheaf* of the preceding harvest is thus sprinkled, to ensure plenteous rain upon the crops of next year, we detect the same idea of continuity which we find expressed when Sceaf comes to land from over the sea: the spirit embodied in the sheaf of last year's harvest returning, and bringing the renewed power of vegetation.

The voyage of the Abingdonian sheaf on the Thames was conducted upon a shield, and it may be that the "vessel without a rower" in which "Sheaf" came to land was, in the original version, a shield. There would be precedent for this. The shield was known by the puzzling name of "Ull's ship" in Scaldic poetry, presumably because the god Ull used his shield as a boat. Anyway, Scyld came to be closely connected with Sceaf and Beow. In Ethelwerd he is son of the former and father of the latter: but in the *Chronicle* genealogies five names intervene between Scyld and Sceaf, and the son of Sceaf is Bedwig, or as he is called in one version, Beowi. *Bedwig* and *Beowi* are probably derived from *Beowius*, the Latinized form of *Beow*. A badly formed *o* might easily be mistaken for a *d*, and indeed *Beowius* appears in forms much more corrupt. In that case it would appear that while some genealogies made Beow the son of Scyld, others made him son of Sceaf, and that the compiler of the pedigree got over the difficulty in the usual way, by adding the one version to the other[570].

But all this is very hypothetical; and how and when Scyld came to be connected with Sceaf and with Beow we cannot with any certainty say. At any rate we find no trace of such connection in Danish traditions of the primitive King Skjold of the Danes. But we can say, with some certainty, that in Beowulf the Dane, the son of Scyld Scefing, in our poem, we have a figure which is identical with Beow, son of Scyld or of Sceldwa and descendant of Sceaf, in the genealogies, and that this Beow is likely to have been an ancient corn-spirit, parallel to the Scandinavian Byggvir. That amount of mythology probably *does* underlie the *Prologue* to *Beowulf*, though the author would no doubt have been highly scandalized had he suspected that his pattern of a young prince was only a disguised heathen god. But I think that any further attempt to proceed, from this, to mythologize the deeds of Beowulf the Great, is pure conjecture, and probably quite fruitless conjecture.

I ought not to conclude this note without reference to the admirable discussion of this subject by Prof. Björkman in *Englische Studien*[571]. This, with the elucidation of other proper names in *Beowulf*, was destined to be the last big contribution to knowledge made by that ripe and good scholar, whose premature loss we all deplore; and it shows to the full those qualities of wide knowledge and balanced judgment which we have all learnt to admire in him.

B. GRENDEL

It may be helpful to examine the places where the name of Grendel occurs in English charters.

A.D. 708. Grant of land at Abbots Morton, near Alcester, co. Worcester, by Kenred, King of the Mercians, to Evesham (extant in a late copy).

Ærest of grindeles pytt on wiðimære; of wiðimære on þæt rēade slōh ... of ðēre dīce on þene blace pōl; of þām pōle æfter long pidele in tō þām mersce; of þām mersce þā æft on grindeles pytt[572].

The valley of the Piddle Brook is about a mile wide, with hills rising on each side till they reach a height of a couple of hundred feet above the brook. The directions begin in the valley and run "From Grindel's 'pytt' to the willow-mere; from the willow-mere to the red morass"; then from the morass the directions take us up the hill and along the lea, where they continue among the downs till we again make our descent into the valley, "from the ditch to the black pool, from the pool along the Piddle brook to the marsh, and from the marsh back to Grindel's 'pytt.'" In modern English a "pit" is an artificial hole which is generally dry: but the word is simply Latin *puteus*, "a well," and is used in this sense in the Gospel translations. Here it is a hole, and we may be sure that, with the willow-mere and the red slough on the one side, and the black pool and the marsh on the other, the hole was full of water.

A.D. 739. Grant of land at Creedy, co. Devon, by Æthelheard, King of Wessex, to Bishop Forthhere.

of doddan hrycge on grendeles pyt; of grendeles pytte on ifigbearo (ivy-grove)...[573].

The spot is near the junction of the rivers Exe and Creedy, with Dartmoor in the distance. The neighbourhood bears uncanny names, *Cāines æcer, egesan trēow*. If, as has been suggested by Napier and Stevenson, a trace of this pit still survives in the name Pitt farm, the mere must have been in the uplands, about 600 feet above sea level.

A.D. 931. Grant of land at Ham in Wiltshire by Athelstan to his thane Wulfgar. Quoted above, p. 43. It is in this charter that *on Bēowan hammes hecgan, on Grendles mere*[574] occur. "Grendel pits or meres" are in most other cases in low-lying marshy country: but this, like (perhaps) the preceding one, is in the uplands—it must have been a lonely mere among the hills, under Inkpen Beacon.

Circa A.D. 957. A list of boundaries near Battersea[575].

Ðis synd ðā landgemǣre tō Batriceseie. Ǣrst at hēgefre; fram hēgefre to gætenesheale; fram gæteneshæle to gryndeles syllen; fram gryndeles sylle to russemere; fram ryssemere to bælgenham....

All this is low-lying land, just south of the Thames. *Hēgefre* is on the river; *Bælgenham* is Balham, co. Surrey. "From Grendel's mire to the rushy mere" harmonizes excellently with what we know of the swampy nature of this district in early times.

A.D. 958. Grant of land at Swinford, on the Stour, co. Stafford, by King Eadred to his thane Burhelm[576].

Ondlong bæces wið neopan eostacote; ondlong dīces in grendels-mere; of grendels-mere in stāncōfan; of stāncōfan ondlong dūne on stiran mere....

A.D. 972. Confirmation of lands to Pershore Abbey (Worcester) by King Edgar[577].

of Grindles bece swā þæt gemǣre ligð....

A.D. 972. Extract from an account of the descent of lands belonging to Westminster, quoting a grant of King Edgar[578].

andlang hagan to grendeles gatan æfter kincges mearce innan brægentan....

The property described is near Watling Street, between Edgware, Hendon, and the River Brent. It is a low-lying district almost surrounded by the hills of Hampstead, Highgate, Barnet, Mill Hill, Elstree, Bushey Heath and Harrow. The bottom of the basin thus formed must have been a swamp[579]. What the "gate" may have been it is difficult to say. A foreign scholar has suggested that it may have been a narrow mountain defile or possibly a cave[580]: but this suggestion could never have been made by anyone who knew the country. The "gate" is likely to have been a channel connecting two meres—or it might have been a narrow piece of land between them—one of those *enge ānpaðas* which Grendel and his mother had to tread. Anyway, there is nothing exceptional in this use of "gate" in connection with a water-spirit. Necker, on the Continent, also had his "gates." Thus there is a "Neckersgate Mill" near Brussels, and the name "Neckersgate" used also to be applied to a group of houses near by, surrounded by water[581].

All the other places clearly point to a water-spirit: two meres, two pits, a mire and a beck: for the most part situated in low-lying country which must in Anglo-Saxon times have been swampy. All this harmonizes excellently with the *fenfreoðo* of *Beowulf* (l. 851). Of course it does not in the least follow that these places were named after the Grendel of our poem. It may well be that there was in England a current belief in a creature Grendel, dwelling among the swamps. Von Sydow has compared the Yorkshire belief in Peg Powler, or the Lancashire Jenny Greenteeth. But these aquatic monsters are not exactly parallel; for they abide in the water, and are dangerous only to those who attempt to cross it, or at any rate venture too near the bank[582], whilst Grendel and even his mother are capable of excursions of some distance from their fastness amid the fens.

Of course the mere-haunting Grendel *may* have been identified only at a comparatively late date with the spirit who struggles with the hero in the house, and flees below the earth in the folk-tale.

At any rate belief in a Grendel, haunting mere and fen, is clearly demonstrable for England—at any rate for the south and west of England: for of these place-names two belong to the London district, one to Wiltshire, one to Devonshire, two to Worcester and one to Stafford. The place-name *Grendele* in Yorkshire is too doubtful to be of much help. (*Domesday Book*, I, 302.) It is the modern village Grindale, four miles N.W. of Bridlington. From it, probably, is derived the surname *Grindle, Grindall* (Bardsley).

Abroad, the nearest parallel is to be found in Transsylvania, where there is a *Grändels môr* among the Saxons of the Senndorf district, near Bistritz. The Saxons of Transsylvania are supposed to have emigrated from the neighbourhood of the lower Rhine and the Moselle, and there is a *Grindelbach* in Luxemburg which may possibly be connected with the marsh demon[583].

Most of the German names in *Grindel-* or *Grendel-* are connected with *grendel*, "a bar," and therefore do not come into consideration here[584]: but the Transsylvanian "Grendel's marsh[585]," anyway, reminds us of the English "Grendel's marsh" or "mere" or "pit." Nevertheless, the local story with which the Transsylvanian swamp is connected—that of a peasant who was ploughing with six oxen and was swallowed up in the earth—is such that it requires considerable ingenuity to see any connection between it and the *Beowulf-Grendel*-tale[586].

The Anglo-Saxon place-names may throw some light upon the meaning and etymology of "Grendel[587]." The name has generally been derived from *grindan*, "to grind"; either directly[588], because Grendel grinds the bones of those he devours, or indirectly, in the sense of "tormentor[589]." Others would connect with O.N. *grindill*, "storm," and perhaps with M.E. *gryndel*, "angry[590]."

It has recently been proposed to connect the word with *grund*, "bottom": for Grendel lives in the *mere-grund* or *grund-wong* and his mother is the *grund-wyrgin*. Erik Rooth, who proposes this etymology, compares the Icelandic *grandi*, "a sandbank," and the common Low German dialect word *grand*, "coarse sand[591]." This brings us back to the root "to grind," for *grand*, "sand" is simply the product of the grinding of the waves[592]. Indeed the same explanation has been given of the word "ground[593]."

However this may be, the new etymology differs from the old in giving Grendel a name derived, not from his grinding or tormenting others, but from his dwelling at the bottom of the lake or marsh[594]. The name would have a parallel in the Modern English *grindle*, *grundel*, German *grundel*[595], a fish haunting the bottom of the water.

The Old English place-names, associating Grendel as they do with meres and swamps, seem rather to support this.

As to the Devonshire stream *Grendel* (now the Grindle or Greendale Brook), it has been suggested that this name is also connected with the root *grand*, "gravel," "sand." But, so far as I have been able to observe, there is no particular suggestion of sand or gravel about this modest little brook. If we follow the River Clyst from the point where the Grindle flows into it, through two miles of marshy land, to the estuary of the Exe, we shall there find plenty. But it is clear from the charter of 963 that the name was then, as now, restricted to the small brook. I cannot tell why the stream should bear the name, or what, if any, is the connection with the monster Grendel. We can only note that the name is again found attached to water, and, near the junction with the Clyst, to marshy ground.

Anyone who will hunt Grendel through the shires, first on the 6-in. ordnance map, and later on foot, will probably have to agree with the Three Jovial Huntsmen

This huntin' doesn't pay,
But we'n powler't up an' down a bit, an' had a rattlin' day.

But, if some conclusions, although scanty, can be drawn from place-names in which the word *grendel* occurs, nothing can be got from the numerous place-names which have been thought to contain the name *Bēow*. The clearest of these is the *on Bēowan hammes hecgan*, which occurs in the Wiltshire charter of 931. But we can learn nothing definite from it: and although there are other instances of strong and weak forms alternating, we cannot even be quite certain that the Beowa here is identical with the Beow of the genealogies[596].

The other cases, many of which occur in *Domesday Book* are worthless. Those which point to a weak form may often be derived from the weak noun *bēo*, "bee": "The Anglo-Saxons set great store by their bees, honey and wax being indispensables to them[597]."

Bēas brōc, *Bēas feld* (*Bewes feld*) occur in charters: but here a connection with *bēaw*, "horsefly," is possible: for parallels, one has only to consider the long list of places enumerated by Björkman, the names of which are derived from those of beasts, birds, or insects[598]. And in such a word as *Bēolēah*, even if the first element be *bēow*, why may it not be the common noun "barley," and not the name of the hero at all?

No argument can therefore be drawn from such a conjecture as that of Olrik, that *Bēas brōc* refers to the water into which the last sheaf (representing Beow) was thrown, in accordance with the harvest custom, and in the expectation of the return of the spirit in the coming spring[599].

C. THE STAGES ABOVE WODEN IN THE WEST-SAXON GENEALOGY

The problems to which this pedigree gives rise are very numerous, and some have been discussed above. There are four which seem to need further discussion.

(I) A "Sceafa" occurs in *Widsith* as ruling over the Longobards. Of course we cannot be certain that this hero is identical with the Sceaf of the genealogy. Now there is no one in the long list of historic or semi-historic Longobard kings, ruling after the tribe had left Scandinavia, who bears a name at all similar. It seems therefore reasonable to suppose that Sceafa, if he is a genuine Longobard king at all, belongs to the primitive times when the Longobardi or Winnili dwelt in "Scadan," before the historic or semi-historic times with which our extant list deals. And Old English accounts, although making Sceaf an ancestor of the Saxon kings, are unanimous in connecting him with Scani or Scandza.

Some scholars[600] have seen a serious difficulty in the weak form "Sceafa," as compared with "Sceaf." But we have the exactly parallel cases of *Horsa*[601] compared with *Hors*[602], and *Hrǣdla*[603] compared with *Hrēdel*[604], *Hrēdel*. Parallel, but not quite so certain, are *Sceldwa*[605] and *Scyld*[606], *Gēata*[607] and *Gēat*[608], *Bēowa*[609] and *Bēaw, Bēo(w)*[610].

I do not think it has ever been doubted that the forms *Hors* and *Horsa*, or *Hrēdel* and *Hrǣdla*, relate to one and the same person. Prof. Chadwick seems to have little or no doubt as to the identity of *Scyld* and *Sceldwa*[611], or *Bēo* and *Bēowa*[612]. Why then should the identity of *Scēaf* and *Scēafa* be denied because one form is strong and the other weak[613]? We cannot demonstrate the identity of the figure in the genealogies with the figure in *Widsith*; but little difficulty is occasioned by the weak form.

(II) Secondly, the absence of the name *Scēaf* from the oldest MS of the *Chronicle* (the *Parker MS, C.C.C.C.* 173) has been made the ground for suggesting that when that MS was written (*c.* 892) Sceaf had not yet been invented (Möller, *Volksepos,* 43; Symons in *Pauls Grdr.* (2), III, 645; Napier, as quoted by Clarke, *Sidelights,* 125). But Sceaf, and the other names which are omitted from the *Parker MS,* are found in the other MSS of the *Chronicle* and the allied pedigrees, which are known to be derived independently from one and the same original. Now, unless the names were older than the *Parker MS,* they could not appear in so many independent transcripts. For, even though these transcripts are individually later, their *agreement* takes us back to a period earlier than that of the *Parker MS* itself[614].

An examination of the different versions of the genealogy, given on pp. 202-3, above, and of the tree showing the connection between them, on p. 315, will, I think, make this clear.

The versions of the pedigree given in the *Parker MS* of the *Chronicle,* in Asser and in *Textus Roffensis I,* all contain the stages *Frithuwald* and *Frithuwulf.* Asser and *Roff. I* are connected by the note about *Gēata*: but *Roff. I* is not derived from that text of Asser which has come down to us, as that text has corrupted *Fin* and *Godwulf* into one name and has substituted *Seth* for *Scēaf* ["Seth, *Saxonice* Sceaf": Florence of Worcester]. *Roff. I* is free from both these corruptions.

Ethelwerd is obviously connected with a type of genealogy giving the stages *Frithuwald* and *Frithuwulf,* but differs from all the others in giving no stages between *Scyld* and *Scēf.*

None of the other versions contain the names *Frithuwald* and *Frithuwulf.* They are closely parallel, but fall into groups showing special peculiarities.

MSS Tib. A. VI and *Tib. B. I* of the *Chronicle* show only trifling differences of spelling. The MSS belong respectively to about the years 1000 and 1050, and are both derived from an Abingdon original of about 977[615].

MS Cott. Tib. B. IV is derived from a copy of the *Chronicle* sent North about 892[616].

MS Cott. Tib. B. V and *Textus Roffensis II* are closely connected, but neither is derived from the other. For *Roff. II* preserves *Tethwa* and *Hwāla,* who are lost in *Tib. B. V; Tib. B. V* preserves *Iterman,* who is corrupted in *Roff. II.* Both *Tib. B. V* and *Roff. II* carry the pedigree down to Edgar, mentioning his three

sons *Ēadweard and Ēadmund and Æþelred æðelingas syndon Ēadgāres suna cyninges.*
The original therefore apparently belongs to some date before 970, when
Edmund died (cf. Stevenson's Asser, 158, note).

Common features of *MS Cott. Tib. B. V* and *Roff. II* are (1) *Eat(a)* for *Geat(a)*,
(2) the omission of *d* from *Scealdwa*, and (3) the expression *se Scēf*, "this Scef."
Features (1) and (3) are copied in the Icelandic pedigrees. *Scealdwa* is given
correctly there, but the Icelandic transcriber could easily have got it from
Scealdwaging above. The Icelandic was, then, ultimately derived either from
Tib. B. V or from a version so closely connected as not to be worth
distinguishing.

Accordingly *Cott. Tib. B. V*, *Textus Roffensis II*, *Langfeðgatal* and *Flateyarbók*
form one group, pointing to an archetype *c.* 970.

The pedigrees can accordingly be grouped on the system shown on the
opposite page[617].

(III) Prof. Chadwick, in his *Origin of the English Nation*, draws wide deductions
from the fact that the Danes traced the pedigree of their kings back to Skjold,
whilst the West-Saxons included Sceldwa (Scyld) in their royal pedigree:

"Since the Angli and the Danes claimed descent from the same ancestor,
there can be no doubt that the bond was believed to be one of blood[618]."

This belief, Prof. Chadwick thinks, went back to exceedingly early times[619],
and he regards it as well-founded:

"It is true that the Angli of Britain seem never to have included themselves
among the Danes, but the reason for this may be that the term *Dene* (*Danir*)
had not come into use as a collective term before the invasion of Britain[620]."

Doubtless the fact that the name of a Danish king *Scyld* or *Sceldwa* is found
in a pedigree of West-Saxon kings, as drawn up at a period certainly not later
than 892, points to a belief, at that date, in some kind of a connection. But
we have still to ask: How close was the connection supposed to be? And how
old is the belief?

Firstly as to the closeness of the connection. Finn also occurs in the
pedigree—possibly the Frisian king: Sceaf occurs, possibly, though not
certainly, a Longobard king. Noah and Adam occur; are we therefore to
suppose that the compiler of the *Genealogy* believed his kings to be of one
blood with the Hebrews? Certainly he did: but only remotely, as common
descendants of Noah. And the occurrence of Sceldwa and Sceaf and Finn in

the genealogies—granting the identity of these heroes with Skjold of the Danes, Sceafa of the Longobards and Finn of the Frisians, might only prove that the genealogist believed in their common (Germanic) race.

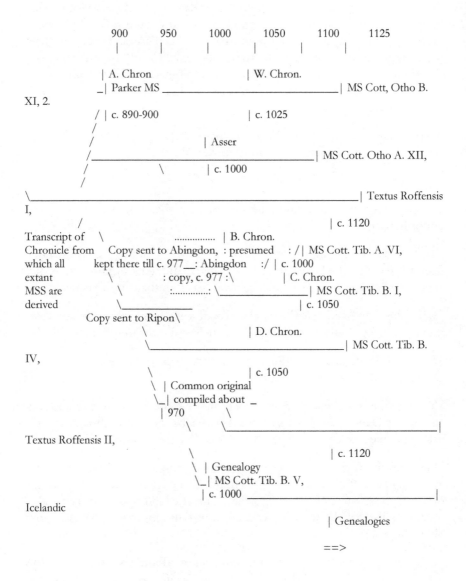

Secondly, how old is the belief? The Anglian genealogies (Northumbrian, Mercian and East Anglian), as reproduced in the *Historia Brittonum* and in the *Vespasian MS*, form part of what is doubtless, as is said above, the oldest extant English historical document. But in this document *there is no mention of Scyld.* Indeed, it contains no pedigree of the West-Saxon kings at all. From whatever cause, the West-Saxon genealogy is not extant from so early a date as are the pedigrees of the Northumbrian, Mercian, East Anglian and Kentish kings[621]. Still, this may well be a mere accident, and I am not prepared to dispute that the pedigree which traces the West-Saxon kings to Woden dates back, like the other genealogies connecting Old English kings with Woden, to primitive and heathen times. Now the West-Saxon pedigree is found in many forms: some which trace the royal house only to Woden, and some which go beyond Woden and contain a list of names by which Woden is connected with Sceaf, and then with Noah and Adam.

(1) The nucleus of the whole pedigree is to be found in the names between Cynric or Cerdic and Woden. These occur in every version. The pedigree in this, its simplest form, is found twice among the entries in the *Chronicle* which deal with the events of heathen times, under 552 and 597. These names fall into verse:

[Cynrīc Cerdicing], Cerdic Elesing,
Elesa Esling, Esla GiWising,
GiWis Wīging, Wīg Frēawining,
Frēawine Friðugāring, Friðugār Bronding,
Brond Bǣldǣging, Bǣldǣg Wōdening.

Like the mnemonic lists in *Widsith*, these lines are probably very old. Their object is clearly to connect the founder of the West-Saxon royal house with Woden. Note, that not only do the names alliterate, but the alliteration is perfect. Every line attains double alliteration in the first half, with one alliterating word only in the second half. The lines must go back to times when lists of royal ancestors, both real and imaginary, had to be arranged in correct verse; times when such things were recorded by memory rather than by writing. They are pre-literary, and were doubtless chanted by retainers of the West-Saxon kings in heathen days.

(2) An expanded form of this genealogy occurs in *MSS C.C.C.C.* 183 and *Cotton Tib. B. V.* Woden is here furnished with a father Frealaf. We know nothing of any Frealaf as father of the All-Father in heathen days, though Frealaf is found in this capacity in other genealogies written down in the ages after the conversion. Frealaf breaks the correct alliterative system. In both MSS the pedigree is brought down to King Ine (688-726): both MSS are ultimately, no doubt, derived from a list current in the time of that king, that is to say less than a century after the conversion of Wessex.

(3) A further expansion, which Prof. Napier has held on linguistic grounds[622] to have been written down as early as 750, is incorporated in a genealogical and chronological note regarding the West-Saxon kings, which is extant in many MSS[623]. *In its present form* this genealogical note is a recension, under Alfred, of a document coming down to the death of his father Æthelwulf. It traces the pedigree of Æthelwulf to Cerdic, but it keeps this district from the rhythmical nucleus, in which it traces Cerdic to Woden, and no further.

(4) Then, in the *Anglo-Saxon Chronicle*, under the year 855, the pedigree is given in its most elaborate form. There the genealogy of Æthelwulf is traced in one unbroken series, not merely through Cerdic to Woden, but from Woden through a long line of Woden's ancestors, including Frealaf, Geat, Sceldwa and Sceaf, to Noah and Adam.

It has been noted above[624] that none of the *Chronicle* pedigrees stop at Sceaf. The *Chronicle*, in the stages above Woden, recognizes as stopping places only Geat (Northumbrian pedigree, anno 547) or Adam (West-Saxon pedigree, anno 855).

(5) The Chronicle of Ethelwerd (*c.* 1000) does, however, stop at Scef[625]. Now it has been argued that Ethelwerd's pedigree is merely abbreviated from the pedigree in the *Anglo-Saxon Chronicle* under 855, and that, in making Scef the final stage, and in what he tells us about that hero, Ethelwerd is merely adapting what he had read in *Beowulf* about Scyld[626]. But this seems hardly possible. Ethelwerd, it is true, borrows most of his facts from the *Chronicle*, from Bede, and other known sources: but there are some passages which show that he had access to a source now lost. Ethelwerd was a member of the West-Saxon royal house, and he wrote his Chronicle for a kinswoman, Matilda, in order, as he says, to explain their common stock and race. They were both descended from Æthelwulf, the chronicler being great-great-grandson of Æthelred, and the lady to whom he dedicates his work being great-great-granddaughter of Alfred. So he writes to tell "who and whence were their kin, so far as memory adduces, and our parents have taught us." Accordingly, though he begins his Chronicle with the Creation, the bulk of it is devoted to the deeds of his or Matilda's ancestors. Is it credible that he would have cut out all the stages in their common pedigree between Scyld and Scef, that he would have sacrificed all the ancestors of Scef, thus severing relations with Noah and Adam, and that he would have attributed to Scef the story which in *Beowulf* is attributed to Scyld, all this simply in order to bring his English pedigree into some harmony with what is told about the Danish pedigree in *Beowulf*—a poem of which we have no evidence that he had ever heard?

To suppose him to have done this, is to make him sacrifice, *without any reason*, just that part of the pedigree in the *Chronicle* under 855 which, from all we know of Ethelwerd, was most likely to have interested him: that which connected his race with Noah and Adam. Further, it is to suppose him to have reproduced just those stages in the pedigree which on critical grounds modern scholars can show to be the oldest, and to have modified or rejected just those which on critical grounds modern scholars can show to be later accretion. When Brandl supposes Ethelwerd to have produced his pedigree by comparing together merely the materials which have come down to us to-day, namely *Beowulf* and the *Chronicle*, he is, in reality, attributing to him the mind and acumen of a modern critic. An Anglo-Saxon alderman could only have detected and rejected the additions by using some material which has *not* come down to us. What more natural than that Ethelwerd, who writes as the historian of the West-Saxon royal family, should have known of a family pedigree which traced the line up to Sceaf and his arrival in the boat, and that he should have (rightly) thought this to be more authoritative than the pedigree in the *Chronicle* under the year 855, which had been expanded from it? Prof. Chadwick, it seems to me, is here quite justified in holding that Ethelwerd had "acquired the genealogy from some unknown source, in a more primitive form than that contained in the *Chronicle*[627]."

But, because the source of Ethelwerd's pedigree is more primitive than that contained in the *Chronicle* under the year 855, it does not follow that it goes back to heathen times. Wessex had been converted more than two centuries earlier.

We are now in a position to make some estimate of the antiquity of Scyld and Sceaf in the West-Saxon pedigree. The nucleus of this pedigree is to be found in the verses connecting Cynric and Cerdic with Woden. (Even as late as Æthelwulf and Alfred this nucleus is often kept distinct from the later, more historic stages connecting Cerdic with living men.) Pedigrees of other royal houses go to Woden, and many stop there; however, in times comparatively early, but yet Christian, we find Woden provided with five ancestors: later, Ethelwerd gives him ten: the *Chronicle* gives him twenty-five. It is evidently a process of accumulation.

Now, if the name of Scyld had occurred in the portion of the pedigree which traces the West-Saxon kings up to Woden, it would possess sufficient authority to form the basis of an argument. But Scyld, like Heremod, Beaw and Sceaf, occurs in the fantastic development of the pedigree, by which Woden is connected up with Adam and Noah. The fact that these heroes occur *above* Woden makes it almost incredible that their position in the pedigree can go back to heathen times. Those who believed in Woden as a god can hardly have believed at the same time that he was a descendant of the Danish king Scyld. This difficulty Prof. Chadwick admits: "It is difficult to believe that in heathen times Woden was credited with five generations of ancestors, as in the *Frealaf-Geat* list." Still less is it credible that he was credited with 25 generations of ancestors, as in the *Frealaf-Geat-Sceldwa-Sceaf-Noe-Adam* list.

The obvious conclusion seems to me to be that the names above Woden were added in Christian times to the original list, which in heathen times only went back to Woden, and *which is still extant in this form*. A Christian, rationalizing Woden as a human magician, would have no difficulty in placing him far down the ages, just as Saxo Grammaticus does[628]. Obviously *Noe-Adam* must be an addition of Christian times, and the same seems to me to apply to all the other names above Woden, which, though ancient and Germanic, are not therefore ancient and Germanic in the capacity of ancestors of Woden.

And even if these extraordinary ancestors of Woden were really believed in in heathen times, they cannot have been regarded as the special property of any one nation. For it was never claimed that the West-Saxon kings had any unique distinction in tracing their ancestry to Woden, such as would give them a special claim upon Woden's forefathers. How then can the ancient belief (if indeed it *were* an ancient belief) that Woden was descended from Scyld, King of Denmark, prove that the Anglo-Saxons regarded *themselves* as specially related to the Danes? For any such relationship derived through Woden must have been shared by all descendants of the All-Father.

Prof. Chadwick avoids this difficulty by supposing that Woden did not originally occur in the pedigree, but is a later insertion[629]. But how can this be so when, of the two forms in which the West-Saxon pedigree appears, one (and, so far as our evidence goes, much the older one) traces the kings to Woden *and stops there*. The *object* of this pedigree is to connect the West-Saxon kings with Woden. The expanded pedigrees, which carry on the line still further, from Woden to Sceldwa, Sceaf and Adam, though very numerous, are all traceable to one, or at most two, sources. It is surely not the right method to regard Woden as an interpolation (though he occurs in that portion of the pedigree which is common to all versions, some of which we can probably trace back to primitive times), and to regard as the original element Scyld and Sceaf (though they form part of the continuation of the pedigree found only in, at most, two families of MSS which we cannot trace back beyond the ninth century).

Besides, there is the strongest external support for Woden in the very place which he occupies in the West-Saxon pedigree. That pedigree is traced in all its texts up to one Baldæg and his father Woden. Those texts which further give Woden's ancestry make him a descendant of Frealaf—they generally make Woden son of Frealaf, though some texts insert an intermediate Frithuwald.

Now the very ancient Northumbrian pedigree also goes up, by a different route, to "Beldæg," and gives him Woden for a father. In some versions (e.g. the *Historia Brittonum*) the Northumbrian pedigree stops there: in others (e.g. the *Vespasian MS*) Woden has a father Frealaf. How then *can* it be argued, contrary to the unanimous evidence of all the dozen or more MSS of the West-Saxon pedigree, that *Woden*, standing as he does between his proper father and his proper son, is an interpolation? There is no evidence whatsoever to support such an argument, and everything to disprove it.

The fact that Sceaf, Sceldwa and Beaw occur above Woden, that some versions of the pedigree stop at Woden, and that in heathen times presumably all must have stopped when they reached the All-Father, seems to me a fatal argument—not against the antiquity of the legends of Sceaf, Sceldwa, and Beaw, but against the antiquity of these characters in the capacity (given to them in the *Anglo-Saxon Chronicle*) of ancestors of the West-Saxon kings, and against the vast deduction concerning the origin of the English nation which Prof. Chadwick draws from this supposed antiquity.

(IV) Precisely the same argument—that Sceaf, Sceldwa and Beaw are found *above Woden* in the pedigree of the English kings, and are not likely to have occupied that place in primitive heathen times, is fatal to the attempt to draw from this pedigree any argument that the myths of these heroes were specially and exclusively Anglo-Saxon. The argument of Müllenhoff and other scholars for an ancient, *purely Anglo-Saxon* Beowa-myth[630] falls, therefore, to the ground.

D. EVIDENCE FOR THE DATE OF *BEOWULF*. THE RELATION OF *BEOWULF* TO THE CLASSICAL EPIC

A few years ago there was a tendency to exaggerate the value of grammatical forms in fixing the date of Old English poetry, and attempts were made to arrange Old English poems in a chronological series, according to the exact percentage of "early" to "late" forms in each. There has now been a natural reaction against the assumption that, granting certain forms to be archaic, these would necessarily be found in a percentage diminishing exactly according to the dates of composition of the various poems in which they occur. The reaction has now gone to the other extreme, and grammatical facts are in danger of being regarded as not being "in any way valid or helpful indications of dates[631]."

Schücking[632], in an elaborate recent monograph on the date of *Beowulf*, rejects the grammatical evidence as valueless, and proceeds to date the poem about two centuries later than has usually been held, placing its composition at the court of some christianized Scandinavian monarch in England, about 900 A.D.

But it surely does not follow that, because grammatical data have been misused, therefore no use can be made of them. And, if *Beowulf* was composed about the year 900, from stories current among the Viking settlers, how are we to account for the fact that the proper names in *Beowulf* are given, not in the Scandinavian forms of the Viking age, nor in corruptions of such forms, but in the correct English forms which we should expect, according to English sound laws, if the names had been brought over in the sixth century, and handed down traditionally[633]?

For example, King Hygelac no doubt called himself *Hugilaikaz*. The *Chochilaicus* of Gregory of Tours is a good—if uncouth—shot at reproducing this name. The name became, in Norse, *Hugleikr* and in Danish *Huglek* (*Hugletus* in Saxo): traditional kings so named are recorded, though it is difficult to find that they have anything in common with the King Hygelac in *Beowulf*[634]. Had the name been introduced into England in Viking times, we should expect the Scandinavian form, not *Hygelād*[635].

Even in the rare cases where the character in *Beowulf* and his Scandinavian equivalent bear names which are not phonologically identical, the difference does not point to any corruption such as might have arisen from borrowing in Viking days[636]. We have only to contrast the way in which the names of Viking chiefs are recorded in the *Anglo-Saxon Chronicle*, to be convinced that the Scandinavian stories recorded in *Beowulf* are due to contact during the age when Britain was being conquered, not during the Viking period three or four centuries later[637].

And the arguments from literary and political history, which Schücking adduces to prove his late date, seem to me to point in exactly the opposite direction, and to confirm the orthodox view which would place *Beowulf* nearer 700 than 900.

Schücking urges that, however highly we estimate the civilizing effect of Christianity, it was only in the second half of the seventh century that England was thoroughly permeated by the new faith. Can we expect already, at the beginning of the eighth century, a courtly work, showing, as does *Beowulf*, such wonderful examples of tact, modesty, unselfishness and magnanimity? And this at the time when King Ceolwulf was forced by his rebellious subjects to take the cowl. For Schücking[638], following Hodgkin[639], reminds us how, in the eighth century, out of 15 Northumbrian kings, five were dethroned, five murdered; two abdicated, and only three held the crown to their death; and how at the end of the century Charlemagne called the Northumbrian Angles "a perfidious and perverse nation, murderers of their lords."

But surely, at the base of all this argument, lies the same assumption which, as Schücking rightly holds, vitiates so many of the grammatical arguments; the assumption that development must necessarily be in steady and progressive proportion. We may take Penda as a type of the unreclaimed heathen, and Edward the Confessor of the chaste and saintly churchman; but Anglo-Saxon history was by no means a development in steady progression, of diminishing percentages of ruffianism and increasing percentages of saintship.

The knowledge of, and interest in, heathen custom shown in *Beowulf*, such as the vivid accounts of cremation, would lead us to place it as near heathen times as other data will allow. So much must be granted to the argument of Prof. Chadwick[640]. But the Christian tone, so far from leading us to place *Beowulf* late, would *also* lead us to place it near the time of the conversion. For it is precisely in these times just after the conversion, that we get the most striking instances in all Old English history of that "tact, modesty, generosity, and magnanimity" which Schücking rightly regards as characteristic of *Beowulf*.

King Oswin (who was slain in 651) was, Bede tells us, handsome, courteous of speech and bearing, bountiful both to great and lowly, beloved of all men for his qualities of mind and body, so that noblemen came from all over England to enter his service—yet of all his endowments gentleness and humility were the chief. We cannot read the description without being reminded of the words of the thegns in praise of the dead Beowulf. Indeed, I doubt if Beowulf would have carried gentleness to those around him quite so far as did Oswin. For Oswin had given to Bishop Aidan an exceptionally fine horse—and Aidan gave it to a beggar who asked alms. The king's mild suggestion that a horse of less value would have been good enough for the beggar, and that the bishop needed a good horse for his own use, drew from the saint the stern question "Is that son of a mare dearer to thee than the Son of God?" The king, who had come from hunting, stood warming himself at the fire, thinking over what had passed; then he suddenly ungirt his sword, gave it to his squire, and throwing himself at the feet of the bishop, promised never again to grudge anything he might give in his charities.

Of course such conduct was exceptional in seventh century Northumbria—it convinced Aidan that the king was too good to live long, as indeed proved to be the case. But it shows that the ideals of courtesy and gentleness shown in *Beowulf* were by no means beyond the possibility of attainment—were indeed surpassed by a seventh century king. I do not know if they could be so easily paralleled in later Old English times.

And what is true from the point of view of morals is true equally from that of art and learning. In spite of the misfortunes of Northumbrian kings in the eighth century, the *first third* of that century was "the Golden Age of Anglo-Saxon England[641]." And not unnaturally, for it had been preceded by half a century during which Northumbria had been free both from internal strife and from invasion. The empire won by Oswiu over Picts and Scots in the North had been lost at the battle of Nectansmere: but that battle had been followed by the twenty years reign of the learned Aldfrid, whose scholarship did not prevent him from nobly retrieving the state of the kingdom[642], though he could not recover the lost dominions.

Now, whatever we may think of *Beowulf* as poetry, it is remarkable for its conscious and deliberate art, and for the tone of civilization which pervades it. And this half century was distinguished, above any other period of Old English history, precisely for its art and its civilization. Four and a half centuries later, when the works of great Norman master builders were rising everywhere in the land, the buildings which Bishop Wilfrid had put up during this first period of conversion were still objects of admiration, even for those who had seen the glories of the great Roman basilicas[643].

Nor is there anything surprising in the fact that this "golden age" was not maintained. On the contrary, it is "in accordance with the phenomena of Saxon history in general, in which seasons of brilliant promise are succeeded by long eras of national eclipse. It is from this point of view quite in accordance with natural likelihood that the age of conversion was one of such stimulus to the artistic powers of the people that a level of effort and achievement was reached which subsequent generations were not able to maintain. The carved crosses and the coins certainly degenerate in artistic value as the centuries pass away, and the fine barbaric gold and encrusted work is early in date[644]."

Already in the early part of the eighth century signs of decay are to be observed. At the end of his *Ecclesiastical History*, Bede complains that the times are so full of disturbance that one knows not what to say, or what the end will be. And these fears were justified. A hundred and forty years of turmoil and decay follow, till the civilization of the North and the Midlands was overthrown by the Danes, and York became the uneasy seat of a heathen jarl.

How it should be possible to see in these facts, as contrasted with the Christian and civilized tone of *Beowulf*, any argument for late date, I cannot see. On the contrary, because of its Christian civilization combined with its still vivid, if perhaps not always quite exact, recollection of heathen customs, we should be inclined to put *Beowulf* in the early Christian ages.

A further argument put forward for this late date is the old one that the Scandinavian sympathies of *Beowulf* show it to have been composed for a Scandinavian court, the court, Schücking thinks, of one of the princes who ruled over those portions of England which the Danes had settled[645]. Of course Schücking is too sound a scholar to revive at this time of day the old fallacy that the Anglo-Saxons ought to have taken no interest in the deeds of any but Anglo-Saxon heroes. But how, he asks, are we to account for such *enthusiasm* for, such a burning interest in, a people of alien dialect and foreign dynasty, such as the Scyldings of Denmark?

The answer seems to me to be that the enthusiasm of *Beowulf* is not for the Danish nation as such: on the contrary, *Beowulf* depicts a situation which is most humiliating to the Danes. For twelve years they have suffered the depredations of Grendel; Hrothgar and his kin have proved helpless: all the Danes have been unequal to the need. Twice at least this is emphasized in the most uncompromising, and indeed insulting, way[646]. The poet's enthusiasm is not, then, for the Danish race as such, but for the ideal of a great court with its body of retainers. Such retainers are not necessarily native born—rather is it the mark of the great court that it draws men from far and wide to enter the service, whether permanently or temporarily, even as Beowulf came from afar to help the aged Hrothgar in his need.

It is this ideal of personal valour and personal loyalty, rather than of tribal patriotism, which pervades *Beowulf*, and which certainly suits the known facts of the seventh and early eighth centuries. The bitterest strife in England in the seventh century had been between the two quite new states of

Northumbria and Mercia, both equally of Anglian race. Both these states had been built up by a combination of smaller units, and not without violating the old local patriotisms of the diverse elements from which they had been formed. At first, at any rate, no such thing as Northumbrian or Mercian patriotism can have existed. Loyalty was personal, to the king. Neither the kingdom nor the *comitatus* was homogeneous. We have seen that Bede mentions it as a peculiar honour to a Northumbrian prince that *from all parts of England* nobles came to enter his service. We must not demand from the seventh or eighth century our ideals of exclusive enthusiasm for the land of one's birth, ideals which make it disreputable for a "mercenary" to sell his sword. The ideal is, on the contrary, loyalty to a prince whose service a warrior *voluntarily* enters. And the Danish court is depicted as a pattern of such loyalty—before the Scyldings began to work evil[647], by the treason of Hrothulf.

Further, the fact that the Danish court at Leire had been a heathen one might be matter for regret, but it would not prevent its being praised by an Englishman about 700. For England was then entirely Christian. In the process of conversion no single Christian had, so far as we know, been martyred. There had been no war of religion. If Penda had fought against Oswald, it had been as the king of Mercia against the king of Northumbria. Penda's allies were Christian, and he showed no antipathy to the new faith[648]. So that at this date there was no reason for men to feel any deep hostility towards a heathendom which had been the faith of their grandfathers, and with which there had never been any embittered conflict.

But in 900 the position was quite different. For more than a generation the country had been engaged in a life-and-death struggle between two warring camps, the "Christian men" and the "heathen men." The "heathen men" were in process of conversion, but were liable to be ever recruited afresh from beyond the sea. It seems highly unlikely that *Beowulf* could have been written at this date, by some English poet, for the court of a converted Scandinavian prince, with a view perhaps, as Schücking suggests, to educating his children in the English speech. In such a case the one thing likely to be avoided by the English poet, with more than two centuries of Christianity behind him, would surely have been the praise of that Scandinavian heathendom, from which his patron had freed himself, and from which his children were to be weaned. The martyrdom of S. Edmund might have seemed a more appropriate theme[649]. The tolerant attitude towards heathen customs, and the almost antiquarian interest in them, very justly, as it seems to me, emphasized by Schücking[650], is surely far more possible in A.D. 700 than in A.D. 900. For between those dates heathendom had ceased to be an antiquarian curiosity, and had become an imminent peril.

If those are right who hold that *Beowulf* is no purely native growth, but shows influence of the classical epic, then again it is easier to credit such influence about the year 700 than 900. At the earlier date we have scholars like Aldhelm and Bede, both well acquainted with Virgil, yet both interested in vernacular verse. It has been urged, as a *reductio ad absurdum* of the view which would connect *Beowulf* with Virgil, that the relation to the *Odyssey* is more obvious than that to the *Æneid*. Perhaps, however, some remote and indirect connection even between *Beowulf* and the *Odyssey* is not altogether unthinkable, about the year 700. At the end of the seventh century there was a flourishing school of Greek learning in England, under Hadrian and the Greek Archbishop Theodore, both "well read in sacred *and in secular* literature." In 730 their scholars were still alive, and, Bede tells us, could speak Greek and Latin as correctly as their native tongue. Bede himself knew something about the *Iliad* and the *Odyssey*. Not till eight centuries have passed, and we reach Grocyn and Linacre, was it again to be as easy for an Englishman to have a first-hand knowledge of a Greek classic as it was about the year 700. What scholarship had sunk to by the days of Alfred, we know: and we know that all Alfred's patronage did not produce any scholar whom we can think of as in the least degree comparable to Bede.

So that from the point of view of its close touch with heathendom, its tolerance for heathen customs, its Christian magnanimity and gentleness, its conscious art, and its learned tone, all historic and artistic analogy would lead us to place *Beowulf* in the great age—the age of Bede.

This has brought us to another question—more interesting to many than the mere question of date. Are we to suppose any direct connection between the classical and the Old English epic?

As nations pass through their "Heroic Age," similar social conditions will necessarily be reflected by many similarities in their poetry. In heroic lays like *Finnsburg* or *Hildebrand* or the Norse poems, phrases and situations may occur which remind us of phrases and situations in the *Iliad*, without affording any ground for supposing classical influence direct or indirect.

But there is much more in *Beowulf* than mere accidental coincidence of phrase or situation.

A simple-minded romancer would have made the *Æneid* a biography of Æneas from the cradle to the grave. Not so Virgil. The story begins with mention of Carthage. Æneas then comes on the scene. At a banquet he tells to Dido his earlier adventures. Just so *Beowulf* begins, not with the birth of Beowulf and his boyhood, but with Heorot. Beowulf arrives. At the banquet, in reply to Unferth, he narrates his earlier adventures. The *Beowulf*-poet is not content merely to tell us that there was minstrelsy at the feast, but like Virgil or Homer, he must give an account of what was sung. The epic style leads often to almost verbal similarities. Jupiter consoling Hercules for the loss of the son of his host says:

stat sua cuique dies, breve et inreparabile tempus
omnibus est vitae; sed famam extendere factis
hoc virtutis opus[651].

In the same spirit and almost in the same words does Beowulf console Hrothgar for the loss of his friend:

Ūre ǣghwylc sceal ende gebīdan
worolde līfes; wyrce sē þe mōte
dōmes ǣr dēaþe; þæt biþ drihtguman
unlifgendum æfter sēlest.

On the other hand, though we are often struck by the likeness in spirit and in plan, it must be allowed that there is no tangible or conclusive proof of borrowing[652]. But the influence may have been none the less effective for being indirect: nor is it quite certain that the author, had he known his Virgil, would necessarily have left traces of direct borrowing. For the deep Christian feeling, which has given to *Beowulf* its almost prudish propriety and its edifying tone, is manifested by no direct and dogmatic reference to Christian personages or doctrines.

I sympathize with Prof. Chadwick's feeling that a man who knew Virgil would not have disguised his knowledge, and would probably have lacked both inclination and ability to compose such a poem as *Beowulf*[653]. But does not this feeling rest largely upon the analogy of other races and ages? Is it borne out by such known facts as we can gather about this period? The reticence of *Beowulf* with reference to Christianity does not harmonize with one's preconceived ideas; and Bishop Aldhelm gives us an even greater surprise. Let anyone read, or try to read, Aldhelm's *Epistola ad Acircium, sive liber de septenario et de metris.* Let him then ask himself "Is it possible that this learned pedant can also have been the author of English poems which King Alfred—surely no mean judge—thought best of all he knew?" These poems may of course have been educated and learned in tone. But we have the authority of King Alfred for the fact that Aldhelm used to perform at the cross roads as a common minstrel, and that he could hold his audiences with such success that they resorted to him again and again[654]. Only after he had made himself popular by several performances did he attempt to weave edifying matter into his verse. And the popular, secular poetry of Aldhelm, his *carmen triviale*, remained current among the common people for centuries. Nor was Aldhelm's classical knowledge of late growth, something superimposed upon an earlier love of popular poetry, for he had studied under Hadrian as a boy[655]. Later we are told that King Ine imported two Greek teachers from Athens for the help of Aldhelm and his school[656]; this may be exaggeration.

Everything seems to show that about 700 an atmosphere existed in England which might easily have led a scholarly Englishman, acquainted with the old lays, to have set to work to compose an epic. Even so venerable a person as Bede, during his last illness, uttered his last teaching not, as we should expect on *a priori* grounds, in Latin hexameters, but in English metre. The evidence for this is conclusive[657]. But, at a later date, Alcuin would surely have condemned the minstrelsy of Aldhelm[658]. Even King Alfred seems to have felt that it needed some apology. It would have rendered Aldhelm liable to severe censure under the Laws of King Edgar[659]; and Dunstan's biographer indignantly denies the charge brought against his hero of having learnt the heathen songs of his forefathers[660].

The evidence is not as plentiful as we might wish, but it rather suggests that the chasm between secular poetry and ecclesiastical learning was more easily bridged in the first generations after the conversion than was the case later.

But, however that may be, it assuredly does not give any grounds for abandoning the old view, based largely upon grammatical and metrical considerations, which would make *Beowulf* a product of the early eighth century, and substituting for it a theory which would make our poem a product of mixed Saxon and Danish society in the early tenth century.

E. THE "JUTE-QUESTION" REOPENED

The view that the Geatas of *Beowulf* are the Jutes (Iuti, Iutae) of Bede (i.e. the tribe which colonized Kent, the Isle of Wight and Hampshire) has been held by many eminent scholars. It was dealt with only briefly above (pp. 8-9) because I thought the theory was now recognized as being no longer tenable. Lately, however, it has been maintained with conviction and ability by two Danish scholars, Schütte and Kier. It therefore becomes necessary once more to reopen the question, now that the only elaborate discussion of it in the English language favours the "Jute-theory," especially as Axel Olrik gave the support of his great name to the view that "the question is still open[661]" and that "the last word has not been said concerning the nationality of the Geatas[662]."

As in most controversies, a number of rather irrelevant side issues have been introduced[663], so that from mere weariness students are sometimes inclined to leave the problem undecided. Yet the interpretation of the opening chapters of Scandinavian history turns upon it.

Supporters of the "Jute-theory" have seldom approached the subject from the point of view of Old English. Bugge[664] perhaps did so: but the "Jute-theory" has been held chiefly by students of Scandinavian history, literature or geography, like Fahlbeck[665], Steenstrup[666], Gering[667], Olrik[668], Schütte[669] and Kier[670]. But, now that the laws of Old English sound-change have been clearly defined, it seldom happens that anyone who approaches the subject primarily as a student of the Anglo-Saxon language holds the view that the Geatas are Jutes.

And this is naturally so: for, from the point of view of language, the question is not disputable. The *Gēatas* phonologically are the *Gautar* (the modern Götar of Southern Sweden). It is admitted that the words are identical[671]. And, equally, it is admitted that the word *Gēatas* cannot be identical with the word *Iuti, Iutae*, used by Bede as the name of the Jutes who colonized Kent[671]. Bede's *Iuti, Iutae*, on the contrary, would correspond to a presumed Old English *Īuti* or *Īutan*[672], current in his time in Northumbria. This in later Northumbrian would become *Īote, Īotan* (though the form *Īute, Īutan* might also survive). The dialect forms which we should expect (and which we find in the genitive and dative) corresponding to this would be: Mercian, *Ēote, Ēotan*; Late West-Saxon, *Ӯte, Ӯtan* (through an intermediate Early West-Saxon *Īete, *Īetan*, which is not recorded).

If, then, the word *Gēatas* came to supplant the correct form *Īote, Īotan* (or its Mercian and West-Saxon equivalents *Ēote, Ēotan, Ӯte, Ӯtan*), this can only have been the result of confusion. Such confusion is, on abstract grounds, conceivable: it is always possible that the name of one tribe may come to be attached to another. "Scot" has ceased to mean "Irishman," and has come to mean "North Briton"; and there is no intrinsic impossibility in the word *Gēatas* having been transferred by Englishmen, from the half-forgotten Gautar, to the Jutes, and having driven out the correct name of the latter, *Īote, Īotan*. For example, there might have been an exiled Geatic family among the Jutish invaders, which might have become so prominent as to cause the name *Gēatas* to supplant the correct *Īote, Ēote*, etc. But, whoever the Geatas may have been, *Beowulf* is their chief early record: indeed, almost all we know of their earliest history is derived from *Beowulf*. In *Beowulf*, therefore, if anywhere, the old names and traditions should be remembered. The word *Gēat* occurs some 50 times in the poem. The poet obviously wishes to use other synonyms, for the sake of variety and alliteration: hence we get *Weder-Gēatas, Wederas, Sǣ-Gēatas, Gūð-Gēatas*. Now, if these Geatas are the Jutes, how comes it that the poet *never* calls them such, never speaks of them under the correct tribal name of *Ēote*, etc., although this was the current name at the time *Beowulf* was written, and indeed for centuries later?

For, demonstrably, the form *Ēote*, etc., *was* recognized as the name of the Jutes till at least the twelfth century. Then it died out of current speech, and only Bede's Latin *Iuti* (and the modern "Jute" derived therefrom) remained as terms used by the historians. The evidence is conclusive:

(*a*) Bede, writing about the time when *Beowulf*, in its present form, is supposed to have been composed, uses *Iuti*, *Iutae*, corresponding to a presumed contemporary Northumbrian **Īuti*, **Īutan*.

(*b*) In the O.E. translation of Bede, made in Mercia perhaps two centuries after Bede's time, we do indeed in one place find "Geata," "Geatum" used to translate "Iutarum," "Iutis," instead of the correctly corresponding Mercian form "Eota," "Eotum." Only two MSS are extant at this point. But since both agree, and since they belong to different types, it is probable that "Geata" here is no mere copyist's error, but is due to the translator himself[673]. But, later, when the translator has to render Bede's "Iutorum," he gives, not "Geata," but the correct Mercian "Eota." There can be no possible doubt here, for five MSS are extant at this point, and all give the correct form— four in the Mercian, "Eota," whilst one gives the West-Saxon equivalent, "Ytena."

Now the *Gēata*-passage in the Bede translation is the chief piece of evidence which those who would explain the Geatas of *Beowulf* as "Jutes" can call: and it does not, in fact, much help them. What they have to prove is that the *Beowulf*-poet could *consistently and invariably* have used *Gēatas* in the place of *Ēote*. To produce an instance in which the two terms are both used by the same translator is very little use, when what has to be proved is that the one term had already, at a much earlier period, entirely ousted the other.

All our other evidence is for the invariable use of the correct form *Īote*, *Īotan*, etc. in Old English.

(*c*) The passage from Bede was again translated, and inserted into a copy of the *Anglo-Saxon Chronicle*, which was sent quite early to one of the great abbeys of Northumbria[674]. In this, "Iutis, Iutarum" is represented by the correct Northumbrian equivalent, "Iutum," "Iotum"; "Iutna."

(*d*) This Northumbrian Chronicle, or a transcript of it, subsequently came South, to Canterbury. There, roughly about the year 1100, it was used to interpolate an Early West-Saxon copy of the Chronicle. Surely at Canterbury, the capital of the old Jutish kingdom, people must have known the correct form of the Jutish name, whether *Gēatas* or *Īote*. We find the forms "Iotum," "Iutum"; "Iutna."

(*e*) Corresponding to this Northumbrian (and Kentish) form *Īote*, Mercian *Ēote*, the Late West-Saxon form should be *Ȳte*. Now *MS Corpus Christi College, Cambridge,* 41, gives us "the Wessex version of the English Bede" and is written by a scribe who knew the Hampshire district[675]. In this MS the "Eota" of the Mercian original has been transcribed as "Ytena," "Eotum" as "Ytum," showing that the scribe understood the tribal name and its equivalent correctly. This was about the time of the Norman Conquest, but the name continued to be understood till the early twelfth century at least. For Florence of Worcester records that William Rufus was slain *in Noua Foresta quae lingua Anglorum Ytene nuncupatur,* and in another place he speaks of the same event as happening *in prouincia Jutarum in Noua Foresta*[676], which shows that Florence understood that "Ytene" was *Ȳtena land,* "the province of the Jutes."

It comes, then, to this. The "Jute-hypothesis" postulates not only that, at the time *Beowulf* was composed, *Gēatas* had come to mean "Jutes," but also that it had so completely ousted the correct old name *Īuti, Īote, Ēote, Ȳte,* that none of the latter terms are ever used in the poem as synonyms for Beowulf's people[677]. Yet all the evidence shows that *Īuti* etc. was the recognized name when Bede wrote, and we have evidence at intervals showing that it was so understood till four centuries later. But not only was *Īuti, Īote* never superseded in O.E. times; there is no real evidence that *Gēatas* was ever *generally* used to signify "Jutes." The fact that one translator in one passage (writing probably some two centuries after *Beowulf* was composed) uses "Geata," "Geatum," where he should have used "Eota," "Eotum," does not prove the misnomer to have been general—especially when the same translator subsequently uses the correct form "Eota."

I do not think sufficient importance has been attached to what seems (to me) the vital argument against the "Jute-theory." It is not merely that *Gēatas* is the exact phonological equivalent of *Gautar* (Götar) and cannot be equivalent to Bede's *Īuti.* This difficulty may be got over by the assumption that somehow the *Īuti,* or some of them, had adopted the name *Gēatas:* and we are not in a position to disprove such assumption. But the advocates of the "Jute-theory" have further to assume that, at the date when *Beowulf* was written, the correct name *Īuti* (Northumbrian *Īote,* Mercian *Ēote,* West-Saxon *Ȳte*) must have so passed into disuse that it could not be once used as a synonym for Beowulf's people, by our synonym-hunting poet. And this assumption we *are* in a position to disprove.

The Jute-theory would therefore still be untenable on the ground of the name, even though it were laboriously proved that, from the historical and geographical standpoint, there was more to be said for it than had hitherto been recognized. But even this has not been proved: quite the reverse. As I have tried to show above, historical and geographical considerations, though in themselves not absolutely conclusive, point emphatically to an identification with the Götar, rather than with the Jutes[678].

The relations of Beowulf and the Geatas with the kings of Denmark and of Sweden are the constant topic of the poem. Now the land of the Götar *was* situated between Denmark and Sweden. But if the Geatas be Jutes, their neighbours were the Danes on the east and the Angles on the south; farther away, across the Cattegat lay the Götar, and beyond these the Swedes. If the Geatas be Jutes, why should their immediate neighbours, the Angles, never appear in *Beowulf* as having any dealings with them? And why, above all, should the Götar never be mentioned, whilst the Swedes, far to the north, play so large a part? Even if Swedes and Götar had at this time been under one king, the Götar could not have been thus ignored, seeing that, owing to their position, the brunt of the fighting must have fallen on them[679]. But we know that the Götar were independent. The strictly contemporary evidence of Procopius shows quite conclusively that they were one of the strongest of the Scandinavian kingdoms[680]. How then could warfare be carried on for three generations between Jutes and Swedes without concerning the Götar, whose territory lay in between?

Again, in the "Catalogue of Kings" in *Widsith*, the Swedes are named with their famous king Ongentheow. The Jutes (*Ȳte*) are also mentioned, with *their* king. And their king is not Hrethel, Hæthcyn, Hygelac or Heardred, but a certain Gefwulf, whose name does not even alliterate with that of any known king of the Geatas[681].

Again, in the (certainly very early) *Book on Monsters*, Hygelac is described as *Huiglaucus qui imperavit Getis*. Now Getis can mean Götar[682], but can hardly mean Jutes.

The geographical case against the identification of Geatas and Götar depends upon the assumption that the western sea-coast of the Götar in ancient times must have coincided with that of West Gothland (Vestra-Götland) in mediæval and modern times. Now as this coast consists merely of a small strip south of the river Götaelv, it is argued that the Götar could not be the maritime Geatas of *Beowulf*, capable of undertaking a Viking raid to the mouth of the Rhine. But the assumption that the frontiers of the Götar about

A.D. 500 were the same as they were a thousand years later, is not only improbable on *a priori* grounds, but, as Schück has shown[683], can be definitely disproved. Adam of Bremen, writing in the eleventh century, speaks of the river Gothelba (Götaelv) as running through the midst of the peoples of the Götar. And the obvious connection between the name of the river and the name of the people seems to make it certain that Adam is right, and that the original Götar must have dwelt around the river Götaelv. But, if so, then they were a maritime folk: for the river Götaelv is merely the outlet which connects Lake Wener with the sea, running a course almost parallel with the shore and nowhere very distant from it[684]. But even when Adam wrote, the Götar to the north of the river had long been politically subject to Norway[685]: and the *Heimskringla* tells us how this happened.

Harold Fairhair, King of Norway (a contemporary of King Alfred), attacked them: they had staked the river Götaelv against him, but he moored his ships to the stakes[686] and harried *on either shore*: he fought far and wide in the country, had many battles *on either side of the river*, and finally slew the leader of the Götar, Hrani Gauzki (the Götlander). Then he annexed to Norway all the land north of the river and west of Lake Wener. Thenceforward the Götaelv was the boundary between Norway and West Gothland, though the country ultimately became Swedish, as it now is. But it is abundantly clear from the *Heimskringla* that Harold regarded as hostile all the territory north of the Götaelv, and between Lake Wener and the sea[687] (the old Ránriki and the modern Bohuslän).

But, if so, then the objection that the Götar are not a sufficiently maritime people becomes untenable. For precisely to this region belong the earliest records of maritime warfare to be found in the north of Europe, possibly the earliest in Europe. The smooth rocks of Bohuslän are covered with incised pictures of the Bronze age: and the favourite subject of these is ships and naval encounters. About 120 different pictures of ships and sea fights are reproduced by one scholar alone[688]. And at the present day this province of Göteborg and Bohus is the most important centre in Sweden both of fishery and shipping. Indeed, more than one quarter of the total tonnage of the modern Swedish mercantile marine comes from this comparatively tiny strip of coast[689].

It is surely quite absurd to urge that the men of this coast could not have harried the Frisians in the manner in which Hygelac is represented as doing. And surely it is equally absurd to urge that the people of this coast would not have had to fear a return attack from the Frisians, after the downfall of their own kings. The Frisians seem to have been "the chief channel of communication between the North and West of Europe[690]" before the rise of the Scandinavian Vikings, and to have been supreme in the North Sea. The Franks were of course a land power, but the Franks, *when in alliance with the Frisians*, were by no means helpless at sea. Gregory of Tours tells us that they overthrew Hygelac on land, and *then in a sea fight annihilated his fleet*. Now the poet says that the Geatas may expect war when the Franks *and Frisians* hear of Beowulf's fall. The objection that, because they feared the Franks, the Geatas must have been reachable by land, depends upon leaving the "and Frisians" out of consideration.

"Now we may look for a time of war" says the messenger "when the fall of our king is known among the Franks and Frisians": then he gives a brief account of the raid upon the land of the Frisians and concludes: "Ever since then has the favour of the Merovingian king been denied us[691]." What is there in this to indicate whether the raiders came from Jutland, or from the coast of the Götar across the Cattegat, 50 miles further off? The messenger goes on to anticipate hostility from the Swedes[692]. To this, at any rate, the Götar were more exposed than the Jutes. Further, he concludes by anticipating the utter overthrow of the Geatas[693]: and the poet expressly tells us that these forebodings were justified[694]. There must therefore be a reference to some famous national catastrophe. Now the Götar *did* lose their independence, and *were* incorporated into the Swedish kingdom. When did the Jutes suffer any similar downfall at the hands of either Frisians, Franks, or Swedes?

The other geographical and historical arguments urged in favour of the Jutes, when carefully scrutinized, are found either equally indecisive, or else actually to tell against the "Jute-theory." Schütte[695] thinks that the name "Wederas" (applied in *Beowulf* to the Geatas) is identical with the name *Eudoses* (that of a tribe mentioned by Tacitus, who *may*[696] have dwelt in Jutland). But this is impossible phonologically: *Wederas* is surely a shortened form of *Weder-Gēatas*, "the Storm-Geatas." Indeed, we have, in favour of the Götar-theory, the fact that the very name of the Wederas survives on the Bohuslän coast to this day, in the Wäder Öar and the Wäder Fiord.

Advocates of the "Jute-theory" lay great stress upon the fact that Gregory of Tours and the *Liber Historiae Francorum* call Hygelac a Dane[697]: *Dani cum rege suo Chochilaico*. Now, when Gregory wrote in the sixth century, either the Jutes were entirely distinct from, and independent of, the Danes, or they were not. If they were distinct, how do Gregory's words help the "Jute-theory"? He must be simply using "Dane," like the Anglo-Saxon historians, for "Scandinavian." But if the Jutes were not distinct from the Danes, then we have an argument against the "Jute-theory." For we know from *Beowulf* that the Geatas *were* quite distinct from the Danes[698], and quite independent of them[699].

It is repeatedly urged that the Geatas and Swedes fight *ofer sǽ*[700]. But *sǽ* can mean a great fresh-water lake, like Lake Wener, just as well as the ocean[701]: and as a matter of fact we know that the decisive battle did take place on Lake Wener, *in stagno Waener, á Vænis ísi*[702]. Lake Wener is an obvious battle place for Götar and Swedes. They were separated by the great and almost impassable forests of "Tived" and "Kolmård," and the lake was their simplest way of meeting[703]. But it does not equally fit Jutes and Swedes.

It is repeatedly objected that the Götar are remote from the Anglo-Saxons[704]. Possibly: but remoteness did not prevent the Anglo-Saxons from being interested in heroes of the Huns or Goths or Burgundians or Longobards, who were much more[705] distant. And the absence of any direct connection between the history of the Geatas and the historic Anglo-Saxon records, affords a strong presumption that the Geatas *were* a somewhat alien people. If the people of Beowulf, Hygelac, and Hrethel, were the same people as the Jutes who colonized Kent and Hampshire, why do we never, in the Kentish royal genealogies or elsewhere, find any claim to such connection? The Mercians did not so forget their connection with the old Offa of Angel, although a much greater space of time had intervened. The fact that we have no mention among the ancestors of Beowulf and Hygelac of any names which we can connect with the Jutish genealogy affords, therefore, a strong presumption that they belonged to some other tribe.

The strongest historical argument for the "Jute-theory" was that produced by Bugge. The *Ynglinga tal* represents Ottar (who is certainly the Ohthere of *Beowulf*) as having fallen in Vendel, and this Vendel was clearly understood as being the district of that name in North Jutland. The body of this Swedish king was torn asunder by carrion birds, and he was remembered as "the Vendel-crow," a mocking nickname which pretty clearly goes back to primitive times. Other ancient authors attributed this name, not to Ottar, but to his father, who can be identified with the Ongentheow of *Beowulf*. This would seem to indicate that the hereditary foes of Ongentheow and the Swedish kings of his house were, after all, the Jutes of Vendel.

But Knut Stjerna has shown that the Vendel from which "Ottar Vendel-crow" took his name was probably not the Vendel of Jutland at all, but the place of that name north of Uppsala, famous for the splendid grave-finds which show it to have been of peculiar importance during our period[706]. And subsequent research has shown that a huge grave-mound, near this Vendel, is mentioned in a record of the seventeenth century as King Ottar's mound, and is still popularly known as the mound of Ottar Vendel-crow[707]. But, if so, this story of the Vendel-crow, so far from supporting the "Jute-hypothesis," tells against it: nothing could be more suitable than Vendel, north of Uppsala, as the "last ditch" to which Ongentheow retreated, if we assume his adversaries to have been the Götar: but it would not suit the Jutes so well.

An exploration of the mound has proved beyond reasonable doubt that it *was* raised to cover the ashes of Ottar Vendel-crow, the Ohthere of *Beowulf*[708]. That Ohthere fell in battle against the Geatas there is nothing, in *Beowulf* or elsewhere, to prove. But the fact that his ashes were laid in mound at Vendel in Sweden makes it unlikely that he fell in battle against the Jutes, and is quite incompatible with what we are told in the *Ynglinga saga* of his body having been torn to pieces by carrion fowl on a mound in Vendel in Jutland. It now becomes clear that this story, and the tale of the crow of wood made by the Jutlanders in mockery of Ottar, is a mere invention to account for the name Vendel-crow: the name, as so often, has survived, and a new story has grown up to give a reason for the name.

What "Vendel-crow" originally implied we cannot be quite sure. Apparently "Crow" or "Vendel-crow" is used to this day as a nickname for the inhabitants of Swedish Vendel. Ottar may have been so called because he was buried (possibly because he lived) in Vendel, not, like other members of his race, his son and his father, at Old Uppsala. But however that may be, what is clear is that, as the name passed from the Swedes to those Norwegian and Icelandic writers who have handed it down to us, Vendel of Sweden was naturally misunderstood as the more familiar Vendel of Jutland. Stjerna's conjecture is confirmed. The Swedish king's nickname, far from pointing to ancient feuds between Jute and Swede, is shown to have nothing whatsoever to do with Jutland.

It appears, then, that *Gēatas* is phonologically the equivalent of "Götar," but not the equivalent of "Jutes"; that what we know of the use of the word "Jutes" (*Īote*, etc.) in Old English makes it incredible that a poem of the length of *Beowulf* could be written, concerning their heroes and their wars, without even mentioning them by their correct name; that in many respects the geographical and historical evidence fits the Götar, but does *not* fit the Jutes; that the instances to the contrary, in which it is claimed that the geographical and historical evidence fits the Jutes but does not fit the Götar, are all found on examination to be either inconclusive or actually to favour the Götar.

F. *BEOWULF* AND THE ARCHÆOLOGISTS

The peat-bogs of Schleswig and Denmark have yielded finds of the first importance for English archæology. These "moss-finds" are great collections, chiefly of arms and accoutrements, obviously deposited with intention. The first of these great discoveries, that of Thorsbjerg, was made in the heart of ancient Angel: the site of the next, Nydam, also comes within the area probably occupied by either Angles or Jutes; and most of the rest of the "moss-finds" were in the closest neighbourhood of the old Anglian home. The period of the oldest deposits, as is shown by the Roman coins found among them, is hardly before the third century A.D., and some authorities would make it considerably later.

An account of these discoveries will be found in Engelhardt's *Denmark in the Early Iron Age*[709], 1866: a volume which summarizes the results of Engelhardt's investigations during the preceding seven years. He had published in Copenhagen *Thorsbjerg Mosefund*, 1863; *Nydam Mosefund*, 1865. Engelhardt's work at Nydam was interrupted by the war of 1864: the finds had to be ceded to Germany, and the exploration was continued by German scholars. Engelhardt consoled himself that these "subsequent investigations ... do not seem to have been carried on with the necessary care and intelligence," and continued his own researches within the narrowed frontiers of Denmark, publishing two monographs on the mosses of Fünen: *Kragehul Mosefund*, 1867; *Vimose Fundet*, 1869.

These deposits, however, obviously belong to a period much earlier than that in which *Beowulf* was written: indeed most of them certainly belong to a period earlier than that in which the historic events described in *Beowulf* occurred; so that, close as is their relation with Anglian civilization, it is with the civilization of the Angles while still on the continent.

The Archæology of *Beowulf* has been made the subject of special study by Knut Stjerna, in a series of articles which appeared between 1903 and his premature death in 1909. A good service has been done to students of *Beowulf* by Dr Clark Hall in collecting and translating Stjerna's essays[710]. They are a mine of useful information, and the reproductions of articles from Scandinavian grave-finds, with which they are so copiously illustrated, are invaluable. The magnificent antiquities from Vendel, now in the Stockholm museum, are more particularly laid under contribution[711]. Dr Clark Hall added a most useful "Index of things mentioned in *Beowulf*[712]," well illustrated. Here again the illustrations, with few exceptions, are from Scandinavian finds.

Two weighty arguments as to the origin of *Beowulf* have been based upon archæology. In the first place it has been urged by Dr Clark Hall that:

"If the poem is read in the light of the evidence which Stjerna has marshalled in the essays as to the profusion of gold, the prevalence of ring-swords, of boar-helmets, of ring-corslets, and ring-money, it becomes clear how strong the distinctively Scandinavian colouring is, and how comparatively little of the *mise-en-scène* must be due to the English author[713]."

Equally, Prof. Klaeber finds in Stjerna's investigations a strong argument for the Scandinavian character of *Beowulf*[714].

Now Stjerna, very rightly and naturally, drew his illustrations of *Beowulf* from those Scandinavian, and especially Swedish, grave-finds which he knew so well: and very valuable those illustrations are. But it does not follow, because the one archæologist who has chosen to devote his knowledge so wholeheartedly to the elucidation of *Beowulf* was a Scandinavian, using Scandinavian material, that therefore *Beowulf* is Scandinavian. This, however, is the inference which Stjerna himself was apt to draw, and which is still being drawn from his work. Stjerna speaks of our poem as a monument raised by the Geatas to the memory of their saga-renowned king[715], though he allows that certain features of the poem, such as the dragon-fight[716], are of Anglo-Saxon origin.

Of course, it must be allowed that accounts such as those of the fighting between Swedes and Geatas, if they are historical (and they obviously are), must have originated from eyewitnesses of the Scandinavian battles: but I doubt if there is anything in *Beowulf* so purely Scandinavian as to compel us to assume that any line of the story, in the poetical form in which we now have it, was *necessarily* composed in Scandinavia. Even if it could be shown that the conditions depicted in *Beowulf* can be better illustrated from the grave-finds of Vendel in Sweden than from English diggings, this would not prove *Beowulf* Scandinavian. Modern scientific archæology is surely based on chronology as well as geography. The English finds date from the period before 650 A.D., and the Vendel finds from the period after. *Beowulf* might well show similarity rather with contemporary art abroad than with the art of earlier generations at home. For intercourse was more general than is always realized. It was not merely trade and plunder which spread fashions from nation to nation. There were the presents of arms which Tacitus mentions as sent, not only privately, but with public ceremony, from one tribe to another[717]. Similar presentations are indicated in *Beowulf*[718]; we find them equally at the court of the Ostrogothic Theodoric[719]; Charles the Great sent to Offa of Mercia *unum balteum et unum gladium huniscum*[720]; according to the famous story in the *Heimskringla*, Athelstan sent to Harold Fairhair of Norway a sword and belt arrayed with gold and silver; Athelstan gave Harold's son Hakon a sword which was the best that ever came to Norway[721]. It is not surprising, then, if we find parallels between English poetry and Scandinavian grave-finds, both apparently dating from about the year 700 A.D. But I do not think that there is any *special* resemblance, though, both in *Beowulf* and in the Vendel graves, there is a profusion lacking in the case of the simpler Anglo-Saxon tomb-furniture.

Let us examine the five points of special resemblance, alleged by Dr Clark Hall, on the basis of Stjerna's studies.

"The profusion of gold." Gold is indeed lavishly used in *Beowulf*: the golden treasure found in the dragon's lair was so bulky that it had to be transported by waggon. And, certainly, gold is found in greater profusion in Swedish than in English graves: the most casual visitor to the Stockholm museum must be impressed by the magnificence of the exhibits there. But, granting gold to have been rarer in England than in Sweden, I cannot grant Stjerna's contention that therefore an English poet could not have conceived the idea of a vast gold hoard[722]; or that, even if the poet does deck his warriors with gold somewhat more sumptuously than was actually the case in England, we can draw any argument from it. For, if the dragon in *Beowulf* guards a treasure, so equally does the typical dragon of Old English proverbial lore[723]. Beowulf is spoken of as *gold-wlanc*, but the typical thegn in *Finnsburg* is called *gold-hladen*[724]. The sword found by Beowulf in the hall of Grendel's mother has a golden hilt, but the English proverb had it that "gold is in its place on a man's sword[725]." Heorot is hung with golden tapestry, but gold-inwoven fabric has been unearthed from Saxon graves at Taplow, and elsewhere in England[726]. Gold glitters in other poems quite as lavishly as in *Beowulf*, sometimes more so. Widsith made a hobby of collecting golden *bēagas*. The subject of *Waldere* is a fight for treasure. The byrnie of Waldere[727] is adorned with gold: so is that of Holofernes in *Judith*[728], so is that of the typical warrior in the *Elene*[729]. Are all these poems Scandinavian?

"The prevalence of ring-swords." We know that swords were sometimes fitted with a ring in the hilt[730]. It is not clear whether the object of this ring was to fasten the hilt by a strap to the wrist, for convenience in fighting (as has been the custom with the cavalry sword in modern times) or whether it was used to attach the "peace bands," by which the hilt of the sword was sometimes fixed to the scabbard, when only being worn ceremonially[731]. The word *hring-mǣl*, applied three times to the sword in *Beowulf*, has been interpretated as a reference to these "ring-swords," though it is quite conceivable that it may refer only to the damascening of the sword with a ringed pattern[732]. Assuming that the reference in *Beowulf is* to a "ring-sword," Stjerna illustrates the allusion from seven ring-swords, or fragments of ring-swords, found in Sweden. But, as Dr Clark Hall himself points out (whilst oddly enough accepting this argument as proof of the Scandinavian colouring of *Beowulf*) four ring-swords at least have been found in England[733]. And these English swords are *real* ring-swords; that is to say, the pommel is furnished with a ring, within which another ring moves (in the oldest type of sword) quite freely. This freedom of movement seems, however, to be gradually restricted, and in one of these English swords the two rings are made in one and the same piece. In the Swedish swords, however, this restriction is carried further, and the two rings are represented by a knob growing out of a circular base. Another sword of this "knob"-type has recently been found in a Frankish tomb[734], and yet another in the Rhineland[735]. It seems to be agreed among archæologists that the English type, as found in Kent, is the original, and that the Swedish and continental "ring-swords" are merely imitations, in which the ring has become conventionalized into a knob[736]. But, if so, how can the mention of a ring-sword in *Beowulf* (if indeed that be the meaning of *hring-mǣl*) prove Scandinavian colouring? If it proved anything (which it does not) it would tend to prove the reverse, and to locate *Beowulf* in Kent, where the true ring-swords have been found.

"The prevalence of boar-helmets." It is true that several representations of warriors wearing boar-helmets have been found in Scandinavia. But the only certainly Anglo-Saxon helmet yet found in England has a boar-crest[737]; and this is, I believe, the only actual boar-helmet yet found. How then can the boar-helmets of *Beowulf* show Scandinavian rather than Anglo-Saxon origin?

"The prevalence of ring-corslets." It is true that only one trace of a byrnie, and that apparently not of ring-mail, has so far been found in an Anglo-Saxon grave. (We have somewhat more abundant remains from the period prior to the migration to England: a peculiarly fine corslet of ring-mail, with remains of some nine others, was found in the moss at Thorsbjerg[738] in the midst of the ancient Anglian continental home; and other ring-corslets have been found in the neighbourhood of Angel, at Vimose[739] in Fünen.) But, for the period when *Beowulf* must have been composed, the ring-corslet is almost as rare in Scandinavia as in England[740]; the artist, however, seems to be indicating a byrnie upon many of the warriors depicted on the Vendel helm (Grave 14: seventh century). Equally, in England, warriors are represented on the Franks Casket as wearing the byrnie: also the laws of Ine (688-95) make it clear that the byrnie was by no means unknown[741]. Other Old

English poems, certainly not Scandinavian, mention the ring-byrnie. How then can the mention of it in *Beowulf* be a proof of Scandinavian origin?

"The prevalence of ring-money." Before minted money became current, rings were used everywhere among the Teutonic peoples. Gold rings, *intertwined* so as to form a chain, have been found throughout Scandinavia, presumably for use as a medium of exchange. The term *locenra bēaga* (gen. plu.) occurs in *Beowulf*, and this is interpreted by Stjerna as "rings *intertwined or locked* together[742]." But *locen* in *Beowulf* need not have the meaning of "intertwined"; it occurs elsewhere in Old English of a single jewel, *sincgim locen*[743]. Further, even if *locen* does mean "intertwined," such intertwined rings are not limited to Scandinavia proper. They have been found in Schleswig[744]. And almost the very phrase in *Beowulf*, *londes ne locenra bēaga*[745], recurs in the *Andreas*. The phrase there may be imitated from *Beowulf*, but, equally, the phrase in *Beowulf* may be imitated from some earlier poem. In fact, it is part of the traditional poetic diction: but its occurrence in the *Andreas* shows that it cannot be used as an argument of Scandinavian origin.

Whilst, therefore, accepting with gratitude the numerous illustrations which Stjerna has drawn from Scandinavian grave-finds, we must be careful not to read a Scandinavian colouring into features of *Beowulf* which are at least as much English as Scandinavian, such as the ring-sword or the boar-helmet or the ring-corslet.

There is, as is noted above, a certain atmosphere of profusion and wealth about some Scandinavian grave-finds, which corresponds much more nearly with the wealthy life depicted in *Beowulf* than does the comparatively meagre tomb-furniture of England. But we must remember that, after the spread of Christianity in the first half of the seventh century, the custom of burying articles with the bodies of the dead naturally ceased, or almost ceased, in England. Scandinavia continued heathen for another four hundred years, and it was during these years that the most magnificent deposits were made. As Stjerna himself points out, "a steadily increasing luxury in the appointment of graves" is to be found in Scandinavia in these centuries before the introduction of Christianity there. When we find in Scandinavia things (complete ships, for example) which we do not find in England, we owe this, partly to the nature of the soil in which they were embedded, but also to the continuance of such burial customs after they had died out in England.

Helm and byrnie were not necessarily unknown, or even very rare in England, simply because it was not the custom to bury them with the dead.

On the other hand, the frequent mention of them in *Beowulf* does not imply that they were common: for *Beowulf* deals only with the aristocratic adherents of a court, and even in *Beowulf* fine specimens of the helm and byrnie are spoken of as things which a king seeks far and wide to procure for his retainers[746]. We cannot, therefore, argue that there is any discrepancy. However, if we do so argue, it would merely prove, not that *Beowulf* is Scandinavian as opposed to English, but that it is comparatively late in date. Tacitus emphasizes the fact that spear and shield were the Teutonic weapons, that helmet and corslet were hardly known[747]. Pagan graves show that at any rate they were hardly known *as tomb-furniture* in England in the fifth, sixth, and early seventh centuries. The introduction of Christianity, and the intercourse with the South which it involved, certainly led to the growth of pomp and wealth in England, till the early eighth century became "the golden age of Anglo-Saxon England."

It might therefore conceivably be argued that *Beowulf* reflects the comparative abundance of early Christian England, as opposed to the more primitive heathen simplicity; but to argue a Scandinavian origin from the profusion of *Beowulf* admits of an easy *reductio ad absurdum*. For the same arguments would prove a heathen, Scandinavian origin for the *Andreas*, the *Elene*, the *Exodus*, or even for the Franks Casket, despite its Anglo-Saxon inscription and Christian carvings.

However, though the absence of helm and byrnie from Anglo-Saxon graves does not prove that these arms were not used by the living in heathen times, one thing it assuredly *does* prove: that the Anglo-Saxons in heathen times did not sacrifice helm and byrnie recklessly in funeral pomp. And this brings us to the second argument as to the origin of *Beowulf* which has been based on archæology.

Something has been said above of this second contention[748]—that the accuracy of the account of Beowulf's funeral is confirmed in every point by archæological evidence: that it must therefore have been composed within living memory of a time when ceremonies of this kind were still actually in use in England: and that therefore we cannot date *Beowulf* later than the third or fourth decade of the seventh century.

To begin with; the pyre in *Beowulf* is represented as hung with helmets, bright byrnies, and shields. Now it is impossible to say exactly how the funeral pyres were equipped in England. But we *do* know how the buried bodies were equipped. And (although inhumation cemeteries are much more common than cremation cemeteries) all the graves that have been opened have so far yielded only one case of a helmet and byrnie being buried with the warrior, and one other very doubtful case of a helmet without the byrnie. Abroad, instances are somewhat more common, but still of great rarity. For such things could ill be spared. Charles the Great forbade the export of byrnies from his dominions. Worn by picked champions fighting in the forefront, they might well decide the issue of a battle. In the mounds where we have reason to think that the great chiefs mentioned in *Beowulf*, Eadgils or Ohthere, lie buried, any trace of weapons was conspicuously absent among the burnt remains. Nevertheless, the belief that his armour would be useful to the champion in the next life, joined perhaps with a feeling that it was unlucky, or unfair on the part of the survivor to deprive the dead of his personal weapons, led in heathen times to the occasional burial of these treasures with the warrior who owned them. The fifth century tomb of Childeric I, when discovered twelve centuries later, was found magnificently furnished—the prince had been buried with treasure and much equipment[749], sword, scramasax[750], axe, spear. But these were his own. Similarly, piety might have demanded that Beowulf should be burnt with his full equipment. But would the pyre have been hung with helmets and byrnies? Whose? Were the thegns asked to sacrifice theirs, and go naked into the next fight in honour of their lord? If so, what archæological authority have we for such a custom in England?

Then the barrow is built, and the vast treasure of the dragon (which included "many a helmet[751]") placed in it. Now there are instances of articles which have not passed through the fire being placed in or upon or around an urn with the cremated bones[752]. But is there any instance of the thing being done on this scale—of a wholesale burning of helmets and byrnies followed by a burial of huge treasure? If so, one would like to know when, and where. If not, how can it be argued that the account in *Beowulf* is one of which "the accuracy is confirmed in every point by archæological or contemporary literary evidence?" Rather we must say, with Knut Stjerna, that it is "too much of a good thing[753]."

For the antiquities of Anglo-Saxon England, the student should consult the *Victoria County History*. The two splendid volumes of Professor G. Baldwin Brown on *Saxon Art and Industry in the Pagan Period*[754] at length enable the general reader to get a survey of the essential facts, for which up to now he has had to have recourse to innumerable scattered treatises. *The Archæology of the Anglo-Saxon Settlements* by Mr E. Thurlow Leeds will also be found helpful.

Side-lights from the field of Teutonic antiquities in general can be got from Prof. Baldwin Brown's *Arts and Crafts of our Teutonic Forefathers*, 1910, and from Lindenschmit's *Handbuch der deutschen Alterthumskunde, I. Theil: Die Alterthümer der Merovingischen Zeit* (Braunschweig, 1880-89), a book which is still indispensable. Hoops' *Reallexikon der germanischen Altertumskunde*, Strassburg, 1911-19, 4 vols., includes a large number of contributions of the greatest importance to the student of *Beowulf*, both upon archæological and other subjects. By the completion[755] of this most valuable work, amid heart-breaking difficulties, Prof. Hoops has placed all students under a great obligation.

Much help can be got from an examination of the antiquities of Teutonic countries other than England. The following books are useful—for Norway: Gustafson (G.), *Norges Oldtid*, 1906; for Denmark: Müller (S.), *Vor Oldtid*, 1897; for Sweden: Montelius (O.), *Civilization of Sweden in Heathen Times*, 1888, *Kulturgeschichte Schwedens*, 1906; for Schleswig: Mestorf (J.), *Vorgeschichtliche Alterthümer aus Schleswig*; for the Germanic nations in their wanderings on the outskirts of the Roman Empire: Hampel (J.), *Alterthümer des frühen Mittelalters in Ungarn*, 3 Bde, 1905; for Germanic remains in Gaul: Barrière-Flavy (M. C.), *Les Arts industriels des peuples barbares de la Gaule du Vme au VIIIme siècle*, 3 tom. 1901.

Somewhat popular accounts, and now rather out of date, are the two South Kensington handbooks: Worsaae (J. J. A.), *Industrial Arts of Denmark*, 1882, and Hildebrand (H.), *Industrial Arts of Scandinavia*, 1883.

Scandinavian Burial Mounds

The three great "Kings' Mounds" at Old Uppsala were explored between 1847 and 1874: cremated remains from them can be seen in the Stockholm Museum. An account of the tunnelling, and of the complicated structure of the mounds, was given in 1876 by the Swedish State-Antiquary[756]. From these finds Knut Stjerna dated the oldest of the "Kings' Mounds" about 500 A.D.[757], and the others somewhat later. Now, as we are definitely told that Athils (Eadgils) and the two kings who figure in the list of Swedish monarchs as his grandfather and great-grandfather (Aun and Egil) were "laid in mound" at Uppsala[758], and as the chronology agrees, it seems only reasonable to conclude that the three Kings' Mounds were raised over these three kings[759].

That Athils' father Ottar (Ohthere) was not regarded as having been buried at Uppsala is abundantly clear from the account given of his death, and of his nickname Vendel-crow[760]. A mound near Vendel north of Uppsala is known by his name. Such names are often the result of quite modern antiquarian conjecture: but that such is not the case here was proved by the recent discovery that an antiquarian survey (preserved in MS in the Royal Library at Stockholm) dating from 1677, mentions in Vendel "widh Hussby, [en] stor jorde högh, som heeter Otters högen[761]." An exploration of Ottar's mound showed a striking similarity with the Uppsala mounds. The structure was the same, a cairn of stones covered over with earth; the cremated remains were similar, there were abundant traces of burnt animals, a comb, half-spherical draughts with two round holes bored in the flat side, above all, there was in neither case any trace of weapons. In Ottar's mound a gold Byzantine coin was found, pierced, having evidently been used as an ornament. It can be dated 477-8; it is much worn, but such coins seldom remained in the North in use for a century after their minting[762]. Ottar's mound obviously, then, belongs to the same period as the Uppsala mounds, and confirms the date attributed by Stjerna to the oldest of those mounds, about 500 A.D.

Weapons

For weapons in general see Lehmann (H.), *Über die Waffen im angelsächsischen Beowulfliede*, in *Germania*, XXXI, 486-97; Keller (May L.), *The Anglo-Saxon weapon names treated archæologically and etymologically*, Heidelberg, 1906 (*Anglistische Forschungen*, XV: cf. Holthausen, *Anglia, Beiblatt*, XVIII, 65-9, Binz, *Litteraturblatt*, XXXI, 98-100); ‡Wagner (R.), *Die Angriffswaffen der Angelsächsischen*, Diss., Königsberg; and especially Falk (H.), *Altnordische Waffenkunde*, in *Videnskapsselskapets Skrifter, Hist.-Filos. Klasse*, 1914, Kristiania.

The Sword. The sword of the Anglo-Saxon pagan period (from the fifth to the seventh century) "is deficient in quality as a blade, and also ... in the character of its hilt[763]." In this it contrasts with the sword found in the peat-bogs of Schleswig from an earlier period: "these swords of the Schleswig moss-finds are much better weapons[764]," as well as with the later Viking sword of the ninth or tenth century, which "is a remarkably effective and well-considered implement[765]." It has been suggested that both the earlier Schleswig swords and the later Viking swords (which bear a considerable likeness to each other, as against the inferior Anglo-Saxon sword) are the product of intercourse with Romanized peoples[766], whilst the typical Anglo-Saxon sword "may represent an independent Germanic effort at sword making[767]." However this may be, it is noteworthy that nowhere in *Beowulf* do we have any hint of the skill of any sword-smith who is regarded as contemporary. A good sword is always "an old heirloom," "an ancient treasure[768]." The sword of Wiglaf, which had belonged to Eanmund, or the sword with which Eofor slays Ongentheow, are described by the phrase *ealdsweord eotenisc*, as if they were weapons of which the secret and origin had been lost—indeed the same phrase is applied to the magic sword which Beowulf finds in the hall of Grendel's mother.

The blade of these ancestral swords was sometimes damascened or adorned with wave-like patterns[769]. The swords of the Schleswig moss-finds are almost all thus adorned with a variegated surface, as often are the later Viking swords; but those of the Anglo-Saxon graves are *not*. Is it fanciful to suggest that the reference to damascening is a tradition coming down from the time of the earlier sword as found in the Nydam moss? A few early swords might have been preserved among the invaders as family heirlooms, too precious to be buried with the owner, as the product of the local weapon-smith was.

See, for a full discussion of the sword in *Beowulf*, Stjerna, *Hjälmar och svärd i Beovulf* (*Studier tillägnade O. Montelius*, Stockholm, pp. 99-120 = *Essays*, transl. Clark Hall, pp. 1-32). The standard treatise on the sword, *Den Yngre Jernalders Svard*, Bergen, 1889, by A. L. Lorange, deals mainly with a rather later period.

The Helmet. The helmet found at Benty Grange in Derbyshire in 1848 is now in the Sheffield Museum[770]: little remains except the boar-crest, the nose-piece, and the framework of iron ribs radiating from the crown, and fixed to a circle of iron surrounding the brow (perhaps the *frēawrāsn* of *Beowulf*, 1451). Mr Bateman, the discoverer, described the helmet as "coated with narrow plates of horn, running in a diagonal direction from the ribs, so as to form a herring-bone pattern; the ends were secured by strips of horn, radiating in like manner as the iron ribs, to which they were riveted at intervals of about an inch and a half: all the rivets had ornamented heads of silver on the outside, and on the front rib is a small cross of the same metal. Upon the top or crown of the helmet, is an elongated oval brass plate, upon which stands the figure of an animal, carved in iron, now much rusted, but still a very good representation of a pig: it has bronze eyes[771]." Helmets of very similar construction, but without the boar, have been found on the Continent and in Scandinavia (Vendel, Grave 14, late seventh century). The continental helmets often stand higher[772] than the Benty Grange or Vendel specimens, being sometimes quite conical (cf. the epithet "war-steep," *heaðo-stēap, Beowulf*). Many of the continental helmets are provided with cheek-protections, and these also appear in the Scandinavian representations of warriors on the Torslunda plates and elsewhere. These side pieces have become detached from the magnificent Vendel helmet, which is often shown in engravings without them[773], but they can be seen in the Stockholm Museum[774]. If it ever possessed them, the Benty Grange helmet has lost these side pieces. Such cheek-protections are, however, represented, together with the nose-protection, on the head of one of the warriors depicted on the Franks Casket. In the Vendel helms, the nose-pieces were connected under the eyes with the rim of the helmet, so as to form a mask[774]; the helmet in *Beowulf* is frequently spoken of as the battle-mask[775].

Both helmet and boar-crest were sometimes gold-adorned[776]: the golden boar was a symbol of the god Freyr: some magic protective power is still, in *Beowulf*[777], felt to adhere to these swine-likenesses, as it was in the days of Tacitus[778].

In Scandinavia, the Torslunda plates show the helmet with a boar-crest: the Vendel helmet has representations of warriors whose crests have an animal's head tailing off to a mere rim or roll: this may be the *walu* or *wala* which keeps watch over the head in *Beowulf*[779]. The helmet was bound fast to the head[780]; exactly how, we do not know.

See Lehmann (H.), *Brünne und Helm im ags. Beowulfliede* (Göttingen Diss., Leipzig; cf. Wülker, *Anglia*, VIII, *Anzeiger*, 167-70; Schulz, *Engl. Stud.*, IX, 471); Hoops' *Reallexikon*, s.v. *Helm*; Baldwin Brown, III, 194-6; Falk, *Altnord. Waffenkunde*, 155-73; Stjerna, *Hjälmar och svärd*, 1907, as above: but the attempt of Stjerna to arrange the helmets he depicts in a chronological series is perilous, and depends on a dating of the Benty Grange helmet which is by no means generally accepted.

The Corslet. This in *Beowulf* is made of rings[781], twisted and interlaced by hand[782]. As stated above, the fragments of the only known Anglo-Saxon byrnie were not of this type, but rather intended to have been sewn "upon a doublet of strong cloth[783]." Byrnies were of various lengths, the longer ones reaching to the middle of the thigh (*byrnan sīde*, Beow. 1291, cf. *loricæ longæ*, *sīðar brynjur*).

See Falk, 179; Baldwin Brown, III. 194.

The Spear. Spear and shield were the essential Germanic weapons in the days of Tacitus, and they are the weapons most commonly found in Old English tombs. The spear-shaft has generally decayed, analysis of fragments surviving show that it was frequently of ash[784]. The butt-end of the spear was frequently furnished with an iron tip, and the distance of this from the spear-head, and the size of the socket, show the spear-shaft to have been six or seven feet long, and three-quarters of an inch to one inch in diameter.

See Falk, 66-90; Baldwin Brown, III, 234-41.

The Shield. Several round shields were preserved on the Gokstad ship, and in the deposits of an earlier period at Thorsbjerg and Nydam. These are formed of boards fastened together, often only a quarter of an inch thick, and not strengthened or braced in any way, bearing out the contemptuous description of the painted German shield which Tacitus puts into the mouth of Germanicus[785]. It was, however, intended that the shield should be light. It was easily pierced, but, by a rapid twist, the foe's sword could be broken or wrenched from his hand. Thus we are told how Gunnar gave his shield a twist, as his adversary thrust his sword through it, and so snapped off his sword at the hilt[786]. The shield was held by a bar, crossing a hole some four inches wide cut in the middle. The hand was protected by a hollow conical boss or umbo, fixed to the wood by its brim, but projecting considerably. In

England the wood of the shield has always perished, but a large number of bosses have been preserved. The boss seems to have been called *rond*, a word which is also used for the shield as a whole. In *Beowulf*, 2673, *Gifts of Men*, 65, the meaning "boss" suits *rond* best, also in *rand sceal on scylde, fæst fingra gebeorh* (*Cotton. Gnomic Verses*, 37-8). But the original meaning of *rand* must have been the circular rim round the edge, and this meaning it retains in Icelandic (Falk, 131). The linden wood was sometimes bound with bast, whence *scyld (sceal) gebunden, lēoht linden bord* (*Exeter Gnomic Verses*, 94-5).

See Falk (126-54); Baldwin Brown, III, 196-204; Pfannkuche (K.), *Der Schild bei den Angelsachsen*, Halle Dissertation, 1908.

The Bow is a weapon of much less importance in *Beowulf* than the spear. Few traces of the bow have survived from Anglo-Saxon England, though many wooden long-bows have been preserved in the moss-finds in a remarkably fine state. They are of yew, some over six feet long, and in at least one instance tipped with horn. The bow entirely of horn was, of course, well known in the East, and in classical antiquity, but I do not think traces of any horn-bow have been discovered in the North. It was a difficult weapon to manage, as the suitors of Penelope found to their cost. Possibly that is why Hæthcyn is represented as killing his brother Herebeald accidentally with a horn-bow: he could not manage the exotic weapon.

See Falk, 91-103; Baldwin Brown, III, 241.

The Hall

It may perhaps be the fact that in the church of Sta. Maria de Naranco, in the north of Spain, we have the hall of a Visigothic king driven north by the Mohammedan invasion. But, even if this surmise[787] be correct, the structure of a stone hall of about 750 A.D. gives us little information as to the wooden halls of early Anglo-Saxon times. Heorot is clearly built of timber, held together by iron clamps[788]. These halls were oblong, and a famous passage in Bede[789] makes it clear that, at any rate at the time of the Conversion, the hall had a door at both ends, and the fire burnt in the middle. (The smoke escaped through a hole in the roof, through which probably most of the light came, for windows were few or none.) The *Finnsburg Fragment* also implies two doors. Further indications can be drawn from references to the halls of Norse chiefs. The Scandinavian hall was divided by rows of wooden pillars into a central nave and side aisles. The pillars in the centre were known as the "high-seat pillars." Rows of seats ran down the length of the hall on each side. The central position, facing the high-seat pillars and the fire, was the most honourable. The place of honour for the chief guest was opposite: and it is quite clear that in *Beowulf* also the guest did not sit next his host[790].

Other points we may note about Heorot, are the tapestry with which its walls are draped[791], and the paved and variegated floor[792]. Unlike so many later halls, Heorot has a floor little, if anything, raised above the ground: horses can be brought in[793].

In later times, in Iceland, the arrangement of the hall was changed, and the house consisted of many rooms; but these were formed, not by partitioning the hall, but by building several such halls side by side: the *stufa* or hall proper, the *skáli* or sleeping hall, *etc.*

See M. Heyne, *Ueber die Lage und Construction der Halle Heorot*, Paderborn, 1864, where the scanty information about Heorot is collected, and supplemented with some information about Anglo-Saxon building. For the Icelandic hall see Valtyr Guðmundsson, *Privatboligen på Island i Sagatiden*, København, 1889. This has been summarized, in a more popular form, in a chapter on *Den islandske Bolig i Fristatstiden*, contributed by Guðmundsson to Rosenberg's *Træk af Livet paa Island i Fristatstiden*, 1894 (pp. 251-74). Here occurs the picture of an Icelandic hall which has been so often reproduced—by Olrik, Holthausen, and in *Beowulf*-translations. But it is a conjectural picture, and we can by no means assume all its details for Heorot. Rhamm's colossal work is only for the initiated, but is useful for consultation on special points (*Ethnographische Beiträge zur Germanischslawischen Altertumskunde*, von K. Rhamm, 1905-8. I. *Die Grosshufen der Nordgermanen*; II. *Urzeitliche Bauernhöfe*). For various details see Hoops' *Reallexikon*, s.v. *flett*; Neckel in *P.B.B.* XLI, 1916, 163-70 (*under edoras*); Meiringer in *I.F.*, especially XVIII, 257 (*under eoderas*); Kaufmann in *Z.f.d.Ph.* XXXIX, 282-92.

Ships

In a tumulus near Snape in Suffolk, opened in 1862, there were discovered, with burnt bones and remains thought to be of Anglo-Saxon date, a large number of rivets which, from the positions in which they were found, seemed to give evidence of a boat 48 feet long by over nine feet wide[794]. A boat, similar in dimensions, but better preserved, was unearthed near Bruges in 1899, and the ribs, mast and rudder removed to the Gruuthuuse Museum[795].

Three boats were discovered in the peat-moss at Nydam in Schleswig in 1863, by Engelhardt. The most important is the "Nydam boat," clinker-built (i.e. with overlapping planks), of oak, 77 feet [23.5 m.] long, by some 11 [3.4 m.] broad, with rowlocks for fourteen oars down each side. There was no trace of any mast. Planks and framework had been held together, partly by iron bolts, and partly by ropes of bast. The boat had fallen to pieces, and had to be laboriously put together in the museum at Flensborg. Another boat was quite fragmentary, but a third boat, of fir, was found tolerably complete. Then the war of 1864 ended Engelhardt's labours at Nydam.

THE GOKSTAD SHIP

THE OSEBERG SHIP

The oak-boat was removed to Kiel, where it now is.

The fir-boat was allowed to decay: many of the pieces of the oak-boat had been rotten and had of necessity been restored in facsimile, and it is much less complete than might be supposed from the numerous reproductions, based upon the fine engraving by Magnus Petersen. The rustic with a spade, there depicted as gazing at the boat, is apt to give a wrong impression that it was dug out intact[796].

Such was, however, actually the case with regard to the ship excavated from the big mound at Gokstad, near Christiania, by Nicolaysen, in 1880. This was fitted both as a rowing and sailing ship; it was 66 feet [20.1 m.] long on the keel, 78 feet [23.8 m.] from fore to aft and nearly 17 feet [5.1 m.] broad, and was clinker-built, out of a much larger number of oaken planks than the Nydam ship. It had rowlocks for sixteen oars down each side, the gunwale was lined with shields, some of them well preserved, which had been originally painted alternately black and yellow. The find owed its extraordinary preservation to the blue clay in which it was embedded. Its discoverer wrote, with pardonable pride: "Certain it is that we shall not disinter any craft which, in respect of model and workmanship, will outrival that of Gokstad[797]."

Yet the prophecy was destined to prove false: for on Aug. 8, 1903, a farmer came into the National Museum at Christiania to tell the curator, Prof. Gustafson, that he had discovered traces of a boat on his farm at Oseberg. Gustafson found that the task was too great to be begun so late in the year: the digging out of the ship, and its removal to Christiania, occupied from just before Midsummer to just before Christmas of 1904. The potter's clay in which the ship was buried had preserved it, if possible, better than the Gokstad ship: but the movement of the soft subsoil had squeezed and broken both ship and contents. The ship was taken out of the earth in nearly two thousand fragments. These were carefully numbered and marked: each piece was treated, bent back into its right shape, and the ship was put together again plank by plank, as when it was first built. With the exception of a piece about half a yard long, five or six little bits let in, and one of the beams, the ship as it stands now consists of the original woodwork. Two-thirds of the rivets are the old ones. Till his death in 1915 Gustafson was occupied in treating and preparing for exhibition first the ship, and then its extraordinarily rich contents: a waggon and sledges beautifully carved, beds, chests, kitchen utensils which had been buried with the princess who had owned them. A full account of the find is only now being published[798].

The Oseberg ship is the pleasure boat of a royal lady: clinker-built, of oak, exquisitely carved, intended not for long voyages but for the land-locked waters of the fiord, 70½ feet [21.5 m.] long by some 16½ feet [5 m.] broad. There are holes for fifteen oars down each side, and the ship carried mast and sail.

The upper part of the prow had been destroyed, but sufficient fragments have been found to show that it ended in the head of a snake-like creature, bent round in a coil. This explains the words *hringed-stefna*[799], *hring-naca*[800], *wunden-stefna*[801], used of the ship in *Beowulf*. A similar ringed prow is depicted on an engraved stone from Tjängvide, now in the National Historical Museum at Stockholm. This is supposed to date from about the year 1000[802].

The Gokstad and Oseberg ships, together with the ship of Tune, a much less complete specimen (unearthed in 1867, and found like the others on the shore of the Christiania fiord) owe their preservation to the clay, and the skill of Scandinavian antiquaries. Yet they are but three out of thousands of ship- or boat-burials. Schetelig enumerates 552 known instances from Norway alone. Often traces of the iron rivets are all that remain.

Ships preserved from the Baltic coast of Germany can be seen at Königsberg, Danzig and Stettin; they are smaller and apparently later; the best, that of Brösen, was destroyed.

The seamanship of *Beowulf* is removed by centuries from that of the (? fourth or fifth century) Nydam boat, which not only has no mast or proper keel, but is so built as to be little suited for sailing. In *Beowulf* the sea is a "sail-road," the word "to row" occurs only in the sense of "swim," sailing is assumed as the means by which Beowulf travels between the land of the Geatas and that of the Danes. Though he voyages with but fourteen companions, the ship is big enough to carry back four horses. How the sail may have been arranged is shown in many inscribed stones of the eighth to the tenth centuries: notably those of Stenkyrka[803], Högbro[804], and Tjängvide[805].

The Oseberg and Gokstad ships are no doubt later than the composition of *Beowulf*. But it is when looking at the Oseberg ship, especially if we picture the great prow like the neck of a swan ending in a serpent's coil, that we can best understand the words of *Beowulf*

flota fāmī-heals fugle gelīcost,
wunden-stefna,

well rendered by Earle "The foamy-necked floater, most like to a bird—the coily-stemmed."

See Boehmer (G. H.), *Prehistoric Naval Architecture of the North of Europe, Report of the U.S. National Museum for 1891* (now rather out of date); Guðmundsson

(V.), *Nordboernes Skibe i Vikinge- og Sagatiden*, København, 1900; [*]Schnepper, *Die Namen der Schiffe u. Schiffsteile im Altenglischen* (Kiel Diss.), 1908; Falk (H.), *Altnordisches Seewesen* (*Wörter u. Sachen*, IV, Heidelberg, 1912); Hoops' *Reallexikon*, s.v. *Schiff*.

G. LEIRE BEFORE ROLF KRAKI

That Leire was the royal town, not merely of Rolf Kraki, but of Rolf's predecessors as well, is stated in the *Skjoldunga Saga*, extant in the Latin abstract of Arngrim Jonsson: *Scioldus in arce Selandiae Hledro sedes posuit, quae et sequentium plurimorum regum regia fuit* (ed. Olrik, København, 1894, p. 23 [105]). Similarly we are told in the *Ynglinga Saga*, concerning Gefion, *Hennar fekk Skjǫldr, sonr Óðins; þau bjoggu at Hleiðru* (*Heimskringla*, udgivne ved F. Jónsson, København, I, 15 [cap. V]).

Above all, it is clear from the *Annales Lundenses* that, in the twelfth century, Dan, Ro (Hrothgar) and Haldan (Healfdene) were traditionally connected with Leire, and three of the grave mounds there were associated with these three kings. See the extract given above, pp. 204-5, and cf. p. 17.

H. BEE-WOLF AND BEAR'S SON

The obvious interpretation of the name *Bēowulf* is that suggested by Grimm[806], that it means "wolf, or foe, of the bee." Grimm's suggestion was repeated independently by Skeat[807], and further reasons for the interpretation "bee-foe" have been found by Sweet[808] (who had been anticipated by Simrock[809] in some of his points), by Cosijn[810], Sievers[811], von Grienberger[812], Panzer[813] and Björkman[814].

From the phonological point of view the etymology is a perfect one, but many of those who were convinced that "Beowulf" meant "bee-foe" had no satisfactory explanation of "bee-foe" to offer[815]. Others, like Bugge, whilst admitting that, so far as the form of the words goes, the etymology is satisfactory, rejected "bee-foe" because it seemed to them meaningless[816].

Yet it is very far from meaningless. "Bee-foe" means "bear." The bear has got a name, or nickname, in many northern languages from his habit of raiding the hives for honey. The Finnish name for bear is said to be "honey-hand": he is certainly called "sweet-foot," *sötfot*, in Sweden, and the Old Slavonic name, "honey-eater," has come to be accepted in Russian, not merely as a nickname, but as the regular term for "bear."

And "bear" is an excellent name for a hero of story. The O.E. *beorn*, "warrior, hero, prince" seems originally to have meant simply "bear." The bear, says Grimm, "is regarded, in the belief of the Old Norse, Slavonic, Finnish and Lapp peoples, as an exalted and holy being, endowed with human understanding and the strength of twelve men. He is called 'forest-king,' 'gold-foot,' 'sweet-foot,' 'honey-hand,' 'honey-paw,' 'honey-eater,' but also 'the great,' 'the old,' 'the old grandsire[817].'" "Bee-hunter" is then a satisfactory explanation of *Bēowulf*: while the alternative explanations are none of them satisfactory.

Many scholars have been led off the track by the assumption that Beow and Beowulf are to be identified, and that we must therefore assume that the first element in Beowulf's name is *Bēow*—that we must divide not *Bēo-wulf* but *Bēow-ulf*, "a warrior after the manner of Beow[818]." But there is no ground for any such assumption. It is true that in ll. 18, 53, "Beowulf" is written where we should have expected "Beowa." But, even if two words of similar sound have been confused, this fact affords no reason for supposing that they must necessarily have been in the first instance connected etymologically. And against the "warrior of Beow" interpretation is the fact that the name is recorded in the early Northumbrian *Liber Vitae* under the form "Biuuulf[819]." This name, which is that of an early monk of Durham, is presumably the same as that of the hero of our poem, though it does not, of course, follow that the bearer of it was named with any special reference to the slayer of Grendel. Now *Biuuulf* is correct Northumbrian for "bee-wolf," but the first element in the word cannot stand for *Bēow*[820], unless the affinities and forms of that word are quite different from all that the evidence has hitherto led us to believe. So much at least seems certain. Besides, we have seen that Byggvir is taunted by Loki precisely with the fact that he *is* no warrior. If we can estimate the characteristics of the O.E. Beow from those of the Scandinavian Byggvir, the name "Warrior after the manner of Beow" would be meaningless, if not absurd. Bugge[821], relying upon the parallel O.N. form *Bjólfr*[822], which is recorded as the name of one of the early settlers in Iceland[823], tried to interpret the word as *Bæjólfr* "the wolf of the farmstead," quoting as parallels *Heimulf, Gardulf*. But *Bjólfr* itself is best interpreted as "Bee-wolf[824]." And admittedly Bugge's explanation does not suit the O.E. *Bēowulf*, and necessitates the assumption that the word in English is a mere meaningless borrowing from the Scandinavian: for *Bēowulf* assuredly does not mean "wolf of the farmstead[825]."

Neither can we take very seriously the explanation of Sarrazin and Ferguson[826] that *Bēowulf* is an abbreviation of *Beadu-wulf*, "wolf of war." Our business is to interpret the name *Bēowulf*, or, if we cannot, to admit that we cannot; not to substitute some quite distinct name for it, and interpret that.

Such theories merely show to what straits we may be reduced, if we reject the obvious etymology of the word.

And there are two further considerations, which confirm, almost to a certainty, this obvious interpretation of "Beowulf" as "Bee-wolf" or "Bear." The first is that it agrees excellently with Beowulf's bear-like habit of hugging his adversaries to death—a feature which surely belongs to the original kernel of our story, since it is incompatible with the chivalrous, weapon-loving trappings in which that story has been dressed[827]. The second is that, as I have tried to show, the evidence is strongly in favour of Bjarki and Beowulf being originally the same figure[828]: and Bjarki is certainly a bear-hero[829]. His name signifies as much, and in the *Saga of Rolf Kraki* we are told at length how the father of Bjarki was a prince who had been turned by enchantment into a bear[830].

If, then, Beowulf is a bear-hero[831], the next step is to enquire whether there is any real likeness between his adventures at Heorot and under the mere, and the adventures of the hero of the widely-spread "Bear's Son" folk-tale. This investigation has, as we have seen above[832], been carried out by Panzer in his monumental work, which marks an epoch in the study of *Beowulf*.

Panzer's arguments in favour of such connection would, I think, have been strengthened if he had either quoted textually a number of the more important and less generally accessible folk-tales, or, since this would have proved cumbersome, if he had at least given abstracts of them. The method which Panzer follows, is to enumerate over two hundred tales, and from them to construct a story which is a compound of them all. This is obviously a method which is liable to abuse, though I do not say that Panzer has abused it. But we must not let a story so constructed usurp in our minds the place of the actual recorded folk-tales. Folk-tales, as Andrew Lang wrote long ago, "consist of but few incidents, grouped together in a kaleidoscopic variety of arrangements." A collection of over two hundred cognate tales offers a wide field for the selection therefrom of a composite story. Further, some geographical discrimination is necessary: these tales are scattered over Europe and Asia, and it is important to keep constantly in mind whether a given type of tale belongs, for example, to Greece or to Scandinavia.

A typical example of the Bear's son tale is *Der Starke Hans* in Grimm[833]. Hans is brought up in a robber's den: but quite apart from any of the theories we are now considering, it has long been recognized that this is a mere toning down of the original incredible story, which makes a bear's den the nursery of the strong youth[834]. Hans overcomes in an empty castle the foe (a mannikin of magic powers) who has already worsted his comrades Fir-twister and Stone-splitter. He pursues this foe to his hole, is let down by his companions in a basket by a rope, slays the foe with his club and rescues a princess. He sends up the princess in the basket; but when his own turn comes to be pulled up his associates intentionally drop the basket when halfway up. But Hans, suspecting treason, has only sent up his club. He escapes by magic help, takes vengeance on the traitors, and weds the princess.

In another story in Grimm[835], the antagonist whom the hero overcomes, but does not in this case slay, is called the Earthman, *Dat Erdmänneken*. This type begins with the disappearance of the princesses, who are to the orthodox number of three; otherwise it does not differ materially from the abstract given above. Grimm records four distinct versions, all from Western Germany.

The versions of this widespread story which are most easily accessible to English readers are likely to prejudice such readers against Panzer's view. The two versions in Campbell's *Popular Tales of the West Highlands*[836], or the version in Kennedy's *Legendary Fictions of the Irish Celts*[837] are not of a kind to remind any unprejudiced reader strongly of *Beowulf*, or of the *Grettir*-story either. Indeed, I believe that from countries so remote as North Italy or Russia parallels can be found which are closer than any so far quoted from the Celtic portions of the British Isles. Possibly more Celtic parallels may be forthcoming in the future: some striking ones at any rate are promised[838].

So, too, the story of the "Great Bird Dan" (*Fugl Dam*[839]), which is accessible to English readers in Dasent's translation[840], is one in which the typical features have been overlaid by a mass of detail.

A much more normal specimen of the "Bear's son" story is found, for example, in a folk-tale from Lombardy—the story of *Giovanni dell' Orso*[841]. Giovanni is brought up in a bear's den, whither his mother has been carried off. At five, he has the growth of a man and the strength of a giant. At sixteen, he is able to remove the stone from the door of the den and escape, with his mother. Going on his adventures with two comrades, he comes to an empty palace. The comrades are defeated: it becomes the turn of Giovanni to be alone. An old man comes in and "grows, grows till his head touched the roof[842]." Giovanni mortally wounds the giant, who however escapes. They all go in search of him, and find a hole in the ground. His comrades let Giovanni down by a rope. He finds a great hall, full of rich clothes and provision of every kind: in a second hall he finds three girls, each one more beautiful than the other: in a third hall he finds the giant himself, drawing up his will[843]. Giovanni kills the giant, rescues the damsels, and, in spite of his comrades deserting the rope, he escapes, pardons them, himself weds the youngest princess and marries his comrades to the elder ones.

I cannot find in this version any mention of the hero smiting the giant below with a magic sword which he finds there, as suggested by Panzer[844]. But even without this, the first part of the story has resemblances to *Beowulf*, and still more to the *Grettir*-story.

There are many Slavonic variants. The South Russian story of the Norka[845] begins with the attack of the Norka upon the King's park. The King offers half his kingdom to whomsoever will destroy the beast. The youngest prince of three watches, after the failure of his two elder brothers, chases and wounds the monster, who in the end pulls up a stone and disappears into the earth. The prince is let down by his brothers, and, with the help of a sword specially given him in the underworld, and a draught of the water of strength, he slays the foe, and wins the princesses. In order to have these for themselves, the elder brothers drop what they suppose to be their youngest brother, as they are drawing him up: but it is only a stone he has cautiously tied to the rope in place of himself. The prince's miraculous return in disguise, his feats, recognition by the youngest princess, the exposure of the traitors, and marriage of the hero, all follow in due course[846].

A closer Russian parallel is that of *Ivashko Medvedko*[847]. "John Honey-eater" or "Bear." John grows up, not by years, but by hours: nearly every hour he gains an inch in height. At fifteen, there are complaints of his rough play with other village boys, and John Bear has to go out into the world, after his grandfather has provided him with a weapon, an iron staff of immense weight. He meets a champion who is drinking up a river: "Good morning, John Bear, whither art going?" "I know not whither; I just go, not knowing where to go." "If so, take me with you." The same happens with a second champion whose hobby is to carry mountains on his shoulder, and with a third, who plucks up oaks or pushes them into the ground. They come to a revolving house in a dark forest, which at John's word stands with its back door to the forest and its front door to them: all its doors and windows open of their own accord. Though the yard is full of poultry, the house is empty. Whilst the three companions go hunting, the river-swallower stays in the house to cook dinner: this done, he washes his head, and sits at the window to comb his locks. Suddenly the earth shakes, then stands still: a stone is lifted, and from under it appears Baba Yaga driving in her mortar with a pestle: behind her comes barking a little dog. A short dialogue ensues, and the champion, at her request, gives her food; but the second helping she throws to her dog, and thereupon beats the champion with her pestle till he becomes unconscious; then she cuts a strip of skin from his back, and after eating all the food, vanishes. The victim recovers his senses, ties up his head with a handkerchief, and, when his companions return, apologizes for the ill-success of his cooking: "He had been nearly suffocated by the fumes of the charcoal, and had had his work cut out to get the room clear." Exactly the same happens to the other champions. On the fourth day it is the turn of John Bear, and here again the same formulas are repeated. John does the cooking, washes his head, sits down at the window and begins to comb his curly locks. Baba Yaga appears with the usual phenomena, and the usual dialogue follows, till she begins to belabour the hero with her pestle. But he wrests it from her, beats her almost to death, cuts three strips from her skin, and imprisons her in a closet. When his companions return, they are astonished to find dinner ready. After dinner they have a bath, and the companions try not to show their mutilated backs, but at last have to confess. "Now I see why you all suffered from suffocation," says John Bear. He goes to the closet, takes the three strips cut from his friends, and reinserts them: they heal at once. Then he ties up Baba Yaga by a cord fastened to one foot, and they all shoot at the cord in turn. John Bear hits it, and cuts the string in two; Baba Yaga falls to the earth, but rises, runs to the stone from under which she had appeared, lifts it, and vanishes. Each of the companions tries in turn to lift the stone, but only John can accomplish it, and only he is willing to go down. His comrades let him down by a rope, which however is too short, and John has to eke it out by the three strips previously cut from the back of Baba Yaga. At the bottom he sees a path, follows it, and reaches a palace where are three beautiful maidens, who welcome him, but warn him against their mother, who is Baba Yaga herself: "She is asleep now, but she keeps at her head a sword. Do not touch it, but take two golden apples lying on a silver tray, wake her gently, and offer them to her. As soon as she begins to eat, seize the sword, and cut her head off at one blow." John Bear carries out these instructions, and sends up the maidens, two to be wives to his companions, and the youngest to be his own wife. This leaves the third companion wifeless and, in indignation, he cuts the rope when the turn comes to pull John up. The hero falls and is badly hurt. [John has forgotten, in this version, to put his iron club into the basket instead of himself—indeed he has up to now made no use of his staff.] In time the hero sees an underground passage, and makes his way out into the white world. Here he finds the youngest maiden, who is tending cattle, after refusing to marry the false companion. John Bear follows her home, slays his former comrades with his staff, and throws their bodies on the field for the wild beasts to devour. He then takes his sweetheart home to his people, and weds her.

The abstract given above is from a translation made by one of my students, Miss M. Steine, who tells me that she had heard the tale in this form many times from her old nurse "when we were being sent to sleep, or sitting round her in the evening." I have given it at this length because I do not know of any accessible translation into any Western language.

Panzer enumerates two hundred and two variants of the story: and there are others[848]. But there is reason in the criticism that what is important for us is the form the folk-tale may have taken in those countries where we must look for the original home of the *Beowulf*-story[849]. The Mantuan folk-tale may have been carried down to North Italy from Scandinavia by the Longobards: who can say? But Panzer's theory must stand or fall by the parallels which can be drawn between the *Beowulf-Grettir*-story on the one hand, and the folk-tales as they have been collected in the countries where this story is native: the lands, that is to say, adjoining the North Sea.

Now it is precisely here that we do find the most remarkable resemblances: in Iceland, the Faroes, Norway, Denmark, Jutland, Schleswig, and the Low German lands as far as the Scheldt.

An Icelandic version exists in an unprinted MS at Reykjavik[850] which can be consulted in a German translation[851]. In this version a bear, who is really an enchanted prince, carries off a princess. He resumes his human form and weds the princess, but must still at times take the bear's form. His child, the Bear-boy (Bjarndreingur), is to be kept in the house during the long periods when the enchanted husband is away. But at twelve years old the Bear-boy is too strong and unmanageable, bursts out, and slays a bear who turns out to be his father. His mother's heart is broken, but Bear-boy goes on his adventures, and associates with himself three companions, one of whom is Stein. They build a house in the wood, which is attacked by a giant, and, as usual, the companions are unable to withstand the attacks. Bear-boy does so, ties the giant's hands behind his back, and fastens him by his beard. But the giant tears himself free. As in *Beowulf*, Bear-boy and his companions follow the track by the drops of blood, and come to a hole. Stein is let some way down, the other companions further, but only Bear-boy dares to go to the bottom. There he finds a weeping princess, and learns that she, and her two sisters, have been carried off by three giants, one of whom is his former assailant. He slays all three, and sends their heads up, together with the maidens and other treasures. But his companions desert the rope, and he has to climb up unaided. In the end he weds the youngest princess.

The story from the Faroe Islands runs thus:

Three brothers lived together and took turns, two to go out fishing, and one to be at home. For two days, when the two elder brothers were at home, came a giant with a long beard (Skeggjatussi) and ate and drank all the food. Then comes the turn of the despised youngest brother, who is called in one version Øskudólgur—"the one who sits and rakes in the ashes"—a kind of male Cinderella. This brother routs the giant, either by catching his long beard in a cleft tree-trunk, or by branding him in the nose with a hot iron. In either case the mutilated giant escapes down a hole: in one version, after the other brothers come home, they follow him to this hole by the track of his blood. The two elder brothers leave the task of plunging down to the youngest one, who finds below a girl (in the second version, two kidnapped princesses). He finds also a magic sword hanging on the wall, which he is only able to lift when he has drunk a magic potion. He then slays the giant, rescues the maiden or maidens, is betrayed in the usual way by his brothers: in the one version they deliberately refuse to draw him up: in the other they cut the rope as they are doing so: but he is discreetly sending up only a big stone. The hero is helped out, however, by a giant, "Skræddi Kjálki" or "Snerkti risi," and in the end marries the princess[852].

In the Norwegian folk-tale the three adventurers are called respectively the Captain, the Lieutenant and the Soldier. They search for the three princesses, and watch in a castle, where the Captain and Lieutenant are in turn worsted by a strange visitor—who in this version is not identical with the troll below ground who guards the princesses[853]. When the turn of the Soldier comes, he seizes the intruder (the man, as he is called).

"Ah no, Ah no, spare my life," said the man, "and you shall know all. East of the castle is a great sandheap, and down in it a winch, with which you can lower yourself. But if you are afraid, and do not dare to go right down, you only need to pull the bell rope which you will find there, and up you will come again. But if you dare venture so far as to come to the bottom, there stands a flask on a shelf over the door: you must drink what is in it: so will you become so strong that you can strike the head off the troll of the mountain. And by the door there hangs a Troll-sword, which also you must take, for no other steel will bite on his body."

When he had learnt this, he let the man go. When the Captain and the Lieutenant came home, they were not a little surprised to find the Soldier alive. "How have you escaped a drubbing," said they, "has not the man been here?" "Oh yes, he is quite a good fellow, he is," said the Soldier, "I have learnt from him where the princesses are," and he told them all. They were glad when they heard that, and when they had eaten, they went all three to the sandheap.

As usual, the Captain and the Lieutenant do not dare to go to the bottom: the hero accomplishes the adventure, is (as usual) betrayed by his comrades, but is saved because he has put a stone in the basket instead of himself, and in the end is rescued by the interposition of "Kløverhans."

What is the explanation of the "sandheap" (*sandhaug*) I do not know. But one cannot forget that Grettir's adventure in the house, followed by his adventure with the troll under the earth, is localized at Sandhaugar. This may be a mere accident; but it is worth noting that in following up the track indicated by Panzer we come across startling coincidences of this kind. As stated above, it can hardly be due to any influence of the *Grettis Saga* upon the folk-tale[854]. The likeness between the two is too remote to have suggested a transference of such details from the one story to the other.

We find the story in its normal form in Jutland[855]. The hero, a foundling, is named Bjørnøre (Bear-ears). There is no explanation offered of this name, but we know that in other versions of the story, where the hero is half bear and half man, his bear nature is shown by his bear's ears. "Bear-ears" comes with his companions to an empty house, worsts the foe (the old man, *den gamle*) who has put his companions to shame, and fixes him by his beard in a cloven tree. The foe escapes nevertheless; they follow him to his hole: the companions are afraid, but "Bear-ears" is let down, finds the enemy on his bed, and slays him. The rest of the story follows the usual pattern. "Bear-ears" rescues and sends up the princesses, his comrades detach the rope, which however is hauling up only the hero's iron club. He escapes miraculously from his confinement below, and returns to marry the youngest princess. In another Danish version, from the South of Zealand[856], the hero, "Strong Hans" (nothing is said about his bear-origin), comes with his companions to a magnificent but empty castle. The old witch worsts his comrades and imprisons them under the trap-door: but Hans beats her and rescues them, though the witch herself escapes. Hans is let down, rescues the princesses, is betrayed by his comrades (who, thinking to drop him in drawing him up, only drop his iron club), and finally weds the third princess.

A little further South we have three versions of the same tale recorded for Schleswig-Holstein[857]. The hero wins his victory below by means of "a great iron sword" (*en grotes ysernes Schwäert*) which he can only wield after drinking of the magic potion.

From Hanover comes the story of Peter Bär[858], which shows all the familiar features: from the same district came some of Grimm's variants. Others were from the Rhine provinces: but the fullest version of all comes from the Scheldt, just over the Flemish border. The hero, Jean l'Ourson, is recovered as a child from a bear's den, is despised in his youth[859], but gives early proof of his strength. He defends an empty castle *un superbe château*, when his companion has failed, strikes off an arm[860] of his assailant *Petit-Père-Bidoux*, chases him to his hole, *un puits vaste et profond*. He is let down by his companion, but finding the rope too short, plunges, and arrives battered at the bottom. There he perceives *une lumière qui brillait au bout d'une longue galerie*[861]. At the end of the gallery he sees his former assailant, attended by *une vieille femme à cheveux blancs, qui semblait âgée de plus de cent ans,* who is salving his wounded arm. The hero quenches the light (which is a magic one) smites his foe on the head and kills him, and then rekindles the lamp[862]. His companion above seeks to rob him of the two princesses he has won, by detaching the rope. Nevertheless, he escapes, weds the good princess, and punishes his faithless companion by making him wed the bad one.

The white-haired old woman is not spoken of as the mother of the foe she is nursing, and it may be doubted whether she is in any way parallel to Grendel's mother. The hero does not fight her: indeed it is she who, in the end, enables him to escape. Still the parallels between Jean l'Ourson and Beowulf are striking enough. Nine distinct features recur, in the same order, in the *Beowulf*-story and in this folk-tale. It needs a more robust faith than I possess to attribute this solely to chance.

Unfortunately, this French-Flemish tale is found in a somewhat sophisticated collection. Its recorder, as Sainte-Beuve points out in his letter introductory to the series[863], uses literary touches which diminish the value of his folk-tales to the student of origins. Any contamination from the *Beowulf*-story or the *Grettir*-story is surely improbable enough in this case: nevertheless, one would have liked the tale taken down verbatim from the lips of some simple-minded narrator as it used to be told at Condé on the Scheldt.

But if we take together the different versions enumerated above, the result is, I think, convincing. Here are eight versions of one folk-tale taken as representatives from a much larger number current in the countries in touch with the North Sea: from Iceland, the Faroes, Norway, Jutland, Zealand, Schleswig, Hanover, and the Scheldt. The champion is a bear-hero (as Beowulf almost certainly is, and as Bjarki quite certainly is); he is called, in Iceland, *Bjarndreingur*, in Jutland, *Bjørnore*, in Hanover, *Peter Bär*, on the Scheldt *Jean l'Ourson*. Like Beowulf, he is despised in his youth (Faroe, Scheldt). In all versions he resists his adversary in an empty house or castle, after his comrades have failed. In most versions of the folk-tale this is the third attack, as it is in the case of Grettir at Sandhaugar and of Bjarki: in *Beowulf*, on the contrary, we gather that Heorot has been raided many times. The adversary, though vanquished, escapes; in one version after the loss of an arm (Scheldt): they follow his track to the hole into which he has vanished, sometimes, as in *Beowulf*, marking traces of his blood (Iceland, Faroe, Schleswig). The hero always ventures down alone, and gets into an underworld of magic, which has left traces of its mysteriousness in *Beowulf*. In one tale (Scheldt) the hero sees a magic lamp burning below, just as he sees the fire in *Beowulf* or the

Grettis Saga. He overcomes either his original foe, or new ones, often by the use of a magic sword (Faroe, Norway, Schleswig); this sword hangs by the door (Norway) or on the wall (Faroe) as in *Beowulf.* After slaying his foe, the hero rekindles the magic lamp, in the Scheldt fairy tale, just as he kindles a light in the *Grettis Saga,* and as the light flashes up in *Beowulf* after the hero has smitten Grendel's mother. The hero is in each case deserted by his companions: a feature which, while it is marked in the *Grettis Saga,* can obviously be allowed to survive in *Beowulf* only in a much softened form. The chosen retainers whom Beowulf has taken with him on his journey could not be represented as unfaithful, because the poet is reserving the episode of the faithless retainers for the death of Beowulf. To have twice represented the escort as cowardly would have made the poem a satire upon the *comitatus,* and would have assured it a hostile reception in every hall from Canterbury to Edinburgh. But there is no doubt as to the faithlessness of the comrade Stein in the *Grettis Saga.* And in Zealand, one of the faithless companions is called *Stenhuggeren* (the Stone-hewer), in Schleswig *Steenklöwer,* in Hanover *Steinspieler,* whilst in Iceland he has the same name, *Stein,* which he has in the *Grettis Saga.*

The fact that the departure home of the Danes in *Beowulf* is due to the same cause as that which accounts for the betrayal of his trust by Stein, shows that in the original *Beowulf*-story also this feature must have occurred, however much it may have become worn down in the existing epic.

I think enough has been said to show that there is a real likeness between a large number of recorded folk-tales and the *Beowulf-Grettir* story. The parallel is not merely with an artificial, theoretical composite put together by Panzer. But it becomes equally clear that *Beowulf* cannot be spoken of as a version of these folk-tales. At most it is a version of a portion of them. The omission of the princesses in *Beowulf* and the *Grettis Saga* is fundamental. With the princesses much else falls away. There is no longer any motive for the betrayal of trust by the watchers. The disguise of the hero and his vengeance are now no longer necessary to the tale.

It might be argued that there was something about the three princesses which made them unsatisfactory as subjects of story. It has been thought that in the oldest version the hero married all three: an awkward episode where a *scop* had to compose a poem for an audience certainly monogamous and most probably Christian. The rather tragic and sombre atmosphere of the stories of Beowulf and Grettir fits in better with a version from which the princesses, and the living happily ever afterwards, have been dropped. On the other hand, it might be argued that the folk-tale is composite, and that the source from which the *Beowulf-Grettir*-story drew was a simpler tale to which the princesses had not yet been added.

And there are additions as well as subtractions. Alike in *Beowulf* and in the *Grettis Saga*, the fight in the house and the fight below are associated with struggles with monsters of different sex. The association of "The Devil and his Dam" has only few and remote parallels in the "Bear's-son" folk-tale.

But Panzer has, I think, proved that the struggle of Beowulf in the hall, and his plunging down into the deep, is simply an epic glorification of a folk-tale motive.

I. THE DATE OF THE DEATH OF HYGELAC.

Gregory of Tours mentions the defeat of Chochilaicus (Hygelac) as an event of the reign of Theudoric. Now Theudoric succeeded his father Chlodoweg, who died 27 Nov. 511. Theudoric died in 534. This, then, gives the extreme limits of time; but as Gregory mentions the event among the first occurrences of the reign, the period 512-520 has generally been suggested, or in round numbers about 515 or 516.

Nevertheless, we cannot attach much importance to the mere order followed by Gregory[864]. He may well have had no means of dating the event exactly. Of much more importance than the order, is the fact he records, that Theudoric did not defeat Chochilaicus in person, but sent his son Theudobert to repel the invaders.

Now Theudobert was born before the death of his grandfather Chlodoweg. For Gregory tells us that Chlodoweg left not only four sons, but a grandson Theudobert, *elegantem atque utilem*[865]: *utilem* cannot mean that, at the time of the death of Chlodoweg, Theudobert was of age to conduct affairs of state, for Chlodoweg was only 45 at death[866]. The Merovingians were a precocious race; but if we are to allow Theudobert to have been at least fifteen before being placed in charge of a very important expedition, and Chlodoweg to have been at least forty before becoming a grandfather, the defeat of Hygelac cannot be put before 521; and probability would favour a date five or ten years later.

There is confirmation for this. When Theudobert died, in 548, he left one son only, quite a child and still under tutelage[867]; probably therefore not more than twelve or thirteen at most. We know the circumstances of the child's birth. Theudobert had been betrothed by his father Theudoric to a Longobardic princess, Wisigardis[868]. In the meantime he fell in love with the lady Deoteria[869], and married her[870]. The Franks were shocked at this fickleness (*valde scandalizabantur*), and Theudobert had ultimately to put away Deoteria[871], although they had this young son (*parvulum filium*), who, as we have seen, could hardly have been born before 535, and possibly was born years later. Theudobert then married the Longobardic princess, in the seventh year after their betrothal. So it cannot have been much before 530 that Theudobert's father was first arranging the Longobardic match. A king is not likely to have waited to find a wife for a son, upon whom his dynasty was to depend, till fifteen years after that son was of age to win a memorable victory[872].

BIBLIOGRAPHY OF *BEOWULF* AND *FINNSBURG*

I remember it was with extreme difficulty that I could bring my master to understand the meaning of the word *opinion*, or how a point could be disputable; because reason taught us to affirm or deny only where we are certain; and beyond our knowledge we cannot do either. So that controversies, wranglings, disputes, and positiveness in false or dubious propositions are evils unknown among the *Houyhnhnms*.... He would laugh that a creature pretending to reason should value itself upon the knowledge of other people's conjectures, and in things, where that knowledge, if it were certain, could be of no use....

I have often since reflected what destruction such a doctrine would make in the libraries of Europe.

Gulliver's Travels.

The following items are (except in special cases) not included in this bibliography:

(*a*) Articles dealing with single passages in *Beowulf*, or two passages only, in cases where they have already been recorded under the appropriate passage in the footnotes to the text, or in the glossary, of my revision of Wyatt's edition.

(*b*) Articles dealing with the emendation or interpretation of single passages, in cases where such emendations have been withdrawn by their author himself.

(*c*) Purely popular paraphrases or summaries.

(*d*) Purely personal protests (e.g., *P.B.B.* XXI, 436), however well founded, in which no point of scholarship is any longer involved.

Books dealing with other subjects, but illustrating *Beowulf*, present a difficulty. Such books may have a value for *Beowulf* students, even though the author may never refer to our poem, and have occasionally been included in previous bibliographies. But, unless *Beowulf* is closely concerned, these books are not usually mentioned below: such enumeration, if carried out consistently, would clog a bibliography already all too bulky. Thus, Siecke's *Drachenkämpfe* does not seem to come within the scope of this bibliography, because the author is not concerned with Beowulf's dragon.

Obviously every general discussion of Old English metre must concern itself largely with *Beowulf*: for such treatises the student is referred to the section *Metrik* of Brandl's Bibliography (*Pauls Grdr.*); and, for Old English heroic legend in general, to the Bibliography of my edition of *Widsith*.

Many scholars, e.g. Heinzel, have put into their reviews of the books of others, much original work which might well have formed the material for independent articles. Such reviews are noted as "weighty," but it must not be supposed that the reviews not so marked are negligible; unless of some value to scholarship, reviews are not usually mentioned below.

The title of any book, article or review which I have not seen and verified is denoted by the sign ‡.

SUMMARY

§ 1. Periodicals.

§ 2. Bibliographies.

§ 3. The MS and its transcripts.

§ 4. Editions.

§ 5. Concordances, *etc.*

§ 6. Translations (including early summaries).

§ 7. Textual criticism and interpretation.

§ 8. Questions of literary history, date and authorship. *Beowulf* in the light of history, archæology[873], heroic legend, mythology and folk-lore.

§ 9. Style and Grammar.

§ 10. Metre.

§ 1. PERIODICALS

The periodicals most frequently quoted are:

A.f.d.A. = Anzeiger für deutsches Alterthum. Berlin, 1876 *etc.*

A.f.n.F. = Arkiv för nordisk Filologi. Christiania, Lund, 1883 *etc. Quoted according to the original numbering.*

Anglia. Halle, 1878 *etc.*

Archiv = Herrigs Archiv für das Studium der neueren Sprachen und Litteraturen. Elberfeld, Braunschweig, 1846 *etc. Quoted according to the original numbering.*

D.L.Z. = Deutsche Literatur-Zeitung. Berlin, 1880 *etc.*

Engl. Stud. = Englische Studien. Heilbronn, Leipzig, 1877 *etc.*

Germania. Wien, 1856-92.

I.F. = Indogermanische Forschungen. Strassburg, 1892 *etc.*

J.(E.)G.Ph. = Journal of (English and) Germanic Philology. Bloomington, Urbana, 1897 *etc.*

Lit. Cbl. = Literarisches Centralblatt. Leipzig, 1851 *etc.*

Literaturblatt für germanische und romanische Philologie. Heilbronn, Leipzig, 1880 *etc.*

M.L.N. = Modern Language Notes. Baltimore, 1886 *etc. Quoted by the page, not the column.*

M.L.R. = The Modern Language Review. Cambridge, 1906 *etc.*

Mod. Phil. = Modern Philology. Chicago, 1903 *etc.*

Morsbachs Studien zur englischen Philologie. Halle, 1897 *etc.*

P.B.B. = Beiträge zur Geschichte der deutschen Sprache u. Litteratur. Halle, 1874 *etc.*

Pub. Mod. Lang. Assoc. Amer. = Publications of the Modern Language Association of America. Baltimore, 1889 *etc.*

Z.f.d.A. = Zeitschrift für deutsches Alterthum. Leipzig, Berlin, 1841 *etc.*

Z.f.d.Ph. = Zachers Zeitschrift für deutsche Philologie. Halle, 1869 *etc.*

Z.f.ö.G. = Zeitschrift für die österreichischen Gymnasien. Wien, 1850 *etc.*

The titles of other periodicals are given with sufficient fulness for easy identification.

§ 2. BIBLIOGRAPHIES

Bibliographies have been published from time to time as a supplement to *Anglia*; also in the *Jahresbericht über...german. Philologie*; by Garnett in his *Translation*, 1882 *etc.*; and will be found in

Wülker's *Grundriss* (with very useful abstracts), 1885, pp. 245 *etc.*

Clark Hall's *Translation*, 1901, 1911.

Holthausen's *Beowulf*, 1906, 1909, 1913, 1919.

Brandl's *Englische Literatur*, in *Pauls Grdr.*(2), II, 1015-24 (full, but not so reliable as Holthausen's).

Sedgefield's *Beowulf*, 1910, 1913 (carefully selected).

An excellent critical bibliography of *Beowulf*-translations up to 1903 is that of Tinker: see under § 6, *Translations*.

§ 3. THE MS AND ITS TRANSCRIPTS

Beowulf fills ff. 129 (132)*a* to 198 (201)*b* of the British Museum MS *Cotton Vitellius A. XV.*

Beowulf is written in two hands, the first of which goes to l. 1939. This hand was identified by Prof. Sedgefield (*Beowulf, Introduction*, p. xiv, footnote) with that of the piece immediately preceding *Beowulf* in the MS, and by Mr Kenneth Sisam, in 1916, with that of all three immediately preceding pieces: the *Christopher* fragment, the *Wonders of the East*, and the *Letter of Alexander on the Wonders of India*. The pieces preceding these, however (the *Soliloquies of S. Augustine*, the *Gospel of Nicodemus, Salomon and Saturn*), are certainly not in the same hand, and their connection with the *Beowulf*-MS is simply due to the bookbinder.

From l. 1939 to the end, *Beowulf* is written in a second hand, thicker and less elegant than the first. This second hand seems to be clearly identical with that in which the poem of *Judith*, immediately following *Beowulf*, is written. This was pointed out by Sievers in 1872 (*Z.f.d.A.* XV, 457), and has never, I think, been disputed (cf. Sisam, p. 337; Förster, p. 31). Nevertheless the two poems have probably not always formed one book. For the last page of *Beowulf* was apparently once the last page of the volume, to judge from its battered condition, whilst *Judith* is imperfect at the beginning. And there are trifling differences, e.g. in the frequency of the use of contractions, and the form of the capital H.

This identity of the scribe of the second portion of *Beowulf* and the *Judith* scribe, together with the identity (pointed out by Mr Sisam) of the scribe of the first portion of *Beowulf* and the scribe of the three preceding works, is important. A detailed comparison of these texts will throw light upon the characteristics of the scribes.

That the three preceding works are in the same hand as that of the first *Beowulf* scribe was again announced, independently of Mr Sisam, by Prof. Max Förster, in 1919. Sievers had already in 1871 arrived at the same result (see Förster, p. 35, note) but had not published it.

It seems to me in the highest degree improbable that the *Beowulf*-MS has lost its ending, as Prof. Förster thinks (pp. 82, 88). Surely nothing could be better than the conclusion of the poem as it stands in the MS: that the casual loss of a number of leaves could have resulted in so satisfactory a conclusion is, I think, not conceivable. Moreover, the scribe has crammed as much material as possible into the last leaf of *Beowulf*, making his lines abnormally long, and using contractions in a way he does not use them elsewhere. The only reason for this must be to avoid running over into a new leaf or quire: there could be no motive for this crowded page if the poem had ever run on beyond it.

There is pretty general agreement that the date of the *Beowulf*-MS is about the year 1000, and that it is somewhat more likely to be before that date than after.

The *Beowulf*-MS was injured in the great Cottonian fire of 1731, and the edges of the parchment have since chipped away owing to the damage then sustained. Valuable assistance can therefore be derived from the two transcripts now preserved in the Royal Library of Copenhagen, made in 1787, when the MS was much less damaged.

A. Poema anglosaxonicum de rebus gestis Danorum ... fecit exscribi Londini A.D. MDCCLXXXVII Grimus Johannis Thorkelin.

B. Poema anglosaxonicum de Danorum rebus gestis ... exscripsit Grimus Johannis Thorkelin. Londini MDCCLXXXVII.

The first description of the *Beowulf*-MS is in 1705 by H. WANLEY (*Librorum Septentrionalium ... Catalogus*, pp. 218—19, Oxoniæ, forming vol. II of Hickes' *Thesaurus*). Two short extracts from the MS are given by Wanley. He describes the poem as telling of the wars *quæ Beowulfus quidam Danus, ex regio Scyldingorum stirpe ortus, gessit contra Sueciæ regulos.* The text was printed by THORKELIN in 1815, and the MS was collated by CONYBEARE, who in his *Illustrations* (1826) issued 19 pages of corrections of Thorkelin. These corrections were further corrected by J. M. KEMBLE in 1837 (Letter to M.

Francisque Michel, in Michel's *Bibliothèque Anglo-Saxonne*, pp. 20, 51-8). Meantime Kemble's text had been issued in 1833, based upon his examination of the MS. The MS was also seen by THORPE (in 1830: Thorpe's text was not published till 1855) and by GRUNDTVIG (pub. 1861). A further collation was that of E. KÖLBING in 1876 (Zur Beóvulf-handschrift, *Archiv*, LVI, 91-118). Kölbing's collation proves the superiority of Kemble's text to Grundtvig's. Line for line transcripts of the MS were those of Holder, Wülker and Zupitza:

1881 HOLDER, A. Beowulf. Bd. I. Abdruck der Handschrift. Freiburg u. Tübingen. (‡1881, from collation made in 1875.) Reviews: Kölbing, *Engl. Stud.* VII, 488; Kluge, *Literaturblatt*, 1883, 178; Wülker, *Lit. Cbl.* 1882, 1035-6.

1882. 2 Aufl.

1895. 3 Aufl. Reviews: Dieter, *Anglia, Beiblatt*, VI, 260-1; Brandl, *Z.f.d.A.* XL, 90.

1881 WÜLKER, R. P. Beowulf: Text nach der handschrift, in Grein's *Bibliothek*, I, 18-148.

1882 ZUPITZA, J. Beowulf. Autotypes of the unique Cotton MS. Vitellius A XV; with a transliteration and notes. *Early English Text Society*, London. Reviews: Trautmann, *Anglia*, VII, *Anzeiger*, 41; Kölbing, *Engl. Stud.* VII, 482 *etc.*; Varnhagen, *A.f.d.A.* X, 304; Sievers, *Lit. Cbl.* 1884, 124.

Further discussion of the MS by

1890 DAVIDSON, C. Differences between the scribes of Beowulf. *M.L.N.* V, 43-4; MCCLUMPHA, C., criticizes the above, *M.L.N.* V, 123; reply by DAVIDSON, *M.L.N.* V, 189-90.

1910 LAMB, EVELYN H. "Beowulf": Hemming of Worcester. *Notes and Queries*, Ser. XI, vol. I, p. 26. (Worthless. An assertion, unsupported by any evidence, that *both* the hands of the Beowulf MS are those of Hemming of Worcester, who flourished c. 1096.)

1916 SISAM, K. The Beowulf Manuscript. *M.L.R.* XI, 335-7. (Very important. Gives results of a scrutiny of the other treatises in *MS Vitellius A. XV* (see above) and shows, among other things, that the Beowulf MS, before reaching the hands of Sir Robert Cotton, was (in 1563) in those of Lawrence Nowell, the Elizabethan Anglo-Saxon scholar.)

1919 FÖRSTER, MAX. Die Beowulf-Handschrift, Leipzig, *Berichte der Sächs. Akad. der Wissenschaften*, Bd. 71. (An excellent and detailed discussion of the problems of the MS, quite independent of that of Mr Sisam, whose results it confirms.) Review: Schröder, *Z.f.d.A.* LVIII, 85-6.

1920 RYPINS, S. I. The Beowulf Codex. *Mod. Phil.* XVII, 541-8 (promising further treatment of the problems of the MS).

The MS of Finnsburg has been lost. See above, p. 245.

§ 4. EDITIONS OF BEOWULF AND FINNSBURG

1705 HICKES, G. Linguarum Vett. Septentrionalium Thesaurus. Oxoniæ. (Vol. I, 192-3, text of Finnsburg Fragment.)

1814 CONYBEARE, J. J. The Battle of Finsborough, in Brydges' *British Bibliographer*, vol. IV, pp. 261-7; No. XV (Text, Latin translation, and free verse paraphrase in English: some brief notes).

1815 THORKELIN, G. J. De Danorum rebus gestis secul. III et IV. Poëma Danicum dialecto Anglo-Saxonica. (Copenhagen, with Lat. transl.) Reviews: See § 7, *Textual Criticism*, 1815, Grundtvig; also *Dansk Litteratur-Tidende*, 1815, 401-32, 437-46, 461-2 (defending Thorkelin against Grundtvig); *Iduna*, vii, 1817, 133-59; *Monthly Review*, LXXXI, 1816, 516-23; ‡*Jenaische Literatur-Zeitung*, 1816, *Ergänzungsblätter*, 353-65 (summary in Wülker's *Grundriss*, p. 252); Outzen in *Kieler Blätter*, 1816, see § 8, below.

1817 RASK, R. K. Angelsaksisk sproglære. Stockholm (pp. 163-6 contain Beowulf, ll. 53-114, with commentary).

1820 Text of Finnsburg, given by GRUNDTVIG in *Bjowulfs Drape*, pp. xl-xlv.

1826 Text of Finnsburg, and of large portions of Beowulf, given in CONYBEARE'S *Illustrations*. See § 5, *Translations*.

1833 KEMBLE, J. M. Beowulf, the Travellers Song, and the Battle of Finnesburh, edited with a glossary ... and an historical preface. London.

1835. Second edit.

1847 SCHALDEMOSE, F. Beo-wulf og Scopes Widsið ... med Oversættelse. Kjøbenhavn. (Follows Kemble's text of 1835: Text and transl. of Finnsburg also given, pp. 161-4.) 1851, Reprinted.

1849 KLIPSTEIN, L. F. Analecta Anglo-Saxonica. New York. (Selections from Beowulf, II, 227-61: Text of Finnsburg, 426-7.)

1850 ETTMÜLLER, L. Engla and Seaxna scopas and bōceras. Quedlinburg u. Leipzig. (Text of large portions of Beowulf, with Finnsburg, pp. 95-131.)

1855 THORPE, B. The A.S. poems of Beowulf, the scop or gleeman's tale, and Finnesburg, with a literal translation ... Oxford. ‡1875, Reprinted.

1857 GREIN, C. W. M. Bibliothek der angelsächsischen Poesie, I. Göttingen (pp. 255—343, Beóvulf, Ueberfall in Finnsburg).

1861-4. Bd. III, IV. Sprachschatz.

1861 RIEGER, M. Alt- u. angelsächsisches Lesebuch. Giessen. (Der Kampf zu Finnsburg, pp. 61-3: aus dem Beovulf, 63-82.)

1861 GRUNDTVIG, N. F. S. Beowulfes Beorh eller Bjovulfs-Drapen. Kiöbenhavn, London. (The Finnsburg Fragment is inserted in the text of Beowulf, after l. 1106.)

1863 HEYNE, M. Beovulf, mit ausführlichem Glossar. Paderborn. (Anhang: Der Ueberfall in Finnsburg.) Reviews: Grein, *Lit. Cbl.* 1864, 137—8; Holtzmann, *Germania*, VIII, 506-7.

1868. ‡2 Aufl. Review: Rieger, *Z.f.d.Ph.* II, 371-4.

1873. 3 Aufl. Review: Sievers, *Lit. Cbl.* 1873, 662-3, brief but severe.

1879. 4 Aufl. [in this, Kölbing's collation of 1876 was utilized; see p. 82]. Reviews: Brenner, *Engl. Stud.* IV, 135-9; Gering, *Z.f.d.Ph.* XII, 122-5.

1867 GREIN, C. W. M. Beowulf, nebst den Fragmenten Finnsburg u. Valdere. Cassel u. Göttingen.

1875 ETTMÜLLER, L. Carmen de Beóvulfi, Gautarum regis, rebus praeclare gestis atque interitu, quale fuerit antequam in manus interpolatoris, monachi Vestsaxonici, inciderat. (Zürich. University Programme. The additions of the "interpolator" being omitted, the edition contains 2896 lines only.) Reviews: Schönbach, *A.f.d.A.* III, 36-46; ‡Suchier, *Jenaer Literatur-Zeitung*, XLVII, 1876, 732.

1876 ARNOLD, T. Beowulf, with a translation, notes and appendix. London. Reviews (unfavourable): Sweet, *Academy*, X, 1876, 588; Wülker, *Lit. Cbl.* 1877, 665-6, and *Anglia*, I, 177-86.

1879 WÜLKER, R. P. Kleinere angelsächsische Dichtungen. Halle, Leipzig. (Finnsburg, pp. 6-7.)

1883 MÖLLER, H. Das altenglische Volksepos in der ursprünglichen strophischen Form. I. Abhandlungen. II. Texte. Kiel. (Containing only those parts of the Finn-story and of Beowulf which Möller regarded as "genuine," in strophic form.) Reviews: Heinzel, *A.f.d.A.* X, 215-33 (important); Schönbach, *Z.f.ö.G.* XXXV, 37-46.

1883 WÜLKER, R. P. Das Beowulfslied, nebst den kleineren epischen ... stücken. Kassel. (In the second edit. of Grein's *Bibliothek der ags. Poesie.*) Review: Kölbing, *Engl. Stud.* VII, 482 *etc.*

1883 HARRISON, J. A. and SHARP, R. Beowulf. Boston, U.S.A. (‡1883, on the basis of Heyne's edition; with Finnsburg.) Reviews: York Powell, *Academy*, XXVI, 1884, 220-1; reply by Harrison, 308-9; by York Powell, 327; Kölbing, *Engl. Stud.* VII, 482; Bright, *Literaturblatt*, 1884, 221—3.

1892. Third edit.

1894. Fourth edit. Reviews: Wülker, *Anglia, Beiblatt*, V, 65-7; Glöde, *Engl. Stud.* XX, 417-18.

1884 HOLDER, A. Beowulf, II. Berichtigter Text u. Wörterbuch. Freiburg u. Tübingen. Reviews: York Powell, *Academy*, XXVI, 1884, 220-1; Wülker, *Lit. Cbl.* 1885, 1008-9; Krüger, *Literaturblatt*, 1884, 468-70.

1899. 2 Aufl. [with suggestions of Kluge and Cosijn]. Reviews: Trautmann, *Anglia, Beiblatt*, X, 257; Wülfing, *Engl. Stud.* XXIX, 278-9; Holthausen, *Literaturblatt*, 1900, 60-2 (important corrections).

1888 HEYNE, M. and SOCIN, A. [Fifth edit. of Heyne's text.] Paderborn u. Münster. Reviews: Koeppel, *Engl. Stud.* XIII, 466-72; Heinzel, *A.f.d.A.* XV, 189-94; Sievers, *Z.f.d.Ph.* XXI, 354-65 (very important corrections); Schröer, *Literaturblatt*, 1889, 170-1.

1898. 6 Aufl. Reviews: Trautmann, *Anglia, Beiblatt*, X, 257; Holthausen, *Anglia, Beiblatt*, X, 265; Sarrazin, *Engl. Stud.* XXVIII, 408-10; Jantzen, *Archiv*, CIII, 175-6.

1903. 7 Aufl. Reviews: Holthausen, *Anglia, Beiblatt*, XVIII, 193-4; Klaeber, the same, 289-91; Kruisinga, *Engl. Stud.* XXXV, 401-2; v. Grienberger, *Z.f.ö.G.* LVI, 744-61 (very full); E. Kock, *A.f.n.F.* XXII, 215 (brief).

1894 WYATT, A. J. Beowulf, edited with textual footnotes, index of proper names, and glossary. (Text of Finnsburg.) Cambridge. Reviews: Bradley,

Academy, XLVI, 1894, 69-70; Wülker, *Anglia, Beiblatt,* V, 65-7; Brenner, *Engl. Stud.* XX, 296; Zupitza, *Archiv,* XCIV, 326-9.

1898. Second edit. Reviews: Trautmann, *Anglia, Beiblatt,* X, 257; Sarrazin, *Engl. Stud.* XXVIII, 407-8.

1902 KLUGE, F. Angelsächsisches Lesebuch. 3 Aufl. Halle. (XXX. Der Überfall von Finnsburuh, pp. 127-8.)

1903 TRAUTMANN, M. Finn u. Hildebrand. *Bonner Beiträge,* VII. (Text, translation and comment on the Episode and Fragment.) Reviews: Binz, *Z.f.d.Ph.* XXXVII, 529-36; Jantzen, *Die Neueren Sprachen,* XI, 543-8; *Neue philol. Rundschau,* 1903, 619-21 (signed -tz- ? Jantzen). Some additional notes by Trautmann, "Nachträgliches zu Finn u. Hildebrand" appeared in *Bonner Beiträge,* XVII, 122.

1904 TRAUTMANN, M. Das Beowulflied ... das Finn-Bruchstück u. die Waldhere-Bruchstücke. Bearbeiteter Text u. deutsche Übersetzung. *Bonner Beiträge,* XVI. Reviews: Klaeber, *M.L.N.* XX, 83-7 (weighty); Eckhardt, *Engl. Stud.* XXXVII, 401-3; Schücking, *Archiv,* CXV, 417-21; Barnouw, *Museum,* XIV, 96-8; *Neue philologische Rundschau* (? by Jantzen), 1905, 549-50.

1905-6 HOLTHAUSEN, F. Beowulf nebst dem Finnsburg-Bruchstück. I. Texte. II. Einleitung, Glossar u. Anmerkungen. Heidelberg. Reviews: Lawrence, *J.E.G.Ph.* VII, 125-9; Klaeber, *M.L.N.* XXIV, 94-5; Schücking, *Engl. Stud.* XXXIX, 94-111 (weighty); Deutschbein, *Archiv,* CXXI, 162-4; v. Grienberger, *Z.f.ö.G.* 1908, LIX, 333-46 (giving an elaborate list of etymological parallels); Barnouw, *Museum,* XIV, 169-70; Wülker, *D.L.Z.* 1906, 285-6; ‡Jantzen, *Neue philologische Rundschau,* 1907, 18.

1908-9. 2 Aufl., nebst den kleineren Denkmälern der Heldensage, Finnsburg, Waldere, Deor, Widsith, Hildebrand. Reviews: Eichler, *Anglia, Beiblatt,* XXI, 129-33; XXII, 161-5; Schücking, *Engl. Stud.* XLII, 108-11; Brandl, *Archiv,* CXXI, 473, CXXIV, 210; Binz, *Literaturblatt,* XXXII, 1911, 53-5: see also Koeppel, *Anglia, Beiblatt,* XXIII, 297.

1912-13. 3 Aufl.

1914-19. 4 Aufl. Reviews: Binz, *Literaturblatt,* XLI, 1920, 316-17; Fischer, *Engl. Stud.* LIV, 404-6.

1908 SCHÜCKING, L. L. Beowulf [8th edit. of Heyne's text]. Paderborn. Reviews: Lawrence, *M.L.N.* XXV, 155-7; Klaeber, *Engl. Stud.* XXXIX, 425-33 (weighty); Imelmann, *D.L.Z.* 1909, 995 (contains important original contributions); v. Grienberger, *Z.f.ö.G.* LX, 1089; Boer, *Museum,* XVI, 139 (brief).

1910. 9 Aufl. Reviews: Sedgefield, *Engl. Stud.* XLIII, 267-9; F. Wild, *Z.f.ö.G.* LXIV, 153-5.

1913. 10 Aufl. Reviews: Klaeber, *Anglia, Beiblatt,* XXIV, 289-91; *Engl. Stud.* XLIX, 424; ‡Degenhart, *Blätter f. gymnasialschulwesen,* LI, 130; E. A. Kock, *A.f.n.F.* XXXII, 222-3; Holthausen, *Z.f.d.Ph.* XLVIII, 127-31 (weighty).

1918. 11, 12 Aufl. Reviews: Björkman, *Anglia, Beiblatt,* XXX, 121-2, 180; Fischer, *Engl. Stud.* LIII, 338-9.

1910 SEDGEFIELD, W. J. Beowulf, edited with Introduction, Bibliography, Notes, Glossary and Appendices. Manchester. Reviews: Thomas, *M.L.R.* VI, 266-8; Lawrence, *J.E.G.Ph.* X, 633-40; Wild, *Anglia, Beiblatt,* XXIII, 253-60; Klaeber, *Engl. Stud.* XLIV, 119-26; Brandl, *Archiv,* CXXVI, 279.

1913. Second edit. Reviews: *M.L.R.* IX, 429; Lawrence, *J.E.G.Ph.* XIV, 609-13; Klaeber, *Anglia, Beiblatt,* XXV, 166-8.

1912 Text of the Finn episode given in MEYER, W., Beiträge zur Geschichte der Eroberung Englands durch die Angelsachsen.

1914 CHAMBERS, R. W. Beowulf with the Finnsburg Fragment, ed. by A. J. WYATT. New edition, revised. Cambridge. Reviews: Jones, *M.L.R.* XI, 230-1: Lawrence, *J.E.G.Ph.* XIV, 609-13; Bright, *M.L.N.* XXXI, 188-9; Schücking, *Engl. Stud.* LV, 88-100.

1915 DICKINS, B. Runic and Heroic Poems (Text of Finnsburg with Notes). Cambridge. Review: Mawer, *M.L.R.* XII, 82-4.

1917 MACKIE, W. L. The Fight at Finnsburg (Introduction, Text and Notes). *J.E.G.Ph.* XVI, 250-73.

1919 SCHÜCKING, L. L. Kleines angelsächsisches Dichterbuch. [Includes Finnsburg Fragment, Finnsburg Episode and "Beowulf's Return" (ll. 1888-2199).] Reviews: Binz, *Literaturblatt,* XLI, 1920, pp. 315-16; Imelmann, *D.L.Z.* XL, 1919, 423-5; Fischer, *Engl. Stud.* LIV, 1920, 302-3.

1920 Text of Finnsburg Fragment and Episode, with commentary, in IMELMANN'S "Forschungen zur altenglischen Poesie."

An edition of Beowulf by Prof. F. KLAEBER is in the press.

§ 5. CONCORDANCES, etc.

1896 HOLDER, A. Beowulf, vol. II*b*, Wortschatz. Freiburg. Review: Brandl, *A.f.d.A.* XXIII, 107.

1911 COOK, A. S. Concordance to Beowulf. Halle. Reviews: Klaeber, *J.E.G.Ph.* XI, 277-9; Garnett, *Amer. Jnl. Philol.* XXXIII, 86-7.

§ 6. TRANSLATIONS (INCLUDING EARLY SUMMARIES)

1881 WÜLKER, R. P. Besprechung der Beowulfübersetzungen, *Anglia*, IV, *Anzeiger*, 69-80.

1886 GUMMERE, F. B. The translation of Beowulf, and the relations of ancient and modern English verse, *Amer. Jour. of Phil.* VII, 46-78. (A weighty argument for translation into "the original metre.")

1891 GARNETT, J. M. The translation of A.S. poetry, *Pub. Mod. Lang. Assoc. Amer.* VI, 95-105. (Agreeing in the main with Gummere.)

1897 FRYE, P. H. The translation of Beowulf, *M.L.N.* XII, 79-82. (Advocating blank verse.)

1898 FULTON, E. On translating A.S. poetry, *Pub. Mod. Lang. Assoc. Amer.* XIII, 286-96. (Recommending an irregular four-accent line.)

1903 GARNETT, J. M. Recent translations of O.E. poetry, *Pub. Mod. Lang. Assoc. Amer.* XVIII, 445-58.

1903 TINKER, C. B. The translations of Beowulf. A critical bibliography. *Yale Studies in English.* New York. Reviews: Klaeber, *J.E.G.Ph.* V, 116-8; Binz, *Anglia, Beiblatt*, XVI, 291-2.

1909 CHILD, G. C. "Gummere's Oldest English Epic," *M.L.N.* XXIV, 253-4. (A criticism advocating prose translation.)

1910 GUMMERE, F. B. Translation of Old English Verse, *M.L.N.* XXV, 61-3. (Advocating alliterative verse.) Reply by CHILD, *M.L.N.* XXV, 157-8. See also reviews of Gummere, under year 1909, below.

1918 LEONARD, W. E. Beowulf and the Niebelungen couplet, *Univ. of Wisconsin Studies in Language and Literature*, II, 99-152.

1805 TURNER, SHARON. History of the manners ... poetry ... and language of the Anglo-Saxons. London. (From p. 398 to p. 408 is a summary, with translations, of Beowulf, Prol.-VIII. Turner was misled as to the subject of the poem, because a leaf had been misplaced in the MS, so that the account of the fighting between Grendel and Beowulf (ll. 740-82) occurred immediately after l. 91. The struggle between Beowulf and an (unnamed) adversary being thus made to follow the account of Hrothgar's court at Heorot, Turner was led to suppose that the poem narrated the attempt of Beowulf to avenge *on Hrothgar* the feud for a homicide he had committed. "The transition," Turner not unreasonably complains, "is rather violent." The correct placing of the shifted leaf is due to Thorkelin.)

1815 THORKELIN, G. J. [Latin version in his edition, q.v.] The reviewers gave summaries of the poem, with translations of portions of it: English in the *Monthly Review*, LXXXI, 1816, 516-23 (less inaccurate than Turner's summary); Danish in the *Dansk Litteratur-Tidende*, 1815, 401-32, 437-46, and by Grundtvig in the *Nyeste Skilderie* (see below, § 7); Swedish in *Iduna*, VII, 1817, 133-59.

1819 GRUNDTVIG, N. F. S. Stykker af Skjoldung-Kvadet eller Bjovulfs Minde, *Dannevirke*, IV, 234-62.

1820 GRUNDTVIG, N. F. S. Bjowulfs Drape, Kjøbenhavn. (Free rhymed translation of Beowulf: Finnsburg rendered into short lines, unrhymed: Introduction and most important critical notes.) Review: J. Grimm in *Gött. Anzeigen*, 1823 = *Kleinere Schriften*, IV, 178-86. For second edit., see 1865.

1820 TURNER, SHARON. History of the Anglo-Saxons ... third edit. London. (Vol. III, pp. 325-48, contains a summary, with translations, of the earlier part of the poem, much less inaccurate than that of 1805.)

1826 CONYBEARE, J. J. Illustrations of Anglo-Saxon poetry. London. (Pp. 35-136 contain a summary of Beowulf, with blank verse transl. and the corresponding text in A.S. and Latin; pp. 175-82, Finnsburg, text with transl. into Latin and into English verse.)

1832 GRUNDTVIG, N. F. S. Nordens mythologi. Anden Udgave. Kiöbenhavn. (Pp. 571-94 give a summary of the Beowulf-stories. This was, of course, wanting in the first edit. of 1808.)

1837 KEMBLE, J. M. Translation ... with ... glossary, preface and notes. London. (The "postscript to the preface" in which Kemble supplemented and corrected the "Historical Preface" to his edition of 1833, is the basis of the mythological explanations of Beowulf as an Anglian god, Beowa.)

1839 LEO, H. [Summary with translation of extracts.] See § 8, below.

1840 ETTMÜLLER, L. Beowulf, stabreimend übersetzt, mit Einleitung und Anmerkungen (Finnsburg, pp. 36-8). Zürich.

1845 LONGFELLOW, H. W. The Poets and Poetry of Europe. Philadelphia. (Pp. 8-10 contain transl. of extracts from Beowulf.)

1847 SCHALDEMOSE, F. [Danish transl. of Beowulf and Finnsburg, in his edit., q.v.]

1849 WACKERBARTH, A. D. Beowulf, translated into English verse. London. (Imitation of Scott's metre.)

1855 THORPE, B. [In his edit., q.v.]

1857 UHLAND, L. [Prose transl. of Finnsburg.] *Germania*, II, 354-5.

1857 GREIN, C. W. M. Dichtungen der Angelsachsen, stabreimend übersetzt. Göttingen. (Vol. I, pp. 222—308, Beowulf, trans. into alliterative verse.)

1883. 2 Aufl. [Incorporating Grein's manuscript corrections, seen through the press by Wülker.] Cassel. Review: Krüger, *Engl. Stud.* VIII, 139—42.

1859 SIMROCK, K. Beowulf übersetzt u. erläutert. Stuttgart u. Augsburg. (Alliterative verse: Finnsburg Fragment inserted after l. 1124.)

1859 SANDRAS, G. S. De carminibus anglo-saxonicis Caedmoni adjudicatis. Paris. (Pp. 8—10 contain extract from Beowulf and Latin transl.)

1861 HAIGH, D. H. (Prose transl. of Finnsburg.) In *Anglo-Saxon Sagas,* pp. 32—3, q.v.

1863 HEYNE, M. Beowulf übersetzt. Paderborn. (Blank verse.) Review: Holtzmann, *Germania*, VIII, 506—7.

1897—8. 2 Aufl. Paderborn. Reviews: Holthausen, *Archiv*, CIII,

373—6; Wülker, *Anglia, Beiblatt*, IX, 1; Jantzen, *Engl. Stud.* XXV,

271—3; Löhner, *Z.f.ö.G.* XLIX, 563.

1915. 3 Aufl. Paderborn.

1865 GRUNDTVIG, N. F. S. Bjovulfs-Drapen. Anden Udgave.

1872 VON WOLZOGEN, H. Beovulf aus dem ags. Leipzig. (Verse.)

1876 ARNOLD, T. [In his edit., q.v.]

1877 BOTKINE, L. Beowulf traduite en français. Havre. (Prose: some omissions.) Review: Körner, *Engl. Stud.* II, 248—51.

1881 ZINSSER, G. Der Kampf Beowulfs mit Grendel [vv. 1—836] als Probe einer metrischen Uebersetzung. Saarbrücken. Reviews: *Archiv,* LXVIII, 446; Krüger, *Engl. Stud.* VII, 370—2.

1881 LUMSDEN, H. W. Beowulf ... transl. into modern rhymes. London. (Some omissions.) Reviews: *Athenæum,* April 1881, p. 587; Garnett, *Amer. Jour. of Phil.* II, 355—61; Wülker, *Anglia,* IV, *Anzeiger,* 69—80.

1883. ‡Second edit. Review: York Powell, *Academy,* XXVI, 1884, pp. 220—1.

1882 SCHUHMANN, G. Beovulf, antichissimo poema epico de' popoli germanici. *Giornale Napoletano di filosofia e lettere.* Anno IV, vol. 7, 25—36, 175—190. (A summary only.)

1882 GARNETT, J. M. Beowulf and the Fight at Finnsburg, translated. Boston, U.S.A. Reviews: *Nation* (New York), No. 919, 1883; Harrison, *Amer. Jour. of Phil.* IV, 84—6, reply by Garnett, 243—6; Schipper, *Anglia,* VI, *Anzeiger,* 120—4; Krüger, *Engl. Stud.* VIII, 133—8, and (second edit.) IX, 151; Bright, *Literaturblatt,* 1883, 386—7.

1885. Second edit., revised.

1900. Fourth edit.

1883 GRION, GIUSTO. Beovulf, poema epico anglòsassone del VII secolo, tradotto e illustrato. In the *Atti della reale Accademia Lucchese,* XXII. (First Italian translation.) Review: Krüger, *Engl. Stud.* IX, 64—77.

1889 ‡WICKBERG, R. Beowulf, en fornengelsk hjältedikt översatt. Westervik.

1914. ‡Second edit. Upsala. Review: Kock, *A.f.n.F.* XXXII, 223—4.

1892 HALL, JOHN LESSLIE. Beowulf translated. (Verse, with notes.) Boston, U.S.A. Reviews: *M.L.N.* VII, 128, 1892 (brief mention); Miller, *Viking Club Year Book,* I, 91—2; Holthausen, *Anglia, Beiblatt,* IV, 33—6; Glöde, *Engl. Stud.* XIX, 257—60.

1893. ‡Student's edit.

1892 (1891) EARLE, JOHN. The deeds of Beowulf. Oxford. (Prose translation, somewhat spoilt by its artificial and sometimes grotesque vocabulary; very valuable introduction, with summary of the controversy to date, and notes.) Reviews: *Athenæum*, 1 Oct. 1892; Koeppel, *Engl. Stud.* XVIII, 93-5 (fair, though rather severe).

1893 HOFFMANN, P. Beówulf ... aus dem angelsächsischen übertragen. Züllichau. (In the measure of the Nibelungenlied; ind. Finnsburg.) Reviews (mostly unfavourable): Shipley, *M.L.N.* IX, 121-3, 1894; Wülker, *Anglia, Beiblatt*, V, 67; Wülker, *Lit. Cbl.* 1894, p. 1930; Glöde, *Engl. Stud.* XIX, 412-5; ‡Detter, *Öster. Literaturblatt*, V, 9; ‡Marold, *Deut. Literaturblatt*, XXIII, 332.

1900. ‡Second edit. Hannover.

1895 MORRIS, W. and WYATT, A. J. The Tale of Beowulf. Kelmscott Press, Hammersmith. (Verse: archaic vocabulary.)

1898. New edit. Review: Hulme, *M.L.N.* XV, 22-6, 1900.

1896 SIMONS, L. Beówulf ... vertaald in stafrijm en met inleiding en aanteekeningen. Gent (*Koninklijke vlaamsche Academie*). Reviews: Glöde, *Engl. Stud.* XXV, 270-1; Uhlenbeck, *Museum* (Groningen), V, 217-8.

1898 STEINECK, H. Altenglische Dichtungen (Beowulf, Elene, u.a.) in wortgetreuer Übersetzung. Leipzig. (Prose, line for line.) Reviews: Binz, *Anglia, Beiblatt*, IX, 220-2; Holthausen, *Archiv*, CIII, 376-8 (both very unfavourable).

1901 HALL, J. R. CLARK. Beowulf and the fight at Finnsburg. A translation into modern English prose. London. Reviews: *Athenæum*, 1901, July, p. 56; *Academy*, LX, 1901, 342; Stedman, *Viking Club Year Book*, III, 72-4; Tinker, *J.E.G.Ph.* IV, 379-81; Holthausen, *Anglia, Beiblatt*, XIII, 225-8; Dibelius, *Archiv*, CIX, 403-4; Vietor, *Die neueren Sprachen*, XI, 439; Wülker, *Lit. Cbl.* 1902, 30-1 ("sehr zu empfehlen").

1911 (q.v.). New edit., with considerable additions.

1902 TINKER, C. B. Beowulf translated out of the Old English. New York. (Prose.) Reviews: Klaeber, *J.E.G.Ph.* V, 91-3; Holthausen, *Anglia, Beiblatt*, XIV, 7.

1903 ‡BJÖRKMAN, E. Swedish transl. (prose) of Beowulf, Part II (in Schück's *Världslitteraturen*, with introd. by Schück).

1903-4 TRAUTMANN, M., in his editions, q.v.

1904 CHILD, C. G. Beowulf and the Finnesburh Fragment translated. London and Boston. Reviews: Grattan, *M.L.R.* III, 303-4 ("a good prose translation which steers an even course between pseudo-archaisms and modern colloquialisms"); Miller, *Viking Club Year Book*, I, 91-2; Klaeber, *Anglia, Beiblatt*, XVI, 225-7; Brandl, *Archiv*, CXXI, 473.

1904 ‡HANSEN, A. Transl. into Danish of Beowulf, ll. 491-924, *Danske Tidsskrift*.

1905 VOGT, P. Beowulf ... übersetzt. Halle. (Text rearranged according to theories of interpolation: Finnsburg Fragment translated, following Möller's text.) Reviews: Binz, *Anglia, Beiblatt*, XXI, 289-91; Eichler, *Z.f.ö.G.* LVII, 908-10; Klaeber, *Archiv*, CXVII, 408-10: Jantzen, *Lit. Cbl.* 1906, 257-8.

1906 GERING, H. Beowulf nebst dem Finnsburg-Bruchstück übersetzt. Heidelberg. (Verse.) Reviews: Lawrence, *J.E.G.Ph.* VII, 129-33 ("thoroughly scholarly"); Jantzen, *Lit. Cbl.* 1907, 64-5; Ries, *A.f.d.A.* XXXIII, 143-7; Binz, *Literaturblatt*, XXXI, 397-8 ("Fliessend und ungezwungen, sinngetreu ..."); ‡Zehme, *Monatsschrift*, XIV, 597-600; v. Grienberger, *Z.f.ö.G.* 1908, LIX, 423-8.

1914. 2 Aufl.

1907 HUYSHE, W. Beowulf ... translated into ... prose ("Appendix: The Fight at Finn's burgh"). London. ("Translation," to quote Clark Hall, "apparently such as might have been compiled from previous translations by a person ignorant of Ags. Some original mistakes.") Reviews: *Athenæum*, 1907, II, 96 ("Mr Huyshe displays sad ignorance of Old English ... but an assiduous study of the work of his predecessors has preserved him from misrepresenting seriously the general sense of the text"); *Notes and Queries*, Ser. X, vol. VIII, 58; Garnett, *Amer. Jnl. Philol.* XXIX, 344-6; Klaeber, *Anglia, Beiblatt*, XIX, 257.

1909 GUMMERE, F. B. The oldest English Epic. Beowulf, Finnsburg, Waldere, Deor and the German Hildebrand, translated in the original metres. New York. Reviews: *Athenæum*, 1909, II, 151; Trautmann, *Anglia, Beiblatt*, XXXIII, 353-60 (metrical debate); Sedgefield, *Engl. Stud.* XLI, 402-3 (discussing possibility of reproducing in Mod. Eng. the Old Eng. alliterative verse-rhythm); Derocquigny, *Revue Germanique*, VI, 356-7; see also above, p. 390.

1910 HANSEN, ADOLF. Bjovulf, oversat af A. Hansen, og efter hans død gået efter og fuldført samt forsynet med en inledning og en oversættelse af brudstykket om kampen i Finsborg, af Viggo Julius von Holstein Rathlou; udgivet ved Oskar Hansen. København og Kristiania. An account of this translation, by v. Holstein Rathlou, in *Tilskueren*, June, 1910, pp. 557-62; Review: Olrik, *Danske Studier*, 1910, 112-13.

1911 CLARK HALL, J. R. Beowulf and the Finnsburg Fragment. A translation into Modern English Prose. London. Reviews: Mawer, *M.L.R.* VI, 542 ("probably the best working translation that we have, enriched by a valuable introduction and excellent appendices"); *Academy*, 1911, I, 225-6; Björkman, *Engl. Stud.* XLIV, 127-8; *Archiv*, CXXVI, 492-3; Binz, *Literaturblatt*, XXXII, 232.

1912 PIERQUIN, H. Le poème Anglo-Saxon de Beowulf. (An extraordinary piece of work; the version mainly follows Kemble's text, which is reproduced, but with many misprints: Kemble's *Saxons in England* is translated by way of introduction. The Finnsburg Fragment is included.) Reviews: *Academy*, 1912, II, 509-10 (seems to regard Pierquin as author of *Les Saxons en Angleterre*); Sedgefield, *M.L.R.* VIII, 550-2; Klaeber, *Anglia, Beiblatt*, XXIV, 138-9; Imelmann, *D.L.Z.* XXXIV (1913), 1062-3 (very unfavourable); ‡Luick, *Mitt. d. inst. f. österr. gesch.-forsch.* XXXVI, 401; ‡Barat, *Moyen Âge*, XXVI (see. ser. XVII), 298-302.

1913 KIRTLAN, E. J. The Story of Beowulf. London. (A fair specimen of the less scholarly translations; nicely got up and not exceedingly incorrect.) Reviews: *Athenæum*, 1914, II, 71; Klaeber, *Anglia, Beiblatt*, XXVII, 129-31.

1914 CLARK HALL, J. R. Beowulf: a metrical translation. Cambridge. (Not so successful as the same writer's prose translation.) Reviews: Sedgefield, *M.L.R.* X, 387-9 (discussing the principles of metrical translation); Klaeber, *Anglia, Beiblatt*, XXVI, 170-2.

1915 OLIVERO, F. Traduzioni dalla Poesia Anglo-sassone. Bari. (Pp. 73-119, extracts from Beowulf.) Review: *M.L.R.* XI, 509.

1916 ‡BENEDETTI, A. La canzone di Beowulf, poema epico anglo-sassone del VI secolo. Versione italiana, con introduzione e note. Palermo.

1918 LEONARD, W. E. [Specimen, Passus IX, of forthcoming transl., in the measure of the Nibelungenlied.] In *Univ. of Wisconsin Studies*, II, 149-52; see above.

A translation of Beowulf into the Norwegian "landsmaal," by H. RYTTER, will appear shortly.

Popular paraphrases of Beowulf are not included in the above list. An account will be found in Tinker's *Translations* of those of E. H. Jones (in COX'S *Popular Romances*, 1871); J. Gibb, 1881-4; Wägner-MacDowall, 1883 *etc.*; Miss Z. A. Ragozin, 1898, 1900; A. J. Church, 1898; Miss C. L. Thomson, 1899, 1904. Mention may also be made of those of ‡F. A. Turner, 1894; H. E. Marshall, 1908; T. Cartwright, 1908; Prof. J. H. Cox, 1910. An illustrated summary of the *Beowulf* story was issued by Mr W. T. Stead in his penny "Books for the Bairns." The versions of Miss Thomson and Prof. Cox are both good. The paraphrase in the *Canadian Monthly*, II, 83 (1872), attributed in several bibliographies to Earle, is assuredly not the work of that scholar: it is an inaccurate version based upon Jones. An account will be found in Tinker of the German paraphrase of Therese Dahn, 1883 *etc.*; mention may also be made of those of J. Arnheim, 1871; ‡ F. Bässler, sec. edit. 1875 (praised highly by Klaeber in *J.E.G.Ph.* V, 118).

§ 7. TEXTUAL CRITICISM AND INTERPRETATION

1815 GRUNDTVIG, N. F. S. Et Par Ord om det nys udkomne angelsaxiske Digt. *Nyeste Skilderie af Kjøbenhavn*, No. 60 *etc.*, cols. 945, 998, 1009, 1025, 1045; Nok et Par Ord om Bjovulfs Drape, 1106, 1121, 1139 (comment upon Thorkelin's text and translation).

1815 THORKELIN, G. J. Reply to Grundtvig in *Nyeste Skilderie*, cols. 1057, 1073. (There were further articles in the same magazine, but they were purely personal.)

1820 GRUNDTVIG, N. F. S. Emendations to Thorkelin's text, added to *Bjowulfs Drape*, 267-312.

1826 CONYBEARE, J. J. Illustrations of Anglo-Saxon poetry. London. (Beowulf and "Finnsborough," pp. 30-182.)

1859 BOUTERWEK, K. W. Zur Kritik des Beowulfliedes, *Z.f.d.A.* XI, 59-113.

1859 DIETRICH, F. Rettungen, *Z.f.d.A.* XI, 409-20.

1863 HOLTZMANN, A. Zu Beowulf, *Germania*, VIII, 489-97. (Incl. Finnsburg.)

1865 GREIN, C. W. M. Zur Textkritik der angelsächsischen Dichter: Finnsburg, *Germania*, X, 422.

1868-9 BUGGE, SOPHUS. Spredte iagttagelser vedkommende de oldengelske digte om Beówulf og Waldere; *Tidskrift for Philologi og Pædagogik*, VIII, 40-78 and 287-307 (incl. Finnsburg, 304-5). Important.

1871 RIEGER, M. Zum Beowulf, *Z.f.d.Ph.* III, 381-416.

1873 BUGGE, S. Zum Beowulf, *Z.f.d.Ph.* IV, 192-224.

1880 KÖLBING, E. Kleine Beiträge (Beowulf, 168, 169), *Engl. Stud.* III, 92 *etc.*

1882 KLUGE, F. Sprachhistorische Miscellen (Beowulf, 63, 1027, 1235, 1267), *P.B.B.* VIII, 532-5.

1882 COSIJN, P. J. Zum Beowulf, *P.B.B.* VIII, 568-74.

1883 SIEVERS, E. Zum Beowulf, *P.B.B.* IX, 135-44, 370.

1883 KLUGE, F. Zum Beowulf, *P.B.B.* IX, 187-92.

1883 KRÜGER, TH. Zum Beowulf, *P.B.B.* IX, 571-8.

1889 MILLER, T. The position of Grendel's arm in Heorot, *Anglia*, XII, 396-400.

1890 JOSEPH, E. Zwei Versversetzungen im Beowulf, *Z.f.d.Ph.* XXII, 385-97.

1891 SCHRÖER, A. Zur texterklärung des Beowulf, *Anglia*, XIII, 333-48.

1891-2 COSIJN, P. J. Aanteekeningen op den Beowulf. Leiden. (Important.) Reviews: Lübke, *A.f.d.A.* XIX, 341-2; Holthausen, *Literaturblatt*, 1895, p. 82.

1892 SIEVERS, E. Zur texterklärung des Beowulf, *Anglia*, XIV, 133-46.

1895 BRIGHT, J. W. Notes on the Beowulf (ll. 30, 306, 386-7, 623, 737), *M.L.N.* X, 43-4.

1899 TRAUTMANN, M. Berichtigungen, Vermutungen und Erklärungen zum Beowulf (ll. 1-1215). *Bonner Beiträge zur Anglistik*, II, 121-92. Reviews: Binz, *Anglia, Beiblatt*, XIV, 358-60; Holthausen, *Literaturblatt*, 1900, 62-4 (important). See Sievers, *P.B.B.* XXVII, 572; XXVIII, 271.

1901 KLAEBER, F. A few Beowulf notes (ll. 459, 847 *etc.*, 1206, 3024 *etc.*, 3171); *M.L.N.* XVI, 14-18.

1902 KLAEBER, F. Zum Beowulf (497-8; 1745-7), *Archiv*, CVIII, 368-70.

1902 KLAEBER, F. Beowulf's character, *M.L.N.* XVII, 162.

1903 KRACKOW, O. Zu Beowulf, 1225, 2222, *Archiv*, CXI, 171-2.

1904 BRYANT, F. E. Beowulf, 62, *M.L.N.* XIX, 121-2.

1904 ABBOTT, W. C. Hrothulf, *M.L.N.* XIX, 122-5. (Abbott suggests that Hrothulf is the name— missing in whole or part from l. 62—of the husband of the daughter of Healfdene. This suggestion is quite untenable, for many reasons: Hrothulf (Rolf Kraki) is a Dane, and the missing husband is a Swede: but the article led to a long controversy between Bryant and Klaeber; see *M.L.N.* XX, 9-11; XXI, 143, 255; XXII, 96, 160. Klaeber is undoubtedly right.)

1904 KRAPP, G. B. Miscellaneous Notes: *Scūrheard*; *M.L.N.* XIX, 234.

1904 SIEVERS, E. Zum Beowulf, *P.B.B.* XXIX, 305-31. (Criticism of Trautmann's emendations.)

1904 KOCK, E. A. Interpretations and Emendations of Early English Texts: III (Beowulf), *Anglia*, XXVII, 218-37.

1904 SIEVERS, E. Zum Beowulf (l. 5, Criticism of Kock), *P.B.B.* XXIX, 560-76. Reply by Kock, *Anglia*, XXVIII (1905), 140-2.

1905 TRAUTMANN, M. Auch zum Beowulf: ein gruss an herren Eduard Sievers, *Bonner Beiträge zur Anglistik*, XVII, 143-74. (Reply to Sievers' criticism of Trautmann's conjectural emendations.) Review: Klaeber, *M.L.N.* XXII, 252.

1905 SWIGGETT, G. L. Notes on the Finnsburg fragment, *M.L.N.* XX, 169-71.

1905 KLAEBER, F. Notizen zur texterklärung des Beowulf, *Anglia*, XXVIII, 439-47 (incl. Finnsburg); Zum Beowulf, the same, 448-56.

1905 KLAEBER, F. Bemerkungen zum Beowulf, *Archiv*, CXV, 178-82. (Incl. Finnsburg.)

1905 HOLTHAUSEN, F. Beiträge zur Erklärung des altengl. epos. I, Zum Beowulf; II, Zum Finnsburg-fragment; *Z.f.d.Ph.* XXXVII, 113-25.

1905-6 KLAEBER, F. Studies in the Textual Interpretation of "Beowulf," *Mod. Phil.* III, 235-66, 445-65 (Most important).

1906 CHILD, C. G. Beowulf, 30, 53, 132 (i.e. 1323), 2957, *M.L.N.* XXI, 175-7, 198-200.

1906 HORN, W. Textkritische Bemerkungen (Beowulf, 69 *etc.*), *Anglia*, XXIX, 130-1.

1906 KLAEBER, F. Notizen zum Beowulf, *Anglia*, XXIX, 378-82.

1907 KLAEBER, F. Minor Notes on the Beowulf, *J.E.G.Ph.* VI, 190-6.

1908 TINKER, C. B. Notes on Beowulf, *M.L.N.* XXIII, 239-40.

1908 KLAEBER, F. Zum Beowulf, *Engl. Stud.* XXXIX, 463-7.

1909 KLAEBER, F. Textual Notes on Beowulf, *J.E.G.Ph.* VIII, 254-9.

1910 VON GRIENBERGER, T. Bemerkungen zum Beowulf, *P.B.B.* XXXVI, 77-101. (Incl. Finnsburg.)

1910 SIEVERS, E. Gegenbemerkungen zum Beowulf, *P.B.B.* XXXVI, 397-434. (Incl. Finnsburg.)

1910 SEDGEFIELD, W. J. Notes on "Beowulf," *M.L.R.* V, 286-8.

1910 TRAUTMANN, M. Beiträge zu einem künftigen "Sprachschatz der altenglischen Dichter," *Anglia*, XXXIII, 276-9 (*gedræg*).

1911 BLACKBURN, F. A. Note on Beowulf, 1591-1617, *Mod. Phil.* IX, 555-66. (Argues that a loose leaf has been misplaced and the order of events thus disturbed.)

1911 KLAEBER, F. Zur Texterklärung des Beowulf, vv. 767, 1129, *Anglia, Beiblatt*, XXII, 372-4.

1912 HART, J. M. Beowulf, 168-9, *M.L.N.* XXVII, 198.

1912-14 GREIN, C. W. M. Sprachschatz der angelsächsischen dichter. Unter mitwirkung von F. Holthausen neu herausgegeben von J. J. Köhler. Heidelberg. Reviews: Trautmann, *Anglia, Beiblatt*, XXIV, 36-43; Schücking, *Engl. Stud.* XLIX, 113-5.

1915 CHAMBERS, R. W. The "Shifted leaf" in Beowulf, *M.L.R.* X, 37-41. (Points out that the alleged "confused order of events" is that also followed in the Grettis saga.)

1916 GREEN, A. The opening of the episode of Finn in Beowulf, *Pub. Mod. Lang. Assoc. Amer.* XXXI, 759-97.

1916 BRIGHT, J. W. Anglo-Saxon *umbor* and *seld-guma*, *M.L.N.* XXXI, 82-4; Beowulf, 489-90, *M.L.N.* XXXI, 217-23.

1917 GREEN, A. An episode in Ongenþeow's fall, *M.L.R.* XII, 340-3.

1917 HOLLANDER, L. M. Beowulf, 33, *M.L.N.* XXXII, 246-7. (Suggests the reading *ītig.*)

1917 HOLTHAUSEN, F. Zu altenglischen Denkmälern—Beowulf, 1140, *Engl. Stud.* LI, 180.

1918 HUBBARD, F. G. Beowulf, 1598, 1996, 2026: uses of the impersonal verb *geweorþan*, *J.E.G.Ph.* XVII, 119.

1918 KOCK, E. A. Interpretations and emendations of early English Texts: IV, Beowulf, *Anglia*, XLII, 99-124. (Important.)

1918 ‡KOCK, E. A. Jubilee Jaunts and Jottings, in the *Lunds univ. årsskrift*, N. F. avd. I, bd. 14, nr. 26 (*Festskrift vid ... 250-årsjubileum*). Reviews: Holthausen, *Anglia, Beiblatt*, XXX, 1-5; Klaeber, *J.E.G.Ph.* XIX, 409-13.

1919 MOORE, SAMUEL. Beowulf Notes (Textual), *J.E.G.Ph.* XVIII, 205-16.

1919 KLAEBER, F. Concerning the functions of O.E. *geweorðan*, *J.E.G.Ph.* XVIII, 250-71. (Cf. paper of Prof. Hubbard above, by which this was suggested.)

1919 KLAEBER, F. Textual notes on "Beowulf," *M.L.N.* XXXIV, 129-34.

1919 BROWN, CARLETON. Beowulf, 1080-1106, *M.L.N.* XXXIV, 181-3.

1919 BRETT, CYRIL. Notes on passages of Old and Middle English, *M.L.R.* XIV, 1-9.

1919-20 KOCK, E. A. Interpretations and emendations of Early English Texts: V (Incl. Beowulf, 2030, 2419-24); VI (Incl. Beowulf 24, 154-6, 189-90, 1992-3, 489-90, 581-3, 1745-7, 1820-1, 1931-2, 2164); VII (Incl. Beowulf, 1230, 1404, 1553-6); *Anglia*, XLIII, 303-4; XLIV, 98 *etc.*, 245 *etc.*

1920 BRYAN W. F. Beowulf Notes (303-6, 532-4, 867-71), *J.E.G.Ph.* XIX, 84-5.

§ 8. QUESTIONS OF LITERARY HISTORY, DATE AND AUTHORSHIP: BEOWULF IN THE LIGHT OF HISTORY, ARCHÆOLOGY, HEROIC LEGEND, MYTHOLOGY AND FOLKLORE

See also preceding section.

No attempt is made here to deal with Old English heroic legend in general: nor to enumerate the references to *Beowulf* in histories of literature. Probably the earliest allusion to our poem by a great writer is in Scott's *Essay on Romance* (1824):

"The Saxons had, no doubt, Romances, ... and Mr Turner ... has given us the abridgement of one entitled Caedmon, in which the hero, whose adventures are told much after the manner of the ancient Norse Sagas, encounters, defeats and finally slays an evil being called Grendel...."

1816 OUTZEN, N. Das ags. Gedicht Beowulf, *Kieler Blätter*, III, 307-27. (See above, p. 4, note.)

1816 (Review of Thorkelin in) *Monthly Review*, LXXXI, 516-23. (Beowulf identified with Beaw Sceldwaing of the West Saxon genealogy; see above, p. 292.)

1817 GRUNDTVIG, N. F. S. *Danne-Virke*, II, 207-89. (Identifies Chochilaicus; see above, p. 4, note.)

1826 GRIMM, W. Einleitung über die Elfen, *Kleinere Schriften*, I, 405, esp. p. 467 (extract relating to Grendel's hatred of song). From ‡*Irische Elfenmärchen*.

1829 GRIMM, W. Die deutsche Heldensage. Göttingen. (Pp. 13-17. Extracts from Beowulf, with translation, relating to Weland, Sigemund, Hama and Eormenric.)

1836 KEMBLE, J. M. Über die Stammtafel der Westsachsen. München. Review: J. Grimm, *Göttingische gelehrte Anziegen*, 1836, 649-57, = *Kleinere Schriften*, V, 240.

1836 MONE, F. J. Zur Kritik des Gedichts von Beowulf (in Untersuchungen zur Geschichte der teutschen Heldensage). Quedlinburg u. Leipzig. (Pp. 129-36.)

1839 LEO, H. Bëówulf ... nach seinem inhalte, und nach seinen historischen und mythologischen beziehungen betrachtet. Halle.

1841 DISRAELI, I. Amenities of Literature. London. (Beowulf; the Hero-Life. Vol. I, pp. 80-92.)

1841 GRUNDTVIG, N. F. S. Bjovulfs Drape, *Brage og Idun*, IV, 481-538. (Discusses the story, with criticism of previous scholars, and especially of Kemble.)

1843-9 GRIMM, W. Einleitung zur Vorlesung über Gudrun [with an abstract of Beowulf]; see *Kleinere Schriften*, IV, 557-60.

1844 MÜLLENHOFF, K. Die deutschen Völker an Nord- und Ostsee in ältester Zeit, *Nordalbingische Studien*, I, 111 *etc.*

1845 A brief discussion of Beowulf in *Edinburgh Review*, LXXXII, 309-11.

1845 HAUPT, M. Zum Beowulf, *Z.f.d.A.* V, 10. (Drawing attention to the reference to Hygelac in the *liber de monstris*; see above, p. 4.)

1848 MÜLLENHOFF, K. Die austrasische Dietrichssage, *Z.f.d.A.* VI, 435 *etc.*

1849 MÜLLENHOFF, K. Sceáf u. seine Nachkommen, *Z.f.d.A.* VII, 410-19; Der Mythus von Beóvulf, *Z.f.d.A.* VII, 419-41.

1849 GRIMM, J. Ueber das Verbrennen der Leichen, *Abhandl. d. Berl. Akad.*, 1849, 191 *etc.* = *Kleinere Schriften*, II, 211-313 (esp. 261-4).

1849 BACHLECHNER, J. Die Merovinge im Beowulf, *Z.f.d.A.* VII, 524-6.

1851 ZAPPERT, G. Virgil's Fortleben im Mittelalter, *Denkschriften der k. Akad. Wien, Phil.-Hist. Classe*, Bd. II, Abth. 2, pp. 17-70. (Gives numerous parallels between Virgil and "Beowulf," somewhat indiscriminately.)

1852 BRYNJULFSSON, G. Oldengelsk og Oldnordisk, *Antikuarisk Tidsskrift*, Kjøbenhavn, 1852-4, pp. 81-143. (An important paper which has been unduly overlooked. Brynjulfsson notes the parallel between Beowulf and Bjarki (see above, p. 61) and in other respects anticipates later scholars, e.g., in noting the close relationship between Angles and Danes (p. 143) and less fortunately (pp. 129-31) in identifying the Geatas with the Jutes.)

1856 BACHLECHNER, J. Eomaer und Heming (Hamlac), *Germania*, I, 297-303 and 455-61.

1856 BOUTERWEK, K. W. Das Beowulflied: Eine Vorlesung; *Germania*, I, 385-418.

1857 UHLAND, L. Sigemund und Sigeferd, *Germania*, II, 344-63 = *Schriften*, VIII, 479 *etc.* (Incl. Finnsburg.)

1858 WEINHOLD, K. Die Riesen des germanischen Mythus, *Sitzungberichte der K. Akad., Wien, Phil-Hist. Classe*, XXVI, 225-306. (Grendel and his mother, p. 255.)

1859 RIEGER, M. Ingaevonen, Istaevonen, Herminonen, *Z.f.d.A.* XI, 177-205.

1859 MÜLLENHOFF, K. Zur Kritik des angelsächsischen Volksepos, 2, Widsith, *Z.f.d.A.* XI, 275-94.

1860 MÜLLENHOFF, K. Zeugnisse u. Excurse zur deutschen Heldensage, *Z.f.d.A.* XII, 253-386. (*This portion* of vol. XII was published in 1860.)

1861 HAIGH, D. H. The Anglo-Saxon Sagas. London. (An uncritical attempt to identify the proper names in Beowulf and Finnsburg with sites in England.)

1862 GREIN, C. W. M. Die historischen Verhältnisse des Beowulfliedes, *Eberts Jahrbuch für roman. u. engl. Litt.* IV, 260-85. (Incl. Finnsburg.)

1864 ‡SCHULTZE, M. Ueber das Beowulfslied. *Programm der städtischen Realschule zu Elbing.* (Not seen, but contents, including the mythical interpretations current at the period, noted in *Archiv*, XXXVII, 232.)

1864 HEYNE, M. Ueber die Lage und Construction der Halle Heorot. Paderborn.

1868 KÖHLER, A. Germanische Alterthümer im Beóvulf, *Germania*, XIII, 129-58.

1869 MÜLLENHOFF, K. Die innere Geschichte des Beovulfs, *Z.f.d.A.* XIV, 193-244. (Reprinted in *Beovulf*, 1889. See above, p. 113 *etc.*)

1870 KÖHLER, A. Die Einleitung des Beovulfliedes. Die beiden Episoden von Heremod, *Z.f.d.Ph.* II, 305-21.

1875 SCHRØDER, L. Om Bjovulfs Drapen. København. (See above, p. 30.)

1876 BOTKINE, L. Beowulf. Analyse historique et géographique. Havre. (Material subsequently incorporated in translation, q.v. § 6.) Review: Körner, *Engl. Stud.* I, 495-6.

1877 SKEAT, W. W. The name "Beowulf," *Academy*, XI (Jan.-June), p. 163. (Suggests Beowulf = "woodpecker"; see above, pp. 365-6, *note*.)

1877 TEN BRINK, B. Geschichte der englischen Litteratur. (Beowulf, Finnsburg, pp. 29-40.)

1877 DEDERICH, H. Historische u. geographische Studien zum ags. Beóvulfliede. Köln. (Incl. Finnsburg.) Reviews: Körner, *Engl. Stud.* I, 481-95; Müllenhoff, *A.f.d.A.* III, 172-82; ‡Suchier, *Jenaer Literatur-Zeitung*, XLVII, 732, 1876.

1877 HORNBURG, J. Die Composition des Beowulf. *Programm des K. Lyceums in Metz.* Full summary by F. Hummel in *Archiv*, LXII, 231-3. See also under 1884.

1877 SCHULTZE, M. Alt-heidnisches in der angelsächsischen Poesie, speciell im Beowulfsliede. Berlin.

1877 SUCHIER, H. Ueber die Sage von Offa u. Þryðo, *P.B.B.* IV, 500-21.

1878 MÜLLER, N. Die Mythen im Beówulf, in ihrem Verhältniss zur germanischen Mythologie betrachtet. Dissertation, Heidelberg. Leipzig.

1879 LAISTNER, L. Nebelsagen. Stuttgart. (See above, p. 46, note.)

1879 SWEET, H. Old English etymologies: I, *Beóhata, Engl. Stud.* II, 312-14. (See above, p. 365.)

1880 GERING, H. Der Beówulf u. die isländische Grettissaga, *Anglia*, III, 74-87. (Important. Gering announced Vigfússon's discovery to a wider circle of readers, with translation of the Sandhaugar episode, and useful comment. The discovery was further announced to American readers by GARNETT in the *American Journal of Philology*, I, 492 (1880), though its importance was there rather understated. See above, p. 54.)

1881 SMITH, C. SPRAGUE. Beówulf Gretti, *New Englander*, XL (N. S. IV), 49-67. (Translation of corresponding passages in Grettis saga and Beowulf.)

1882 MARCH, F. A. The World of Beowulf, *Proceedings of Amer. Phil. Assoc.* pp. xxi-xxiii.

1883 RÖNNING, F. Beovulfs-kvadet; en literær-historisk undersøgelse. København. Review: Heinzel, *A.f.d.A.* X, 233-9. (Rönning criticises Müllenhoff's theories of separate lays. His book and Heinzel's review are both important.)

1883 MERBOT, R. Aesthetische Studien zur Ags. Poesie. Breslau. Reviews: Koch, *Anglia*, VI, *Anzeiger*, 100-3; Kluge, *Engl. Stud.*, VIII, 480-2.

1884 EARLE, J. Anglo-Saxon Literature (The dawn of European Literature). London. (Pp. 120-39 deal with Beowulf. Earle holds Beowulf to be "a genuine growth of that junction in time ... when the heathen tales still kept their traditional interest, and yet the spirit of Christianity had taken full possession of the Saxon mind.")

1884 FAHLBECK, P. Beowulfs-kvädet såsom källa för nordisk fornhistoria, *Antikvar. tidskr. för Sverige*, VIII, 1-87. Review: *Academy*, XXIX, 1886, p. 12. (See above, pp. 8, 333.)

1884 HARRISON, J. A. Old Teutonic life in Beowulf, *Overland Monthly*, Sec. Ser. vol. IV, 14-24; 152-61.

1884 HERTZ, W. Beowulf, das älteste germanische Epos, *Nord und Süd*, XXIX, 229-53.

1884 HORNBURG, J. Die komposition des Beovulf, *Archiv*, LXXII, 333-404. (Rejects Müllenhoff's "Liedertheorie.")

1884 KRÜGER, TH. Zum Beowulfliede. Bromberg. Reviewed favourably by Kölbing, *Engl. Stud.* IX, 150; severely by Kluge, *Literaturblatt*, 1884, 428-9. (A useful summary, which had the misfortune to be superseded next year by the publication of Wülker's *Grundriss*.)

1884 KRÜGER, TH. Über Ursprung u. Entwickelung des Beowulfliedes, *Archiv*, LXXI, 129-52.

1884-5 EARLE, J. Beowulf, in *The Times*, London (Aug. 25, 1884, p. 6 (not signed); Oct. 29, 1885, p. 3; Sept. 30, 1885, p. 3. "The Beowulf itself is a tale of old folk-lore which, in spite of repeated editing, has never quite lost the old crust of its outline.... This discovery, if established, must have the effect of quite excluding the application of the Wolffian hypothesis to our poem.")

1885 WÜLKER, R. Grundriss zur geschichte der angelsächsischen Litteratur. Leipzig. 6. Die angelsächsische Heldendichtung, Beowulf, Finnsburg, 244-315. (An important and useful summary.)

1885 LEHMANN, H. Brünne und Helm im angelsächsischen Beowulfliede. Dissertation, Göttingen. Leipzig. Reviews: Wülker, *Anglia*, VIII, *Anzeiger*, 167-70; Schulz, *Engl. Stud.* IX, 471.

1886 SKEAT, W. W. On the signification of the monster Grendel ... with a discussion of ll. 2076-2100. Read before the Cambridge Philological Society. *Journal of Philology*, XV, 120-31. (Not *American Jour. of Phil.*, as frequently quoted.)

1886 SARRAZIN, G. Die Beowulfsage in Dänemark, *Anglia*, IX, 195-9; Beowa und Böthvar, *Anglia*, IX, 200-4; Beowulf und Kynewulf, *Anglia*, IX, 515-50; Der Schauplatz des ersten Beowulfliedes und die Heimat des Dichters, *P.B.B.* XI, 159-83 (see above, p. 101).

1886 SIEVERS, E. Die Heimat des Beowulfdichters, *P.B.B.* XI, 354-62.

1886 SARRAZIN, G. Altnordisches im Beowulfliede, *P.B.B.* XI, 528-41. (See above, p. 102.)

1886 SIEVERS, E. Altnordisches im Beowulf? *P.B.B.* XII, 168-200.

1886 SCHILLING, H. Notes on the Finnsaga, *M.L.N.* I, 89-92; 116-17.

1886 LEHMANN, H. Über die Waffen im angelsächsischen Beowulfliede, *Germania*, XXXI, 486-97.

1887 SCHILLING, H. The Finnsburg-fragment and the Finn-episode, *M.L.N.* II, 146-50.

1887 MORLEY, H. Beowulf and the Fight at Finnsburg, in *English Writers*, vol. I, 276-354. London.

1887 BUGGE, S. Studien über das Beowulfepos, *P.B.B.* XII, 1-112, 360-75. Important. (Das Finnsburgfragment, pp. 20-8.)

1887 ‡SCHNEIDER, F. Der Kampf mit Grendels Mutter. *Program des Friedrichs Real-Gymnasiums.* Berlin.

1888 TEN BRINK, B. Beowulf. Untersuchungen. (*Quellen u. Forschungen*, LXII.) (Important. See above, p. 113.) Strassburg. Reviews: Wülker, *Anglia*, XI, 319-21 and *Lit. Cbl.* 1889, 251; Möller, *Engl. Stud.* XIII, 247-315 (weighty, containing some good remarks on the Jutes-Geatas); Koeppel, *Z.f.d.Ph.* XXIII, 113-22; Heinzel, *A.f.d.A.* XV, 153-82 (weighty); Liebermann, *Deut. Zeitschr. f. Geschichtswissenschaft*, II, 1889, 197-9; Kraus, *D.L.Z.* XII, 1891, 1605-7, 1846: reply by ten Brink ("Beowulfkritik und *ABAB*"), *D.L.Z.* 1892, 109-12.

1888 SARRAZIN, G. Beowulf-Studien. Berlin. Reviews: Koeppel, *Engl. Stud.* XIII, 472-80; Sarrazin, Entgegnung, *Engl. Stud.* XIV, 421 *etc.*, reply by Koeppel, XIV, 427; Sievers, *Z.f.d.Ph.* XXI, 366; Dieter, *Archiv*, LXXXIII, 352-3; Heinzel, *A.f.d.A.* XV, 182-9; Wülker, *Lit. Cbl.* 1889, 315-16; Wülker, *Anglia*, XI, 536-41. Holthausen, *Literaturblatt*, 1890, 14-16; Liebermann, *Deut. Zeitschr. f. Geschichtswissenschaft*, VI, 1891, 138; Kraus, *D.L.Z.* XII, 1891, pp. 1822-3. (All these reviews express dissent from Sarrazin's main conclusions, though many of them show appreciation of details in his work. See above, p. 101.)

1888 KITTREDGE, G. L. Zu Beowulf, 107 *etc.*, *P.B.B.* XIII, 210 (Cain's kin).

1889 MÜLLENHOFF, K. Beovulf (pp. 110-65=*Z.f.d.A.* XIV, 193-244). Berlin. See above, pp. 46-7, 113-15. Reviews: Schirmer, *Anglia*, XII, 465-7; Sarrazin, *Engl. Stud.* XVI, 71-85 (important); Wülker, *Lit. Cbl.* 1890, 58-9; Heinzel, *A.f.d.A.* XVI, 264-75 (important); Koeppel, *Z.f.d.Ph.* XXIII, 110-13; Holthausen, *Literaturblatt*, 1890, 370-3; Liebermann, *Deut. Zeitschr. f. Geschichtswissenschaft*, VI, 1891, 135-7; Kraus, *D.L.Z.* XII, 1891, pp. 1820-2; Logeman, *Le Moyen Âge*, III, 266-7 ("personne ne conteste plus ... que le poème se composait originairement de plusieurs parties"). Müllenhoff's book, like that of ten Brink, is based on assumptions generally held at the time, but now not so widely accepted; yet it remains important.

1889 LAISTNER, L. Das Rätsel der Sphinx. Berlin. (See above, p. 67.)

1889 LÜNING, O. Die Natur ... in der altgermanischen und mittelhochdeutschen Epik. Zürich. Reviews: Weinhold, *Z.f.d.Ph.* XXII, 246-7; Golther, *D.L.Z.* 1889, 710-2; Ballerstedt, *A.f.d.A.* XVI, 71-4; Fränkel, *Literaturblatt*, 1890, 439-44.

1890 ‡DESKAU, H. Zum studium des Beowulf. Berichte des freien deutschen Hochstiftes, 1890. Frankfurt.

1890 ‡KLÖPPER, C. Heorot-Hall in the Anglo-Saxon poem of Beowulf. Festschrift für K. E. Krause. Rostock.

1891 JELLINEK, M. H. and KRAUS, C. Die Widersprüche im Beowulf, *Z.f.d.A*, XXXV, 265-81.

1891 BUGGE, S. and OLRIK, A. Røveren ved Gråsten og Beowulf, *Dania*, I, 233-45.

1891 JELLINEK, M. H. Zum Finnsburgfragment, *P.B.B.* XV, 428-31.

1892 EARLE, J. The Introduction to his Translation (q.v.) gave a summary of the controversy, with "a constructive essay."

1892 BROOKE, STOPFORD A. History of Early English Literature (Beowulf, pp. 17-131). London. Reviews: McClumpha, *M.L.N.* VIII, 27-9, 1892 (attacks in a letter of unnecessary violence); Wülker, *Anglia, Beiblatt* IV, 170-6, 225-33; Glöde, *Engl. Stud.* XXII, 264-70.

1892 GUMMERE, F. B. Germanic Origins. A study in primitive culture. New York.

1892 FERGUSON, R. The Anglo-Saxon name Beowulf, *Athenæum*, June, 1892 p. 763. See above, p. 368.

1892 HAACK, O. Zeugnisse zur altenglischen Heldensage. Kiel.

1892 ‡KRAUS, K. Hrodulf. (P. Moneta, zum 40 jähr. Dienstjub.) Wien. (p. 4 *etc.*)

1892 OLRIK, A. Er Uffesagnet indvandret fra England? *A.f.n.F.* VIII (N.F. IV), 368-75.

1892 SARRAZIN, G. Die Abfassungszeit des Beowulfliedes, *Anglia*, XIV, 399-415.

1892 SIEVERS, E. Sceaf in den nordischen Genealogien, *P.B.B.* XVI, 361-3.

1892 KÖGEL, R. Beowulf, *Z.f.d.A.* XXXVII, 268-76. (Etymology of the name.) Discussed by Sievers, *P.B.B.* XVIII, 413. See above, p. 367, footnote.

1893 WARD, H. L. D. Catalogue of Romances in the British Museum; Beowulf: vol. II, pp. 1-15, 741-3.

1893 TEN BRINK, B. Altenglische Literatur, *Pauls Grdr.*(1), II, I, 510-50. (Finnsburg, 545-50.)

1894 MCNARY, S. J. Beowulf and Arthur as English Ideals, *Poet-Lore*, VI, 529-36.

1894 ‡DETTER, F. Über die Heaðobarden im Beowulf, *Verhandl. d. Wiener Philologenversammlung*, Mai, 1893. Leipzig, p. 404 *etc.* (Argues that the story is not historical, but mythical—*Ragnarok.*)

1895 SIEVERS, E. Beowulf und Saxo, *Berichte der kgl. sächs. Gesellschaft der Wissenschaften*, XLVII, 175-93. (Important, see above, pp. 90-7.)

1895 BINZ, G. Zeugnisse zur germanischen sage in England, *P.B.B.* XX, 141-223. (A most useful collection, though the significance of many of the names collected is open to dispute.)

1895 KLUGE, F. Zeugnisse zur germanischen sage in England, *Engl. Stud.* XXI, 446-8.

1895-6 KLUGE, F. Der Beowulf u. die Hrolfs Saga Kraka, *Engl. Stud.* XXII, 144-5.

1896 Sarrazin, G. Neue Beowulf-studien, *Engl. Stud.* XXIII, 221-67.

1897 Ker, W. P. Epic and Romance. London. (Beowulf, pp. 182-202. Important. See above, p. 116.) Reviews: Fischer, *Anglia, Beiblatt*, X, 133-5; Brandl, *Archiv*, C, 198-200. New edit. 1908.

1897 BLACKBURN, F. A. The Christian coloring in the Beowulf, *Pub. Mod. Lang. Assoc. Amer.* XII, 205-25. (See above, p. 125.)

1897 SARRAZIN, G. Die Hirschhalle, *Anglia*, XIX, 368-92; Der Balder-kultus in Lethra, *ibid.* 392-7; Rolf Krake und sein Vetter im Beowulfliede, *Engl. Stud.* XXIV, 144-5. (Important. See above, p. 31.)

1897 HENNING, R. Sceaf und die westsächsische Stammtafel, *Z.f.d.A.* XLI, 156-69.

1898 ARNOLD, T. Notes on Beowulf. London. Reviews: Hulme, *M.L.N.* XV, 22-6, 1900; Sarrazin, *Engl. Stud.* XXVIII, 410-18; Garnett, *Amer. Jour. of Phil.* XX, 443.

1898 NIEDNER, F. Die Dioskuren im Beowulf, *Z.f.d.A.* XLII, 229-58.

1899 COOK, A. S. An Irish Parallel to the Beowulf Story, *Archiv*, CIII, 154-6.

1899 AXON, W. E. A. A reference to the evil eye in Beowulf, *Trans. of the Royal Soc. of Literature*, London. (Very slight.)

1899 ‡FURST, CLYDE. "Beowulf" in "A Group of Old Authors." Philadelphia. (Popular.) Review: Child, *M.L.N.* XV, 31-2.

1900 FÖRSTER, MAX. Bêowulf-Materialien, zum Gebrauch bei Vorlesungen. Braunschweig. Reviews: Holthausen, *Anglia, Beiblatt*, XI, 289; Behagel, *Literaturblatt*, 1902, 67 (very brief).

1908. 2 Aufl.

1912. 3 Aufl. Review: Wild, *Anglia, Beiblatt*, XXIV, 166-7.

1901 POWELL, F. YORK. Beowulf and Watanabe-No-Tsema, *Furnivall Miscellany*, pp. 395-6. Oxford. (A parallel from Japanese legend.)

1901 LEHMANN, E. Fandens Oldemor, *Dania*, VIII, 179-94. Repeated ("Teuffels Grossmutter"), *Archiv f. Religionswiss.* VIII, 411-30. (See above, p. 49, note, and p. 381.)

1901 ‡OTTO, E. Typische Motive in dem weltlichen Epos der Angelsachsen. Berlin. Reviews: Binz, *Engl. Stud.* XXXII, 401-5; Spies, *Archiv*, CXV, 222.

1901 OHLENBECK, C. C. Het Béowulf-epos als geschiedbron, *Tijdschrift voor nederlandsche taal- en letterkunde*, XX (N. R. XII), 169-96.

1902 *Gerould*, G. H. Offa and Labhraidh Maen, *M.L.N.* XVII, 201-3. (An Irish parallel of the story of the dumb young prince.)

1902 GOUGH, A. B. The Constance-Saga. Berlin. (The "Thrytho saga," pp. 53-83.) Reviews: Eckhardt, *Engl. Stud.* XXXII, 110-3; Weyrauch, *Archiv*, CXI, 453.

1902 BOER, R. C. Die Béowulfsage. I. Mythische reconstructionen; II. Historische untersuchung der überlieferung; *A.f.n.F.* XIX (N. F. XV), 19-88.

1902 BRANDL, A. Ueber den gegenwärtigen Stand der Beowulf-Forschung, *Archiv,* CVIII, 152-5.

1903 ANDERSON, L. F. The Anglo-Saxon Scop. (*Univ. of Toronto Studies, Phil. Ser. 1.*) Review: Heusler, *A.f.d.A.* XXXI, 113-5.

1903 OLRIK, A. Danmarks Heltedigtning: I, Rolf Krake og den ældre Skjoldungrække. Kobenhavn. (Most important.) Reviews: Heusler, *A.f.d.A.* XXX, 26-36; Golther, *Literaturblatt,* XXVIII, 1907, pp. 8-9; Ranisch, *A.f.d.A.* XXI, 276-80. Revised translation 1919 (q.v.).

1903 ‡BOER, R. C. Eene episode uit den Beowulf, *Handelingen van het 3 nederl. phil. congres.,* p. 84 *etc.*

1903 A Summary of the *Lives of the Offas,* with reproductions of a number of the drawings in *MS Cotton Nero D. I,* in *The Ancestor,* V, 99-137.

1903 HART, J. M. Allotria [on the forms *Bēanstān,* l. 524 and *Þrȳðo,* l. 1931], *M.L.N.* XVIII, 117.

1903 STJERNA, K. Hjälmar och svärd i Beovulf, *Studier tillägnade O. Montelius,* 99-120. Stockholm. See above, pp. 346 *etc.*

1903-4 BOER, R. C. Finnsage und Nibelungen-sage, *Z.f.d.A.* XLVII, 125-60.

1904 RICKERT, E. The O.E. Offa-saga, *Mod. Phil.* II, 29-76 and 321-76. (Important. See above, pp. 34 *etc.*)

1904 HAGEN, S. N. Classical names and stories in Beowulf, *M.L.N.* XIX, 65-74 and 156-65. (Very fantastic).

1904 STJERNA, K. Vendel och Vendelkråka, *A.f.n.F.* XXI (N. F. XVII), 71-80. (Most important: see above, pp. 343-5.)

1904 ‡VETTER, F. Beowulf und das altdeutsche Heldenzeitalter in England, *Deutschland,* III, 558-71.

1905 MOORMAN, F. W. The interpretation of nature in English poetry from Beowulf to Shakespeare. Strassburg. *Quellen u. Forschungen,* 95.

1905 ROUTH, J. E. Two studies on the Ballad Theory of the Beowulf: I. The Origin of the Grendel legend; II. Irrelevant Episodes and Parentheses as features of Anglo-Saxon Poetic Style. Baltimore. Reviews: Eckhardt, *Engl. Stud.* XXXVII, 404-5; Heusler, *A.f.d.A.* XXXI, 115-16; Schücking, *D.L.Z.* 1905, pp. 1908-10.

1905 HEUSLER, A. Lied und Epos in germanischer Sagendichtung. Dortmund. (See above, p. 116.) Reviews: Kauffmann, *Z.f.d.Ph.* XXXVIII, 546-8; Seemüller, *A.f.d.A.* XXXIV, 129-35; Meyer, *Archiv*, CXV, 403-4; Helm, *Literaturblatt*, XXVIII, 237-8.

1905 SCHÜCKING, L. L. Beowulfs Rückkehr. (*Morsbachs Studien*, XXI.) Halle. (Important: see above, pp. 118-20.) Review: Brandl, *Archiv*, CXV, 421-3 (dissenting).

1905 SCHÜCK, H. Studier i Ynglingatal, I-III. Uppsala.

1905 HANSCOM, E. D. The Feeling for Nature in Old English Poetry, *J.E.G.Ph.* V, 439-63.

1905 SARRAZIN, G. Neue Beowulf Studien, *Engl. Stud.* XXXV, 19-27.

1905 STJERNA, K. Skölds hädanfärd, *Studier tillägnade H. Schück*, 110-34. Stockholm.

1905 ‡STJERNA, K. Svear och Götar under folkvandringstiden, *Svenska Förnminnesforeningens Tidskr.* XII, 339-60. (Transl. by Clark Hall in *Essays*. See under 1912.)

1905-6 RIEGER, M. Zum Kampf in Finnsburg, *Z.f.d.A.* XLVIII, 9-12.

1905-6 HEUSLER, A. Zur Skiöldungendichtung, *Z.f.d.A.* XLVIII, 57-87.

1905-6 NECKEL, J. Studien über Fróði, *Z.f.d.A.* XLVIII, 163-86.

1905-7 STJERNA, K. Arkeologiska anteckningar till Beovulf, *Kungl. vitterhets akademiens månadsblad* for 1903-5 (1907), pp. 436-51.

1906 EMERSON, O. F. Legends of Cain, especially in Old and Middle English (see particularly § VI, "Cain's Descendants"), *Pub. Mod. Lang. Assoc. Amer.* XXI, 831-929. (Important.)

1906 SKEMP, A. R. Transformation of scriptural story, motive, and conception in Anglo-Saxon poetry, *Mod. Phil.* IV, 423-70.

1906 DUFF, J. W. Homer and Beowulf: a literary parallel, *Saga-Book of the Viking Club*. London.

1906 MORSBACH, L. Zur datierung des Beowulf-epos, *Nachrichten der kgl. Ges. d. Wiss. zu Göttingen, Phil.-Hist. Klasse*, pp. 252-77. (Important. See above, pp. 107-12.)

1906 PFÄNDLER, W. Die Vergnügungen der Angelsachsen, *Anglia*, XXIX, 417-526.

1906 GARLANDA, F. Béowulf. Origini, bibliografia, metrica ... significato storico, etico, sociologico. Roma. (Slight.)

1906 STJERNA, K. Drakskatten i Beovulf, *Fornvännen*, I, 119-44.

1907 CHADWICK, H. M. Origin of the English Nation. Cambridge. (Important.) Reviews: Andrews, *M.L.N.* XXIII, 261-2; Chambers, *M.L.R.* IV, 262-6; Schütte, *A.f.n.F.* XXV (N. F. XXI), 310-32 (an elaborate discussion of early Germanic ethnology and geography); Huchon, *Revue Germanique*, III, 625-31.

1907 CHADWICK, H. M. "Early National Poetry," in *Cambridge History of English Literature*, vol. I, 19-32, 421-3. Important. See above, pp. 122-6.

1907 HART, WALTER MORRIS. Ballad and Epic. Boston: Harvard *Studies and Notes in Philology and Literature*. (Important: see above, p. 116.) Review: *Archiv*, CXIX, 468.

1907 OLRIK, A. Nordisk Aandsliv i Vikingetid og tidlig Middelalder. København og Kristiania. (Translated into German by W. Ranisch, 1908, as "Nordisches Geistesleben.")

1907 SCHÜCK, H. Folknamnet Geatas i den fornengelska dikten Beowulf. Uppsala. (Important. See above, pp. 8-10, 333 *etc.*) Reviews: Mawer, *M.L.R.* IV, 273; Freeburg, *J.E.G.Ph.* XI, 279-83.

1907 COOK, A. S. Various notes, *M.L.N.* XXI, 146-7. (Further classical parallels to Beowulf, 1408 ff., in succession to a parallel from Seneca quoted in *M.L.N.* XVII, 209-10.)

1907 SARRAZIN, G. Zur Chronologie u. Verfasserfrage Ags. Dichtungen, *Engl. Stud.* XXXVIII, 145 *etc.*, esp. 170-95 (Das Beowulflied und die ältere Genesis).

1907 BRANDL, A. Entstehungsgeschichte des Beowulfepos. A five-line summary of this lecture is given in the *Sitzungsberichte d. k. preuss. Akad. Phil.-Hist. Classe*, p. 615.

1907 HOLTHAUSEN, F. Zur altenglischen literatur—Zur datierung des Beowulf, *Anglia, Beiblatt*, XVIII, 77.

1907 ‡GRÜNER, H. Mathei Parisiensis vitae duorum Offarum, in ihrer manuskript- und textgeschichte. Dissertation, Munich. Kaiserslautern.

1908 BRANDL, A. Geschichte der alteng. Literatur. (Offprint from *Pauls Grdr.*(2): Beowulf, pp. 988-1024; Finnsburg, pp. 983-6; an exceedingly useful and discriminating summary.)

1908 SCHÜCKING, L. L. Das Angelsächsische Totenklagelied, *Engl. Stud.* XXXIX, 1-13.

1908 WEYHE, H. König Ongentheow's Fall, *Engl. Stud.* XXXIX, 14-39.

1908 NECKEL, G. Beiträge zur Eddaforschung; Anhang: Die altgermanische heldenklage (pp. 495-6: cf. p. 376). Dortmund.

1908 KLAEBER, F. Zum Finnsburg Kampfe, *Engl. Stud.* XXXIX, 307-8.

1908 BJÖRKMAN, E. Über den Namen der Jüten, *Engl. Stud.* XXXIX, 356-61.

1908 LEVANDER, L. Sagotraditioner om Sveakonungen Adils, *Antikvarisk Tidskrift för Sverige*, XVIII, 3.

1908 STJERNA, K. Fasta fornlämningar i Beovulf, *Antikvarisk Tidskrift för Sverige*, XVIII, 4.

1908 GRAU, G. Quellen u. Verwandtschaften der älteren germanischen Darstellungen des jüngsten Gerichtes. Halle. (See esp. pp. 145-56.) Review: Guntermann, *Z.f.d.Ph.* XLI, 401-415.

1909 SCHÜCK, H. Studier i Beowulfsagan. Uppsala. Review: Freeburg, *J.E.G.Ph.* XI, 488-97 (a very useful summary).

1909 LAWRENCE, W. W. Some disputed questions in Beowulf-criticism, *Pub. Mod. Lang. Assoc. Amer.* XXIV, 220-73. (Very important.) Review: Brandl, *Archiv*, CXXIII, 473.

1909 EHRISMANN, G. Religionsgeschichtliche Beiträge zum germanischen Frühchristentum, *P.B.B.* XXXV, 209-39.

1909 BUGGE, S. Die Heimat der Altnordischen Lieder von den Welsungen u. den Nibelungen, II, *P.B.B.* XXXV, 240-71.

1909 DEUTSCHBEIN, M. Die Sagenhistorischen u. literarischen Grundlagen des Beowulfepos, *Germanisch-Romanische Monatsschrift*, I, 103-19.

1910 OLRIK, A. Danmarks Heltedigtning: II, Starkad den gamle og den yngre Skjoldungrække. København. (Most important.) Reviews: Heusler, *A.f.d.A.* XXXV, 169-83 (important); Ussing, *Danske Studier*, 1910, 193-203; Boer, *Museum*, XIX, 1912, 171-4.

1910 PANZER, F. Studien zur germanischen Sagengeschichte. I. Beowulf. München. (Most important: see above, pp. 62-8; 365-81. Valuable criticisms and modifications are supplied by the reviews, more particularly perhaps that of von Sydow (*A.f.d.A.* XXXV, 123-31), but also in the elaborate discussions of Heusler (*Engl. Stud.* XLII, 289-98), Binz (*Anglia, Beiblatt*, XXIV, 321-37), Brandl (*Archiv*, CXXVI, 231-5), Kahle (*Z.f.d.Ph.* XLIII, 383-94) and the briefer ones of Lawrence (*M.L.N.* XXVII, 57-60) Sedgefield (*M.L.R.* VI, 128-31) and Golther (*Neue Jahrbücher f. das klassische Altertum*, XXV, 610-13).)

1910 BRADLEY, H. Beowulf, in *Encyclopædia Britannica*, III, pp. 758-61. (Important. See above, pp. 121, 127-8.)

1910 SCHÜCK, H. Sveriges förkristna konungalängd. Uppsala.

1910 CLARK HALL, J. R. A note on Beowulf, 1142-5, *M.L.N.* XXV, 113-14. *(Hūnlāfing.)*

1910 SARRAZIN, G. Neue Beowulf-studien, *Engl. Stud.* XLII, 1-37.

1910 KLAEBER, F. Die ältere Genesis und der Beowulf, *Engl. Stud.* XLII, 321-38.

1910 HEUSLER, A. Zeitrechnung im Beowulf-epos, *Archiv*, CXXIV, 9-14.

1910 NECKEL, G. Etwas von germanischer Sagenforschung, *Germ.-Rom. Monatsschrift*, II, 1-14.

1910 SMITHSON, G. A. The Old English Christian Epic ... in comparison with the Beowulf. Berkeley. *Univ. of California Pub. in Mod. Phil.* (See particularly pp. 363-8, 376-90.)

1911 CLARKE, M. G. Sidelights on Teutonic History. Cambridge. Reviews: Mawer, *M.L.N.* VII, 126-7; Chambers, *Engl. Stud.* XLVIII, 166-8; Fehr, *Anglia, Beiblatt*, XXVI, 19-20; Imelmann, *D.L.Z.* XXXIV, 1913, 1062 *etc.*

1911-19 HEUSLER, A. A series of articles in Hoops' *Reallexikon*: Beowulf, Dichtung, Ermenrich, Gautensagen, Heldensage, Hengest, Heremod, Offa, Skjǫldungar, Ynglingar, *etc.* Strassburg. (Important.)

1911 NECKEL, G. Ragnacharius von Cambrai, *Festschrift zur Jahrhundertfeier der Universität zu Breslau = Mitt. d. Schlesischen Gesellschaft für Volkskunde*, XIII-XIV, 121-54. (A historical parallel between the treatment of Ragnachar by Chlodowech and that of Hrethric by Hrothulf.)

1911 SCHÖNFELD, M. Worterbuch der altgermanischen Personen- und Völkernamen. Heidelberg. See also Schütte, Noter til Schönfelds Navnesamling, in *A.f.n.F.* XXXIII, 22-49.

1911 KLAEBER, F. Aeneis und Beowulf, *Archiv*, CXXVI, 40-8, 339-59. (Important: see above, p. 330.)

1911 LIEBERMANN, F. Grendel als Personenname, *Archiv*, CXXVI, 180.

1911-12 KLAEBER, F. Die Christlichen Elemente im Beowulf, *Anglia*, XXXV, 111-36, 249-70, 453-82; XXXVI, 169-99. (Most important: demonstrates the fundamentally Christian character of the poem.)

1912 CHADWICK, H. Munro. The Heroic Age. Cambridge. (Important: see above, p. 122.) Reviews: Mawer, *M.L.R.* VIII, 207-9; Chambers, *Engl. Stud.* XLVIII, 162-6.

1912 STJERNA, K. Essays on questions connected with the O.E. poem of Beowulf, transl. and ed. by John R. Clark Hall, (Viking Club), Coventry. (Important: see above, pp. 346 *etc.*) Reviews: Klaeber, *J.E.G.Ph.* XIII, 167-73, weighty; Mawer, *M.L.N.* VIII, 242-3; *Athenæum*, 1913, I, 459-60; Brandl, *Archiv*, CXXXII, 238-9; Schütte, *A.f.n.F.* XXXIII, 64-96, elaborate; Olrik, *Nord. Tidskr. f. Filol.* IV, 2. 127; Mogk, *Historische Vierteljahrsschrift*, XVIII, 196-7.

1912 CHAMBERS, R. W. Widsith: a study in Old English heroic legend. Cambridge. Reviews: Mawer, *M.L.R.* VIII, 118-21; Lawrence, *M.L.N.* XXVIII, 53-5; Fehr, *Anglia, Beiblatt*, XXVI, 289-95; Jordan, *Engl. Stud.* XLV, 300-2; Berendsohn, *Literaturblatt*, XXXV (1914), 384-6.

1912 BOER, R. C. Die Altenglische Heldendichtung. I. Béowulf. Halle. (Important.) Reviews: ‡Jantzen, *Z. f. französischen u. englischen Unterricht*, XIII, 546-7; Berendsohn, *Literaturblatt*, XXXV, 152-4; Dyboski, *Allgemeines Literaturblatt*, XXII, 1913, 497-9; Imelmann, *D.L.Z.* XXXIV, 1913, 1062-6 (weighty criticisms); Barnouw, *Museum*, XXI, 53-8.

1912 VON DER LEYEN, F. Die deutschen Heldensagen (Beowulf, pp. 107-23, 345-7). München.

1912 MEYER, W. Beiträge zur Geschichte der Eroberung Englands. Dissertation, Halle. (Finn story.)

1912 LAWRENCE, W. W. The haunted mere in Beowulf. *Pub. Mod. Lang. Assoc. Amer.* XXVII, 208-45. (Important. See above, pp. 52-3.)

1912 SCHÜTTE, G. The Geats of Beowulf, *J.E.G.Ph.* XI, 574-602. (See above, pp. 8, 333 *etc.*)

1912 STEFANOVIČ, S. Ein beitrag zur angelsächsischen Offa-sage, *Anglia*, XXXV, 483-525.

1912 MUCH, R. Grendel, *Wörter u. Sachen*, IV, 170-3. (Deriving *Vendsyssel*, Vandal, and the *Wendle* of Beowulf from *wandil*—"a bough, wand.")

1912 CHAMBERS, R. W. Six thirteenth century drawings illustrating the story of Offa and of Thryth (Drida) from *MS Cotton Nero D. I.* London, *privately printed.*

1913 ‡FAHLBECK, P. Beowulfskvädet som källa för nordisk fornhistoria. (Stockholm, *N. F. K. Vitterhets Historie och Antikvitets Akademiens Handlingar*, 13, 3.) Review: Klaeber, *Engl. Stud.* XLVIII, 435-7.

1913 NERMAN, B. Studier över Svärges hedna litteratur. Uppsala.

1913 NERMAN, B. Vilka konungar ligga i Uppsala högar? Uppsala.

1913 LAWRENCE, W. W. The Breca episode in Beowulf (Anniversary papers to G. L. Kittredge). Boston.

1913 SARRAZIN, G. Von Kädmon bis Kynewulf. Berlin. Reviews: Dudley, *J.E.G.Ph.* XV, 313-17; Berendsohn, *Literaturblatt*, XXXV (1914), 386-8; Funke, *Anglia, Beiblatt*, XXXI, 121-33.

1913 THOMAS, P. G. Beowulf and Daniel A, *M.L.R.* VIII, 537-9. (Parallels between the two poems.)

1913 BELDEN, H. M. Onela the Scylfing and Ali the Bold, *M.L.N.* XXVIII, 149-53.

1913 STEDMAN, D. Some points of resemblance between Beowulf and the Grettla (or Grettis Saga). From the *Saga Book of the Viking Club*, London. (It should have been held unnecessary to prove the relationship yet once again.)

1913 VON SYDOW, C. W. Irisches in Beowulf[874]. (*Verhandlungen der 52 Versammlung deutscher Philologen in Marburg*, pp. 177-80.)

1913 BERENDSOHN, W. A. Drei Schichten dichterischer Gestaltung im Beowulfepos, *Münchener Museum*, II, i, pp. 1-33.

1913 DEUTSCHBEIN, M. Beowulf der Gautenkönig, *Festschrift für Lorenz Morsbach*, Halle, pp. 291-7, *Morsbachs Studien*, L. (Very important. Expresses very well, and with full working out of details, the doubts which some of us had already felt as to the historic character of the reign of Beowulf over the Geatas.)

1913 BENARY, W. Zum Beowulf-Grendelsage, *Archiv*, CXXX, 154-5. (Grändelsmôr in Siebenbürgen: see above, p. 308.)

1913 KLAEBER, F. Das Grändelsmôr—eine Frage, *Archiv*, CXXXI, 427.

1913 BRATE, E. Betydelsen av ortnamnet Skälv [cf. Scilfingas], *Namn och Bygd*, I, 102-8.

1914 MÜLLER, J. Das Kulturbild des Beowulfepos. Halle. *Morsbachs Studien*, LIII. Reviews: Klaeber, *Anglia, Beiblatt*, XXVII, 241-4; Brunner, *Archiv*, CXXXVIII, 242-3.

1914 MOORMAN, F. W. English place-names and Teutonic Sagas, in *Essays and Studies by members of the English Association*, vol. V, pp. 75-103. (Argues that "Gilling" and other place-names in Yorkshire, point to an early colony of Scandinavian "Gautar," who may have been instrumental in introducing Scandinavian traditions into England.)

1914 OLSON, O. L. Beowulf and the Feast of Bricriu, *Mod. Phil.* XI, 407-27. (Emphasises the slight character of the parallels noted by Deutschbein.)

1914 VON SYDOW, C. W. Grendel i anglosaxiska ortnamn, in *Nordiska Ortnamn, hyllningsskrift tillägnad Adolf Noreen*, Uppsala, pp. 160-4=*Namn och Bygd*, II. (Important).

1915 KIER, CHR. Beowulf, et Bidrag til Nordens Oldhistorie. København. (An elaborate and painstaking study of the historic problems of Beowulf, vitiated throughout by quite unjustifiable assumptions. See above, p. 333 *etc.*) Review: Björkmann, *Anglia, Beiblatt*, XXVII, 244-6.

1915 BRADLEY, H. The Numbered Sections in Old English Poetical MSS, *Proc. Brit. Acad.* vol. VII.

1915 LAWRENCE, W. W. Beowulf and the tragedy of Finnsburg, *Pub. Mod. Lang. Assoc. Amer.* XXX, 372-431. (Important. An excellent survey of the Finnsburg problems.)

1915 VAN SWERINGEN, G. F. The main ... types of men in the Germanic Hero-Sagas, *J.E.G.Ph.* XIV, 212-25.

1915-19 LINDROTH, H. Är Skåne de gamles Scadinavia? *Namn och Bygd*, III, 1915, 10-28. Lindroth denied that the two words are the same, and was answered by A. Kock (*A.f.n.F.* XXXIV, 1917, 71 *etc.*), A. Noreen (in ‡*Studier tillegn. E. Tegnér*, 1918) and E. Björkman ("Scedeland, Scedenig," *Namn och Bygd*, VI, 1918, 162-8). Lindroth replied ("Äro Scadinavia och Skåne samma ord," *A.f.n.F.* XXXV, 1918, 29 *etc.*, and "Skandinavien och Skåne," *Namn och Bygd*, VI, 1918, 104-12) and was answered by Kock ("Vidare om Skåne och Scadinavia," *A.f.n.F.* XXXVI, 74-85). Björkman's discussion is the one of chief importance to students of Beowulf.

1915 KLAEBER, F. Observations on the Finn episode, *J.E.G.Ph.* XIV, 544-9.

1915 ANSCOMBE, A. Beowulf in High-Dutch saga, *Notes and Queries*, Aug. 21, 1915, pp. 133-4.

1915 BERENDSOHN, WALTER A. Die Gelage am Dänenhof zu Ehren Beowulfs, *Münchener Museum*, III, i, 31-55.

1915-16 PIZZO, E. Zur frage der ästhetischen einheit des Beowulf, *Anglia*, XXXIX, 1-15. (Sees in Beowulf the uniform expression of the early Anglo-Saxon Christian ideal.)

1916 OLSON, O. L. The relation of the Hrólfs Saga Kraka and the Bjarkarímur to Beowulf. Chicago. (Olson emphasises that the monster slain by Bjarki in the *Saga* does not attack the hall, but the cattle outside, and is therefore a different kind of monster from Grendel (p. 30). But he does not disprove the general equation of Beowulf and Bjarki: many of the most striking points of resemblance, such as the support given to Eadgils (Athils) against Onela (Ali), lie outside the scope of his study.) Review: Hollander, *J.E.G.Ph.* XVI, 147-9.

1916 NECKEL, G. Adel und gefolgschaft, *P.B.B.* XLI, 385-436 (esp. pp. 410 ff. for social conditions in Beowulf).

1917 FLOM, G. T. Alliteration and Variation in Old Germanic name giving, *M.L.N.* XXXII, 7-17.

1917 MEAD, G. W. Wiðergyld of Beowulf, 2051, *M.L.N.* XXXII, 435-6. (Suggests, very reasonably, that Wiðergyld is the father of the young Heathobard warrior who is stirred to revenge.)

1917 AYRES, H. M. The tragedy of Hengest in Beowulf, *J.E.G.Ph.* XVI, 282-95. (See above, pp. 266-7.)

1917 AURNER, N. S. An analysis of the interpretations of the Finnsburg documents. (*Univ. of Iowa Monographs: Humanistic Studies*, I, 6.)

1917 BJÖRKMAN, E. Zu ae. *Eote, Yte,* usw., dän. *Jyder,* "Jüten," *Anglia, Beiblatt,* XXVIII, 275-80. (See above, p. 334.)

1917 ROOTH, E. G. T. Der name Grendel in der Beowulfsage, *Anglia, Beiblatt,* XXVIII, 335-40. (Etymologies. Grendel is the "sandman," a man-eating monster of the sea-bottom. With this, compare Panzer's interpretation of Grendel as the "earthman." See above, p. 309.)

1917 SCHÜCKING, L. L. Wann entstand der Beowulf? Glossen, Zweifel und Fragen, *P.B.B.* XLII, 347-410. (Important. See above, pp. 322-32.)

1917 FOG, REGINALD. Trolden "Grendel" i Bjovulf: en hypothese, *Danske Studier*, 1917, 134-40. (Grendel is here interpreted as an infectious disease, prevalent among those who sleep in an ill-ventilated hall in a state of intoxication, but to which Beowulf, whose health has been confirmed by a recent sea-voyage, is not liable. This view is not as new as its author believes it to be, and a letter from von Holstein Rathlau is added, pointing this out. It might further have been pointed out that as early as 1879 Grendel was explained as the malaria. Cf. the theories of Laistner, Kögel and Golther, and see above, p. 46.)

1917 NEUHAUS, J. Sillende = vetus patria = Angel, *Nordisk Tidsskrift för Filologi,* IV. Række, Bd. V, 125-6; Helges Prinsesse Svåvå = Eider = den svebiske Flod hos Ptolemæos, VI, 29-32; Halfdan = Frode = Hadbardernes Konge, hvis Rige forenes med det danske, VI, 78-80; Vestgermanske Navne i dansk Historie og Sprog, 141-4. The inherent difficulty of the subject is enhanced by the obscurity of the writer's style: but much of the argument (e.g. that Halfdan and Frode are identical) is obviously based upon quite reckless conjectures. The question is complicated by political feeling: many of Neuhaus' arguments are repeated in his pamphlet, *Die Frage von Nordschleswig im Lichte der neuesten vorgeschichtlichen Untersuchungen,* Jena, 1919. His theories were vigorously refuted by G. SCHÜTTE, "Urjyske 'Vestgermaner,'" *Nordisk Tidsskrift för Filologi,* IV. Række, Bd. VII, 129 *etc.*

1917 ‡FREDBORG. Det första årtalet i Sveriges historia. Umeå.

1917 NERMAN, B. Ynglingasagan i arkeologisk belysning, *Fornvännen*, 1917, 226-61.

1917 NERMAN, B. Ottar Vendelkråka och Ottarshögen i Vendel, *Upplands Fornminnesförenings Tidskrift*, VII, 309-34.

1917 BJÖRKMAN, E. Bēowulf och Sveriges Historia, *Nordisk Tidskrift*, 1917, 161-79.

1917-18 ‡VON SYDOW, C. W. Draken som skattevaktare, *Danmarks folkeminder*, XVII, 103 *etc.*

1918 HACKENBERG, E. Die Stammtafeln der angelsächsischen Königreiche, Dissertation, Berlin. (A useful collection.) Reviews: Fischer, *Anglia, Beiblatt*, XXXI, 73-4; Ekwall, *Engl. Stud.* LIV, 307-10; Liebemann, *D.L.Z.* 1 March, 1919.

1918 LAWRENCE, W. W. The dragon and his lair in Beowulf, *Pub. Mod. Lang. Assoc. Amer.* XXXIII, 547-83.

1918 BELDEN, H. M. Beowulf 62, once more, *M.L.N.* XXXIII, 123.

1918 BELDEN, H. M. Scyld Scefing and Huck Finn, *M.L.N.* XXXIII, 315.

1918 KLAEBER, F. Concerning the relation between Exodus and Beowulf, *M.L.N.* XXXIII, 218-24.

1918 BJÖRKMAN, E. Bēow, Bēaw, und Bēowulf, *Engl. Stud.* LII, 145-93. (Very important. See above, p. 304.)

1918 BRANDL, A. Die Urstammtafel der Westsachsen und das Beowulf-Epos, *Archiv*, CXXXVII, 6-24. (See above, p. 200, note.)

1918 BRANDL, A. Die urstammtafel der englischen könige, *Sitzungsberichte d. k. preuss. Akad., Phil.-Hist. Classe*, p. 5. (Five line summary only published).

1918 ‡BJÖRKMAN, E. Bēowulf-forskning och mytologi, *Finsk Tidskrift*, 151 *etc.* (Cf. *Anglia, Beiblatt*, XXX, 207.)

1918 BJÖRKMAN, E. Sköldungaättens mytiska stamfäder, *Nordisk Tidskrift*, 163 *etc.*

1918 V. UNWERTH, W. Eine schwed. Heldensage als deutsches Volksepos, *A.f.n.F.* XXXV, 113-37. (An attempt to connect the story of Hygelac and Hæthcyn with the M.H.G. *Herbort ûʒ Tenelant.*)

1918 NEUHAUS, J. Om Skjold, *A.f.n.F.* XXXV, 166-72. (A dogmatic assertion of errors in Olrik's arguments in the *Heltedigtning*.)

1918 CLAUSEN, H. V. Kong Hugleik, *Danske Studier*, 137-49. (Conjectures based upon the assumption Geatas = Jutes.)

1918 ‡LUND University "Festskrift" contains NORLIND, Skattsägner; VON SYDOW, Sigurds strid med Favne.

1919 OLRIK, A. The heroic legends of Denmark translated ... and revised in collaboration with the author by Lee M. Hollander. New York. (Very important.) Review: Flom, *J.E.G.Ph.* XIX, 284-90.

1919 BJÖRKMAN, E. Bedwig in den westsächsischen genealogien, *Anglia, Beiblatt*, XXX, 23.

1919 BJÖRKMAN, E. Zu einigen Namen im Bēowulf: *Breca, Brondingas, Wealhpēo(w)*; *Anglia, Beiblatt*, XXX, 170-80.

1919 MOGK, E. Altgermanische Spukgeschichten: Zugleich ein Beitrag zur Erklärung der Grendelepisode im Beowulf, *Neue Jahrbücher für das klass. altertum ... und deutsche literatur*, XXXIV, 103-17. (Mogk here abandons his older allegorical interpretation of Grendel as the destroying power of the sea, and sees in the Grendel-story a Germanic ghost-tale, poetically adorned.)

1919 BJÖRKMAN, E. Skialf och Skilfing [edited by E. Ekwall, with a note on Björkman's work], *Namn och Bygd*, VII, 163-81.

1919 LINDERHOLM, E. Vendelshögens konunganamn i socknens 1600-tals-tradition, *Namn och Bygd*, VII, 36-40.

1919 FOG, R. Bjarkemaals "Hjalte," *Danske Studier*, 1919, 29-35. (With a letter from A. Olrik.)

1919 SEVERINSEN, P. Kong Hugleiks Dødsaar, *Danske Studier*, 1919, 96.

1920 IMELMANN, R. Forschungen zur altenglischen Poesie. (IX. Hengest u. Finn; X. *Enge ānpaðas, uncūð gelād*; XII. Þrȳðo; XIII. *Hǣþenra hyht*.) Berlin. (A weighty statement of some original views).

1920 BJÖRKMAN, E. Studien über die Eigennamen im Beowulf. Halle. *Morsbachs Studien*, LVIII. (An extremely valuable and discriminating digest. See above, p. 304.)

1920 BARTO, P. S. The *Schwanritter-Sceaf* Myth in *Perceval le Gallois*, *J.E.G.Ph.* XIX, 190-200.

1920 HUBBARD, F. G. The plundering of the Hoard. *Univ. Wisconsin Stud.* 11.

1920 SCHÜCKING, L. L. Wiðergyld (Beowulf, 2051), *Engl. Stud.* LIII, 468-70. (Schücking, like Mead, but independently, interprets Withergyld as the name of the warrior whose son is being stirred to revenge.)

1920 BJÖRKMAN, E. Hæðcyn und Hákon, *Engl. Stud.* LIV, 24-34.

1920 HOOPS, J. Das Verhüllen des Haupts bei Toten, ein angelsächsisch-nordischer Brauch (Zu Beowulf, 446, *hafalan hȳdan*), *Engl. Stud.* LIV, 19-23.

1920 NOREEN, A. Yngve, Inge, Inglinge [Ingwine], *Namn och Bygd*, VIII, 1-8.

1920 LA COUR, V. Lejrestudier, *Danske Studier*, 1920, 49-67. (Weighty. Emphasizing the importance of the site of Leire in the sixth century.) A discussion on the date and origin of Beowulf, by LIEBERMANN, is about to appear (*Gott. Gelehrt. Gesellschaft*).

§ 9. STYLE AND GRAMMAR

Titles already given in previous sections are not repeated here. General treatises on O.E. style and grammar are recorded here only if they have a special and exceptional bearing upon *Beowulf.*

1873 LICHTENHELD, A. Das schwache adjectiv im ags., *Z.f.d.A.* XVI, 325-93. (Important. See above, pp. 105-7.)

1875 HEINZEL, R. Über den Stil der altgermanischen Poesie. Strassburg. (*Quellen u. Forschungen*, X.) (Important and suggestive: led to further studies on the style of Beowulf, such as those of Hoffmann and Bode.) Review: Zimmer, *A.f.d.A.* II, 294-300.

1877 ‡ARNDT, O. Über die altgerm. epische Sprache. Paderborn.

1877 SCHÖNBACH, A. [A discussion of words peculiar to sections of Beowulf, added to a review of Ettmüller's Beowulf], *A.f.d.A.* III, 36-46. See also Möller, *Volksepos*, 60 *etc.*

1879 NADER, E. Zur Syntax des Béowulf. *Progr. der Staats-Ober-Realschule*, in Brünn. Review: Bernhardt, *Literaturblatt*, 1880, 439-40 (unfavourable: reply by Nader and answer by Bernhardt, 1881, 119-20).

1881 ‡GUMMERE, F. B. The Anglo-Saxon metaphor. Dissertation, Freiburg.

1882 SCHEMANN, K. Die Synonyma im Beówulfsliede, mit Rücksicht auf Composition u. Poetik des Gedichtes. Hagen. Dissertation, Münster. (Examines the use of noun-synonyms in the different sections of the poem as divided by Müllenhoff, and finds no support for Müllenhoff's theories.) Review: Kluge, *Literaturblatt*, 1883, 62-3.

1882 ‡NADER, E. Der Genitiv im Beówulf. Brünn. Review: Klinghardt, *Engl. Stud.* VI, 288.

1882 SCHULZ, F. Die Sprachformen des Hildebrand-Liedes im Beovolf. Königsberg.

1883 NADER, E. Dativ u. Instrumental im Beówulf. Wien. Review: Klinghardt, *Engl. Stud.* VII, 368-70.

1883 HARRISON, J. A. List of irregular (strong) verbs in Béowulf, *Amer. Jour. of Phil.* IV, 462-77.

1883 HOFFMANN, A. Der bildliche Ausdruck im Beówulf u. in der Edda, *Engl. Stud.* VI, 163-216.

1886 BODE, W. Die Kenningar in der angelsächsischen Dichtung. Darmstadt and Leipzig. Reviews: Gummere, *M.L.N.* II, 17-19 (important—praises Bode highly); Kluge, *Engl. Stud.* X, 117; Brandl, *D.L.Z.* 1887, 897-8; Bischoff, *Archiv*, LXXIX, 115-6; Meyer, *A.f.d.A.* XIII, 136.

1886 ‡KÖHLER, K. Der syntaktische gebrauch des Infinitivs und Particips im Beowulf. Dissertation, Münster.

1886 BANNING, A. Die epischen Formeln im Bêowulf. I. Die verbalen synonyma. Dissertation, Marburg.

1887 TOLMAN, A. H. The style of Anglo-Saxon poetry, *Trans. Mod. Lang. Assoc. Amer.* III, 17-47.

1888-9 NADER, E. Tempus und modus im Beowulf, *Anglia*, X, 542-63; XI, 444-99.

1889 KAIL, J. Über die Parallelstellen in der Ags. Poesie, *Anglia*, XII, 21-40. (A *reductio ad absurdum* of the theories of Sarrazin. Important.)

1891 DAVIDSON, C. The Phonology of the Stressed Vowels in Béowulf, *Pub. Mod. Lang. Assoc. Amer.* VI, 106-33. Review: Karsten, *Engl. Stud.* XVII, 417-20.

1892 SONNEFELD, G. Stilistisches und Wortschatz im Beówulf. Dissertation, Strassburg. Würzburg.

1893 TODT, A. Die Wortstellung im Beowulf, *Anglia*, XVI, 226-60.

1898 KISTENMACHER, R. Die wörtlichen Wiederholungen im Bêowulf. Dissertation, Greifswald. Reviews: Mead, *J.(E.)G.Ph.* II, 546-7; Kaluza, *Engl. Stud.* XXVII, 121-2 (short but valuable).

1902 BARNOUW, A. J. Textkritische Untersuchungen nach dem gebrauch des bestimmten Artikels und des schwachen Adjektivs in der altenglischen Poesie. Leiden. (Important, see above, p. 107.) Reviews: Kock, *Engl. Stud.* XXXII, 228-9; Binz, *Z.f.d.Ph.* XXXVI, 269-74; Schücking, *Göttingische gelehrte Anzeigen*, 1905, 730-40.

1902 HEUSLER, A. Der dialog in der altgermanischen erzählenden Dichtung. *Z.f.d.A.* XLVI, 189-284.

1903 SHIPLEY, G. The genitive case in Anglo-Saxon Poetry. Baltimore. Reviews: Kock, *Engl. Stud.* XXV, 92-5; Mourek, *A.f.d.A.* XXX, 172-4.

1903 KRACKOW, O. Die Nominalcomposita als Kunstmittel im altenglischen Epos. Dissertation, Berlin. Review: Björkman, *Archiv*, CXVII, 189-90.

1904 SCHÜCKING, L. L. Die Grundzüge der Satzverknüpfung im Beowulf. Pt. I. (*Morsbachs Studien*, XV.) Halle. (Important.) Reviews: Eckhardt, *Engl. Stud.* XXXVII, 396-7; Pogatscher, *D.L.Z.* 1905, 922-3; Behagel, *Literaturblatt*, XXVIII, 100-2; Grossmann, *Archiv*, CXVIII, 176-9.

1904 HÄUSCHKEL, B. Die Technik der Erzählung im Beowulfliede. Dissertation, Breslau.

1905 KRAPP, G. P. The parenthetic exclamation in Old English poetry, *M.L.N.* XX, 33-7.

1905 SCHEINERT, M. Die Adjektiva im Beowulfepos als Darstellungsmittel, *P.B.B.* XXX, 345-430.

1906 THOMAS, P. G. Notes on the language of Beowulf, *M.L.R.* I, 202-7. (A short summary of the dialectal forms.)

1906 BARNOUW, A. J. Nochmals zum ags. Gebrauch des Artikels, *Archiv*, CXVII, 366-7.

1907 RIES, J. Die Wortstellung im Beowulf. Halle. (An important and exhaustive study by an acknowledged specialist.) Reviews: Binz, *Anglia*, *Beiblatt*, XXII, 65-78 (important); Borst, *Engl. Stud.* XLII, 93-101; Delbrück,

A.f.d.A. XXXI, 65-76 (important); Reis, *Literaturblatt*, XXVIII, 328-30; *Lit. Cbl.* 1907, p. 1474; Huchon, *Revue germanique*, III, 634-8.

1908 KRAUEL, H. Der Haken- und Langzeilenstil im Beowulf. Dissertation, Göttingen.

1908 LORS, A. Aktionsarten des Verbums im Beowulf. Dissertation, Würzburg.

1908 ‡MOUREK, E. Zur Syntax des konjunktivs im Beowulf, *Prager deutsche stud.* VIII.

1909-10 RANKIN, J. W. A study of the Kennings in Ags. poetry, *J.E.G.Ph.* VIII, 357-422; IX, 49-84. (Latin parallels; very important.)

1909 SHEARIN, H. G. The expression of purpose in Old English poetry, *Anglia*, XXXII, 235-52.

1909 ‡RIGGERT, G. Der syntaktische Gebrauch des Infinitivs in der altenglischen Poesie. Dissertation, Kiel.

1910 RICHTER, C. Chronologische Studien zur angelsächsischen Literatur auf grund sprachl.-metrischer Kriterien. Halle. (*Morsbachs Studien*, XXXIII.) Reviews: Binz, *Anglia, Beiblatt*, XXII, 78-80; Imelmann, *D.L.Z.* 1910, 2986-7; Hecht, *Archiv*, CXXX, 430-2.

1910 WAGNER, R. Die Syntax des Superlativs ... im Beowulf. Berlin. (*Palaestra*, XCI.) Reviews: Schatz, *D.L.Z.* 1910, 2848-9; Kock, *A.f.n.F.* XXVIII, 347-9.

1910 SCHUCHARDT, R. Die negation im Beowulf. Berlin. (*Berliner Beiträge zur germ. u. roman. Philol.* XXXVIII.)

1912 BRIGHT, J. W. An Idiom of the Comparative in Anglo-Saxon, *M.L.N.* XXVII, 181-3. (Bearing particularly upon Beowulf, 69, 70.)

1912 EXNER, P. Typische Adverbialbestimmungen in frühenglischer Poesie. Dissertation, Berlin.

1912 GRIMM, P. Beiträge zum Pluralgebrauch in der altenglischen Poesie. Dissertation, Halle.

1913 PAETZEL, W. Die Variationen in der altgermanischen Alliterationspoesie. Berlin. See pp. 73-84 for Beowulf and Finnsburg. (*Palaestra*, XLVIII.) Pt. I. had appeared in 1905 as a Berlin dissertation.

§ 10. METRE

For bibliography of O.E. metre in general, see *Pauls Grdr.* (2), II, 1022-4.

1870 SCHUBERT, H. De Anglosaxonum arte metrica. Dissertatio inauguralis, Berolini.

1884 SIEVERS, E. Zur rhythmik des germanischen alliterationsverses: I. Vorbemerkungen. Die metrik des Beowulf: II. Sprachliche Ergebnisse, *P.B.B.* X, 209-314 and 451-545. (Most important.)

1894 KALUZA, M. Studien zum altgermanischen alliterationsvers. I. Kritik der bisherigen theorien. II. Die Metrik des Beowulfliedes. (Important.) Reviews: Martin, *Engl. Stud.* XX, 293-6; Heusler, *A.f.d.A.* XXI, 313-17; Saran, *Z.f.d.Ph.* XXVII, 539-43.

1905 TRAUTMANN, M. Die neuste Beowulfausgabe und die altenglische verslehre, *Bonner Beiträge zur Anglistik*, XVII, 175-91. (A discussion of O.E. metre in view of Holthausen's edition.) Review: Klaeber, *M.L.N.* XXII, 252.

1908 MORGAN, B. Q. Zur lehre von der alliteration in der westgermanischen dichtung: I. Die tonverhältnisse der hebungen im Beowulf: II. Die gekreuzte alliteration; *P.B.B.* XXXIII, 95-181.

1908 BOHLEN, A. Zusammengehörige Wortgruppen, getrennt durch Cäsur oder Versschluss, in der angelsächsischen Epik. Dissertation, Berlin. Reviews: Dittes, *Anglia, Beiblatt*, XX, 199-202; Kroder, *Engl. Stud.* XL, 90.

1912 TRAUTMANN, M. Zum altenglischen Versbau, *Engl. Stud.* XLIV, 303-42.

1913 SEIFFERT, F. Die Behandlung der Wörter mit auslautenden ursprünglich silbischen Liquiden oder Nasalen und mit Kontraktionsvokalen in der Genesis A und im Beowulf. Dissertation, Halle. (Concludes the dialect of the two poems to be distinct, but finds no evidence on these grounds which is the earlier.)

1914 FIJN VAN DRAAT, P. The cursus in O.E. poetry, *Anglia*, XXXVIII, 377-404.

1918 LEONARD, W. E. Beowulf and the Niebelungen couplet, in *Univ. of Wisconsin Studies in Language and Literature*, II, 98-152. (Important. Pp. 123-46 advocating the "four-accent theory.")

1920 ‡NEUNER, E. Ueber ein- und dreihebige Halbverse in der altenglischen alliterierenden Poesie. Berlin. Review: Bright, *M.L.N.* XXXVI, 59-63.

NOTES

[1] The exact equivalent to *Hróðgar* is found in O.N., in the form *Hróðgeirr*. The by-form *Hróarr*, which is used of the famous Danish king, is due to a number of rather irregular changes, which can however be paralleled. The Primitive Germanic form of the name would have been **Hrōþugaisaʒ*: for the loss of the *g* at the beginning of the second element we may compare *Aðils* with *Ēadgils* (Noreen, *Altisländische Grammatik*, 1903, § 223); for the loss of *ð* before *w* compare *Hrólfr* with *Hrōðwulf* (Noreen, § 222); for the absence of R- umlaut in the second syllable, combined with loss of the *g*, compare O.N. *nafarr* with O.E. *nafugār* (Noreen, § 69).

[2] Corresponding to O.N. *Aðils* we should expect O.E. *Æðgils*, *Æðgisl*. The form *Ēadgils* may be due to confusion with the famous Eadgils, king of the Myrgingas, who is mentioned in *Widsith*. The name comes only once in *Beowulf* (l. 2392) and may owe its form there to a corruption of the scribe. That the O.E. form is corrupt seems more likely than that the O.N. *Aðils*, so well known and so frequently recorded, is a corruption of *Auðgisl*.

[3] It must be remembered that the sound changes of the Germanic dialects have been worked out so minutely that it is nearly always possible to decide quite definitely whether two names do or do not exactly correspond. Only occasionally is dispute possible [e.g. whether *Hrothgar* is or is not phonetically the exact equivalent of *Hroarr*].

[4] See below, pp. 8-10.

[5] *Chochilaicus*, which appears to be the correct form, corresponds to *Hygelac* (in the primitive form *Hugilaikaʒ*) as *Chlodovechus* to *Hludovicus*.

[6] The passages in *Beowulf* referring to this expedition are:

1202 *etc.*. Frisians (adjoining the Hetware) and Franks mentioned as the foes.

2354 *etc.* Hetware mentioned.

2501 *etc.* Hugas (= Franks) and the Frisian king mentioned.

2914 *etc.* Franks, Frisians, Hugas, Hetware and "the Merovingian" mentioned.

[7] The identification of Chochilaicus with Hygelac is the most important discovery ever made in the study of *Beowulf*, and the foundation of our belief in the historic character of its episodes. It is sometimes attributed to Grundtvig, sometimes to Outzen. It was first vaguely suggested by Grundtvig (*Nyeste Skilderie af Kjøbenhavn*, 1815, col. 1030): the importance of the identification was worked out by him fully, two years later (*Danne-Virke*, II, 285). In the meantime the passage from Gregory had been quoted by Outzen in his review of Thorkelin's *Beowulf* (*Kieler Blätter*, III, 312). Outzen's reference was obviously made independently, but he failed to detect the real bearing of the passage upon *Beowulf*. Credit for the find accordingly belongs solely to Grundtvig.

[8] Ongentheow is mentioned in *Widsith* (l. 31) as a famous king of the Swedes. Many of the kings mentioned in the same list can be proved to be historical, and the reference in *Widsith* therefore supports Ongentheow's historic character, but is far, in itself, from proving it.

[9] Strictly *Anganþér*. See Heusler, *Heldennamen in mehrfacher Lautgestalt*, Z.f.d.A. LII, 101.

[10] ll. 2382-4.

[11] ll. 2612-9.

[12] Whether it be accuracy or accident, these names Ottar and Athils come just at that place in the list of the *Ynglinga tal* which, when we reckon back the generations, we find to correspond to the beginning of the sixth century. And this is the date when we know from *Beowulf* that they should have been reigning.

[13] But the accounts are quite inconsistent. Saxo (ed. Holder, pp. 56-7) implies a version in which Athils was deposed, if not slain, by Bothvar Bjarki, which is quite at variance with other information given by Saxo.

[14] Unless they are among the fragments carried off to the Stockholm Museum. Little of interest was found in these mounds when they were opened: everything had been too thoroughly burnt.

[15] See Schück, *Folknamnet Geatas*, 22 *etc.*

[16] See below, p. 98 and Appendix (E); The "Jute-Question."

[17] See below, pp. 45 *etc.*

[18] Olrik (*Heltedigtning*, I, 22 *etc.*). The Danish house—Healfdene, Heorogar, Hrothgar, Halga, Heoroweard, Hrethric, Hrothmund, Hrothulf: the Swedish—Ongentheow, Onela, Ohthere, Eanmund, Eadgils: the Geatic—Hrethel, Herebeald, Hætheyn, Hygelac, Heardred. The same principle is strongly marked in the Old English pedigrees.

[19] ll. 3018 *etc.*

[20] As is done, e.g., by Schück (*Studier i Beowulf-sagan*, 27).

[21] "Dragon fights are more frequent, not less frequent, the nearer we come to historic times": Olrik, *Heltedigtning*, I, 313. The dragon survived much later in Europe than has been generally recognized. He was flying from Mount Pilatus in 1649. (See J. J. Scheuchzer, *Itinera per Helvetiae Alpinas regiones*, 1723, III, p. 385.) The same authority quotes accounts of dragons authenticated by priests, his own contemporaries, and supplies many bloodcurdling engravings of the same.

[22] Cf. on this point Klaeber in *Anglia*, XXXVI (1912) p. 190.

[23] l. 2382.

[24] l. 2393.

[25] Of course, even if Beowulf's reign over the Geatas is not historic, this does not exclude the possibility of his having *some* historic foundation.

[26] Attempts at working out the chronology of *Beowulf* have been made by Gering (in his translation) and by Heusler (*Archiv*, CXXIV, 9-14). On the whole the chronology of *Beowulf* is self-consistent, but there are one or two discrepancies which do not admit of solution.

[27] l. 468.

[28] l. 2161.

[29] *Widsith*, l. 46.

[30] *Beowulf*, l. 2160. Had Hrothulf been a son of Heorogar he could not have been passed over in silence here. Neither can Hrothulf be Hrothgar's sister's son: for since the sister married the Swedish king, Hrothulf would in that case be a Swedish prince, and presumably would be living at the Swedish court, and bearing a name connected by alliteration with those of the Swedish, not the Danish house. Besides, had he been a Swedish prince, he must have been heard of in connection with the dynastic quarrels of the Swedish house.

[31] ll. 1163-5.

[32] ll. 1188-91.

[33] ll. 1180 *etc.*

[34] Doubts are expressed, for example, in Trap's monumental topographical work (*Kongeriket Danmark*, II, 328, 1898).

[35] For example Sweyn Aageson (c. 1200) had no doubt that the little village of Leire near Roskilde was identical with the Leire of story: *Rolf Kraki, occisus in Lethra, qvae tunc famosissima Regis extitit curia, nunc autem Roskildensi vicina civitati, inter abjectissima ferme vix colitur oppida.* Svenonis Aggonis *Historia Regum Daniae*, in Langebek, I, 45.

[36] *Ro ... patrem vero suum Dan colle apud Lethram tumulavit Sialandie ubi sedem regni pro eo pater constituit, qvam ipse post eum divitiis multiplicibus ditavit.* In the so-called *Annales Esromenses*, in Langebek, I, 224. Cf. Olrik, *Heltedigtning*, I, 188, 194. For further evidence, see Appendix (G) below.

[37] We must not think of Heorot as an isolated country seat. The Royal Hall would stand in the middle of the Royal Village, as in the case of the halls of Attila (Priscus in Möller's *Fragmenta*, IV, 85) or Cynewulf (*A.S. Chronicle*, Anno 755).

[38] *Lethram pergitur, quod oppidum, a Roluone constructum eximiisque regni opibus illustratum, ceteris confinium prouinciarum urbibus regie fundacionis et sedis auctoritate prestabat.* Saxo, Book II (ed. Holder, p. 58).

[39] *His cognitis Helgo filium Roluonem Lethrica arce conclusit, heredis saluti consulturus* (p. 52).

[40] *A Roe Roskildia condita memoratur.* Saxo, Book II (ed. Holder, p. 51). Roe's spring, after being a feature of the town throughout the ages, is now (owing perhaps to its sources having been tapped by a neighbouring mineral-water factory) represented only by a pump in a market-garden.

[41] I owe this paragraph to information kindly supplied me by Dr Sofus Larsen, librarian of the University Library, Copenhagen.

[42] It was once believed that, in prehistoric times, the sea came up to Leire also (Forchhammer, Steenstrup and Worsaae: *Undersøgelser i geologisk-antiqvarisk Retning,* Kjøbenhavn, 1851). A most exact scrutiny of the geology of the coast-line has proved this to be erroneous. (Danmarks geologiske Undersøgelse I.R. 6. *Beskrivelse til Kaartbladene Kjøbenhavn og Roskilde,* af K. Rørdam, Kjøbenhavn, 1899.)

[43] The presence at Leire of early remains makes it tempting to suppose that it may have been from very primitive times a stronghold or sacred place. It is impossible here to examine these conjectures, which would connect Heorot ultimately with the "sacred place on the isle of the ocean" mentioned by Tacitus. The curious may be referred to Much in *P.B.B.* XVII, 196-8; Mogk in *Pauls Grdr.* (2) III, 367; Kock in the Swedish *Historisk Tidskrift,* 1895, 162 *etc.*; and particularly to the articles by Sarrazin: *Die Hirsch Halle* in *Anglia,* XIX, 368-91, *Neue Beowulfstudien (Der Grendelsee)* in *Engl. Stud.* XLII, 6-15.

[44] This seems to me much more probable than, as Olrik supposes, that Froda fell in battle against Healfdene (*Skjoldungasaga,* 162 [80]).

[45] *Saga of Rolf Kraki,* cap. IV.

[46] Olrik wishes to read the whole of this account, not as a prediction in the present future tense, but as a narrative of past events in the historic present. (*Heltedigtning,* I, 16; II, 38.) Considering the rarity of the historic present idiom in Old English poetry, this seems exceedingly unlikely.

[47] ll. 2047-2056.

[48] *Verba dei legantur in sacerdotali convivio; ibi decet lectorem audiri, non citharistam, sermones patrum, non carmina gentilium. Quid Hinieldus cum*

Christo? See Jaffé's *Monumenta Alcuiniana* (*Bibliotheca Rer. Germ.* VI), Berlin, 1873, p. 357; *Epistolae*, 81.

[49] Saxo, Book *VI* (ed. Holder, 205, 212-13).

The contrast between this lyrical outburst, and the matter-of-fact speech in which the old warrior in *Beowulf* eggs on the younger man, is thoroughly characteristic of the difference between Old English and Old Scandinavian heroic poetry. This difference is very noticeable whenever we have occasion to compare a passage in *Beowulf* with any parallel passage in a Scandinavian poem, and should be carefully pondered by those who still believe that *Beowulf* is, in its present form, a translation from the Scandinavian.

[50] Saxo, Book VIII (ed. Holder, p. 274); *Helga kviþa Hundingsbana*, II, 19. See also Bugge, *Helge-digtene*, 157.

[51] *Þáttr Þorsteins Skelks* in *Flateyarbók* (ed. Vigfússon and Unger), I, 416.

[52] Similarly, there is certainly a primitive connection between the names of the Geatas (Gautar) and of the Goths: but they are quite distinct peoples: we should not be justified in speaking of the Geatas as identical with the Goths.

[53] Müllenhoff (*Beovulf*, 29-32) followed by Much (*P.B.B.* XVII, 201) and Heinzel (*A.f.d.A.* XVI, 271). The best account of the Heruli is in Procopius (*Bell. Gott.* II, 14, 15).

[54] See also Olrik, *Heltedigtning*, I, 21, 22: Sarrazin in *Engl. Stud.* XLII, 11: Bugge, *Helgi-digtene*, 151-63; 181: Chambers, *Widsith*, p. 82 (note), pp. 205-6.

[55] *Saga of Rolf Kraki: Skjoldungasaga.*

[56] Best represented in Saxo.

[57] See above, p. 15.

[58] ll. 1180-87.

[59] ll. 1188-91.

[60] ll. 1163-5.

[61] ll. 1017-19.

[62] ll. 45-6.

[63] For a contrary view see Clarke, *Sidelights*, 100.

[64] Saxo has mistaken a title *hnøggvanbaugi* for a father's name, (*hins*) *hnøggva Baugs* "(son of the) covetous Baug."

[65] *Langfeðgatal* in Langebek, I, 5. The succession given in *Langfeðgatal* is Halfdan, Helgi and Hroar, Rolf, Hrærek: it should, of course, run Halfdan, Helgi and Hroar, Hrærek, Rolf. Hrærek has been moved from his proper place in order to clear Rolf of any suspicion of usurpation.

[66] l. 1189.

[67] See Olrik, *Episke Love* in *Danske Studier*, 1908, p. 79. Compare the remark of Goethe in *Wilhelm Meister*, as to the necessity of there being *both* a Rosencrantz *and* a Guildenstern (*Apprenticeship*, Book V, chap. V).

[68] ll. 587-9.

[69] ll. 1165-8.

[70] Perhaps such murder of kin was more common among the aristocratic houses than among the bulk of the population (Chadwick, *H.A.* 348). In some great families it almost becomes the rule, producing a state of things similar to that in present day Afghanistan, where it has become a proverb that a man is "as great an enemy as a cousin" (Pennell, *Afghan Frontier*, 30).

[71] This is proposed by Cosijn (*Aanteekeningen*, 21) and again independently by Lawrence in *M.L.N.* XXV, 157.

[72] ll. 467-9.

[73] ll. 2155-62.

[74] See *Widsith*, ed. Chambers, pp. 92-4.

[75] See Rickert, "The Old English Offa Saga" in *Mod. Phil.* II, esp. p. 75.

[76] The common ascription of the *Lives of the Offas* to Matthew Paris is erroneous: they are somewhat earlier.

[77] The identification of *Fifeldor* with the Eider has been doubted, notably by Holthausen, though he seems less doubtful in his latest edition (third edit. II, 178). The reasons for the identification appear to me the following. Place names ending in *dor* are exceedingly rare. When, therefore, two independent authorities tell us that Offa fought at a place named *Fifel-dor* or *Egi-dor*, it appears unlikely that this can be a mere coincidence: it seems more natural to assume that the names are corruptions of one original. But further, the connection is not limited to the second element in the name. For the Eider (*Egidora, Ægisdyr*) would in O.E. be *Egor-dor*: and *Egor-dor* stands to *Fifel-dor* precisely as *egor-stream* (Boethius, *Metra*, XX, 118) does to *fifel-stream* (*Metra*, XXVI, 26), *"egor"* and *"fifel"* being interchangeable synonyms. See note to *Widsith*, l. 43 (p. 204). It is objected that the interchange of *fifel* and *egor*, though frequent in common nouns, would be unusual in the name of a place. The reply is that the Old English scop may not have regarded it as a place-name. He may have substituted *fifel-dor* for the synonymous *egor-dor*, "the monster gate," without realizing that it was the name of a definite place, just as he would have substituted *fifel-stream* for *egor-stream*, "the monster stream, the sea," if alliteration demanded the change.

[78] *The Deeds of Beowulf*, LXXXV.

[79] See below, pp. 105-12, and Appendix (D) below.

[80] Wihtlæg appears in Saxo as *Vigletus* (Book IV, ed. Holder, p. 105).

[81] *Nibelungen Lied*, ed. Piper, 328.

[82] Book IV (ed. Holder, p. 102).

[83] Kemble, *Beowulf, Postscript* IX; followed by Müllenhoff, *etc.* So, lately, Chadwick (*H.A.* 126): cf. also Sievers ('Beowulf und Saxo' in the *Berichte d. k. sächs. Gesell. d. Wissenschaften*, 1895, pp. 180-88); Bradley in *Encyc. Brit.* III, 761; Boer, *Beowulf*, 135. See also Olrik, *Danmarks Heltedigtning*, I, 246. For further discussion see below, Appendix (A).

[84] *Beo—Scyld—Scef* in Ethelwerd: *Beowius—Sceldius—Sceaf* in William of Malmesbury. But in the *Anglo-Saxon Chronicle* five generations intervene between Sceaf and his descendant Scyldwa, father of Beaw.

[85] "Item there is vii acres lond lying by the high weye toward the grendyll": *Bury Wills*, ed. S. Tymms (Camden Soc. XLIX, 1850, p. 31).

[86] I should hardly have thought it worth while to revive this old "cesspool" theory, were it not for the statement of Dr Lawrence that "Miller's argument that the word *grendel* here is not a proper name at all, that it means 'drain,' has never, to my knowledge, been refuted." (*Pub. Mod. Lang. Assoc. Amer.* XXIV, 253.)

Miller was a scholar whose memory should be reverenced, but the letter to the *Academy* was evidently written in haste. The only evidence which Miller produced for *grendel* standing alone as a common noun in Old English was a charter of 963 (Birch, 1103: vol. III, p. 336): *þanon forð eft on grendel: þanon on clyst: grendel* here, he asserted, meant "drain": and consequently *gryndeles sylle* and *grendles mere* in the other charters must mean "cesspool." But the locality of this charter of 963 is known (Clyst St Mary, a few miles east of Exeter), and the two words exist there as names of streams to this day—"thence again along the Greendale brook, thence along the river Clyst." The Grindle or Greendale brook is no sewer, but a stream some half dozen miles in length which "winds tranquilly through a rich tract of alluvial soil" (*Journal of the Archaeol. Assoc.* XXXIX, 273), past three villages which bear the same name, Greendale, Greendale Barton and Higher Greendale, under Greendale Bridge and over the ford by Greendale Lane, to its junction with the Clyst. Why the existence of this charming stream should be held to justify the interpretation of *Grendel* or *Gryndel* as "drain" and *grendles mere* as "cesspool" has always puzzled me. Were a new Drayton to arise he might, in a new *Polyolbion*, introduce the nymph complaining of her hard lot at the hands of scholars in the Hesperides. I hope, when he next visits England, to conduct Dr Lawrence to make his apologies to the lady. Meantime a glance at the "six inch" ordnance map of Devon suffices to refute Miller's curious hypothesis.

[87] It is often asserted that the same Beowa appears as a witness to a charter (Müllenhoff, *Beovulf*, p. 8: Haak, *Zeugnisse zur altenglischen Heldensage*, 53). But this rests upon a misprint of Kemble (*C.D.S.* V, 44). The name is really *Beoba* (Birch, *Cart. Sax.* I, 212).

[88] *Beaf er ver kollum Biar*, in the descent of Harold Fairhair from Adam, in *Flateyarbók*, ed. Vigfússon and Unger, Christiania, 1859,

I, 27. [The genealogy contains many names obviously taken from a MS of the O.E. royal pedigrees, not from oral tradition, as is shown by the miswritings, e.g., *Beaf* for *Beaw*, owing to mistaking the O.E. *w* for *f*.] "This is no proof," Dr Lawrence urges, "of popular acquaintance with Bjár as a Scandinavian figure." (*Pub. Mod. Lang. Assoc. Amer.* XXIV, 246.) But how are we to account for the presence of his name among a mnemonic list of some of the most famous warriors and their horses—mention along with heroes like Sigurd, Gunnar, Atli, Athils and Ali, unless Bjar was a well-known figure?

[89] *en Bjárr [reið] Kerti. Kortr,* "short" (Germ. *Kurz*), if indeed we are so to interpret it, is hardly an Icelandic word, and seems strange as the name of a horse. Egilsson (*Lex. Poet.* 1860) suggests *kertr,* "erect," "with head high" (cf. Kahle in *I.F.* XIV, 164).

[90] See Appendix (A) below.

[91] Müllenhoff derived Beaw from the root *bhū,* "to be, dwell, grow": Beaw therefore represented settled dwelling and culture. Müllenhoff's mythological explanation (*Z.f.d.A.* VII, 419, *etc.,* *Beovulf,* 1, *etc.*) has been largely followed by subsequent scholars, e.g., ten Brink (*Pauls Grdr.* II, 533: *Beowulf,* 184), Symons (*Pauls Grdr.* (2), III, 645-6) and, in general outline, E. H. Meyer (*Mythol. der Germanen,* 1903, 242).

[92] Uhland in *Germania,* II, 349.

[93] Laistner (*Nebelsagen,* 88, *etc.,* 264, *etc.*), Kögel (*Z.f.d.A.* XXXVII, 274: *Geschichte d. deut. Litt.* I, 1, 109), and Golther (*Handbuch der germ. Mythologie,* 1895, 173) see in Grendel the demon of combined storm and pestilence.

[94] E. H. Meyer (*Germ. Mythol.* 1891, 299).

[95] Mogk (*Pauls Grdr.* (2), III, 302) regards Grendel as a "water-spirit."

[96] Boer (*Ark. f. nord. Filol.* XIX, 19).

[97] This suggestion is made (very tentatively) by Brandl, in *Pauls Grdr.* (2), II, i, 992.

[98] This view has been enunciated by Wundt in his *Völkerpsychologie,* II, i, 326, *etc.,* 382. For a discussion see A. Heusler in *Berliner Sitzungsberichte,* XXXVII, 1909, pp. 939-945.

[99] Cf. Lawrence in *Pub. Mod. Lang. Assoc. Amer.* XXIV, 265, *etc.*, and Panzer's "Beowulf" throughout.

[100] The tradition of "the devil and his dam" resembles that of Grendel and his mother in its coupling together the home-keeping female and the roving male. See E. Lehmann, "Fandens Oldemor" in *Dania*, VIII, 179-194; a paper which has been undeservedly neglected in the *Beowulf* bibliographies. But the devil beats his dam (cf. *Piers Plowman*, C-text, XXI, 284): conduct of which one cannot imagine Grendel guilty. See too Lehmann in *Arch. f. Religionswiss.* VIII, 411-30: Panzer, *Beowulf*, 130, 137, *etc.*: Klaeber in *Anglia*, XXXVI, 188.

[101] Cf. *Beowulf*, ll. 1282-7.

[102] There are other coincidences which *may* be the result of mere chance. In each case, before the adventure with the giants, the hero proves his strength by a feat of endurance in the ice-cold water. And, at the end of the story, the hero in each case produces, as evidence of his victory, a trophy with a runic inscription: in *Beowulf* an engraved sword-hilt; in the *Grettis saga* bones and a "rune-staff."

[103] Vigfússon, *Corp. Poet. Boreale*, II, 502: Bugge, *P.B.B.* XII, 58.

[104] Boer, for example, believes that *Beowulf* influenced the *Grettis saga* (*Grettis saga*, Introduction, xliii); so, tentatively, Olrik (*Heltedigtning*, I, 248).

[105] For this argument and the following, cf. Schück, *Studier i Beowulfssagan*, 21.

[106] Even assuming that a MS of *Beowulf* had found its way to Iceland, it would have been unintelligible. This is shown by the absurd blunders made when Icelanders borrowed names from the O.E. genealogies.

[107] Cf. Olrik, *A. f. n. F.*, VIII (N.F. IV), 368-75; and Chadwick, *Origin*, 125-6.

[108] *Pub. Mod. Lang. Assoc. Amer.* XXVII, 208 *etc.*

[109] *Cotton. Gnomic Verses*, ll. 42-3.

[110] *Fornmannasǫgur*, III, 204-228.

[111] Hammershaimb, *Færöiske Kvæder*, II, 1855, Nos. 11 and 12.

[112] A. I. Arwidsson, *Svenska Fornsånger*, 1834-42, Nos. 8 and 9.

[113] Boer, *Beowulf*, 177-180.

[114] ll. 1553-6.

[115] l. 455.

[116] The attacks have taken place at Yule for two successive years, exactly as in the *Grettis saga*. [In *Beowulf* it is, of course, "twelve winters" (l. 147).] Is this mere accident, or does the *Grettis saga* here preserve the original time limit, which has been exaggerated in *Beowulf*? If so, we have another point of resemblance between the *Saga of Rolf Kraki* and the earliest version of the *Beowulf* story.

[117] *Beowulf*, ll. 801-5.

[118] Cf. *Beowulf*, ll. 590-606.

[119] *Beowulf*, l. 679.

[120] *Beowulf*, ll. 1508-9, 1524.

[121] It is only in this adventure that Rolf carries the sword *Gullinhjalti*. His usual sword, as well known as Arthur's Excalibur, was *Skofnungr*. For *Gyldenhilt*, whether descriptive, or proper noun, see *Beowulf*, 1677.

[122] Cf. Symons in *Pauls Grdr.* (2), III, 649: Züge aus dem anglischen Mythus von Béaw-Biar (Biarr oder Bjár?; s. Symons Lieder der Edda, I, 222) wurden auf den dänischen Sagenhelden (Boðvarr) Bjarki durch Ähnlichkeit der Namen veranlasst, übertragen. Cf. too, Heusler in *A.f.d.A.* XXX, 32.

[123] See p. 87 and Appendix (A) below.

[124] *Heltedigtning*, I, 1903, 135-6.

[125] *Beowulf*, 1518.

[126] See Heusler in *Z.f.d.A.* XLVIII, 62.

[127] Cf. on this Heusler, *Z.f.d.A.* XLVIII, 64-5.

[128] Cf. *Skjoldunga saga*, cap. XII; and see Olrik, *Heltedigtning*, I, 201-5; *Bjarka rímur*, VIII.

[129] Similarly *Skáldskaparmál*, 41 (44).

[130] Bärensohn. Jean l'Ours. The name is given to the group because the hero is frequently (though by no means always) represented as having been brought up in a bear's den. The story summarized above is a portion of Panzer's "Type A." See Appendix (H), below.

[131] ll. 704, 729.

[132] ll. 691-6.

[133] In the *Beowulf* it was even desirable, as explained above, to go further, and completely to exculpate the Danish watchers.

[134] From the controversial point of view Panzer has no doubt weakened his case by drawing attention to so many of these, probably accidental, coincidences. It gives the critic material for attack (cf. Boer, *Beowulf*, 14)

[135] ll. 2183 *etc.*

[136] ll. 408-9.

[137] It comes out strongly in the *Bjarki*-story.

[138] It can hardly be argued that Stein is mentioned because he was an historic character who in some way came into contact with the historic Grettir: for in this case his descent would have been given, according to the usual custom in the sagas. (Cf. note to Boer's edition of *Grettis saga*, p. 233.)

[139] P. E. K. Kaalund, *Bidrag til en historisk-topografisk Beskrivelse af Island*, Kjøbenhavn, 1877, II, 151.

[140] The localization in *en stor sandhaug* is found in a version of the story to which Panzer was unable to get access (see p. 7 of his *Beowulf*, Note 2). A copy is to be found in the University Library of Christiania, in a small book entitled *Nor, en Billedbog for den norske Ungdom*. Christiania, 1865. (*Norske Folke-Eventyr ... fortalte af P. C. Asbjørnsen*, pp. 65-128.)

The *sandhaug* is an extraordinary coincidence, if it *is* a mere coincidence. It cannot have been imported into the modern folk-tale from the *Grettis saga*, for there is no superficial resemblance between the two tales.

[141] Cf. Boer, *Beowulf*, 14.

[142] Yet both Beowulf and Orm are saved by divine help.

[143] Panzer exaggerates the case against his own theory when he quotes only six versions as omitting the princesses (p. 122). Such unanimity as this is hardly to be looked for in a collection of 202 kindred folk-tales. In addition to these six, the princesses are altogether missing, for example, in the versions Panzer numbers 68, 69, 77: they are only faintly represented in other versions (e.g. 76). Nevertheless the rescue of the princesses may be regarded as the most essential element in the tale.

[144] I cannot agree with Panzer when (p. 319) he suggests the possibility of the *Beowulf* and the *Grettir*-story having been derived independently from the folk-tale. For the two stories have many features in common which do not belong to the folk-tale: apart from the absence of the princesses we have the *hæft-mēce* and the strange conclusion drawn by the watchers from the blood-stained water.

[145] Ipse Scef cum uno dromone advectus est in insula Oceani, quae dicitur Scani, armis circundatus, eratque valde recens puer, & ab incolis illius terrae ignotus; attamen ab eis suscipitur, & ut familiarem diligenti animo eum custodierunt, & post in regem eligunt.

Ethelwerdus, III, 3, in Savile's *Rerum Anglicarum Scriptores post Bedam*, Francofurti, 1601, p. 842.

[146] See Chadwick, *Origin*, 259-60.

[147] Sceldius [fuit filius] Sceaf. Iste, ut ferunt, in quandam insulam Germaniae Scandzam, de qua Jordanes, historiographus Gothorum, loquitur, appulsus navi sine remige, puerulus, posito ad caput frumenti manipulo, dormiens, ideoque Sceaf nuncupatus, ab hominibus regionis illius pro miraculo exceptus et sedulo nutritus: adulta aetate regnavit in oppido quod tunc Slaswic, nunc vero Haithebi appellatur. Est autem regio illa Anglia vetus dicta....

William of Malmesbury, *De Gestis Regum Anglorum*. Lib. II, § 116, vol. I, p. 121, ed. Stubbs, 1887.

[148] Although Saxo Grammaticus has provided some even earlier kings.

[149] Cf. Müllenhoff in *Z.f.d.A.* VII, 413.

[150] In *Grímnismál*, 54, Odin gives *Gautr* as one of his names.

[151] See below.

[152] Excluding, of course, the Hebrew names.

[153] *Scyld* appears as *Scyldwa, Sce(a)ldwa* in the *Chronicle*. The forms correspond.

[154] See Part II.

[155] *armis circundatus.*

[156] For a list of the scholars who have dealt with the subject, see *Widsith*, p. 119.

[157] *Beovulf*, p. 6 *etc.*

[158] *Pub. Mod. Lang. Assoc. Amer.* XXIV, 259 *etc.*

[159] This objection to the Scyld-theory has been excellently expressed by Olrik—at a time, too, when Olrik himself accepted the story as belonging to Scyld rather than Sceaf. "Binz," says Olrik, "rejects William of Malmesbury as a source for the Scyld story. But he has not noticed that in doing so he saws across the branch upon which he himself and the other investigators are sitting. For if William is not a reliable authority, and even a more reliable authority than the others, then 'Scyld with the sheaf' is left in the air." *Heltedigtning*, I, 238-9, note.

[160] The discussion of Skjold by Olrik (*Danmarks Heltedigtning*, I, 223-271) is perhaps the most helpful of any yet made, especially in emphasizing the necessity of differentiating the stages in the story. But it must be taken in connection with the very essential modifications made by Dr Olrik in his second volume (pp. 249-65, especially pp. 264-5). Dr Olrik's earlier interpretation made Scyld the original hero of the story: *Scefing* Olrik interpreted, not as "with the sheaf," but as "son of Scef." To the objection that any knowledge of Scyld's parentage would be inconsistent with his unknown origin, Olrik replied by supposing that Scyld was a foundling whose origin, though unknown to the people of the

land to which he came, was well known to the poet. The poet, Dr Olrik thought, regarded him as a son of the Langobardic king, Sceafa, a connection which we are to attribute to the Anglo-Saxon love of framing genealogies. But this explanation of Scyld Scefing as a human foundling does not seem to me to be borne out by the text of *Beowulf*. "The child is a poor foundling," says Dr Olrik, "*he suffered distress from the time when he was first found as a helpless child.* Only as a grown man did he get compensation for his childhood's adversity" (p. 228). But this is certainly not the meaning of *egsode eorl[as]*. It is "*He inspired the earl[s] with awe.*"

[161] See below (App. C) for instances of ancestral names extant both in weak and strong forms, like *Scyld, Sceldwa* (the identity of which no one doubts) or *Sceaf, Sceafa* (the identity of which has been doubted).

[162] "As for the name *Scyldungas-Skjöldungar*, we need not hesitate to believe that this originally meant 'the people' or 'kinsmen of the shield.' Similar appellations are not uncommon, e.g., *Rondingas, Helmingas, Brondingas* ... probably these names meant either 'the people of *the* shield, *the* helmet,' *etc.*, or else the people who used shields, helmets, *etc.*, in some special way. In the former case we may compare the Ancile of the Romans and the Palladion of the Greeks; in either case we may note that occasionally shields have been found in the North which can never have been used except for ceremonial purposes." Chadwick, *Origin*, p. 284: cf. Olrik, *Heltedigtning*, I, 274.

[163] Sweyn Aageson, *Skiold Danis primum didici praefuisse*, in Langebek, *S.R.D.* I, 44.

[164] Olrik, *Heltedigtning*, I, 246; Lawrence, *Pub. Mod. Lang. Assoc.* XXIV, 254.

[165] It is odd that Binz, who has recorded so many of these, should have argued on the strength of these place-names that the Scyld story is not Danish, but an ancient possession of the tribes of the North Sea coast (p. 150). For Binz also records an immense number of names of heroes of alien stock—Danish, Gothic or Burgundian—as occurring in England (*P.B.B.* XX, 202 *etc.*).

[166] *Beovulf*, p. 7.

[167] Chadwick, *Origin*, p. 278.

[168] The scandals about King Edgar (*infamias quas post dicam magis resperserunt cantilenae*: see *Gesta Regum Anglorum*, II, § 148, ed. Stubbs, vol. I, p. 165); the story of Gunhilda, the daughter of Knut, who, married to a foreign King with great pomp and rejoicing, *nostro seculo etiam in triviis cantitata*, was unjustly suspected of unchastity till her English page, in vindication of her honour, slew the giant whom her accusers had brought forward as their champion (*Gesta*, II, § 188, ed. Stubbs, I, pp. 229, 230); the story of King Edward and the shepherdess, learnt from *cantilenis per successiones temporum detritis* (*Gesta*, II, § 138, ed. Stubbs, I, 155). Macaulay in the *Lays of Ancient Rome* has selected William as a typical example of the historian who draws upon popular song. Cf. Freeman's *Historical Essays*.

[169] Olrik, *Heltedigtning*, I, 245.

[170] *Origin*, pp. 279-281.

[171] Brand, *Popular Antiquities*, 1813, I, 443.

[172] Henderson, *Folklore of the Northern Counties*, 87-89.

[173] Hone's *Every Day Book*, 1827, p. 1170.

[174] *The Tamar and the Tavy*, I. 330 (1836).

[175] Raymond, *Two men o' Mendip*, 1899, 259.

[176] Miss M. A. Courtney, *Glossary of West Cornwall*; T. Q. Couch, *Glossary of East Cornwall*, s. v. Neck (*Eng. Dial. Soc.* 1880); Jago, *Ancient Language of Cornwall*, 1882, s. v. Anek.

[177] *Notes and Queries*, 4th Ser. XII, 491 (1873).

[178] Holland's *Glossary of Chester* (*Eng. Dial. Soc.*), s.v. *Cutting the Neck*.

[179] Burne, *Shropshire Folk Lore*, 1883, 371.

[180] "to cry the Mare." Blount, *Glossographia*, 4th edit. 1674, s.v. *mare*. Cf. *Notes and Queries*, 5th Ser. VI, 286 (1876).

[181] Wright, *Eng. Dial. Dict.*, s.v. *neck*.

[182] Frazer, *Spirits of the Corn*, 1912, I, 268. The word was understood as = "neck" by the peasants, because "They'm taied

up under the chin laike" (*Notes and Queries*, 5th Ser. X, 51). But this may be false etymology.

[183] Wright, *Eng. Dial. Dict.* Cf. *Notes and Queries*, 5th Ser. X, 51.

[184] *Heltedigtning*, II, 252.

[185] The earliest record of the term "cutting the neck" seems to be found in Randle Holme's *Store House of Armory*, 1688 (II, 73). It may be noted that Holme was a Cheshire man.

[186] Mannhardt, *Mythologische Forschungen*, Strassburg, 1884, 326 *etc.*

[187] Quod dum servi Dei propensius actitarent, inspiratum est eis salubre consilium et (ut pium est credere) divinitus provisum. Die etenim statuto mane surgentes monachi sumpserunt scutum rotundum, cui imponebant manipulum frumenti, et super manipulum cereum circumspectae quantitatis et grossitudinis. Quo accenso scutum cum manipulo et cereo, fluvio ecclesiam praetercurrenti committunt, paucis in navicula fratribus subsequentibus. Praecedebat itaque eos scutum et quasi digito demonstrans possessiones domui Abbendoniae de jure adjacentes nunc huc, nunc illuc divertens; nunc in dextra nunc in sinistra parte fiducialiter eos praeibat, usquedum veniret ad rivum prope pratum quod Beri vocatur, in quo cereus medium cursum Tamisiae miraculose deserens se declinavit et circumdedit pratum inter Tamisiam et Gifteleia, quod hieme et multociens aestate ex redundatione Tamisiae in modum insulae aqua circumdatur.

Chronicon Monasterii de Abingdon, ed. Stevenson, 1858, vol. I, p. 89.

[188] Chadwick, *Origin*, 278.

[189] Olrik, *Heltedigtning*, II, 251.

[190] But is this so? "The word Sämpsä (now sämpsykka) 'small rush, *scirpus silvaticus*, forest rush,' is borrowed from the Germanic family (Engl. semse; Germ. simse)." Olrik, 253. But the Engl. "semse" is difficult to track.

See also note by A. Mieler in *Finnisch-Ugrische Forschungen*, X, 43, 1910.

[191] Kaarle Krohn, "Sampsa Pellervoinen" in *Finnisch-Ugrische Forschungen* IV, 231 *etc.*, 1904.

[192] Cf. Olrik, *Heltedigtning*, II, 252 *etc.*.

[193] I do not understand why Olrik (*Heltedigtning*, I, 235) declares the coming to land in Scani (Ethelwerd) to be inconsistent with Sceaf as a Longobardic king (*Widsith*). For, according to their national historian, the Longobardi came from "Scadinavia" [Paul the Deacon, I, 1-7]. It is a more serious difficulty that Paul knows of no Longobardic king with a name which we can equate with Sceaf.

[194] So, corresponding to O.E. *trīewe* we have Icel. *tryggr*; to O.E. *glēaw*, Icel. *glǫggr*; O.E. *scūwa*, Icel. *skugg-*.

[195] Olrik, *Heltedigtning*, II, 1910, pp. 254-5.

An account of the worship of Pekko will be found in *Finnisch-Ugrische Forschungen*, VI, 1906, pp. 104-111: *Über den Pekokultus bei den Setukesen*, by M. J. Eisen. See also Appendix (A) below.

Pellon-Pecko is mentioned by Michael Agricola, Bishop of Åbo, in his translation of the Psalter into Finnish, 1551. It is here that we are told that he "promoted the growth of barley."

[196] l. 15.

[197] That Heremod is a Danish king is clear from ll. 1709 *etc.* And as we have all the stages in the Scylding genealogy from Scyld to Hrothgar, Heremod must be placed earlier.

[198] Of Grein in *Eberts Jahrbuch*, IV, 264.

[199] A good example of this is supplied by the Assyrian records, which make Jehu a son of Omri—whose family he had destroyed.

[200] This reconstruction is made by Sievers in the *Berichte d. k. sächs. Gesellschaft der Wissenschaften*, 1895, pp. 180-88.

[201] The god *Hermóðr* who rides to Hell to carry a message to the dead Baldr is here left out of consideration. His connection with the king *Hermóðr* is obscure.

[202] On this see Dederich, *Historische u. geographische Studien*, 214; Heinzel in *A.f.d.A.* XV, 161; Chadwick, *Origin*, 148; Chadwick, *Cult of Othin*, 51.

[203] Chadwick, *Cult of Othin*, pp. 50, *etc.*

[204] *puerulus ... pro miraculo exceptus* (William of Malmesbury). Cf. *Beowulf*, l. 7. In Saxo, Skjold distinguishes himself at the age of fifteen.

[205] *omnem Alemannorum gentem tributaria ditione perdomuit.* Cf. *Beowulf*, l. 11.

[206] See above, p. 77.

[207] This relationship of Frothi and Skjold is preserved by Sweyn Aageson: Skiold Danis primum didici praefuisse.... A quo primum.... Skioldunger sunt Reges nuncupati. Qui regni post se reliquit haeredes Frothi videlicet & Haldanum. Svenonis Aggonis *Hist. Regum Dan.* in Langebek, *S.R.D.* I, 44.

In Saxo Frotho is not the son, but the great grandson of Skioldus—but this is a discrepancy which may be neglected, because it seems clear that the difference is due to Saxo having inserted two names into the line at this point—those of Gram and Hadding. There seems no reason to doubt that Danish tradition really represented Frothi as son of Skjold.

[208] Those who accept the identification would regard *Fróði* (O.E. *Frōda*, 'the wise') as a title which has ousted the proper name.

[209] Boer, *Ark. f. nord. filol.*, XIX, 67, calls this theory of Sievers "indisputable."

[210] Sievers, p. 181.

[211] *Beowulf*, 2405. Cf. 2215, 2281.

[212] So Regin guides Sigurd: Una the Red Cross Knight. The list might be indefinitely extended. Similarly with giants: "Then came to him a husbandman of the country, and told him how there was in the country of Constantine, beside Brittany, a great giant".... *Morte d'Arthur*, Book V, cap. V.

[213] *Beowulf*, 895.

[214] l. 2338.

[215] ll. 2570 *etc.*

[216] intrepidum mentis habitum retinere memento.

[217] ll. 2663 *etc.*

[218] Cf. *Beowulf*, 2705: *forwrāt Wedra helm wyrm on middan.*

[219] Cf. *Cotton. Gnomic verses*, ll. 26-7: *Draca sceal on hlǣwe: frōd, frætwum wlanc.*

[220] virusque profundens: *wearp wæl-fȳre*, 2582.

[221]
implicitus gyris serpens crebrisque reflexus
orbibus et caudae sinuosa volumina ducens
multiplicesque agitans spiras.

Cf. *Beowulf*, 2567-8, 2569, 2561 (*hring-boga*), 2827 (*wōhbogen*).

[222] *Volospá*, 172-3 in *Corpus Poeticum Boreale*. I, 200.

[223] Cf. on this Olrik, *Heltedigtning*, I, 305-15.

[224] Panzer, *Beowulf*, 313.

[225] A further and more specific parallel between Lotherus and Heremod has been pointed out by Sarrazin (*Anglia*, XIX, 392). It seems from *Beowulf* that Heremod went into exile (ll. 1714-15), and apparently *mid Eotenum* (l. 902) which (in view of the use of the word *Eotena, Eotenum*, in the *Finnsburg* episode) very probably means "among the Jutes." A late Scandinavian document tells us that *Lotherus ... superatus in Jutiam profugit* (Messenius, *Scondia illustrata*, printed 1700, but written about 1620).

[226] Pointed out by Panzer. A possible parallel to the old man who hides his treasure is discussed by Bugge and Olrik in *Dania*, I, 233-245 (1890-92).

[227] Cf. Ettmüller, *Scopas and Boceras*, 1850, p. ix; *Carmen de Beovvulfi rebus gestis*, 1875, p. iii.

[228] *P.B.B.* XI, 167-170.

[229] Sarrazin, *Der Schauplatz des ersten Beowulfliedes* (*P.B.B.* XI, 170 *etc.*); Sievers, *Die Heimat des Beowulfdichters* (*P.B.B.* XI, 354 *etc.*); Sarrazin, *Altnordisches im Beowulfliede* (*P.B.B.* XI, 528 *etc.*); Sievers, *Altnordisches im Beowulf?* (*P.B.B.* XII, 168 *etc.*)

[230] *Beovulf-Studien*, 68.

[231] Sarrazin has countered this argument by urging that since the present day Swedes and Danes have better manners than the English, they therefore presumably had better manners already in the eighth century. I admit the premises, but deny the deduction.

[232] Sedgefield, *Beowulf* (1st ed.), p. 27.

[233] Schück, *Studier i Beovulfsagan*, 41.

[234] The brief *Fata Apostolorum* is doubted by Sievers (*Anglia*, XIII, 24).

[235] Two of these occur twice: *hātan heolfre*, 1423, 849; *nīowan stefne*, 1789, 2594; the rest once only, 141, 561, 963, 977, 1104, 1502, 1505, 1542, 1746, 2102, 2290, 2347, 2440, 2482, 2492, 2692. See Barnouw, 51.

[236] 74, 99, 122, 257, 390, 412.

[237] *Christ*, 510.

[238] Lichtenheld omits 2011, *se mǣra mago Healfdenes*, inserting instead 1474, where the same phrase occurs, but with a vocative force.

[239] 758, 813, 2011, 2587, 2928, 2971, 2977, 3120.

[240] 1199.

[241] 102, 713, 919, 997, 1016, 1448, 1984, 2255, 2264, 2675, 3024, 3028, 3097.

[242] Saintsbury in *Short History of English Literature*, I. 3.

[243] Morsbach, 270.

[244] Morsbach, 271.

[245] Chadwick, *Heroic Age*, 4.

[246] "Thus in place of the expression *to widan feore* we find occasionally *widan feore* in the same sense, and even in *Beowulf* we meet with *widan feorh*, which is not improbably the oldest form of the phrase. Before the loss of the final *-u* it [*widan feorhu*] would be a perfectly regular half verse, but the operation of this change would render it impossible and necessitate the substitution of a synonymous expression. In principle, it should be observed, the

assumption of such substitutions seems to be absolutely necessary, unless we are prepared to deny that any old poems or even verses survived the period of apocope." Chadwick, *Heroic Age*, pp. 46-7.

[247] *Heroic Age*, 46.

[248] Birch, *Cart. Sax.* No. 81. See Morsbach, 260.

[249] The most important examples being *breguntford* (Birch, *Cart. Sax.* No. 115, dating between 693 and 731; perhaps 705): *heffled* in the life of St Gregory written by a Whitby monk apparently before 713: *-gar* on the Bewcastle Column, earlier than the end of the first quarter of the eighth century and perhaps much earlier: and many names in *ford* and *feld* in the Moore MS of Bede's *Ecclesiastical History* (a MS written about 737).

[250] An English Miscellany presented to Dr Furnivall, 370.

[251] Grienberger, *Anglia*, XXVII, 448.

[252] i.e. *flodu ahof* might stand for *flōd u[p] ǎhōf*, as is suggested by Chadwick, *Heroic Age*, 69.

[253] In the Franks casket *b* already appears as *f*, and the *n* of *sefu*, "seven," has been lost.

[254] Birch, *Cart. Sax.* No. 45.

[255] Chadwick, *Heroic Age*, 67: "In personal names we must clearly allow for traditional orthography." Morsbach admits this in another connection (p. 259).

[256] Lübke's preface to Müllenhoff's *Beovulf*. Both the tendencies specially associated with Müllenhoff's name—the "mythologizing" and the "dissecting"—are due to the influence of Lachmann. It must be frankly admitted that on these subjects Müllenhoff did not begin his studies with an open mind.

[257] "Es ist einfach genug"—*Beovulf*, 110.

[258] Möller, *V.E.* 140: cf. Schücking, *B.R.* 14.

[259] Earle, *Deeds of Beowulf*, xlix (an excellent criticism of Müllenhoff).

[260] Heusler, *Lied u. Epos*, 26.

[261] *Epic and Romance*, Chap. II, § 2.

[262] *Ballad and Epic*, 311-12.

[263] *Beowulfs Rückkehr*, 1905.

[264] e.g. *Genesis*.

[265] Chap. IV, pp. 29-33.

[266] Chap. V, pp. 34-41.

[267] Chap. VI, cf. esp. p. 50.

[268] In the portion which Schücking excludes, we twice have *gǣð* = *gāið* (2034, 2055). Elsewhere in the *Return* we have *dōn* = *dōan* (2166) whilst *frēa* (1934), *Hondsciō* (2076) need to be considered.

[269] 2069.

[270] 2093.

[271] *Satzverknüpfung im Beowulf*, 139.

[272] *Þȳlǣs* = "lest" (1918); *ac* in direct question (1990); *þā* occurring unsupported late in the sentence (2192); *forþām* (1957) [see Sievers in *P.B.B.* XXIX, 313]; *swā* = "since," "because" (2184). But Schücking admits in his edition two other instances of *forþām* (146 and 2645), so this can hardly count.

[273] *hȳrde ic* as introducing a statement, 62, 2163, 2172; *sið ðan ǣrest*, 6, 1947.

[274] A similar use of *þā*, 1078, 1988; cf. 1114, 1125, 2135.

[275] *hæbbe*, 1928; *gēong*, 2019.

[276] *þurfe*, 2495.

[277] Schücking, Chap. VIII.

[278] Cf. Brandl in Herrigs *Archiv*, CXV, 421 (1905).

[279] e.g. Blackburn in *Pub. Mod. Lang. Assoc. Amer.* XII, 204-225; Bradley in the *Encyc. Brit.* III, 760; Chadwick, *H.A.* 49; Clarke, *Sidelights*, 10.

[280] Chadwick, in *Cambridge History*, I, 30.

[281] We may refer especially to the account of Attila's funeral given by Jordanes. [Mr Chadwick's note.]

[282] Chadwick in *The Heroic Age*, 53.

[283] It is adopted, e.g., by Clarke, *Sidelights*, 8.

[284] Yet this is very doubtful: see Leeds, *Archæology*, 27, 74.

[285] Notably in Book VIII (ed. Holder, 264) and Book III (ed. Holder, 74).

[286] 'Fasta fornlämningar i Beowulf,' in *Ant. Tidskrift för Sverige*, XVIII, 4, 64.

[287] See Schücking, *Das angelsächsische Totenklaglied*, in *Engl. Stud.* XXXIX, 1-13.

[288] Blackburn, in *Pub. Mod. Lang. Assoc. Amer.* Cf. Hart, *Ballad and Epic*, 175.

[289] Clark Hall, xlvii.

[290] Blackburn, as above, p. 126.

[291] Chadwick, in *Cambridge History*, I, 30.

[292] Clark Hall, xlvii. See, to the contrary, Klaeber in *Anglia*, XXXVI, 196.

[293] This point is fully developed by Brandl, 1002-3. As Brandl points out, if we want to find a parallel to the hero Beowulf, saving his people from their temporal and ghostly foes, we must look, not to the other heroes of Old English heroic poetry, such as Waldhere or Hengest, but to Moses in the Old English *Exodus*. [Since this was written the essentially Christian character of *Beowulf* has been further, and I think finally, demonstrated by Klaeber, in the last section of his article on *Die Christlichen Elemente im Beowulf*, in *Anglia*, XXXVI; see especially 194-199.]

[294] Cf. *Beowulf*, ll. 180 *etc.*

[295] Bradley, in *Encyc. Brit.*

[296] Bradley, in *Encyc. Brit.* III, 760-1.

[297] Blackburn, 218.

[298] See Finnur Jónsson, *Den Norsk-Islandske Skjaldedigtning*, B. ii. 473-4.

[299] MS A, followed by Magnússon, makes Glam *bláeygðr*, "blue-eyed": Boer reads *gráeygðr*, considering grey a more uncanny colour.

[300] MS A has *fonᵐ* or *fenᵐ*, it is difficult to tell which. Magnússon reads *fenum*, "morasses."

[301] Immediately inside the door of the Icelandic dwelling was the *anddyri* or vestibule. For want of a better word, I translate *anddyri* by "porch": but it is a porch inside the building. Opening out of this 'porch' were a number of rooms. Chief among which were the *skáli* or "hall," and the *stufa* or "sitting room," the latter reached by a passage (*gǫng*). These were separated from the "porch" by panelling. In the struggle with Glam, Grettir is lying in the hall (*skáli*), but the panelling has all been broken away from the great cross-beam to which it was fixed. Grettir consequently sees Glam enter the outer door; Glam turns to the *skáli*, and glares down it, leaning over the cross-beam; then enters the hall, and the struggle begins. See Guðmundssen (V.), *Privatbolegen på Island i Sagatiden*, 1889.

[302] The partition beams (*set-stokkar*) stood between the middle of the *skáli* or hall and the planked daïs which ran down each side. The strength of the combatants is such that the *stokkar* give way. Grettir gets no footing to withstand Glam till they reach the outer-door. Here there is a stone set in the ground, which apparently gives a better footing for a push than for a pull. So Grettir changes his tactics, gets a purchase on the stone, and at the same time pushes against Glam's breast, and so dashes Glam's head and shoulders against the lintel of the outer-door.

[303] So MS 551 *a*. Magnússon reads *dvaldist þar* "he stayed there."

[304] Meaning that an attack by the evil beings would at least break the monotony.

[305] A passage (*gǫng*) had to be traversed between the door of the room (*stufa*) and the porch (*anddyri*).

[306] MSS *bælt*. Boer reads *bolat* "hewn down."

[307] A night troll, if caught by the sunrise, was supposed to turn into stone.

[308] *Skúta* may be acc. of the noun *skúti*, "overhanging precipice, cave"; or it may be the verb, "hang over." Grettir and his companion see that the sides of the ravine are precipitous (*skúta upp*) and so clean-cut (*meitil-berg: meitill*, "a chisel") that they give no hold to the climber. Hence the need for the rope. The translators all take *skúta* as acc. of *skúti*, which is quite possible: but they are surely wrong when they proceed to identify the *skúti* with the *hellir* behind the waterfall. For this cave behind the waterfall is introduced in the *saga* as something which Grettir discovers *after* he has dived beneath the fall, the fall in front naturally hiding it till then.

The verb *skúta* occurs elsewhere in *Grettis saga*, of the glaciers overhanging a valley. Boer's attempt to reconstruct the scene appears to me wrong: cf. Ranisch in *A.f.d.A.* XXVIII, 217.

[309] The old editions read *fimm tigir faðma* "fifty fathoms": but according to Boer's collation the best MS (A) read X, whilst four of the five others collated give XV (*fimtán*). The editors seem dissatisfied with this: yet sixty to ninety feet seems a good enough height for a dive.

[310] *ok sat þar hjá*, not in MS A, nor in Boer's edition.

[311] The two poems are given according to the version of William Morris.

[312] On his first arrival at Leire, Bjarki had been attacked by, and had slain, the watch-dogs (*Rímur*, IV, 41): this naturally brings him now into disfavour, and he has to dispute with men.

[313] Reading *kappana*.

[314] The MSS have either *Sandeyar* or *Saudeyar* (*Sauðeyar*). But that *Sandeyar* is the correct form is shown by the name Sandø, which is given still to the island of Dollsey, where Orm's fight is localized (Panzer, 403).

[315] Literally "she-cat," *ketta*; but the word may mean "giantess." It is used in some MSS of the *Grettis saga* of the giantess who attacks Grettir at Sandhaugar.

[316] See Sweet, *Oldest English Texts*, 1885, p. 170.

[317] See *Catalogue of MSS. in the Library of Corpus Christi College, Cambridge* by Montague Rhodes James, Camb., 1912, p. 437.

[318] See *Publications of the Palæographical Society*, 1880, where a facsimile of part of the *Vespasian MS* is given. (Pt. 10, Plate 165: subsequently Ser. I, Vol. II.)

[319] So Zimmer, *Nennius Vindicatus*, Berlin, 1893, pp. 78 etc., and Duchesne (*Revue Celtique*, XV, 196). Duchesne sums up these genealogies as "un recueil constitué, vers la fin du VIIe siècle, dans le royaume de Strathcluyd, mais complété par diverses retouches, dont la dernière est de 796."

[320] This is shown by one of the supplementary Mercian pedigrees being made to end, both in the *Vespasian* genealogy and the *Historia Brittonum*, in Ecgfrith, who reigned for a few months in 796. See Thurneysen (*Z.f.d.Ph.* XXVIII, 101).

[321] Ed. Mommsen, p. 203.

[322] Anno 626: a similar genealogy will be found in these MSS and in the Parker MS, anno 755 (accession of Offa II).

[323] Zimmer (*Nennius Vindicatus*, p. 84) argues that this *Geta-Woden* pedigree belongs to a portion of the *Historia Brittonum* written down A.D. 685. Thurneysen (*Z.f.d.Ph.* XXVIII, 103-4) dates the section in which it occurs 679; Duchesne (*Revue Celtique*, XV, 196) places it more vaguely between the end of the sixth and the beginning of the eighth century; van Hamel (*Hoops Reallexikon* s.v. *Nennius*) between much the same limits, and clearly before 705.

[324] Zimmer (p. 275) says A.D. 796; Duchesne (p. 196) A.D. 800; Thurneysen (*Zeitschr. f. Celtische Philologie*, I, 166) A.D. 826; Skene (*Four Ancient Books of Wales*, 1868, I, 38) A.D. 858; van Hamel (p. 304) A.D. 820-859. See also Chadwick, *Origin*, 38.

[325] Bradshaw, *Investigations among Early Welsh, Breton and Cornish MSS. in Collected Papers*, 466.

[326] See above, p. 196.

[327] Cf. *Bretwalda*.

[328] The genealogies have recently been dealt with by E. Hackenberg, *Die Stammtafeln der angelsächsischen Königreiche*, Berlin,

1918; and by Brandl, (Herrig's *Archiv*, CXXXVII, 1-24). Most of Brandl's derivations seem to me to depend upon very perilous conjectures. Thus he derives *Scēfing* from the Gr.-Lat. *scapha*, "a skiff": a word which was not adopted into Old English. This seems to be sacrificing all probability to the desire to find a new interpretation: and, even so, it is not quite successful. For Riley in the *Gentleman's Magazine*, August, 1857, p. 126, suggested the derivation of the name of Scef from the *schiff* or *skiff* in which he came.

[329] For a list of the Icelandic versions, see Heusler, *Die gelehrte Urgeschichte im altisländischen Schrifttum*, pp. 18-19, in the *Abhandlungen d. preuss. Akad., Phil. Hist. Klasse*, 1908, Berlin.

[330] The names are given as in the Trinity Roll (T), collated with Corpus (C) and Moseley (M). For Paris (P) I follow Kemble's report (*Postscript to Preface*, 1837, pp. vii, viii: *Stammtafel der Westsachsen*, pp. 18, 31). All seem to agree in writing *t* for *c* in Steph and Steldius, and in Boerinus, *obviously, as Kemble pointed out, r is written by error for p = Beowinus* [or *Beowius*]; Cinrinicius T, Cinrinicus C, Cininicus P, Siuruncius M; Suethedus TCP, Suechedius M; Gethius T, Thecius M, Ehecius CP; Geate T, Geathe CM, Geathus P.

[331] I follow the spelling of the Moseley roll in this note.

[332] *Dacia* = "Denmark": *Dacia* and *Dania* were identified.

[333] *uocabitur*, Gertz; *uocatur*, all MSS.

[334] This account of the peaceful reign of Ro is simply false etymology from Danish *ro*, "rest."

[335] Note that Ro (Hrothgar), the son of Haldanus (Healfdene), is here represented as his father. Saxo Grammaticus, combining divergent accounts, as he often does, accordingly mentions two Roes—one the brother of Haldanus, the other his son. See above, pp. 131-2.

[336] *cum piratica classe*, Langebek; the MSS have *cum pietate* (!) with or without *classe*.

[337] *post quem*, Holder-Egger, Gertz; *postquam*, all MSS.

[338] Snyo: the viceroy whom Athisl had placed over the Danes.

[339] *in* added by Gertz; omitted in all MSS.

[340] A scribal error for *transalbinas*, "beyond the Elbe."

[341] Assembly.

[342] Island.

[343] I have substituted *u* for *v*, and have abandoned spellings like *theutones, thezauro, orrifico, charitas, phas* (for *fas*), *atlethas, choercuit, iocundum, charum, fœlicissima, nanque, hœreditarii, exoluere.*

The actual reading of the 1514 text is abandoned by substituting: p. 130, l. 3 *ingeniti* for *ingenitis* (1514); p. 132, l. 22, *iacientis* for *iacentis*; p. 134, l. 2, *diutinæ* for *diutiuæ*; p. 136, l. 11, *fudit* for *fugit*; p. 136, l. 20, *ut* for *aut*; p. 137, l. 8, *ammirationi* for *ammirationis*; p. 137, l. 16, *offert* for *affert*; p. 137, l. 17, *Roluoni* for *Rouolni*; p. 137, l. 27, *ministerio* for *ministros*; p. 137, l. 33 *diuturnus* for *diuturnius*; p. 206, l. 22, *diutinam* for *diutina*; p. 207, l. 3, *ei* for *eique*; p. 207, l. 5, *destituat* for *deficiat*; p. 209, l. 2, *latere* for *latera*; p. 209, l. 5, *conscisci* for *concissi*; p. 209, l. 14, *defoderat* for *defodera.*

[344] *Above this heading* B *has* Gesta Offe Regis mercior*um*.

[345] A *repeats* sibi *after* constitueret.

[346] Hic Riganus binomin[i]s fuit. Vocabat*ur* eni*m* alio nomine Aliel. Rigan*us* ue*r*o a rigore. Huic erat fili*us* Hildebrand*us*, miles strenuus, ab ense sic d*ic*t*us*. Hu*n*c uoluit pat*er* p*r*omouere: *Contemporary rubric in* A, *inserted in the middle of the sketch representing Riganus demanding the kingdom from Warmundus.*

[347] optat, B.

[348] celebri, B; celibri, A.

[349] hoc, B.

[350] ueheement*er*, A.

[351] ueheementi, A.

[352] eciam, B.

[353] *Added in margin in* A; *not in* B.

[354] hec *omitted*, B.

[355] *Added in margin in* A; *not in* B.

[356] dereliquerunt, B.

[357] precipue *omitted,* B.

[358] ei *omitted,* B.

[359] Qualmhul *vel* Qualmweld *in margin,* A.

[360] planies, A: planicies, *perhaps corrected from* planies, B.

[361] blodifeld, B.

[362] Gloria triumphi, *in margin,* A.

[363] tripudium, B; tripuduum, A.

[364] scis, A, B.

[365] menbra, A.

[366] gracias, B.

[367] hosstibus, A.

[368] romotis, A.

[369] congnouerunt, A.

[370] Warmandi, A.

[371] habenas *repeated after* regni *above in* A, *but cancelled in* B.

[372] exaggeret, B.

[373] pulcritudinis, B; pulchritudini, A.

[374] ingnota, A.

[375] euuangelii, B.

[376] consingnatas, A.

[377] *from* B, *written over erasure.*

[378] scribitur, B.

[379] Epistola, *in margin,* A.

[380] in*co*ngnita, A.

[381] dicebant, B.

[382] frustratim, A, B.

[383] ossium, B.

[384] co*n*gnouit, A.

[385] hoc *omitted,* B.

[386] co*n*gnic*i*one, A.

[387] sui, A.

[388] obtemp*er*are, B.

[389] menbra, A.

[390] qui, AB; quae, Wats.

[391] reco*n*gnosce, A.

[392] sancte *et* dulcissime, B.

[393] ut *added above line,* A, B.

[394] scenobium, A; *the* s*i* s *erased in* B.

[395] deo, B

[396] tuinfreth, B.

[397] scenobio, A; s *erased* B.

[398] de tiran*n*ide Beormredi reg*is* Mercie, B.

[399] fecerat, *wanting in* A; *added in margin,* B.

[400] Pinefredum, B; Penefredum, A, *but with* i *above in first case.*

[401] uariis *repeated,* A; *second* variis *cancelled,* B.

[402] considerans, B, *inserted in margin; omitted,* A.

[403] Marcelline, A; Marcell, B.

[404] vixisset, B, *inserted in margin; omitted,* A.

[405] Alberto, *etc. passim*, B.

[406] virtutibus, *in margin, later hand,* A; *in* B, *over erasure.*

[407] est *in margin,* A.

[408] et *omitted,* B.

[409] innotuerunt, B.

[410] in pietatis manu, B.

[411] præmissimis, A.

[412] sinistrum, B.

[413] quam *in margin,* A; *over erasure,* B.

[414] *Space for cap. left vacant,* A.

[415] aucmentu*m*, A.

[416] facinoris, B.

[417] co*n*gnouit, A.

[418] celeriter, B.

[419] cum *in* A *is inserted after* peruenisse*t, instead of before: and this was probably the original reading in* B, *although subsequently corrected.*

[420] *per,* B.

[421] *corrected to* nullaten*us* dormire quasi suspecta*m* pe*r*misit, B.

[422] Justa Vindicta, A, *in margin.*

[423] Mr Mackie, in an excellent article on the *Fragment* (*J.E.G.Ph.* XVI, 251) objects that my criticism of Hickes' accuracy "is not altogether judicial." Mackie urges that, since the MS is no longer extant, we cannot tell how far the errors are due to Hickes, and how far they already existed in the MS from which Hickes copied.

But we must not forget that there are other transcripts by Hickes, of MSS which *are* still extant, and from these we can estimate his accuracy. It is no disrespect to the memory of Hickes, a scholar to whom we are all indebted, to recognize frankly that his transcripts are not sufficiently accurate to make them at all a satisfactory substitute for the original MS. Hickes' transcript of the *Cottonian Gnomic Verses* (*Thesaurus*, I, 207) shows an average of one error in every four lines: about half these errors are mere matters of spelling, the others are serious. Hickes' transcript of the *Calendar* (*Thesaurus*, I, 203) shows an average of one error in every six lines. When, therefore, we find in the *Finnsburg Fragment* inaccuracies of exactly the type which Hickes often commits, it would be "hardly judicial" to attribute these to the MS which he copied, and to attribute to Hickes in this particular instance an accuracy to which he has really no claim.

Mr Mackie doubts the legitimacy of emending *Garulf* to *Garulf[e]*: but we must remember that Hickes (or his printer) was systematically careless as to the final *e*: cf. *Calendar*, 15, 23, 41, 141, 144, 171, 210; *Gnomic Verses*, 45. Other forms in the *Finnsburg Fragment* which can be easily paralleled by Hickes' miswritings in the *Calendar* and *Gnomic Verses* are

Confusion of *u* and *a* (*Finn.* 3, 27, perhaps 44) cf. *Gn.* 66.
    "   " *c* " *e* (*Finn.* 12) cf. *Cal.* 136, *Gn.* 44.
    "   " *e* " *æ* (*Finn.* 41) cf. *Cal.* 44, 73, *Gn.* 44.
    "   " *e* " *a* (*Finn.* 22) cf. *Cal.* 74.
    "   " *eo* " *ea* (*Finn.* 28) cf. *Cal.* 121.
    "   " letters involving long down stroke, e.g., *f, s, r, þ, w,* þ
(*Finn.* 2, 36) cf. *Cal.* 97, 142, 180, 181, *Gn.* 9.
Addition of *n* (*Finn.* 22) cf. *Cal.* 161.

[424] *Heimskringla*, chap. 220.

[425] It has been suggested that the phrase "Hengest himself" indicates that Hengest is the "war-young king." But surely the expression merely marks Hengest out as a person of special interest. If we *must* assume that he is one of the people who have been speaking, then it would be just as natural to identify him with the watcher who has warned the king, as with the king himself. The difficulties which prevent us from identifying Hengest with the king are explained below.

[426] Garulf must be an assailant, since he falls at the beginning of the struggle, whilst we are told that for five days none of the defenders fell.

[427] Very possibly Guthere is uncle of Garulf. For Garulf is said to be son of Guthlaf (l. 35) and a *Guth*ere would be likely to be a brother of a *Guth*laf. Further, as Klaeber points out (*Engl. Stud.* XXXIX, 307) it is the part of the uncle to protect and advise the nephew.

[428] Koegel, *Geschichte d. deut. Litt.* I, i, 165.

[429] Klaeber (*Engl. Stud.* XXXIX, 308) reminds us that, as there are two warriors named Godric in the *Battle of Maldon* (l. 325), so there may be two warriors named Guthlaf here. But to this it might possibly be replied that "Godric" was, in England, an exceedingly common name, "Guthlaf" an exceedingly rare one.

[430] Finn is called the *bana*, "slayer" of Hnæf. But this does not necessarily mean that he slew him with his own hand; it would be enough if he were in command of the assailants at the time when Hnæf was slain. Cf. *Beowulf,* l. 1968.

[431] The idea that Finn's Frisians are the "North Frisians" of Schleswig has been supported by Grein (*Eberts Jahrbuch*, IV, 270) and, following him, by many scholars, including recently Sedgefield (*Beowulf*, p. 258). The difficulties of this view are very many: one only need be emphasized. We first hear of these North Frisians of Schleswig in the 12th century, and Saxo Grammaticus tells us expressly that they were a colony from the greater Frisia (Book XIV, ed. Holder, p. 465). At what date this colony was founded we do not know. The latter part of the 9th century has been suggested by Langhans: so has the end of the 11th century by Lauridsen. However this may be, all the evidence precludes our supposing this North Friesland, or, as Saxo calls it, Fresia Minor, to have existed at the date to which we must attribute the origin of the Finn story. On this point the following should be consulted: Langhans (V.), *Ueber den Ursprung der Nordfriesen*, Wien, 1879 (most valuable on account of its citation of documents: the latter part of the book, which consists of an attempt to rewrite the Finn story by dismissing as corrupt or spurious many of the data, must not blind us to the value of the earlier portions): Lauridsen, *Om Nordfrisernes Indvandring i Sønderjylland, Historisk Tidsskrift*, 6 R, 4 B. II, 318-67, Kjøbenhavn, 1893: Siebs, *Zur Geschichte der Englisch-Friesischen Sprache*, 1889, 23-6: Chadwick, *Origin*, 94: Much in *Hoops Reallexikon*, s.v. *Friesen*; and Bremer in *Pauls Grdr.* (2), III, 848, where references will be found to earlier essays on the subject.

[432] The theory that Hnæf is a captain of Healfdene is based upon a rendering of l. 1064 which is in all probability wrong.

[433] The view that the *Eotenas* are the men of Hnæf and Hengest has been held by Thorpe (*Beowulf*, pp. 76-7), Ettmüller (*Beowulf*, 1840, p. 108), Bouterwek (*Germania*, I, 389), Holtzmann (*Germania*, VIII, 492), Möller (*Volksepos*, 94-5), Chadwick (*Origin*, 53), Clarke (*Sidelights*, 184).

[434] "And therefore, said the King ... much more I am sorrier for my good knights' loss, than for the loss of my fair queen. For queens I might have enow: but such a fellowship of good knights shall never be together in no company." Malory, *Morte Darthur*, Bk. XX, chap. ix.

[435] The argument of Bugge (*P.B.B.* XII, 37) that the Eotens here (l. 1088) must be the Frisians, is inconclusive: but so is Miss Clarke's argument that they must be Danes (*Sidelights*, 181), as is shown by Lawrence (*Pub. Mod. Lang. Assoc. Amer.* XXX, 395).

[436] I say "son" in what follows, without prejudice to the possibility of more than one son having fallen. It in no wise affects the argument.

[437] For example, it might well be said of Achilles, whilst thirsting for vengeance upon the Trojans for the death of Patroclus, that "he could not get the children of the Trojans out of his mind." But surely it would be unintelligible to say that "he could not get the child of the Achaeans out of his mind," meaning Patroclus, for "child of the Achaeans" is not sufficiently distinctive to denote Patroclus. Cf. Boer in *Z.f.d.A.* XLVII, 134.

[438] In the *Skjoldunga Saga* [extant in a Latin abstract by Arngrim Jonsson, ed. Olrik, 1894], cap. IV, mention is made of a king of Denmark named Leifus who had six sons, three of whom are named Hunleifus, Oddleifus and Gunnleifus—corresponding exactly to O.E. *Hūnlāf*, *Ordlāf* and *Gūðlāf*. That Hunlaf was well known in English story is proved by a remarkable passage unearthed by Dr Imelmann from *MS Cotton Vesp. D. IV* (fol. 139 *b*) where Hunlaf is mentioned together with a number of other heroes of Old English story—Wugda, Hama, Hrothulf, Hengest, Horsa (*Hoc testantur gesta rudolphi et hunlapi, Unwini et Widie, horsi et hengisti, Waltef et hame*). See Chadwick, *Origin*, 52: R. Huchon, *Revue Germanique*, III, 626: Imelmann, in *D.L.Z.* XXX, 999: April, 1909. This disposes of the translation "Hun thrust or placed in his

bosom Lafing, best of swords," which was adopted by Bugge (*P.B.B.* XII, 33), Holder, ten Brink and Gering. Hun is mentioned in *Widsith* (1. 33) and in the Icelandic *Thulor.*

That Guthlaf, Ordlaf and Hunlaf must be connected together had been noted by Boer (*Z.f.d.A.* XLVII, 139) before this discovery of Chadwick's confirmed him.

[439] The fragment which tells of the fighting in the hall is so imperfect that there is nothing impossible in the assumption, though it is too hazardous to make it.

[440] Cf. *Beowulf,* ll. 1900 *etc.*

[441] *Das Altenglische Volksepos,* 46-99.

[442] C. P. Hansen, *Uald' Söld'ring tialen,* Møgeltønder, 1858. See Möller, *Volksepos,* 75 *etc.*

[443] See Müllenhoff in *A.f.d.A.* VI, 86.

[444] So Möller, *Volksepos,* 152.

[445] See *Beowulf,* ed. Wyatt, 1894, p. 145.

[446] *Volksepos,* 71 *etc.*

[447] e.g., Sedgefield, *Beowulf,* 2nd ed., p. 258. So 1st ed., p. 13 (*Hoc* being an obvious misprint).

[448] On the poet's use of plural for singular here, see Osthoff, *I.F.* XX, 202-7.

[449] I have thought it necessary to give fully the reasons why Möller's view cannot be accepted, because in whole or in part it is still widely followed in England. Chadwick (*Origin,* 53) still interprets "Eotens" as "Danes"; and Sedgefield (*Beowulf* (2), p. 258) gives Möller's view the place of honour.

[450] The treachery of Finn is emphasized, for example, by Bugge (*P.B.B.* XII, 36), Koegel (*Geschichte d. deut. Litt.* 164), ten Brink (*Pauls Grdr.* (1), II, 545), Trautmann (*Finn und Hildebrand,* 59), Lawrence (*Pub. Mod. Lang. Assoc. Amer.* XXX, 397, 430), Ayres (*J.E.G.Ph.* XVI, 290).

[451]
syþðan morgen cōm

ðā hēo under swegle gesēon meahte, *etc.*

[452] l. 36. The swords flash *swylce eal Finnsburuh fȳrenu wǣre*, "as if all Finnsburg were afire." I think we may safely argue from this that the swords are flashing near Finnsburg. It would be just conceivable that the poet's mind travels back from the scene of the battle to Finn's distant home: "the swords made as great a flash as would have been made had Finn's distant capital been aflame": but this is a weak and forced interpretation, which we have no right to assume, though it may be conceivable.

[453] *Beowulf,* ll. 1125-7. I doubt whether it is possible to explain the difficulty away by supposing that "the warriors departing to see Friesland, their homes and their head-town" simply means that Finn's men, "summoned by Finn in preparation for the encounter with the Danes, return to their respective homes in the country," and that "*hēaburh* is a high sounding epic term that should not be pressed." This is the explanation offered by Klaeber (*J.E.G.Ph.* VI, 193) and endorsed by Lawrence (*Pub. Mod. Lang. Assoc. Amer.* XXX, 401). But it seems to me taking a liberty with the text to interpret *hēaburh* (singular) as the "respective homes in the country" to which Finn's warriors resort on demobilisation. And the statement of ll. 1125-7, that the warriors departed from the place of combat to see Friesland, seems to necessitate that such place of combat was not in Friesland. Klaeber objects to this (surely obvious) inference: "If we are to infer [from ll. 1125-7] that Finnsburg lies outside Friesland proper, we might as well conclude that *Dyflen* (Dublin) is not situated in Ireland according to the *Battle of Brunanburh (gewitan him þā Norðmenn ... Dyflen sēcan and eft Īraland).*" But how could anyone infer this from the *Brunanburh* lines? What we *are* justified in inferring, is, surely, that the *site of the battle of Brunanburh* (from which the Northmen departed to visit Ireland and Dublin) was not identical with Dublin, and did not lie in Ireland. And by exact parity of reason, we are justified in arguing that Finnsburg, the site of the first battle in which Hnæf fell (from which site the warriors depart to visit Friesland and the *hēaburh*) was not identical with the *hēaburh*, and did not lie in Friesland. Accordingly the usual view, that Finnsburg is situated outside Friesland, seems incontestable. See Bugge (*P.B.B.* XII, 29-30), Trautmann (*Finn und Hildebrand,* 60) and Boer (*Z.f.d.A.* XLVII, 137). Cf. Ayres (*J.E.G.Ph.* XVI, 294).

[454] See below, p. 289.

[455] So Brandl, 984, and Heinzel.

[456] Or just as the attack on the Danes began at night, we might suppose (as does Trautmann) that it equally culminated in a night assault five days later. There would be obvious advantage in night fighting when the object was to storm a hall: Flugumýrr was burnt by night, and so was the hall of Njal. So, too, was the hall of Rolf Kraki. It would be, then, on the morning after this second night assault, that Hildeburh found her kinsfolk dead.

[457] *Beowulf*, l. 1831: cf. l. 409.

[458] Leo (*Beowulf*, 1839, 67), Müllenhoff (*Nordalbingische Studien*, I, 157), Rieger (*Lesebuch; Z.f.d.Ph.* III, 398-401), Dederich (*Studien*, 1877, 96-7), Heyne (in his fourth edition) and in recent times Holthausen have interpreted *eoten* as a common noun "giant," "monster," and consequently "foe" in general. But they have failed to produce any adequate justification for interpreting *eoten* as "foe," and Holthausen, the modern advocate of this interpretation, has now abandoned it. Grundtvig (*Beowulfes Beorh*, 1861, pp. 133 *etc.*) and Möller (*Volksepos*, 97 *etc.*) also interpret "giant," Möller giving an impossible mythological explanation, which was, at the time, widely followed.

[459] Like *oxnum*, *nefenum* (cf. Sievers, § 277, Anm. 1).

[460] I do not attach much importance to the argument which might be drawn from the statement of Binz (*P.B.B.* XX, 185) that the evidence of proper names shows that in the Hampshire district (which was colonized by Jutes) the legend of *Finnsburg* was particularly remembered. For on the other hand, as Binz points out, similar evidence is markedly lacking for Kent. And why, indeed, should the Jutes have specially commemorated a legend in which their part appears not to have been a very creditable one?

[461] p. 97, note 225.

[462] See above, p. 200. Zimmer, *Nennius Vindicatus*, 84, assumes that the Kentish pedigree borrowed these names from the Bernician: but there is no evidence for this.

[463] Among those who have so held are Kemble, Thorpe (*Beowulf*, pp. 76-7), Ettmüller (*Beowulf*, 1840, p. 23), Bouterwek (*Germania*, I, 389), Grein (*Eberts Jahrbuch*, IV, 270), Köhler (*Germania*, XIII, 155), Heyne (in first three editions), Holder

(*Beowulf*, p. 128), ten Brink (*Pauls Grdr.* (1), II, 548), Heinzel (*A.f.d.A.* X. 228), Stevenson (*Asser*, 1904, p. 169), Schücking (*Beowulf*, 1913, p. 321), Klaeber (*J.E.G.Ph.* XIV, 545), Lawrence (*Pub. Mod. Lang. Assoc. Amer.* XXX, 393), Moorman (*Essays and Studies*, V, 99), Björkman (*Eigennamen im Beowulf*, 21).

So too, with some hesitation, Chadwick (*Orgin*, 52-3): with much more hesitation, Bugge (*P.B.B.* XII, 37). Whilst this is passing through the press Holthausen has withdrawn his former interpretation *eotena*, "enemies," in favour of *Eotena=Ēotna*, "Jutes" (*Engl. Stud.* LI, 180).

[464] *P.B.B.* XII, 37.

[465] The cognate of O.E. *fǣr* (Mod. Eng. "fear") in other Germanic languages, such as Old Saxon and Old High German, has the meaning of "ambush." In the nine places where it occurs in O.E. verse it has always the meaning of a peril which comes upon one suddenly, and is applied, e.g. to the Day of Judgement (twice) or some unexpected flood (three times). In compounds *fǣr* conveys an idea of suddenness: "*fǣr-dēað*, repentina mors."

[466] *Volksepos*, 69.

[467] It has been surmounted in two ways. (1) By altering *eaferum* to *eaferan* (a very slight change) and then making *fǣr* refer to the *final* attack upon Finn, in which he certainly *was* on the defensive (Lawrence, 397 *etc.*, Ayres, 284, Trautmann, *BB.* II, Klaeber, *Anglia*, XXVIII, 443, Holthausen). (2) By making *hīe* refer to *hæleð Healf-Dena* which follows (Green in *Pub. Mod. Lang. Assoc. Amer.* XXXI, 759-97); but this is forced. See also below, p. 284.

[468] Cf. Tacitus, *Germania*, XIV.

[469] For examples of this see pp. 278-82 below.

[470] *Fragment*, 40-1.

[471] See above, p. 30.

[472] Book II (ed. Holder, p. 67).

[473] *P.B.B.* XII, 34.

[474] For a discussion of the interpretation of the difficult *forþringan*, see Carlton Brown in *M.L.N.* XXXIV, 181-3.

[475] *J.E.G.Ph.* XVI, 291-2.

[476] *Ib.* 293-4.

[477] I wish I could feel convinced, with Ayres, that the person whom Guthlaf and Oslaf blame for their woes is Hengest rather than Finn. Such an interpretation renders the story so much more coherent; but if the poet really meant this, he assuredly did not make his meaning quite clear.

[478] See below, pp. 276, 288-9.

[479] Ne hūru Hildeburh herian þorfte Eotena trēowe.

[480] Ayres, in *J.E.G.Ph.* XVI, 286. So Lawrence in a private communication.

[481] ll. 2910, *etc.*

[482] We can construct the situation from such historical information as we can get from Gregory of Tours and other sources. The author of *Beowulf* may not have been clear as to the exact relation of the different tribes. We cannot tell, from the vague way he speaks, how much he knew.

[483] I have argued this at some length below, but I do not think anyone would deny it. Bugge recognized it to be true (*P.B.B.* XII, 29-30) as does Lawrence (392). See below, pp. 288-9.

[484] We can never argue that words are synonymous because they are parallel. Compare Psalm cxiv; in the first verse the parallel words are synonymous, but in the second and third not:

"When Israel came out of Egypt and the house of Jacob from among the strange people" [Israel = house of Jacob: Egypt = strange people].

"Judah was His sanctuary and Israel His dominion." [Judah is only one of the tribes of Israel.]

"The sea saw that and fled: Jordan was driven back." [The Red Sea and Jordan are distinct, though parallel, examples.]

[485] *J.E.G.Ph.* XVI, 288.

[486] *Pub. Mod. Lang. Assoc. Amer.* XXX, 430.

[487] Plummer, *Two Saxon Chronicles Parallel*, II, 47.

[488] *Njáls Saga*, cap. 45.

[489] *Pauls Grdr.* (2), II, 524.

[490] Helmhold.

[491] I know of only one parallel for such assumed adoption of a name: that also concerns the Jutes. The Angles, says Bede, dwelt between the Saxons and Jutes: the Jutes must, then, according to Bede, have dwelt north of the Angles, since the Saxons dwelt south. But the people north of the Angles are now, and have been from early times, Scandinavian in speech, whilst the Jutes who settled Kent obviously were not. The best way of harmonizing known linguistic facts with Bede's statement is, then, to assume that Scandinavians settled in the old continental home of these Jutes and took over their name, whilst introducing the Scandinavian speech.

Now many scholars have regarded this as so forced and unlikely an explanation that they reject it, and refuse to believe that the Jutes who settled Kent can have dwelt north of the Angles, in spite of Bede's statement. If we are asked to reject the "Scandinavian-Jute" theory, as too unlikely on *a priori* grounds, although it is demanded by the express evidence of Bede, it is surely absurd to put forward a precisely similar theory in favour of "Frisian-Jutes" upon no evidence at all.

[492] Koegel (164), Lawrence (382).

[493] Björkman (*Eigennamen im Beowulf*, 23) interprets the *Eotenas* as Jutist subjects of Finn. This suggestion was made quite independently of anything I had written, and confirms me in my belief that it is a reasonable interpretation.

[494] Ayres in *J.E.G.Ph.* XVI, 288.

[495] e.g. *Njáls Saga*, cap. 144: *Laxdæla Saga*, cap. 51.

[496] Of course a primitive stage can be conceived at which homicide is regarded as worse than murder. Your brother shoots *A* intentionally: he must therefore have had good reasons, and you fraternally support him. But you may feel legitimate annoyance if he aims at a stag, and shooting *A* by mere misadventure, involves you in a blood-feud.

[497] *Heimskringla, Ól. Tryggv.* K. 111; *Saga Olafs Tryggvasonar,* K. 70 (*Fornmanna Sǫgur,* 1835, X.)

[498] Saxo Grammaticus (ed. Holder, p. 67).

[499] *Heimskringla, Ól. Tryggv.* K. 41.

[500] *lýsti vígi á hendr sér. Laxdæla Saga,* cap. 49.

[501] Cap. 55.

[502] Cap. 85.

[503] *Anglo-Saxon Chronicle,* anno 755.

[504] *Njáls Saga,* cap. 158.

[505] *Fragment,* ll. 40-1.

[506] p. 213 (ed. Holder).

[507] Finn may perhaps be holding a meeting of chieftains. For similar meetings of chieftains, compare *Sǫrla þáttr,* cap. 4; *Laxdæla Saga,* cap. 12; *Skáldskaparmál,* cap. 47 (50).

[508] There is assuredly a considerable likeness between the Finn story and the Nibelungen story: this has been noted often enough. It is more open to dispute whether the likeness is so great as to justify us in believing that the Nibelungen story is *copied* from the Finn story, and may therefore safely be used as an indication how gaps in our existing versions of that story may be filled. See Boer in *Z.f.d.A.* XLVII, 125 *etc.*

[509] The fact that both sides have suffered about equally facilitates a settlement in the Teutonic feud, just as it does among the Afridis or the Albanians at the present day.

[510] The situation would then be parallel to that in *Laxdæla Saga,* cap. 60-5, where the boy Thorleik, aged fifteen, is nominally in command of the expedition which avenges his father Bolli, but is only able to accomplish his revenge by enlisting the great warrior Thorgils, who is the real leader of the raid.

[511] Bugge (*P.B.B.* XII, 36) interpreted this *swylce* as meaning that sword-bale came upon Finn in like manner as it had previously come upon Hnæf. But this is to make *swylce* in l. 1146 refer back to the death of Hnæf mentioned (72 lines previously) in l. 1074.

Möller (*Volksepos*, 67) tries to explain *swylce* by supposing the passage it introduces to be a fragment detached from its context.

[512] f, r, s, þ, w, p (ϝⲛⲅþⲣⲣ), all letters involving a long down stroke, are constantly confused. For examples, see above, p. 245, and cf. e.g. *Beowulf*, l. 2882 (*fergendra* for *wergendra*); *Crist*, 12 (*cræstga* for *cræftga*); *Phoenix*, 15 (*fnæft* for *fnæst*); Riddles III (IV), 18 (*þyran* for *þywan*); XL (XLI), 63 (*þyrre* for *þyrse*); XLII (XLIII), 4 (*speoþ* for *spēow*), 11 (*wæs* for *pæs*); LVII (LVIII), 3 (*rope* for *rōfe* or *rōwe*), etc.

[513] p. 392.

[514] p. 431.

[515] *Nennius Interpretatus*, ed. Mommsen (*Chronica Minora*, III, 179, in *Mon. Germ. Hist.*)

[516] "De norske oldsager synes at vidne om, at temmelig livlige handelsforbindelser i den ældre jernalder har fundet sted mellem Norge og de sydlige Nordsøkyster." Undset, *Fra Norges ældre Jernalder* in the *Aarbøger for Nordisk Oldkyndighed og Historie*, 1880, 89-184, esp. p. 173. See also Chadwick, *Origin*, 93. I am indebted to Chadwick's note for this reference to Undset.

[517] *Ravennatis anonymi cosmographia*, ed. Pinder et Parthey, Berolini, 1860, pp. 27, 28 (§ I, 11).

[518] The modern Wijk bij Duurstede, not far from Utrecht, on the Lower Rhine.

[519] An account of the numerous coins found among the ruins of the old town will be found in the *Forschungen zur deutschen Geschichte*, IV (1864), pp. 301-303. They testify to its commercial importance.

[520] So Adam of Bremen, following Alcuin. Concerning "Heiligland" Adam says: "Hanc in vita Sancti Willebrordi Fosetisland appellari discimus, quae sita est in confinio Danorum et Fresonum." Adam of Bremen in Pertz, *Scriptores*, VII, 1846, p. 369.

[521] Alcuin's *Life of Willibrord* in Migne (1851)—Alcuini *Opera*, vol. II, 699-702.

[522] See above, pp. 199-200.

[523] It had been disputed by Skeat, Earle, Boer, and others, but never with such strong reasons.

[524] I use below the form "Beow," which I believe to be the correct one. "Beaw" is the form in the *Anglo-Saxon Chronicle*. But as the name of Sceldwa, Beaw's father, is there given in a form which is not West-Saxon (*sceld*, not *scield* or *scyld*), it may well be that "Beaw" is also the Anglian dialect form, if it be not indeed a mere error: and this is confirmed by *Beo* (Ethelwerd), *Beowius* (William of Malmesbury), *Boerinus* (for *Beowinus*: Chronicle Roll), perhaps too by *Beowa* (Charter of 931) and *Beowi*, (*MS Cott. Tib. B. IV*). For the significance of this last, see pp. 303-4, below, and Björkman in *Engl. Stud.* LII, 171, *Anglia, Beiblatt*, XXX, 23.

[525] Vol. LXXXI, p. 517.

[526] It has indeed been so argued by Brandl: "Beowulf ... ist nur der Erlöser seines Volkes ... und dankt es schliesslich dem Himmel, in einer an den Heiland gemahnenden Weise, dass er die Seinen um den Preis des eigenen Lebens mit Schätzen beglücken konnte." *Pauls Grdr.* (2), II, l. 1002.

[527] *Encyclopædia Britannica*, 11th edit., III, 760-1.

[528] l. 2039, where a capital O occurs, but without a section number.

[529] *Moore, Namur, Cotton.*

[530] *Cotton Tiberius B. XI.*

[531] *Hatton*, 20.

[532] See above, pp. 92-7.

[533] See above, pp. 43-4.

[534] Ethelwerd.

[535] *Chronicle.*

[536] Boer, *Beowulf*, 135, 143: *Arkiv f. nord. Filologi*, XIX, 29.

[537] *Heroic Age*, 126.

[538] *Postscript to Preface*, p. ix.

[539] *Postscript*, pp. xi, xiv.

[540] See *Lokasenna* in *Die Lieder der Edda*, herausg. von Sijmons u. Gering, I, 134.

Byggvir kvaþ:
"[Veiztu] ef [ek] øþle ættak sem Ingunar-Freyr,
ok svá sǽllekt setr,
merge smǽra mølþak [þá] meinkrǫ́ko
ok lemþa alla í liþo."

[541] Lines corresponding to these of Burns are found both in the Scotch ballad recorded by Jamieson, and in the English ballad (Pepys Collection). See Jamieson, *Popular Ballads and Songs*, 1806, II, 241, 256.

[542]
Loki kvaþ:
"Hvat's þat et lítla, es [ek] þat lǫggra sék,
ok snapvíst snaper?
at eyrom Freys mont[u] ǽ vesa
ok und kvernom klaka."

[543] Jamieson, II, 239. So Burns: "John Barleycorn was a hero bold," and the ballad

John Barleycorn is the wightest man
That ever throve in land.

[544]
Byggvir kvaþ:
"Byggver ek heite, en mik bráþan kveþa
goþ ǫll ok gumar;
því emk hér hróþogr, at drekka Hrópts meger
aller ǫl saman."

[545]
Loki kvaþ:
"þege þú, Byggver! þú kunner aldrege
deila meþ mǫnnom mat;
[ok] þik í flets strae finna né mǫ́tto,
þás vǫ́go verar."

[546] This follows from the allusive way in which he and his wife are introduced—there must be a background to allusions. If the

poet were inventing this figure, and had no background of knowledge in his audience to appeal to, he must have been more explicit. Cf. Olsen in Christiania *Videnskapsselskapets Skrifter*, 1914, II, 2, 107.

[547] p. 87.

[548] See Olrik, "Nordisk og Lappisk Gudsdyrkelse," *Danske Studier*, 1905, pp. 39-57; "Tordenguden og hans dreng," 1905, pp. 129-46; "Tordenguden og hans dreng i Lappernes myteverden," 1906, pp. 65-9; Krohn, "Lappische beiträge zur germ. mythologie," *Finnisch-Ugrische Forschungen*, VI, 1906, pp. 155-80.

[549] See Axel Olrik in *Festgabe f. Vilh. Thomsen*, 1912 (= *Finnisch-Ugrische Forschungen*, XII, 1, p. 40). Olrik refers therein to his earlier paper on the subject in *Danske Studier*, 1911, p. 38, and to a forthcoming article in the *Germanisch-Romanische Monatsschrift*, which has, I think, never appeared. See also K. Krohn in *Göttingische gelehrte Anzeigen*, 1912, p. 211. Reviewing Meyer's *Altgermanische Religionsgeschichte*, Krohn, after referring to the Teutonic gods of agriculture, continues "Ausser diesen agrikulturellen Gottheiten sind aus der finnischen Mythologie mit Hülfe der Linguistik mehrere germanische Naturgötter welche verschiedene Nutzpflanzen vertreten, entdeckt worden: der Roggengott Runkoteivas oder Rukotivo, der Gerstengott Pekko (nach Magnus Olsen aus urnord. Beggw-, vgl. Byggwir) und ein Gott des Futtergrases Sämpsä (vgl. Semse od. Simse, 'die Binse')." See also Krohn, "Germanische Elemente in der finnischen Volksdichtung," *Z.f.d.A.* LI, 1909, pp. 13-22; and Karsten, "Einige Zeugnisse zur altnordischen Götterverehrung in Finland," *Finnisch-Ugrische Forschungen*, XII, 307-16.

[550] As proposed by K. Krohn in a publication of the Finnish Academy at Helsingfors which I have not been able to consult, but as to which see Setälä in *Finnisch-Ugrische Forschungen*, XIII, 311, 424. Setälä accepts the derivation from *beggwu-*, rejecting an alternative derivation of Pekko from a Finnish root.

[551] This is proposed by J. J. Mikkola in a note appended to the article by K. Krohn, "Sampsa Pellervoinen < Njordr, Freyr?" in *Finnisch-Ugrische Forschungen*, IV, 231-48. See also Olrik, "Forårsmyten hos Finnerne," in *Danske Studier*, 1907, pp. 62-4.

[552] See note by K. Krohn, *Finnisch-Ugrische Forschungen*, VI, 105.

[553] See above, p. 87, and M. J. Eisen, "Ueber den Pekokultus bei den Setukesen," *Finnisch-Ugrische Forschungen*, VI, 104-11.

[554] See M. Olsen, *Hedenske Kultminder i Norske Stedsnavne*, Christiania *Videnskapsselskapets Skrifter*, II, 2, 1914, pp. 227-8.

[555] See above, p. 84.

[556] Mannhardt, *Mythologische Forschungen*, 332.

[557] In view of the weight laid upon this custom by Olrik as illustrating the story of Sceaf, it is necessary to note that it seems to be confined to parts of England bordering on the "Celtic fringe." See above, pp. 81, *etc.* Olrik and Olsen quote it as Kentish (see *Heltedigtning*, II, 252) but this is certainly wrong. Frazer attributes the custom of "crying the mare" to Hertfordshire and Shropshire (*Spirits of the Corn*, I, 292 = *Golden Bough*, 3rd edit., VII, 292). In this he is following Brand's *Popular Antiquities* (1813, I, 443; 1849, II, 24; also Carew Hazlitt, 1905, I, 157). But Brand's authority is Blount's *Glossographia*, 1674, and Blount says *Herefordshire*.

[558] Brand, *Popular Antiquities*, 1849, II, 24.

[559] Frazer in the *Folk-Lore Journal*, VII, 1889, pp. 50, 51; *Adonis, Attis and Osiris*, I, 237.

[560] Frazer, *Adonis, Attis and Osiris*, I, 238 (*Golden Bough*, 3rd edit.).

[561] Frazer, *Spirits of the Corn and of the Wild*, I, 143-4.

[562] Frazer in the *Folk-Lore Journal*, VII, 1889, pp. 50, 51.

[563] Mannhardt, *Forschungen*, 317.

[564] Frazer, *Spirits of the Corn*, I, 138.

[565] Mannhardt, 323; Fraser, *Adonis*, I, 238.

[566] Mannhardt, 330.

[567] Mannhardt, 24; Frazer, *Adonis*, I, 238.

[568] Frazer, *Adonis*, I, 237.

[569] Frazer, *Spirits of the Corn*, I, 217.

[570] See Björkman in *Anglia, Beiblatt*, XXX, 1919, p. 23. In a similar way Sceaf appears twice in William of Malmesbury, once as Sceaf and once as Strephius.

[571] Vol. LII, p. 145.

[572] *MS Cott. Vesp. B. XXIV*, fol. 32 (Evesham Cartulary). See Birch, *Cart. Sax.* I, 176 (No. 120); Kemble, *Cod. Dipl.* III, 376. Kemble prints *pæt æft* for *pā æft* (MS "þ‾ æft"). For examples of "þ‾" for *pā*, see *Ælfrics Grammatik*, herausg. Zupitza, 1880; 38, 3; 121, 4; 291, 1.

[573] There are two copies, one of the tenth and one of the eleventh century, among the Crawford Collection in the Bodleian. See Birch, *Cart. Sax.* III, ..7 (No. 1331); Napier and Stevenson, *The Crawford Collection* (*Anecdota Oxoniensia*), 1895, pp. 1, 3, 50.

[574] *MS Cotton Ch. VIII*, 16. See Birch, *Cart. Sax.* II, 363 (No. 677); Kemble, *Cod. Dipl.* II, 172.

[575] A nearly contemporary copy: *Westminster Abbey Charters*, III. See Birch, *Cart. Sax.* III, 189 (No. 994), and W. B. Sanders, *Ord. Surv. Facs.* II, plate III.

[576] A fourteenth to fifteenth century copy preserved at Wells Cathedral (*Registr. Album*, f. 289 *b*). See Birch, *Cart. Sax.* III, 223 (No. 1023).

[577] *MS Cotton Aug. II*, 6. See Birch, *Cart. Sax.* III, 588 (No. 1282).

[578] *Brit. Mus. Stowe Chart.* No. 32. See Birch, *Cart. Sax.* III, 605 (No. 1290).

[579] Cf. the *Victoria History*, Middlesex, II, p. 1.

[580] "*Grendeles gate* har väl snarast varit någon naturbildning t. ex. ett trångt bergpass eller kanske en grotta": C. W. von Sydow, in an excellent article on *Grendel i anglosaxiska ortnamn*, in *Nordiska Ortnamn: Hyllningsskrift tillägnad A. Noreen*, Upsala, 1914, pp. 160-4.

[581] Près du *Neckersgat molen*, il y avait jadis, antérieurement aux guerres de religion, des maisons entourées d'eau et appelées *de hoffstede te Neckersgate*: Wauters (A.), *Histoire des Environs de Bruxelles*, 1852, III, 646.

[582] Peg Powler lived in the Tees, and devoured children who played on the banks, especially on Sundays: Peg o' Nell, in the Ribble, demanded a life every seven years. See Henderson (W.), *Notes on the Folk-Lore of the Northern Counties of England*, 1879 (*Folk-Lore Society*), p. 265.

[583] See Kisch (G.), *Vergleichendes Wörterbuch der siebenbürgischen und moselfränkischluxemburgischen Mundart, nebst siebenbürgischniederrheinischem Ortsund Familiennamen-verzeichnis* (vol. XXXIII, 1 of the *Archiv des Vereins f. siebenbürg. Landeskunde*, 1905).

[584] See *Grindel* in Förstemann (E.), *Altdeutsches Namenbuch*, Dritte Aufl., herausg. Jellinghaus, II, 1913, and in Fischer (H.), *Schwäbisches Wörterbuch*, III, 1911 (nevertheless Rooth legitimately calls attention to the names recorded by Fischer in which *Grindel* is connected with *bach*, *teich* and *moos*).

[585] There is an account of this by G. Kisch in the *Festgabe zur Feier der Einweihung des neuen evang. Gymnasial Bürger- und Elementarschulgebäudes in Besztercze (Bistritz) am 7 Oct. 1911*; a document which I have not been able to procure.

[586] Such a connection is attempted by W. Benary in Herrig's *Archiv*, CXXX, 154. Alternative suggestions, which would exclude any connection with the Grendel of *Beowulf*, are made by Klaeber, in *Archiv*, CXXXI, 427.

[587] A very useful summary of the different etymologies proposed is made by Rooth in *Anglia, Beiblatt*, XXVIII (1917), 335-8.

[588] So Skeat, "On the significance of the monster Grendel," *Journal of Philology*, Cambridge, XV (1886), p. 123; Laistner, *Rätsel der Sphinx*, 1889, p. 23; Holthausen, in his edition.

[589] So Weinhold in the *SB. der k. Akad. Wien, Phil.-Hist. Classe*, XXVI, 255.

[590] Cf. Gollancz, *Patience*, 1913, Glossary. For *grindill* as one of the synonyms for "storm," see *Edda Snorra Sturlusonar*, Hafniae, 1852, II, 486, 569.

[591] This will be found in several of the vocabularies of Low German dialects published by the *Verein für Niederdeutsche Sprachforschung*.

[592] See *grand* in Falk and Torp, *Etymologisk Ordbog*, Kristiania, 1903-6.

[593] See Feist, *Etymol. Wörterbuch der Gotischen Sprache*, Halle, 1909; *grunduwaddjus*.

[594] With Grendel, thus explained, Rooth would connect the "Earth man" of the fairy-tale "Dat Erdmänneken" (see below, p. 370) and the name *Sandhaug*, *Sandey*, which clings to the Scandinavian *Grettir-* and *Orm*-stories. We have seen that a *sandhaug* figures also in one of the Scandinavian cognates of the folk-tale (see above, p. 67). These resemblances may be noted, though it would be perilous to draw deductions from them.

[595] *Schweizerisches Idiotikon*, II, 1885, p. 776.

[596] See above, pp. 43, *etc.*; below, p. 311.

[597] Duignan, *Warwickshire Place Names*, p. 22. Duignan suggests the same etymology for *Beoshelle*, *beos* being "the Norman scribe's idea of the gen. plu." This, however, is very doubtful.

[598] *Engl. Stud.* LII, 177.

[599] *Heltedigtning*, II, 255. See above, pp. 81-7.

[600] Binz in *P.B.B.* XX, 148; Chadwick, *Origin*, 282. So Clarke, *Sidelights*, 128. Cf. Heusler in *A.f.d. A.* XXX, 31.

[601] *A.-S. Chronicle.*

[602] *Historia Brittonum.*

[603] "hrædlan" (gen.), *Beowulf*, 454.

[604] "hrædles," *Beowulf*, 1485.

[605] *A.-S. Chronicle.*

[606] *Beowulf*, Ethelwerd.

[607] Geata, Geta, *Historia Brittonum*; Asser; *MS Cott. Tib. A. VI*; *Textus Roffensis.*

[608] *A.-S. Chronicle.*

[609] Charter of 931.

[610] *A.-S. Chronicle*, Ethelwerd.

[611] *Origin*, 273.

[612] *Origin*, 282.

[613] Some O.H.G. parallels will be found in *Z.f.d.A.* XII, 260. The weak form *Gēata*, Mr Stevenson argues, is due to Asser's attempt to reconcile the form *Gēat* with the Latin *Geta* with which he identifies it (Asser, pp. 160-161). See also Chadwick, *Heroic Age*, 124 footnote. Yet we get *Gēata* in one text of the *Chronicle*, and in other documents.

[614] This is the view taken by Plummer, who does not seem to regard any solution as possible other than that the names are missing from the *Parker MS* by a transcriber's slip (see *Two Saxon Chronicles Parallel*, II, p. xciv).

[615] Plummer, II, pp. xxix, xxxi, lxxxix.

[616] Plummer, II, p. lxxi. Note *Beowi* for *Bedwig*.

[617] This table shows the relationship of the genealogies only, not of the whole MSS, of which the genealogies form but a small part. MS-relationships are always liable to fluctuation, as we pass from one part of a MS to another, and for obvious reasons this is peculiarly the case with the *Chronicle* MSS.

[618] *Origin*, 295.

[619] *Origin*, 292.

[620] *Origin*, 296.

[621] The absence of the West-Saxon pedigree may be due to the document from which the *Historia Brittonum* and the *Vespasian MS* derive these pedigrees having been drawn up in the North: Wessex may have been outside the purview of its compiler; though against this is the fact that it contains the Kentish pedigree. But another quite possible explanation is, that Cerdic, with his odd name, was not of the right royal race, but an adventurer, and that it was only later that a pedigree was made up for his descendants, on the analogy of those possessed by the more blue-blooded monarchs of Mercia and Northumbria.

[622] See *M.L.N.* 1897, XII, 110-11.

[623] It is prefixed to the *Parker MS* of the *Chronicle*, and is found also in the Cambridge MS of the Anglo-Saxon Bede (*Univ. Lib. Kk.* 3. 18) printed in Miller's edition; in *MS Cott. Tib. A. III,* 178 (printed in Thorpe's *Chronicle*): and in *MS Add.* 34652, printed by Napier in *M.L.N.* 1897, XII, 106 *etc.* There are uncollated copies in *MS C.C.C.C.* 383, fol. 107, and according to Liebermann (Herrig's *Archiv,* CIV, 23) in the *Textus Roffensis,* fol. 7 *b.* There is also a fragment, which does not however include the portion under consideration, in *MS Add.* 23211 (*Brit. Mus.*) printed in Sweet's *Oldest English Texts,* p. 179. The statement, sometimes made, that there is a copy in *MS C.C.C.C.* 41, rests on an error of Whelock, who was really referring to the *Parker MS* of the *Chronicle* (*C.C.C.C.* 173).

[624] p. 73.

[625] See above, p. 70.

[626] Brandl in Herrig's *Archiv,* CXXXVII, 12-13.

[627] *Origin,* p. 272.

[628] So Ethelwerd (*Lib.* I) sees in Woden a *rex multitudinis Barbarorum,* in error deified. It is the usual point of view, and persists down to Carlyle (*Heroes*).

[629] *Origin,* p. 293.

[630] *Beowulf,* p. 5. For a further examination of this "Beowa-myth" see Appendix A, above.

[631] Cf. Tupper in *Pub. Mod. Lang. Assoc. Amer.* XXVI, 275.

[632] *P.B.B.* XLII, 347-410. A theory as to the date of *Beowulf,* in some respects similar, was put forward by Mone in 1836: *Untersuchungen zur Geschichte der teutschen Heldensage,* p. 132.

[633] See above, p. 103; and Brandl in *Pauls Grdr.* (2) II, 1000, where the argument is excellently stated.

[634] See Olrik, *Sakses Oldhistorie,* 1894, 190-91.

[635] See Björkman, *Eigennamen im Beowulf,* 77.

[636] Sarrazin's attempt to prove such corruption is an entire failure. Cf. Brandl in Herrig's *Archiv,* CXXVI, 234; Björkman, *Eigennamen im Beowulf,* 58 (*Heaðo-Beardan*).

[637] A few Geatic adventurers may have taken part in the Anglo-Saxon invasion, as has been argued by Moorman (*Essays and Studies*, V). This is likely enough on *a priori* grounds, though many of the etymologies of place-names quoted by Moorman in support of his thesis are open to doubt.

[638] *P.B.B.* XLII, 366-7.

[639] *History of England to the Norman Conquest*, I, 245.

[640] *Heroic Age*, 52-6. I have tried to show (Appendix F) that these accounts of cremation are not so archaeologically correct as has sometimes been claimed.

[641] Oman, *England before the Norman Conquest*, 319.

[642] Bede, *Hist. Eccles.* IV, 26.

[643] "Nunc qui Roma veniunt idem allegant, ut qui Haugustaldensem fabricam vident ambitionem Romanam se imaginari jurent." William of Malmesbury, *Gesta Pontificum*, Rolls Series, p. 255.

[644] Baldwin Brown, *The Arts in Early England*, II, 1903, p. 325.

[645] p. 407.

[646] *Beowulf*, ll. 201, 601-3.

[647] Cf. *Beowulf*, l. 1018.

[648] Bede, *Eccles. Hist.* III, 21.

[649] See Oman, pp. 460, 591, for the honour done to this saint by converted Danes.

[650] p. 393.

[651] *Æneid*, X, 467-9.

[652] In the two admirable articles by Klaeber (*Archiv*, CCXVI, 40 *etc.*, 399 *etc.*) every possible parallel is drawn: the result, to my mind, is not complete conviction.

[653] Chadwick, *Heroic Age*, 74.

[654] "Litteris itaque ad plenum instructus, nativae quoque linguae non negligebat carmina; adeo ut, teste libro Elfredi, de

quo superius dixi, nulla umquam aetate par ei fuerit quisquam. Poesim Anglicam posse facere, cantum componere, *eadem apposite vel canere vel dicere*. Denique commemorat Elfredus carmen triviale, quod adhuc vulgo cantitatur, Aldelmum fecisse, aditiens causam qua probet rationabiliter tantum virum his quae videantur frivola institisse. Populum eo tempore semibarbarum, parum divinis sermonibus intentum, statim, cantatis missis, domos cursitare solitum. Ideo sanctum virum, super pontem qui rura et urbem continuat, abeuntibus se opposuisse obicem, quasi artem cantitandi professum. Eo plusquam semel facto, plebis favorem et concursum emeritum. Hoc commento sensim inter ludicra verbis Scripturarum insertis, cives ad sanitatem reduxisse." William of Malmesbury, *De gestis pontificum Anglorum*, ed. Hamilton, *Rolls Series*, 1870, 336.

[655] "Reverentissimo patri meaeque rudis infantiae venerando praeceptori Adriano." *Epist.* (Aldhelmi *Opera*, ed. Giles, 1844, p. 330).

[656] Faricius, Life, in Giles' edition of Aldhelm, 1844, p. 357.

[657] Letter of Cuthbert to Cuthwine, describing Bede's last illness. "Et in nostra lingua, hoc est anglica, ut erat doctus in nostris carminibus, nonnulla dixit. Nam et tunc Anglico carmine componens, multum compunctus aiebat, *etc.*" The letter is quoted by Simeon of Durham, ed. Arnold, *Rolls Series*, 1882, I, pp. 43-46, and is extant elsewhere, notably in a ninth century MS at St Gall.

[658] "quid Hinieldus cum Christo."

[659] "Þæt ænig prēost ne bēo ealuscop, ne on ænige wīsan glīwige, mid him sylfum oþþe mid ōþrum mannum"—Thorpe, *Ancient Laws and Institutes of England*, 1840, p. 400 (Laws of Edgar, cap. 58).

[660] "avitae gentilitatis vanissima didicisse carmina." This charge is dismissed as "scabiem mendacii." *Vita Sancti Dunstani*, by "B," in *Memorials of Dunstan*, ed. Stubbs, *Rolls Series*, 1874, p. 11. Were these songs heroic or magic?

[661] *The Heroic Legends of Denmark*, New York, 1919, p. 32 (footnote).

[662] *Ibid.* p. 39.

[663] Thus, much space has been devoted to discussing whether "Gotland," in the eleventh century Cotton MS of Alfred's Orosius, signifies Jutland. I believe that it does; but fail to see how it can be argued from this that Alfred believed the Jutes to be "Geatas." Old English had no special symbol for the semi-vowel J; so, to signify *Jötland*, Alfred would have written "Geotland" (Sievers, *Gram.* §§ 74, 175). Had he meant "Land of the Geatas" he would have written "Geataland" or "Geatland." Surely "Gotland" is nearer to "Geotland" than to "Geatland."

[664] *P.B.B.* XII, 1-10.

[665] See above, p. 8. Fahlbeck has recently revised and re-stated his arguments.

[666] *Danmarks Riges Historie*, I, 79 *etc.*

[667] *Beowulf*, übersetzt von H. Gering, 1906, p. vii.

[668] See above, also *Nordisk Aandsliv*, 10, where Olrik speaks of the Geatas as "Jyderne." His arguments as presented to the Copenhagen *Philologisk-historisk Samfund* are summarized by Schütte, *J.E.G. Ph.* XI, 575-6. Clausen also supports the Jute-theory, *Danske Studier*, 1918, 137-49.

[669] *J.E.G. Ph.* XI, 574-602.

[670] *Beowulf, et Bidrag til Nordens Oldhistorie* af Chr. Kier, København, 1915.

[671] This is admitted by Bugge, *P.B.B.* XII, 6. "*Geátas* ... ist sprachlich ein ganz anderer name als altn. *Jótar, Jútar*, bei Beda *Jutae*, und nach Beda im *Chron. Sax.* 449 *Jotum, Jutna* ... Die *Geátas* ... tragen einen namen der sprachlich mit altn. *Gautar* identisch ist."

[672] From a presumed Prim. Germ. **Eutiz, *Eutjaniz*. The word in O.E. seems to have been declined both as an *i*-stem and an *n*-stem, the *n*-stem forms being used more particularly in the gen. plu., just as in the case of the tribal names, *Seaxe, Mierce* (Sievers, § 264). The Latinized forms show the same duplication, the dat. *Euciis* pointing to an *i*-stem, the nom. *Euthio* to an *n*-stem, plu. **Eutiones*. For a discussion of the relation of the O.E. name to the Danish *Jyder*, see Björkman in *Anglia, Beiblatt*, XXVIII, 274-80: "Zu ae. *Eote, Yte*, dän. *Jyder* 'Jüten'."

[673] I regard it as simply an *error* of the translator, possibly because he had before him a text in which Bede's *Iutis* had been corrupted in this place into *Giotis*, as it is in Ethelwerd: *Cantuarii de Giotis traxerunt originem, Vuhtii quoque*. (Bk. I: other names which Ethelwerd draws from Bede in this section are equally corrupt.)

Bede's text runs: (I, 15) *Aduenerant autem de tribus Germaniae populis fortioribus, id est Saxonibus, Anglis, Iutis. De Iutarum origine sunt Cantuarii et Victuarii*; in the translation: "Comon hi of þrim folcum ðam strangestan Germanie, þæt [is] of Seaxum and of Angle and of Geatum. Of Geata fruman syndon Cantware and Wihtsætan": (IV, 16) *In proximam Iutorum prouinciam translati ... in locum, qui uocatur Ad Lapidem*; "in þa neahmægðe, seo is gecegd Eota lond, in sume stowe seo is nemned Æt Stane" (Stoneham, near Southampton). *MS C.C.C.C.* 41 reads "Ytena land": see below.

[674] *Two Saxon Chronicles*, ed. Plummer, 1899. *Introduction*, pp. lxx, lxxi.

[675] *The O.E. version of Bede's Ecclesiastical History*, ed. Miller, II, xv, xvi, 1898.

[676] Florentii Wigorn. *Chron.*, ed. Thorpe, II, 45; I, 276.

[677] It cannot be said that this is due to textual corruption in our late copy, for the alliteration constantly demands a G-form, not a vowel-form.

[678] See pp. 8, 9 above, §§ 2-7.

[679] Just as, for example, in *Heimskringla: Haraldz saga ins hárfagra*, 13-17, the Götar are constantly mentioned, because the kingdom of Sweden is being attacked from their side.

[680] Procopius tells us that there were in Thule (i.e. the Scandinavian peninsula) thirteen nations, each under its own king: βασιλεῖς τέ εἰσι κατὰ ἔθνος ἕκαστον ... ὧν ἔθνος ἓν πολυάνθρωπον οἱ Γαυτοί εἰσι (*Bell. Gott.* ii, 15).

[681] On this alliteration-test, which is very important, see above, pp. 10-11.

[682] *Geta* was the recognized Latin synonym for *Gothus*, and is used in this sense in the sixth century, e.g. by Venantius Fortunatus and Jordanes. And the Götar are constantly called *Gothi*, e.g. in the formula *rex Sueorum et Gothorum* (for the date of

this formula see Söderqvist in the *Historisk Tidskrift*, 1915: *Ägde Uppsvearne rätt att taga och vräka konung*); or Saxo, Bk. XIII (ed. Holder, p. 420, describing how the *Gothi* invited a candidate to be king, and slew the rival claimant, who was supported by the legally more constitutional suffrages of the Swedes); or Adam of Bremen (as quoted below).

[683] *Folknamnet Geatas*, p. 5 *etc.*

[684] Speaking of the Götaelv, Adam says "Ille oritur in praedictis alpibus, perque *medios Gothorum populos* currit in Oceanum, unde et Gothelba dicitur." Adami Canonici Bremensis, *Gesta Hamm. eccl. pontificum*, Lib. IV, in Migne, CXLVI, 637. Modern scholars are of the opinion that the borrowing has been rather the other way. According to Noreen the river Götaelv (Gautelfr) gets its name as the outflow from Lake Væner. (Cf. O.E. *gēotan, gēat*, "pour.") Götland (Gautland) is the country around the river, and the Götar (Gautar) get their name from the country. See Noreen, *Våra Ortnamn och deras Ursprungliga Betydelse*, in *Spridda Studier*, II, 91, 139.

[685] The Scholiast, in his commentary on Adam, records the later state of things, when the Götar were confined to the south of the river: "Gothelba fluvius a Nordmannis Gothiam separat."

[686] *Heimskringla*, cap. 17.

[687] "Hann [Haraldr] er úti á herskipum allan vetrinn ok herjar á Ránríki" (cap. 15). "Haraldr konungr fór víða um Gautland herskildi, ok átti þar margar orrostur tveim megin elfarinnar.... Síðan lagði Haraldr konungr land alt undir sik fyrir norðan elfina ok fyrir vestan Væni" (cap. 17). *Heimskringla: Haraldz saga ins hárfagra*, udgiv. F. Jónsson, København, 1893-1900.

[688] Baltzer (L.), *Glyphes des rochers du Bohuslän, avec une préface de V. Rydberg*, Gothembourg, 1881. See also Baltzer, *Några af de viktigaste Hällristningarna*, Göteborg, 1911.

[689] Guinchard, *Sweden: Historical and Statistical Handbook*, 1914, II, 549.

[690] See Chadwick, *Origin*, 93; *Heroic Age*, 51.

[691] ll. 2910-21. See Schütte, 579, 583.

[692] ll. 2922-3007.

[693] ll. 3018-27.

[694] ll. 3029-30.

[695] pp. 575, 581.

[696] The reason for locating the *Eudoses* in Jutland is that the name has, very hazardously, been identified with that of the Jutes, *Eutiones*. Obviously this argument could no longer be used, if the *Eudoses* were the "Wederas."

[697] See e.g. Schütte, 579-80.

[698] *Beowulf*, 1856.

[699] *Beowulf*, 1830 *etc.*

[700] *Beowulf*, 2394. See Schütte, 576-9.

[701] *Sēo ēa þǣr wyrcþ micelne sǣ.* Orosius, ed. Sweet, 12, 24.

[702] See above, p. 7.

[703] As Miss Paues, herself a *Geat*, points out to me.

[704] Kier, 39; Schütte, 582, 591 *etc.*

[705] See above, pp. 99, 100.

[706] *Vendel och Vendelkråka* in *A.f.n.F.* XXI, 71-80: see *Essays*, trans. Clark Hall, 50-62.

[707] This grave mound is mentioned as "Kong Ottars Hög" in *Ättartal för Swea och Götha Kununga Hus*, by J. Peringskiöld, Stockholm, 1725, p. 13, and earlier, in 1677, it is mentioned by the same name in some notes of an antiquarian survey. That the name "Vendel-crow" is now attached to it is stated by Dr Almgren. These early references seem conclusive: little weight could, of course, be carried by the modern name alone, since it might easily be of learned origin. The mound was opened in 1914-16, and the contents showed it to belong to about 500 to 550 A.D., which agrees excellently with the date of Ohthere. See two articles in *Fornvännen* for 1917: an account of the opening of the mound by S. Lindqvist entitled "Ottarshögen i Vendel" (pp. 127-43) and a discussion of early Swedish history in the light of archaeology, by B. Nerman, "Ynglingasagan i arkeologisk belysning" (esp. pp. 243-6). See also Björkman in *Nordisk*

Tidskrift, Stockholm, 1917, p. 169, and *Eigennamen im Beowulf*, 1920, pp. 86-99.

[708] See Appendix F: *Beowulf* and the Archæologists, esp. p. 356, below.

[709] By the Early Iron Age, Engelhardt meant from 250 to 450 A.D.: but more recent Danish scholars have placed these deposits in the fifth century, with some overlapping into the preceding and succeeding centuries (Müller, *Vor Oldtid*, 561; Wimmer, *Die Runenschrift*, 301, *etc.*). The Swedish archæologists, Knut Stjerna and O. Almgren, agree with Engelhardt, dating the finds between about 250 and 450 A.D. (Stjerna's *Essays*, trans. Clark Hall, p. 149, and *Introduction*, xxxii-iii).

[710] *Essays on questions connected with the O.E. poem of Beowulf*, trans. and ed. by John R. Clark Hall, (Viking Club), Coventry. (Reviews by Klaeber, *J.E.G.Ph.* XIII, 167-73, weighty; Mawer, *M.L.N.* VIII, 242-3; *Athenæum*, 1913, I, 459-60; *Archiv*, CXXXII, 238-9; Schütte, *A.f.n.F.* XXXIII, 64-96, elaborate.)

[711] An account of these was given at the time by H. Stolpe, who undertook the excavation. See his *Vendelfyndet*, in the *Antiqvarisk Tidskrift för Sverige*, VIII, 1, 1-34, and Hildebrand (H.) in the same, 35-64 (1884). Stolpe did not live to issue the definitive account of his work, *Graffältet vid Vendel, beskrifvet af* H. Stolpe och T. J. Arne, Stockholm, 1912.

[712] Also added as an Appendix to his *Beowulf* translation, 1911.

[713] Clark Hall's *Preface* to Stjerna's *Essays*, p. xx.

[714] *J.E.G.Ph.* XIII, 1914, p. 172.

[715] *Essays*, p. 239: cf. p. 84.

[716] p. 39.

[717] *Germania*, cap. XV.

[718] ll. 378, 470.

[719] Cassiodorus, *Variae*, V, 1.

[720] Walter, *Corpus juris Germanici antiqui*, 1824, II, 125.

[721] *Heimskringla, Haraldz saga*, cap. 38-40.

[722] "The idea of a gold hoard undoubtedly points to the earlier version of the *Beowulf* poem having originated in Scandinavia. No such 'gold period' ever existed in Britain." *Essays*, p. 147.

[723] *Cottonian Gnomic Verses*, ll. 26-7.

[724] l. 14.

[725] *Exeter Gnomic Verses*, l. 126.

[726] Baldwin Brown, III, 385, IV, 640.

[727] *B.* l. 19.

[728] l. 339.

[729] l. 991.

[730] Cf. Falk, *Altnordische Waffenkunde*, 28.

[731] I would suggest this as the more likely because, if the ring were inserted for a practical purpose, it is not easy to see why it later survived in the form of a mere knob, which is neither useful nor ornamental. But if it were used to attach the symbolical "peace bands," it may have been retained, in a "fossilized form," with a symbolical meaning.

[732] Most editors indeed do take it in this sense, though recently Schücking has adopted Stjerna's explanation of "ring-sword." In l. 322, Falk (27) takes *hring-īren* to refer to a "ring-adorned sword," though it may well mean a ring-byrnie.

[733] Actually, I believe, more: for two ring-swords were found at Faversham, and are now in the British Museum. For an account of one of them see Roach Smith, *Collectanea Antiqua*, 1868, vol. VI, 139. In this specimen both the fixed ring and the ring which moves within it are complete circles. But in the Gilton sword (*Archæologia*, XXX, 132) and in the sword discovered at Bifrons (*Archæologia Cantiana*, X, 312) one of the rings no longer forms a complete circle, and in the sword discovered at Sarre (*Archæol. Cant.* VI, 172) the rings are fixed together, and one of them has little resemblance to a ring at all.

[734] At Concevreux. It is described by M. Jules Pilloy in *Mémoires de la Société Académique de St Quentin*, 4ᵉ Sér. tom. XVI, 1913; see esp. pp. 36-7.

[735] See Lindenschmit, "Germanisches Schwert mit ungewöhnlicher Bildung des Knaufes," in *Die Altertümer unserer heidnischen Vorzeit*, V Bd., V Heft, Taf. 30, p. 165, Mainz, 1905.

[736] Salin has no doubt that the Swedish type from Uppland (his figure 252) is later than even the latest type of English ring-sword (the Sarre pommel, 251) which is itself later than the Faversham (249) or Bifrons (250) pommel. See Salin (B.), *Die Altgermanische Thierornamentik*, Stockholm, 1904, p. 101. The same conclusion is arrived at by Lindenschmit: "Die ursprüngliche Form ist wohl in dem, unter Nr. 249 von Salin abgebildeten Schwertknopf aus Kent zu sehen"; and even more emphatically by Pilloy, who pronounces the Swedish Vendel sword both on account of its "ring" and other characteristics, as "inspirée par un modèle venu de cette contrée [Angleterre]."

[737] The Benty Grange helmet; see below, p. 358.

[738] Depicted by Clark Hall, Stjerna's *Essays*, p. 258.

[739] Clark Hall's *Beowulf*, p. 227.

[740] "Von Skandinavien gibt es aus der Völkerwanderungszeit und Wikingerepoche keine archäologischen Anhaltspunkte für das Tragen des Panzers, weder aus Funden noch aus Darstellungen," Max Ebert in Hoops' *Reallexikon*, III, 395 (1915-16). But surely this is too sweeping. Fragments of an iron byrnie, made of small rings fastened together, were found in the Vendel grave 12 (seventh century). See *Graffältet vid Vendel, beskrifvet af* H. Stolpe och T. J. Arne, pp. 49, 60, plates xl, xli, xlii.

[741] 54-I. Liebermann, p. 114.

[742] *Essays*, 34-5.

[743] *Elene*, 264.

[744] Engelhardt, *Denmark in the Early Iron Age*, p. 66.

[745] *Andreas*, 303.

[746] l. 2869.

[747] "Few have corslets and only one here and there a helmet" (*Germania*, 6). In the *Annals* (II, 14) Tacitus makes Germanicus

roundly deny the use of either by the Germans: *non loricam Germano, non galeam.*

[748] See above, p. 124.

[749] See Chifflet, J. J., *Anastasis Childerici I ... sive thesaurus sepulchralis*, Antverpiæ, *Plantin*, 1655.

[750] That *both* sword and scramasax were buried with Childeric is shown by Lindenschmit, *Handbuch*, I, 236-9: see also pp. 68 *etc.*

[751] l. 2762-3.

[752] Worsaae, *Nordiske Oldsager*, Kjøbenhavn, 1859; see No. 499; Roach Smith, *Collectanea Antiqua*, 1852, II, 164; Montelius, *Antiq. Suéd.* 1873, No. 294 (p. 184).

[753] *Essays*, p. 198. See also above, p. 124. Mr Reginald Smith writes to me: "Unburnt objects with cremated burials in prehistoric times (Bronze, Early and late Iron Ages) are the exception, and are probably accidental survivals from the funeral pyre. In such an interpretation of *Beowulf* I agree with the late Knut Stjerna, who was an archæologist of much experience."

[754] Forming vols. 3 and 4 of *The Arts in Early England*, 1903-15.

[755] It was, however, necessary to leave over for a supplementary volume some of the contributions most interesting from the point of view of the archæology of *Beowulf*: e.g. spatha, speer, schild.

[756] B. E. Hildebrand, *Grafhögarne vid Gamla Upsala, Kongl. Vitterhets Historie och Antiqvitets Akademiens Månadsblad*, 1875-7, pp. 250-60.

[757] *Fasta fornlämningar i Beovulf*, in *Antiqvarisk Tidskrift för Sverige*, XVIII, 48-64.

[758] *Heimskringla: Ynglingasaga*, cap. 25, 26, 29.

[759] See B. Nerman, *Vilka konungar ligga i Uppsala högar?* Uppsala, 1913, and the same scholar's *Ynglingasagan i arkeologisk belysning*, in *Fornvännen*, 1917, 226-61.

[760] *Heimskringla: Ynglingasaga,* cap. 27.

[761] A discovery made by Otto v. Friesen in 1910: see S. Lindqvist in *Fornvännen*, 1917, 129. Two years earlier (1675) "Utters högen i Wändell" is mentioned in connection with an investigation into witchcraft. See Linderholm, *Vendelshögens konunganamn*, in *Namn och Bygd*, VII, 1919, 36, 40.

[762] For a preliminary account of the discovery, see *Ottarshögen i Vendel*, by S. Lindqvist in *Fornvännen*, 1917, 127-43, and for discussion of the whole subject, B. Nerman, *Ottar Vendelkråka och Ottarshögen i Vendel*, in *Upplands Fornminnesförenings Tidskrift*, VII, 309-34.

[763] Baldwin Brown, III, 216.

[764] 213.

[765] 218.

[766] So Baldwin Brown, III, 213; Lorange, *Den Yngre Jernalders Sværd*, Bergen, 1889, passim.

[767] Baldwin Brown, III, 215.

[768] It is somewhat similar in Norse literature, where swords are constantly indicated as either inherited from of old, or coming from abroad: cf. Falk, 38-41.

[769] *Beowulf*, 1489, *wægsweord*; cf. *Vægir* as a sword-name in the *Thulur*. In ll. 1521, 1564, 2037, *hringmæl* may refer to the ring in the hilt, and terms like *wunden-* are more likely to refer to the serpentine ornament of the hilt. This must be the case with *wyrmfäh* (1698) as it is a question of the hilt alone. Stjerna (p. 111 = *Essays*, 20) and others take *äter-tänum fäh* (1459) as referring to the damascened pattern (cf. *eggjar ... eitrdropom innan fápar; Brot af Sigurðarkviðu*). It is suggested however by Falk (p. 17) that *tän* here refers to an edge welded-on: the Icelandic *egg-teinn*.

[770] The only certainly Anglo-Saxon helmet as yet discovered: traces of what may have been a similar head-piece were found near Cheltenham: Roach Smith, *Collectanea Antiqua*, II, 1852, 238.

[771] *Coll. Ant.* II, 1852, 239; Bateman, *Ten Years' Diggings*, 30; *Catalogue of the Antiquities preserved in the Museum of Thomas Bateman*, Bakewell, 1855.

[772] A very good description of these continental "Spangenhelme" is given in the magnificent work of I. W. Gröbbels, *Der Reihengräberfund von Gammertingen*, München, 1905. These helms had long been known from a specimen (place of origin uncertain) in the Hermitage at Petrograd, and another example, that of Vézeronce, supposed to have been lost in the battle between Franks and Burgundians in 524. Seven other examples have been discovered in the last quarter of a century, including those of Baldenheim (for which see Henning (R.), *Der helm von Baldenheim und die verwandten helme des frühen mittelalters*, Strassburg, 1907, cf. Kauffmann, *Z.f.d.Ph.* XL, 464-7) and Gammertingen. They are not purely Germanic, and may have been made in Gaul, or among the Ostrogoths in Ravenna, or further east.

[773] Stjerna, *Essays*, p. 11 = *Studier tillägnade Oscar Montelius af Lärjungar*, 1903, p. 104: Clark Hall, *Beowulf*, 1911, p. 228.

[774] See also *Graffältet vid Vendel, beskrifvet af* H. Stolpe och T. J. Arne, Stockholm, 1912, pp. 13, 54; Pl. v, xli.

[775] ll. 396, 2049, 2257, 2605; cf. *grīmhelm*, 334.

[776] 2811, 304, 1111 (cf. Falk, 156).

[777] 1453-4 (cf. Falk, 157-9).

[778] *securum etiam inter hostes praestat. Germ.* cap. 45.

[779] 1031 (cf. Falk, 158).

[780] 1630, 2723. Cf. *Exodus*, 174, *grīmhelm gespēon cyning cinberge*, and *Genesis*, 444. (See Falk, 166.)

[781] Cf. ll. 1503, 1548, 2260, 2754.

[782] Cf. ll. 322, 551, 1443.

[783] Bateman, *Ten Years' Diggings*, 1861, p. 32.

[784] Cf. *Beowulf*, 330, 1772, 2042.

[785] "ne scuta quidem ferro neruoue firmata, sed ... tenuis et fucatas colore tabulas," *Annals*, II, 14; cf. *Germania*, 6, "scuta tantum lectissimis coloribus distinguunt."

[786] *Njáls Saga*, cap. XXX.

[787] It is the guess of A. Haupt, *Die Älteste Kunst der Germanen*, p. 213.

[788] ll. 773-5, 998.

[789] *Hist. Eccl.* II, 13. The life of man is compared to the transit of a sparrow flying from door to door of the hall where the king sits feasting with his thanes and warriors, with a fire in the midst.

[790] ll. 617-24, 2011-3.

[791] 995.

[792] 725.

[793] 1035 *etc.*

[794] *Proc. Soc. Ant., Sec. Ser.* II, 177-82.

[795] Jonckheere (É.), *L'origine de la Côte de Flandre et le Bateau de Bruges*, Bruges, 1903.

[796] Engelhardt (H. C. C.), *Nydam Mosefund*, Kjöbenhavn, 1865.

[797] Nicolaysen (N.), *Langskibet fra Gokstad*, Kristiania, 1882.

[798] *Osebergfundet. Udgit av den Norske Stat, under redaktion av* A. W. Brøgger, Hj. Falk, H. Schetelig. Bd. I, Kristiania, 1917.

[799] *Beowulf*, ll. 32, 1131, 1897.

[800] 1862.

[801] 220.

[802] Noreen, *Altschwedische Grammatik*, 1904, p. 499.

[803] All these places are in Gotland. The Stenkyrka stone is reproduced in Stjerna's *Essays*, transl. Clark Hall, fig. 24.

[804] The same, fig. 27.

[805] Reproduced in Montelius, *Sveriges Historia*, p. 283.

[806] *Deutsche Mythologie*, 3te Ausgabe, 1854, pp. 342, 639.

[807] *Academy*, XI, 1877, p. 163.

[808] *Engl. Stud.* II, 314.

[809] *Beowulf*, p. 177.

[810] *Aanteekeningen op den Beowulf*, 1892, p. 42.

[811] *P.B.B.* XVIII, 413.

[812] *Z.f.ö.G.* LVI, 759.

[813] *Beowulf*, p. 392.

[814] *Engl. Stud.* LII, 191. Among the many who have accepted the explanation "bee-wolf," without giving additional reasons, may be mentioned R. Müller, *Untersuchungen über die Namen des Liber Vitae*, 1901, p. 94.

[815] Both Grimm and Skeat suggested the woodpecker, which feeds upon bees and their larvae: Grimm appealing to classical mythology, Skeat instancing the bird's courage. But nothing seems forthcoming from Teutonic mythology to favour this interpretation. Cosijn, following Sijmons, *Z.f.d.Ph.* XXIV, 17, thought bees might have been an omen of victory. But there is no satisfactory evidence for this. The term *sigewīf* applied to the swarming bees in the *Charms* (Cockayne's *Leechdoms*, I, 384) is insufficient.

[816] *Tidskr. f. Philol. og Pædag.* VIII, 289.

[817] *Deutsches Wörterbuch*, 1854, I, 1122.

[818] "Das compositum Beóvulf, wie Gôzolf, Irminolf, Reginolf, und andre gebildet, zeigt nur einen helden und krieger im geist und sinn oder von der art des Beówa an. Ihm entspricht altn. Biôlfr." (Müllenhoff, in *Z.f.d.A.* XII, 284.) But certainly this interpretation is impossible for O.N. *Biólfr*. "warrior of Beowa" would be **Byggulfr*, which we nowhere find. See Björkman in *Engl. Stud.* LII, 191. Müllenhoff at this date, whilst not connecting *Bēowulf* directly with *bēo*, "bee," did so connect *Bēowa*, whom he interpreted as a bee-god or bee-father. But there is no evidence for this, and the *w* of *Bēowa* tells emphatically against it. Müllenhoff subsequently abandoned this explanation.

[819] It is actually written *Biuᵘulf*.

[820] *Biu* in *Biuuulf* cannot stand for *Bēo* [older *Beu*] because in Old Northumbrian *iu* and *eo* are rigidly differentiated, as an examination of all the other names in the *Liber Vitae* shows. As

Sievers points out, if *Biuuulf* is to be derived from **Beuw (w)ulf*, then it would afford an isolated and inexplicable case of *iu* for *eo[eu]*, unique in the *Liber Vitae*, as in the whole mass of the oldest English texts: "Soll ein zusammenhang mit st. *beuwa*- stattfinden, so muss man auch diesen stamm für einen urspr. s-stamm erklären, und unser *biu*- auf die stammform *biuwi(ʒ)*- nicht auf *beuwa(ʒ)*- zurückführen." (Sievers, *P.B.B.* XVIII, 413.) The word however is a neut. *wa*-stem, whether in O.E. (*bēow*), Old Saxon (*bēo*) or Icelandic (*bygg*): see Sievers, *Ags. Grammatik*, 3te Aufl. § 250; Gallée, *Altsächsische Grammatik*, 2te Aufl. § 305; Noreen, *Altisländische Grammatik*, 3te Aufl. § 356. The word is extant in Old English only in the Glossaries, in the gen. sing., "handful beouaes," *etc.*, and in Old Saxon only in the gen. plu. *beuuo*. It is thought to have been originally a *wu*-stem, which subsequently, as e.g. in O.E., passed into a *wa*-stem. (See Noreen, *A.f.n.F.* I, 166, arguing from the form *begg* in the Dalecarlian dialect.) The presumed Primitive Norse form is *beggwu*, whence the various Scandinavian forms, Icel. *bygg*, Old Swedish and Old Danish *biug(g)*. See Hellquist in *A.f.n.F.* VII, 31; von Unwerth, *A.f.n.F.* XXXIII, 331; Binz, *P.B.B.* XX, 153; von Helten, *P.B.B.* XXX, 245; Kock, *Umlaut u. Brechung im Aschw.* p. 314, in *Lunds Universitets årsskrift*, Bd. XII. The proper name *Byggvir* is a *ja*-stem, but *Bēow* cannot have been so formed, as a *ja*-stem would give the form *Bēowe*. Cosijn (*Aanteekeningen*, 42) was accordingly justified in pointing to the form *Biuuulf* as refuting Kögel's attempt to connect *Bēowulf* with *Bēow* through a form **Bawiwulf* (*A.f.d.A.* XVIII, 56). Kögel replied with a laboured defence (*Z.f.d.A.* XXXVII, 268): he starts by assuming that *Bēow* and *Bēowulf* are etymologically connected, which is the very point which has to be proved: he has to admit that, if his etymology be correct, the *Biuuulf* of the *Liber Vitae* is not the same form as *Bēowulf*, which is the very point Cosijn urged as telling against his etymology: and even so his etymological explanations depend upon stages which cannot be accepted in the present state of our knowledge (see especially Sievers in *P.B.B.* XVIII, 413; Björkman in *Engl. Stud.* LII, 150).

[821] *Tidskr. f. Philol og Pædag.* VIII, 289.

[822] First pointed out by Grundtvig in Barfod's *Brage og Idun*, IV, 1841, p. 500, footnote.

[823] "Lodmundr hinn gamli het madr enn annarr. Biólfr fostbrodir hans. Þeir foru til Islands af Vors af Þvlvnesi" (Voss in Norway). See *Landnámabók*, København, 1900, p. 92.

[824] Noreen, *Altisländische Grammatik*, 3te Aufl. p. 97. See also Noreen in *Festskrift til H. F. Feilberg*, 1911, p. 283. Noreen seems to have no doubt as to the explanation of *Bjólfr* as *Bý-olfr*, "Beewolf."

[825] Bugge, has, however, been followed by Gering, *Beowulf*, 1906, p. 100.

[826] Ferguson in the *Athenæum*, June 1892, p. 763: "Beadowulf by a common form of elision (!) would become Beowulf." Sarrazin admits "Freilich ist das eine ungewöhnliche verkürzung" (*Engl. Stud.* XLII, 19). See also Sarrazin in *Anglia*, V, 200; *Beowulf-Studien*, 33, 77; *Engl. Stud.* XVI, 79.

[827] This incompatibility comes out very strongly in ll. 2499-2506, where Beowulf praises his sword particularly for the services it has *not* been able to render him.

[828] See above, pp. 60-1.

[829] Olrik, *Heltedigtning*, I, 140: F. Jónsson, *Hrólfs Saga Kraka*, 1904, *Inledning*, XX.

[830] *Hrólfs Saga Kraka*, cap. 17-20.

[831] The trait is wanting in the *Grettis saga*: Grettir son of Asmund was too historical a character for such features to be attributed to him.

[832] See pp. 62-7.

[833] No. 166. Translated as "Strong Hans." (*Grimm's Household Tales, trans. by M. Hunt, with introduction by A. Lang*, 1884.)

[834] As, for example, by Cosquin, *Contes populaires de Lorraine*, I, 7. A comparison of the different versions in which the "strange theme" is toned down, in a greater or less degree, seems to make this certain.

[835] No. 91.

[836] Edinburgh, 1860, vol. I, No. XVI, "The king of Lochlin's three daughters": vol. III, No. LVIII, "The rider of Grianaig."

[837] London, 1866: p. 43, "The Three Crowns."

[838] Notably by von Sydow.

[839] Asbjørnsen og Moe, *Norske Folkeeventyr*, Christiania, 1852, No. 3.

[840] *Popular Tales from the Norse* (third edit., Edinburgh, 1888, p. 382).

[841] Visentini, *Fiabe Mantovane*, 1879, No. 32, 157-161.

[842] "fino a che col capo tocca le travi." Cf. Glam in the *Grettis Saga.*

[843] "e qui vede il gigante seduto, che detteva il suo testamento."

[844] p. 153. This is Panzer's version 97.

[845] "A fabulous creature, but zoologically the name Norka (from *nora*, a hole) belongs to the otter," Ralston, *Russian Folk Tales*, p. 73.

[846] Afanasief (A. N.), *Narodnuiya Russkiya Skazki*, Moscow, 1860-63, I, 6. See Ralston, p. 73.

[847] Afanasief, VIII, No. 6.

[848] For example, "Shepherd Paul," in *The Folk-Tales of the Magyars*, by W. H. Jones and L. L. Knopf, *Folk-Lore Society*, 1889, p. 244. The latest collection contains its version, 'The Story of Tāling, the Half-boy' in *Persian Tales, written down for the first time and translated* by D. L. R. and E. O. Lorimer, London, 1919.

[849] Cf. von Sydow in *A.f.d.A*. XXXV, 126.

[850] Ión Arnason's MSS, No. 536, 4°.

[851] Rittershaus (A.), *Die Neuisländischen Volksmärchen*, Halle, 1902, No. 25.

[852] *Færøske Folkesagn og Æventyr*, ed. by Jakob Jakobsen, 1898-1901, pp. 241-4 (*Samfund til Udgivelse af gammel Nordisk Litteratur.*)

[853] This folk-tale is given in a small book, to be found in the Christiania University Library, and no doubt elsewhere in Norway: *Nor, en Billedbog for den norske Ungdom* (Tredie Oplag, Christiania, 1865). *Norske Folke-Eventyr og Sagn*, fortalte af P. Chr.

Asbjørnsen. A copy of the story, slightly altered, occurs in the *Udvalgte Eventyr og Sagn for Børn*, of Knutsen, Bentsen and Johnsson, Christiania, 1877, p. 58 *etc.*

[854] pp. 66-7.

[855] Berntsen (K.), *Folke-Æventyr*, 1873, No. 12, pp. 109-115.

[856] Grundtvig (Sv.), *Gamle Danske Minder*, 1854, No. 34, p. 33: from Næstved.

[857] *Hans mit de ysern Stang'*, Müllenhoff, *Sagen, Märchen u. Lieder* ... 1845, No. XVI, p. 437.

[858] Colshorn (C. and Th.), *Märchen u. Sagen*, Hannover, 1854, No. V, pp. 18-30.

[859] Cf. *Beowulf*, ll. 2183-8.

[860] Cf. *Beowulf*, ll. 815 *etc.*

[861] Cf. *Beowulf*, ll. 1516-17; cf. *Grettis Saga*, LXVI.

[862] Cf. *Grettis Saga*, LXVI, *hann kveikti ljós*; cf. *Beowulf*, 1570.

[863] *Contes du roi Cambrinus*, par C. Deulin, Paris, 1874 (I. *L'intrépide Gayant*). The story is associated with Gayant, the traditional hero of Douai.

[864] Cf. Schmidt, *Geschichte der deutschen Stämme*, II, 495, 499, *note* 4.

[865] III, 1.

[866] II, 43.

[867] Παῖς ... νέος ἦν κομιδῇ, καὶ ἔτι ὑπὸ παιδοκόμῳ τιθηνούμενος, Agathias, I, 4: *parvulus*, Gregory, IV, 6.

[868] Gregory, III, 20.

[869] III, 22.

[870] III, 23.

[871] III, 27.

[872] Many recent historians have expressed doubts as to the conventional date, 515, for Hygelac's death. J. P. Jacobsen, in the Danish translation of Gregory (1911) suggested 525-30: following him Severinsen (*Danske Studier*, 1919, 96) suggested c. 526, as did Fredborg, *Det första årtalet i Sveriges historia*. L. Schmidt (*Geschichte der deutschen Stämme*, II, 500, *note*, 1918) suggested c. 528.

[873] Archæological works bearing less directly upon *Beowulf* are enumerated in *Appendix F*; that enumeration is not repeated here.

[874] Most students nowadays will probably agree with v. Sydow's contention that the struggle of Beowulf, first above ground and then below, is a folk-story, one and indivisible, and that therefore there is no reason for attributing the two sections to different authors, as do Boer, Müllenhoff and ten Brink. But that the folk-tale is exclusively Celtic remains to be proved; v. Sydow's contention that Celtic influence is shown in *Beowulf* by the inhospitable shamelessness of Unferth (compare that of Kai) is surely fanciful. Also the statement that the likeness of Bjarki and Beowulf is confined to the freeing of the Danish palace from a dangerous monster by a stranger from abroad, and that "das sonstige Beiwerk völlig verschieden ist" surely cannot be maintained. As argued above (pp. 54-61) there are other distinct points of resemblance.

v. Sydow's statement no doubt suffers from the brevity with which it is reported, and his forthcoming volume of *Beowulf studien* will be awaited with interest.

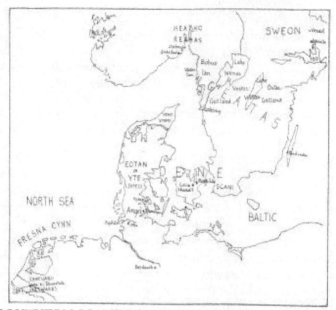

SOUTHERN SCANDINAVIA IN THE SIXTH CENTURY

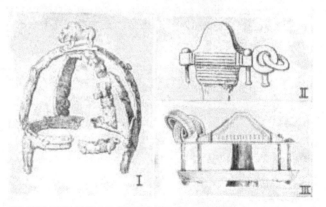

ENGLISH BOAR-HELMET AND RING-SWORDS

I. Benty Grange Helmet (Roach Smith, *Collectanea Antiqua*, II, 238).

II. Pommel of Ring-Sword from Faversham, Kent (*Ibid.*, VI, 139).

III. Pommel of Ring-Sword from Gilton, Kent (*Archæologia*, XXX, 132).

Printed in the USA
CPSIA information can be obtained
at www.ICGtesting.com
LVHW091514210624
783653LV00045B/851